The Thelemic Initiations

Being Book M

Vol I.

0° - Petitioner

I-III° M∴M∴

I° - magician

III-XIII° M∴M∴

II° - Knight of the Rose Cross

XII -XIIX° M∴M∴

Delivered to

Sib. Z. Arrhenothelus

Edited by

Tau Isodaetes
Tau Babalon

Dedicated to

Many an Holy Bard

Table of Contents

Foreword

The Inception of the Thelemic Initiations

In this foreword to the first edition, I have taken the time to set out some of the circumstances regarding how Rebecca Doll and myself came to be in a collaboration with Sibling *Z. Arrhenothelus* to produce the Thelemic Initiations. I use the term "collaboration," loosely. The majority of the creative work is that of Z. and the majority of the editing is by Tau Babalon. My work was coordination, fact-checking, stage directions, and formatting.

Enter William Blake Lodge

While it had once been a major center of my life, throughout the first decade of the 2000's I had fallen away from the practice, pursuit, and perfection of esoterica.

Several things happened around 2010, and immediately afterward, which changed this. The first was I met, and became partners with, Rebecca Doll. Deeply burned by an abusive family and by her experiences with the hypocrisy of middle-American Christianity, she had some need for a spiritual dimension in her life. The second was that my wife, Stephanie Olmstead-Dean became first an Officer, then the Master, of William Blake Lodge, O.T.O., in Baltimore Maryland, most often referred to as "Blake" and written as "WBL" by its members.

I enthusiastically recommended Rebecca to the Lodge, and especially with Stephanie's growing role became more involved myself. It was grueling work over several years. We did not live particularly close to Baltimore. A round trip, for us, was about five hours of travel. The closest viable hotel was almost 25 minutes away in normal traffic, and the cost of booking full weekend hotel rooms for roughly half of the weekends out of the year was prohibitive. Weekends at the Lodge meant camping slumber party style on the Lodge floor, usually on a dubious and back-wrenching air mattress, and waking, ready or not, an hour before anyone arrived to ensure the place was ready and breakfast prepared for volunteers.

If the work wasn't easy it eventually became rewarding. The move under a previous Master from a small-town street in Catonsville to Carrolton Ridge, literally one of the most economically disadvantaged neighborhoods in the city of Baltimore, had driven away many of the Lodge's suburban supporters. At one early event, the three of us were the only attendants. Over her years as an officer, and most especially during her Mastership, Stephanie managed to rebuild a thriving membership based on a core value of Thelema: "We are infinitely tolerant, save of intolerance." Among other things, WBL was accepting of kink and heavily populated by queer-identifying individuals. Everyone was welcome there, provided they could embrace the above message.

When Stephanie took charge, there were a handful of relatively new members whose adherence to the Lodge had more to do with the desire to pass through the O.T.O. Grade system than to find a loving spiritual home. They didn't like having a woman as Master, and they didn't like the new people who Stephanie brought in. They were neither kink nor queer accepting, and some of them tried various pressure to remove Stephanie or alienate her supporters from the Lodge, but this went nowhere. In the short term, we were triumphant, and the Lodge presented at local Pagan Pride and Baltimore Pride, grew, and held events and rituals.

Through the perspective of years, it is probably an accident that the Lodge flourished as it did during the years of Stephanie's Mastery. While she did nothing in violation of O.T.O. policy, Stephanie's unwillingness to kowtow to privileged middle-aged white men, or to shame anyone whose presence threatened their outspoken monogamy and heterosexuality, went against the de facto prevailing norm. Stephanie held innovative events, inviting speakers from as far away as California and the UK to present at the Lodge. WBL also tapped into the "grimoire revival" and the renewal of interest in traditional magic, holding classes that featured mainstream pagan teachers and subjects relevant to the wider magical community. Many of the events were co-hosted by other local Pagan groups, from a variety of backgrounds. The performance of the *Liber XV* mass was pushed to its limits, with as much innovation as was allowed.

While this may not have formally broken any rules, in practice, the policy of the O.T.O. was to use its Sovereign Grand Inspector Generals (S.G.I.G.), who also held the automatic rank of Bishop in the Ecclesia Gnostica Catholica or E.G.C., to keep a tight leash on Lodges. Presenters and Magick from outside O.T.O. were viewed with suspicion. Magickal theory was fine, but though the Program Synopsis of the U.S. Grand Lodge theoretically called for "instruction in Hermetic Science, Yoga, and Magick," this was usually not much encouraged outside of having senior lodge members present on their specialties. Groups outside of O.T.O. were typically viewed as competition, not as partners. Festival or ritual events with other local groups were uncommon in most quarters.

It would be unfair to suggest that no other lodges had done the things that WBL did. It is more the case that such things were usually seen as a "big deal" and the exception, rather than the rule. Most O.T.O bodies had probably done a few of the things WBL did that fell outside the O.T.O. mainstream, but we were not aware of any that did as many of them, nor as often. Part of the reason was that we lived in the center of a large urban corridor with a ton of local groups and resources, and had easy access to prominent speakers from both inside and outside O.T.O.

WBL had always been bold, experimental, and decidedly not prude. Early rituals had involved open exploration of sex magick. During the time that Stephanie was an officer, though not yet Master, WBL had pioneered "modern music masses," a concept that the conservative Roman Catholic Church had embraced in the 1960s, and which was endorsed by the local S.G.I.Gs. As part of a progressive group handling Blake's scheduling, Stephanie had a hand in creating WBL's "Katy Perry Mass" which became the cause célèbre of the Thelemic Right. Apparently, putting the producer of the "Raggedy Ragtime Girls'" Mass to a fun, upbeat, contemporary score was beyond the pale. Reactionary elements within O.T.O. had the ear of the international leadership, and shortly after this senior leadership handed down a rule outlawing lyrics in music used at public Mass, universally understood at the time as a direct rebuke to WBL.

The official reasoning given was that lyrics might be "confusing," as if some modern-day person might not grasp the idea of a soundtrack, but the impact was to stop a wildly popular event at WBL which had been a powerful tool for attracting "new blood." Once slapped down, the local S.G.I.Gs. had been largely unwilling to rock the boat. Stephanie had pushed to continue the modern music masses as private, restricted, events, a practice discouraged but still officially allowed. Once she became Master, Stephanie began the process of reviving modern music masses. Since public masses were banned from using tracks with lyrics, Stephanie began experimenting with karaoke tracks which carried the melody, but not the actual lyrics, in order to revitalize what had been an enormously successful program in regards to generating public interest. The driving force behind these attempts to "spice up" *Liber XV* was a feeling that we needed to break out of a loop in which we engaged in endless repetition of the same ritual without allowance for any sort of variation to prevent stagnation.

A Golden Era at Blake

The Golden era at WBL was an accident. Stephanie's inspired leadership happened to coincide with a series of health and personal issues that largely sidelined the local S.G.I.G.'s. Over years Stephanie had developed a wide network of acquaintances and, when she became first Secretary and later Master, she put her influence to work building exciting programs.

As I grew more active, I grew more curious and interested in our work. WBL was working actual magic, not merely doing endless replications of a century-old ritual. As Stephanie promoted the growth of the Lodge, Rebecca was rapidly becoming an experienced and noteworthy spirit worker and, with my esoteric studies largely dormant since the very early 2000s, I had catching up to do.

This led to a renewal of acquaintance and conversation with Z., who I had always looked to for expertise and what some people might term "spiritual guidance." I had once worked on several projects quite closely with Z., and they had been a significant guiding force in my life. But we had fallen out of regular touch after 2010, and I was pleased, if hardly surprised, to find that they had gained a great deal of knowledge and wisdom in the intervening years. Over the course of our collaboration, Z. has managed to teach me a great deal about the realities of attainment. Whether or not Z. can be said to have attained is a matter of opinion, and they make no such claim. In their behavior, however, they model what is expected of a Master of the Temple. What is clear is that they have a firm grasp on the road map and the necessary teaching to allow an individual to follow it.

The tarot cards that bring change also imply a certain level of chaos and upheaval. It is often only in retrospect that what seemed to be a disaster appears as a blessing.

On the eve of the inception of The Thelemic Initiations, we still believed heavily in a promise of Thelema that seemed to emanate from the leadership in the Obama era. The Thelemic world we had been promised was one where rules concerning gender in the rituals (which dated only to the recent past) would soon be erased and the rest of the Thelemic world would catch up with the work we were doing at WBL. We were not a "problem lodge," but a shining example of what a successful lodge could be when it shared with other local groups. Nothing at WBL was *entirely* unique, but Blake was too *many* things at once. It was too kinky, too queer, too magick heavy, too pagan, too close to non-O.T.O. groups, and too willing to challenge authority by playing at the edge of tolerance in areas like the presentation of *Liber XV*.

Ultimately, sexuality and gender were the straws that broke the camel's back. The O.T.O. had some reason, coming out of the "Satanic Panic" in the 1960s, to fear too much open discussion of sex and, certainly, in some regions, there was still good reasons for caution. But efforts to downplay the existence of sex on-premises and consensual sex between partners as an adjunct to celebratory rituals made the local S.G.I.G. resistant to adopting a consent policy that directly referenced sex, which is the first line of defense in making spaces safer. Likewise, while O.T.O. was theoretically tolerant of polyamory, kink, and gender expression, in practice leadership usually insisted such things be "toned down" to not alienate members who were intolerant or threatened by those things.

If those issues had only been local, perhaps WBL would have been tolerated as an "oddball" lodge. Unfortunately, as nonbinary and trans rights began to catch up with gay rights, the international leadership of O.T.O. found itself in a pitched battle. The O.T.O. had long taken an "either/or" approach to the roles of Priest and Priestess which mandated that individuals had to choose a role and stick to it, for life, allowing a potential one-time, non-revocable switch for individuals who came out as transgender, thus limiting which roles could be taken by an individual in

The Thelemic Initiations

Liber XV. This had seemed reasonable, and even somewhat tolerant in the early 2000s, but it was increasingly at odds with a world in which understanding of nonbinary gender was a daily reality for many people.

Still, on the eve of the inception of the Thelemic Initiations, all seemed well. As the Lodge that Stephanie built became increasingly organized and sophisticated, Rebecca worked magic, while I built closets, shelves, and eventually a shower. If I occasionally talked esoterica late at night, that was not my *job*. I mastered the sets for initiation and made vast improvements on them, allowing them to be staged in a manageable time. I made sure we had a viable First Aid kit. My business was the practical, not the spiritual.

Unite the Right v. Thelema

In August 2017 we drove to O.T.O.'s Biennial Convention in Orlando Florida to hear a message from the leadership that rebuked white supremacy and seemed to promise an end to arbitrary discrimination against nonbinary people within an organization founded by a Prophet who wrote stridently of his own nonbinary identity. Only hours before the delivery of that message on Saturday evening, August 12, 2017, a white supremacist and neo-nazi in Charlottesville, Virginia attending a "Unite the Right" rally ran down and killed Heather Heyer. Racial tensions had been increasing for some time. Deep fractures of privilege and entitlement in Western culture were highlighted by issues such as Brexit and the political ascendance of Donald Trump on a provocatively white nationalist agenda. Key members of the international O.T.O. leadership had expressed admiration for Trump, and there were uncomfortable rumors that some of them had seriously considered putting the arguably negligible weight of the Thelemic "establishment" behind him.

None of us believed that Thelema was about political parties, political candidates, Democrats, Labor, or agricultural subsidies. Yet we understood that it was antithetical to Fascism, to white supremacy, and to intolerance. It might be impossible to list all the potential beliefs that are Thelemic, but it is quite possible to identify those things which were, definitively, its polar opposites. We wanted to exemplify Thelemic opposition to Fascism, white nationalism and, most of all, intolerance and, in response to the emergent threats, we boosted our message.

There was no battle line along which to confront the senior leadership for admiring Trump. If members of the senior circle spoke out, the actual heads of the organization remained quiet. The battle concerning gender became symbolic, a push against a tainted establishment that had lost touch with its roots. At this point, we were not ready to reject O.T.O. wholesale. We believed the message put forward by the United States Grand Lodge leadership at Orlando, and believed we were providing the energy that moderate leaders needed to force change on the unwilling senior international leadership.

A New Mass

The degree to which *Liber XV*, dominated the business of the lodge had always been a frustration to me. We were obligated to two performances a month, 24 annually, and E.G.C. policy was obsessive on the subject of conformity. In Texas, a group that used to shout joyfully during their Mass performances had been told to be quiet because shouts of joy weren't in the rubric. The ritual was old and needed updating, but changing so much as a line of it was not allowed. "Memorize and duplicate" was the focus.

My failure to engage with *Liber XV* ate at me, and on one occasion brought Stephanie to tears. Her frustration with me was fair and I felt awful. Within the narrow confines of the E.G.C. rubric, she had done everything humanly possible to bring life to that single, tired ritual. WBL hosted an annual "Massapalooza," where Thelemites from across the country came to present as many as fourteen Masses in a weekend, each exchanging their knowledge. Private masses during that period allowed for greater freedom of expression. There had been Mardi Gras Mass, Victorian Mass, and pajama masses. Stephanie had even gone through the laborious process of getting authorization to use a variant anthem for *Liber XV*, yet the problem remained the same - you could dress up the trappings, but the core ritual and its performance were set, not in stone, but rather in recent, highly artificial, concrete. I focused on the initiations and other rituals, but *Liber XV* was inescapable. The E.G.C. drove the weekly activities of O.T.O. and any sort of advancement in the organization was closely tied to participation as clergy.

The issue of a "new mass" was also a somewhat divisive one. *Liber XV* was the focus of the battle for nonbinary rights. The deepest issue of gender discrimination within O.T.O. was a prohibition against nonbinary clergy representing their gender in the performance of *Liber XV*. Working from the Old Aeon viewpoint of two fixed genders, the leadership had ordained that clergy needed to pick one with no understanding that this was deeply problematic to those who did not spiritually identify with only the male or female principles. When nonbinary clergy pushed for changes they were told they should write a nonbinary mass.

This was problematic in two regards. First, anyone who understood Thelema understood that *Liber XV* was already nonbinary, as was Thelema itself, making the idea of a "separate but equal" mass repugnant.

> *This constitutes a profound Riddle of Holiness. Those only understand it who combine in themselves the extremes of Moral idea, identifying them through transcendental overcoming of the antinomy. They must have gone further yet, beyond the fundamental opposition of the sexes. The male must have completed himself and become androgyne; the female, and become gynander. This incompleteness imprisons the soul. To think "I am not woman, but man," or vice versa, is to limit one's self, to set a bar to one's motion. It is the root of the "shutting-up" which culminates in becoming "Mary inviolate" or a "Black Brother."[1]*

Second, any suggestion about a "new mass" was also a sort of administrative Catch-22. E.G.C. exercised wide authority over the use of any language from *Liber XV*. Even in private rituals, there were strong rules against appropriating language from *Liber XV*. No "separate but equal" mass could ever be publicly performed because, to the extent it used any of the text from *Liber XV*, it would contravene the draconian rules on presentation and be forbidden. To write a mass that couldn't be presented was a fool's errand. In all probability, if it drew heavily on *Liber XV*, it wouldn't be allowed even in private. Further, by forcing the memorization of *Liber XV*, E.G.C. made it ubiquitous. It was hard for a lot of people to master and, after having done so, many had little interest in memorizing another, similar mass.

Liber XV, while beautiful in its day, was dated, but most known attempts to create a new mass had focused on a narrow revision of it. James Eshelman had published the "Thelemic Mass," adding female saints, but the Mass itself preserved the same dated 19th-century writing style, designed to convey a subtle secret to an early 20th-century audience that could be imprisoned for speaking it aloud. I began to wonder: What if there were an *entirely* new mass? One which used little of the language of *Liber XV*, but incorporated the core ideas of Thelema which Crowley and Reuss had been forced to shroud in layers, which apparently still confounded the middle-aged men that ran O.T.O?

The Magic of the Mass

One recurrent theme at WBL was that we did magic. We rolled up our sleeves and got our hands dirty. We did spirit magic. We summoned a familiar for the Lodge and bound it in a jar. We held Bacchanals and Orphic rituals. We learned and flourished. In the end, this would be a key to our downfall.

The Thelemic Initiations

Official representations aside, the O.T.O. leadership was still fighting the battles of the "satanic panic" of two decades past. The last thing they wanted an O.T.O. Lodge doing was summoning demons or working with Lilith or Hecate. These things were firmly a part of Thelema and Crowley's writing and work but the O.T.O. was more concerned about its public image and deference to some theoretical "norm" than appeal to people who might actually be willing to get involved with Thelema if they thought it included *anything* relevant to their existing practice.

While I had begun brushing up, my magical learning was at least a decade out of date. I was not up to the task of creating a major new ritual on my own. I needed someone who could deliver such a thing, someone who knew Thelema and its ideals well, and who had a gift for writing that merged the classical feel of *Liber XV* with a clear modern form that could be readily understood by anyone living in the 21st century.

If Stephanie had exhausted what was humanly possible, perhaps we needed what was inhumanly possible? Rebecca was gaining confidence and experience as a spirit worker. I turned to my old associate Z.

Z. had never been particularly involved in O.T.O. And, while most definitely a Thelemite, had overwhelming reservations about our association with the organization. I plead our case. Between Rebecca and myself, we had the editing and presentation skills to put together final drafts. Even before the first of the disruptions that brought an end to our time at WBL, I was well along toward commissioning Z. to write an entirely new mass.

The Hammer Falls

Z. liked the idea but was busy. I was also busy. If all things had remained the same, the idea of a new mass could have been a back-burner project for years. As often happens, a series of rapid blows came in quick succession, changing all our plans and leaving us with the need to commit to a course of action.

Within the O.T.O. promotion to the invitational grades above IV° relied largely on patronage. The only way to get invited was to do work for the higher-ups who did the inviting. Thus the organization had, at any time, a decent body of individuals willing to do "service" for free, in hope of attracting attention and being allowed to advance. One common employment was to ask them to go act as spies on other bodies. The presence of an S.G.I.G. raised alarm bells and, like an officer on deck, everyone knew to snap to attention and behave. A visit from someone of mid-degree was less likely to garner attention.

If we were only beginning to truly understand the moral dereliction of the senior leadership, Stephanie and WBL had a ton of institutional knowledge about the normal and mid-grade operations of O.T.O. We knew about the practice of spying because members from WBL had been part of it, and it wasn't entirely onerous. There had been issues of abuse and non-consent within the organization and, in theory, this practice could be and had been on occasion used to gain real knowledge to curb abuses. We knew WBL was being spied on, but we didn't care. We had nothing to hide, in fact, we aspired to be an example for other Lodges. When V° and VI° members showed up unexpectedly on short notice, we cheerfully invited them in.

Aside from reading like a recounting of the Cuban Missile Crisis, I don't think there is much to be gained from a blow-by-blow of the rapidly escalating debacle from June 15 to December 21, 2019. The intention of this article is not to drag a tired organization that lost its way through the mud, but to convey a feeling for the currents that led to the inception of the Thelemic Initiations. The O.T.O. is incidental but, just as one cannot understand Crowley's magical work leading up to the reception of *Liber AL* without understanding the collapse of the Isis-Urania Temple of the Golden Dawn, it would be hard to understand the forces that predicated the reception of a new set of initiations without some description of the environment.

The collapse came quite quickly after two years of prosperity and building, most of it in a matter of weeks.

By June 15, there was already a whispering campaign against WBL, attempting to whip perceptions of the leaders' sexuality, polyamory, kink, and gender expression into scandal. Nebulous charges were brought forward but never documented, repeated on the phone but nowhere written down. Eventually, the rumors became an official inquiry. There were phone calls to Stephanie about something that had taken place at a goetic ritual hosted by the Lodge. Exactly what was supposed to have happened was never revealed.

We knew who the spy was as it happened that the ritual, though it had an interestingly diverse group of attendees, was fairly small. Every single person, and every event of the evening, could be easily accounted for, except for an out-of-town guest who had visited on short notice. Stephanie anticipated this would be cleared up at the organization's biennial conference, held in Cleveland that year, in early August, but the matter was ignored throughout the weekend by the quasi-democratic body with authority to act on it. With most of the guests broken up and on their way home, at the very point where we were preparing to go get a final drink and declare victory, thinking the rumors apparently hadn't warranted official action, Stephanie was called into a secret meeting and dismissed peremptorily on nebulous emergency executive authority.

She was, frankly, devastated. She'd had a great deal of confidence in her friends, in the general sanity of the organization, and dismissal on trumped-up and, as we'd show, unsustainable charges that vilified her friends and metamours was not the ending she had expected. Already battling health issues, the unexpected reality that the organization she had labored for tirelessly, slept on floors for, risen before dawn for, cooked prepared, and cleaned for, would round on her without actually hearing her case was enough to leave her momentarily out of energy and ideas. Realizing that the powers-that-be had chosen the course they did specifically to circumvent any real democratic consideration, Rebecca, I, and the Lodge's Deputy Master back in Baltimore began working social media. By the next morning, the first battle had been won. Pressure was brought to bear and dismissal had been revised to suspension pending a meeting in October.

Another Blow

Stephanie urged patience. The issue would be cleared up. The wheels of sober reason which she had learned to depend upon would eventually grind to a satisfactory conclusion. This was alarmism and incompetence, not actually part of an ongoing coup within the organization designed to silence voices calling for change. The next blow fell quickly, though it took a while to sink in.

It had been anticipated that the crowning point of the Cleveland conference would be the rollback of the regressive gender policy regarding the *Liber XV*, in fulfillment of the promise made in 2017. It was already known that it would not be a complete rollback, but certainly, it would be an improvement. The senior leadership knew by then that what was coming was unpalatable, and chose to make a vague announcement toward the end of the weekend about a "new position" without actually releasing the written language. The announcement was fairly dismal but left everyone hoping the published version would be better than what had been articulated at the event.

It wasn't.

Published in late August, the policy instead rolled back compromises made in writing in the early 2000's and disguised the segregation and isolation of nonbinary Clergy as a "promotion." Those who didn't *look* adequately male enough to fulfill the role of Priest or female enough to fulfill the role of Priestess would no longer have even a one-time choice, but be relegated to the neutral role of Deacon which had been promoted from junior status to a nebulously separate-but-equal rank. However, those who did meet those arbitrary Old Aeon standards could pursue both the Deaconate as well as Priest or Priestess as long as their gender presentation fit within the "appropriate" binary.

Victory in California

It was at that point that I began following up on the idea of a new mass in earnest. We'd need one if we were to continue operation as anything more than just a random ceremonial magic coven. I admit I was through with the O.T.O. at that point. I went on the record advocating leaving O.T.O. altogether and operating as William Blake Lodge, Baltimore, Maryland, Independent. My loyalty was to my family, friends, and magic not to a rather ordinary bunch of boomers a few years older than me who happened by virtue of proximity to fall into the inheritance of the title to Thelema.

It may be surprising that it took from August to December for us to leave O.T.O. altogether, but the reality was much like a slow slide towards confrontation, each day bringing hope of reconciliation before being met with some new indignity or injury. There was optimism that the almost universal unpopularity of the new pronouncement would garner a retraction, or at least that practical compromises might be added. Instead, when challenged, the leadership doubled down. There was also the pending case against Stephanie. Whether or not we left O.T.O., the charges that were leveled not only against her, but whispered about all of us, needed to be resolved before a fair tribunal.

The recidivist gender policy of late August was Malcolm Gladwell's tipping point. Despite a genuine desire to continue to work with a number of the people in O.T.O., there was no way to look back without seeing an organization that was not only willing to alienate large chunks of its entire millennial and post-millennial membership, but which genuinely could not see the incompatibility of a core set of values which esteemed the individual identity while imposing arbitrary outside standards based on assigned or perceived gender.

The senior leadership was obsessed with ensuring the accommodation of conservative populists, rather than concerns of people who had been born in the last thirty years. While not necessarily radicals themselves, they framed advocates for gender equality and white nationalists with a false equivalence, considering both "extremists" who might damage their book sales or warrant extra hours of administration. The Law was for All, provided "All" was aging white men or adequately supportive white women. Being gay was okay...as long as one was orthodox in all other regards.

By the time Stephanie flew to California in October, I knew there was very little chance that we could remain in the O.T.O. On the other hand, I didn't see how the break was going to come. I was fairly certain the case against her would fail. I had literally buried the tribunal in evidence, and the instigators had made a strategic miscalculation in choosing to make allegations about conduct at a ritual which was relatively short and in which virtually every element had been witnessed by a variety of individuals with a broad array of backgrounds, ages, and gender identifications. Whatever their allegations...and ultimately we got only intimations...I knew "there was no there there." In California, Stephanie was restored to her position as Lodge Master; her opponents getting no more satisfaction than a pronouncement that she should put forward a formal alcohol policy, something we'd already moved toward doing. To that we also added a consent policy, this time without asking for permission.

The Shape of a New Order

I have always believed in working on multiple tracks at once. On one hand, Stephanie was working towards reconciliation. I had no faith that the campaign against us, which had by this time taken on the form of direct ad hominem personal attacks by senior officers in O.T.O., was going to stop, despite our victory. If all the membership of WBL had been willing to leave O.T.O., then the entire matter might not have come to much more than a footnote. We'd have had our fun, done brilliant magical work, and operated an exciting Lodge in Baltimore. *The Triune Mass* would have been prepared, but it is questionable we would have developed a new set of initiations for ourselves. I had the legal know-how to ensure that we maintained control of the property if that is what the membership wanted to do.

There were members, friends of ours, however, who had their own good reasons for sticking it out and there was no desire in our hearts to fight with them. I was sick to lose the building space we'd struggled to maintain and improve and the library - a large portion of which I had donated. In the long run, peace and fellowship were more important than a meeting space. We were about respect for personal choice and that meant supporting the choice of others to continue to work within O.T.O. Freed from the need to figure out how to maintain, run, and pay for a property in Baltimore, I could think about the scope that was needed to put together a functional international organization. The point wasn't to challenge, or even replace, the O.T.O. The point was to promulgate Thelema in an entirely new way.

The debacle of the charges against WBL's leadership had resulted in everyone taking a hard look at the realities of operating within the O.T.O. structure, and the degree to which simply being affiliated with the organization brought more drag and complexity than it did reward. The national organization offered no benefits. It did not advertise, did not promote, and did not offer any free materials aside from dog-eared photocopies of ritual scripts that had been published since 1973. It did offer fellowship, but when that fellowship came with such onerous terms its value had to be questioned. Its membership had flat-lined over the past decade, with about as many people leaving each year as new members came in. The reason was obvious. It was an organization that ground up and spit out volunteers. It wasn't rewarding to work for. The O.T.O. was comparatively tiny; its entire membership was smaller than my home county's biggest high school. It owned Crowley's copyrights, but many of those were already in the public domain in Europe, if not in the United States.

November became a go/no-go period. Despite victory in California, it was increasingly clear that there was no future within O.T.O., merely a long wait to be singled out and defeated in detail, divided, and conquered. We had won the battle, but through attrition, we would lose the war. If it had merely been a matter of continuing to work and do the things we wanted the situation might have been workable. But with victory came constraint. We'd had two years of comparative freedom, but now the excitement of any new event would be shadowed by waiting for the other shoe to drop.

There were, of course, signs, indications, and portents from small coincidences to major events. Perhaps one of the most significant was the sudden delivery of another new mass *Liber DCLXVI*, to educator, author, and Ordeal Priestess Thista Minai while visiting WBL on a speaking engagement. It has been stated that when you are acting on your true will, it feels like the universe is moving with you, and the more the new structure developed the more the universe seemed to be pushing for it to be born.

What I didn't want to do was to create a McOTO. A "separate but equal" organization for queer and progressive people. While there might be some merit in the idea, as it was certainly closer to the original vision of people like Crowley and Parsons, it was a diminutive task born more of grievance than the desire to promulgate Thelema. This was a chance to do things right from the ground up. I knew why NPOs failed, and I had the business and management skills to file the paperwork and build a structure that could last while also bringing a democratic form of leadership that washed away the tradition of government by upper degrees. A new order needed its own central mystery, not merely a rehash of the century-old mysteries put forward by Reuss and Crowley. That mystery needed to convey the essence of Thelema in a way that the old mysteries did not. By the time I saw the draft of *The Triune Mass*, I knew it was a core on which to build a new organization – not merely different but better; the real New Aeon version of the thing that could not be fully envisioned, let alone executed, in 1910, 1924 or even the 1980s.

The Old Initiations

I had conversations in September and October about the idea of new initiations, both with Z. and with others. By that time I had seen drafts of the *Triune Mass* and was working on the formatting of *Liber DCLXVI*. but these were external rituals and, as valuable as they were, the heart of an order was a path to attainment. I couldn't deliver that because I didn't know what the path to attainment was.

To produce entirely new initiations was a huge undertaking. An obvious step would be to use the existing ones. The O.T.O. might not like it, but they had no real means to stop it. O.T.O. might own the U.S. copyrights to Crowley's work, already lapsed in Europe, but his initiations had been published in the 1970s by esotericist and journalist Francis X. King. However, the more I looked at the initiations the more dismal the idea of running them became. They had three issues:

1) They were politically insensitive. Playing dress-up as Saladin would be seen as harmless fun in the early 1900s, but in the 21st century, it smacked of cultural appropriation and imperialism. In general form, they reflected a sensibility from before the era in which Fascism had been sharply defined. At the time they were written, the model for a despot was Napoleon, not Stalin or Hitler, and the idea of benign despotism was widely seen as acceptable. Ultimately, they were written to support a cult of personality.

2) They reflected a very early version of Thelema. The rituals as written clearly dated from just before or after the First World War, and simply did not reflect the evolved conceptualization of Thelema that came afterward. For all they incorporated Thelema, it felt in some ways incidental to them.

3) They assumed that most initiates were Freemasons or familiar with Freemasonry. They blithely deliver vast Masonic honors with little real explication of the significance and meaning of Freemasonry, Rosicrucianism, and Neo-Templarism, something which would have been well known at least by word of mouth to initiates at the time, but is poorly understood today.

4) They use thickly veiled language and assume that disclosure of the sexual nature of the mysteries below the very highest degrees would be disastrous. This was not a trivial matter. Prosecution for indecency was a very real possibility. Today, these mysteries are frankly discussed in books and media. The effect is that they present less real initiatory information than numerous minor books. They are the equivalent of a 1970s basic course in "what is computing" for people who live with a phone in their pocket, their actual wealth concealed in a ton of irrelevant and dated material that is bluntly obvious.

Whether or not I wished to throw down for the rights to use the material, the fact was that it was unusable. I did not have initiations.

The New Initiations

There is a difference of opinion between myself and Z. on who got who to agree to produce the initiations. They maintain that they cleverly led me to the idea. I maintain I'd already looked in several other directions before I resolved to screw up the courage to feel them out about the prospect.

It was a big undertaking for myself and Rebecca Doll. I was to be the integrator, taking the material and massaging it into final form, consulting on the realities of running an initiation, while Rebecca Doll would act as editor. There was more as well. I was informed that Z. could not produce all the initiatory material, particularly the high-grade material by themselves. Some of it would require contact with people or things who were not strictly speaking alive and while they Z. has done their own spirit-work, Rebecca Doll's involvement and emergent competence as a spirit worker was part of what attracted them to the idea.

While the world of instantaneous communication is a wonder, due to their lifestyle and mine Z. could not be in constant contact with myself and Rebecca Doll. There might be periods, even substantial periods when we were out of contact. And with the emergence of the COVID pandemic, face-to-face meetings, always a difficulty, would become no easier.

The Triune Mass told me this was a writer who understood Thelema on a level that had thus far eluded me, that they were capable of producing good work in their own time, and that we saw eye to eye on the importance of integrating history and tradition with a modern attitude and mindset. Of showing not how to live in the past, but rather how idealists and freethinkers in the past had built the world in which we lived, and how it was their mindset and approach, not what they happened to believe at the time, that we should take to heart.

Like myself, Z. believed that Thelema dictated a world in which everyone was free to pursue their will and that by equipping them with sufficient resources to do so they would, in general not collide. They believed that a refusal to change, whether by embracing new ideas or surrendering privilege, was a cancer that prevented us from reaching for that accessible future. They also believed that the argument "it has always been so," resounds with natural fear and mistrust, yet that weak argument finds a hiding place and camouflage in the apparent traditionalism of the esoteric world. By teaching the truth of our traditions, not only of Thelema, but of the Masonic, Rosicrucian, Gnostic, and Hermetic roots which are its genetic makeup, we can make it clear that our Traditions are about change rather than allowing them to be conscripted as ill-fitting foot soldiers in the hapless struggle to perpetuate the Old Aeon.

We also shared a belief that Thelema could not be understood either as a one-line aphorism or through *Liber AL* alone. Thelema was a complex revelation, with several distinct inspired sources beyond *Liber AL*, the most powerful and obvious of which was *The Vision and the Voice*. Failure to initiate into the whole of Thelema – failure to comprehend the entirety of the revelation – was the flaw in those who somehow could reconcile gender essentialism or Fascism with Thelema. We also agreed that it was unlikely most modern people would read the entirety of the Thelemic revelation. We needed to communicate the essence of the vast revelation, not just the starting point. Initiations distill the essence of a series of beliefs into a set of passion plays that allowed those ideas to be not just intellectually understood, but emotionalized. If we were to produce initiations, they would not stop at *Liber AL*, but initiate into the entirety of Thelema.

I had questions about whether or not this was the time to set out on our own. What I could not know was that the world was edging towards a breaking point that would separate the past from the future for a generation. The signs were there. If portents and coincidences were definitive we could have no doubt. We received encouragements strange and unexpected.

The Thelemic Initiations

The gender policy was an attack on Rebecca's core identity, even if she was told it wasn't because she "looked like a woman." By December of 2019, she had resigned from O.T.O. With the California question settled, Stephanie had come to terms with the reality that while WBL might have survived the challenge to its existence, there was no place within O.T.O. for the spirit of exploration, dynamicism, and acceptance that had distinguished the Golden Era of WBL. I filed incorporation papers for a non-profit organization in December of 2019, and by the end of the year, The Thelemic Order had emerged into existence. Stephanie had agreed to work with the organization as soon as she had overseen an orderly transfer of power at WBL in January and filed her paperwork to transfer Mastery the night before our announcement. We were saved the problem and several weeks of administrative work. The O.T.O. was not given to graceful partings of the way and she was peremptorily fired, though she was not named in our announcement and had not at that point been involved in more than the discussion of the new organization. As someone who had experienced not just magical, but spiritual revelations, she had a spiritual dimension that I lacked. I immediately asked her to act as Chief Prelate of the new organization.

Deadline and Disaster

In choosing to put together initiations, our work had just begun. I had reckoned aggressively that by dropping everything in my life except for my day job if Z. could deliver initiations by April of 2020, I could perform them in May. However, as borders shut down and the COVID pandemic emerged, it felt at first as if we were being opposed at every turn. Where the wind had been at our back, it suddenly seemed to be blowing in our face. I was bitter at having to cancel initiations not long after they were announced. It was here that Z. once again gave me perspective, making the point, though I do not recall the exact words, that while they could have produced initiations in three months they would produce much better and richer initiations with more time available. It was not that the disaster was good, but that we had been led to throw our gauntlet on its cusp by a current larger than ourselves. The disaster we had been spared loomed large. Unable to hold events or fundraisers we'd have been financially flayed to the bone or forced to give up the Baltimore Lodge.

We agreed to a relaxed timeline and the first set of drafts were delivered in 2020, though the final form would not shape until the summer of 2022. While I had been disappointed, I was forced to agree. Looking over even the rough draft, there was no question that it was better than what we could have accomplished in even the three most compulsive months.

I had some guilt about our schedule as well. I'd rather have done the work and lost sleep than have a ruinous pandemic. But the pandemic was something epochal and beyond our control; an era-defining event. I came to understand that we had been guided as we were to be poised to emerge at the end of it. The pandemic was not giving us time, we were simply being prepared in advance for a role in the new, more dangerous world when it had abated. Had we waited even a few months rather than acting on our resolve, our ties to O.T.O. might have simply melted away in social distancing, and the new initiations would never have been born into the world.

During our long preparation, some expectations changed. I needed to be open to change and compromise. I had originally been insistent that the Initiations could be performed by a single initiator, and I quarreled with Z. when they told me, simply that they could not produce initiations that would function that way, and have the other qualities we assessed. Z. slowly brought me around to the idea that this could not be the case, and suggested ways in which a single initiator might still be able to initiate. Initiation, they pointed out, was social, and it was best presented in a social context. I learned a great deal, including just how much more I have to learn.

Inspiration and Perspiration

If I said that initiations are 1% inspiration, and 99% perspiration, Z. and possibly Rebecca Doll might disagree. Inspiration does play a major role. But as Rebecca Doll has also proven they are a lot of perspiration. For my part I have never minded any of it as I have been fortunate to be working with some of the best beings I could imagine. If Z. has been an inspiration, Rebecca Doll has been a constant reminder both of why these initiations are important and to keep my eyes above any issues in the past and focus clearly on the magic and purpose of these initiations, for they will be around when these circumstances of their invention are antiquarian footnotes.

Stephanie has also been a rock and support, handling all the work of establishing a church while I focused primarily on the initiatory track. As well, she has from time to time reminded me of practical facts. I went around with Z. for some weeks and did a lot of reading in regards to the decision to make the Cathar Court the central fixture for our initial plays. On one hand, it made perfect sense. Where Salah al-Din is the principal figure from the legend of a culture orthogonal to the traditions that produce Thelema, the Occitan court is closely knit with that of Norman England, the Cathar tradition the literal and specific root of the Gnostic tradition of Doinel and Reuss. It is the cultural stem of a vast font of Western esotericism. Yet, Occitania exists today as a discreet culture, and it is not where I was raised nor the language I speak. Was not this a form of appropriation? It was at this point that Stephanie, who spends a lot of time doing genealogy, casually mentioned that she was a literal descendant of Jeanne, Queen of Sicily, and Countess of Toulouse. Z., when told this fact, could only say "of course," as if they had known all along that this mystery was intimately tied to one of our own.

The initiations are seen here in their first public form. Z. stressed that they should be living documents, revised from time to time to retain their relevance and that no hand of tradition should prevail to keep them from being changed, in an orderly fashion, to better lead the people to their goal. Welcome to the Thelemic Initiations. I hope this thorough exploration of the initial three grades will be as fruitful as your initial experience of them.

- James Gordon, February 2022

Overview

In the following pages, we'll provide some framing for the initiation scripts presented later in this work. We'll look at three principle areas:

Introduction – the ideas thinking and concepts behind these particular initiations.

Topics of Interest – these are areas where we believe questions are likely to be raised about these initiations. Sovereign Initiators are going to be asked questions on these topics by initiates and others and we want you to be able to respond with authoritative information where possible.

Presentation and Techniques – these are the technical aspects of initiation. The scripts present the "what" but not the "how." This covers not only elements within the initiations, such as properties, but the framing around the initiations, including negotiation.

Notes – notes about the form, and content of the initiations.

Introduction

The Changing Cycle of Initiations

Every century sees its cycles of initiation. The cycle of initiations traceable from the Edinburgh House Register and the early 18th century sources of Freemasonry lead directly from the Strict Observance and Scottish Rite of the mid 17th century to the 19th-century explosion of esoteric mysteries that included the Rite of Misraim of 1813, the Esoteric initiations of the Brotherhood of Luxor, and the Golden Dawn in the late 19th century, the O.T.O. in the early 20th century, and Wicca in the mid 20th century.

Certainly, each of these initiations included new ideas and new material. As learning increased, and our view of the breadth of what constituted an initiatory experience broadened, there were drastic changes. The Golden Dawn initiations would seem blasphemous and pagan to the Mason of 1721, yet all these initiations carried a spark of Western Hermeticism and Ceremonial magick, haltingly joining that tradition to others around the world.

Initiation in the 21st Century

The 21st century is a time of profound change. Humans living today have unprecedented access to information. Conversations traverse long-established walls of culture and distance in the blink of an eye. While we cannot yet quite erase the barrier of language in regards to higher conversation, translation of simple ideas and mechanical concepts chips away at that last barrier between humans.

Yet there are also vast disparities of wealth, resources, and opportunity. War is prolific. Authoritarian regimes hold sway over vast segments of the world's population, and around the world slavery, in fact, if not in name, is the state of millions.

Ideologically the struggle between the concept of individual determination versus the subjugation of the individual to authoritarian rule is a burning issue.

Currently, the battle is not going well for individualism. Authoritarian thought grows and prospers both in places that have long had some form of totalitarian rule, and within cultures that have previously been disposed toward individual freedom.

Would-be tyrants seeking their own economic or political advantage have taken advantage of inequality in education and opportunity to mislead vast swathes of the population into upholding dangerous and self-defeating practices as emblems of their "freedom," literally expressing their liberty by cutting off their noses to spite their face. The tyrants are not, themselves, opposed to authoritarianism and are thus able to achieve a double victory – profiting in the short term while undermining the legitimacy of the concept of self-determination, helping to entrench their positions. Even those who have long supported individual freedom, too, call for laws and a strong leader to curb public idiocy and self-destructive behavior.

This is nothing new. Throughout the history of the West, bad ideas have been entwined with good. People who do not understand the world around them may be misled, particularly by those who claim superior knowledge, most especially through some divine means. While we would like to remember the witchcraft persecutions as something driven by a medieval church, the fact is that they pertain more to the period we refer to as the "Enlightenment," and were driven as much by nominally egalitarian institutions such as Protestant town councils as by the Roman

Catholic Church. It has been very reasonably suggested that the witch trials were a byproduct of an increasing understanding of science. As it became more clear that the universe operated not by the direct hand of God, but through a set of natural laws which were generally inviolate, actions that had previously simply been attributed to divine wrath seemed to require a proximate cause. If the work of God required human agents working in obedience to fixed laws of nature, then so must the supposed Devil have agents working ill through laws occult, but no less predictable.

The Thelemic Vision

Thelema envisions a world of powerful individuals, each moving forward in their course without collision with others, supplied with all they need and want, governed by an intelligent recognition of their self-interests. The language of the early 20th century was not always enough to express this concept with perfect clarity, nor was it always clear under which political model imagined in the early 20th century this might be best accomplished, but the core understanding that this is what the Thelemic world looks like is unmistakable. While there are musings here and there to clashes of will, the overwhelming focus is on the idea that in a world where everyone follows their true will perfectly, clashes will not exist.

Initiation as Politics

Initiation is apolitical in the sense that it is not aligned with any specific party or narrow ideology. It is not Labor or Conservative, not Republic and Democrat, nor Christian Democrat, nor Socialist.

Yes, initiation is and always has been *political*. Politics is how human beings relate to each other. And initiation is not about *ourselves*, but rather about *understanding our place in the universe*, and that means our place among other people.

Initiation is political and always has been. The Mithraic initiations upheld the far-flung military brotherhood of the Roman Empire, the very invention of Freemasonry was based on the assertion by tradesmen of ancient privilege before a Royal Government. Rosicrucianism the actual Bavarian Illuminati, and 18th century Freemasons were all political organizations that promulgated philosophies antithetical to the rule of Kings, the concept of divine right, and the Ancien Régime. It is no coincidence that "Liberté, égalité, fraternité," is the motto, not only of Republican France, but of the French Masonic Grand Orient and Grand Lodge.

There are indeed places where Crowley argued against democracy. He had watched the elected government of Britain blunder and grind its way through history's most catastrophic and pointless war in Europe, the rise of Mussolini through Constitutional means and intimidation, and evangelism-driven American populist "democracy." He wasn't wrong to see republican systems that could put someone such as Hitler in power as a problem with the "democracy" of the day, and his arguments against democracy, when analyzed, focus primarily on a recognition of the dangers of populism, manipulation, and ignorance. Yet, if the rise of Hitler points to a weakness in democracy, it also underscores the bankruptcy of any attempt to find a "strong man" ruler who will impose a fair and evenhanded law.

Taken in context, Crowley's complaints are justified and focus on those things we see as dangers in our own day – the enthusiasms and intolerance of populism and the manipulation of sentiment. Unfortunately, he was not a political scientist and therefore presents no specific solutions. However, there have been enormous advances in the understanding of political philosophy and science since the 1920s. The systems that provided some degree of an answer to Crowley's legitimate concerns emerged largely in the 1950s and 1960s, though they remain imperfect even where implemented, today.

Thelema does not exist to promote any specific form of government, but since its fundamental principles are light, life, love, and liberty, it is the opposite and foe of authoritarianism, ignorance, repression, and slavery. It is likely the case that none of the extant economic or political models in our world entirely support Thelema, but in practical terms, enlightened and educated democracy is among the systems most *welcoming* to Thelema, while rigid authoritarianism of any sort is that most *opposed*. That is only true, however, of *enlightened* democracy. Unenlightened democracy, or 'mob rule' is nearly as antithetical to Thelema as totalitarianism, perhaps in some cases moreso, for a tyrant can be somewhat enlightened as in the case of Napoleon, while ignorance never fails to be repressive.

The Thelemic Initiations are irrefutably progressive in character. They focus on the concept of "one star in the company of stars," on our interconnection to all things, and on the concept of liberty and personal freedom. Yet we understand these things not as a carte-blanche for selfishness, but rather as imposing a great yoke of responsibility in regards to their use – to create a world in which "Everyone, whatever his ambition, will feel that he can rely on the whole force of the state to assist him; for all ambitions alike will be respected by all, with the single proviso that they shall not tend to restrict the equal right of the rest."[2]

The concept of liberty is enshrined as one of the core values of Thelema alongside love itself, and liberty is fundamentally impossible without equality. As we see above, true liberty must imply equality; one is not truly free if, as Orwell bleakly puts it in *Animal Farm*, "some animals are more equal than others."[3] Freedom is the fruit of liberty, but to use freedom to take that same fruit from others is an abuse and an abomination; the definition of the Abyss. Yet, the Magus must have perspective. We champion not ruthless individual freedom at the cost of others, but rather a responsible exercise of freedom that allows for "the equal right of the rest." To date, democracy is the best device available to achieve egalitarian government.

Initiation as Science

Despite some attempts to frame it that way, the history of occultism and esoteric thought is not a story of a war in opposition to science. The people who created science were also mystics, from Pythagoras and Paracelsus to Sir Isaac Newton and Carl Jung. They sought to explore the inner universe in harmony with the outer universe. Every tradition and discipline valued ancient knowledge and wisdom. If there is a single core to the idea of initiation it is to fully comprehend and experience, rather than merely be told about, the harmony between our deepest inner self and the universe in which we exist.

Science in its true form is about accepting the evidence of the physical universe around us. Magick is about exploring its unseen laws and how we relate to the universe we live in on both a microcosmic and macrocosmic scale. The concept of initiation is indivisible from magick, and discussion of it is woven throughout *magick, Liber ABA, Book 4* (hereafter "*Book Four*")[4] - the Thelemic magnum opus on magical operation.

Science versus Faith

In *Eight Lectures on Yoga*, we are told: We place no reliance

> *On Virgin or Pigeon;*
>
> *Our method is science,*

Our aim is religion.[5]

The full import of this concept is well developed by Rodney Orpheus in his essay titled "The Method of Science, the Aim of Religion."[6]

> "in order to properly examine our experiences and to truly reconnect we need to reject 'belief' - because belief will blind us to the deeper reality that we are trying to find, test, and understand. We may hypothesize about the existence of gods, demons, secret chiefs etc. but we must not believe in them. Not only that, we can only hypothesize insofar as those hypotheses themselves are falsifiable. It is not enough to say 'they exist because I think they exist, and therefore everyone else must believe they exist because I say so'…. Unless we can continually test our hypotheses by observation and prediction, they are not useful."

Orpheus summarizes the principles of science. We cannot "prove" anything with science, merely disprove things. If something cannot be tested we cannot apply the method of science. Orpheus continues:

> The human mind is a great deceiver and our desire for the "religious experience" often blinds us to the reality of it when it happens. Someone goes to a Christian church, prays, and feels an outpouring of transcendent love. Result: they believe that it was because of Jesus, therefore Jesus must exist, therefore he must be immortal if he still exists after death, and therefore he must be invisible if I can feel his presence but no-one else can see him, and so on. So from the flawed attempt at comprehending that mind-blowing transcendent experience flows a whole heap of reasoning that appears on the surface to be logical and coherent, but is actually completely nonsensical. The primary religious experience is "true" inasmuch as the person experiences it, but the secondary beliefs have no validity beyond that, and are likely as not to be "false."

To Orpheus' musings on religion, we'll add George Orwell's classic description of doublethink:

> His mind slid away into the labyrinthine world of doublethink. To know and not to know, to be conscious of complete truthfulness while telling carefully constructed lies, to hold simultaneously two opinions which cancelled out, knowing them to be contradictory and believing in both of them, to use logic against logic, to repudiate morality while laying claim to it, to believe that democracy was impossible and that the Party was the guardian of democracy, to forget whatever it was necessary to forget, then to draw it back into memory again at the moment when it was needed, and then promptly to forget it again: and above all, to apply the same process to the process itself. That was the ultimate subtlety: consciously to induce unconsciousness, and then, once again, to become unconscious of the act of hypnosis you had just performed. Even to understand the word 'doublethink' involved the use of doublethink.[7]

When evangelical Christian leaders demand that their faithful believe in the Old Testament as written, they are perfectly aware that it contains events that never happened. Despite dramatic 1970s conspiracies, the world wasn't flooded up to the altitude of a high mountain in Turkey within historical times, and if there is a giant boat there, it is not because a great flood carried it. There were great floods of course, and the truth of them was passed down in legend. But despite "creation science" and other equivocation, the root of evangelical Christian belief isn't about finding evidence that the Bible is right. It is about believing the stories as written even though one knows they are wrong.

To force acceptance of a known untruth is the first step in building a compliance ladder in which one accepts whatever the Church authorities say. In individual relationships, we call this sort of behavior "gaslighting" after a 1944 movie in which the Charles Boyer character fakes evidence to convince his wife, played by Ingrid Bergman, that she is going insane. As she accepts each instance of proof that she is losing her mind, her belief is deepened, moving closer to Boyer's evil endgame in which she will come to believe herself insane, and therefore disqualify the evidence of her eyes and ears.

Christian fundamentalists use belief in miracles as part of their training in doublethink. Unlike the Charles Boyer character, they can't afford to have their followers be fully delusional. They need them to believe enough to be scared and responsive to the Church message, but also lucid enough to continue to earn a paycheck, even though Christ is supposed to return in the near future. Ancient miracles are a first step in training the believer to "hold simultaneously two opinions which canceled out, knowing them to be contradictory and believing in both of them."

Thelema, and its system of magick, is not about doublethink. It is not about the kind of esotericism which invites belief in a wild variety of unlikely things; a deepening spiral that ends up in a state that invites belief in wild conspiracy theories or fundamental denial of the laws of causality in the universe. Thelemites are skeptical, and they remain skeptical. The path to Thelemic attainment is not one of deepening belief but of parsing away wrong answers until only probability remains. To that end, we don't need to believe that Cagliostro traveled to Egypt and preserved an unbroken strain of initiation which was passed down from Heliopolis, or that Freemasonry preserves a legend that emanates from the time of Solomon. What we do know is that Cagliostro's Egyptian Masonry, and High Degree Craft Masonry, preserve *traditions* that can tell us something important about Western thought, and magick.

This is what distinguishes the seeker of attainment from the simple person of faith. The faithful have no desire or *need* to understand. If the idea of a heavenly throne and city of gold is ridiculous by standards of their day-to-day experience, they simply accept that it will come to pass in some way, because someone said so. By the same token, they accept that this or that charismatic leader will fix things. They hear familiar words and accept them on faith.

Among esotericists, the faithful would prefer to believe in a literal line of transmission from master to initiate from Hermes Trismegistus, even if there never was any such specific person, with all evidence indicating that claims of a direct line to the ancient past are frayed in all directions. Faith in a secret society is easier and less demanding than understanding a tortured set of relationships from Harranians in the 9th century and Paulicians in the 11th century to 12th-century poets and 17th-century pastors. And once one has accepted such a patent falsehood, how much easier to digest the orders of its leadership as truths?

It may be noted that the Foreword to this edition alluded to, but did not give much detail about, the various coincidences and revelations through magick that led to the creation of these initiations. It is not because they did not happen or are not important. Rather it is because they are *unprovable*, and our strident claims that they happened are equally unprovable. The initiate must judge the power of these initiations by their own experience, not by our insistence that this path is, *must be*, of great importance because it is so ordained and spoken.

It may be the case that, having learned to understand the difference between legend, symbol, and fact, we choose to leverage the process of doublethink informedly in our favor, using certain sets of symbols to achieve clarity or states of consciousness that serve us. There is nothing wrong with this. Doublethink is a negative word for the abusive use by outsiders of a property of plasticity that is natural to the human mind. To live hidebound in a black and white world of supposed "fact" can be just as delusive as the wildest flights of fancy associated with faith, and every bit as dangerous. Inability to conceptualize two opposed ideas at once can poison the imagination. It is our work as adepts to ensure this particular plasticity serves us, rather than making us the unintended servants of another.

Initiation as Magick

Magick, understood to be the science of life, is the means to initiation. Perhaps it might be better in the modern period to say that magick is the empirical study of all those things which are not strictly defined by a formal scientific discipline, or which have qualities that exceed current scientific understanding. That includes, at present, our mindscape and the meaning of consciousness. Even if the scientific mechanism of consciousness were perfectly explained, the experience of consciousness is subjective. Science is a process; magick an exploration – yet the two are not incompatible.

As we touch on above, there is much question and argument today over whether magick is objective and real, or whether it is primarily a mental discipline; a tool for psychological mastery of the self. Thelema may embrace both points of view and it is not necessary to take a side to appreciate the importance of magick as the core of initiation. Meditation and contemplation are only the first part of *Book Four* which leads smoothly into a core understanding of these initiations. The book is about magick, and it is magick that is core to attainment.

Thelema is complete in "Do what thou wilt…" in the same way that Einstein's Theory of Special Relativity is "complete" in E=MC2. The single element suggests it – may even sometimes come to stand for it – but it is not the whole thing, or even the simplified expression of the whole thing. "Do what thou wilt…" is incomplete without the recognition that every person is a star. Likewise, *Liber AL* is not the entirety of Thelema, though it may be understood to be its foundation.

Thelema does not exist in a vacuum. The core of its ideals existed before Crowley and as he identifies them with Rabelais, connecting it to all the thought between Rabelais and Crowley himself. The magical systems and symbols of Thelema, even those core to it rather than passing references, are derived from myriad sources. Most importantly, Thelema embraces a specific set of increasingly complex and murky revelations. If we credit any Crowley's statement that Aiwass dictated *Liber AL*, and thereby it is inspired work, we must credit his insistence that Aiwass was a hand or influence in all of his work. All the inspired, prophetic, or prophesied work must be interpreted as core to Thelema, though we may question whether it is foundational or clarifying. This includes even *Book Four*, which was predicated by the Abul-ul-diz working. Thus we must see *Book Four* not as a mere technical manual, but as a key element in the Thelemic revelation, one which the author explicitly intended to be illustrated by a system of initiations.

Teaching magick

We cannot teach magick, per se, in two-hour initiations. That said, we include some degree of working, or basic instruction on a working, in most of the initial rituals and it is fair to ask why?

We make it clear that magick is an important part of initiation; that it is the key to attainment. Yet, it is our experience that a phenomenal number of Thelemites have done little or no magick themselves. There are several reasons for this. One is that they have been told by those better read in Thelemic magick that they "aren't ready." This is often more a matter of self-aggrandizement than basic safety. Another is that they don't have any coherent overview of how the various common Thelemic rituals fit together or form the basis for a regular practice.

We cannot teach magick, but we can give a taste of it, and make sure that no one passes to II° without having ever worked *any* actual ritual. We can also endeavor to link a series of key rites that can form the backbone of a core practice. By giving some magick instruction in a group setting, we introduce magick to our initiations and open the minds of our initiates to the boundless possibilities of what we can do. Most of all, we convey permission to do magick. It is one thing to say "go and do this," but that becomes difficult when an initiate is told that a given ritual is "dangerous," that they are "not advanced enough," and so forth. By literally walking the initiate through a given ritual, we give the initiate permission to go forth and do in a way more powerful than mere exhortation.

The Meaning of Initiation

There is a widespread misconception that attainment is about apprehending deity, or the self as deity, or perhaps the interconnectedness of everything – that it is about attaining a state for which we borrow the Yogic term "Samadhi," a state of apprehension of the absolute undiluted by ego. While something of this sort may have been true for medieval Gnosticism, it is not true for modern Thelema. A brief reading of the Thelemic source materials reveals that this state, even the ability to hold this state for lengthening periods, is not itself attainment, but rather a discipline that may lead to attainment.

In the modern era, this mental state which could previously be reached only through contemplation, often with training mandating extreme asceticism, can be reached fairly easily by anyone who is able to safely use one of many entheogenic substances, which include psilocybin. If you want to call such usage a "shortcut" or "cheating," you can, but the fact is that the pioneers of Thelema did not hesitate to use such means as an aid. In any case, the point here is that reaching an ego-free state is not the core of attainment, but rather its first practical step.

The goal of a 21st-century initiation is to harness the good of our traditions while placing them in the context of our present-day culture, particularly those concepts embedded in Thelema such as freedom of gender expression, respect for the natural order, and respect for all people, which have also become core elements of progressive thought. We do not aspire to a "universal" initiation that incorporates every system from every culture because those cultures and traditions are not our properties. Instead, we present a basis for respectful exploration of other traditions, while focusing on those traditions that led directly to Thelema.

The Work of Attainment

Seeing oneself as a star among stars may be important, but it is not the end goal of initiation or attainment. It is rather a tool that can help reach attainment. The primitive Gnostics thought that we were trapped in flesh by an evil creator and that our role was to escape this world of misery. Thelema teaches nothing of the sort and explicitly rejects the Buddhist model of a world of sorrows. If the point of attainment were no more than to transcend the material universe, why do it at all? We are here to act out our will not, as the ancient Gnostics thought, to escape from a prison.

True attainment is not transcending our world or apprehending the divine, or even becoming the divine. It is using that to impact our world and to fully implement our will. It is *the accomplishment of our will*. That is the difference between a mere contemplative ascetic and a true magician – one who conforms the world about them to their own will, and in doing so improves it.

In the introductory discussion to *Liber 418, The Vision and the Voice*, the revelations following the invocation of the fifteenth Aethyr describes examination by an assembly of adepts and admission to the Second Order: the Grade of Babe of the Abyss, a Master of the Temple. The following invocation – that of the fourteenth Aethyr – led to a ritual of sex magick and ensuing events, during which "Mine Angel whispered the secret words whereby one partakes of the Mysteries of the Masters of the Temple." From it, we learn:

> *My mind and body, deprived of the Ego which they had hitherto obeyed, were now free to*
> *manifest according to their nature in the world, to devote themselves to aid mankind in its*

evolution. In my case I was to be cast out into the Sphere of Jupiter. My mortal part was to help humanity by Jupiterian work, such as governing, teaching, creating, exhorting men to aspire to become nobler, holier, worthier, kinglier, kindlier, and more generous.[8]

While there might be many different courses of such devotion, there is no path whereby selfishness prevails. There may be limited room for "tough love," and Crowley certainly believed in such a thing, but our current understandings of science and human behavior indicate that such behaviors are usually narcissistic and counterproductive – merely excuses to gratify the ego by lashing out while pretending to be "helpful." It seems unlikely that there is a great deal of "tough love" required of those who attain.

While tough love may be a matter for debate, it is beyond debate that those who attain have work to do. Moreover, that work is not some minor effort from the shadows, but strong proactive roles "exhorting." Despite Crowley's misgivings about "being kind" in the narrow sense of Christian hypocrisy, we are here told unambiguously that the work of the Master of the Temple is to increase kindness and generosity. We may disagree on the mechanisms or best courses, but we cannot suggest that it involves sitting in quiet contemplation. The Master of the Temple is by no means a perfected Adept, but rather has many steps yet in learning to wield their newfound power.

The Elements of Initiation

The Thelemic Initiations present a very specific worldview and path which is Thelema. They have historical elements, and they teach a lot about where we came from because it is necessary to have a solid foundation if one wants to build a tower that reaches the stars. Yet, they also infuse a certain worldview that is not always common in esotericism, but should be common in Thelema. They embody skepticism, pragmatism, and a respect for the inflexible laws of nature because any supposed initiation that cannot survive in the real world is of no use to us. Unless our will happens to be to sit and vegetate, and that seems unlikely to represent anyone's true will, initiation that does not afford us the means to accomplish our will is not truly initiation at all.

The Thelemic Initiations are not a light undertaking. They are packed with symbolism, history, and knowledge, though they unfold in a way that puts more emphasis on the overview rather than the details. In most cases, the idea is more to convey the arc of previous systems of initiation and allow the Adept to recognize how they relate to our own than to force the assimilation of great levels of detail. For example, passing reference is made to Cornelius Agrippa's *Passing the River* script. Knowing it exists and being able to identify concepts which the script embodies – from the fact that it is based on the Hebrew alphabet to the key metaphor of "passing over" and its connection to crossing the Abyss – may be useful in seeing relationships between our initiations and other traditional sources. Learning to write the script itself, while it may be a fascinating skill, is unlikely to be necessary to achieve attainment. We focus more on general awareness than excessive memorization or detailed study of any specific body of writing or esoterica.

It is often repeated among authors and dramatists that there are only a handful of basic stories. Yet, those stories must be retold again and again, in ways that speak to a contemporary audience. *Jaws*, with its beach town threatened by a shark, may be more meaningful to contemporary people than *Beowulf* with its mead hall. Most of us have probably seen more beach towns than mead halls. In this way, the Thelemic Initiations are a melding of antiquity to the present day and the future; of the Hermetic past to the New Aeon.

The focus on History

A focal element of the Thelemic Initiations is the actual history of our traditions, which is largely absent in the initiations of the 20ᵗʰ century. This is important for three reasons.

Firstly, we are proportionately more remote from those teachings. It is not the case that most anyone likely to undertake an initiation is already somewhat familiar with the Masonic mystery of the Arch of Enoch, or has read the *Fama Fraternitatis*.

Secondly, many of our traditions are incomplete or have been eroded in their transmission. Historical stories originally presented as true secrets in the 18ᵗʰ and 19ᵗʰ centuries were exposed by scholarship as transparently false, leading them to seem somewhat hokey and embarrassing, as with the story of George Washington and the cherry tree. In continuing to present these stories with the understanding that they are legend, there was a tendency in many traditions to gloss them; to omit the details as if telling an old child's fairy story one is self-conscious to admit to remembering, and certainly does not wish to be mistaken for taking seriously. It is hard to present Hiram or the Lost Mark strongly if one knows they are recent fabrications. Crowley's choice of Salah ad-Din is reflective of this. From his introduction onward, the character is clearly metaphorical.

We endeavor to reclaim the core meaning of these stories while associating them with legitimate historical facts to the best of our understanding according to the archaeology and anthropology of our day. There is much in them that is fabricated, but those fabrications served the point of illustrating ancient truths. A suburban father might be slightly embarrassed to even know the story of "Jack-and-the-Beanstalk," but we look at it with reverence, siding with folklorists who link it to Aarne-Thompson-Uther Folklore Index as story ATU 328 "The Boy who Stole the Ogre's Treasure" and the Cornish tradition of "Jack tales," ultimately tracing the core back over five millennia.

Thirdly, the 21ˢᵗ century has seen a resurgence of what may be broadly termed "European Traditional magick." The term "Grimoire Revival" has been widely used in reference to this movement, but that narrow term fails to account for the return or revitalization of other non-grimoire strands of magick. Thousands of books of magick that were nearly unknown have become accessible and, in many cases, edited and published with commentary. This phenomenon also extends to non-European sources; particularly, the Greek magical Papyri (PGM) texts which have become far more widely available. Thus, the secrets of 17ᵗʰ century magick, a subject considered so remote as to be of only marginal interest to the occultists of 1922, may be of significant relevance to the occultist of 2022. Without the knowledge to tie the rich trove of "discovered" material to Thelema, it may seem as if the modern magical renaissance has left Thelema behind, even where it is rooted in texts from the first to 18ᵗʰ centuries.

The Process of Initiation

The Thelemic Initiations are an exploration of the Thelemic Tradition. They serve two classic purposes of initiation:

Initiation into the Community

In the first place, going through them makes one a functional, as well as symbolic, member of the Thelemic community. You not only aspire to be a Thelemite, but you know the things which it is appropriate to know and understand those things on a level adequate to explain them to others.

The Thelemic Initiations

Initiation into the Mysteries

In the second place, the Thelemic Initiations unfold the mysteries of Thelema and a path to attainment in a Thelemic context. Like the suggestion that "Osiris is a Black God," these mysteries are hardly unknown. They are articulated throughout the Thelemic writings. The Initiations create an emotional context for personalizing them and understanding them; for living and experiencing them.

The length and difficulty of presentation affect the ability of any initiation to grow. It might be ideal to take a week, or even a month, for a single initiator to initiate a single Petitioner, but it is in no way practical. It is not a thing that can happen in our current society outside of a select few individuals. Certainly, the general length of Crowley's ritual is about correct. A ritual running two to three hours is manageable and easy enough to propagate. The Law is for All; not just for those who can afford to take a month away from work. However, this generates the necessity for what might be called "homework." The Initiatory ritual begins the alchemical process of transformation, concentrates its ingredients. But there is no time for the whole process to take place within the framework of a single ritual.

In practical terms, we realize that single initiatory moments may be part of the process, may contribute to it, or may be a distracting byproduct. Above, we quoted Rodney Orpheus: "Someone goes to a Christian church, prays, and feels an outpouring of transcendent love. Result: they believe that it was because of Jesus, therefore Jesus must exist, therefore he must be immortal if he still exists after death, and therefore he must be invisible if I can feel his presence but no-one else can see him, and so on." This is no less true of initiatory experiences. One has a moment within or, more likely, in the weeks after initiation and decides uncritically to believe that everything repeated in initiation is true. It is for this reason we repeat, many times, that not everything within the initiation is literally or objectively true. The problem with the focus on single experiences is that they may make the initiate less inclined to continue to search the initiatory material and the events which come after initiation for those shreds of meaning that are the signposts to attainment.

Profound experiences during or after initiation should be taken as part of the overall larger process. They may be moments in which profound change is revealed, like the sudden slip of a melting glacier into the sea, even though the melting began long ago and will continue after.

Topics of Interest

Questions, Controversies, and Misunderstandings

Every cycle of initiation prompts questions and, without answers, the initiation may accumulate controversy and misunderstanding. Sovereign Initiators have taken the Oath of the Rose Cross Knight and serve as guides along the initiatory path. Just as any guide must understand the roads, the road signs, and the dangers of a region, so the Sovereign Initiator must understand the areas in which questions will be asked.

This section is eclectic by design. We look at how the Thelemic Initiations differ from the historical initiations put forward through the O.T.O. by Reuss and Crowley, at the influence of Kabbalah, at issues such as gender, at the use of Cathar history, and at other subjects which are likely to raise questions.

Thelema and Western Culture

Why Do We Care about a Tradition

There is no universal agreement on what "initiation" means. We use it in a sense defined as "admission into a secret group," yet the word itself comes from the Latin verb for beginning. To initiate is to begin. When Crowley says of the Golden Dawn "In short, the Order failed to initiate,"[9] he doesn't mean they failed to open the doors, run rituals, or admit candidates. There is something deeper intended.

Historically, initiation into mystery cults was designed to produce a profound change or elevation in the individual. They would move forward along some "path" because they learned a key "mystery" that told them something they didn't know about life. As we mentioned in passing above, Eliphas Levi claimed that, in the Eleusinian Mysteries, the final secret told to the initiate is "Osiris is a Black God."[10] The intimation is that the God of Life was the God of Death; a sentiment echoed by Crowley in his *Liber XV*[11] "I am Life, and the giver of Life, yet therefore is the knowledge of me the knowledge of death." This isn't a piece of random information such as "the bus station is by the railway depot," or even a piece of life advice such as "don't make assumptions." It is intended to be transformative; to change how the individual thinks about life and death.

Levi may or may not have been accurate about the core of the Eleusinian mysteries, but he certainly gets the general idea. The initiate was expected to walk away with a fundamentally different understanding of the universe and their place in it, not simply to say "huh I didn't know Osiris moonlighted…" This type of initiation is "Gnostic" in the sense that it triggers a deep change that reveals the connection of the self to the infinite. The core of revived mysteries in Europe through Rosicrucianism, Cagliostro's lines of Esoteric Freemasonry, Doinel's Gnostic Church, and so forth focused on a core Gnostic revelation: the true nature of God which is, in the Thelemic sense, both the self and all others.

The problem is that there are literally no major tropes of Western philosophical thought which are not well known. "God is life and death" is the summary of dozens of short stories, novels, and movies. Far from being a cult secret, the core of the Eleusinian mysteries is also at the heart of David Bowie's final album "Black Star" which has sold two million copies worldwide. The idea that sex can be used to establish a conduit to the infinite is known to anyone who has spent more than twenty minutes in an esoteric book store. Even the core Thelemic idea that we are God "I am alone, there is no God where I am," can be found throughout media and pop psychology.

Given the ready availability of the "true secrets," one might think that everyone would be a walking Bodhisattva, dispensing the wisdom of the ages. But the path is still crooked. In Crowley's day, it was crooked because it was still hard for people of average means to come by the knowledge. In our day, there is a profusion of information, penetrating to levels of society it did not reach a hundred years ago. Where there was famine now there is feast. The modern seeker is awash in ideas.

That it is possible to be a Thelemite for 20 years and have assimilated little more than the rudimentary philosophy of Thelema will not be a shock to many. Certainly, Thelema is no worse than Christianity, where a vast swath of adherents seems to somehow have missed the very essence of their own religion. "A new commandment I give unto you: That you love one another, as I have loved you, that you also love one another."[12]

We could level endless critique at the descendants of Crowley's initiatory model, but it is enough to say that in many or most cases they "fail to initiate." Our work is to create a new system that *does* initiate; to approach Thelema as a whole tradition, not as little more than DWTW and *Liber AL* while relying on a presumption of A∴A∴ initiation for any true instruction. It means to present the entirety of the Thelemic system in a coherent manner. Still, it is impossible to include all of it. Z. observed that:

> "Initiations have a lot in common with writing screenplays from full-length novels. The author has a huge work to distill that needs to be reduced to a script that must run not much more than two hours. It is all about what to leave in and what to leave out. There is a lot of hinting and throwing in small details. Too many details and the screenplay doesn't hold together – it's just a confusing swirl of parts. That was the failure with the G.D. initiations. Too few details and the screenplay doesn't convey the original work. That seems to be the problem with Crowley's original initiations."

The Roots of Thelema

Thelema is a genuine and legitimate religion, older than quite a few of the world's faiths, and where it deeply incorporates borrowed ideas, it does so to a purpose. It is not an attempt to re-brand some culture's faith and resell it rather, to create a syncretic new practice, unlike any predecessor. For example, there are certain yogic principles and terms, such as "Samadhi" deeply woven into Thelema, but they have a unique interpretation in Thelemic context. Crowley was not a hipster who bought a few books off of Amazon and set up a retreat for wealthy influencers. What he learned was principally from Allan Bennett who studied Hatha Yoga under the yogi Ponnambalam Ramanathan. Whatever else one can say, his thirst to learn other systems of belief was genuine and his belief in his mission to integrate them into a new faith was quite sincere.

There is no serious debate that Crowley's system of magick was derived principally from the Hermetic Order of the Golden Dawn which attempted to syncretize the major strains of European and Near-Eastern Tradition. Where it differs markedly, it shows the influence of Theosophy, as well as Bennett and Crowley's travels in Asia and America. While the system of magick is not the whole of Thelema, it is the key to attainment and, therefore, critical to our purpose. We could add that, where Thelema manifests shortcomings as a philosophy, it is because the missing parts were intended to be filled by the experience of Knowledge and Conversation, or whichever of the numerous terms provided one prefers to use. Thelema is Gnostic because the missing elements in its ideology are meant to be revealed through practice.

In terms of the traditions from which Thelema emanated, we focus on those which are closely and indisputably linked to the organizations and writers who provided the foundation on which it was erected: Gnosticism and Neo-Gnosticism, Hermeticism, Hermetic Qabalah, Rosicrucianism, Esoteric Freemasonry, and those elements of Eastern thought specific to Thelema, most heavily those emanating from Blavatsky and Bennett. In regards to all of these, we give due regard to the sources from which they emanated, including classical Paganism, Judaism, and Christianity. In particular, we try to portray the degree to which Paganism, Hermeticism, Judaism, Islam, and Christianity represent a spectrum of interrelated beliefs; a core idea of Theosophy which was, itself, a major influence on Thelema.

The closer we get to the present strains, the harder it is to differentiate ideas from organizations and individual people. One does not associate Johannes Valentinus Andreae with Rosicrucianism the way one associates Helena Blavatsky with Theosophy. We can call out the work of Paschal Beverly Randolph, the Hermetic Brotherhood of Luxor, the Theosophical Society, the Golden Dawn, and the Gnostic Catholic Church of Doinel and Papus, but in doing so we leave out dozens of other groups and authors, esoteric and secular, which influenced Thelema.

What to Leave In and What to Leave Out?

To tie Thelema to its historical roots is a delicate balancing act. It is not intended to be European, white, or even Western. It is a practice for all and that vision is core to it. Thelema is syncretist, meaning that it seeks to combine different forms of belief and practice to promote the concept of a universal shared dignity among all peoples. By necessity, syncretic religions do not remain within any one narrow path.

Some will turn up their nose at our concern over cultural appropriation as mere posturing or political correctness. Ironically some of those same individuals are most obsessed with establishing "legitimate" succession and agonize over the matter of a "direct connection" to Crowley. The fact is that the issue of appropriation is the true core of legitimacy; the yardstick of what is and is not ours to teach.

There is a very difficult and circular issue here that we have to acknowledge. No one would question that it is wildly inappropriate for us to use the character of an Evenk Saman or a Mescalero Apache Medicine Man as a foil in our tradition. We live in an era when we recognize the rights of peoples to their own traditions, as well as the imperialistic nature of the appropriation of the stories of others. The alternative is just as bad. If we refuse to acknowledge influences and disciplines other than a few narrow traditions from Western Europe, West Asia, and North Africa, we run the risk of continuing a form of cultural imperialism that suggests that only white European traditions have real merit or depth. Caught between a desire not to represent traditions that are not ours to represent, and the fear of over-representing the traditions which are definitely our rightful heritage, we might well abandon the idea of presenting any historical tradition at all.

Certainly, that has been done. Scientology is probably the best known and most successful take on a completely sterile new tradition. L. Ron Hubbard was a member of Agape Lodge and could be said to share the same basic esoteric background as Phyllis Seckler, the founder of the College of Thelema. He saw there was a profit to be made in recycling the traditions of Western esotericism in a completely new, branded, wrapper. If Scientology is the most noxious example, it is not unique. There are any number of "New Age" flavored movements which have stripped all past tradition away, or neutered it to the point of insipidity. We favor present-day syncretism – including the willingness to incorporate modern elements of esoterica that fall under the general category of "high weirdness" into our practices. Yet, there is a fundamental difference in picking up the present as we find it and putting a new coat of paint on the past and calling it our own.

The Disconnection of Thelema

The disciples of Crowley certainly had better and less rapacious intent than Hubbard, but they fell victim to some of the same fallacies. Crowley certainly thought highly of his writing, but he encouraged broad reading in numerous disciplines. He assumed that learned esoteric readers would have read not only his work but a variety of other authors.

This has not always been the case. There are Thelemites who read little, if any, in the way of esoteric which was not written by Crowley. The result is a form of Thelema that has been, not entirely jokingly, called "Crowleyism," in which his central corpus is regarded as an end-all and be-all. Not unexpectedly, the work of authors other than those either annotating Crowley, or at least writing primarily only in reference to his body of work, is deprecated.

There are a lot of reasons this occurs. Crowley wrote quite a lot and never owned a computer. While he made efforts at centralizing his knowledge, e.g. *magick Without Tears*,[13] he lacked the resources to do so in a comprehensive way. He lived at a time when media was more expensive and less pervasive than the present day, and he reasonably assumed anyone truly interested in the esoteric had a lot of time to read. Resultingly, studying his entire body of work is exhausting and, once someone has mastered it, they are rightfully proud and tend to be resistant to taking in additional giant bodies of knowledge and practice. Thus they define everything in terms of Crowley. Their interest in cross-pollination is, in many cases, limited or nonexistent. Less admirably there are those with personal relationships to Crowley, legitimate or largely symbolic, who called on those relationships for status within the Thelemic world. They had little or no interest in encouraging reading or thinking outside of the "Crowleysphere" and passed this principle along to their own disciples.

The result is a form of Thelema that has lost a connection with the rest of the esoteric world. This might not be a problem if it actually *were* Scientology – a behemoth that provides for all needs, however badly. But Thelema does nothing of the sort and ends up alienating many Thelemites in the process. Much existing Thelemic culture makes it easy to either have no day-to-day practice of magick at all or to become immersed in a *Liber XV* obsessed system of Thelemic practice that does no more than scratch the surface of the Thelemic corpus. Crowley's publication of Mathers' translation of the *Lemegeton* may have been seminal in Goetia, but Goetia has no place in much systemic modern Thelemic Practice.

An exacerbating factor is the over-reliance on *Liber AL* which, though it is rightly the beginning of the Thelemic revelation, is not its endpoint. There is a vast wealth of other material – some inspired, some partially inspired and some merely technical – that is available but is stressed only within the narrow confines of A∴A∴; a specialized structure of teachers and students that is outside our scope. It is enough to note that most of those who have promulgated Thelema, including several popular writers, have had a vested interest in one of the multiple, generally rival, A∴A∴ "lineages" and that interest may have narrowed their inclination to teach beyond the basics. Whatever function any of the A∴A∴ lineages serve, and it is impossible to categorize them broadly as they have very different qualities. Their system of lengthy individualized teaching means are not going to be the way that the vast *majority* of Thelemites interact with Thelema, nor is membership in any branch of A∴A∴ necessary to the accomplishment of Will.

For reference, neither Z. nor the editors of this work are, or have ever been, members of any A∴A∴ structure or organization, and have no interest in the promotion of any of its branches. While there are branches of A∴A∴ that are quite reputable, we do advise anyone interested to look carefully at the written work, history, and character of the leaders of any group they are interested in joining.

A Magical Renaissance

There is another equally pressing reason not to abandon our ties to the past and that is that the past has never been more present. The decades of widespread online presence have led to a completely new element in magical practice and tradition. As libraries, museums, and collectors around the world began to digitize source material and systems like WorldCat emerged to classify and list existing material, the accessibility of ancient materials began to emerge. MacGregor Mathers put a mark on the esoteric world for more than a century with the release of one relatively obscure magical treatise, *The Book of the Sacred magick of Abramelin the Mage*,[14] which he found in manuscript edition at the Bibliotheque de l'Arsenal in Paris. Mathers also worked with Crowley to bring out an edition of the *Lemegeton* or *Lesser Key of Solomon*.[15] In this case, the work was not unknown, but had been incorporated in haphazard and garbled fashion into many more recent sources. While neither of these editions is perfect, Mathers proved that the release of older material could have an impact on modern practice.

The volume of material released since the turn of the century is a thousand times what Mathers released. In the immediate frame, it has brought about a revival of European Traditional magick, practices based on the Greek Magical Papyri (PGM), and other branches of magick. The phenomenon has been written about and commented on narrowly as the "grimoire revival," but is more broadly an information-driven paradigm shift in access to all historical materials.

As time goes by, an obsession with the exact reconstruction of authentic tradition will give way to a balanced incorporation of that tradition into modern work. In practice, most of the revivalist authors have engaged in at least some syncretic incorporation of ancient into modern practice, but this is not a simple fad that will blow away. The centuries of material released, in many cases in excellent well-commented new editions, is not going to go back in the box. A generation of magicians is learning this material and it is not going to be forgotten any more than Mathers' *Goetia*.

Given the seminal role of Crowley's publication of Mathers' *Goetia* and his own investment in the Abramelin working, one would think that Thelema would stand at the forefront of this powerful intellectual movement to recover the traditions from which it emerged. In sad fact, mainstream Thelema has done little to embrace this movement, though many individual Thelemites are, of necessity, involved with it. One result has been an exodus of ex-Thelemites who were led to an interest in European Traditional magick through Thelema but, in the end, could not see any real relevance of the Thelemic system to their traditionalist practice, grimoire-based or otherwise.

The late 18th and 19th centuries saw an increased awareness in Europe of a sort of cultural sterility. A driving reason for this was that the rise of the hegemonic medieval papacy, followed by the reactionary Protestant and Counter-Reformation movements which, in some ways, mirrored Scientology. In the interest of taking power from old traditions, new leaders literally destroyed those traditions, sterilizing them in the name of a purified Christianity that served the interests of the governing elite. While arguably well-intentioned, Protestants were among the most ardent "purifiers."

The late 18th and 19th centuries saw Europeans, especially Protestant Europeans, recognizing the hollowness and superficiality of their traditions, and this can be seen in thousands of places. The interest of the Romantics in Catholicism says less about an ardent dedication to the papacy than a desire to connect with a spiritual past that had not been scoured to bare boards. The Romanticism of Shelley or Rossetti mixed with numerous branches of pagan revivalism such as the forgery-based Secret Societies of Iolo Morganwg. This coincided with nascent anthropology which, albeit in an imperfect and flawed fashion, began the process of understanding the value in all cultures and spirituality.

The Thelemic Initiations

If 19th century saw Westerners come to understand that cultures other than their own had much to offer, their privileged response was often to simply seize the trappings of those cultures, as if by doing so they could also assimilate their resilience and values. The peoples of those cultures were often subjected to treatment that ranged from patronizing to genocidal. For that reason alone, the rediscovery of European Traditional magick and North African and West Asian Traditions is healthy for everyone. Rather than asserting the *primacy* of European traditions, it places them in *perspective*. It provides an authentic way for those who have European roots of any kind to explore ancestral tradition, without the need to lay claim to traditions that are not their own. Safe in having a rich tradition, they can approach other cultures with curiosity, respect, and reverence.

The Conundrum of Syncretism

Not all Thelemites are European, nor did Crowley see Thelema as a principally European/North African/West Asian Tradition. Thelema contains intimations of West African Tribal magick, as well as strong Buddhist and Yogic elements, and influences from dozens of other sources. Yet, Crowley did not learn magick in West Africa or, for the most part, in Southeast Asia.

We cannot pretend that Thelema, with its heavily Western magical system, is not descended principally from European, North African, and West Asian sources. To do so is to create another sterilizing fiction. We must be honest about the roots of Thelema. This may argue for the development of different initiations, forms, and expressions of Thelema by those who have a legitimate claim on traditions which the present authors do not, and such evolutions should be celebrated. As we provide a starting point, others will hopefully come to add respectful elements which continue to syncretize other traditions.

There will never be agreement between all people on what is and is not appropriative. Even discussing the issue is anathematic to those who would slam a hard black and white shutter down on any interpretation that is not their own. For those people, no discussion will be productive, but the answer to such a reaction is not to veer to the opposite extreme of intolerance and declare that we don't care about issues of cultural sensitivity. We most certainly do, and we represent the moderate norm. In our case, we balance the issue of cultural sensitivity with genuine and authentic religious, philosophical, and spiritual beliefs.

We feel that there is a difference between a respectful decision to enter into a culture and a desire to take its trappings. The work done by Allan Bennett in learning and then acting as a missionary for Theravada Buddhism differs intrinsically from a New York Lawyer who opens a "sweat lodge" after paying an impoverished indigenous person to teach him the rudiments of his culture. For absolutists this idea is contemptible, but Thelema is not about absolutes. Within the world of art and literature, there is a value placed on the difference between those who work with a genuine vocation and passion, and those who simply want to collect a paycheck. The difference is subjective, but that doesn't make it any less real.

There is a difference between broad practices which have, for centuries, been written about and widely promulgated, such as Buddhism, and practices that are the ancestral rites of an indigenous people, particularly if those people have been victimized. In determining the nature of a given culture in this regard, one (but not the only) factor we take into account is initiation. We do not need to concern ourselves with the legitimacy of any *individual's* initiation. There are certainly people who have bought, extorted, or coerced the outward sign of initiation, but there are also those who earn initiation through respect, devotion, and work. Whatever the case, that which can only be shared through initiation tied to a single people is not ours to teach unless it is part of our heritage.

It goes without saying that any attempt to extend this prohibition to modern syncretic traditions such as the Golden Dawn or Thelema is ludicrous. "Thelemites" are not an indigenous people. Nonetheless, someone will surely raise the quibble that we reference the IX° secret, which Crowley often referred to as the IX° O.T.O., when we are not, and make no pretense to be, the O.T.O. To be clear, we do not and cannot grant the IX° of the Ordo Templi Orientis or the Typhonian Order or any other such organization, just as we cannot grant the Royal Arch Degree of the United Grand Lodge of England. We grant the Royal Arch Degree of M∴M∴ which shares the same core secret, but is part of a different tradition.

That the secret exists apart from the organization is beyond question. Crowley records that Reuss at first thought he had stolen it and then concluded he had come into the secret on his own. It is derived from Paschal Beverly Randolph's Ansairetic Mystery Secret. We do not present it as part of any one specific degree, but rather unfold it slowly, throughout all the Thelemic Initiations, as would doubtless have been the case if Crowley and Reuss had not worked within a framework where its exposure was likely to bring ostracization at least and legal action at worst. The IX° O.T.O. is the property of that specific organization, but the secret itself is common to the core thread of Western Esotericism.

We finally note that there is a considerable difference between referencing something and teaching something. We reference many things which are not ours to teach. We reference Sufism, Jewish Kabbalah, and West African Tribal Religion because it is important to understand their influence on Thelema and to demonstrate our respect. It is further important to empower those who have a legitimate connection to those things to incorporate them into Thelema to enrich themselves and others, but that is work the current authors cannot do. It is quite possible, probable even, that this is not the only set of Thelemic Initiations even today, and it is certain that the future will see new cycles of initiations put together by those who have grown up in an environment that constructively syncretized traditions which it is not the wherewithal of the current recipients to incorporate. Those approaching Thelema with a primary background in Tao or Yi Jing, or West African Tribal Religion might create an entirely different set of initiations. The initiations laid out here are the initiations which it is given to us to create and it is our intention to act authentically, leaving Thelema neither adrift and rootless nor claiming roots it does not really have.

We teach those things which are core to the traditions we have inherited, either because they are part of Traditional European, North African and West Asian magick, or because they were deeply integrated into Thelema by people who learned them appropriately. We proclaim nothing as the one true way, though the corollary is not true. The fact that many paths lead to the destination does not mean that *all* paths lead to the destination. There are beliefs and fallacies that we can concretely express to be wrong. The best example might be the idea of one truth and one path as applied to Thelema. Thelema is heterodox and eclectic.

In the Thelemic Initiations, we set out the rich tradition of Thelema, from the distant mists of time to *Liber AL* and the complex revelations that followed it. Those who initiate have earned it as their legacy wherever their roots happen to be, but we do not pretend it is something that it is not. In doing so, we take exceptional pains to present the warts and blemishes of the past. We do not hate our traditions, but we do not pretend they are perfect or that the people who moved them forward through the centuries were without failings. We present them realistically so that they can be valued for what they are, not for what they are not.

The Initiations of Reuss and Crowley

In this discussion, we attempt to balance some concern for discretion in regards to a system that is still being worked in earnest by some groups with the necessity of a broad conversation about the future of Thelemic initiation. For that reason, there are references to the published works that may constitute "spoilers." Just as it would be difficult to write about Crowley's system without reference to the G.D. it is difficult to write about our own system without reference to his.

That we have Crowley's rituals is not a matter of theft, accident, or coincidence. Gerald Yorke, as well as providing a considerable amount of direct support to Crowley in his career, was the principal collector of his papers both before his death and posthumously. Along with Israel Regardie, he was one of the two living authorities regarded by Grady McMurtry as the "Eyes of Horus" when McMurtry sought validation of his efforts to restart Crowley's O.T.O. in the 1960s.

If we credit Yorke as an eye, we must credit him with possessing some of the foresight of Horus. Certainly, no one knew Crowley's inclinations or the fragility of his reputation better. Yorke chose to release most of Crowley's initiatory material to journalist and occultist Francis X. King, who published it as *The Secret Rituals of the O.T.O.* in 1973[16] (hereafter noted as "King" in this text). The only element which Yorke either withheld or did not have was a document ambiguously titled *IX° Emblems and Modes of Use* which details Crowley's conceptualization of sex magick. This has been widely published online and can be found most recently in the excellent collection *Amor Divina, Writings on the Sexual Praxis of Ordo Templi Orientis.*[17]

That the rituals published by King are genuine is beyond question. Jerry Cornelius, one of the long time core members of McMurtry's re-founded O.T.O., noted that McMurtry, who certainly knew the outline of initiations, "did openly use it for years while acting as a Saladin," and that "When I received my own Charter to Initiate through the O.T.O. in the late seventies Grady told me to use King's book and he'd send me the originals later."[18] While it could be argued that McMurtry himself was not familiar with the initiatory rituals, Phyllis Seckler, then married to McMurtry, had been at Agape Lodge, was certainly familiar with their framework, and expressed no reservations about the authenticity when she commented on the publication of King's work.[19]

Crowley's Ideas on Initiation

Crowley had opinions on what an initiation should be, and while we have already referenced them in passing his assessment of the Golden Dawn initiations from "The Temple of Solomon The King" *Equinox* vol. 1, no. 2, is worth quoting at length:

> To even the most casual student it must be apparent, once he has finished reading these rituals, that though they contain much that is scholarly and erudite, besides much that is essential and true, they, however, are bloated and swollen with much that is silly and pedantic, affected and misplaced, so much so that wilful obscurity taking the place of a lucid simplicity, the pilgrim, ignorant as he must be in most cases, is spontaneously plunged into a surging mill-race of classical deities and heroes, many of whom thrust themselves boisterously upon him without rhyme or reason.
>
> Ushered as it were into a Judgment Hall in which the law expounded to him is not only entirely unknown but is written in a language which he cannot even read, he is cross-questioned in a foreign tongue and judged in words which at present convey not a symptom of sense to him. As the Rituals proceed it might be expected that these difficulties would gradually lessen, but this is far from being the case; for, as we have seen, the complexities already involved by the introduction of Ancient Egyptian deities, concerning whom it is probable the candidate has but little knowledge, are further heightened by a general intrusion on the part of Hebrew, Christian, Macedonian and Phrygian gods, angels and demons, and a profuse scattering of symbols; which,

unitedly, are apt either so to bewilder the candidate that he leaves the temple with an impression that the whole ritual is a huge joke, a kind of buffoonish carnival of Gods which in the sane can only provoke laughter; or, on account of it being so utterly incomprehensible to him, his ignorance makes him feel that it is so vastly beyond him and above his own simple standard of knowledge, that all that he can do is to bow down before those who possess such an exalted language, concerning even the words and alphabet of which he can get no grasp or measure.

The result of this obscurity naturally is that in both cases the Rituals fail to initiate—in the first case they, not being understood, are jeered at; in the second they, though equally incomprehensible, are however revered. Instead of teaching the Alphabet by means of simple characters they teach it by grotesque and all but impossible hieroglyphics, and in the place of giving the infant adept a simple magick rag doll to play with, intrust to his care, with dire prognostication and portent of disaster, a gargoyle torn from the very roof of that temple on the floor of which he, as a little child, is as yet but learning to crawl. The result being, as it proved in most cases, as disastrous as it was lamentable.[20]

The Crowley-Reuss Initiations

As he became involved in establishing an English branch of Theodor Reuss' O.T.O., Crowley put himself to the work of developing a new set of initiations, later published by King. Precisely how much influence Reuss' previous work had on the initiations is unclear and a thorough discussion of the suppositions is outside the parameters of this work.

Drawing on source materials from various systems of Continental Masonry and/or the Scottish Rite, Crowley developed a set of initiations that have been in use, to a greater or lesser extent, for more than a century. It should be noted that our discussion of these initiations is, as our regard of the Golden Dawn rituals, based upon their place in the evolution of Thelema. The discussion of Crowley's work stops with the published version of 1973 and is not meant to be seen as a discussion of the value, relative merits, or any other characteristics of any organization which, through whatever initial source or pedigree, use those initiations or revisions upon them today. There will always be a place for the maintenance of historic traditions.

Great familiarity with the details of the system established by Reuss and Crowley and published by King is not an absolute necessity for an Initiator within our Sovereign Sanctuary, nor is a detailed working knowledge of the Golden Dawn initiations or those of the Hermetic Brotherhood of Luxor, of Craft, York, and Scottish Rite Freemasonry, or of Rosicrucianism and Esoteric Freemasonry, including Memphis and Misraim. Yet the study of all of these systems, as well as Gerald Gardner's more recent initiatory systems in their modern forms, provides a strong basis for understanding the tradition as it has existed up to this point and is recommended.

Crowley was not a theatrical producer, though he had produced several theatrical pieces – both his exhibitions of the "Raggedy Ragtime Girls" and the "Rite of Eleusis." Both relied heavily on the talents of the performers and the second also on the presence of entheogens. What is key is to take away are the core values that Crowley projected. Initiation should not be a matter of pompous demonstration or attempting to awe the initiate with the depth of knowledge. It should be simple, straightforward, and explain itself.

The Thelemic Initiations

The Issues with Crowley's Initiations Today

If the Golden Dawn initiations were too complex, Crowley's can be seen as perhaps overly streamlined. It is possible to see them as perfectly adequate for Crowley's needs in the early 20ᵗʰ century, yet problematic in our own era.

The Initiations Do Not Present a Complete System

Probably the first issue is the sparsity of content. The O.T.O. was not Crowley's first creation nor was it actually "his" until about 1923/24. Crowley's principal investment was in his Golden Dawn spin-off organization; the A∴A∴. His O.T.O. track does not seem to have truly been intended as a full "magical" initiation in the sense of G.D. or A∴A∴ but, rather, exactly as Reuss intended, a catch-all replacement for Lodge Freemasonry – covering the Royal Arch at IV° and abstracted from various degrees to which Crowley and Reuss believed they were entitled.

Crowley awarded the upper "sex magick" degrees based on recognition of the secrets, just as Reuss had awarded him such a degree. Every indication is that there were few actual rituals developed for the higher degrees. It is questionable that Crowley intended anyone to attain solely through his O.T.O. degrees because they do not teach magick, though magick is the core tool for initiation. To some extent, the lower degree system emerges as much as a "feeder" for A∴A∴, while the higher degrees are more awarded for recognition of initiation already accomplished.

Without a doubt, Crowley's initiations occupy an important place in the history of Ceremonial magick. They carried forward the general ideas of sex magick from Paschal Beverly Randolph and the questionable Hermetic Brotherhood of Luxor and welded them to the more generalized system of the G.D. It enshrined the concept of the replacement of the birth/death/rebirth formula of the Old Aeon with the ongoing birth cycle of the New Aeon; an inherent departure from our history of glorification of violence and suffering.

The Initiations Do Not Put the Sex Mysteries in Their Proper Place

That the higher degree focus is on the IX° Sex Mystery, certainly inherited from Reuss, is particularly problematic, not because there is anything challenging about the mystery itself, but because there is not. Anyone who has seen a cup and dagger ritual knows precisely what the IX° secret is. In tamest form it has been widely portrayed in mainstream media and featured in novels. There is nothing "secret" about it in our time, but the rituals were written for an audience to whom sex was still, for the most part, genuinely scandalous. Part of the function of the initiations was simply to move people with Victorian sensibilities into a mindset where they were receptive to the blasphemous and incredible idea that an act of sexual penetration may be a literal liminal state, in which humans can access the infinite.

In *The Secret Instructions of the Seventh, Eight and Ninth Degrees,* Crowley asks "What is the tent of Saladin but the Phallus? And the First Word as the last is ON, the Sun. But were the Minerval to suspect this truth, would he not turn to flee in terror from the Camp and be cut down by the Black Guard that wardeth even the outmost marches of the Kingdom of the Most Holy and Most High Lord God Almighty?"

That was a bit dramatic even for the 1920s; a time when journalists complained that people could talk of nothing but Freud and sex at cocktail parties but, even if the text was hyperbolic, the point was well-taken. Your average businessman about town probably wouldn't want to join an order with a sex secret and, when such groups came to light, they were likely to be hounded by police and prosecutors. That's not the case now. It is unlikely that more than a handful of people take initiation without knowing the outline of the IX° concept from some form of media, and anyone put off by the idea of sex secrets probably isn't going to be brought round to the concept no matter how timorously it is introduced.

The initiations introduced a relatively obscure turn of the century concept and provided a springboard for the development of sex mystery in the XI° which stepped beyond old Aeon concepts of gender and sexuality into a queer ethos, exploring the ramifications of queer sexuality in sex magick. Old Aeon thinking about the XI° mystery has underplayed its central importance in Crowley's life, thinking, and work. In the 20th century, Thelemic leaders with cisgender and heterosexual sensibilities were mildly embarrassed by the IX° mystery and reduced the XI° to a "side degree for gay men" about which, in their opinion, the less was said, the better.

Even Crowley's limited writing about the XI° makes it profoundly clear that it is queer in the modern sense; not as a segregate ritual for people who are not "straight," but rather as an exploration into the non-existence of conformist gender and the ability of the individual to construct their own gender, as Crowley certainly did.

> *"This constitutes a profound Riddle of Holiness. Those only understand it who combine in themselves the extremes of Moral idea, identifying them through transcendental overcoming of the antinomy. They must have gone further yet, beyond the fundamental opposition of the sexes. The male must have completed himself and become androgyne; the female, and become gynander. This incompleteness imprisons the soul. To think "I am not woman, but man," or vice versa, is to limit one's self, to set a bar to one's motion. It is the root of the "shutting-up" which culminates in becoming 'Mary inviolate' or a 'Black Brother.'"*[21]

If Crowley ever produced a written XI° ritual, it was repressed, with only fragmentary references surviving, most notably an extract made by Cosmo Trelawney. Patrick King, who was acknowledged by Grady McMurtry, then Caliph of O.T.O., as the founder and Chief of the Rite of Shiraz XIth degree Ordo Templi Orientis, produced some papers supporting his XI° concept, notably *Liber Qadosh*.[22] Patrick King's rite was repressed by McMurtry's successor shortly after his accession in 1986.

The sex mysteries are key to the initiatory concept but are held back artificially, not because they're particularly difficult to master or because it is most sensible to present them starting at VII°, but because presenting them to people who were not already very committed to your group could be disastrous. Even if Crowley never accomplished much in the way of establishing a system of operative lodges, he certainly meant to. His practical experience from Detroit and elsewhere had taught him that his most likely audience was middle class Freemasons, and talking to the average businessman-freemason about penises was likely to get one referred on a criminal complaint. So the place of sex within the initiations is wildly distorted because it is linked, not in the best or most obvious way, but in the one least likely to create trouble with police in an era not far past the Keystone Cops.

Idealistic Assumptions About "Decency"

For all his wickedness, Crowley believed in a basic code of decency throughout his life; one attached to his British middle-class values and sense of self. The idea may prove hard to swallow on two levels. On one hand, Crowley willingly wore the reputation of "the wickedest man in the world." In this sense, he saw himself as a rebel against the narrow and prosaic morality of Victorian and Edwardian England. On the other hand, he did things which were neither generous nor decent. He hurt and turned his back on partners and colleagues and he took money without any serious prospect for repaying it. These certainly are failings, and very human ones at that. Like most humans, he justified them within his ethical code and excused in himself what he would excuse in others.

Still, falling short of one's own code isn't the same as not having one. He admitted and discussed his shortcomings, albeit defensively, in his diaries. The very fact that he was defensive and felt the need to justify his flaws illustrates that Crowley was never proud of, nor happy about, failing to meet his own standards. For all of his deficiencies, many of his long-term friends remembered him best for his hospitality, generosity, and basic decency.

Crowley lived in a time that is difficult for most middle-class Westerners to understand, though we are only a few generations removed from it. Artists and poets were not "superstars" defining the social scene, but an isolated lower class, surviving on the patronage of "betters" or the thin dime of those in the middle class who could afford entertainment. The interwar and post-war periods changed this, but the real change by which a queer literary icon such as Truman Capote could be ascendant over noted social figures came in the two decades after Crowley's death. Crowley was, at one point, a wealthy and privileged brat and, at another, destitute and desperate, and both extremes brought out bad behavior. He borrowed money and spent it entertaining or paying prostitutes so that he could appear generous and have the sexual outlet he justified as being necessary to his work.

Crowley is also often excoriated for the fact that he wrote off several partners as insane, the presumption being that he dismissed them out of convenience or drove them mad. Neither option is particularly likely. The demi-monde around the art world was often the refuge of those who could find no work elsewhere because they did not "fit in." In a time before the existence of any treatment other than talk therapy for mental illness, that could mean a lot of things, but often it denoted sexual non-conformity, as in Crowley's case, or mental illness in the case of some of his partners.

Still, Crowley's generosity and general dedication to the ideal human decency show through in his writing and that of others about him. If his wit could be cruel, it was turned toward those whom he thought deserved it. His veneration of customs of hospitality he found in North Africa and elsewhere indicates a deep commitment to the ideals of kindness and generosity. His demonstrations against "charity" must be framed against the holier than thou "Salvation Army" mentality of his time, whereby helping the poor meant rubbing their noses in their own poverty in the interests of feeling superior, which he loathed as hypocrisy.

Crowley had come close to a Byronic exile for being outspokenly queer, had been ostracized, surveilled by the police, and had his work seized. He would eventually face being destitute, alone, and exile even from exile. It is no surprise that throughout his life he drew lines between "his people" and "all others" and wrote his rituals to reinforce the interdependence of the Thelemic Community. Still, his goal was not to create a cabal of mutual villainy but to bring the Law to all. Those he excluded were only "those parasites of society who feed upon the troubles caused by Restriction: officials, lawyers, financiers, and the like. Ill disposed people — that is, those whose failure to understand their own true Will of Freedom leads them to seek to interfere with others."[23]

Crowley assumed that most people shared his values and was consistently astonished when they did not. His experience cannot be defined by cultural imperialism. His concept of "decency" came out of middle-class England, but he recognized it with pleasure in Africa and Asia. Some of his writing suggests a neurodivergence that may have made it more difficult for Crowley to understand why others didn't think as he did, and made it easier for him to misunderstand their actions when they acted in ways that seemed wrong to him. He got along well with other seminally kind people such as Nancy Cunard, who were moved by a deep regard for others, and the essential decency of his nature is the one characteristic attested by those friends he kept for life. As early as 1923, he was concerned with the idea that people could interpret "True Will" in ways that were incompatible with basic human decency.

There seems to be much misunderstanding about True Will ... The fact of a person being a gentleman is as much an ineluctable factor as any possible spiritual experience; in fact, it is possible, even probable, that a man may be misled by the enthusiasm of an illumination, and if he should find apparent conflict between his spiritual duty and his duty to honour, it is almost sure evidence that a trap is being laid for him and he should unhesitatingly stick to the course which ordinary decency indicates. Error on such point is precisely the "folly" anticipated in CCXX, I, 36, and I wish to say definitely, once and for all, that people who do not understand and accept this position have utterly failed to grasp the fundamental principles of the Law of Thelema."[24]

Crowley's initiations do make a real effort to teach decency. If anything, that is their central fixture. They are neo-masonic and, rather than teaching the commonweal of all humankind which he certainly believed in, he focused on the duty to other members of his Secret Society. That it was "us against the world" was clear to Crowley, yet to read his writing is to understand that his "brothers and sisters" weren't just those sworn to his particular Order, but everyone else who shared the self-awareness and dangerously insecure freedom that he did. The behavior he teaches in his initiations is meant to embrace all Thelemites, declared or not. Unfortunately, it is easy to misunderstand that and instead come away with the idea of a crypto-Masonic "mutual defense pact" in which those to be trusted and aided are only the specific individuals with whom one happened to share initiation, regardless of their personal character, rather than all people who share the goals and ideals core to Thelema.

The Controversial Elements

Mansur Al-Hallaj

The introductory cycle of Crowley's initiations, as publicly available, are framed by the characters of Saladin and of Mansur Al-Hallaj. We won't go into extreme detail on the framing here as it does constitute the core surprise of Crowley's script. If you'd like to know more and haven't taken the initiations as offered by one of the organizations that still works them, we suggest reading the initial degrees in King to see their development.

Mansur Al-Hallaj (c. 858-922) was a historic person. Born to a Sunni family with a Zoroastrian grandfather, he is a major figure in the Sufi mystical tradition, though he was rejected by other Sufis during his lifetime. He is identified with the quote "I am the truth," also rendered as "There is nothing wrapped in my turban but God." Fundamentally, Al-Hallaj was evoking the mystical idea that the self is God and his quote can be seen as either a mystical statement about the submersion of the ego or a declaration of personal divinity. The prevailing idea is common across many faiths, including esoteric Christianity, but the concept of personal divinity is especially strong in Thelema.

Masonic writer, spiritualist, and prophet J.S.M. Ward (notably also a close friend of Gerald Garder) believed the central figure of the masonic legend of the Lost Master's Word, Hiram Abiff, was a sort of cipher for Mansur Al-Hallaj. The figure of Hiram Abiff has always been problematic for Freemasonry. Despite being core to the Masonic mystery, there is no real agreement on who the figure represents, allegorically or otherwise. Ward's overall view of Masonry was syncretic, seeing it as a secret tradition that preserved the knowledge and tradition of other ancient faiths through the Christian era. His views are not anthropologically sound, nor were they accepted by the English Grand Lodge, but they were popular and are absolutely an influence on Crowley and Reuss.

Crowley was a profound Islamophile. While he certainly shared the admixture of colonial thought that also distinguishes Richard Francis Burton or T.E. Lawrence, there is no question that his respect and admiration for

Islamic culture and its ideals was deep and genuine. Nor was his veneration that of a distant fan who reveres the ancient culture, but thinks nothing of the struggles of the modern people. His choice to name his son "Attaturk" after the progressive and reformist Turkish nationalist leader indicates that he was politically aware of the changing tides within the Islamic world and did not support some romanticized version of Islam at the expense of its modern adherents. Crowley's lifelong sympathies in Islam seem to have been those which we would respect today, supporting rational self-determination and the rights of indigenous tribes over colonial authorities.

Crowley's use of Islamic icons in his work was certainly considered both an homage and a reflection of the very real presence of Islamic ideals in Western culture, both through the long Islamic presence in Iberia and through the fact that almost all of the initial Hermetic material brought to Europe was translated or maintained by writers under a strong Islamic influence. Islamic mysticism, like Gnostic Christian mysticism, was shaped heavily by its immediate predecessors and thus is, in a very real way, a link with "ancient traditions." As with the Russian Orthodox practice which inspired *Liber XV*, Crowley saw in Islam a faith that was less out of touch with its historical antecedents than 19th century Protestant Christianity. In addition to the references above, Crowley was very consciously following the arc of sex magick established by Paschal Beverly Randolph. While Randolph traced his ideas to the Shia Alawis or Nusayri sect, which was radically opposed by the Sunni Sufis, the links themselves are fictitious and understandings of the nuances of the groups involved were poor.

It becomes easy then to see why both Reuss and Crowley could see Al-Hallaj as a seminal symbol – an eruption point of the modern Gnostic concept – and wanted to identify Al-Hallaj with Hiram. Both Crowley and Ward agreed that the original Lost Master's Word, or Masonic Secret, was the true nature of God and that the nature of God is personal divinity.

We have abandoned the concept of wrapping this concept around Al-Hallaj for several reasons. The first and most obvious is that we are not a Sufi tradition, nor are we heirs to one. Sufism is an influence on our tradition but we are at best a distant cousin, not a descendant. Sufism is a worldwide movement with millions of adherents. Modern Sufism has a complex relationship with Sunni practice and with the politics of Islamic reform. To give Al-Hallaj our deep regard for his contributions to thought and practice is respectful. To take his story for our own diminishes our understanding of his place in world culture.

Secondly, the use of Al-Hallaj is highly ahistorical. By wedding his story with Hiram's it becomes pure fiction, making him the victim of the three assassins of Hiram and stripping his own story of leadership in the reformist uprising in 908 and his subsequent death by torture and burning at the hands of the 18th Abbasid Caliph in Baghdad in 922. This is not innocent historical fiction or allegory. Rather, it is stripping Al-Hallaj of much that makes him Al-Hallaj. To teach his name, without his actual story, is something which we can understand, in our era, to be an insulting wrong.

Saladin

If Crowley's use of the figure of Al-Hallaj is an homage to an ideal, his use of Saladin falls little short of blatant hero-worship. That Crowley idolized Saladin is without doubt; the character features in the final line of his 1910 tragic play "The Scorpion," which takes place against the backdrop of the Crusades.

If Al-Hallaj is presented ahistorically, Salah al-Din is not presented at all. Rather what is presented is more a symbol out of legend than the actual personage. If Salah al-Din were a legend of our tradition we might let the use of his name stand, as it is clearly metaphorical. It is understood that historical figures are often presented not as their actual human selves, but more as symbols of certain powers or ideals. But Salah al-Din is again, at best, a distant cousin – one whose memory rightly belongs to millions of people from Kurdistan to Egypt and across the Islamic world and beyond.

It could be suggested that Crowley saw the historical Saladin as a radical and iconoclastic solution to the cloying framework of Christianity that surrounded the Golden Dawn and Rosicrucianism. By focusing on a Saladin who is presented throughout the vast majority of Western European history as an "adversary" and best remembered for his breaking of the Crusades at Hattin, Crowley makes a strong point. "We're not Christians, and this is not the Medieval Christian Church." By presenting an Islamic figure in a strong and vibrant light, he could be seen as promoting Islamic culture.

There was reason to seek tolerance. Crowley could not have been unfamiliar with nationalist uprisings against Britain in Egypt, or the Denshawai incident of 1906. Within his lifetime the Ottoman Empire was collapsed, the Balfour Declaration made, and a wave of Colonial misrule instigated which would throw West Asia into a century of turmoil. In the years since, the restoration and overthrow of the Shah of Iran, the Iranian hostage crisis, the rise of Saddam Hussein, the Iran-Iraq War, the US overthrow of the Iraqi Government, the Arab-Israeli conflict, even the Syrian Civil War have been the legacy of that Colonialism.

The ethical framework that separates respect for other cultures from appropriation was little evolved in Crowley's time. To imitate respectfully was seen as flattering and promoting tolerance. That is not today's world. Imitation without context and understanding is no longer flattering, and tolerance is better encouraged through respect and acknowledgment. At a time when Islamic persons in the US and Europe are profoundly at risk of violence because of a rising tide of Islamophobia, we can understand Crowley's turn of the century use of the figure as a tribute and still see that, in light of our current understandings of culture and ethics, it would be misguided and inappropriate to continue doing so ourselves.

Moving beyond Crowley's Initiations

Crowley's initiations also use archaic language, including the use of some commonplace English words in a sense which is not the one most current in the modern era. Shades of meaning are lost. In the world of modern media, the world runs on an accelerated time cycle. Crowley's mysteries, completed before even the tinny blare of radio had penetrated into the average living room, are paced for those with leisure and long evenings to contemplate. We can appreciate the beauty of things past and even bemoan the loss of the time to fully engage with them, while understanding that they are not the world in which we live.

In building new initiations, we wished to focus on a Thelemic worldview consistent with the broad passion of Thelemic work and the attitude and understandings of modern Thelemites – one which leaves no room for tolerance of intolerance or fascism, and which makes unmistakable the essential Thelemic thesis that every person is a star.

Reclaiming our Traditions through Thelema

In presenting a complete modernization of the Thelemic Initiations, we have sought to reach back to connect ancient traditions with the modern. We begin with a presentation of the core mystery of Hiram. While we do not agree with Ward and Crowley on the vehicle of Mansur Al-Hallaj, we do agree on the core idea that the Lost Master's Word is a lesson about the nature of God. Exploring it gives us us our first chance to look into a concept that will be continually referenced over and over again in the Thelemic Initiations. Likewise, we embrace and double down on Crowley's concept of actual theater, rather than a limp pageant, as the delivery mechanism for initiation. We create a mystery play that has multiple levels because stories are more memorable than lectures.

Where we have drawn on history we have chosen history that has a direct connection to the people, places, and things that feed most directly into our tradition. Because no past culture is the same as ours today, we are always open to accusations of appropriation, but we have chosen settings that are relevant to our mysteries, traditions that are core to our own.

Historical Realism

Many would argue that the trend towards a truthful depiction of the past runs contrary to the Western Tradition, much of which is built on legend. And, of course, we cannot truthfully depict the past except as it comes to us through archaeology, records, research, and in some cases, inspiration.

Romanticizing the Past Leads to Misunderstanding of the Present

To deal with the past primarily from legend is to whitewash and romanticize it. We have learned in the modern era that doing so has a terrible consequence. The belief in some idealized past "when things were better" drives ideological intransigence – resistance to change – which is the fundamental opposition to the New Aeon. Thelema is rich in tradition, but no part of it is about clinging to the relics of the Old Aeon. By stripping the past of its brutality, ignorance, and cruelty, it becomes possible to believe that it was a much better and nobler time, playing into the hands of those who wish to hold power by shaming us for changes while playing to "traditional values."

The unconditional veneration of medieval kings, or male military leaders in general, has less to do with nobility and chivalry than it does with perpetuating a status quo where powerful middle-aged white men make the decisions. The past was uniformly unequal and those without money – women, minorities, and those whose sexuality did not conform to perceived norms – usually received the short end of the stick. "If the past was better," goes the logic of the romanticist, "then clearly doing things as in the past is better. If that means repressing others, it is the price we must pay." The romanticist themselves may or may not believe their stories, but they sell them to those a little further down the ladder as a rationale and to their peers as a sop for any feelings of guilt.

To us, traditions are valuable because they are a chronicle of ongoing change. They are the story of the arrival of the New Aeon; of those who worked and sacrificed to shake off the shackles of the old. We choose to challenge those who would make the Western Tradition which, since Ficino and Rabelais has been about the triumph of respect for human dignity and the balance of individual choice with the commonweal, about the championship of tyranny, even when that masquerades as the blind ascendance of the individual over the collective. The Western Tradition values individualism, but it does not glorify an anarchistic valuation of the self above all others in a zero sum game of king of the hill. We are social animals and our traditions are social; our core values revolving around *"exhorting men to aspire to become nobler, holier, worthier, kinglier, kindlier, and more generous."*

Truth is More Interesting than Fiction

When we embrace things we know to be untrue because they seem "cool" we blind ourselves to things that are *actually* true and are in some cases cooler. For example, we make a strong presentation of the concept that Asherah, who can be soundly etymologically and symbolically linked to the Thelemic "Babalon" was, *in fact*, worshiped at the Temple of Solomon. Cagliostro? He likely didn't initiate into a tradition that dated back to the 2nd or 3rd century

CE, yet he represents a renewal of interest in that material and likely did come across others doing Egyptian rites based on their recreation of Hermetic tradition.

If we construct a false Eurocentric version of Hermeticism, we miss the fascinating line of preservation of Hermetic texts that runs through the Harranians and establishes a real, not feigned, connection to Islam.[25] We also miss very real ties between the worship of YHWH and the Egyptian deities. In short, when we make things up we short ourselves very real richness. If we construct a fanciful Richard Lionheart, we not only erase his brutality but his fascinating willingness to ignore prevailing Christian norms in offering to marry his sister to al-Adil, the brother of Salah ad-Din. If we make up a grandiose grail legend around the Cathars we miss the amazing reality of the battle for Toulouse in which, on 25 June 1218 Simon IV de Montfort, leader of the anti-Cathar crusade, fell when "a stone arrived just where it was needed and struck Count Simon on his steel helmet, shattering his eyes, brains, back teeth, forehead and jaw," such that "Bleeding and black, the count dropped dead on the ground." And that this stone was thrown by a siege engine manned by "noblewomen, by little girls and men's wives" of Toulouse.

Of course, in the Thelemic Initiations, we construct drama and our drama is fiction. We don't know what the characters of Azalais or Hiram actually said or did. But we attribute them to their appropriate place and time and frame them to the best of our knowledge of their world. Our initiates understand they are watching a play and our protagonists remind them of this fact. We tell no lies. In the plays, we clarify, to some extent, what is speculation and what is a fact. In this, we do nothing against the core understandings of magick. If Azalais were to reach through the centuries to speak to us, we can be certain she would not remember a fictionalized Toulouse.

Controversial Elements

At least one of our team of collaborators may be a Fool, but we are not fools in the generic sense and must anticipate that, in discussing the issue of appropriation in the context of Crowley's initiation, our initiations will similarly come under scrutiny. Here we discuss our treatment of some of the more controversial of our material.

Judaism

The issue of Judaism is particularly difficult. It is important to understand that both the Golden Dawn and Thelema share strong Jewish influences. A number of their prominent thinkers and writers were culturally Jewish though, for the most part, they were secular in regards to Judaism as a religion.

The difficulty comes from the fact that antisemitism is on the rise in the world, and Jews have long been a punching bag in regard to occult conspiracies. Well before the fabricated and defamatory *Protocols of the Elders of Zion* was published, Jews had been accused of a wide range of evils throughout European history. This places on us a heavy responsibility to be both honest about the incorporation of Jewish material and to do everything possible to combat the antisemitic ideas that dog some occultism circles.

In our narratives, we take exceptional pains not to whitewash the history of Jews in Europe. We pick for our champions those who were, generally, tolerant, yet we admit and call attention to atrocities and neglect on the part of European leaders. We also remind Thelemites that we have a duty to all persecuted peoples; that those who are deprived of those rights of humankind are our partners in the struggle to bring the Law of light, life, love, and liberty to all.

Kabbalah, Cabbala, Qabbalah

Hermetic Qabbalah is derived principally from Christian Cabbala, which is derived from Jewish Kabbalah. A full exploration of the relationship between these systems is outside the scope of our initiation, however, we want to discuss frankly two concepts. First, we'll address the idea Kabbalah was stolen from the Jews and that, therefore, Hermetic Qabbalah is illegitimate. Second, we'll address attempts to source Hermetic Qabbalah directly into Jewish Kabbalah, rather than the Christian Cabbala from which it principally derived.

There can be no question that Jews in Europe were often at the mercy of powerful Christian magnates, when they were tolerated at all. It is easy to envision forced cultural exchanges, such as those where Native Americans were effectively forced to "sell" their traditions in shows in order to survive. We cannot rule out that books were sold or lessons given out of the necessity to pay fines or move, but we can say there is little evidence this a major line of transmission for Christian Cabbala.

Nor were the individuals who were interested in ideas such as Cabbala generally those interested in the persecution of Jews. While there are exceptions, the majority of scholars and philosophers encouraged tolerance toward Jews. Christian thinkers, as a matter of necessity, at least formally advocated conversion, even when, like Giovanni Pico della Mirandola, they also expressed admiration for Jewish thought and philosophy. The idea that everyone should be Christian was implicit and unquestioned in Medieval Christianity. By the standard of the day, tolerance was the concept that such conversion should be sought by peaceful and philosophical, rather than militaristic, means. If thinkers such as Mirandola and Reuchlinn wanted, in the abstract at least, to Christianize the Jews, they also wanted to paganize and Judaize the Christians, citing the Kabbalah in particular as a link to an honorable past that included Hermeticism and Pythagoreanism. Without forswearing, on pain of death, Christianity, these thinkers did much to cut at the roots of Christianity as a monolithic institution. Pointedly, Reuchlinn elevated Jewish thought by suggesting that it supplied the intellectual core of Pythagoreanism and implicitly much other classical pagan thought.

Nor was the exchange one-way – a simple matter of Christians appropriating Jewish material. Moshe Idel, Emeritus Max Cooper Professor in Jewish Thought at the Hebrew University in Jerusalem, cites 13th-century Jewish authors who translated Latin works and drew from contemporary philosophical developments within the Christian community in the Italian peninsula. Idel concludes that "Christian Kabbalah influenced not only a few forms of Christian theology but also European culture in general."[26] Ultimately his work supports a narrative of scholarly collaboration and influence.

We take exceptional pains to make clear three things:

1) Hermetic Qabbalah is descended from Jewish Kabbalah through Christian Cabbala

2) Christian Cabbala dates at least to the 15th century, and probably somewhat earlier, and is a significant and historical tradition. It is rooted in the exchange of ideas among thinkers and flourished with tolerance, rather than with subjugation, of Jewish culture.

3) Jewish people have been subject to racist violence and prejudice throughout most of European history, and we cannot forget that or ignore it.

Kabbalah is a tradition of Jewish origin which has been practiced by various others, Christian and non-Christian, for at least five centuries. Kabbalah is European, emanating from the areas that are today Italy, Portugal, Spain, Catalonia, France, and Germany. Jewish Kabbalah, as it diverged into Christian Cabbala and then into Hermetic

Qabbalah, formed a core strand of the Western esoteric tradition because, despite persecution and mistreatment, Jewish culture remains an undeniable element of European culture and produced an indelible mark on Thelema.

The Temple of Solomon the King

The story of the Temple of Solomon the King has been a core element of Western Tradition for at least ten centuries and comes with its own complexities.

The Facts

The site of Solomon's Temple is a holy site in Judaism. Destroyed in 587 BCE during the conquest of Judah, the Second Temple was built on the same site sometime in the closing days of the same century. It was rededicated after the Maccabean revolt, resulting in the association with Hanukkah. The temple complex was vastly expanded by Herod the Great and destroyed in the 70 CE revolt against Roman Rule. One of the retaining walls of the Temple Mount remains today as the Western Wall and is a Jewish Holy site. The Al-Aqsa Mosque, the third holiest site in Islam, was built on top of the Temple Mount, with construction starting in the 7th century. It was destroyed by an earthquake and rebuilt several times.

Of Jerusalem in the First Crusade, former Haifa University professor Sylvia Schein says, "After its capture, which involved the almost complete annihilation of its non-Christian inhabitants, the once flourishing and populous city became a small town whose entire population probably numbered no more than a few hundred."[27] The nascent Kingdom of Jerusalem had no budget for large-scale civic construction and repurposed the captured Al-Aqsa Mosque, believed to have been built on the site of the Temple of Solomon, as the Palace of the Kings of Jerusalem. In 1119, the southern part of the Al-Aqsa site, referred to as the Temple or Palace of Solomon, was granted by Baldwin II to a community of knights headed by Hughes de Payens. The building was quite dilapidated at this point. It had been plundered during the conquest and Baldwin I had stripped the lead from its dome to pay his bills.

When the new knighthood was recognized as a military order nine years later, economic improvements led Baldwin II to move to a new Palace near the Citadel; likely a renovation of the former residence of the Fatimid governor. This left the Al-Aqsa site to be associated with the new military order, which would be remembered as the Templars, and they undertook a restoration of the site, raising a complex of new buildings.

The Temple and the Crusades

The story of the place of the Temple of Solomon in the heart of Christian legend is complex, as are the Crusades themselves. The Crusades are characterized as an arbitrary determination on the part of European Christians to seize the Holy Lands from Muslims as if Christian Europe woke up in 1095 and resolved to go take something that had not been theirs since the early days of the Byzantine Empire.

In fact, the events were part of a series of geopolitical upheavals. Muslims originally took Jerusalem in 683 CE. During the early period, there was broad religious tolerance and many Christian pilgrimages. In the early 11th century, the Fatimid ruler ordered widespread destruction of churches, probably in response to increasing internal instability. Atsiz ibn Uwaq, a Khwarezmian Turkish mercenary serving the conquering Seljuk Empire, captured Jerusalem from the Fatimids twice, in 1073 and again in 1077, and committed a large-scale slaughter on the second occasion. The Seljuk rulers of Jerusalem seem to have been generally less tolerant of pilgrims, leading to stories of mistreatment in Europe. The Byzantines had been defeated by Seljuks in 1071 and, despite the Great Schism of

1054 which separated the Eastern Church from the Roman Catholic, both the Empire and the Christian Kingdom of Armenia had asked for intervention from Western Europe.

The point here is not to justify the Crusades, but to establish that they were military operations typical of the period driven by shifting alliances in a four-way power game between the Byzantine Empire, Frankish Crusaders, Seljuk Turks, and Egyptian Fatimids. At the level of leadership, there were wide motives beyond religious fervor and, even among the rank-and-file, they did not have the flavor of a genocidal war against Muslims. The Crusaders who eventually captured Jerusalem after an abortive treaty with the Fatimids committed a barbaric slaughter but, as shown by ibn Uwaq's 1077 attack, such actions were not unusual. We cannot like any slaughter, yet there is very little to be gained by judging a medieval military action by contemporary standards.

Our Use of the Temple and the Templars

It would perhaps be best to stay away entirely from the subject of the Temple and the Templars. After all, some white supremacists have identified with the Templars and the Temple itself casts a long and confusing shadow. Unfortunately, if we are to cut to the core of the Western esoteric tradition, we do not have that luxury. Solomon's Temple is core to our tradition. It is referenced in the oldest known Masonic Ritual, the Register House MS, which is dated to 1696. Nor is the interest in the Temple limited to Masons or Neo-Templars. It pervades the Western Tradition.

Respected Mormon writer and historian Hugh Nibley, writing in *The Jewish Quarterly Review* in 1959, coined the term "Christian Envy of the Temple."[28] In later writing, he expanded on this thought.

> *The moral of our tale is that the Christian world has been perennially haunted by the ghost of the temple—a ghost in which it does not believe. If the least be said for it, the temple has never lost its power to stir men's imaginations and excite their emotions, and the emotion which it has most often inspired in Christian breasts has certainly been that of envy, a passion the more dangerous for being suppressed. The temple has cast a shadow over the claims and the confidence of the Christian church from early times, a shadow which is by no means diminishing in our ownday. If we seem to have labored the obvious in pointing this out, it is only because the obvious has been so long and so resolutely denied or ignored in high places.*[29]

In exploring the Templars, we do not condone slaughter or colonialism of any kind. Instead, we look at people caught at a difficult, politically nuanced, time and place in history. We attempt to draw lessons from the humiliation and defeat that they eventually enudred and relate their legend to our own experiences and time. Our exploration embodies many of the techniques used by film in the 1960s and 1970s to explore the impacts of war on the individual.

The Templars were already the subject of legend before they were extinguished. Their incorporation into Parzival, written by Wolfram von Eschenbach in the early 13th century, is the source of their connection to the grail and Solomon. While we raise fair and interesting questions about von Eschenbach's stated sources, we also try and portray the surprisingly sophisticated world of prose and poetry in the Middle Ages. If von Eschenbach's claim of having access to an Arabic manuscript from Moorish Toledo through Kyot of Provence seems something which must be true because of the naivete of the era, our look at the Troubadour Courts should make it clear that this was not a period of "folk stories around the fire," but one in which complex fictions were composed for notoriety and commission.

Where we investigate the relationship of the Templars to Baphomet and other darker legends which remain to be explored, we are cautious. There can be no provable knowing, yet our citations are drawn almost exclusively from the extant trial records. Whatever our conjectures, they are at least based on the evidence.

The Temple of Solomon of Masonic Rituals could be seen to have little to do with the man who served as King of the United Kingdom of Israel and reigned roughly 970-931 BCE and most likely built a permanent temple at the site of Jerusalem. Our portrayal of the Temple of Solomon is strongly anchored in the historic era of pagan Israel and Judah, emphasizing the well-documented kinship between the Temple's God, El, and the related deities, Ba'al, Hadad, and Asherah. Our intent here is not trivial. The cudgel with which Christianity is able to beat modern paganism – and Thelema is as pagan as it is anything else – is the presumption of the essential truth of the Christian God, of YHWH. The core story of one God and one Truth coming out of ancient Israel is critical to the legitimacy of Evangelical Christianity. In the context of Christian faith, monotheism – knowledge of one, eternal, God dating to the dawn of history – was revealed to Moses, and that God was the literal father of Jesus. If we can understand that for centuries after the time of Moses there was not one God but many, that the God who would become the Father of the New Testament had a sister and mother, was in fact simply one God in a pantheon…then the special nature of the Christian faith evaporates. Christian monotheism ceases to be some special revelation and instead is simply the reflection of a larger cultural drift seen equally in Neo-Platonism. To place Babalon on the Temple Mount beside El in the place of YHWH, rewrites the script that most of us, growing up in a country where Christianity is the most common religion, have inside our heads.

The Cathars

The reflection of Thelema in Al-Hallaj's work is not coincidental. Hallaj was identified as a Sunni Muslim, but, through his brother-in-law, he had contact with Shi'a ideology and he studied at the Sahl al-Tustari school, which was one of the birthplaces of Sufi mysticism. Perhaps, more importantly, his grandfather was Zoroastrian and there are strong suggestions of Zoroastrian ideology in Hallaj's recorded thought. There is debate as to whether Manichaeism developed out of or co-evolved alongside Zoroastrianism, but both faiths ultimately influenced the Christian heresy of Marcionism, which is the direct ancestor of Paulicianism. The Paulicians, named for a 3rd Century Bishop of Antioch, preserved some late Hellenic, Neoplatonist ideals. Forcibly transplanted by the Byzantine Empire to Europe from Asia Minor, the Paulicians became the Bogomils.

There was likely already a Gnostic movement in the West when the Bogomil Bishop Nicetas arrived at the Council of Saint-Felix in 1167, or it is unlikely that a Council would have taken form. Yet Nicetas' consecration of Cathar Bishops at that council was the explosion point of Western Gnosticism. Suppressed within about a Century, the Cathar (or Albigensian) Heresy lived as an intellectual idea to be embraced by nonconformist Protestants and by a rising generation of Pagan thinkers in the 19th century.

The Modern Gnostics and L'Eglise Gnostique

Jules Doinel based his L'Eglise Gnostique (known by several similar names) of 1890 on spiritual experiences of 1888-1889. While doing spirit-work with Lady Caithness he received various messages, including a communication from Helene-Ennoia, the "Divine Androgyne," and instruction from the martyred Cathar Bishop Guilhabert de Castres, both of whom commanded him to re-found the Cathar Succession. Doinel used existing knowledge of Cathar rituals to establish his church.

The Thelemic Initiations

The idea of continuity of ideas over 2500 years often seems strange to Westerners, partially because of the general presentation of Christianity. In the West, we receive the message that Christianity was a sudden and drastic departure from the past, marking a clean break from paganism. We are also typically given the impression that Christianity, as it was practiced at the Table of the Last Supper, was not ideologically much different from Christianity as it is practiced at the local Evangelical Church. The only difference admitted in the minds of many Christians between the Jerusalem-based Church of James brother of Jesus, and the First Baptist Church of Lumberton, NC is that primitive Christians were cinematically persecuted for the first few hundred years by Roman Emperors and did not sit in pews.

Of course, this is very much mistaken. Christianity is a welter of influences embodying every faith and philosophy which came before it. By the late classical period paganism had already metamorphosed almost unrecognizably into a variety of Mystery Cults, State Cults, Neo-Platonism, Hermeticism, and so on. It is not surprising that the ideas of Gnosticism survived the end of the Classical era and seeped into Europe via the Bogomils and, potentially, Crusader contact with Paulicians. If anything, evidence of various heresies in Burgundy in the century before the flourishing of the Cathar Church suggests that seeds fell on already fertile ground.

As to the choice to use the Cathar principals, Raimond, his Countess Jeanne, sister Azalais, his daughter Guillemette, and son Raimond d'Alfaro, as well as their kinswoman, Esclarmonde, the connections to the specific strain of Gnosticism that led to Crowley's conception of the one Gnostic and Catholic Church is explicit. "Guilhabert de Castres…Esclamonde de Foix, Roger de Foix, Raymond de Toulouse," were explicitly honored in Doinel's Chivalric Order of The Dove of the Paraclete as martyrs. One of Doinel's original Bishops, or "Sophias" as female Bishops were termed was Marie Chauvel de Chauvigny, who took the Episcopal name "Esclarmonde."

Despite all such history Z. would likely say, simply, that they insisted on inclusion, about which more detail is offered in the section on Received Information regarding inspired content.

Cathar Influences on the Kabbalah

It is also worth considering that the Kabbalah itself may bear Cathar influence. It is no coincidence that the period during which the group of Cabbalist authors that Gershom Scholem[30] refers to as the Iyyun Circle flourished overlaps heavily with that period of permissiveness that allowed the flourishing of Aristotelean Philosophy and Catharism, both in time and geography. The relatively liberal government of the region did not lend itself to persecution and allowed thought and writing to grow and thrive. We do not invent facts when we recount that the Lord of Beziers hired Jews in the role of Bailiff.

Scholem's attribution of the Iyyun Circle texts largely to Provence has been questioned, but the fact that at least some of the texts emanated from Toulouse is attested, and more recent theories place the central point of emanation in nearby Castile. One of the earliest suggestions of a relationship between Kabbalah and Catharism was Moses Gaster in 1894;[31] in the modern era Scholem gives some credence to the possibility. The concept has been visited in more detail by Shulamith Shahar,[32] who sees "mutual influence between the Cathars and Kabbalists," and points out specific examples of syncretism between the *Book Bahir* and the Cathar version of the Bogomil *Cena Secreta*.

The point here is not to suggest any primacy of Cathar material in the Kabbalah. If anything, Catharism presents another axis by which Kabbalistic material was fused into the Western Tradition. The mere fact that Shahar's suggestions are plausible indicates the existence of a vibrant European culture of Esoterica which flourished wherever the Roman Catholic Church failed to support its doctrinal hegemony by force of arms and law. Where this culture existed, it needs must inform and influence, leading incrementally to the explosion of esotericism in the 18th-20th century.

Occitania and the Occitans

A final point must address the issue of the appropriation of Cathar culture. While Americans and even Britons may see a monolithic France, awareness of the Occitan-speaking region of modern France as a separate people and culture is important. Modern estimates have about half a million to a million Occitan speakers in southern France, Catalonia, Monaco, and Italy. The terms *Occitan* and *Occitania*, themselves, date from the mid 13th century. Numerous groups promoting Occitan history, cultural festivals, language, and politics exist, though the language itself was repressed by the French. Are we not merely appropriating the identity of another persecuted culture?

Here we must make decisions. The same could be argued for a vast swath of European traditions. If we show an interest in the Gorsedd of Bards or the Mabinogion, are we appropriating Welsh Culture? For that matter, if we revive Saxon traditions are we not appropriating the culture of a people repressed by the Danes and Normans? The decision on where to draw the line might be considered arbitrary. Is it based on blood alone? The first Chief Prelate of TTO is a lineal descendant of Jeanne, Queen of Sicily, and Countess of Toulouse. Yet such a distant connection to a Native American or West African ancestor would not embolden us to speak for their culture.

There is no perfect solution, however, we must attempt to discern "parentage" from "relationship." All the world's ideas and cultures are related. The culture of liberalism which thrived in Southern France in the 12th century was heavily defined by the story cycles of the Troubadours and included the growth of Catharism as an alternative to Catholicism. Ideas from and regarding the Cathars moved forward along dozens of lines, through France, Burgundy, Lombardy, and Britain, to directly influence the modern Western Tradition that produced the Golden Dawn and Thelema. Catharism is the most direct of several lines through which Gnosticism was handed down to become modern Neo-Gnosticism. We do not claim to be from Occitania or represent its modern people. Neither do we claim to be from London or Berlin. But we do not need to be a native, raised in London, to write about it, nor do we hesitate to represent those places or the people from them as part of our shared history.

In regards to the Court of Toulouse itself, we have been generally historical, though in several cases we are faced with riddles or indefinite historical information, such as those regarding the children of Raimond V, and we have used a combination of inspiration and creativity to flesh out the details, which resolved in a remarkably symmetrical fashion. Where we mention dates or events they are, to the best of our ability, factual.

Gender

Gender in History

Because historical people used gender as a concept, the characters of the Thelemic Initiations manifest gender. They consider themselves "men" and "women," just as they consider themselves "knights" or "clergy." This gender matters in terms of presentation because it explains why they believe or act certain ways towards each other.

In the play-within-a-play section of the 0° initiation, misogyny, as well as transphobia, is a significant element and, again, this cannot be understood outside of the cultural paradigm of gender. This does not mean that the characters need to be "gender-matched" to people who present as the same gender that they historically were. *It is very important that Sovereign Initiators do not restrict participation in the mysteries based on gender.* It does mean that, particularly in the play-within-a-play, the characters be portrayed as gendered. The elements of misogyny and transphobia become incoherent if it is not understood that the *characters* think of themselves as male or female.

In general, the dialog conveys this through the use of gendered words "I am a man," or words that historically have been attached to gender such as "Queen." While the use of gendered costuming is fine, care should be taken to portray gender with respect. Likewise, the presentation of the individual roles should be left to the performers. Outside of the play-within-a-play, how the performers choose to evoke their gender should be left to their discretion. Even historically the matter is open. Jeanne of England and Sicily is presented as a Queen and written of as a woman, but she led a siege – an activity most commonly reserved to men.

Some of the roles might at once seem to lend themselves to a Monty-Pythonesque take on performance. It is important to understand that the intent of the initiation is serious even where parts of it may be amusing. The spirit of Ludus should not lead into disrespectful portrayals which could be seen as mocking.

Gender outside of History

Within the larger sense of the ritual, we have done our best to choose non-gendered terms where possible. In the case of some words (e.g. master), the widely-accepted gender neutral option is unfortunately identical to one of the gendered options. At the time of this publication, there are no better options within the common lexicon for a gender neutral variant, so we have chosen to use the best options we have available with the understanding that they are not to be treated as indicating the gender of the individual in question. Thus the formal title "Master of the Temple" should never be corrected to "Mistress of the Temple," or so forth. We take either those words which have been stripped of their gender, or those words which are most connotative, but we do not divide initiates by gender. Likewise, it should never be suggested that they should prefer a given role or practice because of their perceived or assigned gender. If they have a preference of any kind they will assert it, but it is not our role as Initiators.

A Summary of Controversy

Likely, there will always be someone unhappy with any set of choices we make about what material to present and how. We can say only that where we have made decisions about what to present and what not to, those decisions have been made with as much respect and care as possible, no decision has been undertaken lightly, and we have tried to give some account of our thought process for posterity. In some cases, material was included because it was fitting and necessary. Yet, when some element was revealed to us as important, it was seldom presented with staging and framing applied and, even if it were, we cannot stand on inspiration alone. We have tried above to illustrate the reasons for our choices in our attempt to create a coherent central narrative that seeks to strengthen the understanding of Thelema and to prevail against those misinterpretations of it which are most injurious to the individual or Thelemic Community.

The Masonic Superstructure

The Rectified Rite of the Ancient and Primitive Mystery of Memphis and Misraim

It has long been customary for Esoteric Degrees to be connected to and convey certain Degrees within Esoteric Freemasonry. Rosicrucianism, Neo-Templarism, and Neo-Gnosticism form core elements of the Western Esoteric Tradition. These make up the outward structures through which Hermeticism, Paganism (whether ancestral or revival), and Qabbalah are most often presented to general western audiences. Those organizations which did not explicitly grant Masonic titles often aped the style, custom, and terminology without specifically acknowledging it, in some cases because the operators did not wish to compromise their membership in existing bodies. For example, the Hermetic Order of the Golden Dawn had links to the Mark Master Masons' Lodge which operates the Royal Arch Degree, and the Societas Rosicruciana in Anglia. Theodor Reuss attempted to amalgamate an array of existing orders into his Ordo Templi Orientis, though it must be understood he did not acquire the *sole* rights to the traditions he worked to integrate.

A Note about "Regular" Freemasonry

By the early 20th century organized Masonry had become staid and somewhat monolithic. Freemasonry existed mostly as a social organization, and references to the esoteric were heavily diluted or altogether missing. Most of the rites collected by Yarker or consolidated by Reuss were considered fringe or clandestine at best, and spurious at worst, by serious Masons. In practical fact, they all have their own histories and lineage, as interesting and culturally distinctive as any more mainstream practice. The Rectified Rite of the Ancient and Primitive Mystery of Memphis and Misraim provides a sort of structural external framework to the Degrees of the Thelemic Order.

We have respect for those who work Masonic degrees today, and have no desire to represent ourselves as anything other than we are. That said, some perspective is called for.

There is a tendency to dismiss the various Esoteric Masonic Groups which do not belong to the United Grand Lodge of England, or to the Grand Orient of France, or some other Grand Lode body, as "Irregular." The term is inherently prejudicial, and in writing that does not emanate from one of the major masonic bodies terms such as "not real Masons" are frequently thrown around. In practical fact, the Speculative Lodges themselves, in deciding to dispense with the need for Sponsorship of a Master Mason, were "irregular."

Operant Masonry, that is organizations of actual Stone-Masons are well attested in the 17th century. Elias Ashmole joined a Masonic Lodge in Warrington Cheshire in 1646, and is often cited as the first "speculative" Mason, that is a Member who was accorded the privilege of membership without actually being a Stone mason.

> One of the earliest recorded initiations of an English Freemason was in 1646, when Elias Ashmole (1617–1692), an antiquarian, was initiated into a lodge at his father-in-law's house wherein there was not one stonemason present. This seemed to become the norm with more and more 'accepted' brethren, i.e. non-stonemasons, frequenting the Lodges....the early 1700s were becoming known for an increase in convivial social meetings, whether in the clubs or the coffee shops of the time, therefore it would seem logical that a social and moral club would be of great interest to those men of standing. Such were the members of the four lodges who came together to 'reform' Freemasonry on that day in the Goose and Gridiron. The unification of the lodges caused a definitive split between 'operative' or working masons and 'speculative' or non-trade Masons (the term 'speculative' pertaining to their speculation as to what the rituals, working tools, and symbolism of the stonemasons may have meant). Now it was no longer necessary for lodges to be made up of both stonemasons and non-Masons as described in documents as early as the 1660s whereby it was stipulated that a lodge must be properly consisted of at least five accepted brothers and a minimum of one who was an active master of the trade. In the constitutions laid down in 1723, the charges do not stipulate this; they do, however, state that a lodge can only be deemed to be 'regular' if under the jurisdiction of a Grand Lodge, or

> specifically the directorate of the Grand Master or his deputies. A certificate would then be issued and the lodge documented in Grand Lodge's records.[33]

Thus a group of people who did not actually practice the Craft of Masonry, and were presumably running out of active Masons to sponsor them, decided that the criteria for being a "regular" lodge was not in fact having an active master of the Trade, but rather their approval. The "Ancients" wished to maintain a connection to the Operant Lodges, and did not wish to make changes to the traditional ritual. The Ancients left the Grand Lodge of England, formed in 1717, in 1751. They eventually reunited after a generation to form the United Grand Lodge of England in 1813.

This is all fascinating, but it has little to do with our Masonic background. While the Ancients and "Moderns" were quarreling in Britain, Schroeder, Mesmer, Pasqually, Cagliostro, Hund, Koppen, de Negre were forming Rosicrucian and Masonic groups on the Continent. The Grand Orient of France, which absorbed the Grand Lodge of France in 1773, seems to never have had quite the pretensions of the 19th century English, and regards itself as the "largest" body of French Masons, having no illusion about exclusivity.

We have no quarrel with any of the existing Grand Lodges. In the U.S. a curious structure called the "Grand College of Rites" was created in 1932 with the principal purpose of controlling "abandoned and unauthorized" rituals in the United States.

The Memphis tradition has been around for at least two centuries, is contemporary with the United Grand Lodge of England, and has rich antecedents. It is not "regular" in the sense of participating in any of the Grand Lodge systems, however it also has no quarrel with these systems, however it also does not embrace the term "regular" as it is an internal term applicable only to those structures. It is as "regular" as any other branch of Rosicrucianism or Freemasonry, in the sense that it is a living tradition descended from deep Hermetic Roots.

Why Have a Masonic Structure?

It may be a legitimate question to ask why we would bother to have a Masonic Superstructure at all. It is not necessary to Thelema, any more than it is to Wicca or any other religion or philosophy which stands on its own. The reason is that these are initiations, and the Freemason and Rosicrucian traditions stand as the core of the Western initiatory tradition. As such, the structure of a Masonic organization provides a link to the traditions of the past and a sort of continuity. It is an acknowledgment of those Ancestors in spirit who worked to bring the concept of initiation forward to the present day.

Why Memphis and Misraim?

There are several reasons we have selected to operate M∴M∴ as the principal Masonic structure or backbone of this order. First, it very simply provides a convenient manner for the Thelemic Initiations to be operated externally. The true name of the Order of the Thelemic Initiations is a secret and, for purposes of reserving space, holding meetings, even organizing rituals within an existing TTO Lodge or Sanctuary, using the outer name of the Rite may be easier. Likewise, initiates of the Thelemic Order may use the structure of M∴M∴ to conduct public rites and gatherings, etc.

Second, M∴M∴ is French in origin and has always been egalitarian, revolutionary, and progressive in character. It was associated with Revolutionary activities during the 19th century and credibly accused of Socialist affiliations in the 20th. It also has a substantial history of ethnic diversity. It has always been somewhat clandestine and esoteric in nature and has never been predominantly associated with that 20th-century manifestation of Freemasonry which may be seen primarily as a manifestation of white and upper-middle-class privilege.

Third, Crowley had some significant interest in it; enough to take a hand in it and eventually to become at least the putative head of the branch of the tradition operated by Reuss. While he did not write glowingly of the degrees he was handed by Yarker, he saw some value to the overall structure that such an organization could bring to esoteric rites. For the record, we do not claim to operate the Reuss branch of M∴M∴. The tradition is widespread and has evolved along many parallel axes. A lengthier discussion of M∴M∴ may be found in the Appendix.

Some Initiates within the Thelemic Order will already hold the highest degrees of M∴M∴, particularly if they were passed along as part of an Apostolic Succession as has been common since at least the first half of the 20th century. The Thelemic Order otherwise conveys these degrees through its initiations. In practical terms, we also "work" the degrees in that their pageants or stories are incorporated into the Thelemic degrees. It would be wrong, however, to say that this or that Thelemic degree *is* a given degree of masonry. The I° may incorporate certain degrees of M∴M∴ and, more generally, the core stories of Western Masonry and Rosicrucianism, but they are only a part of its overall lesson.

Received Information

In regards to the content of these rituals, there has been much research but also some degree of communication by means of which certain elements were "received" from a variety of sources. From a magical perspective, this is certainly a legitimate method of research. Many of the major works of esoterica, including Liber AL, were received. Doinel actively sought to do spirit-work with Lady Caithness. Crowley repeatedly sought out mediums as partners in his work.

That said, the fact that a work is received does not necessarily make it viable or important. Received material is, by nature, enigmatic and speculative. Material has only been included in these rites if, in the opinion of the authors, it formed a reasonable and legitimate element of the arc and fit with the dramatic goal, which is to facilitate initiation. In every case, extensive contextual correlative use was made of evidence-based materials, including a great deal of scholarship surrounding the ancient cultures of Tyre, Sidon, and Jerusalem, and sources such as Tobias Churton's well-researched *The Lost Pillars of Enoch*.[34]

The Cathar Principals

This is, perhaps, the one place where inspiration played a key and indisputable part in the choices of presentation in these mysteries. The link to the modern Gnostic Church should not be understated. These individuals were not merely in proximity to the Cathar Church, but were certainly well known to and, in some cases, patrons of Guilhabert de Castres. Cathar Bishops had two assistants, called *filius maior* and the *filius minor*, and Zoe Oldenbourg cites de Castres as *filius maior* to the Cathar Bishop of Toulouse from around 1205.[35] He was likely a force in Toulouse long before that. Born around 1165, he would have been well known to the individuals we portray. The de facto Cathar House in Toulouse in the 1220s was the impressive house of the Roaix family, which served as the Palace of Raimond VI in 1215.[36] That these secular figures have chosen to speak to us and through us carries the message that the ideals of the Gnostic Church are larger than the narrow interests of the clergy. We must recall, too, that it was not Guilhabert de Castres alone who spoke through Lady Caithness to Jules Doinel and shaped the modern Gnostic Church.

One might question why the scions and relations of Raimond VI rather than, with the exception of Esclarmonde de Foix, significant members of the Cathar Clergy have been selected to convey this story. One can surmise that the Initiatory Arm is not the Heterodox Gnostic Church. The story arc of Initiation is closer to the Knighthood which protected the Cathars, many of whom never formally or fully professed to Gnosticism, than the Cathar faith itself.

The Feast of the Child of the Prophet

The intimations regarding the Child of the Prophet are firmly rooted in an understanding of a broad array of Thelemic writing. We are told repeatedly that "Children" are the result of the various sex magick workings, including the IX° or XI°. Specifically, "the 'Child' of such a love is a third person, an Holy Spirit, so to speak, partaking both natures, et boundless and impersonal because it is a bodiless creation of a wholly divine nature. Connected with this, there is a Formula of Practical Magick by which the consciousness conceives...and then creates accordingly."[37] When the traditional role of Tahuti in the Osiris myth, providing the formula by which life is brought to the inanimate, is considered, the odd conjunction of Tahuti and the Child of the Prophet begins to fall into perspective.

When secrecy is invoked, one might recall that workings of sex magick of any kind were not the stuff of public discourse in 1904. One might be inclined to further speculate regarding Crowley's tendency to engage in homosexual, i.e. XI°, workings as a seed for his major undertakings; not merely in a focused situation with a disciple, such as Neuburg in the Paris Working, but in a manner that would seem to outsiders rather casual, with partners having no specific background in magick, such as with Shabmodar in Tunis.[38] However, barring some hitherto undisclosed documentary evidence, this must remain in the sphere of speculation. The identification of the Child of the Prophet with his work, as well as the suggestion that the later intentional or unintentional use of "Children" in Liber XV[39] indicates a broadening of that work, is not one which need be accepted at face value to appreciate or participate in the Initiations. It is inherently unprovable and suggestive rather than dogmatic. It is not the way of a heterodox organization to become bound up in forcing a single element of dogma. Conversely, its omission would lessen the relationships drawn in the initiatory text.

Whatever the original intent or historical facts, the symmetry of the particular symbolism is indisputable and is at least *one* sense in which the text may be taken. To directly quote Z.: "There is room for different readings as we have written it. However you read it is powerful and symbolic."

The Techniques of Initiation

Initiation as Theater

There is an absurd idea that initiations are somehow separate from theater. In practical fact, the tradition of initiations is heavily aligned with theater. The Cult of Dionysus, for example, revolved around theater with the Great Dionysia, a festival honoring Dionysus Eleuthereus, organized around a series of plays. To a considerable extent, drama emerged from religious initiation and initiation continued to evolve hand-in-hand with drama.

In the post-classical era, mystery plays had been common since the 5th-century in Europe, though a 1210 Papal edict by Innocent III forbid clergy from staging them. This had the effect of transferring the responsibility for their staging and organization to the trade guilds or towns. These plays are well attested in several cycles in England. In York, we have a well-documented cycle of plays presented on Corpus Christi by the Trade Guilds. We know that, by the 1370s, the use of movable stages or "pageant wagons" was common, making for something like a medieval Macy's Parade, where the stages would stop and perform at twelve different points. The Mason's Play from the York Cycle is the "Coming of the Three Kings to Herod," but this appears to have been dictated by the overall structure of the festival. Various Masonic scholars believe that the core mystery of Hiram Abif harnessed for Freemasonry was originally a mystery play performed by one or more Guild companies of Masons in the British Isles. Certainly, it was likely performed as a mystery play within the Lodges.

If the various mysteries of Freemasonry and Rosicrucianism were presented flamboyantly, the esoteric orders of the late 19th century went above and beyond. The Golden Dawn presented its Rosicrucian mysteries in a specially constructed space. Far from avoiding the bleeding edge of special effects, the Vault of the Adepts was lit with an electric light – a novelty at the time – which ran off a rechargeable battery.

Presentation

Our ideal is not to stage a vast theatrical spectacle. We are not Wagner presenting *Parzival*. To that end we have focused on two devices: Dialog and engagement.

Dialog

While a certain amount of monologue is endemic to initiation, we feel that it has two weaknesses. First, it is dull and tends to lose the listener. Secondly, it leaves the modern mind to answer back. While a few listeners may fall completely and powerfully under the sway of majestic words, the vast majority of us will have a hard time suppressing a tendency to questioning, imagining smart remarks, and so forth. Instead, we have chosen to present much of our initiation as a dialog, with the Fool as the "everyman" character. The Fool also plays a role as a sort of intermediary for the initiates, and provides a practical source of counseling should they have trouble with the initiation.

Exposition through dialog is the primary format for most modern drama. We learn things in shows because the characters talk to each other. Our Fool can ask questions and provoke a response, but also be able to throw back objections. If those objections are not already boiling in the mind of the candidate during initiation, they certainly would at some point afterward. While there will be those who consider this a very modern device, it is the device used by many ancient texts. Plato's work takes the form of dialogues, as does the *Poimandres*, and other elements of the *Corpus Hermeticum*.

Engagement

Our own presentations rely heavily on the principle of engagement. We sacrifice a perfect and crisp presentation by involving the initiates in the presentation of the ongoing drama, ensuring that they will carry a strong memory of at least their own part in the initiations. The reason behind this choice is simple – the most brilliantly staged presentation cannot begin to have the impact of participation. By encouraging many of the initiates to participate we attempt to ensure they will have a powerful and memorable experience. Furthermore, while we do not deal in draconian ordeal at these stages, it is worth noting that, even for the experienced dramatist, sight-reading tends to be difficult, so there is certainly the presumption that the reading will add a certain background of tension, at least in the first initiation.

Pronunciation

Initiates are generally not called upon to sound out particularly difficult words unless they are being initiated by Brevet. Initiations do not ride on correct pronunciation and, as we will investigate with other errors below, it is seldom beneficial to disrupt the initiation by correcting them.

Many of the words and names in the initiations are pronounced in more than one way depending on the region or nationality of the speaker, particularly some which are sounded differently in British English. Where possible, we have given the variants. Otherwise, we have tried to give the most widely used pronunciation. Where pronunciations are given inline they are stylized for ease of reading on the fly and use the most common pronunciation.

There is endless potential for argument. For example, the Latin Passage is likely to be read differently by actual Latin Speakers, those who are familiar with Medieval Church-Latin, and modern Latin speakers. Sovereign Initiators are free to use any pronunciation they find ground for and may teach any pronunciation that seems right to them, provided it is not intentionally contrary or absurd. They may not, however, insist on the use of certain pronunciations. For individuals who have learned to pronounce a name one way, the nuisance of changing it on the fly to meet the expectations of this or that Initiator may take them out of the moment and detract from the initiation at hand.

Handling Misreadings or Errors

There are many points where a reader may misspeak. The Sovereign Initiator is expected to have the text in front of them and be prepared to prompt if someone gets lost or freezes. However, in general, they should not interrupt the initiates. Any interruption to the flow of the proceedings creates a powerful disruption in the train of cognition. Far from aiding in understanding, it may derail the natural facilities of contextualization that allow us to make sense of speech in which individuals occasionally misspeak or even say the opposite of what they meant to. Error also breeds error, and one correction snapped by a Sovereign Initiator may breed ten stumbles as other readers overthink their parts.

As a rule, initiates should not be corrected unless they are clearly fishing for a line or a cue. For instance, in the case that they hesitate over a difficult word, the Sovereign initiator should supply the pronunciation quietly and gently without further comment. If someone becomes flustered or embarrassed, the Sovereign Initiator may and should comfort them ad. lib., and encourage them to continue. There may be the very occasional error that requires *gentle* correction. When this is the case, to be less than disruptive, the Sovereign Initiator should add in a firm but soft tone something like "I believe you meant to say 'I have no right' there," and allow the proceedings to continue. If the reader begins to apologize, they may add "please continue." Likewise, new readers should be schooled not to restart unnecessarily, or apologize for misreadings. A set of lines read imperfectly will generally carry enough context to be understood. Continued restarts or apologies create a "harried" feel and disrupt the ability to process the initiation. The initiate may begin to engage more with the reader's sense of self and discomfort and be taken out of the mind to engage fully with the initiation itself.

Techniques that harm more than help:

> Shotgun – prompts in which a speaker who is slow to begin speaking is instantly prompted, giving the effect that they are slow, or doing a poor job. Some individuals take a moment to process. A natural silence is more desirable than the constant prompting of someone who simply begins a moment or two later than the Sovereign Initiator would prefer.

> School Teacher – prompts in which pointless corrections are made. *The initiation is not a rehearsal, and corrections are usually counterproductive.* The initiations are not read in a vacuum. They carry enormous context and humans have strong abilities to contextualize.

In most cases, even if a *key* word is omitted, the context is reasonably clear. For example, "We make no claim to be better or worse than any other true path, and it may be that our path is not the one which fits you best" read as "We make no claim to be better or worse than any other true path, and it may be that our path is the one which fits you best" muddies the meaning, but is a less than disastrous omission and not worth correcting. Likewise, "we do not ask free men to swear oaths to us as vassals" and "we ask free men to swear oaths to us as vassals" *does* change the meaning, but it is still very likely that the context will carry and, if not, it merely creates a momentary bit of confusion soon ironed out in the exposition, similarly making it not important enough to bring the train of presentation crashing to a halt.

Negotiations

Sovereign Initiators are subject to the guidance of the Supreme Senate of the Initiatory Order III° and to the Cancellarius of the Order. The Supreme Senate may, from time to time, issue guidance which clarifies the latitude available to Sovereign Initiators in making decisions regarding initiations. Where not *specifically* clarified or reserved, all final decisions regarding an individual initiation rest with the Sovereign Initiator. In the case that more than one Sovereign Initiator is present, one Sovereign Initiator should be identified as the lead. In the case that two or more Sovereign Initiators have determined to work together, they should resolve for themselves in advance which is to be considered the lead. The lead initiator shall be the one answerable to the Cancellarius for any irregularities or other issues. Failure to designate authority appropriately, creating difficult to resolve issues for the Supreme Senate of the Initiatory Order III°, may become grounds for suspension of Charter to Initiate.

What Do We Negotiate?

When we talk about negotiation before initiation we are typically looking at three related areas:

> **Ordeals** – we negotiate in terms of any element that might be considered an ordeal or challenge because these have the potential to disrupt initiation for everyone.

Accommodations – specifically in reference to persons with disabilities. In the United States, the Americans with Disabilities Act (ADA) passed in 1990 defines a person with a disability as a person who has a physical or mental impairment that substantially limits one or more major life activity. This includes people who have a record of such an impairment, even if they do not currently have a disability. TTO uses this definition. In the past, there was some resistance to the use of the term "disability." However, we take our cues from the wider disability community which has generally rejected alternative terms. In keeping with that, we prefer to avoid euphemisms that avoid reality and trivialize an important part of the identity of people with disabilities, robbing them of dignity.

Remedies – not every issue that may take someone out of the appropriate headspace in initiation is a disability. Stage fright is not a disability but it may make sight-reading in an impromptu play unpleasant to the point of being counterproductive.

"Negotiation" is a term that comes from the business and diplomacy. However, we pick up the use primarily from the consensual power exchange community where it is used in the context of "negotiating a scene." In this context, one individual is ceding a degree of control to another and the negotiation details what is and is not allowed in order to assure the physical and emotional safety of each individual within their risk profile. A risk profile is an evaluation of a given individual's willingness and ability to take risks, and may include parameters for various types and degree of risk.

Initiation is a consensual power exchange in a way that going to a theater is not. Even if we do not state that someone may not leave, there is incredible social onus brought to bear in the framework of an initiation which creates a coercive environment. There is strong peer pressure to remain within an initiation, even if the individual concerned is not in a receptive state. To try to "undo" this compulsion is to undercut a core element of initiation – that participation is a decision which represents a commitment. Saying "you can leave any time you want, no problem," even if we would not in any way restrain someone from leaving, undercuts the legitimacy of the experience and is likely to be a lie. We cannot protect against the social ramifications in terms of peer disapproval of someone who walks out of an initiation.

Instead we must understand our responsibility in creating a consensual situation. This means acting with due diligence beforehand to ensure that every participant knows the basic outline of what may happen in the initiations, and is able to evaluate the planned experience with reference to their personal risk profile. Most people won't know what a risk profile is, so it is up to the initiator to guide them using the principle of informed consent. That is to say that they need to be aware on a high level of the realities of what is likely to happen.

In negotiations we do not necessarily make a verbal distinction between Accommodations and Remedies to candidates. However, we should be aware that we are required, in all circumstances possible, to accommodate disabilities. We have somewhat more discretion in how to handle remedies. Still, in negotiating for initiation we must be pro-active. We must look not only at any potential issues that the initiate has flagged, but evaluate any stated preferences or issues against what we know of the initiation.

Why Do We Negotiate?

The point of initiations is to offer an emotional/magickal experience which creates or catalyzes change within the individual, immediately or in the ensuing time-frame. In order to do this, we must provide a somewhat uniform experience. For example, let us theorize an initiation in which a live, caged, tarantula was introduced into the room. For most initiates, the experience would be one of curiosity mixed with some degree of fear. Provided the cage was

Vol. I, 0° Petitioner - II° K.R.C.　　　45

not opened nor was any threat made to open it, it would create a tension and some anxiety, which might be desirable. Some initiates, perhaps those from regions where tarantulas are fairly common, might feel no anxiety at all, but provided there were several such points producing limited anxiety, the basic structure of the initiation would not be undone. If they experienced nothing they would at least be no worse off. For a few individuals who experience arachnophobia the presence of a tarantula might create not mild anxiety, but terror. In this case they are not experiencing the initiation as it was intended but, rather, experiencing a "house of horrors" that has little to do with the intent of the initiations. Negotiations allow us to identify the metaphorical "tarantulas" in the initiation and ensure that they do not create an experience that bears no resemblance to our intent – one which, rather than supporting initiation, in fact overwhelms it.

Pre-Negotiation

It is fairly important to engage in pre-negotiation in regards to the initiations. Sovereign Initiators are given a wide latitude in working up their own process for pre-negotiation. We supply application forms or petitions in this edition, however these may be updated by the Supreme Senate of the Initiatory Order III° through the Cancellarius of the Initiatory Arm. The Supreme Senate of the Initiatory Order III° will set specific rules as to whether or not certain forms must be used, whether or not dated forms can be used, and whether or not Sovereign Initiators may deviate from the process.

There is no set time-frame for pre-negotiation, however, it should ideally be carried out far enough in advance to ensure that candidates:

- Have time to collect costuming and required supplies
- Have time to think through any potential trigger issues and ensure their own comfort level
- Have ample time to feel they have been able to discuss and talk through any second thoughts

It is the responsibility of the Sovereign Initiator to meet the needs of the candidate in terms of negotiation. Some candidates may have trouble negotiating online, where typed messages make it hard for them to gauge tone, and may tend to respond badly to written messages. Other candidates may have a hard time with phone or verbal communications, preferring the time to write and think. The Sovereign Initiator must develop some degree of facility in all forms of communication in order to meet the initiate where they are comfortable. Typically, we expect to see two phases of negotiation: one taking place through online communication and another taking place in a final consultation, in person, before initiation actually occurs. It is important that no Sovereign Initiator be too busy on the day of to actually consult and complete negotiations.

Privacy in Negotiation

It should go without saying, though we will restate it here, that negotiations regarding initiation are a private and sacred trust between candidate and Sovereign Initiator. From the perspective of TTO as a church, this is considered to be religious counseling by a qualified layperson and subject to all legal provisions of confidentiality implied therein. The communication and retention of records regarding negotiation is subject to privacy regulations set in place by the Inspector General of The Thelemic Order, in cooperation with the Supreme Senate of the Initiatory Order III°. The specifics of privacy requirements will be handled through specific circulars. However, we can give a brief overview of the meta-concepts.

- Records of negotiations for 0°-III° are never shared with anyone but a duly authorized representative of the Supreme Senate of the Initiatory Order III° as confirmed by the Cancellarius of the Initiatory Arm. This includes records of negotiations where the candidate eventually declined to initiate, or was refused initiation. This includes law enforcement. Any requests from law enforcement are to be referred immediately to the Inspector General of The Thelemic Order, who will handle them through the organization's legal counsel. In the event that any records are confiscated by law enforcement for any reason, the Inspector General of The Thelemic Order must be informed immediately.

- Records of negotiations for 0°-III° are never shared with other Sovereign Initiators or individuals of higher degrees unless specifically authorized by a representative of the Supreme Senate of the Initiatory Order III° as confirmed by the Cancellarius of the Initiatory Arm.

- Records of negotiations for 0°-III° are stored in a safe, encrypted, environment. This may mean an electronic service which provides licensed commercial services for communication or on a duly encrypted device.

- Records of negotiations for 0°-III° are never to be stored in a shared environment where other individuals may access them. This includes accounts which significant others have access to, etc.

- Details of negotiations for 0°-III° may be shared with staff at a given initiation to the degree the Sovereign Initiator deems necessary to ensure that any accommodations and remedies are safely carried out. The Sovereign Initiator will not communicate any additional information about the attitudes, mindset, other options or choices, concerns, etc. of the candidate, except to such extent as may be necessary to ensure safety.

- Staff will be charged on their oaths not to repeat any details regarding remedies or accommodations in reference to any specific individual.

- From time to time Sovereign Initiators my come to feel that they are not the best qualified to handle a specific situation requiring remedy or accommodation and may suggest an alternative Sovereign Initiator to the candidate. In this case, with the permission of the candidate, they may discuss their negotiations with another Sovereign Initiator, including explicit information regarding the initiate's identity.

- Sovereign Initiators may discuss with those with a need to know., e.g. other Sovereign Initiators in a training situation, other leaders, etc., the general details of any situations involving remedies or accommodations, in the interest of promoting safety. In all cases, every effort shall be made to withhold personally identifying information about a given candidate.

Initiation Without Pre-Negotiation

The goal of the Initiatory Arm is to promulgate the law of Thelema through initiation. Within the limitations of any specific orders of the Supreme Senate of the Initiatory Order III°, the Sovereign Initiator is given broad latitude to conduct initiations, even under irregular circumstances. This may lead to situations where it becomes expedient to initiate on short notice. Probably the most common situation will be the potential addition of a last minute extra party to a planned initiation. While additional guidance will be forthcoming from the Supreme Senate of the Initiatory Order III°, in any situation where initiation is performed without pre-negotiation, exceptional care must be taken to ensure that informed consent exists. This may mean allocating extra time, etc. The life experience and esoteric experience of a candidate should be a major area of consideration in any decision along these lines.

Negotiation and Ordeals

The Initiatory Ordeals are not the Ordeals of Thelema

While there are many interpretations of the lines in *Liber AL* that regard ordeals, most interpretations suggest that they will not come out of initiation rituals written down on paper. While it is true, we are told of the Prophet, "He must teach; but he may make severe the ordeals."[40] We can agree that the ordeals left in the initiations by Reuss and Crowley are not particularly severe. There are many other references to ordeals, such as the "ordeals of my knowledge!"[41] but these references seem to be to the sempiternal ordeals implicit in Thelema, not playing with wrist cuffs or thumbscrews in a Masonic Lodge.

Challenges as Ordeal

For this reason, we draw a line between challenges issued by human beings in ritual and ordeals which are experienced by the Adept in their journey. In higher degrees, when non-human entities play a more direct part, these concepts may merge. Certainly, the ritual performed by Crowley and Neuburg on Da'leh Addin[42] was a both challenge and ordeal, but it was an inspired ritual of a different magnitude. What is critical to appreciate is that, at Da'leh Addin, the challenge did not come from Crowley or Neuburg themselves, clever trick devices, clumsily made wooden furniture, or any human agency. We affirm the Thelemic Initiations are inspired and, as the Adept advances, they may be invited to similar undertakings. Yet, the first three workings of a degree system is not the place for ordeals of that magnitude.

Traditionally, there has been a great deal of emphasis on the idea of a challenge in degree work. The idea is that this challenge provides an ordeal so significant that it is life changing and effectively causes initiation. Perhaps, in the days when Roman Soldiers worked the Mithraic Initiations, this was true but it has the case for centuries. In practical fact, initiatory challenges are a Grand Guignol which act to scare some candidates disproportionately while having no impact on others. Certainly, for the initiate who has never faced anything but the comforts of a suburban home, having a knife placed at the breast might be discomfiting, even potentially life-changing. Yet, for most initiates, secure in the knowledge that the Lodge has operated for some time without being the subject of a massive murder investigation, such threat is minimal.

For example, take a challenge common to a certain initiation from the early 20th century which has been published and discussed for decades: the candidate is tipped into a dunking tank in a questionable lesson about trust. For most of those who participated, the general outline of the experience was no secret and the whole thing was more or less a charade; mostly annoying for having to stand around in wet clothing after. For a few, it was a safety hazard. And, for a few who have issues with falling, balance, or a fear of water, it was a diabolic torment. Surely those experiences are not in any way equal.

It is nearly impossible for a challenge designed by human beings to be equal for all people. One person's greatest fear is another's minor inconvenience. In the distant past, it may have been the case that initiations could pose an actual threat to life and limb. However, our ethics do not permit this. Therefore, as we do not live a time when one can place a bare gladius at the throat without full intention of using it, we must acknowledge that most attempts to create a true ordeal within the framework of initiations are inherently defective. If they are severe, it is by accident. If they are not, then they mean little. We have chosen instead to deliver certain challenges which are designed, not to be true ordeals, but rather to prepare the initiate for those ordeals which they will most certainly experience in life as they become cognizant of the significance of initation.

The Thelemic Initiations

Challenges as Winnowing

Another approach concedes these challenges are not truly life changing ordeals, but sees them as obstacles to keep the unworthy and unfit from participating in our initiations. In the late 19th century, when Europe had known no great wars for decades and most initiates could be assumed to be middle class Victorian men with similar education and backgrounds, perhaps this idea had some merit. At the same time, Europe was in the sway of the cult of "muscular Christianity" and this sort of challenge was designed to weed out those who were not neurotypical; who were not sufficiently "strong" in a sort of middle-school sense that implies more about being able to sit comfortably through a slasher flick than any real resilience or inner strength.

Challenges as a method of culling out those who "don't fit" is a mechanism for elitism which favors neurotypical people with secure middle class backgrounds. It discriminates against those who have experienced trauma and those who process information or experiences in a way that does not conform to assumptions about what is "normal." Some elements tend to be more impactful on minorities. For example, situations which require stripping or bondage are likely to be disproportionately impactful to women or transpeople. These are elements which might legitimately trigger issues around sexual violence and numerous studies show women and transpeople to have been far more likely than men to have experienced attempted or completed sexual violence.

Legitimate Uses of Challenges

If using challenges as a winnowing mechanism is self-defeating and unethical and the idea that challenges within initiations are "ordeals" in the sense they are spoken of in *Liber AL* simply wrong, then what is the point of initiatory challenges? Are there any legitimate uses?

Some Challenge is Inevitable

Even if initiations were no more than sitting and listening to a lecture, that would be a challenge for someone. Because experience is so broad, what may be a standard part of initiation for one person may constitute a challenge to someone else. For example, theater is used within the initiations not as a challenge per se, but as a means of increasing of participation. We must regard it as a challenge, however, for people with stage fright, or difficulties reading.

These challenges are land mines. That is to say they do not appear to be very formidable, but may destroy the experience of the initiation for someone who is vulnerable to them. As initiators, it is our role to guide people to initiation and part of our job is to guide our initiates around and keep their experience from being wrecked by land mines. We try to allow for these challenges to be bypassed to give a more uniform experience.

Some Challenge Creates a Receptive Mindset

Anyone who has passing familiarity with the work of Milton Erickson is aware that most religious ceremonies (as well as most public ceremonies and most commercials) create what he referred to as a "hypnotic modality." This is not hypnosis in the stage sense, but rather a natural learning state in which people become receptive to taking in new ideas and new information. Most classrooms construct a hypnotic modality. The Roman Catholic Mass is a profound example of creating a hypnotic modality. A strange setting, elevated ceilings, a wealth of complex decoration, reading from an elevated position, and even the use of incense all work to mildly overwhelm the senses. These elements can also be seen in political speeches, academic presentations, and so forth.

The point of a hypnotic modality is not to completely overwhelm the individual but, rather, to create a receptive state. The Catholic Mass would likely fail if the organ were ramped up to arena concert levels or the hall-filled with choking incense. Thus, the sweet spot is one where there is mild anxiety and a slight overwhelming of the senses. We see this in any movie.

Music, sudden cuts, and even jump scares are used to create tension and amp up our receptivity to the plot. There's nothing underhanded about this. Its stagecraft, pure and simple, from the earliest days of theater. Most traditional initiations were designed to accomplish this for the target audience. The Golden Dawn initiations with their complex props, staging, and dialog aim for this, but Crowley thought that they did so at the cost of clarity. His take on initiations focused on a compelling story with embarrassment or physical duress creating the underlying tension.

Humor Versus Hazing

Saying things which intimidate candidates or lead to them being more scared is not productive. At the best, it can ratchet up tension and, at the worst, it can constitute a sort of hazing. On the other hand, a dogmatic preoccupation with this can demoralize the participants in initiation and suck the spontaneity out of it, leaving initiation joyless and sterile. Remember that The Thelemic Initiations encourage repetition through participation. Having the presenters of the initiation take no pleasure in it will discourage this.

The Value of Humor

Humor is a natural part of human conduct. Even if Plato didn't much care for it, Aristotle certainly acknowledged the value of wit.[43] As much as it can be used to emphasize power differentials and legitimize longstanding inequalities, humor is also the first weapon in breaking down inequalities and double standards. The incongruity theory of humor suggests that humor violates our mental expectations. As such, it is a leveling device used for breaking down established norms; a function which cleaves close to that of Thelema itself. Often, the first step in an attack on the status quo is jokes. In authoritarian states such as the Communist Soviet Union of the previous century, covert jokes were often one of the only forms of authentic expression, leading the breakdown of the state. It could be argued that, despite justification, many authorities who have repressed humor did so more because it challenged their established status quo than because it was actually disrespectful.

An older theory of humor dating from the early 18th century suggests that it provides a sort of relief. While this is observably untrue of all humor, relief may more appropriately be considered one social function of humor. In situations such as initiations, humor can serve the purpose of breaking up and relieving tension on two levels. While a certain level of anticipatory anxiety is usually desirable in candidates, an excess of it is generally counterproductive, especially in the Foundational Degrees. To that end, humor can moderate anxiety. Just as importantly, an initiation is most often a situation where a group of amateurs will perform a piece of emotional theater for an audience which may contain people they care about or wish to impress. Their amateur status often renders them very anxious and that may lead to short tempers, argument, and stoke any existing social conflicts. Shared humor can be a bonding element. It introduces a sense of proportion. Initiations should be taken seriously, but taking them too seriously will seldom improve the quality. Rather, it will sour the process making it miserable for everyone involved.

Liber AL leaves very little doubt as to where Thelemites fall on the issue of humor. "Beauty and strength, leaping laughter and delicious languor, force and fire, are of us. "[44] Of the mocking laughter of others we are told to "fear not at all."[45] The first of the Thelemic Initiations talks to us of *Ludus,* which is a kind of playful love. Laughter that principally exists to mock does not really become us. It is the role of the Sovereign Initiator in preparation to gently reign in any mocking humor and channel it to absurdity. It is important to ensure the initiates are comfortable and feel a part of the fun, or that they shall soon be made a part of the fun, rather than mocked. Yes, the difference can be subtle, yet if a Sovereign Initiator cannot recognize and explain the difference between mocking and absurd humor, how can they possibly master the multitude of other subtleties in Thelema itself?

Certainly, there are places where humor does not belong. Before the law, in some professional proceedings, and certain types of work or business matters are all inappropriate. But the initiations are not a lawsuit or a business meeting. Initiations are intensely intimate and personal. To deny humor in and around our initiations is to deny *Ludus*, one of the forms of love that we explore. Where we remove love, any part of love, we shortchange the Law. Humor must then be a part both of our initiations and our overall initiatory experience.

For the initiator we see two core skills in differentiating between humor and hazing: sensitivity and consent.

Sensitivity

Sensitivity to the content of humor and who it is being directed at is important. One element for this is determining if there is a historic axis of inequality. White men making jokes at the expense of other white men is much different than white men making jokes at the expense of historically marginalized groups, including women and BIPOC individuals. This is not to say that one cannot joke around anyone who represents a minority or that only historically marginalized people are allowed to joke. It does mean that consideration should be given to issues of tone and privilege.

Jokes and humor should carry some awareness of trauma within our population. People approaching initiation may be in a highly suggestible state and more sensitive to such things than they otherwise would be. The "Curse of Knowledge" - the tendency of people to overestimate what outsiders may easily know or deduce – may lead initiators to deem absurd and innocuous something which may not be seen as such.

It should go without saying that someone's marginalized identity, disability, gender, or sexuality should never be the basis for jokes. Making jokes at the expense of someone's race, gender, or sexual orientation is seldom appropriate, even if they claim they are "cool with it" or if they lead in it themselves. Likewise, in regards to jokes that carry a sexualized context, even in a rather absurd and unlikely context, remember that the marginalized groups who bear a disproportionate burden of sexual assault may find such jokes off-putting or even traumatizing.

Consent

Groups and individual Sovereign Initiators will have their own "feel" and traditions. That said, Sovereign Initiators are expected to sublimate their needs and style to meet the needs and style of candidates. We are not a society of the "wise" who exist to inflict on those "lesser" than ourselves our own experience and understandings of initiations. By giving the ability to initiate to those only a few grades farther along than those being initiated, we frame the role of the Sovereign Initiator as guide and mentor rather than master to student, and the guide respects the needs and preferences of those whom they are guiding.

Gaining consent and making sure that candidates understand the meaning of jokes and humor is a part of that mentorship. This starts out with making sure the candidates are informed so that they can decide whether or not to consent. Saying early on in the process something to the effect of, "In our initiatory practices we sometimes joke around, in particular sometimes we tease about the upcoming challenges. I want you to know that if you have real questions, I'll try to answer them and that, joking aside, we won't spring anything on you which has not been negotiated. And if any of the jokes make you uncomfortable, it is my responsibility to make sure that stops and does not hurt your initiatory experience. That is important to me."

This approach accomplishes several things. First, it gives an opportunity to express discomfort in advance. Second, it makes it clear that self-advocacy on the part of the initiate will be respected and acted upon. Furthermore, by making it clear that there is the potential for damage to the initiatory experience it gives some leverage to the candidate. Rather than feeling they are being "bad" by requesting restraint, they can feel they are being "good" by working with the Initiator to secure a successful initiatory experience. Is this an ideal consent framework between equals? No. The fact is that initiation is not an inherently egalitarian experience, though it is a process of elevation. Rather than ignoring that paradigm, we have to respect it and enable self-advocacy within the initiatory framework.

Remedies and Accommodations

About Accommodations

In the United States, the Americans with Disabilities Act (ADA) makes it illegal to discriminate against disabled individuals in both hiring practices and public accommodations. The ADA defines a person with a disability as a person who has a physical or mental impairment that substantially limits one or more major life activity. Title III of ADA requires that businesses and publicly accessible areas make reasonable accommodations to serve people with disabilities. This may include modification of buildings or renovation of spaces. However "Religious entities are exempt from the requirements of title III of the ADA." In practical fact, that exemption is because religious entities cannot always renovate spaces or afford the rental of accessible public spaces. Still, as Thelemites, we believe that the Law is for all and, thus, we have an ethical obligation to make initiation available to everyone.

It is the obligation of the Sovereign Initiator to make every effort to accommodate individuals with disabilities. This may include, but is not limited to:

- Considering alternative venues
- Enlisting the aid of facility management or authorities to provide accessibility (e.g. in one situaiton a space was inaccessible, but the building management was able to provide access via a staff elevator).
- Making reasonable alterations to existing space
- Making any any all changes necessary to staging, expectations for movement, etc.

Essentially, *no barrier that is within our control* should stand between any person and initiation on the basis of disability. Furthermore, every effort should be made to accommodate disability within the framework of an existing initiation. In some cases, issues of access may create so formidable a barrier as to necessitate an alternative initiation for a person with disabilities. Socially, to be separated is demeaning to human dignity. As a last resort in extreme cases, a separate accommodation may be necessary. However, it is better to make changes to or move an existing initiation than to create a separate initiation ritual.

Exceptions

There are extremely rare circumstances in which disabilities may create a significant barrier to initiation.

Consent – In the case of people with mental disabilities, there may be legitimate question of whether or not the person involved can give informed consent. This would be outstandingly unusual. However, this might occur if, for example, someone was presented for initiation by a guardian. That said, we believe in respecting, to the greatest degree possible, the agency and autonomy of all individuals. Outside of the ability to provide informed consent, mental disabilities should not be a barrier to initiation. This does not mean, however, that evidence of previous violent or unsafe behavior cannot be taken into account in evaluating whether or not an individual is to be allowed initiation, even if that behavior was a result of mental disability.

Safety – in some cases there may not be a safe way to get someone who has a disability into an initiation site. While alternative venues should be considered, they are not always available. We must balance the desire to accommodate initiating everyone within the same social setting along with the safety of the individual.

About the Remedies and Accommodations

What are the Remedies?

Where we list potential remedies for issues, they are listed in order from the ones which change the candidate's experience least to those remedies which will change their experience the most. Understand that these aren't a list of best to worst. On one hand, we want to preserve as much of the experience as possible. On the other, people for whom a given situation, such as jump scares, is a hard limit are not going to get the intended experience. They are going to get a completely different experience that bears no resemblance to it.

How to Present the Remedies

Before presenting any remedies, it is important to tell the candidate that there are several *possible* remedies which can be adjusted to their level of comfort and ask if they would like to hear them all before making a decision. In a minority of cases, there may be only one remedy and that needs to be explained as well.

Language should never be used which indicates either that some choices are better or worse, or that they require more or less work on the part of the Initiator. Such language may make the candidate feel compelled to make a poor choice for themselves which lessens their chance of initiating successfully. Focus on the concept that initiation is about mindset. Candidates may feel ashamed or defensive about having to ask for exceptions. Affirm that doing so is a good and valuable choice because it helps keep them in the correct mindset.

Take negotiation seriously, but keep a fairly light tone. The more that someone feels it is very important, the more they are likely to agonize, freeze up, and overthink. For 0°-IV°, it is possible to say something like "The challenges at these grades are very secondary to the content. It is better that you choose the most comfortable option to make sure you are not distracted from the core of the initiation." This gives the candidate permission to feel they are making a good choice in choosing a more comfortable accommodation, rather than cheating themselves of an experience or imposing on others.

Good Language
- I have a list of possible choices to adjust the ritual to help you maintain the proper mindset

- Preserving your mindset during the initiation is the most important thing. Let's talk about what changes you can choose from to make sure that you are able to stay in the initiatory mindset.

Bad Language
- I have some choices, some of which are better, and some of which are worse

- There are some changes we can make, some of which are harder than others

- There are choices you can make, some of which take you further from the intent of the initiation than others.

Helping them Choose

Part of the art of being an initiator is helping guide people to good choices. Often, a candidate will ask the initiator what they think would be best or ask them to make the choice. While we want everyone to advocate for themselves, letting someone more experienced choose for them is in some cases a rational form of self-advocacy.

There is an easy method to making the choice. In most cases, if they are wavering between two choices, they are seeking permission to take the easier of the two. Choose that for them. If you make the easier choice and they resist, then you can offer the more difficult. It is better to let them talk you into the more personally challenging option than for them to feel that you talked them into something they didn't want. The initiator who pushes someone for "their own good" puts themselves at risk. There is an adage which spans several categories of performative interaction that states "it is better to leave them wanting more than they got, than sorry they got what they did." Remember, the initiations are tiered, and the challenges at the Foundational Grades not intended to be incredibly intense. They mostly exist to allow the candidate to get a feel for the initiations and have enough information to make better choices. If someone is forced to undergo a challenge in a foundational initiation and then fails to return, you have not helped them at all.

There may be special cases. For example, someone who has self-doubt may truly want a meaty reading role, but be afraid to ask for it. If you believe this is the case, rather than making a snap judgment, ask probing questions. "Have you enjoyed getting to perform in the past?" You could ask them to do a brief sight-reading from the script (a minor revelation will do no lasting harm) and then ask them how they felt about it. In some cases they will vacillate. Make the easier choice and say "let's do it like this this time. If you feel you need to be challenged more, then we can work on that at the next grade." That gives both of you a graceful out.

Alternative Remedies

A Sovereign Initiator is not limited to the remedies listed in the description of the ritual. There may be other potential remedies that make sense in a given context and the Sovereign Initiator is given broad discretion to modify the ritual in any way which does not damage the basic fabric in order to achieve a reasonable remedy.

The Oath Challenges and Unwritten Remedies

A major challenge in the initiations is a series of points during which the initiates are asked to swear oaths of fealty. These challenges perform several functions. They simulate the lure of the abyss – the desire to conform, to "make a deal with the devil," or to otherwise become mired in using newly gained powers not for the fulfillment of will, but at another's behest. They create some dramatic tension and also allow the initiates to leave feeling good about themselves. The challenges are generally set up to win and, if the initiates lose, it is a soft loss. They're training bouts, not make-or-break challenges to prevent forward motion. That sort of challenge doesn't exist in the framework of the foundational initiations, except as it is provided by the initiations themselves. Someone who cannot show up and be appropriately and safely social might well eliminate themselves. Someone highly offended at sexual or queer content might drop out. Still, for the most part, the early initiations are trainers.

We don't list these challenges in the things that may be triggers, but they could be. An individual who is particularly sensitive about failure or about any feeling they are being tricked might take these elements badly. So why don't we advertise them? First, in terms of potential issues, we discuss things that are not a part of normal life experience. Hearing a tirade about queer people being evil or women not knowing their place *shouldn't* be a part of normal life experience. If it is, we consider that someone is in a fairly abusive situation. Likewise, jump scares or loud noises right behind you aren't things people should expect in day to day life. However, being pushed into conformity or being told one must give allegiance to some person or cause that has no legitimate claim on us is not unusual. Neither is having to say "no." It is a standard social engagement most of us repeat dozens of times a day as we respond to advertising, employers, and even friends and family members. Learning to put our will front and center and not be told by others what our imperatives should be is a part of life. We warn candidates that these things may happen when we warn that the Initiations are not a stage show to passively watch.

Nevertheless, the Sovereign Initiator must know that these confrontations have the potential to be problematic. In the process of negotiation with candidates, if there is a feel that they may take these challenges badly, it is up to the Sovereign Initiator to attempt to prepare them without undue advance coaching. There is no one quality that may lead to taking these elements badly, however anyone who suggests they are strongly sensitive, that they become angry easily, or that they have trouble understanding social exchanges may be someone who could benefit from extra support in these situations. During the Initiations, it is up to the Fool to defuse any problems that do occur. This is the primary reason the Sovereign Initiator should most often be the Fool. If the role of the Fool is handed off, make sure the performer knows what is expected of them in this regard.

When to Say "No"

The Law is for All, but the Thelemic Initiations may not be. Disability needs to be accommodated where possible. Other issues should be remedied when reasonable, however it must be remembered that a negotiation includes the right of either party to say "no." Every Sovereign Initiator has the right to decide on the basis of negotiation that they are not willing to take on a given initiate.

There are, of course limits, to this. No refusal should *ever* be based in any violation of TTO's non-discrimination policy, which includes the bases of ethnicity, ancestry, appearance, gender, gender identity, gender expression, sexuality, sexual identity, sexual expression, international origin, age or, as previously stated, disability. In the case of a request to initiate as part of a group, the overall welfare of the group must be considered. If someone has a dozen hard limits and is not satisfied with those remedies which largely preserve the experience for others, they may not be suitable for initiation as part of a group. For those individuals it may be better to pursue a different path. Other reasons for refusing initiation include concerns that an individual will behave safely or basic incompatibility with the ideals the Sovereign Initiator knows are put forward through the initiations.

How to Say No

While every Sovereign Initiator has the right to decline a candidate, they do not have the right to be impolite or to humiliate or denigrate any candidate. Sovereign Initiators should observe the following rules:

- Declining should take place well before initiation, if possible. The pre-negotiation phase should be used to determine if there are any issues likely to result in declining to initiate.

- Day-of declination of candidates accepted in advance should be an absolute last resort used only in the case where there is some major last minute disagreement or unsafe behavior, including the candidate being in a state unsuitable for initiation (e.g. drunk, belligerent).

- Candidates who ask for last minute inclusion can be declined on the basis of prior preparations without prejudice and encouraged to apply in advance for a later initiation.

- The Sovereign Initiator should, in most cases, refund any monies collected. If part of the Initiation fee for site, etc., is non-refundable, this must be clearly spelled out in advance. Amounts that are not refunded must represent actual purchases or non-refundable payments. Any situation in which individuals are consistently declined for initiation without a full refund may lead to investigation by the Cancellarius of the Initiatory Arm.

- The Sovereign Initiator should speak politely and in a businesslike fashion. They should refrain from any ad hominem or negative characterizations or statements regarding the declined candidate. Unless the issue is one of basic safety, they should state that they are unable to work with the situation as presented, but not preclude the possibility that a different Sovereign Initiator might be able to.

A general rule is that, to the greatest extent possible, we do not want to send people away angry. If someone simply is not in the right headspace at the current time, or has some rethinking to do, we do not want to make an enemy of them. Likewise, there is nothing to be gained by fighting with people who will never be suitable to initiate. Focusing them on our organization does no one any favors.

There will be people who become angry and will not disengage, becoming belligerent or antagonistic, through online communications or in person. It is the role of the Sovereign Initiator to keep calm, remember they represent the Initiatory Arm, and move on without stooping to their level. Any level of initiation should be represented with dignity and grace in all cases. Likewise, no Sovereign Initiator should allow themselves to be bullied into an initiation that they do not think is safe.

Alternative Presentations

Alternative presentation is different from accommodation or remedies. *Alternative Presentation* means to present the initiatory ritual outside the normal framework of initiation. Alternative Presentations will be used most often when either the Initiation is in a distant or new area where there is as of yet no initiatory body or when an initiation that people have paid to travel to must either move ahead without some personnel or be canceled resulting in losses.

Circumstances for Alternative Presentation

Generally, Alternative Presentation is made in two circumstances:

- Developing Areas: The power of the initiation is carried in its Logos, for which the Sovereign Initiator serves as vehicle. While guidance will change annually it is intended that a single Sovereign Initiator can carry the spark of the Logos to a distant area. Some Sovereign Initiators who travel widely may frequently be forced to use Alternative Presentation. It is assumed that, as the Initiations are more widely distributed, Alternative Presentation for this reason will become less common.

- Emergencies: Scheduled initiations may move forward in the event of a shortage of personnel at the discretion of the Sovereign Initiator. This might occur if, for example, an illness or travel delay caused a group of people to miss an initiation, however there was a strong desire to present it for those who were able to be present.

The Thelemic Initiations

Informed Consent

In the case of an Alternative Presentation, the candidates must be told that the presentation is being done in an alternative fashion and given the opportunity to withdraw and await a more regular initiation. It is imperative that the initiates be told, roughly, what is going on. For example, "normally we have four people, but today we are presenting a version where I will read two roles." Honesty balances mystery and most initiates will be sympathetic to any difficulties if the presentation is made under difficult circumstances. The initiates should also be strongly encouraged to go through the initiation as observers or performers in the future, in order to ensure they catch all nuances of the experience.

Properties

A lack of properties could occur for any number of reasons. Props could have been lost in transit, An initiation could have been arranged at the last minute because certain people are available. Properties are very helpful, but they are not the heart and soul of the initiations. Symbolic props should be used where possible, and pantomimed where not possible. Likewise, minimal symbolic costuming may be used, though it may be better to forgo costuming entirely. A ritual should not stop for lack of properties, however it is the role of the Sovereign Initiator to do everything possible to ensure that regular and high quality properties are available.

Voices

There are two methods for handling a lack of personnel in the ritual. One is double-reading, in which one Initiator reads multiple parts. The second is brevet, in which one of the initiates reads the role of one of the principals, in a fashion explored more thoroughly below.

The preference for method lays, to some extent, with the Sovereign Initiator. Two matters should be given consideration:

- Is there an initiate available who has the skill and facility to read two parts and keep them well-defined? Alternatively, is there someone capable of playing the Fool with facility, allowing the Sovereign Initiator to read two principal roles?
- Is there a candidate who is well qualified to read the role of a Principal via brevet (discussed below)? In practical fact, many experienced esotericists will already have advanced through some other system of initiation or may have some experience with acting. Such initiates may appreciate the core of The Thelemic Initiations even more if they experience them while reading one of the performer roles while only stepping out of it long enough to take the oath of the degree.

Qualification for Brevet

Many persons who come to 0°-II° in our Sovereign Sanctuary will be fully qualified to initiate to a higher degree. That is to say they will have already undergone the ordeals of some of the Foundational Grades through initiation with G.D., Wicca, or some other initiatory organization, or through their own life experience. While they may have been advanced studies in the previous century, the materials and concepts of 0°-II° are fairly well known in the modern era and the life experiences and ordeals are those which many persons of middle age will already be familiar with.

We feel that the Thelemic Initiations provide a unique experience, unlike any other initiation. We believe firmly that even those who have already done considerable initiatory work will find things to take away from this experience. We cannot deny, however, that persons with more initiatory and or life experience will take away *different* lessons. While we state the initiations may be experienced repeatedly on different levels, we also concede that the initial grades are introductory. To that end, experiencing them initially as an officer rather than a candidate is not likely to significantly lessen them for many experienced and qualified persons.

No one may be forced or coerced to take initiation as a brevet. For some individuals, brevetting will be a small matter and have little impact on their reception of the grade. For others, it may tremendously weaken or lessen the experience. Determining the likely impact and choosing well is the job of the Sovereign Initiator. It is important that this not be presented as a matter of rank or bragging rights. Brevetting is a matter of necessity and, while it does indicate a certain degree of trust, it should never be suggested that it is better than any other mode of initiation.

When to Brevet

With this in mind, it may be considered better to brevet one or more well-experienced candidates in order to perform a full initiation than to struggle with an initiation in which there are not sufficient officers. It is worth considering that the initiations are designed with the idea that the candidates will be performing at least part of the time, so initiating while performing a role is not intrinsically threatening to the mindset, though it may be more difficult when performing a major role.

The discretion to brevet in regards to the initiations 0°-II° rests with the Sovereign Initiator. It is useful if individuals brevetted experience the initiations as an observer or performer later in order to pick up on details they may have missed due to focus on their role. It is not the intention of the Sovereign Sanctuary that this should be a *common* means of initiation. The Thelemic Initiations are not merely the extension of the Thelemic egregore to be conveyed, but an experience that is carefully crafted and designed to facilitate initiation.

How to Brevet

Our system of brevet and "reading-in" is a compromise and improvement over the Classic system whereby a reasonably qualified Adept might be handed a sheaf of initiation papers after being "recognized" at a high degree. It is meant to ensure that the Mysteries can be presented widely and rapidly, while at the same time ensuring that everyone connected with the Mysteries has, in fact, gone through them. In general, the principle reason for initiation by reading-in is to prepare a candidate for performance as a brevet in an initiation in the immediate future. Where there is no pressing need, reading-in should not stand in for a regular initiation and it may be better to defer initiation until a more regular initiation can be arranged.

Reading-In – the initiation is read by the Initiator, or with the prospective brevet, who voices all of the characters, discerning them by stating who is speaking. While there are no specific guidelines, this should not be done in a comic or disrespectful fashion – particularly one which mocks the traditionally female roles with a poor imitation. If the reader is especially competent and can respectfully differentiate the voices by moderation, they may use that method provided the characters are quite distinct. In this mode, it is imperative that the recipient be aware of who is supposed to be speaking.

If the intention is for the person being read-in to perform the next day in one of the roles, they may follow along with the manuscript. While the candidate who is read-in is held to be prepared to act as a Brevet Officer in the initiation indefinitely, they are not considered to be possessed of the grade until they have actually been through the ritual.

Brevet without Reading-In – where possible a brevet should be read-in, however an experienced esotericist and dramatist might be allowed to sight read the initiation at the discretion of the Sovereign Initiator. This would typically be the case only for a last minute brevet.

Electronic and Online Initiations

Currently, the Supreme Senate of the Initiatory Order III° does not allow for initiation through virtual means. However, as the ability to simulate physical presence increases, we must consider the possibility. As of this publication, no use of remote participants is considered acceptable in the Initiations. In the future, consideration may be given to allowing some readers to be present via some form of telepresence. It is arguable that a disembodied-but-remote voice might be no more disruptive than someone having to read two roles in as an emergency remedy but, because physical engagement is part of initiation, telepresence for candidates (e.g. flatscreen presence through Zoom, etc.) is not satisfactorily immersive. It may also be possible at some future point to allow initiations conducted in a fully immersive 3D space. This would require a setting where all participants appear to be functionally present, can communicate, and share in the emotion of the occasion.

The Supreme Senate will review technology annually and entertain any such proposals, issuing new guidance as technology evolves. As of this publication, there is no regular provision for electronic presence and any exception must come, in writing, from the Cancellarius.

Entheogens in Initiations

We have no specific beliefs or teachings regarding the use of entheogens in initiation. Certainly, mind altering substances have been used for initiation throughout history. Crowley's willingness to administer entheogens to his audience at the "Rite of Eleusis" raises the question of whether or not he assumed his initiations would be administered in the same way. There is no evidence that Crowley specifically intended his initiatory system to be assisted by entheogens, however, given his championship of such substances, it is not unreasonable to believe he considered the possibility. We do have unquestionably reliable accounts of a notable Thelemic author, still living, going through the Crowley-Reuss initiations while significantly altered. Multiple accounts confirm that in the 1970s and 1980s, such undertakings were far from uncommon. In general, it is the case that the sort of information-rich initiatory experience we enshrine here is not optimal for an altered state, however individual experience varies.

The use of medically prescribed substances does not figure into our policies. However, if, in the estimation of the Sovereign Initiator, any candidate is in an unsafe state, they may be denied initiation.

Our set policy on the use of entheogens which are not medically prescribed is that it:
- Requires fully informed consent on the part of *all* participants – Fully informed consent means that everyone present knows not only what is going to happen, but has the learning and knowledge to understand the ramifications of what is going to happen. "All participants" includes not only the Sovereign Initiator, but all other candidates and participants.
- Should be in compliance with prevailing law – Within the United States, because of the conflict between US federal, state, and local law, this can be rather unclear. In general, we focus on local law as enforced. See the *TTO Handbook - Vision and Mission, Polices and Procedures, and Membership*, for further details.

- Should be done in a safer fashion – This implies that multiple parties present should have experience in the use of the entheogens to be used. While there are no professional certifications in the use of entheogens, it is well within the rights of a Sovereign Initiator to decline to allow them on the basis that they themselves do not have enough information to determine if they are being appropriately and safely used.

This policy, current as of this printing, may be supplemented or changed at any time by action of the Supreme Senate of the Initiatory Order III°.

Notes

About the Initiation Text

Disclosure for Sovereign Initiators

There is a rich amount of detail in this supporting text which is not in the initiations themselves. It is supplied with the idea that Sovereign Initiators should be educated in and able to explain the initiations and may require some supporting text to do so. The question may arise in discussion and debate where this supporting material may be quoted without violating degree secrets. Arguably none of the information is a "secret," however some of it, if published, (e.g. the list of Toulousian characters, in order) would yield considerable information about the structure of the initiations.

The following guidelines would be applicable:

- It is preferable not to quote this book as a source. Numerous end notes are given to allow the sources of most elements of it to be found and many of these are available online. Quote the source in preference to this text, particularly in regards to Thelemic texts.

- It is preferable to paraphrase this text rather than quote it when possible. By putting the ideas in your own words, you will also retain them better. This text exists for the benefit of the Sovereign Initiator. Close paraphrasing of this text is definitively **not plagiarism** and is encouraged for teaching purposes.

- If it is necessary to quote this book, keep quotes brief and avoid sections which directly reference the initiatory contents.

- It will become known in time that certain characters or mythologies are used within the initiations. Just as Freemasons do not publish their rituals but may write historically about Hiram Abiff, we'd rather that you engaged in scholarship around these points than were overly secretive about them.

- The association of the Mysteries with the Gnostic Church founded by Doinel and with the Memphis-Misraim material is not secret. Therefore, subjects which touch on those interests (e.g. Cathars, Templars, etc.) are not secret provided their role within the initiations is not described in great detail. Likewise the YHWH formula is exposited in Thelemic writing. It is not necessary or desirable to feign disinterest in elements which form the core of our initiations.

- At the discretion of the Author and Editors, certain elements of this Book, most especially the Foreword, may be published publicly with degree specific information redacted. Close paraphrases of sections of this work may also be published. In that case, it is preferential to quote from the published version.

- In discussing the initiations with 0° and I° Initiates, it is permissible to allow them to read or to copy short sections for them, provided those are not sections which contain degree-specific information, or from which the outline of the degrees can easily be deduced. Discretion is encouraged.

Geographical Terms

It is impossible to entirely disentangle geographic terminology from colonialist terminology, however we have tried where possible without creating gross confusion.

We have used the modern term "West Asia" in reference to the region which has historically been called the "Near East" or "Middle East." The concept of "The East" carries an inherent element of Eurocentrism, whereas East and West Asia are simply descriptors, like "Western Europe."

References to a "European Tradition" tend to focus on Celtic, Norse, or other traditions that were predominantly practiced within Europe. The Hermetic Tradition emanated from Hellenized Egypt, and propagated throughout the Selucid, Ptolemaic, and bordering Hellenic empires back into Greece and Italy. Nor are the traditions we draw from those regions strictly Hermetic. For example Hermetic Qabalah has roots in West Asia and North Africa before it was perfected in Iberia. We have taken pains to be clear that our Traditions are principally rooted in West Asia, North Africa, and Europe and worked where possible to break the perception of Eurocentrism. We have no objection to describing later Grimoire traditions confined almost exclusively to Europe as a "European Tradition" because, denoted in particular, they are. However, our overall tradition is much larger than that small cross section from the late Middle Ages and Early Modern Europe.

We have used the term "Levant" in historical context. The term used by Venetian and Genoese merchants from the 13th century and is a relatively neutral term compared to others such as Outremer or The Holy Land. It is accepted today as an archaeological and historical term for the region and its use in recent historical writing about the Crusades is prolific. We give a specific description of the area we intend in the 0° Initiation. We typically designate Anatolia and Egypt separately.

We have retained the phrase "of the East" in "Temple of the East" because this is a historical title and does not carry any particularly strong pejorative context.

We have used the term "Eastern Roman Empire" and "Eastern Church" in keeping with generally understood references.

References to the Initiates

For ease of reference, every line in which the candidates or initiates respond is labeled as "initiates." In some cases, this is before the point in the ritual where they technically cease to be candidates, however dividing the labels would make it harder to search by line and more confusing. This should not be taken as inferring that candidates are fully initiated before taking the oaths, etc.

Citations and Sources

In editing, we have used several conventions in regards to the end notes. Throughout we have tried to think of what would be most helpful to the Sovereign Initiator working to assimilate this information.

- Where a work is cited from a specific source, we have given the conventional citation, using a slightly modified Chicago style. In particular, in some cases, additional identifying information is appended, such as identifying the Golden Dawn Z.1 document from the Regardie collection.

- In the case of religious or classical works that have numerous published versions (e.g. the Bible, *Liber AL*, etc.) and which have existing reference conventions, we have used the existing conventions (e.g. chapter and verse citations) without citing a specific edition, in order to make it easier to find the relevant text.
  - Format for citation of The Book of the Law is *Liber AL book.verse*
  - Format for citation of the Comment is *Comment Name book.verse*
- With numbered works by Crowley, we have tried where possible to refer to the earliest extant version, and whenever possible this is generally the version referenced. In particular, we have tried to reference those works originally published in *The Equinox* to that source. The reason for this is that the vast majority of Crowley's work, particularly his earlier work, is out of copyright and available freely in the public domain. All issues of *The Equinox* are available in PDF. We do not wish to encourage anyone to feel they need to pay for a modern copy, unless they truly value the work of the editor and commentators.
- There are a number of common and widely available versions of *Vision and the Voice*, several of which that are readily available online. For this reason, we have chosen not to cite any one version's page numbers, but rather to format citation of the *Vision and the Voice* by page number to the introduction and by *Aethyr No. / Enochian Name* to the text.
- In referencing *Liber ABA, Book Four*, where not otherwise specified, the page numbers are for the 2021 Stephen Skinner edition by Watkins. The Skinner edition is cited because it is still in print and available at a more reasonable price point than the out-of-print editions and is available for Kindle.
- Where the Hebrew or Christian Bible is cited, the citations are generic, except in a few cases where the Latin Vulgate or Greek Septuagint is cited explicitly.
  - Chapter and verse is given in the form of Douay-Rheims/King James Version, with the KJV chapter and verse in parentheses in the cases where it differs. Most Catholic Bibles will follow chapter verse from Douay-Rheims, while most Protestant Bibles will follow chapter verse from the KJV.
  - In these cases the exact version is not of significance, though the older text may be slightly preferential. Numerous online sites offer multiple versions in side-by-side format.
- In referencing public domain works which are readily available as PDF files online, through Project Gutenberg, the Open Library, etc., the original out-of-print volume has been cited, as these are the most inexpensively available and accessible editions. As URLs and sources change and these are photographic reproductions, these have been cited as print books.

End Notes

- We have, in cases where we were certain of the identification of a given individual, generally attempted to include a note with their dates of birth and death and full name in order to make it easier for the student to identify the person being referenced. In cases where the identification is conjectural, we have noted such.
- Where an individual has an entry in the Concordance, we have noted that in preference to listing dates.
- In cases where material is suggestive of specific Thelemic work, or seems to relate to it, but is not quoted, we have generally included a cf. note. We have not done this in cases where (a) the number of Thelemic sources cited would be overwhelmingly large, (b) the discussion does not seem to reference any specific text (e.g. a generic reference to Hadit), (c) we are not certain of the identification.
  - In most cases if we identify a given reference there is some specific basis for that identification based on conversation with the author, either through having a passage specifically called to our attention or having asked about the relevance.

- We have intentionally withheld notes in some cases where we believe they would compromise the III° or IV° material.

Recording the Time of Initiation.

Some Initiates may want the time of their initiation recorded, and it is useful to keep a record. The time may be noted on the initiation certificate below or after the date. There is a cue within the scripts for the timekeeper to record the moment of initiation.

On this basis, the Sovereign Initiator may wish to appoint an official Timekeeper whose duty is to have a timepiece of some sort available, discreetly, as well as pen and paper to note down the time of Initiation.

Opening of the M∴M∴ Temple

Officers of the Sovereign Sanctuary

The Rectified Rite of the Ancient and Primitive Mystery of Memphis and Misraim (R.R. of A&P.M. of M∴M∴) provides a sort of structural external framework to the degrees of the Thelemic Order. One might think of it as a "super structure." It is not, strictly speaking necessary.

If the organization of TTO which is sponsoring the initiation operates a regular Lodge of the R.R. of A&P.M. of M∴M∴, the local Officers may open. Otherwise, the Sovereign Initiator may convene a Lodge of Occasion and appoint officers. The Sovereign Initiator may, at their discretion, convey the requisite degrees of M∴M∴ necessary to open the working Lodge prior to the Thelemic initiation or may open the Lodge silently as a sole Master.

The Ceremony of Opening calls for a minimum of four officers.

- Sovereign Master
- Grand Secretary
- Senior Warden
- Tyler

The following rite is used to open and close the temple before and after each initiation. All Siblings who are initiates of M∴M∴ *and also of appropriate degree within the Initiatory Arm* may attend the opening rite.

TTO Initiation to be Performed	Sovereign Sanctuary of TTO Current Degree to Attend Opening	Degree of M∴M∴ for opening
0° Petitioner	0° Petitioner	Master 3°
1° magician	College of the Initiatory Order 1°	Royal Arch 13°
2° Knight of the Rose Cross	Chapter of the Initaitory Order 2°	Knight of the Rose Cross 18°

The precise form of opening the M∴M∴ Temple is not a requirement of the initiations. Anyone who holds 97° from the Independent and Rectified Rite of the Ancient and Primitive Mystery of Memphis and Misraim and the appropriate degree in the Sovereign Sanctuary of TTO may write their own opening ritual, provided it allows for appropriate Tyling.

The Position of the Properties

The specific layout for the properties for Opening of the Temple is the same as that given in the degree rituals, save those implements which are specified as starting on the sideboard and being moved to the Altar are in their sideboard positions. See the diagram in the instructions for each ritual for the layout of the Altar.

- Hammer
- Compass
- Ruler
- Candle of hours – remains on the sideboard
- Lighter – remains on the sideboard or in another convenient place

The Tyling

Tyling may occur either before the Temple is opened but within the precincts or at the door. The Tyler must ensure that every individual is appropriately tyled as Masons, using the Masonic password, but not giving the sign of their grade within TTO's Sovereign Sanctuary. The Tyler should, before the ceremony, confer with each Sibling individually and help ensure that they recall the correct signs which will be required. Any gross irregularities (that is, individuals who do not seem to have known the signs or to be properly initiated) must be reported to the Sovereign Initiator at once.

The Ritual of the Opening of the Temple

Sovereign Master: *knocks loudly.*

Salutations on all points of the Triangle, and Honor to the Order. Grand Secretary, what is the first duty of the Grand Secretary in Lodge?

Grand Secretary:

Sovereign Master, to assure the regular operation of the Lodge.

Sovereign Master:

Grand Secretary, how many Officers has the Lodge?

Grand Secretary:

Three and Seven and again Three.

Sovereign Master:

Grand Secretary. This differs from the number of Officers upon the Rolls. I would ask you to explain.

Grand Secretary:

The answer may not be given in the company of these siblings, for it lies under the shroud of the Night of Pan, under the seal of the Gate Keeper of the City of Pyramids.

Sovereign Master:

Let it remained sealed then. So mote it be. Grand Secretary, what is the first duty of the Senior Warden?

Grand Secretary:

Sovereign Master, to assure themselves that all the Initiates present are protected from profane indiscretion.

Sovereign Master:

Grand Secretary, assure yourself that this is so.

Grand Secretary:

Senior Warden, assure yourself that we are secure.

Senior Warden: *partly opens the door.*

Tyler, please enter and report.

Tyler: *enters and closes the door.*

The approaches to the Temple are deserted, the echo remains silent, and we are duly tyled.

Senior Warden:

Grand Secretary, the inviolability of our Mysteries are assured, we are duly tiled, and the Profane are set apart.

Sovereign Master:

Grand Secretary, what is the second duty of the Warden in a Lodge?

Grand Secretary:

Sovereign Master, it is to assure ourselves that all present are indeed true and regular fellows of craft within this operative Lodge.

Sovereign Master:

Grand Secretary, assure yourself that this is so.

Grand Secretary:

Senior Warden, assure yourself that all present are indeed true and regular fellows of craft within this Lodge.

Senior Warden: *confers with the Tyler and determines if it is the case that all present are Siblings. If any are not, they are duly tyled.*

Grand Secretary, the inviolability of our Mysteries are assured, we are duly tiled, and the Profane are set apart.

Grand Secretary:

Senior Warden we are about to

For 0°

Open this Lodge in the degree of Master Masons, in order to Initiate Petitioners into the Sovereign Sanctuary of The Thelemic Order. It is moot therefore that all present should be not only master Masons, but Petitioners, at least, to the Sovereign Sanctuary. Assure yourself that this is so:

For 1°

Open this Lodge in the degree of the Royal Arch, in order to Initiate magicians into the Sovereign Sanctuary of The Thelemic Order. It is moot therefore that all present should be not only master Masons, but Magicians of the First Degree, at least, of the Sovereign Sanctuary. Assure yourself that this is so:

For 2°

Open this Lodge in the degree of the Rose Cross, in order to Initiate Knights of the Rose Cross into the Sovereign Sanctuary of The Thelemic Order. It is moot therefore that all present should be not only master Masons, but Knights of the Rose Cross, at least, of the Sovereign Sanctuary. Assure yourself that this is so:

Senior Warden:

Tyler please ensure that all present have proved themselves to be (Petitioners, Magicians, Knights of the Rose Cross).

Tyler:

Please form ranks left and right.

The Tyler will ensure that the Company is evenly divided into ranks left and right. They will then ask, regarding the relevant Grade, and choosing randomly between the ranks:

- *One rank for the Formula*
- *The other rank for its Elaboration*
- *All shall then be asked to face the Grand Secretary and deliver the Sign*
  If any do not know the tokens, they will be taken to the side or outside the door by the Tyler, who will refresh them, until they are able to return and give the signs as required.

Tyler:

All present have proven themselves to be (Petitioners, Magicians, Knights of the Rose Cross).

Senior Warden:

Grand Secretary, all have been duly tyled.

Grand Secretary:

Sovereign Master, all have been duly tyled.

Sovereign Master:

Then let the Temple be opened. Ineffable Wisdom, O Unknown God of the Temples of Memphis, Thou that art One, our Lord in the Universe the Sun, whose name is Mystery of Mystery, O secret of secrets that art hidden in the being of all that lives, let the First Light be!

The Thelemic Initiations

Grand Secretary: *GS causes the Candle of Hours on the sideboard to be lit. The lighting may be done by the Grand Secretary or by any selected officer.*

This is the flame that burns in every human heart, and in the core of every star.

Sovereign Master:

My Siblings, the Work of Architecture which was entrusted to us at the Dawn of Time and is accomplished with the aid of three Tools which carry the beautiful name of "Jewels of the Lodge". These are the Hammer, the Square Rule, and the Compass.

The Compass invokes the all, encompassing all. The Hammer strikes a single point with great energy. The Square Rule is the manner by which the infinite may be measured, and divided, for the sake of Union.

Without them, we could achieve nothing. Because of this, let us make manifest these three Symbols.

Grand Secretary: *ensures that the Hammer, the Square Rule, and the Compass are on Altar in their proper place and order*

Sovereign Master, the Three Jewels shine forth at the center of the Nous.

Sovereign Master:

Grand Secretary, what is your time?

Grand Secretary:

More than eleven years.

Sovereign Master:

Warden, at what hour were the Masons of Egypt accustomed to open their works by the ceremony of the Stretching of the Cord?

Senior Warden:

When the sun was at its highest over the sands of Memphis, when it was high noon, and shadows at their shortest, then the Masons of Egypt would hold the ritual of beginning their great works, Sovereign Master.

Sovereign Master:

Since the Temple of Egyptian Wisdom is right and perfect, and since it is the Hour and we are of the correct time.

gives three hard knocks

I declare this Lodge of the Independent and Rectified Rite of the Ancient and Primitive Mystery of Memphis and Misraim, and of the Sovereign Sanctuary of the Gnosis of the Thelemic Order duly opened in the Degree of (Master Masons, the Royal Arch, Knights of the Rose Cross).

The Ritual of Closing the Temple

Sovereign Master:

Our Business is done. Grand Secretary, you will now poll the Siblings of this Lodge to speak now if they have anything to propose for the good of the Order in general, and for this Worthy Lodge in particular.

Grand Secretary:

My Siblings, I ask you on behalf of the Sovereign Master if you have anything to propose for the good of the Order in general, and for this Worthy Lodge in particular.

In general, only points of significance and formality would be raised, and those by prearrangement. This might be an occasion to thank anyone who has contributed greatly to the work of the initiation.

Senior Warden:

Sovereign Master, the announcement has been made, and the rank and file of the assembled initiates are silent.

Sovereign Master:

Fellows of Craft, the only manner for an Initiate to exemplify the path of the Adept is to conduct themselves before the whole world with wisdom, discerning true will, and rejecting false will, acknowledging with reverence all stars in the company of stars, and exemplifying that tolerance of all things other than intolerance, thus exemplifying the divine.

Senior Warden, has this rule been perpetuated today in the heart of Masons of the Memory of Memphis?

Senior Warden:

Sovereign Master, the Fellows of Craft who have worked beneath the shadow of the columns have labored upon the Square each according to their Will.

Sovereign Master:

Senior Warden, for how long do Apprentice Masons labor in the Temple of Wisdom?

Senior Warden:

From High Noon until Midnight Clear, Sovereign Master.

Sovereign Master:

Grand Secretary, what is the hour?

Grand Secretary:

Midnight Clear, Sovereign Master. Night reigns over the Temple, and the Company of Stars bathe the sleeping Sanctuaries with their light.

Sovereign Master:

Please rise and come to Order.

All rise and stand attentive, hands at rest

Sovereign Master:

As we suspend our Works, may the veil of Falsehood, Error and Prejudice fall from our eyes and illuminate within and between us the bonds of Light, Life, Love and Liberty. Let us rejoice in our Fellowship together. Grand Secretary, let us extinguish the lights.

Grand Secretary: *selects an officer to extinguish the Lights. As they do the Secretary repeats:*

It is dark. From the Night of Pan we will walk out into the world, carrying with us the word and double mystery of Horus the Child of the Aeon.

Sovereign Master:

So mote it be.

All:

So mote it be.

0° - Petitioner - Instructions

Major Properties

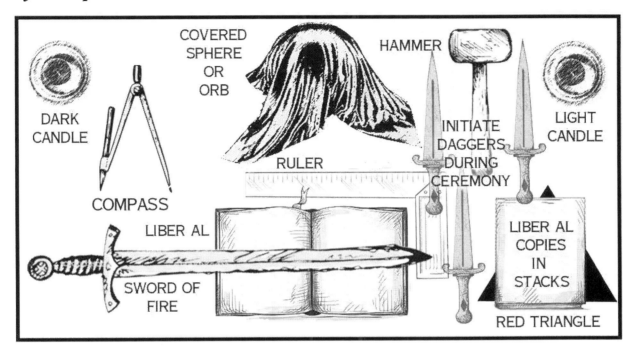

THE SETTING OF THE PRINCIPAL ALTAR

See the appendices for a printable checklist of Properties by location

The Altar Elements

- **The Orb** is rather large, the size of a large upright and oval about 8-10 inches high and 6-8 inches side to side It is never seen and so it could be made from any object, or even a bundle of cloth and duct tape.

- **Cloth Cover for Orb** – large enough to completely cover the orb, leaving no part of it exposed

- **Two Altar candles** – these may be pillar candles, or may be glass jar (novena) candles.
    - Right candle – white or light
    - Left candle – black or dark

- **Masonic Tools** – to the degree possible, the tools should be "archaic" - the sort that can be easily purchased at antique stores or online. It would be best if these were large enough not to seem comical as weapons.
    - Hammer
    - Compass
    - Ruler

- **Daggers** – these are placed during the ceremony. The placement above is suggested, and a reminder to leave room for them. They may also be placed alongside the sword or in any other viable location.

It may be desirable not to use these as props for the play, but to have a larger or more harmless set of properties for the staging of the play. In extremis, however, these may be taken from the altar and used as part of the performance.

- **Sword of Fire** – this does not need to be a large sword, but should be somewhat larger than a dagger.

- **Display copy of *Liber AL*** – This may be a larger or more handsome edition than the ones being distributed to initiates.

- **Copies of *Liber AL* for distribution** – a preference would be for editions which do not carry information regarding O.T.O. inside the front, however until such time as TTO prints its own editions, these are acceptable if necessary. The page to which *Liber AL* is laid open is at the discretion of the Sovereign Initiator.

- **Red Triangle** – made of cardboard, paper, or cloth. It may be sewn onto a table cloth or merely laid beneath the books. It should be somewhat larger so that the points show, or should be exposed at one corner if it is smaller.

Other Ritual Elements

- **Candle of the Hours** – On the Sideboard. This is lit during the M∴M∴ Opening

- **Bowl** – Sufficient for hand-washing.

- **Hyssop** – for water to be used for hand-washing. Hyssop water could also be bottled in advance.

- **Tracing Board** – Prepared according to the Illustration. Ideally, the board would be hand painted, but it may be copied and pasted onto cardboard.

- **Pitcher** – For pouring water over hands

Readings

- **Readings** on printed cards or sheets

Properties for the Play

- **The Weapons** – it is possible to use the Compass, Ruler, and Hammer from the altar. However, if very heavy historic tools are used these may be dangerous within the context of a play. Remember that the play is meant to be an actual performance by medieval players, so the props may be rather rudimentary (e.g. a painted wooden cut out). If the props from the altar are used, exceptional care must be taken to insure everyone is instructed in how to use them so as to cause no injury.

- **Ring of Hiram** – this should be a ring which bears the inscription YHWH on the inside or reverse. An archaic and rich look is preferred, but any ring could be used with the inscription written on tape on the inside.

- **Staff of Hiram** – This is a theatrical prop so the quality may be minimal.

- **Broken Staff of Hiram** – two pieces that closely resemble Hiram's walking staff. *As this is only alluded to, it may be omitted.*

- **Prop for Well** (may be a chair or table) - this is not truly a property as it is an element of the "play within a play." For that reason, it may be contrived on the occasion, even by moving the third chair into the center of the playing area, or by moving a small table. This is not a real well, but a stage property, and a decorated cardboard box would also be fine.

- **Scripts for the Play** – these should be ready to read. Readability is favored over authenticity so these should not be printed in a historic font. Ideally, they can be presented in neat black binders.

- **Bread and Salt** – the bread and salt from the sideboard may be reused, or additional may be set aside with other theatrical properties.

- **Wine in a cup** – should be prepared and set aside to be carried by the Villains.

The Books

These are not really books, but binding covers for scripts. In general, a binder from an office supply company, covered with decorative paper, leather or fabric, is preferential for ease of use. The binders should be neat and easy to use and not kept cluttered with unrelated material. A larger binder may be used for carrying multiple scripts. Note that many companies sell binders with "slip in" covers which may be used to present several different initiations simply by rotating the covers. Keep in mind that Enochian is written from right to left. See the examples at the end of this book for the correct lettering for the covers.

It is possible to make use of this bound book, using a folded paper or cloth cover, however it is suggested that the Sovereign Initiator photocopy the scripts from this book or make use of such downloads as may be made available to Chartered Sovereign Initiators.

Book AMBZ – binder containing script – orange cover with the Enochian letters AMBZ in dark violet print for Azalais -

ꝑᴠᴇꙅ

Book ABFMA – binder containing script - red cover with the Enochian letters ABFMA in blue print for Raimond –

ꙅᴇᴀᴠꙅ

Book AN – binder containing script – reddish brown or blood red cover with the letters Enochian letters AN in black print for Jeanne

ꙅ

Book Black – binder containing script – black cover with no inscription for the Fool

Generic Properties

These properties should be fairly easy to come by at a given locale or purchase from a store.

- **Lighter** – A reliable grill lighter, or high quality long matches should be used. A search on "candle lighter with bell snuffer" will reveal a number of church-style lighters which run on a replaceable wick. These can be lit from the Candle of the Hours after the initial Temple opening. A small lighter in the 18" range is generally best, unless one is dealing with a particularly large Temple space.

- **Three Chairs** – Three chairs together, with the one to the right, as one stands facing them, somehow visibly denoted as a throne, either by being larger, more elevated, etc.

- **Sideboard** – This may be any small or medium-sized table at the side of the room, which is used for various implements when they are not being used on the altar. It is also used for a candle and so should be safe and away from any sources of combustion.

- **Altar** – This must be large and sturdy enough to accommodate a sword, the implements, and two candles without being in danger of tipping. In general, a size of 40"-50" and a depth of 14-18" or larger is preferable.

- **Towels** – adequate to dry hands of all initiates, clean and fresh.

- **Timepiece** - a timepiece to record the time of initiation

- **Note Paper and Writing Implement** - to record the time of initiation

The Feast Food

The minimum symbolic elements are **Bread, Honey**, and **Salt.** Ideally, these will have antique or exotic plates and containers, however, that is secondary.

- **Bread**
- **Honey**
- **Salt**
- **Additional Feast Food**

The cost of the feast should be budgeted as part of the overall initiation.

Items for Gifts

These items are described in *Book 4*, Part II, Chapter IV "The Scourge, The Dagger, and the Chain," and in a perfect world they would be identical. In practice, that is unlikely to be possible. For initiation purposes, they are essentially symbols or suggestions of the magical tools.

- **Scourges** – small flails or scourges. These can be handmade of knotted leather, wire or fiber. A common item sold as "fringe leather tassel" can stand in for this. As of this publication they are available for about $2.00 apiece.

- **Chains** – these may be used to hang charms or worn as a reminder of the initiation. Jewelry chains can be purchased at a craft store, or somewhat larger chain at a chain hardware store. Searching "bulk" or "wholesale" chains may be helpful in sourcing fairly large numbers of chain necklaces cheaply. Alternatively, one could buy a large amount of chain and clasps and make their own.

- **I° Initiation Petitions**

The total cost of these items may be included in the fees for initiation and as of this publication should be no more than $25.00.

In order to avoid resentment, the quality of items presented to all initiates at any given initiation should be roughly the same. If an initiator wishes to present a special piece as a gift, they should either arrange a separate initiation or pass the gift along afterward privately. In no situation should an initiate see another receiving gifts of much different or better quality. The one exception to this is when a late initiate has been added to an initiation, and there are not enough prepared items to go around. In this case, the Initiator should discuss in advance the existence of the gifts within the ritual, and let the late initiate know that as a result of the late addition, their gifts will be imparted at a later date.

Dramatis Personae (Principals)

- The Fool
- Azalais (ah-zuh-lie-ees)
- Raimond I
- Jeanne (Joan of England)

The above roles of the Principals may be filled by anyone who is already initiated to 0°. In general, the Sovereign Initiator will take the role of The Fool or Azalais for this initiation, according to their Will, as those roles have the greatest ability to "guide" the experience. Technically speaking, the Sovereign Initiator is not obligated to take *any* speaking part, however this would only tend to be the case in a situation where new Initiators were being trained. The roles of Players in the play-within-a-play, except for the role of Hiram, are preferentially filled by the initiates, but any remaining roles may be played by any other attendees or by other principals.

Initiation Team Negotiations

Castration/Penectomy

It is important to remember that the Performer of the role of the Fool/Hiram must be involved in negotiations for the castration/penectomy scene in the play-within-a-play. The penectomy should be explicitly negotiated with the person playing Apophrasz. One reason for the Fool to play Hiram Abif is that the person portraying the Fool should be an experienced initiatory officer and thus able to be understanding if there is some accident. That said, it is imperative that no one be injured. There is no latitude given for more "imaginative" portrayals of the penectomy that may in any way involve actual exposure or the risk of injury. Apophrasz should be encouraged not to strike fast but rather to pantomime a sawing action, preferably against the outside of the hip, or against the lower thigh. The Sovereign Initiator may wish to take Apophrasz from the room and rehearse.

It goes without saying that there is no need for actual exposure of the penis or any sort of touching or physical contact between individuals. Any contact with the prop should be outside of the clothing and at a safe distance.

Initiate Negotiations

These are the general issues which should be disclosed, and which may require negotiations. At a minimum, the Sovereign Initiator should review with each candidate for initiation their application, and ensure that they do not have any issues or concerns.

Hand-washing

- If a common bowl is to be used, the initiates should be polled to insure they do not have concerns. Remedies would include providing a separate bowl, wet towel, pouring water from a pitcher, etc.

  ○ This is only a concern if a common bowl is used, pouring water from a pitcher is preferential if possible.

Play-within-a-Play

- This ritual contains a portion in which a "play-within-a-play" occurs, in which initiates may be asked to take a script and play act with others. No memorization is required.

- Potential Limits/Problems

  ○ Stage fright, issues with reading, or reading aloud

  ○ The ritual play-within-a-play contains a violent castration/penectomy

  ○ The ritual play-within-a-play contains elements of homophobia and transphobia, though these are presented as villainous. It still may be uncomfortable for some people to perform the roles.

- Possible remedies – stage fright, reading aloud

  ○ Candidate may be specifically given a part which has fewer lines (see roles below)

  ○ Candidate may choose not to read a role at all

- Possible remedies – Violence/Penectomy – *The ritual murder is the literal culmination of the play and may not be omitted. The element of penectomy is symbolic on multiple levels and may not be omitted.*

  ○ Candidates who have issues with genital violence should not be selected for the role of Hiram, or Apophrasz for the play.

  ○ If someone believes they will be triggered by the very idea, ask if it would help to explain in advance exactly what happens. If they agree, explaining that the scene is pantomimed, clothed, during a play-within-a-play which depicts a brutal murder may be enough to make them feel comfortable. Further disclosure is at the discretion of the Sovereign Initiator, however in general the scene is tame enough it will generally be possible for someone to decide to sit through it.

  ○ In extremis, someone may be excused from the play, or the end of the play, and merely told the story of what happens or allowed to read the section.

- Possible remedies – homophobic and transphobic language

  ○ Explain that the roles in which this language is used involve the portrayal of a villain, and are intentionally strongly-stated in order to get the point across.

  ○ Anyone still not comfortable with this language should be excused from playing one of the three villains.

  ○ In extremis, someone may be excused from the play, or the end of the play, and merely told the story of what happens or allowed to read the section.

Roles Within the Play

The Principal for the grade, Azalais, assigns the roles, answering any basic questions that do not give away the entire plot. The Principal should act in conference with the Sovereign Initiator if they are playing the Fool and may simply ask the Fool to "help cast the play."

In general, some thought should have been given to casting in advance, though if there are no special considerations, there is no particular harm in simply handing out the parts somewhat at random.

Any attendees or officers may take roles not taken by initiates.

Despite having a plan for casting, the Sovereign Initiator should give great consideration to those requests or preferences of the initiates themselves. In the end, what is most important is that they are as satisfied as possible with their roles.

There must be separation between the Sovereign Initiator's thoughts on the best possible casting, and what is said to the initiates. On no account should the Initiator give even minor slight by suggesting someone is not competent to read a given part because of their clarity of speech and reading.

The parts of Apophrasz and Besz may be played by the same persons as Ahiman and Abiychazah as they are only briefly present in once place, and have fairly few exchanges together. However, if this is done, make sure the players differentiate which characters they are reading, perhaps by draping the villains with a black hood.

Casting Imperatives

Hiram Abif – The Fool should be chosen by Azalais to play Hiram Abif. This is a matter of symbolism, not mere convenience.

Iam, Besz, and Apophrasz – must all be able to feign a "strike" with their weapons safely. It is best if this is rehearsed briefly during the Feast. See the above note on negotiations with Apophrasz.

If the Sovereign Initiator is not the Fool, an extra layer of negotiation exists. Exceptional care needs to be taken to ensure that all strikes are negotiated carefully and that no one is injured.

The Roles

- **King Solomon** – no particular warnings attach to this role
- **Hiram Abif** – Hiram the Father – The role of Hiram Abif is generally played by the Fool, but anyone performing that role should be made aware of the penectomy by the Sovereign Initiator.
- **Ahiman** – The Master Architect and Stonemason – this is a fairly light speaking part
- **Abiychazah**[46] - The Priestess of Asherah
- **Iam** – a craftsman and villain – all of the villains engage in murderous violence, and are misogynistic, homophobic, and transphobic.
- **Apophrasz**[47] - a craftsman and villain – all of the villains engage in murderous violence, and are misogynistic, homophobic, and transphobic, however this character is responsible for the penectomy/castration
- **Besz** – a craftsman and villain – all of the villains engage in murderous violence, and are misogynistic, homophobic, and transphobic.
- **Shallum** – this is a minor role, which has only a few lines of reading

- **Akkub** – this is a minor role, which has only a few lines of reading
- **Talmon** – this is a minor role, which has only a few lines of reading

Safety Concerns

- Check for dietary issues regarding the snack
- Check for allergies to hyssop or any incense planned for use during the initiation
- Hand-washing – In general we feel that, under normal circumstances, there is little danger in symbolic washing of hands in a common bowl, though it does not meet the CDC standards for hand-washing. For increased safety, *particularly if anyone present is immunocompromised:*
  - It may be advisable to ask all initiates to wash their hands in a modern fashion (e.g. with running water and soap) before beginning.
  - Water may be poured from a pitcher over their hands, using the bowl only as a catch basin.
  - Small individual bowls may be used.
- Standard Fire Safety
  - Extinguisher
- Standard Medical Safety
  - First Aid Kit
  - Certified First Aid Training

0° Initiation – Script – First Section

Prologue

Speech to the Candidate

This is delivered outside the initiation space or, if that is not possible because there is only one space, before the initiation candidates have been excused to open the Temple. This may overlap with the Opening of the Lodge, though it may take somewhat longer.

The Fool:

> You have come here with the intention of initiating into our most terrible and secret order. I am here to give you one last opportunity to turn away.

> Let us be clear: We have no license on the truth, nor does anyone else, and there are other true paths. We make no claim to be better or worse than any other true path, and it may be that our path is not the one which fits you best. If that is the case we will wish you peace and success, but we cannot be a tradition other than our own.

> We all know the magical world is full of fantasy, and that for each true path there are a dozen...no, a hundred… easy roads which make a gentle climb to a suburban cul-de-sac where you can park and announce to all who care that you have ascended. They confer *respectability*. If no one will much care that you have ascended, no one will argue the point either because you can point to a degree, or number, or magical garment and say indisputably that you have done the thing. These paths imply no responsibility, for they exist to feed the ego and to satisfy the outward appearance of the seeker. They are worn to impress your friends.

> I will tell you now: You cannot unknow. If you persist on this path and do not turn aside, you will be changed and every revelation will draw you further towards knowledge of the self of self.

> Before you begin it is fair that I tell you a few things about what will and will not be.

> First, the Oaths:

> We demand no oath upon anything but the self and honor. The implicit penalty of the violation of such an oath is injury to faith in the self, and to the public perception of the self. To the true Adept, such Obligation, freely undertaken, is far more potent than any litany of imaginary punishments, and to the cowardly or faithless seeker, no oath can carry meaning regardless of its content.

> We further demand no oath of obedience to any living person or organization outside of that of basic respect for the secrecy of the Initiations. Nor do we collect oaths of obligation to forces or principles which you have not had the opportunity to fully explore and understand, so that you may decide advisedly whether or not you wish to be so obligated.

> The concepts of these initiations, including their symbolism, may be discussed. In most cases, the elements are centuries or even millennia old, and to forbid discussing them would be as foolish as to prohibit you to

speak of Orpheus or Dionysus. It is also not your duty to repress the knowledge of their contents. Those who wish to spoil secrets will most often find a way.

We ask that you refrain in act and in spirit from:

○ giving out in written or in verbal form the exact words of the initiations, though where they quote from ancient sources those may be freely discussed.

○ describing in synoptic detail the general course and outline by part, or the specific roles and speeches of the characters within the initiations.

○ transmitting in any way the various words and signs of the degrees. These are important because they do serve to some extent as guarantors that someone attending an initiation has been exposed to this talk and others, and is thus duly informed as to safety and behavior.

○ acting as an initiator into these specific mysteries, as written, without the due authorization of the Sovereign Sanctuary.

○ We further ask that you please remember: that in deciding how to speak you err on the side of caution and, when in doubt, embrace the fourth power of the Sphinx which is silence.

○ We remind you that it is your role only to police your own speech and that the obedience of other initiates to these oaths must be judge by themselves.

With that understanding, you have been informed in advance of the following oath:

> On my name, upon the deepest identity and understanding of my self, and upon my honor I do swear to maintain the secrets of this Sovereign Sanctuary both in adherence to the word of my oath and the spirit of my action, as it has been fairly and diligently explained to me.
>
> I will not reveal the words as they are written in whole or part;
>
> I will not reveal the general course and form of the initiation by part, or the specifics of the characters within;
>
> I understand that transmitting the words and signs outside of the path of initiation may endanger others and I will refrain utterly from doing this;
>
> I will not act as an initiator into these mysteries, in whole or in part, without the due authorization of this Sovereign Sanctuary;
>
> I will not violate the privacy of other initiates, including disclosing their initiatory status or details about their initiation, including their grade of initiation, without their explicit consent;
>
> When considering how I speak I will err towards silence;
>
> I understand that it is my duty to police only myself and that I am neither obliged nor empowered to school others in their adherence to this oath;
>
> So mote it be.

External power or authority may be conferred by laying on of hands, but no human can truly initiate another. We present initiations but we do not, ourselves, initiate you. The only true source of true initiation is within. Even when we say the Gods may initiate, that does not, as you shall learn if you do not already know, change our assertion. We may plant a seed, but we cannot make the seed grow.

The function of this external initiation is to open you to internal initiation. We may open the door and provide a map, but if you do not step across the threshold and follow the markings you will not truly be initiated. We have some faculties for looking into your mind and dissuading you from undertaking those steps for which you are not prepared, but if you are more determined than wise, you may take every step and understand nothing. For that reason let me emphasize that the choice to take further initiations is not a race or contest. If you pile on one initiation after another you will cheat yourself of the benefit that comes only with reflection and experience.

In these initiations you will be told many lies which are truths. You will also come to understand that some truths are in fact lies. This may seem confusing and unclear now, but before you are done you will understand it intimately.

We cannot say for certain that if you walk every step of this path, you will attain. It may be that there is no one true path for all persons, or it may be that you cannot find the right pace to walk this road. It is our intent to make the road as flat and easy as possible, but at best there are many twists and sudden turns.

We cannot claim that you will learn magick. There are lessons on magick embedded in these initiations, but they alone are not enough to make you a magician. The Platonic School of magick is the Order General, where you may learn one from another, and only through experience and practice will you be able to put the lessons of your initiations to good use.

These initiations are not intended to harm you, yet they contain the possibility of harm. The intent in all cases is to limit the possibility of inadvertent harm, but you may sustain physical harm if you do not follow the directions as they are given.

Emotionally, it is not possible for initiation to occur without profound challenge to the ego. It may even be said that the ego must "die" in order for initiation to occur. The true ordeal comes not during our ceremony but in your life afterwards, in the interval between initiations when the lesson works its way into your life.

In many traditional initiations, a sword is presented to the candidate and they are told that it is better that they thrust themselves upon its tip than undertake the initiation unprepared. Each initiation lays the foundation and prepares the mind for the next. The first three initiations you may undertake at once, for they are related, and most of the ordeals you have already faced in life.

We warn that the sword at your breast will be waiting beyond the exit door. Once the veil has been lifted from your eyes, you cannot escape the ordeals that will come as a result. Nor can you return here to initiate further until you have, in your own way and time, come through them. Even if you depart feeling nothing, you cannot unsee or unknow and, as consequence ensues, you will come to know.

While we do not aim to deceive you, the masks of the players are a kind of lie and candidates may be subject to various tricks and traps. The goal of these is not to humiliate or belittle, but rather to build both a tolerance for the blows of bad fortune and a tendency to consider all angles of one's choices. All fiction is deceit. Mythology may be an untruth which conceals the truth, while a literal truth may be stated so as to constitute a lie.

Leave to Depart

Having come to this threshold, if it is not your will to initiate now, you may depart without prejudice. You are welcome to return at a future time. No one will question your decision, nor ask you to explain yourself. If you continue beyond the Threshold, it is with the expectation that you have read and reviewed the Oaths and intend to give them on your honor. Since you will not be refused Initiation at some future time, if you have any doubt that it is your will to initiate now, I urge you to excuse yourself.

That said, this is an introductory degree, and save agreeing to secrecy, it creates no lasting bond, nor mandates any ordeal.

The Fool may explain what provisions have been made for anyone who wishes to leave, whether there is a waiting area, etc. In general, it is best if there is one person who can remain outside with anyone who chooses to leave the ritual if they are not also leaving the premises.

The Fool may explain how any refund is to be issued. The terms of initiation should be explained in advance.

The Fool may take a moment to ensure as to needs, creating a pause in which anyone who chooses not to take initiation may leave without attracting undue attention. Some things to remind candidates.

- Make sure you are hydrated
- Make sure you have anything you need to keep with you
- Make sure you have used the restroom

The Fool:

I conduct you now to a place that is a story, or a story that is a place. I will be Virgil to your Dante, your confidant and guide. If you have questions or ought occurs that troubles you, you may pull me aside and ask only of me. For all else that you will see is not as it seems. The people are not people and the places not places, and like the pages of a book they are fragile and may be torn. But I am made of the same stuff as you.

Welcome

*At the front are three Chairs. They are for, from left to right, Azalais, Jeanne, and Raimond. The **Altar** may be situated behind them, or to one side. Jeanne, and Raimond are already seated, while Azalais stands about halfway through the hall.*

Azalais: *(ah-zuh-lie-ees)*

I am Azalais, Countess of Burlats (*BEE-or-lah*). I greet you on this day as hostess and Chatelaine for my brother, Raimond, the Sixth Count of Toulouse, and his Countess, Jeanne.

You, jongleur, whom have you discovered and brought before my brother's court?

The Fool:

Now is when you introduce yourself. I could make a flowery answer for you, but it won't make sense. Much of the time we speak in riddles or obscure codes. Or you could just answer for yourself, though that won't make much sense either.

Initiates: *May introduce themselves. Once they are finished, or by way of introduction if they demur, the Fool will also deliver the following introduction.*

The Fool:

These are travelers who have been turned away from the gate of Heliopolis (*HEE-lee-OP-uh-lis*) , and sent to Memphis, thence to Thebes, where they were also denied instruction. They seek shelter and the path to the unknowable city.

Azalais: *The following Canso of Welcome may be recited, chanted, or sung based on the performer's preference.*

I welcome you with a Canso (*KAN-soh*),[48] as is our tradition. It is not one which I composed, but which I learned in my youth in a place far away.

Exordium

    Petitioner, practitioner

    From far away came calling

    Traditioner, auditioner

    From hunger nearly falling

    Circling our gate while seeking fate

    A cross upon their surcoat[49]

    Blazon'ed Star with Sword and Snake[50]

    Sought our gate past circling moat

Verses

    A noble peer and cavalier

    Called aloud from whence come thou?

    From Heliopolis a tear

    Turned away did stain my brow

    From Memphis too and Thebes at last

    Into subterranean depth[51]

    A darkened tomb where I was cast

    The universe in full breadth

    There on the highest mountaintops

    I did behold a city

    Sunset of blood and white snowdrops[52]

    All mercy without pity

    Balance restored and gateway arch[53]

    On a mount of silver fir[54]

    Of Kneph endless as knew Plutarch[55] [56]

    Lignum Aloes, Sandal, Myrrh[57]

Envois

    The Castellan then raised the gate

    And let pass the weary knight

> "Beyond you'll find the road is straight
> Serpent heart, immortal light"[58]

We are hospitable, but cautious of travelers, for our rich and pleasant principality of Toulouse (*too-LOOZ*) lies at the center of four Kingdoms, and thus through no fault of our own we have until recently seen numerous hostilities in our troubled realm.

Yet if you be of good disposition towards us you shall find that in Court of my brother, song and story, meat and drink and tenderness of the flesh are valued above War, and so would say even those who do not know him as I have.

The Fool:

What are these four Kingdoms of which you speak?

Raimond:

Closest to us and manifest to the north[59] is the Kingdom of the Franks, whose king is our Uncle Louis, who now pretentiously calls himself "King of France." Our mother came from Paris,[60] and she was intolerant of Cathar and Jew, and of his many loves she was jealous. My father gave her leave to return to Paris and broke the oaths that bound him to Louis.

Azalais:

To the south[61] lay the great Kingdom of Castile (*KASS-teel*) which lives by the sword. On this day, Castile is at peace with us but they are rapacious and their loyalty shifts with the wind, always seeking advantage. It is in Castile that the seed of fate is sewn, and that the seers foretell the agent of our fate is already born.[62]

Jeanne:

To the west[63] is Anjou (*AHN-zhoo*) and farther, England, a single Angevin (*ANN-juh-vin*) Realm unified by my father Henry King of England.[64] Before I was Countess here, I was widowed as Queen of Sicily, for I am the sister of Richard, who is called Lionheart, and when he went to the Levant to challenge Salah-ad-Din and made a pact over Jerusalem,[65] he took me there. He made peace and now rules in England and in Anjou, ally of this Court through my marriage to its Count. Richard is a famed lord, clever beyond the wiles of most fighting men and able to turn disadvantage to advantage through imagination. A patron of the arts, he himself is terse, and he has two natures. In generosity, none exceeds him, yet his capacity for cruelty, though dispassionate, is more awful than the vengeful rage of lesser men.

Azalais:

Finally in the sunny and hot lands to our south[66] lies the Kingdom of Aragon. There has King Alfonso the Troubadour, facetiously called "the chaste," only recently passed into the night. I knew him well, for he wooed me in many songs at the court of my late husband, and was much angered that I preferred to give myself to other Troubadours. My husband sided with Alfonso in his many wars but, out of spite and jealousy at my rejection, Alfonso bestowed rich cities and lands which ought to have belonged to myself and my son on our rivals - such a betrayal that it is a matter of song. Even so, I cannot question that his was the model of the Court of Troubadours, the archetype of song and story, and none shall ever burn as bright again.

The Fool: *turns to the initiates*

As you may learn from this recital, here all words carry secrets. For as Azalais stands astride four Kingdoms, so also do you. Each thing said unto you, even those which seem trivial, may tend to conceal a double meaning or refer to some occluded truth. This, as experienced travelers, you should know, so from here on I shall not belabor.

turns to the dais

Now, worthy folk, I beg and invoke on behalf of these travelers, and by right of old, your vaunted hospitality.

The Challenge

Azalais:

You shall have our hospitality and more. My brother is a strong supporter of the rights of free peoples both in the cities and in the countryside. In this realm, we are guided by paratge (*pah-RAHD-jay*), the spirit of balance and generosity, and we do not ask free men to swear oaths to us as vassals, or to render fealty in the way of the Capetians (*KUH-peesh-uhns*) to the north. Thus, I ask only that, in respect for hospitality and being named as our honored guest, you swear to uphold the privacy of this court, for we are pressed on many fronts and our enemies would seek advantage over us.

The Fool:

What is this about partridges?

Azalais:

We have, here in the lands of the South, a notion of paratge (*pah-RAHD-jay*). It has its root in our word for peerage, but is valued as much by the low-born jongleurs, such as yourself, as by the noble troubadours. It is a way of life that sees nobility as being expressed only in generosity decency, and in consideration for others. It rejects the idea of vassalage and the service of men who are not free, and of all serfdom and slavery, in favor of contracts and agreements. It means, too, that all have food in plenty, that there are games and dances, finery, seemly manners, kindness, and poetry so that life is filled with beauty.

Raimond:

A Lord who would uphold paratge must defend the rights of the Town and its Councils as zealously as their own patrimony. Paratge is the vice of Kings.

The Fool:

That sounds nice enough. I'm not sure it's very Thelemic.

Azalais:

The concept of paratge is about having all things moving in harmony, as the stars in their courses move in harmony when all act in accordance with their will. One might wonder if it is our concept of paratge, more even than our proximity to the mysteries of the Templars and the Gnostics, that has led our Court to be chosen as the exemplar of your first traverse through the four worlds.

Raimond:

I will share with you at the outset words of the Master Therion, which might have been written by a Troubadour in explanation of our noble concept of paratge, that you have no misunderstanding of the character of our our Knighthood.

"There seems to be much misunderstanding about True Will ... The fact of a person being a gentleman is as much an ineluctable (*in-ELECT-able*) factor as any possible spiritual experience; in fact, it is possible, even probable, that a man may be misled by the enthusiasm of an illumination, and if he should find apparent conflict between his spiritual duty and his duty to honour, it is almost sure evidence that a trap is being laid for him and he should unhesitatingly stick to the course which ordinary decency indicates. Error on such point is precisely the 'folly' anticipated in..." *The Book of the Law, Liber AL, Chapter I Verse 36* "...and I wish to say definitely, once and for all, that people who do not understand and accept this position have utterly failed to grasp the fundamental principles of the Law of Thelema."[67]

One might find in our concept of paratge a somewhat more universal statement of that Edwardian concept of a "Gentleman."

The Fool:

How is it that you quote Crowley? Or for that matter know anything about Thelema?

Azalais:

Your poet Crowley is a mortal man, but the Master Therion (*THAY-ree-uhn*) is ageless and exists through all time. And we, my good Fool, are as much metaphors as you; each a symbol for an element of one key mystery.

The Fool:

Well, whatever you are, you can't put one over on me or my friends here. I know that nobody can tell me what Thelema is, or how to do it. And that it's not about being nice to people.

Raimond: *adamantly*

This is the initiation of the Most Ancient Order of the Defenders of the Temple of the East and of the Hermetic Fellowship of Light, and we are those who are chosen to conduct the initiates through the first four worlds.

Azalais:

We are the advocates of one Gnostic and Catholic Church of Light, Life, Love and Liberty, the Word of whose Law is THELEMA, for we are the progenitors of that Church.

Jeanne:

It is true that no one can tell you precisely what Thelema means or tell you explicitly how to observe that Law. Yet, that Law has guiding principles and is, illustrated by a series of revelations of which *Liber AL* is but the first. The Law is not merely a word, infinitely mutable, to which any passion may be conveniently attached. It is a complex worldview, supported by additional revelations, those of the Holy Books of Thelema, Vision and the Voice, The Paris Working , the Ab-ul-Diz working, and of others.

Azalais:

Few who learn Thelema go beyond baby steps. These initiations will take you to the core of the heart girt with a serpent, and beyond. If you fear to plunge into that depth, then it is best you leave now and take no oath.

Jeanne:

You may disagree with some of what is said or even the specific teachings of we, its exemplars; for, where all things have been divided for love's sake, there are many reflections and none will echo perfectly your will. But, if it is your will to determine that Thelema is no more than a convenient word for your momentary fancy, bereft of structure, worldview, or meaning, then it is best you leave now and take no oath.

Raimond:

There is nothing nice about this path. It is savage and fraught with peril, the violation of taboos, and perversity. Yet, if you reject that Thelema is the word of Light, Life, Love, and Liberty, and seek Thelema as nothing more than an outlet for rage; a conduit to rationalize your contempt for all about you, it is best you leave now and take no oath.

The Fool:

If any of you choose to leave, I will conduct you safely outside of this space.

If anyone chooses to leave they are conducted safely outside the space.

Azalais:

Now, the oath. As you may know I am studied in the ways of the Good People, who are sometimes called the Cathars, and do not take oaths upon the name of God in the manner of the followers of Priests who look to Celestine[68] in Rome. Therefore, I would have you swear only on your honor, though their mysteries make that to be an oath upon God.

Fool, would you read the oath?

The Fool:

Wait!? What if they prove faithless? What…what if you prove faithless!?

Azalais:

As my Father and Brother have proved, oaths between mortal beings are agreements, and, regardless of invocation or relic, are binding only if they are kept on both sides. To say otherwise would be to shackle the wrists of those who have honor and allow the dishonorable the power of blocking them from the accomplishment of their wills. We promise, on our part: hospitality, generosity, and an offer to share our secrets; and further agree that we will give warning of any dangers we know to be present in our realm. Provided that we honor our commitments, to breach our trust will serve as its own punishment.

The Thelemic Initiations

The Oath

The Fool, echoed by the initiates: *leads in a reading of the Oath, reading each phrase and allowing it to be repeated.*

On my name, upon the deepest identity and understanding of my self, and upon my honor I do swear to maintain the secrets of this Sovereign Sanctuary both in adherence to the word of my oath and the spirit of my action, as it has been fairly and diligently explained to me.

I will not reveal the words as they are written in whole or part;

I will not reveal the general course and form of the initiation by part, or the specifics of the characters within;

I understand that transmitting the words and signs outside of the path of initiation may endanger others and I will refrain utterly from doing this;

I will not act as an initiator into these mysteries, in whole or in part, without the due authorization of this Sovereign Sanctuary;

I will not violate the privacy of other initiates, including disclosing their initiatory status or details about their initiation, including their grade of initiation, without their explicit consent;

When considering how I speak I will err towards silence;

I understand that it is my duty to police only myself and that I am neither obliged nor empowered to school others in their adherence to this oath;

So mote it be.

The Ritual of Purification

Azalais:

Now that the first step has been taken, let us welcome you. You are not yet Petitioners in Full, yet you will be received.

Raimond:

Child of my father's seed, this room is not well lit, for there is but one small candle which marks this hour. If there is to be merriment and true hospitality, I bid you chase away the shadows with light.

Azalais:

Let this palace of our meeting be made beautiful and sacred with the kindling of fire.

Azalais takes fire from the Candle of Hours which is burning on the Sideboard and lights the dark candle

This is the flame that burns in every human heart...

Azalais lights the light candle

...and in the core of every star.[69]

Jeanne:

Oh Prince. These travelers still wear the dust and discomfort of the road. Before they join us in our Revels, should they not be made comfortable?

Azalais, who hath borne my husband's seed, fetch for them a bowl of water made pure with hyssop and towels that they may wash away all that is behind them,[70] and turn themselves to revelry with abandon, as is the custom here.

Symbolic Washing of Hands

Jeanne:

Let the dust of your journey be washed down into nothing.

Azalais: The performer should make a point of obviously reading the following:

As your coming was witnessed from the watchtowers which stand at the four corners of this City, so a feast is already being prepared. It is our way here that no feast is undertaken without some revelry or entertainment, of times the songs of the noble troubadours or the performances of their jongleurs, at others recitals or dramas. I take you to be people of refinement and taste, for you travel with a fool who must be both your respite and guide.

The Challenge and Presentation

The Fool: gives Azalais a pointed look

Wait…enough. Stop. I have been tolerant but now I must protest.

The Fool turns to the initiates.

This is no true initiation. See you why?

Azalais:

Why, O Fool of the Earth?

The Fool:

Look. She is reading from a book. Everyone knows that to be a true initiation, the words must be memorized.

Azalais:

Why again, O Fool of the Earth?

The Fool:

That is how it must be. Someone important said so. By memorizing the words the initiator becomes…able to convey…the awesome and puissant power of initiation. It is like a magick spell.

The Thelemic Initiations

Azalais:

There is a gulf between you and understanding of magick, O Fool. And you travelers are well-warned that the Fool as a guide is prone to enthusiasms, and can no more be trusted than you trust yourselves.

This book I bear is the book of the Good People, which is a great secret unto the scores of years. In any case, I am not an initiator, I am one who holds the hooded lantern by the gate of initiation and casts a light for the feet to tread.

Raimond: *raises his hand for silence*

Perhaps because you have walked backwards you have begun to think backwards, O Fool. The skills which make a good magician and a good actor do not always overlap, nor does memorization connote understanding. You said yourself that the words bear double meanings. How are they preserved if not in writing? From whence does initiation emanate, from my living mouth, or from the Logos?

The Fool:

Even the lowest form of Fool knows that within the choices named the answer must be the Logos, though perhaps that is not the final answer. I am in check, I surrender the board.

Azalais:

Indeed. You said truly all our words bear double power. Outside of the book they are ephemeral, and may become dilute.

The Fool:

What book then?

Azalais:

By that which lies within me, the Realm of Fire knows but one Book, that book having four parts. Even Eusebius[71] (*AY-oo-SEB-ee-oos*) knew, by way of Sanchuniathon (*SAN-chu-nee-AH-thun*) of Beirut, that Thoth first revealed the true nature of Kneph (*NEF*), which has been veiled to us, and so the Logos was written in that Book of Thoth called by some the Emerald Tablet. Yet, the Good People admit to no name for it.

Azalais holds up their book which is bound in Orange and on it in Dark Violet are the Enochian initials AMBZ[72]

I name it "The Forthsaying of the New Aeon" and its words are the Revelation of Destruction. It was handed down to me from our Grandfather.[73]

The Fool: *dismissive tone:*

It is but a child's story.

Azalais:

You speak truth, O Fool. It is the story of a child.

Raimond:

Behold *The Book of Opening of the New Aeon.* It was given to me by my sister as a Gift from the Good People who could not read it themselves.

Raimond holds up their book which is bound in Red and on it are the Enochian initials ABFMA[74] in Blue

The Fool:

That is no story for children.

Jeanne: *knocks three times: !!!*

During the time that I was in Acre (*AH-ker*), my brother sold the Isle of Cyprus to the Templars for the value of forty thousand gold bezants (*BEH-zant* or *bez-UNT*) advance. Along with the coin were some objects of value, including a book which had been the property of a certain Lord of Sidon whom, after its fall, took the Templar Cross.

This is the Book of the Scorpion which is the Book of Pain and Failure and the downfall of the Old Aeon. Of its discovery, I will tell at some other time.

The Book displayed is of a ruddy color and has on it the letters AN[75] in Enochian

Raimond:

Within these books there is surpassing danger.

The Fool:

You mock us with warnings for children. What fear have we? Do you threaten us with monsters and ghosts?

Raimond:

Monsters and ghosts, yes. Those who read from the Book of the Rain of Blood[76] and cannot pour out their own blood will become no more than shells; things of the qlippoth, (*KLI-fath*), empty vessels.

Too, they shall become monsters, though they shall breathe that they are free people in the same moment they offer their wrists eagerly for shackles. They will put chains upon others and believe that they are not slaves, but Kings, mistaking the chain around their neck for a crown upon their head.

Within them is the power to suborn every sacred thing, to twist the sun itself.[77] They forsake the company of stars, and wreck the orbits of all those whom they cross.

Jeanne:

Beware lest ye follow them into the abyss, thinking it a Royal Palace. There would you wallow in satisfaction at your accomplishments, full of self-justification and knowing-best, and the certainty that you are more than one star in the company of stars. There would you hoard shattered stars to ensure their light is not rekindled.

Azalais:

There would you know not love.

The Thelemic Initiations

Raimond:

> Come before me now and I will give you a pass-word so that you may enjoy the Freedom of the Commune of the City of Toulouse and yet return to our Hall. .

Raimond knocks five times, by 3 and 2 thus: !!! !!

The Fool: *bids the initiates advance before the dais.*

Raimond:

> The password is Ludus, which is fitting for a court of love and mirth. Its meaning is playful love – that which passes without guilt or second thought; the joy of children.
>
> Now, repeat it to me.

Initiates:

> Ludus.

Raimond:

> Its meaning?

Initiates: *Must give some satisfactory response regarding playful love.*

Raimond:

> Carry it with you and you shall not grow old for it is written: "All is a never ending Play of Love wherein our Lady Nuit and her Lord Hadit rejoice; and every Part of the Play is Play."[78]

Azalais:

> These travelers are children now or they would not follow the Fool into our court. Yet they are also aged, or they would fly in fear from these deepening mysteries.

The Fool:

> Three books? Is there not then a fourth. That, at least, you have sealed up, for it cannot be heard nor spoken.

Raimond:

> The angel which guards it presents unto each generation its darkest and deepest shadow. Only through that fearsome darkness can be found the silence. I have it here upon the altar.

The books sit on the altar, stacked or ordered on a Triangle of red which may be sewn on the cloth or cut and placed beneath it. Raimond rises and walks to the altar

> I offer you this book as a host gift, freely and with a glad heart. It is the Rapture of Ineffable Union. But this book I cannot read to you, for I may not speak it and you may not hear it. It is the manifestation of the revelation of the new Aeon, yet it is but a door. I would ask that as you take your book you rest upon the altar those blades which you have brought which are to be consecrated to your purpose as a Magician. These shall rest on the Altar through the rite of your initiation and afterwards you shall carry them forth into the world.

Initiates: *Each should take a book, and leave their dagger upon the Altar, or hand it over to be placed upon the Altar.*

Raimond:

This book which is called "The Book of the Law," is a door. If you step through the door, you will be beset with your greatest fears and sorrows, yet it is a beginning not an end. If you do not pursue the entire story and choose to remain on the threshold, you may be lost to the Abyss.

More sorrowful still, you will not know yourself to be lost, but think rather that you have attained greatly, and you shall shut out the terror of the angel to a tiny sliver of doubt and fear at the back of your mind.

The Fool:

He means you may make yourself at home in a trough filled with pig shit and call it a palace.

Raimond:

I now give you a further sign. Hold the book in your left hand and extend it outward. Now place your right hand upon the book and make with it an angle of ninety degrees. This is the pass-sign of the Petitioner.

The Fool:

What is this of Petitions? My friends here are not your subjects. And they're not yet under contract.

The next line should be said humorously.

I'm their agent, I should know.

On the Mystery of Initiation

Azalais:

Those who have sought hospitality here may Petition for initiation into these great secrets which are the birthright of all peoples. Before our guests leave, they will be handed a Petition and, should they choose, they may return, signing their name upon it to signify their readiness to explore the Great Work. As we refresh ourselves, is well at this time that I should tell you something of the structure of our Mysteries. At the outermost edge are those such as yourselves, Our Guests, who have been received and may Petition for entrance to our Sovereign Sanctuary.

Some see initiation as a ladder by which one climbs to a height. Still others see each initiation as its own unrelated story which might as well be a ring, experienced in any order.

In truth, there is a progression and those who leap to the greater initiations without benefit of the foundational initiations do not benefit much. So, too, initiations are cyclical, in that they may often be repeated with deepening effect.

Too, we learn that the grades above the Foundational are not necessarily attained in strict order, or to the same extent for each individual. Because this upends the entire idea of a strict hierarchy, lest this seem to be some unique doctrine to our Order, I will mention that it has been part and parcel from the beginning for it is written "It should be stated that these Grades are not necessarily attained fully, and in strict consecution, or manifested wholly on all planes. The subject is very difficult..."[79]

The Thelemic Initiations

The Fool:

If you repeat initiations does that mean you have to go through the ordeals again?

Azalais:

It is the case that rituals of initiation and the ordeals are separate. Of old, there was an attempt to integrate them, so you might be bound, or threatened.

We understand on one hand that these things may open the mind for initiation and make limited use of such dramatics here and there, but even if we made them quite draconian, they would still not be true ordeals. Those, most particularly Ordeal X, come to the individual. Each of you must learn to recognize the Ordeals in your own life, and also to choose when to accept the challenges given you in life as Ordeals.

It would be neat and convenient if there were an easy pattern...initiation, ordeal, initiation, ordeal...one after the other. In the world of matter, these things may come out of order, or be repeated if the lesson does not take, or is not learned completely, or even if it is to be deepened. Some may have already experienced the ordeal of a given initiation and have no need of it. Too, ordeals are not always ills; they may be any strong experience.

Raimond:

It is permitted to take some of our degrees closely together, as they are complementary, or their ordeals interlinked. It is well for you to know now that there are no degrees of the Thelemic Order which are busywork. All these degrees have been presented as "Higher" mysteries in past times, for there is no slow road in the New Aeon. Likewise there is no Novice rank. The Thelemic Order is designed for leaders, for Kings, and those who Petition must be ready to become magicians.

Azalais:

This is the only "introduction" you shall receive. This is no system for the faint, nor are even the First and Second degrees for the casual dilettante. Each of the Foundational degrees is a great mystery, and the road progresses quickly into the heart of Thelema and the Aeon.

But, for now, our guests have been purified and received handsome gifts, and have yet to eat and drink.

The Revels

Raimond:

Let the Revels begin. Let there be bread and honey.

Jeanne:

First, as I learned in the Levant, let us share bread and salt with our guests that there may be a bond of amity and a memory of promises given and received for all time.

The Fool: If the meal is mostly symbolic the Fool says as an aside:

It's a symbolic feast.

The Fool may also add a bit of Ludus breaking the fourth wall extempore here e.g. "We'll order pizza later," or something else amusing and relevant. Be careful though not to imply that it is the responsibility of the initiates to buy food for, or feed the initiators later, because this is not our tradition.

Either way, the following should be spoken to the Initiates:

> I will give you one fair warning. All that is read from the book here is Holy and has meaning upon meaning. But the revels are a time of jest. There may be that said which is irreverent, even intentionally contrary, by way of Ludus, jest, levity, and even careless speech. From this you may take the lesson that even among the Adepts not every spoken word is a gem of wisdom.

The Symbolic Meal

The guests go to the tables, or the food is brought in to the guests. At a minimum if possible some form of salt and bread, or salty bread is broken and eaten. Too, there should be honey.

Because this is a time when Initiates are allowed to Ad Lib it is possible that they will say things which are misleading or confusing. While the Fool and principals may explain or even correct some of these things, for the most part the warning should be allowed to stand and this should be a time for free and relaxed speech. It is not particularly important that the speech be "in period" in the sense of the setting of the initiation as if it were a historical drama, but it is best if those who are not being initiated on this day refrain from talking about their day to day business and personal matters, gossip, or news, outside the setting. It is useful to reflect upon Liber AL, its history, and import if the Initiates do not yet know it.

The Sovereign Initiator should guide rather than proscribe or order. If someone insists on continually breaking the "fourth wall," the Sovereign Initiator may speak to them quietly, privately and compassionately, to urge them to maintain the spirit of the initiation.

Once everyone has gathered food, and is within earshot, after a reasonable pause for conversation, Azalais should continue.

The Staging of the Tragedy

Azalais:

> For your entertainment and edification, following our revels shall be a performance. Listen as we refresh ourselves, and I will tell you how I came to learn of it, though you may travel through three other Kingdoms and I may come into the City of Pyramids before you shall know the import of my story.

> This is a story which was known to the Knights of the Temple and of the Hospital of St. John. When our grandfather took our father to join in the ill-fated Crusade to retake Edessa he traveled East by way of the Roman Court at Constantinople. After, he sailed to Caesarea along the coast by way of the Gulf of Satalia, where he was beset by storm, and came at length to Acre where he was poisoned.[80]

Raimond:

> It is said by some by my mother-in-law, Eleanor of Aquitaine.[81]

Jeanne:

> It is said by others by Queen Melisende of Jerusalem[82]… not that mother wouldn't.

The Thelemic Initiations

Raimond:

Whatever the truth, it is more than half a century past. I learned this story from my father,[83] though my sister tells me that it is found as well in the Secret Book of the Good People.

Azalais:

Now it is known that the Secret Book of The Good People was brought from the Levant by the Bishop Nicetas (*nee-KAY-tass*) of Constantinople,[84] who convened the Council of Saint-Felix (*SAHN-fay-Leeks*) and debated against our mother here, in this very city, at a meeting called by our father in that same year.

And the sect of Nicetas came, first from Thrace but, before that, from Armenia, where they were some centuries ago dispossessed of their lands by the Eastern Roman Emperor in Byzantium. In Armenia, they had been rightly called Paulician Gnostics after an ancient Bishop of Antioch. Their way was older than that of the Church at Constantinople or the Patriarch of Jerusalem, and much of their teaching was far older than that of the Church of Christ. They knew much of old of the Sabians of Harran who had no use for Jesus and revered Hermes Trismegistus (*HUR-meez triz-MUH-giss-tus* or *triz-MUH-jiss-tus the US favors a soft g, the UK a hard g*), whom they called Enoch or Idris (*ID-riss* or *EED-riss*), as their Prophet.

Many of these Gnostics remained in the Levant and Anatolia and still kept their faith, hiding in the mountains or amongst the crowds in the cities.

When the Crusades came to contest with the Seljuks (*SELL-jukes*), some of these Gnostics hired themselves as mercenaries, hoping that new rulers would bring better treatment. From them, our father received stories and ancient words by night. Some fought on the side of the Seljuks, but neither did the Frankish Crusaders flinch to hire them, even though they called them heretics.

Jeanne:

And so they were, by account of the authorities both East and West.

Azalais:

You do not approve of these stories, I think?

Jeanne:

Why should I disapprove? The Good People, I do not dislike per se, but they bring contention and an excuse for your uncle, the Capetian King, to rally Christian Princes against the legacy which pertains to the child of my flesh. Myths are just that and nothing more.

Azalais:

Do not these things conflict with the Doctrine of Rome?

Jeanne: *scornful*

You do me injustice. Do you think I care a thing for Popes? Am I my father's daughter? I keep allegiance to Rome for my own reasons. I am pragmatic, not prude. Have I raised an eyebrow over having Cathar Bishops at my table? At Lydda (*LEE-duh, or LOAD*), my brother shared a great feast with Salah ad-Din (*sal-AH-ahd-een*) and proposed that I should marry Sayf ad-Din (*sa-EEF-ahd-een*) and be with him co-ruler of Jerusalem. Why should the mere recitation of a heretical story scandalize me?

Azalais:

I heard that you would not turn from Christendom to marry Sayf ad-Din.

Jeanne:

How long and fruitful do you think such a dynasty would have been? Do you think that the pale skinned men of the Empire, of England, the Franks...even you of Toulouse would have honored it for long? My brother is monstrous and practical, yet strangely naive. Having contempt for all peoples equally, with little understanding of those who act from conviction, he was a fool to think the Crusaders had the breadth or depth to tolerate it. When I bore a child whose countenance did not reflect their own? Perhaps I lacked bravery in refusing to consider this great union of peoples, but I fear the ideal of harmony would not hold up to the intolerance of those fired with the zeal to kill and conquer in the name of Christ.

Azalais:

You speak like a heretic, for you seem to care little for differences between the faiths. If you do not believe in the Holy Father in Rome, or his church, why have a God?

Jeanne:

The God of Salah ad-Din is the God of Pope Celestine. So says even Salah ad-Din. I do not think that God cares a fig for either of them. Yet people need a God. Freed of his gaze, they would strip the lands for their passions to feed their whimsy. Charity for the poor? Why not let them labor as slaves? The Good People hold that we, ourselves, are God. Pray, you, that my brother Richard never decides that he is God, so that what little restraint lay upon him vanishes. Without that faint flicker of fear, he would put Nero and Caligula to shame. The Good People are children who would pry the lock off Pandora's Box.

Azalais:

It is fortunate that the road is narrow which leads to understanding of the mystery of God within. The Good People speak it, but to those who cannot see the road for themselves, such talk means nothing.

Jeanne:

Those who know not where the road ends, or even where it begins may serve as highwaymen upon it, waylaying others and tempting them to ruin. I'll turn my eyes to Rome, yet. It is safer and I have seen the injury men do when they lack wisdom and understanding. Perhaps my brother already secretly vies with God, he still conspired to marry me to a Prince who is not a Christian.

Raimond:

I have not said I am not a Christian. I have given much to the Knights of the Hospital and of the Temple. f I have doubts about Rome, I am also not a Cathar. Nothing about the base rivalry of faith suits paratge. Nor can the Good People answer all questions. My sister may very well be God, but then so I am too, and the man who mucks the barns as well. So Jeanne, Countess and Queen, you do not object to my sister's story?

Jeanne:

Why should I? A story is a myth. My father commissioned a Troubadour, a certain Benoit (*BIN-wah*), to compose a great epic, the Romance of Troy, [85]which speaks freely of the Gods and Goddesses, yet no one in the Royal Court of Anjou was moved to sacrifice to Jupiter by the hearing of it. When it comes to ancient histories, we might yet chance to learn from them. Here and there, the Gods of old had more reverence for things pastoral than the arts of war.

Raimond:

And sometimes more veneration for war than commerce. A mixed lot, those old Gods.

Jeanne:

The new one is a mixed lot too.

Azalais:

You'll see why soon. We may hereticate you yet.

Jeanne:

Doubtful. But I'm not easily shocked. Being Queen of Sicily wasn't a job for the faint of heart.

Raimond:

You got overthrown by your dead husband's bastard cousin. And your brother let him have the kingdom and took you off to try to marry you to the brother of Salah-ad-Din.

Jeanne:

There's one in every family. Two in mine apparently. In his defense, my brother did sack Messina on my behalf.

The Fool:

Well at least he assuaged family honor! I'm sure the citizens there were delighted to serve as sacrifice.

Jeanne: looks directly at the Fool

I did say *two* in every family. The situation was complicated. And having my husband take a dig at me is one thing, but have one more go at me, Fool, and I'll take a lesson from my brother and storm that fourth wall of yours. I'll not be held to blame for the entire political tenor of Medieval Europe. If you don't want them to take our mysteries as worship of the past, it's best they know how blighted and savage we are, that they may appreciate how immensely their world has improved. If they hold the changes at nothing and romanticize us, how are they to walk backwards from the pinnacle without tripping as you are wont to do, O Fool?

Jeanne then looks to Azalais to continue speaking

Now if we are to enact the story I suspect, it may be that I should give some knowledge of geography to our travelers, for they may not have traveled in the Levant and know its particular features and history.

Azalais:

You know the land better than I. By all means.

Jeanne:

First, let me give an outline of the Levant, and all that which lies around it. The coast which we call Levantine reaches north to the Gulf of Satalia is dotted with ports. In order: Jaffa, Caesarea, Acre, Tyre, Sidon, Beirut, and Tripoli. Then, further north and bordering on the Kingdom of Armenia, Maraclea. The city of Antioch lays from there a little inland, and further yet Edessa.

Neighboring the Levant, to the West and South from Edessa but not yet to Baghdad lays that strange region where neither Islam or Christianity nor even   have wholly penetrated, with the city Harran where Hermes is revered to this day as Enoch, and the Festival of the Moon God still held each year. North and east of Edessa lie Armenia, Anatolia, and all the remains of the Roman Empire of the East which answers to the Emperor in Byzantium.

It is well that you know that Jerusalem, is an inland city, toward very south of the Levantine coast, reached by the roads which go up from the coast through valleys into the mountains. Now, in the days of the Kingdom of Solomon, the Tribes of Israel occupied the mountains above Tyre and Sidon and there Solomon made his capital at Jerusalem and built his Temple, from whence the Order of Templars took its name, for the Muslims raised a mosque there, which Baldwin the First took as his palace, and gifted it to them when he moved closer to the Citadel.

In the days of Solomon, the coastal cities were the home of great sailors, ancestors of Carthage - the great rival of Rome – Caananites, as we would say. Solomon aspired to build a great capital in the mountains but, at that time, Tyre and Sidon were already mighty cities.

As King Solomon had much trade with Tyre and great friendship, he sent to Hiram, its King, and asked him for a builder, so that he might build a Temple as magnificent as those of the Coast.

Azalais:

It is well they know the outline of the land for though our forefathers journeyed there, I have not. While you finish eating I will organize our play. I would have some among you take the roles of this pageant. Now, Fool, travelers, I'll ask for your assistance. I will describe the roles, then you can tell me who would play them. You all read, do you not?

The Fool:

They read.

The Fool then does a double take at Azalais, as if surprised.

You Read?

Azalais:

We of Toulouse are shockingly literate for Medievals.

The Fool:

No wonder the Church has dark looks for you. What sort of play is it?

The Thelemic Initiations

Azalais: *Gives the Fool a stern look.*

> Mind that wall you keep chipping at, Fool. If you break it completely, you'll have to find some Masons to build it back up.
>
> As for the play it is a tragedy, but it may be played with a bit of Ludus as a balm to lessen the tears.

The Fool: *To the Initiates*

> It's like a Murder Mystery, only it's the 12th century and things are simpler. So it's just 'a murder.'

Azalais:

> We have a Great King, a Master Architect and Stonemason, a Priestess, and three villains. They're buffoons, so you may play them with a bit of ludus, though the third of them is a bit clever and grasping, so give him a twist of cruelty. The Priestess may be played by anyone, but respectfully. You, O Fool, shall play a role I have in mind!
>
> On this are lines which you will read to the best of your ability when prompted.

The parts are then assigned as described in the notes to the degree.

The Tragedy of Hiram Abif

Dramatis Personae: Necessary

- **King Solomon** – King of the United Kingdom of Israel and Judah, c. 970-931 BCE

  Hiram Abif – (*HEE-rahm AHH-beef* or *HI-rim ABB-iff*) Hiram the Father

  Ahiman – (*ah-HEE-mon* or *Am-mon*) The Master Architect and Stonemason

  Abiychazah – (*uh-BEE-shah-ZAH* or *uh-BEE-shuh-ZUH*) The Priestess of Asherah

  Iam – (*EE-am*) a craftsman and villain

  Apophrasz – (ap-OPH-razz) a craftsman and villain – trigger issue with penectomy/castration

  Besz – (*BEZZ or BES*) a craftsman and villain

Auxiliary

- **Shallum** (SHA-loom)

  Akkub (ah-KOOV)

  Talmon (tal-MON0

Direction

The specific directions for the play, including the stations, the entries and exits, and the location of props will be clarified before the time of performance.

If the roles of Shallum, Akkub, and Talmon are not filled by players, then their lines are either ignored, or read by the name in parentheses afterwards.

Note that it would go against the spirit of the entertainment for those who are to be "offstage" to leave the room so that they could not hear the performance. Thus some area should be designated as the "stage" or the play should be played in the round with the players who are active standing at the center of the room.

Act the First

Solomon is seated or standing at one end of his hall, flanked by all the other cast present, which constitute his Court. Hiram Abif enters, escorted by Shallum or if Shallum is not played, escorted by Ahiman.

Shallum (Ahiman):

> I introduce to you O King a great and distinguished visitor, who has come up this very day from the Great City of Tyre on the Coast!

Hiram Abif:

> I am the Father of Hiram, sent by Hiram, King of Tyre, for thee O Solomon King I have brought gifts from the Lord of Tyre, which are borne by your noble gatekeepers and porters.

Akkub (Hiram):

> A fine hawk for the King, keen of sight and vision.

The Thelemic Initiations

Talmon (Hiram):

And as well a trained hunting dog for Solomon King, subtle of scent.

Solomon:

Full welcome are you, Father. I shall set you over all of my Architects, and Masons, and Casters in Bronze, and Laborers, that you be Chief Architect of our Great Temple.

Besz:

Forgive my question, O King, I am a warrior old and stooped ere I became a Master of Laborers and my ways are simple. Is this stranger among us the Father of the King of Tyre, or a workman sent by him?

Abiychazah:

Hush, unworthy fool. He is called Father as I am called Mother, for he is Great in the ways of the Lord El, and he is of the Household of Hiram in the same way that I am of the Household of Solomon.

Apophrasz:

Then may we know his name?

Hiram Abif:

My true name I shall write for you someday as it may prove difficult for you to speak.

Ahiman: *To Apophrasz, Besz, and Iam*

Silence! All your questions shall be answered in time.

Solomon:

Allow me to present to you, Father, Abiychazah (*uh-BEE-shah-ZAH*): Holy One of Asherah (*uh-SHEE-rah*), a mighty seer, and senior of all the Holy Ones of Asherah within our walls. Since our last High Priest conspired with my brother so that I was forced to send him into exile, the Holy One of Asherah has provided great guidance and knowledge of the traditions of our forebears.

Shallum (Solomon):

Indeed she has done much to train Zadok who shall serve as the High Priest in our new Temple, even to instruction in the ways of seeing, so that he may use the Urim (*YOO-rim*) and Thummin (*TOO-mim*).

Hiram Abif:

In the name of El, and of Hadad the Son of El, greetings to our spouse and mother.

Solomon:

I would present to you also, Father, Noble Ahiman, Architect and Master of my Masons. Like yourself is descended from Bezalel (*BAY-sal-el*) who was given the secret flame of knowledge to build the Tabernacle, the Sanctuary of the Ark which contained the word of El.

Ahiman:

It is my honor to meet the Noble Father. I mean no disrespect to our worthy guest, but we are full of knowledge in the ways of the Gods, most particularly of Lord El. I request respectfully, as a matter of my duty, to have account of the qualifications of a Tyrian who would be set over us in the completion of our Great Work.

Solomon:

Know you, worthy Ahiman, that it is the Father Hiram who taught me the subtle craft both of the creation of spirits and the discerning of their names and natures, such that many were realized in a great bronze vessel which I cast under his guidance.

Ahiman:

I defer then gladly to the Father in the matter of casting. But architecture is also building in stone. The cord must be stretched, the great cornerstone must be laid, then all the others, and the roof supported.

Hiram Abif:

I have traveled to the City of the Sun, Heliopolis, in the secret realm built above Mount Abiegnus (*ABI-ayn-us*) beyond the headwaters of the Nile, from whence the Gods came and will return. I have learned the formulae which are the essence of life itself and the secret identity of the Gods. And far from being stingy with these gifts, I would bestow them upon you.

Iam:

I am eager then, when shall these great secrets be disclosed to us? For I would have the secret of life itself, if thou knowest it?

Ahiman:

A third time, silence! Thou knowest nothing of this craft! A mark of wisdom is knowing what one does not know. I welcome the Architect Father who has been sent to us by Hiram of Tyre, and would patiently learn his secrets. Allow the introduction of my Assistants.

Shallum (Ahiman):

This is worthy Apophrasz a foreman of laborers, who measures their work - you may know him by the metal rule he carries; worthy Besz a Master of Stonecutters who was before a Soldier - you may know him by his hammer; and, finally, who last spoke out of turn, worthy Iam an Architect of the Temple, who carries at all times the compass that is his tool and emblem of his station.

Abiychazah:

Come Noble Ahiman. Let us go from this hall, before there can be further display of ignorance. We will later take counsel with the Father on how best to proceed with this great project.

Exeunt Abiychazah followed by Ahiman, Apophrasz, Besz, Iam. Solomon continues once they are alone.

Solomon:

Speak to me, if you would, of these great secrets, for I am most anxious to learn.

Hiram Abif:

I give you my word, Solomon King, that they cannot be revealed at once, for to comprehend each step is a matter of time and labor. I carry with me on a signet a sacred word. It cannot be spoken for it is not truly a word. It is a formula, not superior in itself, yet the understanding of which ties all other formulae together. I carry with me Ten and Three remaining words, each meaningless to the uninitiated. These you must learn by and by.

Solomon:

On the strength of your past generosity and great wisdom, I defer to you to teach these matters as is befitting. I am most anxious then that the work on our Great Temple begin. What work is most important?

Hiram Abif:

First you, O King, must preside over the Stretching of the Cord, under her gaze. Then must be set up three Poles of Asherah.

Solomon:

Would not one do? I have a satisfactory beam, the greatest of cedars, not from the coast, but brought by the Great Queen of the South who, with it, brought riddles and much knowledge. But I have not two more beams of such magnificence.

Hiram Abif:

Have you bronze?

Solomon:

Deep into the desert land of the Edomites we have ventured and there fortified great mines which produce copper in quantity.

Hiram Abif:

Then I will cast them in bronze, one burnished to reflect the Sun in the South, the other the infinite darkness, and all the world shall wonder at their magnificence, pillars of dark and of light. The Tree of Life grows from the belly of Asherah, source of life, and the pillars are her children.

Solomon:

Is not El the spark of life?

Hiram Abif:

You could have asked 'is not El' oh subtle King. Or 'is El not.' If Asherah is infinite and El a single spark, yet the spark of El is contained within and springs from Asherah. She is the egg, but that egg is winged and coiled by the serpent lion.

Solomon:

Are they not opposites: one endless potential, the other limitless possibility?

Hiram Abif:

Take up thy sword, O King, and I will teach thee in simplest terms.

Solomon: *picks up his sword*

Hiram Abif:

Hold it up first as if you meant to deal me a deadly blow?

Solomon:

I would feign no such violence to a guest, for fear that the shadow of violence might open the gate to ill happenings.

Hiram Abif:

All gates are open now, O King. There is little time and much to lose. And there is no blow, even from your flaming sword, which can strike me dead.

Solomon:

So be it.

He turns his blade edge perpendicular to the floor, aimed at Hiram.

Hiram Abif:

Now based only on what you can discern before you, tell me is the blade of the sword wide or narrow?

Solomon:

It is narrow, of surpassing thinness.

Hiram Abif:

Then, if it please you, O King, turn the blade as if you intended to bestow upon me some great honor.

Solomon:

It pleases me far more than to feign harm to you, great friend.

He rotates the blade so it is parallel to the floor, still aimed at Hiram.

Hiram Abif:

Again, using only the evidence before you, is it wide or narrow?

Solomon:

It is wide and formidable.

Hiram Abif:

Then rest your sword, O King, and hear me. So it is with the infinite that is all and the infinite that is nothing.

Solomon:

It is but a point of view?

Hiram Abif:

Even so, the Mystery of the Egg and Serpent.

Solomon:

Then they are as some of my workers say, one, and we might do away with all the other names and call the one 'El.'

Hiram Abif:

No more than you might win a great victory against enemies with the flat of your blade, and reward your allies by cleaving their skulls O King. And there is yet a third, a twin child covered with lilies and roses.[86] Prince and Princess to their King and Queen.

Solomon:

Child or children? How named? And which Prince and which Princess?

Hiram Abif:

Among the Egyptians they are named in Heliopolis in many ways. Ra, and Horus of the Horizon, and Hathor, Cobra of Ra, also lightbringer of the new year.

Solomon:

But which is which? Is the babe a manchild, or womanchild?

Hiram Abif:

The babe is the Sun and Moon commingled. As, if it were fully revealed, are the parents. The sign of the babe is the five pointed star of light.[87]

Solomon:

Then what dwells beyond, inside the Great Building in the Sacred Space beyond the veil? Is not that the house of El?

Hiram Abif:

If thou truly be a King, then it is thy own Palace. This and more I shall teach to you in time. And the secret even of the children.

Solomon:

What secret?

Hiram Abif:

How by passing your seed through the fire you may create new life.

Solomon:

The uneducated would say the sacrifice of babes, but I know more whereof you speak. This is then, a manly mystery.

Hiram Abif:

Your understanding, O King, is greater than that of the workmen and even the architects who would bare the throats of babes over the altar if they thought it would bring them life everlasting. But you are still too fixed. It is a mystery of the Egg and the Serpent. It is elegant in its simplicity and yet hides itself coiled at the center of a labyrinth with many blind ends.

Solomon:

I am patient. For now I am satisfied that my Kingdom shall prosper and grow greater, not through the arts of war as by my father, but through trade and industry, and due respect to the peoples and all the gods, though they be numerous as the company of stars. The peoples of the hills and the coast shall be as one for trade and shared secrets shall bind us more closely than the divisions of land or dialect part us. Share as you can with me and my Masters, both the Master Architect, and the Master of the Mysteries of Asherah who dwells in the House of Asherah.

Hiram Abif:

It shall be as you wish, O King.

Act the Second

Enter Apophrasz, Besz, Iam. They gather beside the Well. Besz carries bread, Iam has a small bag with salt, and Apophrasz is drinking wine from a cup.

Iam:

Share with me, brothers, under the secrecy of our bond as Fellow Craftsmen. Do you not bristle at this Tyrian who usurps our dignity? I, too, am born of Egypt and learned great craft there, but I have made Jerusalem my home. Our own Master of Masons, noble Ahiman, reduced in dignity to Assistant next to this prodigy of Tyre, this so called "Hiram?" And if this Hiram knows mysteries, why does he not speak them plain? Why does he speak of the Cup of Hapocrates as a high mystery? Why does he withhold the sacred word? There is no mystery but the Circle and the Cross, Cup and Chalice!

Here the player may make an obscene pantomime, with a finger penetrating a hole made by the other hand.

I would learn the secrets of the Great Work, of how to pass the seed of my manhood through the fire and thus gain immortality. I tire of riddles and lessons. The seed of man alone is the beginning and the end of life, and woman but fertile ground. I would have the word!

Apophrasz:

I will tell you my grievances without reserve. I have worked long to become a Foreman of Laborers, and carry the measure. Since the time of the Tabernacle, has not the House of the Lord been for El, and his wife Asherah surrogate and supporter, subordinated to the forecourt? Did not Solomon exile Abiathar the rightful High Priest of El, and strip from him the Lamen? Take from him the Urim and Thummim.

Besz:

I, too, have grievances. I have worked long to become a Master of Stonecutters, and to carry the hammer, and to be a Man among Men. I have no grievance with the hearty cult of the potent and warlike God, whether he be named El, Hadad, or otherwise. But since the coming of the Queen of the South has not Solomon King forsaken the hunt and manly arts for perfumes and the company of women, and men who pose as women? The House of Asherah is painted and proud. There, now, perfumed men wear the sacred finery that was reserved for the daughters of Asherah alone.

Apophrasz:

Is not El the Great Lord of our nation, while Asherah is worshiped by wives and daughters in the household shrines? What attendance men may give to the House of Asherah should be a secret of the night, and no business of our wives if we go there. Now the place is painted and lit and there is no going to it secretly. My venom for these perversions knows no bounds. Tell me when and where, for I ache to strike!

Besz:

When women knew their place and men were men, the House of Asherah did serve a purpose. But now it is become a place of corruption, and men and women mix there with no distinction among them, so that "boys" whom I will not call men wear the sacred garments reserved for the Priestesses. Solomon King consorts with them and heeds their oracles. When I looked upon the body of David there was a man, but Solomon King sickens me. I would see the Asherah pole pulled down and their garments burned and these prostitutes driven from among us with knot and cord upon their backside.

Iam:

I hear your grievances, Brothers. I have worked long to become a Fellow Craftsman among Architects and carry the compass. Solomon has abrogated his authority by deposing the rightful Priest of El. Solomon has taken wives from many lands, and he talks of honoring their Gods and Goddesses alongside El. Where the Gods of Egypt trod, so soon will its armies, that I well know. Solomon is a weakling and is made a cuckold.

Besz:

If Asherah be wife of El, then he must put her away as must any man whose wife is unfaithful or disobedient – As Solomon King should with his wives of many lands!

Apophrasz:

This Father Hiram subverts the obedience of our wives. He must be restrained!

Besz:

This Father Hiram subverts the very nature of men and women. He must be halted!

Iam:

Restrained? Halted? Fools! You have no perception![88] Think, you, that Solomon King would take kindly if we chased him back to Tyre? Think, you, that Solomon would not publish our villainy and strip us of all that we have earned? Think, you, that the word would then be given to us? Hiram the Father must die!

Apophrasz:

Yea, and we shall throw down the Asherah Pole of wood and cut it into many pieces!

Besz:

And, once Hiram is gone, we shall go into the House of Asherah and thereby establish the obedience of the Priestesses and strip from men the robes of women and burn them.

Iam:

And throw down the metal poles that are the glory of Hiram's work!

Besz:

The metal poles you shall not touch, for they are of great value and mighty symbols of our potency, moreso even than the Brass Sea. They are beloved of me and I will defend them with my life, and you do not wish to trifle with me for there is not in all these lands not one more a man than I. I shall see them dedicated to El alone. We shall say that we were so instructed by Hiram before he died. One shall be called "He Establishes," the other "He is Strong."

Iam:

And we shall have the secret word which shall grant us life everlasting, so that we may use the word directly without dilution of our selves or principles. It is on a ring around his finger! That alone is the source of all life.

Apophrasz:

I care not for the word. The only name which has meaning is the name of El. How then shall this be accomplished?

Besz:

I am strong, but I would not slay him alone. We must share in this treason.

Iam:

Wait! Call it not treason, for we are faithful to El, who is Lord of Gods. As to the accomplishment of his destruction, be not blind. Besz you were once a warrior and your hammer is heavy. Apophrasz, you carry the sharp-edged ruler. I carry the sharp-pointed compass. Now, it is his custom to come every day at high noon and take water from the well here. Besz, you shall stand against the edge like so and offer him bread. Here put on it some of this salt, which I carry for flavoring of meet as is due my station.

He hands the salt to Besz.

Now bread is made salty so, when he has eaten, his mouth shall be dry and you, Apophrasz, will offer him wine. While he is distracted by its consumption, Besz, you shall step behind him and strike him with your hammer. It shall then be a small matter to end his life.

Apophrasz:

It is well planned then.

The Thelemic Initiations

Besz:

And just in time! See, he comes!

Iam: *steps back as the other two take their places*

Hiram Abif: *Enters, walking, with his staff.*

How now brothers?

Besz:

Well, but just recently come from our labors. I would share this bread with you, for you must hunger. Set your staff aside, that I might sit beside you.

Hiram Abif: *Sits his staff to his side, away from Besz.*

If it is thy will, then I shall eat of it that you may know we are of one flesh.

Eats the bread.

Apophrasz: *Approaches and moves Hiram's staff further away to stand on the side of Hiram opposite Besz.*

You must be thirsty, for the bread is salty. I would share this wine with you, for you must thirst.

Hiram Abif: *Turns his back on Besz and accepts the bread.*

If it is thy will, then I shall drink of it that you may know we are of one blood.

Besz: *should be positioned behind Hiram and raise his hammer, but visibly hesitate*

Iam:

Strike, fool!

Besz:

I am well positioned now, Father of Hiram, to deal you a mortal blow. But if you agree to surrender to us the true word of power and go quietly from this country, telling no-one and swearing a mighty oath to your silence, I shall not take your life.

Hiram Abif:

In truth, I would yield the word to you my siblings though you already have it, for it is your name as well as mine. It is graven on the ring around my finger. But it is a cipher, and the other formulae are the key, and those you must learn else it be meaningless. Nor could I make such an oath to you, for an oath against the truth, extracted by force, cannot bind a Magus. Such bindings would shatter at the first utterance. Know you, too, that though you pervert the tools of peace into weapons of war, it is not given to you to slay me. Now, I shall turn my back on you all and drink again, this time of water from the well. If you are gone ere my thirst is quenched then all shall be forgiven and we will speak not of this day.

Iam:

He speaks riddles to confuse us. This was not in our plan! Strike!

Hiram Abif: *Turning towards the well.*

Do what thou wilt shall be the whole of the Law.

Besz: *Feigns a strike at Hiram on the back of the head with the hammer.* **Note that it is far more important to ensure no injury occurs or can occur than for this strike to appear "realistic."** *The blow drives Hiram to his knees.*

Now strike him, that I be not alone in this.

Apophrasz: *Places the ruler between Hiram's legs, pantomiming castration within the pre-negotiated bounds of the participants. The way in which this occurs should be pre-negotiated.* **Note that it is far more important to ensure no injury occurs or can occur than for this strike to appear "realistic."**

There, good Besz. I have made him less a man than you. If he so loves the Temple of Asherah, he may be a woman there.

Iam:

Fool! He must not live! Else all will know our infamy!

Iam stands over the now prostate Hiram and feigns driving the compass into his back. **Note that it is far more important to ensure no injury occurs or can occur than for this strike to appear "realistic."**

With the sharp tip of my compass, I give him a third hard blow, and pierce his heart!

Apophrasz:

Your act is no infamy, but Holy in the sight of El. A sacrifice.

Iam:

Take, first, the ring from his finger! Read us the word!

Besz: *removes the ring from Hiram's finger*

I have it! Upon the back of it are the characters Yod Heh Vau Heh.

Apophrasz:

Only that? What is their meaning!?

Iam:

Yod Heh Vau Heh. I speak them but I feel no different. Am I become a God?

Besz:

They are the secret name of El. That and no more. Let us break his staff and cast it into the well, and then his body, and let us begone. He is no more a man.

He takes the ring from the puzzled Iam and casts it into the well, while the other two pantomime breaking Hiram's staff and throwing his body into the well.

Act the Third

Solomon is in his hall with Shallum, Akkub, Talmon and Ahiman.

Solomon:

> My worthy friends, what have you discovered pertaining to the disappearance of the noble Father Hiram of Tyre?

Shallum (Ahiman):

> I have sent our Gatekeepers out to to search the roads wast and west, north and south.

Akkub (Ahiman):

> He has not been seen east or west.

Talmon (Ahiman):

> Nor has he been seen north or south.

Ahiman:

> No word has come of him in the City, alone or in company. Two days past, we called off the search.

Abiychazah:

> For the past twelve days, since the noble Father vanished, has the water of the well been bitter and low. Today, a woman of the House of Asherah was drawing up water from the well and in her bucket came his ring. Immediately was a descent arranged, but at the bottom was found only an old skull, showing a blow upon the back. As well were the two parts of his walking staff, which had been shattered. No body was found, thus the mystery is deepened rather than resolved.

Solomon:

> The skull is his?

Shallum (Ahiman):

> It has been examined, but none can say with certainty.

Solomon:

> Why would anyone strike down such nobility?

Ahiman:

> I know not for certain, but I can hazard a guess. Many resented his Mastery. Some are young and raised in comfort. They do not remember past struggles and believe that Mastery should come easily. Others are old and resent that, in opening our city in the hills to the world, you have exposed them to much challenging and novel.

Solomon:

> I have brought no custom to this place that was not known to our forebears.

Abiychazah:

That may be true, O King. But you know much of our history, and read even the characters of Tyre and Sidon. Outside the Court where records are written and customs remembered, the people they are ignorant of all but their father's generation. In this way they mistake the customs of their childhood, or stories of their father, for all of history. Jerusalem is yet, compared to Tyre, a small town, and was smaller in the days of David, your father. Many of those who have come here were raised in the countryside. Since their memories do not embrace the House of Asherah, they believe it is a new thing, and raise hatred against my House and all those in it.

Ahiman:

Whatever their motivation, they have made strange claims as to the last orders given them by Hiram and, without my knowledge, taken axes to the great cedar which was to serve as the Asherah Pole, cutting it into sections. Too, they have given names to the metal poles which they claim to have been ordered by Hiram.

Solomon:

This is most grave, for surely some foul play has occurred. I fear that my Kingdom will bear the stain of this iniquity.

Ahiman:

This falls not upon you, O King, or even upon the peoples of this place. If he was undone, it was a matter of jealousy and sloth, and these are known among all generations and all peoples. Your hands and those of your people are cleaned by our diligent search and attempts to do justice. I have suspicions.

Shallum (Ahiman):

Those who are suspected will say nothing, but perhaps being dragged before Solomon King and put to the question would loosen lips. If not they might still be killed. Thus there would be no stain, for blood would avenge blood.

Solomon:

The course of justice must not be driven by hearsay or speculation. A strong king is a just king. Better for the guilty to go free than the innocent to be unfairly punished.

Abiychazah:

Be that as it may, I have become in fear for my life and the lives of those who reside in the House of Asherah. It is my intention to remove us to Damascus, for I do not believe now that Solomon King can guarantee our safety.

Solomon:

This is a heavy blow, but just. I will set up a new Asherah pole even in your absence. I would ask that you give me the ring, that I may understand its secrets.

Abiychazah:

Willingly, O King. It is not thou with whom we have quarrel, nor even with this place, rather the few who have corrupted many. In time, perhaps, you will bring them to heel.

Solomon:

Let the fragments of the Asherah pole be placed in the foundations of the Temple. But let a section be turned, along with the end of the staff of Father Hiram, that the two be joined into a wand of double power which shall lay across my knees, paired beside my sword. So mote it be.

Ahiman:

So mote it be.

Abiychazah:

So mote it be.

The Fool: lead in applause for all the players

0° Initiation – Script – Second Section

The Discussion

Raimond:

And all this we have seen? It is truth?

Jeanne:

I have no quarrel with it. The ancient Scriptures themselves bear out its truth. In the Latin Vulgate, in the Eleventh Chapter of the First Book of Kings, it is written "Sed colebat Salomon Astharthen deam Sidoniorum,"[89] that Solomon worshiped Ashtoreth the God of Sidon. Certainly, Tyre and Sidon were one people, and Hiram King a worshipper of El the Lord, known also to the people of Caanan as Ba'al and Ashtoreth. During his long and stable reign Manasses, who was the sixteenth King in line from Solomon, planted a grove and made a graven image to Astarte which he set in the Temple.[90] Of course, the eighteenth King, Josiah, had the groves cut down and burned their keepers and the had the shrines to Astarte filled with the bones of the dead.[91]

The Fool:

You know much of the Kings of Jerusalem.

Jeanne:

No more than the Greek Septuagint Bible and the Latin Vulgate Bible tell us. My brother spent years trying to win that city, and contemplated my betrothal as its Queen. It seemed a subject of some relevance.

Azalais:

So even the Churches, East and West, cannot doubt the gist of the story?

Jeanne:

It is written that Solomon and many of the Kings before and after him worshiped Asherah, whom the Greeks called Astarte. She is the Venus of the "Romance of Troy" as well, and called out in the Revelation of John as the "Whore of Babalon." All that said, I suspect the Bishop from Rome might prefer not to dwell on the apostasy of Solomon in worshiping pagan Gods.

Azalais:

The true apostasy was to elevate El, the Vice-regent of the Sun upon the Earth, above the station of his consort and put him in place of the secret and ineffable Lord whose name cannot be known to another. Our play would be as true were it told of the Secret Society of the Dionysian Artificers, or set in the Athens of the architects Ictinus (*IK-tie-nuss*) and Callicrates (*kuh-LICK-ruh-tees*), or any other place where the Inspiration of Thoth was passed down.

The Thelemic Initiations

Raimond:

Even so, the Temple and the Skull are special to us and, through the inspiration of Bezalel, who is the shadow of God, we have some special affinity for this particular story which our travelers will come to understand in time.

Azalais:

Even so, I warrant not that it happened just so. Yet, this story reminds us that, for all the pretensions of the Christians, it is their story that is the crude twist upon the truth. A divine trinity exists, dictated not by dynasties of Gods but visible in Natural law, worshiped in the Temple of Solomon as much as in our Temple.

The infinite circle and all potential, the descending blue triangle: Nuit, Asherah, Astarte, Venus.

The infinite point, having no dimension, the principle of energy and action, ascending red triangle: Hadit or Set, undying Hadad or El.

The child of their union, the golden Tau in the midst of their marriage: the Child Horus or Heru-ra-ha, divided upon itself as Hoor-pa-kraat, and also Ra-Hoor-Khuit, Lord of the Aeon and Crowned and Conquering Child.

Below the Abyss, these are manifest to us as Chaos, Babalon, and Baphomet.

Through many thousand years, it has been useful for those who would restrict others to eliminate the boundless, Nuit, to take for themselves the principle of action, Hadit, and to restrict the understanding of Ra-Hoor-Khuit and of the principle of Love. Through fire and rebuilding they were stripped even from Solomon's Temple, but to understand and experience that they were there is our proof that it is we who are the holders of the true tradition.

These myths belong to us. These are our birthright as magicians and priests; an ancient truth which has been revealed in some form since primitive magicians first daubed paint on the walls of deep places of the earth and contemplated what lay beyond their next meal.

The Fool:

What is the difference between a myth and a lie?

Jeanne:

A lie is false.

Raimond:

I would say, rather, a lie is deceitful, for lies may be built of misleading truths. A myth is a story which might be untruthful, but is told with no intention to deceive.

Jeanne:

I have no objection to a good story. Though, your Solomon seemed at exceptional pains to make sure that no hard feelings were taken towards the Jews in your play.

Azalais:

I will not deny it is so. It was long the tradition of my late husband and my son, who now rules as Count, to treat the same – Christian, Good People, and Jew alike – often employing Jews as bailiffs of the court on account of their education. But, when they have gone on the Count's business to settle accounts with the monasteries, the monks have oft times shown Christian goodwill by beating them. Now, those godly monks send missives to Paris and Rome calling stridently for preachers, soldiers, and fire to burn away the 'heresy' that is tolerance.

Jeanne:

There was, indeed, much slaughter of the Jews when my brother came to the throne, terrible and bloody. To his credit, my brother punished the worst offenders. Those who committed such murders held themselves Christian and excused their violation of the simplest of their own teachings on a grudge that the Jews slew the Messiah a thousand years before. I have seen the True Cross, and will aver such devices were Roman. It might be an irony that those same who howl for the blood of Jews brag of a Roman pedigree for their town or even for their family. For my own part, if I ever have to have the sins of my father or brother counted against me, I shall indeed be a villain.

Azalais:

The Good People question even that the true Messiah died at all, and account the Cross but a cipher which, along with the circle, answers to one of our Foundational mysteries. It has made me, in the teaching of myths, over cautious not to churn poison. The setting of the Temple of Solomon brings to mind the Jews, for we know it through the scripture which is the history of their Kingdoms, though the people of that time are hardly those we know today. Nor is the story truly about them, or indeed about any one King or Temple. It is about every state and holy place through all of time, from the first Kings who drove their herds to worship on the plain of Edessa, to the halls of the Lateran Palace.

Raimond:

It is written "The savage babe being born is taught the myths of his tribe, that uncorrupted are beautiful enough; the civilised child, the myths of his nation, that corrupted are merely bestial, and are as rigid as the former are elastic."[92] Those who lack the free air and privilege of our towns, the spacious halls and nobility of our Palaces, will twist any story, no matter how noble, to justify the torment of others. The fault is ours as well as theirs. They strike down at those below them because they cannot strike up, and save we elevate them to stand with us, they will hallow ignorance. To the Jews, we owe much, for they have taught to us the secrets of the Tree of Life and the Qlippoth, and it is in our lands and those near us where they have been most free to write and think.

Jeanne:

In truth, husband, you have made yourself into a model for the persecuted people of the scripture, for powerful monarchs scheme to destroy all that you protect.

Raimond:

This I must refute, we are not a persecuted people. Not you, not I, nor any of us who have the privilege of nobility.

Jeanne:

Do not the Pope and the Capetian King now strive to raise ire against, not only you, but the other Lords of this region – your sister's son, the Count of Carcassonne,[93] and as well your vassal the Count of Foix,[94] and his sister, Esclarmonde,[95] both of whom bear the stigma of overmuch association with the Cathars? Is not the wind such that the Lords of Saint-Felix have been emboldened to make threat of seizure of castles which belong, by rights, to you, my husband?

Raimond:

The Pope has some reason left in him. There are those who fan the flames, and see every instance in which some noble relation takes counsel with the Good People as an occasion to cry heresy. The rash and avaricious contemplate war upon us for our tolerance, yet I will bend far to avoid it, as did my father.

Azalais:

The threat upon our pleasant and prosperous lands has damped at least our rivalries amongst ourselves. For our father and my late husband[96] were oft at odds.

Raimond:

Whatever threat faces us, we have, by accident of birth, sword and horse and wall of stone, which the Good People and the Jews and all others who depend on us for protection, whether they would or no, do not. They have no recourse but to suffer what is visited upon them, whether it be fury or tyranny.

When those with nobility and privilege believe themselves martyrs, it is seldom more than a justification for inaction, for the role of Knights is struggle.

If we are truly knights, then all those who would live in peace, abjuring hatred and avoiding bloodshed save in direct defense of their freedom, become our siblings.

When they are hunted or hated, it is ours to protect and defend the roads they walk, but one cannot be both master and martyr. From this point on you choose your path. You are not yet magicians or knights but, if you choose to return to this place and Petition, so shall you become, and assume the sacred duty of safeguarding the path to Attainment with mercy and with balance. And, so now, the cost of initiation is known to you.

The Fool:

To keep the unworthy off the path?

Azalais:

You know better, Fool. The Law is for all. To ease the hardship of the road with meat and drink and revelry. To show the way, but not to lead.

The Fool:

And what reward to these travelers for absorption of these ancient ideas.

Azalais:

Travelers, what do you gather from our performance?

The travelers are bid to speak. Only the Sovereign Initiator, or one they designate, may respond to their comments. In general, it is best to leave the comments of the initiates to stand. If one is very much in error, the Sovereign Initiator may make gentle corrections, but this is a time for honoring what understandings they have gained, however complete or incomplete.

Azalais:

What you have said has much wisdom. Let us clear the tables from our refreshment, and I will ask my brother to proceed with the conferral of those dignities to which you have become entitled.

The Conferral of Dignities

Raimond:

So mote it be. Now, it is moot that I should convey to you some dignities which you have earned here as a recognition of what you have seen and come to understand.

It is not our way to visit dignities which are not explicitly ours to convey. You have been made aware that, under the Sovereign Sanctuary of the Gnosis of the Thelemic Order, is operated the Independent and Rectified Rite of the Ancient and Primitive Mystery of Memphis and Misraim - one of many manifestations of that Rite, which is itself one of many manifestations of Masonry, Rosicrucianism, Neo-Templarism, and Neo-Gnosticism. This is not, as will have been explained to you, the system of Thelemic Initiation, but rather a framework which not only connects us to the past, but reminds us that our past was, by rights, progressive, with our siblings in the vanguard of that change which led to humanity and tolerance.

In particular, it is understood that the Mystery of Memphis and Misraim had a character, above all other rites, which was both progressive and revolutionary, tied as it was not only to the Revolutions of the late 18th century, but to those continuous revolutions of the 19th century which sought to erase the Ancien (*ahn-CEE-en*) Regime and throw down the Tyranny of wealth to create an egalitarian order upon the face of Europe and the World.

It cannot be said now, or even in the past, that this Mystery answers to any one political party or philosophy; rather, it is written by the Master Therion:

> At the very head of the Book stands the great charter of our godhead: "Every man and every woman is a star." We are all free, all independent, all shining gloriously, each one a radiant world. Is not that good tidings?[97]

Thus our order is not servant to any agenda but the Law of Love itself and always we keep in mind the word "every," and recall the divinity of all people. Too we are reminded that it is implied in that Book that the True Will of every person is "essentially noble."[98]

Rather, our members support, according to their Will and understanding, those causes and persons which happen, by coincidence or intent, to bring the Law closer to all. It is our job, not to encourage our initiates to follow this or that leader or doctrine but, rather, to supply the tools by which they may, as magicians, discern the best choices for themselves and the world around them.

The Thelemic Initiations

The tradition of Esoteric Masonry manifested many degrees. However, some are understood to represent the core stories of the Western Tradition, while others provide interesting, but secondary, narrative. Within our tradition, you will find that this introductory degree is related to the foundational three Degrees of Craft Masonry and, as such, contains the true Secret of the Lost Master's Word. You will find that each degree above contains one of the core mysteries, which shall become clear to you as they are taken. In this, we answer to no other structure, but there are no degrees for novices, nor placeholder degrees. In this Order, rather, each degree is a major unfolding of our tradition.

I bear, among other titles, that of Knight of the Rose Cross and, as such, I may confer upon you lesser grades within this outer and historic order.

Raimond knocks nine times in a series of 3 x 3 x 3; thus: !!! !!! !!!

As has been revealed to you the truth of the Lost Master's Word, I hereby grant and confer upon you the first three degrees of our Tradition; those of Apprentice, Companion, and Master. We do not claim to bestow these degrees from any Tradition other than our own. It is my earnest hope that you will seek out further learning regarding these progressive and humanitarian traditions of which we have preserved the esoteric core. Now, as your time here grows short, there is a further lesson to be imparted to you.

In order that you may be proven to be Masters, I ask my sister to give you instruction in the Masonic Password of a Master within our Tradition.

Azalais:

This is our Tracing Board. You may not be familiar with such tools, for were known only among the earliest of orders when it was their way to meet in secret places; the back rooms of public houses, cellars, or upper rooms.

The board itself is said to represent the pavement of the Court of the Temple of Solomon. The Border to represent a Cord with Tassels stretched around the Court, which we know is a reference to the Cord of the Egyptians sacred to Sothis who is identified as we shall explain later, with Babalon.

As the halls of the Orders grew, the Tracing Board fell out of use. We have preserved it here.

Across the top you will read: Yod Heh Vau Heh

Azalais points at the letters in turn, from right to left.

This is the pass-word of the Third Degree of our Masonic Tradition. Please repeat it to me?

Initiates:

Yod Heh Vau Heh

Raimond:

Welcome, Masters of the Craft. Yet you are not yet accepted as Initiates of the Thelemic Order, with the right to Petition for Admission to the First, Foundational, Grade.

The Instruction

Preliminary Instruction – The Kabbalistic Cross

Azalais:

Let us clear the tables, then I shall expound on a mystery which was referenced in our play. The Child Horus is described as a five pointed star of light. It is well then that you know that this symbol is the key to a ritual which is a building block of our mysteries. We have promised gifts and great gifts have we bestowed on you, though you may not yet sense how great. Yet we would not send you away without another token to remember us. Therefore, since learning is both precious and eternal, I shall teach you this ritual.

First, you must learn the Kabbalistic Cross.

The Fool:

I'd guess most of them are already acquainted.

Azalais:

Most likely. But in order to initiate in our tradition, it is important not only to know the words and general sense, but to connect with the ancient form and evolution of our mysteries. We aim to create complete magicians not magicians of the hour.

Those things we teach in classical form we teach to a point. But we present them as examples. The magician who truly understands the evolution and history of the mysteries will interpret for themselves, and never find themselves bound to someone else's dogma or interpretation. In fact we earnestly charge you not to dutifully reproduce these or any rituals, but rather to master the principles behind them, that you may own them and make them your tools, altering them as you will, that they should best serve you.

To this extent, the analogy of architecture is accurate. We must have a firm foundation, lest we find ourselves building a great edifice on shifting sands.

The Fool:

That would characterize no small part of the world of the spiritual and mystical that my travelers will return to. Icarus wings....or castles prone to falling over and sinking into a swamp.

Azalais: Gives the Fool a dark look.

You have a knack for undermining walls yourself, do you not?

Azalais turns back to the initiates.

As my sister-by-law has said, our goal is not to engender a worship of the past. If you are to truly understand where you are going, you must fully understand the nature of the tools and their design. It is no good to allude to secrets if they are not eventually carefully explained.

The ritual itself comes from the Tree of Life, which has been given form by the Jewish Scholars who have found refuge in Provence, in Castile, and in our own lands – most particularly, those recent writers who have taught us the harmony of the ten and the thirteen. Too, it comes from the sign of the cross which, as witnessed by those who have traveled in Egypt, was a symbol of life long before the Romans used it as an engine of death.

Let us have the instruction.

The Instructor may be any Principal, Attendee, or in some cases even an Initiate who has a great familiarity with the subject matter, and is comfortable with the role.

Instructor:

Now, in regards to this ritual, there are many ways to perform it, and many arguments about which is correct. We shall, for our exhibition, teach a slightly updated version of that the most basic and primitive form of the Kabbalistic Cross, written by that incarnation of the Master Therion which cast Baphomet into modern form.[99] It is not that this form is superior rather, like our rite, it is primitive, and thus all else is built upon it.

The Instructor demonstrates the gestures, explaining

The hand is raised to touch the forehead, and it is said, "For thine,"

The hand is touched to the breast and it is said, "is the kingdom,"

The hand is touched to the left shoulder and it is said, "the justice,"

The hand is touched to the right shoulder and it is said, "and the mercy,"

Then the hands are dropped to cover the reins and it is concluded, "Through the Aeon, AUMGN."[100]

I would ask that you follow me now in this most primitive form, though I expect you may never use it again. You shall find many opinions, most having some merit, about which words and phrases best summarize the meaning of this most basic of our rituals. The phrases are most commonly rendered in Hebrew, which is pointless if one does not know their meaning first. There are methodologies for adding the name of the Holy Guardian Angel or for some other personal element that can be incorporated later.

The instructor repeats, having the students recite and follow along.

Now that word at the end AUGMN is not from our older source, but from Master Therion.

Reference AUGMN etc. on the Tracing Board

Preliminary Instruction – The Meaning of AUGMN[101]

Instructor:

In the New Aeon, it is intoned as AUGMN which has a more sophisticated meaning. For a full explanation, you are commended to certain explicit readings. However, in short: A is the Holy Spirit who conceives God in flesh upon the Virgin. A is also the babe in the egg thus produced, the dawning of the Kneph. Thus A is bisexual and self-begetting, the original force — Zeus Arrhenothelus (*air-HEN-oh-THEE-lus*), Bacchus Diphues (*dee-FOO-ay*), or Baphomet.

This word AUM is held to be the true name of the City of the Sun, Heliopolis, the City of Pyramids which was and shall be.

Upon the Tracing Board are scribed three emblems associated with the sacred principle of the Kneph; the serpent and egg or winged egg. In the modern era, the association with sperm and egg seems both prescient and unmistakable. Among the Gnostics in late antiquity the Lion-headed serpent Chnoubis (*KUH-noob-iss*) was associated with the late classical Agathodaemon (*ah-GOTH-oh-DYE-muhn*) or Abraxas (*ah-BRAX-us*). In Thelema it is retained as a symbol of the energy of creation reflected in physical sperm.

To these, we add the Cadeuceus, (*kuh-DOO-shus*) the staff of Hermes. This is an ancient symbol known to the Mesopotamians before the Greeks, the symbol of their Lord of the Good Tree, who passed into the underworld and returned; the precursor to Persephone. The staff of Hermes, and associated with Alchemical Mercury. Because of this association It is sometimes found as a symbol of medicine, but it differs from the traditional symbol, the Rod of Asclepius, which has but one snake. It has been used to signify learning and printing as well as commerce and was said to have the power to restore life unto the dead. If we can extrapolate the serpent lion to signify our modern understanding of sperm, then in the Cadeuceus we needs must extrapolate the true and greater mystery of life, the double helix.

U or V is the child thus manifest, which has the seal of the hexagram - the two triangles interlocked, representing the nature of the Logos as divine and human. The Seal of the Child is the five pointed star, but as we shall soon come to see, at the center of that star is the six rayed star. Six is also the first number of the Sun, whose last number is 666 the "number of a man."

M is the conclusion; the Hanged Man. The individual called forth from the absolute is terminated in death. Together, they express the formula of the old Aeon - a catastrophe and rebirth; the formula of the Slain God.

In the Aeon of Horus, we recognize that those who wait for the end times wait futilely - that there is no universal apocalypse; no single moment of catastrophe. Nature proceeds by undulations. Thus, we often "do not see the forest for the trees;" failing to comprehend the catastrophe in front of us because we expect some glorious pageant instead of ongoing decay and rot.

This formula is represented in the Kabbalah by the letter N. which refers to Scorpio, whose triune nature combines the Eagle, Snake, and Scorpion. These symbols embody the spiritual formula of incarnation.

The letter G is another triune formula which expresses aspects of the moon and describes the nature of our existence in another way. The moon has no light of its own, but appears to have light because of the sun. The sun is still there, even if the moon is not reflecting it, or the reflection cannot be seen from earth.

Thus each of our incarnations is lit by the individual star which is ourselves and that star remains regardless of whether it is currently throwing light on a body which can be seen by others.

The root GN suggests both knowledge as in the root of "Gnosis" and generation, even the sound nasal and suggesting the breath of life.

This moved the Master Therion to replace the M of the old formula with the compound letter MGN. In this way what followed Vau was changed from silence and death into a vibration of the nature of generation and knowledge. Further the symbols of the Virgin moon and Serpent operate as a "commemoration of the legend so grossly deformed in the Hebrew legend of the Garden of Eden, and its even more malignantly debased falsification in that bitterly sectarian broadside, the Apocalypse."

The Fool:

Genesis and the Apocalypse of John? For not being Christian we've talked an awful lot of Bible.

Azalais:

If we were sending you from here to walk into a world where people grow up invoking the *Avesta* night and day and use it to justify everything from sexual repression to genocide, we'd probably talk a lot more about Zarathustra. As you will be charged, you must create your world, and it must include those things which are poisonous to you. You have learned of the Lost Master's Word and the historic purge or subordination of the divine feminine to the divine masculine. Without the understanding of that corruption, you will be hard pressed to even set out on the road to attainment.

Instructor:

Now that you have been shown the pattern of the Kabbalistic Cross, we move into our formal instruction, which is the ritual of the Five Pointed Star.

The Instruction

The instruction may be delivered by the most qualified and confident presenter in the room, though it is generally best if this is not also the Fool. The quality of instruction is more important than the attribution to any of the archetypes.

The Lesser Banishing Ritual of the Pentagram[102]

Instructor:

This ritual is also known as the Lesser Banishing Ritual of the Pentagram. There are many versions and all have some merit. However, we ask for today that you follow along with the version which we have selected, as it is specifically used to most readily illustrate the basic nature of the ritual.

Once you are on your own, you are welcome to add or change it as you like. And in this we speak with the voice of the Master Therion:

> "But I feel bound to observe that they must be studied merely as classics, just as a musician studies Bach and Others. He cannot compose by copying or combining their works; they serve him only as indications of the art of expression. He must master the technique, theory and practice, of music, til the general principles are absorbed, and he has command of the language, to use it to express his Will.
>
> So with Magick; the student must understand and assimilate the basic propositions, and he must be expert in the drill of the practical details.
>
> But that is merely ground-work: he must then conceive his own expression, and execute it in his own style." [103]

Now, in this ritual, you will find yourself on the Tree of Life, or among the spheres.

The Fool should act as a model for each of the following demonstrations while the Instructor speaks and points to Tree of Life on Tracing Board, showing the location in Yesod, then indicates the corresponding spheres.

Instructor:

Below you is the Foundation, the Moon, and below it the Earth, from which you have advanced. To your right is Netzach, Victory or Venus, and to your left is Hod, Splendor or Mercury. Before you shines Tiphareth the Sun.

This is an elemental ritual. With the greater ritual you will use the other pentagrams to banish or invoke, but we begin with the Banishing Pentagram of Earth. Upon completing the Kabbalistic Cross, you will turn, first, to the East and make a Pentagram, sweeping your hand with your forefinger extended, or with the proper tool, from your left hip to your head, then down to your right hip, then up to your left shoulder, then across to your right shoulder, and finally sweeping back down to return to your original starting point.

Now it is our goal to imagine vividly, or to visualize, the pentagram quite naturally in flame, so vividly that we might expect someone else present to see it.

Sign of Osiris Slain

Sign of Horus the Enterer

With every pentagram you create, you will also vibrate a name. Once you have traced the pentagram, stand with arms outstretched in this fashion (*demonstrate*), which is the sign of the Old Aeon, of Osiris or the Slain God.

Take in your breath through the nose, imagining that you are breathing in the name and letting it pass down through your heart, the core of your body, your belly, your sex, and then to your feet. When it reaches your feet, advance your left foot in this way (*demonstrate*), comfortably not overlong, let your hands come forward into the sign of the New Aeon of Horus, and simultaneously feel the name rushing up through your body while you breathe it out. Vibrate the name as you do so – a thing which is neither quite speech nor quite singing. How it feels to you matters more than how it sounds. You may come to find it makes you grow hot and feel great exertion, and that you will hear it echoed as if by the voice of the Universe itself. You then shall withdraw your foot and place your finger onto your lips in the sign of Horus the Child or Hapocrates.

Now these are called God Names, yet think of them neither as Gods in the sense the Romans thought of Venus as some being remote from themselves, only more powerful, nor as God in the sense of the Christians – that is, to say, a creator with whom one might share a connection or an image; a perfect father. If our goal was nothing more than to replicate those mysteries, we would have no need of initiation. You may already grasp the meaning of God implied by Thelema, but through initiation you will come to be that meaning.

The first name, in the East, is that of I-H-V-H, which is pronounced Ye-ho-wau, which you may recognize as Jehovah. It is a cognate of Yod-heh-vau-heh, most associated by us with Air, but that incestuous formula we will unravel more at a later point. It is a story, the main character of which is yourself.

Next, in the South, you shall vibrate A-D-N-I, which is pronounced Ah-doe-nai and is associated by us with Earth. This may be taken as "The Lord" but it has a deeper sense of "to be." Herein lies a great clue to the key of the mystery.

Then, to the West, turn and say A-H-I-H which is pronounced "Eh-yeh," and completes the thought "I am," so that it may be taken in implication from Adonai as "I am that I am," and together they make a statement which is a great key.

Finally then, in the North, is said A-G-L-A pronounced "Ahh-gah-lah" which is a Kabbalistic cipher for "Thou, O Lord, art mighty forever," though it also has an older meaning. This, again, should be taken in light of our understanding of the nature of the divine. It completes the statement of our present mystery.

Then, extending the arms again in the form of the Cross, say:

> Before me Raphael
> Behind me Gabriel
> On my right hand Michael
> On my left hand Auriel

Now these powers you should consider in light of what is implied before, and where they stand in relation to you.

Then say:

> For about me flames the Pentagram
> And in the Column stands the six rayed star

Here we make a note:

In the original concept of this ritual, as put forward by the Hermetic Order of the Golden Dawn and before, the six-rayed star shone behind and outside of us, but in our conception as Thelemites we stand within the star, for every one of us is a star. As the Master Therion says "It flames both above and beneath the magus, who is thus in a cube of 4 pentagrams and 2 hexagrams, 32 points in all. And 32 is AHIHIHVH (*Eh-Yeh-Ye-ho-wau*), the sacred word that expresses the Unity of the Highest and the Human."

And this is the key to not only this ritual, but all secrets.

When it is done, you again make the Kabbalistic Cross as I showed you.

Now if you will follow me, we shall each complete this simple ritual. It matters not if you do it correctly, as it may take several tries. Nor does it matter if you ever use exactly this form again...it is not expected that you will. What is important is that you understand its meaning and import.

Here, the Instructor leads the ritual, as follows, while the Fool and the initiates practice along with them.

touch the forehead

     For thine

touch the breast

     is the kingdom

touch the left shoulder

     the justice

touch the right shoulder

     and the mercy

hands are dropped to cover the reins

     Through the Aeon, AUMGN

Sign of Osiris Slain

Turn to each of the cardinal points. At each point

- *Make a pentagram*
- *Makes the **sign of Osiris Slain***
- *Vibrate the appropriate name*
  - *East: IHVH (ye-HO-wau)*
  - *South: ADNI (ah-DOH-nie)*
  - *West: AHIH (Ehyeh/Eheieh or AY-yah)*
  - *North: AGLA (Ahh-gah-lah)*
- *Make the sign of Horus*

Again extend arms outward to form a cross

     Before me Raphael

     Behind me Gabriel

     On my right hand Michael

     On my left hand Auriel

     For about me flames the Pentagram

     And in the Column stands the six rayed star

touch the forehead

     For thine

touch the breast

     is the kingdom

touch the left shoulder

     the justice

touch the right shoulder

     and the mercy

hands are dropped to cover the reins

     Through the Aeon, AUMGN

Instructor:

Now this ritual has many variations, and there are many arguments. There are even those who suggest that the well known instructions are a blind, designed to keep the unworthy from the path.

The Thelemic Initiations

The Fool:

> Some people like to go around in circles. You may find that teaching in Book O to be most useful, and you will be provided with a copy, but it has been much elaborated on.

Azalais:

> A "blind" may be anything which does not serve you, but the blinds on the path to Mount Abiegnus and the City of Pyramids are simple and manifest. They are those things which thwart you from your true will. If you have learned the meaning behind these rituals, you may change them as you will, as seems more useful and elegant to you so that they serve you better. If you have not, there is no correct formulation which will sweep you on your path.

The Presentation of Gifts

The Fool:

> Their time is short. Let us hasten to the final secret.

Azalais:

> In a moment, we shall present you with our parting gifts. For now, we wish that you should claim from the altar your daggers, which were placed there during the time of your Initiation, and we shall reveal to you the secret of these tools which are now dedicated for your use as a Magician.
>
> The Dagger is the first of three magical implements, representing Mercury, which is the symbol of the mind: it is used to calm too great heat, by the letting of blood; and it is this weapon which is plunged into the side or heart of the magician to fill the Holy Cup. Those faculties which come between the appetites and the reason are thus dealt with.

The daggers are reclaimed from the altar

The Fool:

> A warning: Master Therion has said "This is why those who seek to buttress up religion are so anxious to prove that the universe has no real existence, or only a temporary and relatively unimportant one; the result is of course the usual self destructive....muddle. ....Here then, are we, finite beings in a finite universe; time, space, and causality themselves finite"[104]
>
> Which is to say that if you plunge your finite knife into your finite heart, in a non-metaphorical sense, you will wind up dead. We offer no rule or law of magick by which you may circumvent this causality.
>
> However unimportant that may be in the scheme of the universe, it means that any utility that this finite incarnation has to you will come to an abrupt and sudden end.
>
> Do not misunderstand for one second in relation to this or any other physical act that we have told you otherwise, or encouraged you to end this presumably useful incarnation.
>
> There are times and places where a magician may choose to let their own blood, as detailed in "Liber III vel Jugorum"[105] and other sources, if it be their will. We advise that any instinct towards sacrifice of blood be well-balanced with the laws of causality and point out that other fluids, just as efficacious and safer to extract, may be used in place of living blood in most circumstances.

Put more directly, don't injure yourselves unless you know exactly what you are doing.

Azalais:

First, gifts. It is our belief that you have the makings of a magician. In order that you may better find your way, I share with you two remaining tools. You may of course make better tools for yourself, but these shall serve as a symbolic start and a reminder of your commitment.

If you choose to Petition for admission to the Foundational Mysteries of our Sovereign Sanctuary, you shall be asked at each stage to provide a piece of equipment or regalia for yourself.

The Fool: *passes these out as they are being described, or summons the initiates forward to receive them*

Azalais:

The Scourge is sulfur, the symbol of the spirit: its application excites our sluggish natures; and it may further be used as an instrument of correction, to castigate rebellious volitions. It is applied to the Nephesh (*NEF-ish*), the Animal Soul, the natural desires. This symbolic scourge will remind you of the need to analyze your passions and bring them under conscious control

The scourges are distributed.

Azalais:

Next, I present you with this chain, the symbol of salt, which represents the body. While the ancient Gnostics saw the body as a prison, to Thelemites, it is part of a triad, integral and valuable. If it is agreeable to you, I shall place it around your neck; else you may hold out your hand. It serves to bind the wandering thoughts; and for this reason is worn about the neck of the magician, where Daath is situated.

The chains are distributed

You may be inclined to rush forth and make for yourself, or procure, elaborate magician's tools, and if it be thy will then by all means do. But to paraphrase the Master Therion: "Remember that magick includes all acts soever. Anything may serve as a magical weapon. To impose one's Will on a nation, for instance, one's talisman may be a newspaper, one's triangle a church, or one's circle a Club. To win a partner at romance, one's pantacle may be a necklace; to discover a treasure, one's wand may be a dramatist's pen, or one's incantation a popular song."

Finally, I present to you a Petition, or the key to a Petition to take the First Degree, that of magician, within our Sovereign Sanctuary.

The Petitions are distributed

Now is the moment when you have received all signs and tokens that will denote you as one who is entitled to Petition for Admission to the First, Foundational, Grade of the Thelemic Initiations. With the reception of the Word, you shall become, truly and fully, Petitioners to our Order.

Should you choose to Petition for Admission, you will be asked to bring to your Initiation a Pantacle. The instructions for this you may find in Chapter IX of Book 4, Part II.[106] It may be made of wax or ought else, but you should bear in mind this advice as it is printed in that source: "The Neophyte will perhaps do well to make the first sketches for his Pantacle very large and complex, subsequently simplifying, not so much by exclusion as by combination, just as a Zoologist, beginning with the four great Apes and Man, combines all in the single word 'primate.'

It is not wise to simplify too far, since the ultimate hieroglyphic must be an infinite. The ultimate resolution not having been performed, its symbol must not be portrayed."

The Fool:

The time grows shorter still.

The Word of the Aeon

Azalais:

In parting then; you have the pass-word of the grade.

Initiates, guided by The Fool:

Ludus.

Azalais:

You have been given the sign of the grade.

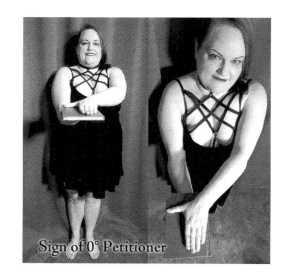

Sign of 0° Petitioner

Initiates, guided by The Fool: Place their left hand on the book at an angle of 90 degrees, right hand under the book

Azalais:

Now I will give you the formula of the grade. It is written here upon the Tracing Board ABRAHADABRA and you will find it in the book which you carry. It is the word of the Aeon, and represents the Great Work which you may Petition to begin to undertake within our Sovereign Sanctuary, and is therefore the "archetype of all other operations." It is the word of Double Power, and like the union of IHVHAHIH (*Ye-ho-wau-eheieh*), it represents the unification in you of the Microcosm and the Macrocosm, that which is above and that which is below.

It is the uniting of the five and six, the rose and cross. It is the Pillar of Asherah that is established in the forecourt of the Temple, so too is it the Pyramid and the Phallus in the City of The Sun. It is the Reward of Ra Hoor Khu and the number of the divine Triads. It's number is 418 and, from that, may much meaning be taken.

I would commend you earnestly, both now and in your first Grade work here, to make careful study of this word. I commend to you as well the Book of the Cairo Working which you hold.

So now if you are asked the Formula of the Petitioner Grade you shall respond ABRAHADABRA, and if asked to elaborate further your response shall be 418. And with the reception of this Mystery, you are received as Petitioners. Timekeeper, mark the time at which these Initiates were received.

Timekeeper:

So mote it be.

Azalais:

I would ask that you Petitioners repeat for me the Formula of the Grade

Initiates:

> ABRAHADABRA

Azalais:

> Its elaboration?

Initiates:

> 418

The Fool:

> Time is come to an end. Some of you were given readings beforehand...if you can turn to those now, I will call on you in turn.

The Fool should indicate if these are on cards, are bookmarked in the copies of Liber AL, etc.

The Reading

First Reading

> From *The Book of the Law, Liber AL vel Legis*, The Third Chapter, First Verse

> ABRAHADABRA the reward of Ra Hoor Khut. (AL III: 1)

Second Reading

> From *The Book of the Law, Liber AL vel Legis*, the Third Chapter, Forty Seventh Verse

> This book shall be translated into all tongues: but always with the original in the writing of the Beast; for in the chance shape of the letters and their position to one another: in these are mysteries that no Beast shall divine. Let him not seek to try: but one cometh after him, whence I say not, who shall discover the Key of it all. Then this line drawn is a key: then this circle squared in its failure is a key also. And ABRAHADABRA . It shall be his child & that strangely. Let him not seek after this; for thereby alone can he fall from it. (AL III: 47)

Third Reading

> From *The Book of the Law, Liber AL vel Legis*, the Third Chapter, Seventy Fifth Verse

> The ending of the words is the Word ABRAHADABRA. (AL III: 75)

The Fool: *indicates by gestures or by whispers if necessary that the Initiates should process from the Temple*

The Presenters remain and close the Temple. Even though the new initiates are of the proper grade, the dramatic effect of their departure overrides any interest in remaining.

I° - Magician - Instructions

Major Properties

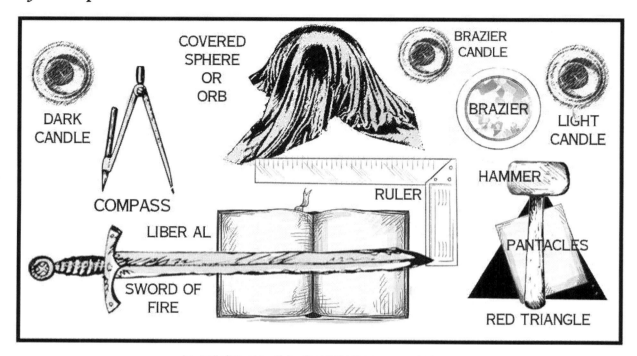

THE SETTING OF THE PRINCIPAL ALTAR

See the appendices for a printable checklist of Properties by location

The Altar Elements

- **The Orb** is rather large, the size of a large upright and oval about 8-10 inches high and 6-8 inches side to side It is never seen and so it could be made from any object, or even a bundle of cloth and duct tape.

- **Cloth Cover for Orb** – large enough to completely cover the orb, leaving no part of it exposed

- **Two Altar candles** – these may be pillar candles, or may be glass jar (novena) candles.
    - Right candle – white or light
    - Left candle – black or dark

- **Masonic Tools** – to the degree possible, the tools should be "archaic" - the sort that can be easily purchased at antique stores or online. It would be best if these were large enough not to seem comical as weapons.
    - Hammer
    - Compass
    - Ruler

- **Brazier** – this needs to look convincingly like it might be intended to burn paper, but it does not have to actually be safe to burn paper in, as no actual paper will be burned. It may sit on a wood, metal, or ceramic protective disk for the appearance of utility. This should not immediately suggest itself as comically too small to burn the pantacles in, but there is no need to go overboard on "selling" it either.

- **Brazier Candle** – this may be a taper as it only needs to be lit for a brief period. The point of this is to create a plausible threat that the Pantacles will be lit on fire and dropped into the brazier. It is extinguished at the end of the challenge.

Other Ritual Elements

- **Tracing Board** – Prepared according to the Illustration. Ideally the board would be hand painted but it may be copied and pasted onto cardboard.

Readings

- **Readings** on printed cards or sheets

Properties for the Play

- **Scripts for the Play** – these should be ready to read. Readability is favored over authenticity so these should not be printed in a historic font. Ideally they can be presented in neat black binders

Optional Suggested Play Properties for Color

- **Crown** - for the King
- **Fishnet** - for the fisherman
- **Solar Crown** - for Isis, Cow Horns and Solar Disk
- **Ankh or Tyet** - for Isis
- **Pschent Crown or Hawk Headpiece** - for Horus
- **Military Hats or Jackets** - for Officers, NCO
- **Rope** - for Soldiers
- **Old style flashlight**- for Soldiers
- **Old Poster for Cafe Dorian Gray** - for Soldier cache
- **Broken Wall**
- **Fake Book Cover** - *The Scented Garden of Abdullah the Satirist of Shiraz*
- **Fake Book Cover** - *Berlin's Third Sex*. By Doctor Magnus Hirschfeld
- **Fake Book Cover** - *The Equinox* Volume One, Number Five

The Books

These are not really books, but binding covers for scripts. In general a binder from an office supply company, covered with decorative paper, leather or fabric, is probably preferential for ease of use. The binders should be neat and easy to use and not kept cluttered with unrelated material. A larger binder may be used for carrying multiple scripts.

Book of the Left Hand/Sempiternal *Liber AL* – This is described at one point as a "Great Book." It bears no legend upon its cover and may be black or may show some fitting design. This may be understood as a likely reference to Liber CDXVIII , the 16th Aethyr LEA, in which it is clarified that the Angel is that of the Beast himself, and the Book Liber AL. Isis suggests some sort of sempiternal Liber AL which exists above the veil of manifestation and is equivalent to the Emerald Tablet, the sum of all knowledge. Isis also suggests this is also the same book as that in the 13th Aethyr, ZIM in which the Blind Adept writes of NEMO.

Generic Properties

These properties should be fairly easy to come by at a given locale or purchase from a grocery store.

- **Chessboard** – While it is *not required* it may be desirable to have a chessboard on a small table near Raimond's seat. He will gesture to this during his "chess" explanation.

- **Lighter** – A reliable grill lighter, or high quality long matches should be used. A search on "candle lighter with bell snuffer" will reveal a number of church-style lighters which run on a replaceable wick. These can be lit from the Candle of the hours after the initial Temple opening. A small lighter in the 18" range is generally best, unless one is dealing with a particularly large Temple space.

- **Three Chairs** – Three chairs together, with the one to the right, as one stands facing them, somehow visibly denoted as a throne, either by being larger, more elevated, etc.

- **Sideboard** – This may be any small or medium-sized table at the side of the room, which is used for various implements when they are not being used on the altar. It is used for a candle and so should be safe and away from any sources of combustion.

- **Altar** – This must be large and sturdy enough to accommodate a sword, the implements, and two candles without being in danger of tipping. In general, a size of 40"-50", and a depth of 14-18" or larger, is preferable.

- **Timepiece** - a timepiece to record the time of initiation

- **Note Paper and Writing Implement** - to record the time of initiation

The Feast Food

There is no specific food ordained for this feast, however those foods which are Venusian or appropriate to Eros might be considered ideal. Ideally, these will have antique or exotic plates and containers; however, that is secondary.

The cost of the feast should be budgeted as part of the overall initiation.

Dramatis Personae (Principals)

- The Fool
- Azalais (ah-zuh-lie-ees)
- Raimond I
- Jeanne (Joan of England)

The above roles of Performers may be filled by anyone who is already initiated to I°. In general, the Sovereign Initiator will take the role of The Fool or Raimond for this initiation, according to their Will, as those roles have the greatest ability to "guide" the experience. Technically speaking, the Sovereign Initiator is not obligated to take *any* speaking part, however this would only tend to be the case in a situation where new Initiators were being trained. The roles of Players in the play-within-a-play are preferentially filled by the initiates, but any remaining roles may be played by any other attendees or by other principals.

Initiation Team Negotiations

Touching Jeanne's Belly

The character of Raimond must touch or gesture towards Jeanne's "pregnant" belly; their child. The degree of touch that is acceptable should be explicitly negotiated, and it is the role of the Sovereign Initiator to ensure this has occurred and not make assumptions. It is fine to merely gesture, or hold the hand a little away.

The person performing as Jeanne must be comfortable having their pregnancy indicated in public.

Initiate Negotiations

These are the general issues which should be disclosed, and which may require negotiations. At a minimum the Sovereign Initiator should review with each candidate for initiation their Petition, and ensure that they do not have any issues or concerns.

Play within a Play

- This ritual contains a portion in which a "play within a play" occurs, in which you may be asked to take a script and play act with others. No memorization is required.

- Potential Limits/Problems

  ○ Stage fright, issues with reading, or reading aloud

  ○ The ritual play-within-a-play contains elements of homophobia and transphobia, though these are presented as villainous. It still may be uncomfortable for some people to perform the roles.

- Possible remedies – stage fright, reading aloud

  ○ Candidate may be specifically given a part which has fewer lines (see roles below)

  ○ Candidate may choose not to read a role at all

- Possible remedies – homophobic and transphobic language

  ○ Explain that the roles in which this language is used involve the portrayal of a villain, and are intentionally strongly-stated in order to get the point across.

  ○ Anyone still not comfortable with this language should be excused from playing one of the three villains.

  ○ In extremis, someone may be excused from the play, or the end of the play, and merely told the story of what happens or allowed to read the section.

Casting Imperatives

The characters of the Sergeant and Bellisario have homophobic lines and behaviors.

For purposes of casting, no characters overlap in acts, nor do the narrators. Thus, the entire play could be performed with only four performers.

The Roles

- **Narrators**
  - **Isis/Babalon** – a narrator character with a fair number of lines
  - **Horus** – a narrator character with a fair number of lines
- **Act I**
  - **King** – a principal with a fair number of lines
  - **Architect** – a principal with a fair number of lines
  - **Fisherman** – a minor character with very few lines
- **Act II**
  - **Marsilio Ficino** – a principal with many lines
  - **Francesco** – a principal with a fair number of lines
  - **Bellisario** – a young man of Florence, homophobic lines and behaviors
  - **Alessandro** – a principal with a fair number of lines
- **Act III**
  - **Tech Corporal** – a principal with a fair number of lines
  - **Sergeant** – an Allied Military Officer, homophobic lines and behaviors
  - **Lieutenant** - a minor character with somewhat fewer lines

Safety Concerns

- Check for dietary issues regarding the snack
- Check for allergies to any incense planned for use
- Standard Fire Safety
  - Extinguisher
- Standard Medical Safety
  - First Aid Kit
  - Certified First Aid Training

I° Initiation – Script – First Section

Prologue

Speech to the Candidate

This is delivered outside the Initiation space, or if that is not plausible before the Initiation candidates have been excused to open the Temple. This may overlap with the Opening of the Lodge, though it may take somewhat longer.

The Sovereign Initiator should assure themselves upon arrival that each Initiate has their pantacle, and their Petition. If not, a copy of the instruction should be provided, along with materials necessary to complete the task. If the Initiate has not completed the pantacle, they should be encouraged to rethink it after the initiation and to continue work on it.

The Fool:

If you remember from your previous initiation there was a lengthy discussion of initiation. You have come here today after having petitioned to initiate as a magician into our Sovereign Sanctuary. In the past other Ceremonial orders have claimed that such initiations create a magical tie "to the Order." That is not untrue, in that initiation, with intent, with group of like minded people does create a magical bond which is real.

That is not the thrust of our warning, however. What we warn here is that you will begin to experience changes in your life through this initiation. As subtle as these initiations are, they have a magical potency through the ideas invoked and through the magical lines of tradition which they open. You will begin to feel the inexorable pressure as you are pushed forward. We believe that most people who have had some life experience are ready for the experience of initiation to the first, and second, degrees, however that does not suggest these will be easy. You may feel as if your life which has previously run in snarls and coils is being snapped tight as a rope which is suddenly stretched straight. The experience may be disorienting. This may be true even if we are quite experienced in Ceremonial magick and magical work.

We will briefly recap what you have been told before:

We do not represent any one true path, however we know that this initiation represents a viable path to attainment.

We do not initiate you. Living people cannot truly initiate other living people. Initiation is not a serum which can be injected against the will. Initiation is an internal process, and living people can act only to open doors and remove barriers to initiation.

These initiations are not intended to harm you, yet they contain the possibility of harm. The intent in all cases is to limit the possibility of inadvertent harm, but you may sustain physical harm if you do not follow the directions as they are given.

Emotionally, it is not possible for initiation to occur without profound challenge to the ego. It may even be said that the ego must "die" in order for initiation to occur. The true ordeal comes not during our ceremony but in your life afterwards, in the interval between initiations when the lesson works its way into your life.

This is not an order for those who would collect degrees. If you do not intend to fulfill the Oath of the Magician, and walk the path of the Magician it is better that you should leave now than bring these forces into your life unprepared.

Unlike other Orders, our higher degrees exist only for the purpose of attainment, and do not grant wide or sweeping temporal powers of leadership. The leadership of this order rests primarily in the Supreme Senate of the Third Degree, and by advancing to the First Degree you may reasonably expect, within a few years or less, to be a member of the Supreme Senate if you continue to advance. There will be no prolonged childhood, you will be thrust into a role of guidance and leadership. You will not be asked to initiate to the Second or Third Degree until you are ready, but understand that taking the First Degree puts you on a path where many factors in your life, internal and external will drive you inexorably towards those initiations.

We do not ask for an Oath to any living being, or Organization, including our Sovereign Sanctuary, except in regards to basic privacy and secrecy.

Your Oath of secrecy regarding the initiations still holds, and I am asked by the Supreme Senate of the Third Degree to remind you of this oath. .

We ask that you refrain in act and in spirit from:

○ giving out in written or in verbal form the exact words of the initiations, though where they quote from ancient sources those may be freely discussed.

○ describing in synoptic detail the general course and outline by part, or the specific roles and speeches of the characters within the initiations.

○ transmitting in any way the various words and signs of the degrees. These are important because they do serve to some extent as guarantors that someone attending an initiation has been exposed to this talk and others, and is thus duly informed as to safety and behavior.

○ acting as an initiator into these specific mysteries, as written, without the due authorization of the Sovereign Sanctuary.

We further ask that you please remember: that in deciding how to speak you err on the side of caution and, when in doubt, embrace the fourth power of the Sphinx which is silence. We remind you that it is your role only to police your own speech and that the obedience of other initiates to these oaths must be judge by themselves.

Now we shall review of the oath.

Initiates should repeat after the Fool as this is stated.

I _____ do solemnly promise on my self of self in the sight of the one secret and ineffable Lord, and in the sight of all stars in the company of stars that I shall do these things to the best of my understanding:

○ I shall walk the path of the magician

○ I shall seek my true will

○ I shall seek the understanding of love which is Agape

○ I shall invoke the Aeon of Horus in fact as well as theory

       ○   I shall embody the energies of the Aeon of Horus

I shall try in every circumstance to better understand these matters, both unflinching and incisive pursuit of knowledge of myself, and in eager and anxious acceptance of all experience.

Within the Pantacle that is my world, I will include not only those things favorable to me, but those things which are poisonous to me, that my world not be folly and lead me to a false will.

That I shall strive in every way to increase my understanding that I may better walk the path of the magician.

So mote it be.

Leave to Depart

The Fool:

Having come to this threshold, if it is not your will to initiate now, you may depart without prejudice. You are welcome to return at a future time. No one will question your decision, nor ask you to explain yourself. If you continue beyond the Threshold, it is with the expectation that you have read and reviewed the Oaths and intend to give them on your honor. Since you will not be refused Initiation at some future time, if you have any doubt that it is your will to initiate now, I urge you to excuse yourself.

The Fool may explain what provisions have been made for anyone who wishes to leave, whether there is a waiting area, etc. In general, it is best if there is one person who can remain outside with anyone who chooses to leave the ritual if they are not also leaving the premises.

The Fool may explain how any refund is to be issued. The terms of initiation should be explained in advance.

The Fool may take a moment to ensure everyone has had water, used the restroom, etc., creating a pause in which anyone who chooses not to take initiation may leave.

As before I conduct you now to a place that is a story, or a story that is a place. I will be for these foundational degrees Virgil to your Dante, your confidant and guide. Because this initiation is garbed as a story, it may be that you shall be inclined to take its lessons lightly. Let me assure you that starting at this point, the time of Ludus is passed and that all which transpires will be in deadly earnest. As before it is important that you do not disrupt outright the story. If you need, you may take me aside. But...The people are not people and the places not places, and like the pages of a book they are fragile and may be torn. Yet, I am made of the same stuff as you.

The Welcome

Raimond:

I bid you welcome to my Court once again, O travelers. I open my gate to you, though a shadow looms behind you, for today is a day of celebration and a Great Feast – perhaps the last we shall know in peace and serenity.

The Thelemic Initiations

The Fool:

Strange, Prince, that you answer your own door. Is the budget tight or is all the help out fighting your adversaries?

Raimond:

I wait upon my own door for reasons you shall come to understand if you prove yourselves friends.

The Fool:

Then let us enter and thereby be tried.

Raimond:

Before you step across this threshold, know that it would be better for you to fall upon my sword than to enter into this place with a false intention.

The Fool:

You threaten the violence of the sword?

Raimond:

Do I raise my blade, O Fool? I make no threat, but a statement of fact; of a truth which I can no more change than I may stay the stars in their courses. The statement is clearly metaphorical, as is the feast, for the most part.

The Fool:

That's a bit disappointing. A metaphorical feast sounds less than delicious.

Raimond:

You will find food and drink enough. But this feast is not one merely of the palate, but of the most sensual pleasures.

The Fool:

I see why it's a secret.

Raimond: *gesturing sharply*

Come!

The Fool:

It sounds like that's the point. But let us not tax the patience of this doorward Prince further, let us venture within.

The Challenge

*At the front are three Chairs, the same as in 0°. They are for, from left to right, Azalais, Jeanne, and Raimond. The **Altar** may be situated behind them, or to one side. Azalais and Jeanne are already seated, while Raimond stands in the entrance to the room, or in a foyer if one is available.*

Raimond takes up a station near the Altar, standing vigilant.

The Fool:

You do not take your throne.

Raimond:

The throne is left for you, O Fool, and eventually for them. You will recall those whom you met in your recent visit: my noble wife, Jeanne, the daughter of Henry late King of England and Prince of Anjou, sister of Richard, King of England who is called the Lion Heart mother to my heir, and my sister Azalais, Countess of Burlats who has borne also a daughter of my line.

The Fool:

That arrangement would be hard to forget. I trust they remember you.

As they speak the fool makes his way to the throne and sits in it, his bearing showing a certain unfamiliarity, either awkward or presumptuous or both in turn.

Azalais:

Fitting, perhaps, that you arrive on this, the Night of our most precious and erotic feast.

Jeanne:

Even on a night such as this, it seems unwise to entrust the throne to the Fool.

Raimond:

So it is, by our tradition, that we must.

Jeanne:

Who are these, O Prince, who come before our Sovereign Court?

Raimond:

Petitioners who seek the wisdom of our Court and the path to the Rose Cross knighthood and, beyond, the road to the City of Pyramids.

Azalais:

They would do well to flee back whence they came; from Heliopolis or Memphis or some other nameless suburb. To accept the knighthood of this court is to face near certainty of death. Brother, you are known for your fairness. Speak truth to them of our circumstance, that they may be dissuaded and not lay down their life in our lost cause.

Raimond:

Oh noble guests, you have arrived amongst us at a time of grave concern, when superstition, tyranny and oppression seem poised to deliver the decisive blow against freedom.[107]

The Thelemic Initiations

The Fool:

You are beset then. Under what banners march these forces of tyranny and oppression which would destroy this realm of tolerance, learning, and poetry which you have here created?

Raimond:

Under the banners of freedom.

The Fool:

I may be a Fool, but your words seem nonsensical. How can the forces that march to destroy you fly the very same banners you, yourself, raise?

Raimond:

May not brother be turned against brother by ignorance and fear? Well you know that "freedom is a two-edged sword, of which one edge is liberty and the other, responsibility. Both edges are exceedingly sharp and the weapon is not suited to casual, cowardly, or treacherous hands."[108] Yet think not for one moment that such hands hesitate to pick it up and wield it.

The Fool:

How can such hands wield such a weapon if it is not suited to them?

Raimond:

As any footman may, upon finding the sword of a knight discarded in the heat of battle, wield it with some effect as a club. The footman lays about with strength and power and against others who have no sword and may achieve some great effect. With every blow the footman blunts the blade, damaging it at some point beyond repair. Yet, even when it shatters, the shards may be sharp and dangerous. Arm very many ignorant persons with swords and you may challenge even knights; these chattel footmen fighting with the zealous knowledge that they strike for freedom, certain that their possession of a sword means that they are not the vassals of the tyrants who send them forth.

The Fool:

Slaves to ignorance remain as unfree as those who bear shackles, even if they fancy themselves Kings. But these enemies. They are metaphorical, I hope, like you and the Feast?

Raimond:

To these travelers, if they are fortunate, the war will be metaphorical.

Jeanne:

To us, not so much.

Azalais:

It is, at least, our way. From the time I was wed in oath, if not body, in my childhood, our father, the old Count, and my husband were more often at war than peace. Though I bore my spouse an heir who is this day Lord of Carcassone, my spouse was never much friend to me, nor I to him. I kept my own court of Troubadours, was wooed by kings and kept company with my brother.

Jeanne:

Who also quickened you some years past.

Azalais:

I bore of my body an heir to him in spirit as you may get an heir-in-law, though such is a secret only fit for such Holy Occasion as this feast.

Jeanne:

And that heir-in-law, grandson of Henry King of England, should by rights hold his entire realm as Raimond, the Seventh Count of that name, to rule Toulouse. Yet even now we are beset and there is no true peace. The avarice of the Capetian King and the Pope's intolerance for the Good People have cast a shadow over our realm and emboldened our neighbors to seize some castles of my husband and your brother…

speaking impetuously

…I have a mind to go and get them back.

Raimond:

You shall betake yourself to a monastery and there on consecrated ground surrounded by Christian monks give birth to my heir, that there may be no argument or trickery of the Pope to claim he is hereticated and thereby revoke his claims.

Jeanne:

So you say.

Azalais:

Have we made of you a heretic?

Jeanne:

I am, as I ever was, the daughter of my mother. It is not my will to sit idly by and let the storm crash down around the legacy of my children.

Azalais:

Our span of years is almost past, but my brother, the Count, will live to see the storm crash down upon us. Within the decade, the thunder will fall upon our children. Fire and stones shall rain down upon this very house. I shall not live to see it, but my daughter shall, as will your son by my brother, Countess, the rightful heir to Toulouse. So you see, these travelers should be dissuaded from joining our cause for in it there is little glory and much suffering as we are ground under the heel of pride and hatred respectively.

Jeanne:

Speak for yourself my sister-by-law. I shall do some grinding ere all is done. And so shall your kinsfolk and blood of your blood. Skulls shall be shattered and blood spilled by the hands of women and children.

The Thelemic Initiations

The Fool:

Metaphorical brains and blood I hope?

Jeanne:

For our travelers, perhaps. For us, most assuredly not. Remember that when you hold light the significance of what we did, for if we had surrendered or been led away to our executions like sheep no-one would remember us. And it is our memory that kept alive that two-edged sword which is the flame of the West, which is passed to you...And these travelers shall not, I think, shy from our cause. What say you?

The Fool:

In truth, they must die.

Jeanne:

So must we all. Better to do it with a sword in hand fighting against injustices.

The Fool:

What if the cause truly is lost and they fail?

Jeanne:

The better still to die masters of their own destiny. No one who dies in the pursuit of their pure will truly dies.

Raimond: *to the travelers*

If it is your will to pursue this path, I shall test the sincerity of your Petition.

The Fool: *stopping for a moment and considering it before responding, then raises a hand in casual salute to Jeanne and speaks significantly*

So mote it be.

Raimond:

I will solve for you, then, the mystery of my presence receiving you. On this Feast Day, the most holy and secret of our calendar, are all things perverted and turned upside down. Today, we celebrate the violation of all those restrictions and prohibitions visited upon us, like Romans of old. Yet, even in turning upside down society, we do not overturn the ways of paratge, for that is not a custom or tradition, but the expression of our nature. Thus, Fools and travelers are Kings, and princes made doormen.

The Fool:

But these Petitioners *are* Kings.

Azalais:

Let them prove themselves Petitioners and friends.

Raimond: *In asking for the signs, the order in which they are requested should be varied, so that if possible each Initiate is called on to answer for some part of them. If an initiate does not remember the answer they may be prompted by the Fool with a hint.*

Very well. When you became Honored Guests of this Court, you were given a password. I ask now that you convey it to me.

Initiate:

Ludus.

Raimond:

And, you, what is its meaning?

Initiate: *Any reasonable answer signifying "playful love" is acceptable.*

Raimond: *raises the book from the Altar, holding it toward the initiates*

Come forward and show me the sign which you were given.

Initiates: *Each initiate should be directed to place their hands upon the book each in turn and give the sign.*

Raimond:

Now, *you*, what is the Formula of the Grade?

Initiate:

ABRAHADABRA.

Raimond:

And you would tell me its elaboration?

Initiate:

418.

Raimond:

The Petitioners have proven themselves to be worthy and honored guests and, also, by their understanding of the Formula of ABRAHADABRA, true petitioners, seeking enlightenment and attainment. Finally, I shall ask them for a token of not only of their seeking, but of their diligence and willingness to work toward attainment, that it may be proven that they have the strength to undertake the path.

At your previous Initiation, you were instructed to manufacture a pantacle, according to the provisions of the Book which was mandated by the Ab-ul-Diz working, and was named ABA, and numbered Four. I invite you, now, as a token of your diligence to come forward and place your pantacle upon the altar. If it is your will, you may also say a few words about it or the process by which you were led to it.

The Thelemic Initiations

Initiates: Come forward and lay their pantacles on the altar, speaking a few words about them as is their will.

Raimond:

> These petitioners have shown that they have not only zeal, but willingness to entertain the work of a magician. Let them then be subjected to the first test of initiation. Let the candle for the brazier be lit.

Azalais: The brazier candle is lit. The appearance should be that Azalais intends to light the Pantacles on fire, one at a time as they are handed over, then drop them into the brazier to burn to ash. The method used should be fairly similar to the lighting of the Altar Candles.

> You know, or long suspect, that these orders are driven by invisible powers. Now you will come face-to-face with them. Well you know also that, throughout the history of the Esoteric Orders, those which offer wisdom and attainment exact a high price. Now you must be prepared to pay this price. Are you prepared?

Offers a chance for the Petitioners to say "yea" or "nay," but this is a "magician's choice." If they object Azalais will command they wait until all is said. If they agree, or offer no objection, continuing:

> The Pantacle is, at this point, the closest thing to a representation of your self of selves.
>
> Now you shall each come in turn and hand unto me that which you have made, and it shall be offered into the flames then dropped into the brazier to be consumed to ash. With it you will release all that you have put into it. Every hope, every intent, every dream. You have been told that your ego must die, and so it shall. You renounce this identity that you have claimed for yourself and give yourself up as a wax tablet on which the most awful Secret and Invisible Chiefs of this Order would scribe their will, forging you into a potent and puissant weapon in the battle to establish the Law. In this matter, as in many others, they who would come first shall have the greatest reward.

Ideally, the Petitioners demur. If they do not advance, Azalais shall say:

Azalais:

> By the powers of the Secret Chiefs and the most awful and invisible hand of this order, you are sworn to this place and this cause and I command you come forth and give over your self to be bound to their will and reborn in the fire of the cauldron.

The Fool: *The Fool shall accord them every chance to reject the offer of their own accord. At any point where one begins to advance the Fool shall move to intercept them saying*

> Wait. Do what **thou** wilt shall be the whole of the Law.

The term "thou" should be emphasized. The Fool may further counsel:

> Thou hast no right but to do thy will...are you certain that this is your own will?

Speech if the Offer is rejected

Azalais: Should they reject the offer, even if the Fool was required to dissuade them, Azalais will say:

> "The word of Sin is Restriction."[109] For as it is written, "There is no bond that can unite the divided but love: all else is a curse. Let it be that state of manyhood bound and loathing. So with thy all; thou hast no right but to do thy will. Do that, and no other shall say nay."[110]

You have passed this test. While there may come times that you wish to make free association with others, or undertake mutual obligation, there is no power in the universe which has the right to suborn your will. No invisible or secret chiefs. No supposed superiors. No earthly chiefs or order. You may at times need to give solemn promise. But understand always that such promise is a contract, and obligates you only inasmuch as another accepts as well their own obligation. The purpose of undertaking an obligation is to follow the course of your pure Will, and to accept obligation without receiving what is expected in return is restriction in that it hinders you in your pursuit of Will. There may, of course, be times it may even suit your sense of honor, which is the measure of how others perceive you, to keep your promise when others abrogate theirs, but you do so then because it is in line with your Will to be seen as reliable, not through fear of some imagined consequence.

As a magician the fulfillment of your will rests solely upon your shoulders. The failure of another to fulfill their contract to you is no excuse for allowing your Will to remain unfulfilled.

Let your Pantacle remain on the altar throughout our celebration then take it forth as a reminder of the sacredness of your will and of this test of your Will. They have completed the Test!

Speech if the Offer is entertained or there is the appearance of acceptance

In general, any eventual rejection, even with much help from the Fool, should be credited as a rejection. Should they insist on attempting to accept the offer Azalais will extinguish the flame saying:

Azalais:

You have somewhat to learn before you shall be ready to advance to the next Grade of Attainment by petitioning for admission to the Second Degree of our Order. There is no harm in this, for the purpose of our earthly tests here is like a practice fight. The point of our limited ordeals is not to accomplish initiation, but rather to help to identify those weaknesses which may, in battle, prove your undoing.

I commend to you, then, the diligent pursuit of this lesson. There is no power in the universe which has the right to suborn your will. No invisible or secret chiefs. No supposed superiors. No earthly chiefs or order. No earthly chiefs or order. You may at times need to give solemn promise. But understand always that such promise is a contract, and obligates you only inasmuch as another accepts as well their own obligation. The purpose of undertaking an obligation is to follow the course of your pure Will, and to accept obligation without receiving what is expected in return is restriction in that it hinders you in your pursuit of Will. There may of course be times it may even suit your sense of honor, which is the measure of how others perceive you, to keep your promise when others abrogate theirs, but you do so then because it is in line with your Will to be seen as reliable, not through fear of some imagined consequence.

As a magician the fulfillment of your will rests solely upon your shoulders. The failure of another to fulfill their contract to you is no excuse for allowing your Will to remain unfulfilled.

"The word of Sin is Restriction." For as it is written, "There is no bond that can unite the divided but love: all else is a curse."[111]

"Let it be that state of manyhood bound and loathing. So with thy all; thou hast no right but to do thy will. Do that, and no other shall say nay."[112]

Let your Pantacle remain on the altar throughout our celebration then take it forth as a reminder of the sacredness of your will. They have completed the Test!

The Oath

Raimond:

It is proper at this time that you should follow me in the Oath of The First Degree or magician. You should give as your name that name with which you identify yourself, and repeat after me:

Raimond reads line by line, permitting time to respond.

I, "state your name," do solemnly promise on my self of self in the sight of the one secret and ineffable Lord, and in the sight of all stars in the company of stars that I shall do these things to the best of my understanding:

- I shall walk the path of the magician
- I shall seek my true will
- I shall seek the understanding of love which is Agape
- I shall invoke the Aeon of Horus in fact as well as theory
- I shall embody the energies of the Aeon of Horus

I shall try in every circumstance to better understand these matters, both unflinching and incisive pursuit of knowledge of myself, and in eager and anxious acceptance of all experience.

Within the Pantacle that is my world, I will include not only those things favorable to me, but those things which are poisonous to me, that my world not be folly and lead me to a false will.

That I shall strive in every way to increase my understanding that I may better walk the path of the magician.

So mote it be.

The Bringing of Light

Jeanne:

Then I bid you welcome. You are not yet made Magicians unto the Logos, but you shall be received as such.

Raimond:

It is well that they should understand the occasion on which they have arrived.

Azalais:

On this night we celebrate the Feast of Thoth, whose name is also spoken as Tahuti, creator of language of music and medicine, patron of the scribes, and the recorder of the verdict of balance, author of the first book. Thoth, the Ibis who laid the egg from which Ra or Khephri was delivered. Thoth, father and self of Seshat, Scribe of the Seven Pointed Star. Thoth, who was known to the Hellenes as Thrice Great Hermes, author of all of these mysteries, both Foundational and their explication in the Greater Mysteries.

Raimond:

Thoth, the first architect, master of all architects, who recorded his sacred book on two pillars that it might survive the ages.

Jeanne:

On this night we celebrate the Feast of the Children of the Prophet which is a secret you shall come to understand.

The Fool:

It's "A feast for Tahuti and the child of the Prophet--secret, O Prophet!" From the Book of the Law which you gave us last time, chapter two, verse thirty-nine.

Jeanne:

How strange it should be printed otherwise by Master Therion. Twice. But no doubt the Fool knows best. As to the secret, it is the core of this degree. It weds the Eros of our Feast with the legacy of that God who was known to the Egyptians as Djehuti or Tahuti, but better known to us as Thoth.

The Fool:

But of all the Gods, Thoth is the least erotic. Most commonly Thoth is self-begotten, bornless, and has no children. Strange you should have him sharing a feast with children of the Prophet, and talk of Eros.

Azalais:

As you pointed out yourself, O Fool, it is not our saying. And as regards Thoth, sometimes Seshat is made his daughter, wife, or both. But it is not mine to speak of Children. And I am not sure if my Christian sister-by-law wishes much to speak of Thoth.

Jeanne:

As I said once before, to talk of ancient legends is no more than any Troubadour may do. Thoth is the Ibis-billed God of the moon and that alone might suggest much. Yet Thoth has much to do with children, for he gave to Isis the magical formula which allowed her to restore the phallus and life of Osiris, thus enabling the engenderment of Horus, who is the Crowned and Conquering Child.

The Fool:

Well enough then for Thoth. But what of the Child of the Prophet?

Jeanne:

You shall learn soon enough how Children are made.

The Fool:

I feel like they probably know that.

Azalais:

Not how Magickal Children are made. Perhaps my brother will give them the password of this Feast and, to this, the first Grade of Thelemic attainment.

Raimond:

Stand before me.

Waits for them.

First I give you the sign appropriate to this Grade.

Raimond shows Grand Salute of Royal Arch

GRAND SALUTE OF THE ROYAL ARCH

This is the Grand Salute of the Royal Arch, which meaning shall become clear to you over the course of the hour. Note for now its resemblance to the sign Vir (*Veer* or *Weer*), that of the Beast. It may be taken to symbolize two pillars making an arch, however the thumbs give a suggestion of horns which may be seen as two coming together to make a thing which is not of themselves.

Now, the password appropriate to this feast, and to this Grade is *Eros* which is sensual or passionate love. It is the source of your word erotic, and while it can be extended to embrace all arousal it most significantly deals with the arousal of sex.

Azalais:

Most directly it may pertain to those acts of carnality and desire which produce fluids. The quality of fluid, however, is an attribute which may exceed the apparent and physical.

Jeanne:

By extension, Eros embraces all erotica, even the most abstract self-love or love of the infinite, which may in fact be the same. Eros is the creative force in love, but by itself it has no shape or form.

The Fool:

Are they to be debauched then? Plunged into an orgy. What is this "feast?"

Raimond: *humorously*

I do not know that we would object. But they shall not be debauched this night, nor any other without their full awareness and consent, for they are free people who know better than to let themselves be forced either by overt chains or such covert badgerings as shame or the pressure of their peers. Tonight we celebrate the fruit of Eros: the birth of the Child of the Prophet, most Secret. Let us light the lamps of the Festival!

Azalais:

"At the Ending of the Night:

At the Limits of the Light:

Thoth stood before the Unborn Ones of Time

Then was formulated the Universe:

Then came forth the Gods thereof:

The Aeons of the Bornless Beyond:

Then was the Voice vibrated:

Then was the Name declared.

Lights Dark Candle

"At the Threshold of the Entrance,

Between the Universe and the Infinite,

In the Sign of the Enterer, stood Thoth,

As before him were the Aeons proclaimed.

Lights Light Candle

In Breath did he vibrate them:

In Symbols did he record them:

For betwixt the Light and the Darkness did he stand"[113]

The Preliminary Instruction

Jeanne:

Let them be instructed!

The Fool:

Doesn't the instruction come after dinner and the show?

Exegesis of the Mystery of Sex Magick

Azalais:

We've changed the format in the sequel, O Fool. Keep up! These initiations are not mere repetition, or a plodding series of petty truths. In this initiation alone we shall reveal much of the circle and the cross, which was of old accounted a great mystery. The New Aeon accomplishes in a single news cycle what in the Old Aeon took a year or a century.

Azalais walks to the altar and picks up the cup. She gives a significant nod to Raimond who thrusts the dagger into it.

Petitioners, know you what this signifies?

Initiates: are allowed to speculate until one answers with something approaching sex.

Raimond:

In truth yes, it means fucking. The implication is the exchange of semen into the body of another. By extension the idea that the act of creation and union within the visible universe are sexual in nature.

Azalais:

So too is the meaning of the circle and the cross. A cock and a hole. And this basic imagery of the common phenomenon of sexual reproduction is as far as many aspirants ever go.

The Thelemic Initiations

Raimond: *If a chessboard is present, then Raimond may indicate it.*

    Do you play chess?

Initiates: *respond as they will*

Raimond:

    They say of the game that it can be learned in a few minutes, but that mastery of it takes a lifetime. So, too, with the Foundational sexual mysteries we lay bare here before you. If you recognized the dagger in the chalice you know the outline of them already.

    The inference is obvious but in ancient times this was shocking stuff. Even the Catholics held procreation sacred. The mystery was that the act of sexual procreation is one in which we, as a people, may engender life.

The Fool:

    How will they know when they have really understood the mystery?

Raimond:

    How does the lutist know when they have mastered the lute.

Azalais:

    When they feel mastery.

Jeanne:

    When the audience stops wincing when they play.

Raimond:

    A little of both perhaps, but it will come. In the meantime, we will endeavor to supply you with the basic knowledge and outline of the Foundational sex mysteries. Understand that no statement of these mysteries is complete.

    The true secrets or mysteries are formulate, like that of YHVH, and they may go under many names. We have named them for convenience according to the most common references in esoteric writing.

    Beyond these mysteries are techniques, which amount to no more than personal alchemical formulae, though in the past they were celebrated as the core of the initiatory rites. They may be of more or less use to a given individual, but they are but the operations of the formulae, and should not be mistaken for the things themselves.

    Sister, declare the Mysteries.

Azalais:

    Before all, the Mystery of the Circle and the Cross
    First the Mystery of the Serpent and the Egg
    Secondly the Mystery of the White Eagle and the Red Lion
    Thirdly the Mystery of the Dwarf-homunculous

Understand we make no claim to provide a complete course in the Sex Mysteries, nor do we offer you partnership to explore, though if you make a study of the true ethics of Thelema it may aid you in finding others whom trust you to explore the mysteries with them. What we offer up is the cipher, a single ring holding the scattered keys by which you may read and learn for yourselves with neither restriction nor condemnation, and as holder of that ring of keys feel permission to explore those mysteries and find which expression of them is most suited to your unique will.

Jeanne:

By offering the outline of these mysteries on this occasion of the Feast most Sacred to Eros, we begin the process of your understanding of the nature of the Child of the Prophet, that you may not remain mired in the Foundational Mysteries, but proceed into the Greater.

The Fool:

Wait! You can't teach them these things. It's not right!

Raimond:

How do you mean, O Fool?

The Fool:

You can't just lay the core of the Sex Mysteries out in the First Degree initiation! That's insane! You're supposed to string them along for a decade, making the grub for every morsel of detail, dropping opaque hints about crosses and eagles, and then reveal it to them at a high degree when they are ready for such a shocking revelation!

Jeanne:

And what if we do?

The Fool: *looks confused*

They will undermine civilization. They will engage in endless debauchery. They will throw morality and caution to the winds! It will be chaos! Disaster!...They might tell someone!

Jeanne:

You mean they might do sex magick?

The Fool:

Well...yes.

Raimond:

The whole system of slowly revealing the sexual nature of the mysteries seems somewhat like teaching someone to read while hiding the shape of the letters. "The word Cat begins with a letter of which I cannot speak, but it resembles the Crescent moon." If it was ever a good system it has lost all utility now that people truly have the knowledge of the Universe at their fingertips. Withholding the mysteries is supposed to protect the initiate, but the danger of sex magick was more of criminal prosecution or social ostracization for those who taught them.

The Thelemic Initiations

Azalais:

> The slow trickling out of the mysteries breeds a form of darkness.
>
> At best, it makes our mysteries seem ridiculous and antiquated, as we tease hints of things which our initiates already know well.
>
> At worst it is frustrating, and fosters bile, and bile opens the path to becoming what, in the old writing, would have been called a "Black Brother," though we might now better say "Dark Adept." Those who pass into the abyss and have no inclination to move, instead destroying and suffocating all around them.

The Fool:

> But how are you going to keep them coming back if you do not trickle the mysteries out in tiny hints?

Azalais:

> By providing that which is true and valuable, and engendering a slow explosion in the lives of those who initiate. Why should we not respect the time of these initiates by giving them respect and value in return?

The Fool:

> They're initiates. I'm pretty sure it's a commandment or something. I think Crowley wrote something about it!

Azalais:

> Yes well. *The internet* wasn't a thing in Crowley's day.

In the 1990s and early 2000s we might have said "the web." As time moves on this term may be modified to reflect the closest approximation to the information technology that houses, and provides access to, the world's knowledge. This is to ensure that this reference does not become dated. The intention is a shock, a sudden reference to the real and immediate world of the petitioners.

The Fool:

> What do you know about *the internet?*

Azalais:

> You missed the part where we're metaphors? You're the one who keeps breaking the fourth wall. The concept is not new. The Book of Thoth, the Emerald Tablet of Hermes, contained all wisdom and knowledge whatsoever.

The Fool:

> Wait a minute. Are you saying that the internet is the Book of Thoth?

Azalais:

> Perhaps not precisely. But the New Aeon is heralded by Thoth and Thoth is the God of the Tablet, of all knowledge. Think you that the New Aeon is a metaphorical fiction, or that the flood of knowledge so powerful it begins to erode the pillars of the world's social structures is a coincidence? Think you the emergence of these rites is mere coincidence? We...

Azalais moves their hand to indicate the Performers

...spring from the need to understand all that has been made known in order to navigate all that will come. You may think our voices are mere metaphors, but think well on our nature, and our proximity to the mystery of the founding of Doinel's Gnostic Church, under the charge of by Guilhabert de Castres, whose is well known to us.

Our identity is are no accident or literary convention. We are recalled into existence to guide the New Aeon, and have a life as real as those you shall come to create. The New Aeon is no fantasy, it is upon you, and if you cannot learn to swim in it you will drown!

Exegesis of the Mysteries of Eros

The Preliminary Mystery of the Cup and Dagger or Circle and Cross

Raimond:

The preliminary mystery of the Cup and Dagger or Circle and Cross you already recognize. These are not true Mysteries, but historic intimations of the very idea of sacred sexuality, symbolizing on a rather crude level, the act of procreation. In each progressive Mystery more possibility is opened.

Jeanne:

Also more false and misleading constraints. "The Word of Sin is Restriction."[114]

The Fool:

But why sex and, if it has to be sex, why now? Couldn't you teach them about tracing pentacles or meditating?

Azalais:

These mysteries are full of blinds and dead ends, O Fool. Not the largely fictional type of blind where one explains an inconsistency in some great writer by saying they left some deliberate misstatement to trap the unwary. Rather the very real kind of blind in which a writer or authority, however great, found one method or sympathy that worked for them, and then savagely upheld that it was the only course which would work for others.

The Fool:

Oh yes, Crow...Master Therion did that a lot.

Azalais:

Less than you might think. His statements are more often than not open-ended. It is disciples that have imposed rigidity. I don't suppose that sounds familiar to you, O Fool?

Raimond:

Let us declare at once upon our own Holy and Profound Authority, under the Seal of our Sovereign Sanctuary that part of the Law of Love which we shall, for the sake of giving it a single name, call Sacred Sex, or Eros. There is no human sexuality or asexuality which is incompatible with the mysteries of Sacred

Sex nor can there be any person who is barred from its expression by any part of their nature. This has of course already been stated. "Thou hast no right but to do thy will."[115]

Azalais:

It is impossible to apprehend the mysteries by this path without an understanding of their sexual nature, and that understanding should be Foundational. We read that "There is a single definition of the object of all magical Ritual. It is the uniting of the Microcosm with the Macrocosm. The Supreme and Complete Holy Ritual is therefore the Invocation of the Holy Guardian Angel; or in the language of mysticism, Union with God."[116]

Raimond:

This is the core of the Great Work of love under will, the ability to unite with all outside the Ego...indeed to annihilate the Ego. It is written "The Perfect and the Perfect are one Perfect and not two; nay, are none! Nothing is a secret key of this law."[117] There are many paths, not mutually exclusive, whether through Union with another, or with their self-of-self, or with their self-of-self which is the divine. It is given to us to ensure that those Adepts who leave our house have a map of all the many branching paths that they may travel in accordance with their pure Will, so that as they travel they might purify their Will.

The Mystery of the Egg and the Serpent

Jeanne:

Let us speak now of the First Mystery, that of the Serpent and the Egg [118]

The Fool:

I recognize this at least. The Serpent is the poignant power of the erect phallus! Or perhaps the sperm itself. And the egg just the passive recipient. The female nature which should be grateful she gets to play a part in the whole thing. But I suppose everyone else is out of luck? Clearly those who have no penis, no living ejaculate, no erection, no desire for intercourse with another or even with themselves may not be magicians!

Raimond:

The shout of the abyss. Truly thou art the Fool. The expression of Eros is universal, its expression within the individual varied. The Serpent is "the principle of immortality, the self-renewal through incarnation of persistent will." It might be identified perhaps with the Serpent-Lion, which symbol was in the past identified with the phallus, and later when science had progressed to a sufficient point, with the sperm. Yet it is not truly bound to any of these. Would you instruct this Fool on both points of their error?

Jeanne:

Firstly, sex magick is engenderment and there are none who lack the power to engender. Do not bodies constantly spin out new life, and cast off dead shards?

The Fool:

But the phallus is Hadit! Source of life, force of energy, fire of motion![119]

Jeanne:

And all of that does not come out of the male penis. The literal human phallus is but one hieroglyph of the serpent force, and perhaps an overly simple and lazy one. An easy symbol for those who happen to have a penis of their own, but alienating for those who don't.

The Fool:

Yet the idea of the Lion with the Serpent's tail as the force of life presaged sperm, though no one in the days of the worship of Hermes had seen it! It is not truly the force of life?

Azalais:

Did it truly? Or did those whose science had grown to the point that they could distill the source of life as far as sperm choose the Lion Headed Serpent over the Man-Headed Fish or the Faun because it fit the discovery? But it is not the only source of life. If we could modify the posits of the ancients on the basis of the invention of the microscope in Delft, we must modify it again for the discovery of the true source of life in the helix which resides in every one of us.

Jeanne:

And perhaps the ancients knew that better than you think. Consider that the serpent of the caduceus (*kuh-DOO-see-us*) of Hermes mimics the double helix that is the source of all life, which potential lies in everyone who lives. The active principal of Hadit is shared by all. To believe it limited is a hyper-literal failure of the imagination. Think you I am some mere receptacle, no clay tablet to be imprinted. The wand and the sword belong to all.

Raimond:

And still, though the making of new life is a sacred act, it is but a reflection. It is written "We are then particularly careful to deny that the object of love is the gross physiological object which happens to be Nature's excuse for it. Generation is a sacrament of the physical Rite, by which we create ourselves anew in our own image, weave in a new flesh-tapestry the Romance of our own Soul's History. But also Love is a sacrament of trans-substantiation whereby we initiate our own souls; it is the Wine of Intoxication as well as the Bread of Nourishment."[120]

The Mystery of the White Eagle and the Red Lion

Jeanne:

As we have come to the gross and physiological, it would be best for them if we parsed for them the Mystery of the White Eagle and the Red Lion.

The Fool:

Isn't that just the same? The White Eagle the Egg, the Red Lion the enraged serpent of the Phallus, full of potential. The "wand" of the magician?

Raimond:

There are many ways in which the concepts could be sliced, and every division but a shorthand. We take the Mystery of the Serpent and the Egg to be the underlying principle, the mystery which we highlighted in your previous initiation, symbolized by the Kneph. With this refinement we build on it. We are told of "the principle of immortality, the self-renewal through incarnation, of persistent will, inherent in the 'Red Lion' who is, of course the operator."[121] That will is said to swim in the "Blood of the Red Lion," so one might equate it more to sperm than to the phallus itself. A rather modern take on the "Lion Serpent."

Jeanne:

One is told to "impose the image of your particular Will upon the actually existing physical serpents which you possess."

The Fool:

So whatever high-minded ideas you have, it boils down to the admixture of human fluids! Sperm from a Phallus? A thoroughly masculine mystery. Clearly those serpents are sperm and if one does not possess them...

Raimond:

Patience, Fool, for we must again resolve two errors. First, is the presumption which we have already begun to dispel, that the Red Lion is exclusive to those who posses a literal human phallus made of flesh. The second is that the White Eagle or the Red Lion needs be literal at all.

Jeanne:

Lest it be understood that, in classical form, this magical operation is completed by the co-mingling of the literal fluids of the human body, and it is this admixture which is in so much of the Thelemic work, and in more ancient texts, referred to as the Philosopher's Stone, the Quintessence and the Elixir of Life. It must according to the method put forward by Master Therion for the operation be taken up by suction and ingested, shared between the partners. Semen alone, embodying as it was thought the Red Lion, was held to have some virtue on its own, yet it was the Elixir which characterizes this Mystery.

The Fool:

So the Red Lion is the important part. The stuff of engenderment. And that comes from...phalluses!

Jeanne:

Let us correct the first of these errors. Speak to me, O Fool. Tell me of that place where it is writ that the fire of engenderment, the spirit of the serpent lion, swims only in the blood of a man?

Fool:

A trick question. It does not need to be stated. It's obvious. The phallus creates life.

Azalais:

Yet it does not. It was thought in the day of the writing of these mysteries that the sperm was the all encompassing seed, and the womb but fertile ground. Yet you know that not to be true. As our understandings of science change, so do our understandings of the mysteries.

Fool:

The mysteries are traditional and eternal and should not be profaned with anything so new and base as science!

Jeanne:

The mysteries *are* science, O Fool. "The Method of science the Aim of Religion"[122] The laws of nature are declared. If you do not believe me, go argue with Paracelsus or Hermes himself. We are sternly warned: "God himself is not found to interfere arbitrarily with the course of nature, but to work within his laws...Let the Adept not act otherwise."[123] Thus no matter what was thought in the past, we know that both elements of the Elixir perform an active role and both perform a receptive role, interlinking, each with the other, and later in his life the Master Therion came to understand this as well.[124]

Azalais:

Furthermore, many of the classical alchemists presumed the male fluid to have no more function than that of quickening the female egg, with all other heritage of life residing within the egg. The Master Therion understood that both fluids contributed to conception, but it was only toward the end of that mortal incarnation with which you are familiar that the mechanisms were exposed. He was wise enough to realize his understanding was imperfect and left the matter open ended, writing only that it is "not so easy to be made effective by Woman initiates," and subsequently "Of what may be the result of a development parallel to that indicated above among the Noble and Chaste Ladies of the Order, it is at present impossible for us to declare." [125]

Jeanne:

Such imbalance speaks more of the prohibitions of the day by which women might not pick up sword and lead an army into battle, than any magical limitation. It is stated timorously. I shall state with certainty!

"Isis art thou, and from thy life are fed
All showers and suns, all moons that wax and wane"[126]

Azalais:

Let us go further for much of this writing predates the revelation of Babalon:

> But now the darkness is riven through
> and the robes of sin are gone,
> And naked she stands as a terrible blade
> and a flame and a splendid song
>
> Her mouth is red and her breasts are fair
> and her loins are full of fire,
> And her lust is strong as a man is strong
> in the heat of her desire.[127]

Jeanne:

Too it is written:

> This is the Mystery of Babylon, the Mother of abominations, and this is the mystery of her adulteries, for she hath yielded up herself to everything that liveth, and hath become a partaker in

its mystery. And because she hath made herself the servant of each, therefore is she become the mistress of all. Not as yet canst thou comprehend her glory.[128]

Azalais:

Having established that the serpent fire is found in all blood, it would be well for you to recall, Fool, that among adepts are annulled both male and female. We recall that "The male must have completed himself and become androgyne; the female, and become gynander."[129]

Jeanne:

Shall we speak then, Fool, no more of woman solely as passive and receptive, and man as the sole force of fire and force of spirit? For the Adept must be of both natures, and this is reflected in the human alchemy. Or if you doubt I lack force of fire, shall I get a sword and demonstrate?

Fool:

That isn't...necessary. Your point is taken. Yet it is still a matter of physical fluids is it not?

Azalais:

We do not deny that for some the fluids may be potent, yet there are many forms of Union which produce no physical fluids, and we shall dispel all assertions of their necessity in a single stroke. We told in reference to another ritual "It is to be noted that persons of powerful imagination, will, and intelligence have no need of these material symbols."[130] and more directly of these mysteries "Certain truly magical aids to the physiological experiments indicated above have always been held worthy."[131]

Fool:

This all seems a bit heavy for them. This is First Degree. What if we scare them off talking about sperm and sex? Shouldn't we be going over elemental magick or life lessons or something more..." his voice trails off.

The "Secrets" of the Nine and Eleven

Raimond:

With all things it is best to start at the beginning. Now before we continue to our third and final mystery it is necessary that we speak of those erstwhile secrets which are known by the numbers Nine and Eleven.

Azalais:

We have stated that, in the century before your own, there was much use of ciphers in the teaching of these secrets. The Foundational secret was, before the time of the revelation of Thelema, known, completely or partially, under various names. Called by some the Ansairetic Mystery,[132] and known in other terms to the Hermetic Brotherhood of Luxor and certain offshoots of the Golden Dawn. The Master Therion most often wrote of it as the secret of the Ninth Degree, for that is where it had been placed by that Gnostic Saint Theodor Reuss within his initiatory system. It is no more than the combination of those mysteries of sacred sex, in whole or in part, which we have unfolded thus far under the names of the Serpent and the Egg, and the Eagle and the Lion.

Jeanne:

The Master Therion went beyond these historic formulae, following his own will, which did not allow for conformity to sexual norms. He plumbed those mysteries which could produce no child of flesh. Those penetrations by which no conception could occur upon our most usual plane of existence all of which were then, and until the early years of our own century, criminalized under the general misnomer of "Sodomy." Criminal regardless, but most stridently outlawed when they passed between those deemed by society to be "male," these carried real danger of broken reputations, commitment, imprisonment, or worse. Despised even by some of Master Therion's close associates, all references to these operations were thickly veiled in code and hidden meanings during his lifetime.

Azalais:

This secret was attributed to the Eleventh degree of the Master's prevailing system of initiation, however as this was understood to be a technique, not the fabric of a degree, was divorced from it in practical fact, such that it was stated "Of the Eleventh Degree, its powers, privileges, and qualifications, nothing whatever is said in any grade. It has no relation to the general plan of the Order, is inscrutable, and dwells in its own Palaces." The attribution of Eleven was sensible because of its identification with Kether, and as we shall clarify, we recognize the aptness of that number even if we do not hide the secrets at such an arbitrarily remote point in our initiations.

Fool:

Finally then...then is a truly manly mystery, for it involves sodomy and we know what that is.

Raimond:

Sodomy, Fool, was all sex which could not result in procreation. The distinction of Eleven is really an evolution, for here the Master Therion first broke away from the concept of sex as a function of gender. Yet there is no mandate to homosexuality, or its converse.

Raimond:

Yes. We are reminded as well "Nor is he for priest designed Who partakes only in one kind."[133] Thus we know that there may be mixture of gender, or even its overturning. One may extrapolate from that point that the variations are infinite and subtle. "We therefore heartily cherish those forms of Love in which no question of generation arises; we use the stimulating effects of physical enthusiasm to inspire us morally and spiritually. Experience teaches that passions thus employed do serve to refine and to exalt the whole being of man or woman. Nuit indicates the sole condition: 'But always unto me.'"[134]

Azalais:

The energies of Eleven are described most specifically as the Magus, as the Yod-He, providing energy and the substance of the Pantacle, while the Virgin He Vau received and interpreted it, also expressing it intellectually and impressing that idea upon the coin, while Aiwass was Shin, harmonizing and inspiring all.[135]

The Thelemic Initiations

Raimond:

To us, the nine and eleven are but arbitrary divisions on a long and winding road. Nor did this road end with Master Therion. Yet you are not wrong to think that Master Therion often referred to penetration of the anus, the distribution of the Red Lion within the Eye or Chalice of Horus being the foremost symbol you may encounter. This may lend clarity to any number of otherwise mysterious works. It is good as well for you to know that this work was neither perfected by, nor does it end with, the Master Therion, who was still learning of it at the end of his life. There are many other writings of more or less authority issued in the years since Master Therion last wrote which you may explore armed with the sword of this outline.

Azalais:

Nor need you restrict your explorations to those recent documents, for all of these techniques are, if one is able to read them through the ciphers that conceal them, of some antiquity.

The Mystery of the Dwarf-homunculous

Raimond:

Let us proceed on that note to a great and practical secret of the magician, a third Mystery of Eros, which is the creation of life, the Dwarf-homunculous, and we shall see one way in which the energies of the Eleven may be put to use.

Fool:

I honestly thought that one was just a joke. Dwarfs? Like in a fantasy novel?

Raimond:

Literally, the homunculous was the first scientific conception of the human embryo, from Zosiums and Paracelsus, who created such a "little man." It was thought first that an egg within the female carried such a little man, then that the head of the sperm carried such a creature. By the time of Master Therion's writing this was known to be a literal untruth. Yet it held figurative and alchemical truth. Now, we all know that Eros can create real and tactile human life within the womb.

Raimond stands and reaches out toward Jeanne's belly. She gives a nod of assent and he touches it. The nod of assent is important. Even though the two are partnered, it reminds the Initiates of the importance of consent in all cases.

Yet those acts of eros which do not have the potential to create physical life may yet create children, the fruit of the Will of the magician and it is this which is our interest, for this is the process of manifesting our pure will into the world.

Jeanne:

We are told, "The 'Child' of such a love is a third person, an Holy Spirit, so to speak, partaking both natures, yet boundless and impersonal because it is a bodiless creation of a wholly divine nature. Connected with this, there is a Formula of Practical Magick by which the consciousness conceives...and then creates accordingly."[136]

Thus the homunculous is the magical child, taking form as an Elemental, or some other form, and thus aid in making manifest the will of the Magician in the living world. Along with this go warnings. which may be taken more or less seriously, that such magical children, created without adequate thought, may do harm to the Magician or others.

Fool:

So it's a little spell for making Elemental servants. That seems almost disappointing after all the buildup.

Raimond:

That it is simple makes it no less miraculous. We are told that "Man is God therefore can create Spirits by ceremonial masturbation on talismans as God first did."[137] The whole of the mystery revolves around that divine nature within ourselves and our ability to create life. Nor are these things to be created lightly, but rather with focus and intent, for they are not mere toys or playthings, but rather avatars to aid us in the completion of our Will, children and extensions of our selves. To conceive them for trivial purpose is to poison our will.

Fool:

Were you going to warn them about that!?

Azalais:

If they do the reading to understand these methods they will find the warnings present and perhaps even somewhat over-dramatized. But none should not be constrained by what is written, and each should read it for themselves. In the New Aeon these mysteries encompass not merely of life but of consciousness and the creation of consciousness and the recognition of consciousness in all things.

Jeanne:

We have told them much which may stretch credulity. Should we not proceed to our Feast and its entertainments? In that way, may the outline of our teaching be fleshed out and made clear.

Raimond:

In benediction, I declare again most solemnly and upon the authority of my charge that part of the universal Law of Love "There is no human sexuality or asexuality which is incompatible with the mysteries of Sacred Sex nor can there be any person who is barred from its expression by any part of their nature." Understand that this is no simple doctrine or prohibition on my part, rather a simple statement of inherent universal law based on the nature of that which liveth. And now The Secret Feast. So mote it be!

Raimond knocks 11 times in the following series: !   !!!   !!!   !!!   !

The Revels

The food of the feast is brought in, or all go out to it, or to some sideboard where it is prepared. Some time is given, as previously, for conversation and discussion extempore. It is well, however, that unless much time has been allowed for this initiation, that the time for conversation be limited, and that once all have been served, the reading continue, covering the story of The Pillars of Thoth as the feast is consumed.

The Thelemic Initiations

It may be desirable, if an entire day or evening has been set aside for this initiation, for the adjournment to Feast to be a full meal and, if this is the case, then a somewhat more relaxed schedule may be followed.

Raimond:

As is the tradition at our revels there has been prepared an entertainment. As this Feast is to Tahuti, or Thoth, the subject of our Tragedy is the Pillars of Thoth, which is also at times called the Royal Arch of Enoch.

Jeanne:

As in the Angevin retelling of the Romance of Troy, some liberties have been taken by our Troubadour to make a work of drama which is captivating to those who are not fascinated by high-blown and lofty histories. The story of the Lost Master's Word is well known, but to travelers from afar, the story of the Royal Arch of Enoch or the Pillars of Thoth may be obscure. It may bear therefore to tell the story straight, as it has long been known to the Defenders of the Temple and the followers of the Rose Cross.

Raimond:

The story is told of Thoth in Egypt or of Enoch in the Levant, for their legend long ago merged to become as one. In the simplest form it is told how this ancient architect gathered or was given all the world's knowledge, and devised the first system of writing by which it might be recorded. Understanding that a great catastrophe loomed, Thoth devised two great pillars, one which was made of brick to survive fire, the other of stone to survive flood. And upon these pillars was carved all the knowledge of the world, that it might survive the catastrophe. The location of the pillars varies. The ancient historian Josephus gives us a riddle. Some read it to be Syria, which well might be, for my father saw with his own eyes a very ancient Temple from before the deluge, upon the plains above Edessa. But others take it to be from the land of the Dog Star, Sirius, who in Egypt was the Goddess Sothis.

Azalais:

It may be of interest to them to know that Sothis is identified with Seshat, who we said before was daughter and self of Thoth. Too, Sothis was identified as I.S.I.S., an acronym which leads us to Nuit, whose secret name, as was revealed to the Master Therion, is Babalon.[138] It cannot be coincidence that Sothis was omnipresent at the ceremony of the stretching of the cord, which was the architectural start to any great new work of the Egyptians, where the King even if she were a queen such as Hatshepsut, would lay the corner stones. Thus we carry over from our previous drama the understanding of the identification of Great Kings with architecture.

Jeanne:

Sothis was Anubis as well.

The Fool:

It's most confusing these deities all being one another. Why can't they stay sorted out and be themselves.

Azalais:

A good question, O Fool. Understand the answer and you will have covered half the distance to attainment. Perhaps you should give it a try yourself sometime.

Raimond:

In whatever event, these great pillars were raised and at the time of the Roman Empire one was said to still be standing. The mystery however often is presented as a group of Knights of the Temple, or of the Cross of Ruby delving into a subterranean vault wherein the pillars are preserved. They are in this case supporting an arch, thus titled the Royal Arch of Thoth-Hermes, or through attribution, the Royal Arch of Enoch.

Azalais:

Is anyone else warm?

Jeanne:

Even in a castle the space may grow close and hot. Blow out the candles and perhaps it will cool a bit.

Raimond:

Drama proceeds best in darkness.

Raimond snuffs out the candles upon the altar.

The Casting

Sovereign Initiator: Proceeds with casting the play with the help of Raimond or Azalais, generally along lines already planned. The list of parts can be read out and assigned based on preferences for lines.

The Players are organized in groups. As before, this should be played on a stage in the front, or in the round.

The characters in Act II should be given a few moments to read over the names they are to pronounce and say them aloud to make sure they have them.

The Tragedy of the Royal Arch of Enoch

Dramatis Personae

Narrators

Isis/Babalon

Horus

Act I

King

Architect

Fisherman

Act II

Marsilio Ficino (mar-SEE-lee-oh fi-CHEE-noh)

Francesco (frahn-CHEZZ-koh)

Bellisario (BAY-lee-SAHR-ee-oh)

Alessandro (owl-lay-SAHN-druh)

Act III

Tech Corporal

Sergeant

Lieutenant

Prologue

Isis/Babalon:

Give heed, my son Horus; for you shall hear secret doctrine, of which our forefather the Secret God of the Black Rite. It happens that I have this teaching from that which is known as Kamephis; self-engendered eldest of all our race whose seed and self was Thoth-Hermes, the writer of records, who taught me the way by which your father was made whole and is thus spirit of your flesh.

Horus:

Tell me, Mother, for I thirst for the knowledge of our fathers.

Isis/Babalon:

Once upon a time there was a great king…

Isis gestures to one side of the "stage" area where the Players for Act I stand.

The Thelemic Initiations

Act the First – The Peloponnese c. 2500 BCE

King:

I have summoned you before me, architect, to give you instruction.

Architect:

I am well pleased that you have summoned me, for it is my wish to give you benefit of my wisdom as I did your father. But as you are King, I shall of course hear your instruction first.

King:

First, I wish it to be well known that I am pleased with those latest towers you have built for us. Thus completed, our walls are a great wonder of the world. An obsidian merchant who sailed from the Cyclades (*SICK-luh-dees*) and has also sailed to Egypt says that the Pyramid of Khufu (*KOO-foo*) is no greater than your work. More urgently, I am well pleased with our granaries which have allowed us to take advantage of the recent warm summers to store up grain for several years.

Architect:

It is that of which I wish to speak to you, O King. The summers give me concern. I have brought with me a fisherman with whom I have had discourse and would have you hear what he has to say.

King:

A fisherman before the king? Well, let it not be said that I am not tolerant of all of our people. Bring him in and let him speak.

Fisherman: *enters.*

Architect:

Tell our noble and sage King all that you have told me regarding the port and harbor.

Fisherman: *looks nervous*

Only that, with the warm years, the water is higher now than it has ever been. Large fish are caught now within sight of the towers, and the shore fishers set their traps far above where they were set in my father's day. At high tide, the sea laps nearly even with the great stone quays, where in my childhood it was a fearsome jump into my father's boat.

King:

The waters do as they will. Are you suggesting, Architect, that we must raise the quay?

Architect:

I am suggesting, O King, that within the lifespan of a man this city may be drowned and all within it. That it must be rebuilt far inland well above the line of tide.

King:

I do not deny your wisdom, old man, or the great council that you have given my father. But here I think you overreact to fisherman's tales. I looked at the sea this morning and it was no different than yesterday, nor the day before. The waters may rise and fall but the sea itself does not move. And if, by chance, you be right, then there are many years in which we may act.

Architect:

It is not so, O King. Periodically, as you know, the dea is tormented to ferocity and expends its full savagery upon us. By storm to be sure, but also when those smokings and fires among the islands cause upheaval and the sea is thrown upon the land. Of old, our walls were proof against disaster. It would be long before the daily tide consumed us. Rather, the risk is that the sea might overwhelm our walls and lay waste our houses and store of grain in one savage and terrible night.

King:

I think age has brought you, not wisdom, but that shrill fear that is why men of war should not live too long. In any case, discussion of this must wait. I am off to battle.

Architect:

Battle? But there is peace in the land!

King:

There has been so far but, each year, there are more savages come from the north or the sea. The quality of their weapons is nothing to our fine bronze swords, and spears, and armor, but they eye our fertile lands and stores of grain. I intend to deal them a savage blow that will see them fleeing back across the isthmus and away from our fair land.

Architect:

Is that wise, O King? We have our walls to protect us and our granary to feed us, and they have better cause to barter with us than to assault that which they cannot possibly take. Why risk our men and troops in battle?

King:

I will leave my son the strongest city in the world. He will be a king greater than Khufu. These savages cannot stand against us, for I am a great king and we have fine weapons. We will win much land where our children shall farm. We shall make slaves of them and they shall till for us.

Architect:

What if your army is defeated? The walls of this city stand only if there are strong defenders. If your host is swept away, then those same raiders, enraged by your assault, shall storm our walls and our children shall be slaughtered or enslaved, and the city of your father burnt to ash. We have great store of grain. Are they not herders? Why not sell them food in return for their herds, which we could then slaughter, salting them for store of meat and strengthening our people?

King:

Hush, old man. I once valued your wisdom, but I see that you have become a dotard. A king must win battles. The sea is eternal. It is settled. Take your fisherman for company and tell him your tales of woe. Begone! If you have wit left, plan a great monument for my victory!

The fisherman and the Architect walk away, talking.

Fisherman:

Whatever the king may say, it still moves. What will you do now?

Architect:

The King has given me leave to build a monument. I will endeavor to build that which will survive both flood and fire, for I know not which calamity will be visited upon us first. Upon it, I will inscribe images of our city and its accomplishments that perhaps those shall not be lost to all time.

Interlude

Horus:

Did the architect's stories survive, Mother? What happened to his city?

Isis/Babalon:

It lies nameless at the bottom of a bay, though whether it was drowned or burned first mortal men have not yet divined. His message, perhaps, survived at least in the form of ruins which impressed those who wondered at them later, even to provide a kernel of legend.

Horus:

But I thought that the architect preserved ancient wisdom? All the knowledge of building and the arts, of writing and science?

Isis/Babalon:

Child, what do you think the architect knew of those things that did not come after? He did not know the arch. He had not even the hieroglyphs of the Egyptians of his day, only the grandeur of scale.

Horus:

What point then to his preservation?

Isis/Babalon:

Mortals have not changed very much. The ancient architect knew the futility of vanity, the danger of rashness, and the benefit of generosity. If his monument marked nothing but that, it would not be in vain.

Horus:

What of the great secrets of the pyramids, unknown even today?

Isis/Babalon:

The secrets of the building of Khufu's pyramids are known, even to mortals. Levers, and the best of food. There may of course be tricks the architects of Khufu could teach to later builders but, for the most part, with each year the works of engineering and the sciences grow greater.

Horus:

Were not the pyramids built by slaves?

Isis/Babalon:

Mortals have discovered much writing left by the victuallers of the pyramids and found they were built by free peoples, lured from poverty, enticed with good cuts of meat and bread jars. But when men preserve knowledge, it is not science or the techniques of building. It is rather something about themselves. Even those most ancient standing stones which were raised by people who had neither copper nor writing, send us a message of yearning and aspiration; of dissatisfaction with a life that was no more than a cycle of eat, drink, and death.

Horus:

Then the ineffable knowledge is not a fact, or a magick spell, but an ideal?

Isis/Babalon:

Let me tell you another story. Long ago there was a very wise man, who had spent a long life translating ancient wisdom...

Act the Second – Outside the City of Florence, 1497

Names

Alcibiades (owl-SIBBY-ahh-deez)

Alessandro (owl-lay-SAHN-druh)

Bellisario (BAY-lee-SAHR-ee-oh)

Bernardo del Nero (bear-NAHR-duh de NARE-oh)

Francesco (frahn-CHEZZ-koh)

Gemistos Plethon (juh-MEE-stos PLEE-thon)

Lorenzo (*lohr-EHN-zuh*)

Marsilio Ficino (mar-SEE-lee-oh fi-CHEE-noh)

Medici (MED-uh-chee)

Pico de la Mirandola (PEEK-oh yela meer-AHN-dole-uh)

Piero (pee-AIR-uh)

Rodrigo Borgia (rode-REE-go BOR-ja)

Savonarola (SAH-von-ah-role-uh)

Socrates (sock-RUH-teez)

Ficino:

I am pleased that two young men do me the honor of climbing the hill of Monte Vecchio and dining with me here, overlooking the troubled city below us with its starvation, plague, and turmoil. Alessandro (*owl-lay-SAHN-druh*), I have ever counted you among my *confabulatores*, my familiar friends and conversationalists, and remember many pleasant hours with you in my gymnasium where we spoke of so many things. You will find my board quite humble, but perhaps the excellence of company and the conversation will compensate. I already have another guest, but you two are most welcome.

Francesco:

Marsilio Ficino (*mar-SEE-lee-oh fi-CHEE-noh*), well met. I had heard that your house is always open. Is that wise? There is much plague in the city and the deaths have never been greater. Too, since winter, mobs of the country folk, destitute and starving, have swollen the city seeking bread. Do you not fear that some ragged men might climb your hillside and lay hands upon your person?

Ficino:

It is not my way to fear. Yet Alessandro knows I am well protected. The vast Villa of the Medici (MED-uh-chee) lies just below me, for as you know this little farm was given to me by Lorenzo[139] (*lohr-EHN-zuh*) in thanks for my translation of the Corpus Hermeticum so long ago. Those who would transgress on my land transgress also on that great Villa and, even with the Medici heir, Piero[140] (*pee-AIR-uh*), in exile, many strong men guard that great estate. But come, let me make introductions.

Ficino guides them inside where Bellisario is waiting. He gestures to each person in turn to ensure the audience recognizes them.

I would introduce you to Allessandro, a poet and fine young talent of Florence, whom I recommended in his first flush of fortune to Lorenzo, who became his patron. With him is young Francesco (*frahn-CHEZZ-koh*), whose name and face I recognize as a rising young lawyer and whose father has served several times as a Prior of the Signoria, our governing Council. He has been a strong supporter of the Republic, which has been resurgent since the exile of Piero, and of the Great Council.

This is young Bellisario (*BAY-lee-SAHR-ee-oh*), whose father as you may know is one of the War-Office Council of Ten, who direct our foreign affairs. He has come up the hill to seduce me into signing the petition which is to go to Roderic Borgia Pope Alexander the Sixth,[141] asking him to rescind the Excommunication of our Friar of San Marco, Savonarola (*SAH-von-ah-role-uh*).[142]

Alessandro:

Outrage that you can entertain such a notion! Savonarola is as much the murderer of your great friend Bernardo del Nero(*bear-NAHR-duh de NARE-oh*)[143] as if he had personally chopped off his head.

Francesco:

The Friar himself might have done a better job. It took five whacks, secretly, in the dead of night, and I have heard one took off his chin before he was well slain.

Bellisario:

For treason, Alessandro! For scheming to admit your former Master – the exiled former ruler of this city, Piero di Medici – to our walls when he came before them with guns and cavaliers!

Ficino:

Stop! There shall be no bitterness nor rancor within these walls. I am unclear what help an old man may be to either side, but here, if you wish my aid, you shall have respect for my years and behave, and we shall have civilized discourse. Now, I have heard of the execution of my good friend, Bernardo del Nero, for treason, which was done in the dead of night. But I also know much of the Friar Savonarola, and admire many of the things he stands for.

Alessandro:

How can you admire him? He has burned your books!

Francesco:

I told you it would be no use. He is taken by the Friar's tongue and manner just as Botticelli[144] and as del Mirandola[145] (*PEEK-oh yela meer-AHN-dole-uh*) before his death!

Ficino:

Stop! Much has changed in the world. In the year of my birth, the first printing press had barely begun to spit out paper. Now, the world is buried in a torrent of pages and debate rages over every matter and all things move with the swiftness of Hermes. The stability of the past is washed away in ink and blood. But there is much to be said for sitting and talking. So I shall hear from each of you what it is you have to say.

Now, save Alessandro, who was a fledgling poet, all of you were still boys when my brilliant friend, Pico – who opened eyes to the common threads of Islam, of the Kabbalah of the Jews, and of Hermes – convinced Lorenzo, our patron, to invite Savonarola to Florence. Lorenzo wished a strong spiritual leader in the Dominican House of San Marco, and Pico was stung with the Pope's rejection and destruction of his many theses and plans for a great conference which could have changed the very nature of the Church.

Then, Savonarola was both learned and dynamic and had a way with words to make men realize their venality. We all loved him then and, though he began to preach against the hypocritical Clergy and the wealthy, Lorenzo himself called Savonarola to his bedside when he lay dying and was consoled by him.

Bellisario:

And it was exposed at trial that your good friend, the brilliant Pico was murdered by the Medici for his support of Savonarola. Such do the wealthy reward service.

Alessandro:

That is a black lie.

Ficino:

Alessandro. I know enough medicine to know the young Count Pico was felled by poison. He had become, as had I, quite devoted to Savonarola.

Alessandro:

...who had carried out a coup against Piero di Medici and driven Piero from our city.

Francesco:

Even I must agree that Piero was a terrible ruler, and it was a Republican coup that drove him out. If they were motivated by Savonarola, it was because Piero was everything he despised. Alessandro! Well you know that Piero loved luxury and spent more time cavorting in sport and showing off his handsome build, playing games in the square and racing horses, than he did attending to the government he had inherited.

Alessandro:

And Savonarola and your Republic? When the French King Charles invaded Italy, instead of joining with every other state and the Pope to resist him, you hailed him as a new Cyrus and the mad monk prophesied his great victory. Charles is fled and does not return, and all Italy is united against us. We have lost the port of Pisa, and the Pope threatens interdiction for the antics of this Friar.

Bellisario:

Which is to say the Pope opposes the Great Council and the Republic and would have us managed under some Prince again. Can you not see? This has little to do with Savonarola, who has ever advocated what all men of good character do – the care of the poor, the feeding of the starving, government by the people, jobs, and devotion to God. In the meantime, the Pope in Rome plays games while immersed in luxury and simony, making foreign policy according to who will give principalities to his bastard heirs. He is no Saint!

Ficino:

The Dominican Friar has called for a great reform of the Church. Is that not what our dear departed Pico also wanted? I do not mind a few luxuries, but Plato did not treasure luxury above the good of men. When the wealthy drip with jewels and the poor of the countryside drip with sores and throng the city begging because they have no bread, how is this right?

Alessandro:

Savonarola cares no more for the poor than he does for anyone. They are his excuse to rouse the citizens. He methodically subverts the youth. When the young men of the city who might once have read your translation of Plato fled to the suburbs in the rising plague, he had printed letters to send to them. It is not a matter of some impassioned preaching. He has a program and a machine which supports that program with propaganda.

Bellisario:

You do great injury to say the Friar is not sincere. He lives even as he speaks, and he seeks to bring about a charitable kingdom of heaven upon earth. He cares greatly about the poor and would see them turn their faces to Christ and receive great charity. He abhors violence. He is a most gentle man if you but spoke to him. He had no part in the overthrow of Piero, but stepped in to encourage amnesty, that there would not be a great slaughter of the Medici supporters...which might have included both our revered Master Ficino here and your father, Alessandro.

Francesco:

Yet the hand that withheld the axe when he came to power did nothing to save Nero, nor any of the others falsely condemned. At a word from him for mercy, the Signoria would have backed down. This Carnival, he had boys in the streets – the flower of youth – and they went door to door demanding the "vanities" of the people of Florence to consign to a great bonfire. It brought tears to my eyes, Master Ficino, to see copies of your Corpus Hermeticum, and of the fine editions of your Plato, cast into the flames.

Alessandro:

On that we are agreed.

Francesco:

He might as well have called Plato a pagan and you a heretic, Master Ficino. He has said, "We need to be aware that Plato is Plato, Aristotle is Aristotle, and that they are not Christians simply because they are not, because the difference between Plato and a Christian is much as between sin and virtue, and the difference between Plato's doctrine and Christ's doctrine is as deep as the difference between darkness and light."

Alessandro:

You know he has copied out passages of Mirandola's work disputing your interpretation of Plato?

Ficino:

Ahh, and there is the beauty of it, you see?

Alessandro:

How is it beautiful that he implies that those of us who treasure Plato are outcast and unclean?

Bellisario:

You exaggerate. He keeps books of their work to reference in his sermons.

Ficino:

And that there is the part which is beautiful. In my lifetime, Plato, once lost to us, is as enmeshed in the fabric of Christianity as Aristotle or of the Apostle Paul. His ideas are like that new French disease which has ravaged of late in the wake of the King's army, transmitted by the act of love. Where I fused Christianity to Plato, neither Pico nor Savonarola can be rid of him. They may treat the symptoms of Plato. But they cannot hide his ravages upon the primitive Christianity of Augustine.

Alessandro:

If you talked like that in front of Savonarola he would have you in chains or worse.

Ficino:

Preach against me perhaps. But it is the Pope, not the Friar, who advocates the burning of heretics.

Alessandro:

He has had two young poets cast into prison for the art of poetry.

Bellisario:

The poets of Florence are known for a scorpion sting. They were not making art, but scurrilous songs attacking the Friar and the government.

Francesco:

Savonarola propagates new laws against sodomy that amount to little more, for he equates that supposed sin with a love of Plato.

Bellisario:

Supposed? Would you dispute the word even of the Holy Father that it is among the gravest of sins? And one for which Florence is broadly and darkly famous. Though the secular laws have never been enforced before, so we shall see if these new laws are any different.

Alessandro:

These new laws he means to be enforced. What we well know to be the beauty of Plato, he sees as the darkest sin and he would see bodies reduced to ash because of it; would see Master Ficino's body, whom you claim to love.

Bellisario:

The Friar is a gentle man. And he has done much that is good. He emphasized justice...

Francesco:

...yet did not intervene when the Signoria, in the case of Nero, refused to honor the law that he himself had promulgated – that all men condemned to death, that greatest restriction, should have right of appeal to the Grand Council. Instead, they claimed emergencies of state and a crisis and did their foul work of death in the dark, and Savonarola smiled at them.

Ficino:

Savonarola is right about many things. It is hard to care for fine things when people starve. It is hard to have faith in doctors and medicine when the plague rages. He is right to be angry about the treatment of people. He is right to be angry about the corruption of the Pope and Rome, though the man himself is no more than the product of a system which created him. He is right, even as Pico before him, to want to turn the world upside down and reform the church.

Alessandro:

Then you will sign this petition!? Advocate for him to remain among us!

Bellisario:

It is as I said...he has been vigilant for those who would destroy our Republic. He has worked to see women renounce immodest dress which courts the French disease, and to see our children educated, most especially in the lives of the Saints that they may learn from their example.

Ficino:

I have been called a pagan for many years, though I have never called myself other than a Christian, yet I see an unbroken chain of great philosophers – Hermes Trismegistus, Orpheus, Pythagoras, and Plato most of all. This ancient system of theology was harmonious and sufficient in all regards. My old friend Gemistos Plethon (*juh-MEE-stos PLEE-thon*)[146] arrived at a new cosmology which removed entirely that Christian name of God, though he substituted Zeus and other powers. That was true reform to wash away all those names that have been put by Rome and San Marco on the divine, and to use those ancient names which are as true as any other.

Alessandro, recall you my first disagreement over Plato with our dear, departed Pico?

Alessandro:

Hazily, for it transpired when I was still learning of these things. I know that it revolved around the questions of love and a poem.

Ficino:

That much is true. Well you know...though, perhaps, you, my good Bellisario do not...that in the *Symposium*, Socrates discusses love? Socrates explanation of love, taught to him by the Priestess Diotima, was to see it as a ladder. We start out in youth loving all beautiful bodies, particularly those like our own, and then love of those bodies unlike ours, then to the beauty of souls, and then to ideas and traditions, then something higher still. Through our initial love of the body; our embrace of eros, we come to love all things and, indeed, see all things as equally beautiful.

Pico saw that the ladder led away from touch and affairs of the flesh and, in a general way, he was right. Now some of you at least may know that the final section of the *Symposium* is a drunken eulogy by Alcibiades[147] (owl-SIBBY-ahh-deez) which is rather earthy and openly discusses his desire for Socrates. It's often dismissed as a sort of comic epilogue; not really related to the theme.

Yet, I saw that the two were very much related because, in his narration of Alcibiades' base desires – his physical yearning for Socrates – the whole thing comes back around. We're reminded that his burning need is as much a part of the whole process as that highest pinnacle. No part is better or worse. They simply are.

This was a bit indelicate for our young Pico. In Plato's day as in our own, one might have to talk around whether or not that yearning was ever assuaged by the body of Socrates or elsewhere. Yet it came too close to the flesh for our young friend who wanted to keep his mind firmly focused on the divine and not acknowledge those urges from below with which we all have been afflicted.

Bellisario:

Rightly in the marriage bed! All else is sin. Our good Florentines may like stories of antique pagans enough, from painters and poets and their learned men. But they do not pray to Hermes, nor do they look for succor to the Ein Sof of Pico. They look to Jesus and the Virgin Mary.

Ficino:

Of course, my dear Bellisario. We speak only of beauty and eros.

Alessandro:

I knew a time when you upheld the virtues of "beauty" somewhat more avidly, my dear Ficino. Has age changed your heart?

Bellisario:

Well, how now Master Ficino? You have said much positive of Savonarola. Do you uphold this repudiation of the basal flesh which our departed Pico so insisted upon?

Ficino:

I, like Savonarola, believe a cleansing must come. And I understand in principle that gold and finery and other rich things are an oppression of sorts. They are not merely vanity but, when they are amassed at the expense of the poor; at the expense of the good of the realm, they are objectively bad. They may be comely in form, but prettiness and beauty are not the same thing, and so many of them are disposable or trivial. One may say they are beautiful because all things are beautiful, but on the level we live at, where my cock throbs at the sight of a pretty ass, they are ugly and detestable. Even my books, when they are purchased more to show others one's prosperity or supposed learning than to absorb their contents, are a vanity.

Francesco:

Then you reject the flesh and side with the Friar?

Bellisario:

You will lend your name to our missive to the Pope!?

Ficino:

No, that is precisely why I cannot sign your petition. For Savonarola has slain beauty, and thus slain love.

Bellisario:

But you said those things are ugly.

Ficino:

They are. But the answer to them is not to destroy all beauty. That is the model of the Gnostics who said that God is an evil being who hid men in flesh that they might not see the light. If the God of the Gnostics was a fiction, Savonarola has created him. To fight fear of tyranny, he has approved of tyranny. To fight those who care not about those qualities which are truly beautiful, he makes war and razes beautiful things. He sets the lives of the Saints, who often teach no more than that humans can be quite stubborn, above the lives of those who actually thought and wrote; mere passion above substance.

I will tell you a great secret. At my age what harm can it do? The Friar can come, if he is not too busy with other fish to fry, and make me drink hemlock if he likes. But in the work of Plato and in the universe of God, the physical love of the flesh and all the storm and fury that accompanies it is so central that it cannot be ignored. That is why Plato circles back to it. It cannot be laid on a shelf or brushed aside, for it is the nature of humankind. Love is Beauty and Beauty is Love.

Bellisario:

What will become of our Friar?

Ficino:

He will continue to knock down doors and fight an increasingly bitter and desperate fight as those who are extreme in their views do when they cannot back down. Pope Alexander is corrupt and venal and I find it hard to love him. Yet he is also subtle and better at politics than your Friar. If your Friar does not apologize – and I think he will not, for he is full of his own righteousness – he will get his own cup of hemlock or worse. He has painted himself into a corner and, even if I loved him, I might wonder what can happen now but to drag the misery out.

I respect his rebellion. Pico rebelled, but lacked conviction. He had a coherent thesis for a great change of faith to embrace all peoples, as did my friend Plethon, and put it away, discouraged at the word of a corrupt Pope. But Savonarola is all passionate intensity, and his real conviction is nothing more than that something is wrong. He sees nothing wrong with burning down the world because it does not suit him and, because he has lost touch with feelings of the flesh and lives entirely in the beauty of the divine, the cost of his actions means little to him.

Bellisario:

Is that not what even Plato wanted? To reach that level of divinity where all things are beautiful?

Ficino:

Perhaps. But Socrates used it to help the young men around him and, in doing so, he was not averse to some degree of practicality, for he was brave as a warrior and knew something of the earthly concepts of love. Savonarola, in deciding to belittle his great education and put away the philosophers behind the Saints, has made himself nothing but passion. He shall have a great legacy perhaps, but it shall be as much a warning as an example of what happens when humans mistake mere passion for true will. He could not believe himself a part of God, thus he could never truly see God in others, hard as he might try.

Interlude

Horus:

What happened to Savonarola?

Isis/Babalon:

He was hanged and burned at the Pope's order. But the Pope was merciful and, after subjecting him to the agony of fire, let him go to heaven on an indulgence, so...at least in theory...everyone was happy in the end.

Horus:

And the wise old man?

Isis/Babalon:

He is remembered mostly by those who revere the name of Hermes. His murdered friend Pico is far more famous, and perhaps more daring.

Horus:

I thought his book was burned?

Isis/Babalon:

He lived in the first generation to build printing presses. When he was born there was but one book printed in Europe. By the time he died there were nine million books for only sixty million people.

The Thelemic Initiations

Horus:

> Then his work did become immortal! Did he write all the secrets of Hermes, the Emerald Tablet, all the science and knowledge of the world?

Isis/Babalon:

> There is no such book. At least not one which tells how to move mountains and great stones and may be written in hieroglyphs. Mortals in his day wrote about the dangers of all the information beings spread, and much of it was false. Yet books are the only way that thoughts may be made immortal. That is why our initiations come from the book.

Horus:

> What book does this initiation come from, Mother?

Isis/Babalon:

> The book of the Left hand of the Angel of the Beast which has the face of Man and Woman, of which the Child of the Prophet is only a reflection upon this plane.[148] It is the book to which the Book of Enoch is but prologue. As well it is the book in which the secrets of NEMO are written[149] and in which it is written that by Union is exalted the daughter to the throne of the mother.[150]

Horus:

> I shall not be exalted then for I am told that I am your son and not your daughter.

Isis/Babalon:

> Thou knowest not, my child, of what thou speaketh.

> Let me tell you another story. Once upon a time there was a great Tyrant who waged a war against all of his neighbors. Like all tyrants, he claimed a righteous cause: that his people needed "elbow room" to live. In the end, three quarters of his capital was burned to ash and millions of people killed. This is the story of some Architects who wandered through the ruins, looking for a stable place for their Captain.

Act the Third – Berlin Germany, 1945

Sergeant:

> Steady now, Tech Corporal. This place looks alright but the rest of the block got leveled by one of our bombers, so it might fool ya. Don't need to lose a good man after the war is done!

Tech Corporal:

> The landlady on the next block said this house was in good enough shape. It was a private house back in the day, but the owner was arrested not long after the fighting broke out and some Nazi Officers lived here during the war. A bomb took down the rest of the block but this place was barely touched.

Sergeant:

> Sounds chancy to me. I'm surprised it didn't take this building too.

Tech Corporal:

It was detached with a little garden. It looks in good enough shape. I know a little about these things. I was in engineering school back home, before the war.

Sergeant:

Engineering school? That's fancy. I worked at a sandwich shop outside a factory back at home. I'm surprised you didn't get a deferment.

Tech Corporal:

I enlisted. I guess I had romantic ideas about war. Do my part to stop Tojo and Hitler, fight with the Allies and all. I'm not sorry I got into the fight, but I'm not a romantic anymore. I've seen things I wished I hadn't. I think this place is sound enough to make a Command Post.

Lieutenant:

Inspect it all the same, Tech Corporal. Can't have an Allied Commander in an unsafe building. Half the buildings in Berlin are burned down and half the ones still standing are as likely to collapse as not. We'll have some luck if we've found a solid place on this street. Remember, there were Officers staying here, so if you find any papers secure them in case they're valuable.

Tech Corporal:

Yes, Sir. I'm going in. I've got a light and a rope.

The Tech Corporal proceeds some distance away from the others and then calls out:

The downstairs is safe enough, but there's a collapsed wall in the cellar I need to take a closer look at. Come in here, Sergeant ,and hold the light while I climb over it.

The Sergeant joins the Tech Corporal the building, where he holds the light as the Tech Corporal proceeds through a broken section of wall.

Sergeant:

What do you see?

Tech Corporal:

It's interesting. This wall collapsed because it wasn't original in the first place. It's thrown together – just some lathe and a few boards. Someone made a cache here.

Sergeant:

Better grab anything you find and bring it out for the Lieutenant.

Lieutenant: *moves to join the other two*

I'm here, Tech Corporal. What is it? Reich government documents? Bank information?

Tech Corporal:

> Nothing like that. Honestly doesn't seem to be much of value. There's an old poster here... some place called Cafe Dorian Gray.

Sergeant:

> Is that what was here? It looked like an apartment house.

Tech Corporal:

> No, that was on the Bülowstrasse. (*BOO-low-strahss*). I'm not exactly certain where that is anymore but I know it's not right here. There's a moldy leather satchel with some books and papers in it.

Sergeant:

> Better bring those out to the Lieutenant.

Tech Corporal: *brings out several documents and lays them down*

Lieutenant:

> Enumerate what you've found Tech Corporal.

Tech Corporal:

> Well there are a couple of books and some pictures... Ohhh...looks like some sort of French postcard type pictures.

Sergeant:

> Give those here. We can barter them to the Supply Corps for some beer!

Tech Corporal:

> I'm not so sure about that Sergeant. They're kinda...weird.

Lieutenant:

> Let's see them, Tech Corporal.

Tech Corporal:

> Well, this one is a couple of men. And this one is a couple of girls, but I'm not sure what this one is.

Sergeant:

> Well damn. Might as well burn 'em. They won't trade for that.

Lieutenant:

> Not so fast, Sergeant. Someone went to an awful lot of trouble to preserve these.

Sergeant:

> Some pervert hiding their filth I'd say.

Lieutenant:

What are the books Tech Corporal?

Tech Corporal:

This one is poetry I think. *The Scented Garden of Abdullah the Satirist of Shiraz.*[151] Translated by a Major Lutiy...in the Indian service I suppose. It's old, 1910, back before the last war.

Lieutenant:

Interesting. What else?

Tech Corporal:

Berlin's Third Sex by a Doctor Magnus Hirschfeld. Also not new...old, dated 1905. In German. Third Sex? That's odd. Am I translating that correctly, Sir?

Sergeant:

See, Sir? Perversions.

Lieutenant:

I think you are, Tech Corporal. What is the last book?

Tech Corporal:

It says *The Method of Science and the Aim of Religion.* I think it's poetry too, Sir...advertisements for poetry books anyway. *The Triumph of Pan.* Some sort of magazine for spiritualists back before the war. Here it is. *The Equinox Volume One, Number Five.*[152] A very weighty book, Sir.

The Tech Corporal flips to a random page.

"And the ring of the horizon above her is a company of glorious Archangels with joined hands, that stand and sing: This is the daughter of Babalon the Beautiful, that she hath borne unto the Father of All."[153]

He thumbs a few more pages and reads at random.

"And this is the Mystery of the incest of Chaos with his daughter."[154] More poetry I think. It reads like poetry anyway.

Sergeant:

And ungodly ones at that.

Lieutenant:

You're not much for poetry, are you, Sergeant?

Sergeant:

God no, Sir.

Lieutenant:

We'll keep these books. Someone who lived in this house went to a lot of trouble to keep them safe.

The Thelemic Initiations

Sergeant:

More like keep them hidden, Sir. This is the sort of perverted filth we came over here to fight, Sir.

Lieutenant:

Just the opposite, Sergeant. This place was very different before Hitler came. These sort of books might get you a visit from a Postal Inspector back home, but here? Once Hitler was in charge I suspect they'd get you sent to one of those death factories they've found. Someone risked their life...maybe lost it...to preserve these books when the night fell on this city. I think the least we owe them is not to pay for their diligence by casting them into a furnace.

Sergeant:

Do what with them then, Sir? I can't trade them and they're not intelligence.

Lieutenant:

Just so, Sergeant, I know a few people who might find these things interesting. Poetry and psychology. I might even be able to get you a beer for them, Sergeant.

Sergeant:

Well if you think so, Sir.

Lieutenant:

Is there any book plate or name in any of them, Tech Corporal? There is perhaps the slimmest chance that the owner yet lives.

Sergeant:

Doubtful, Sir.

Tech Corporal:

There is no name, but there is writing on the first page of the poetry book. It is in a cipher script though, some sort of code I suppose.

Lieutenant:

Let me look, Tech Corporal. Yes it is a cipher but one I recognize.

Tech Corporal:

From military intelligence, Sir?

Lieutenant:

From long before that. It is made of angles; a geometric cipher. There is some inconsistency in its application. Yet I believe I can read this.

The Lieutenant may take his finger or a pencil to the text as if deciphering it.

Boaz broken,

Jachin gone,

Freely spoken

Jahbulon,

All above

Is overthrown

For the love

Of Babalon.[155]

Sergeant:

More poetry, Sir? What's it about?

Lieutenant:

From the Bible, Sergeant, more or less. Even you can only be so disapproving. It's the chorus of a little song. It has verses.

Tech Corporal:

With your permission, Sir, I'd like to keep this thick one. It's kind of strange but seems an interesting read. I feel like there might be something to it.

Lieutenant:

As you will, Tech Corporal. You found this hidden cache. You should get first pick of its treasure.

Epilogue:

Horus:

What happened to the man who hid the books, Mother?

Isis/Babalon:

You always want to know the unknowable, O child of your father. It is likely he died in the camps where the Nazis killed all their victims. But perhaps he fled far away before they came for him.

Horus:

Why did he hide the books? If the Nazis were going to kill him for having them shouldn't he have thrown them away.

Isis/Babalon:

Sometimes, O child, an idea is something we cannot part with, and we treasure even the representation of it in picture or writing. "Let there be no difference made among you between any one thing & any other thing; for thereby there cometh hurt."[156] Sometimes to destroy an idea...even the image of an idea... is to do violence against ourselves. Too, the gift of Thoth is writing, and writing is a sort of immortality. Through writing the Logos may transcend one life.

Horus:

What is the point of saving anything at all then?

Isis/Babalon:

It is the greatest proof of all that humans are as immortal as ourselves. For truly without them we have no life. A declaration of identity that transcends an individual lifetime. The urge to propagate not only the legacy of the flesh but of creativity, the spark of eros. They have carved their wisdom and images upon golden disks and flung them into the stars.

Horus:

That is the root of it then? The urge to immortality. What do they get from it?

Isis/Babalon:

Their continuation which is our continuation.

Horus:

Do they create us then?

Isis/Babalon:

No. We are the laws within their universe, the laws and forces of Nature that bind them all. If the universe is their house, we are its walls. Maybe they made us once upon a time, but whereas they may divide for the sake of union eternal, we are omnipotent, omnipresent and so on; our wills immutable and absolute.[157]

Horus:

They are always changing?

Isis/Babalon:

It is their nature. They dug beneath the ice in the deepest north to hide seeds in the cold and ice against some great catastrophe, then heated the planet until the place was awash and the ice melted away. For those who see these monuments, it is on one hand, proof that humans have faced adversity and that however overwhelmed they were, they eventually triumphed. On the other hand proof that all is not well and that even in the most secure and glorious circumstances their undoing may be not far away. One of their poets wrote of it:

> I met a traveler from an antique land,
> Who said—"Two vast and trunkless legs of stone
> Stand in the desert. . . . Near them, on the sand,
> Half sunk a shattered visage lies, whose frown,
> And wrinkled lip, and sneer of cold command,
> Tell that its sculptor well those passions read
> Which yet survive, stamped on these lifeless things,
> The hand that mocked them, and the heart that fed;
> And on the pedestal, these words appear: My name is Ozymandias, King of Kings;
> Look on my Works, ye Mighty, and despair!
> Nothing beside remains. Round the decay

Of that colossal Wreck, boundless and bare
The lone and level sands stretch far away."[158]

I° Initiation – Script – Second Section

The Formal Instruction

Raimond:

> The lesson of the Arch of Enoch, or the Pillars of Thoth, is with us still and always. We recall it with the pillar candles on our Altar and the pillars in some Temples. It is sharp and poignant for your time as well as ours. It is a message at once of alarm and hope.

> In the New Aeon, there is great threat of calamity; on one hand brought about through harnessing nature without completely understanding it, and on another through the false will of the ignorant who deplore learning and knowledge in favor of momentary satisfaction in strong emotions. The Pillars remind us of the need to preserve knowledge and wisdom. Yet they also provide a promise that knowledge is immortal, and that through it, we ourselves become immortal.

> Fools imagine that somewhere there is a book which they can find which will contain on its pages all the world's knowledge. There is perhaps an ultimate book, but it is a teaching on how to think, not a set of facts. That abstract form you have already been given, encoded in final form in that Book which is labeled *AL*. As that record was of the Cairo Working, we will, in this First Grade of the Thelemic Order, commend to you most especially that desert working which is known as *Liber 418*, or the *Vision and the Voice*, as well as those inspired texts published by Master Therion in the collection titled *Thelema*. Further, we commend to your continuing study that exemplification of the *Book of Thoth*[159] which is the commentary upon the tapestries of that noble Saint, Lady Frieda Harris.

> The lesson of the two pillars is for us as well as you. Within our principality of Toulouse, we prepare for grievous blows aimed at ourselves and others of our region – the Count of Carcassonne, son of our sister Azalais; and our vassal Raimond-Roger Count of Foix, whose sister Esclarmonde, has been attentive to the word of the Good People. Yet, through song and writing, it is our hope that the spirit of the peaceful realm we have made here will serve our memory well; that in some strange and far-off vault our own images may be graven.

> Now, I am given to understand that you would petition this Court, now that you understand more of its nature, for admission to the mysteries and for reception as a Magician. Know that the reception of this petition entails as part of your acceptance the broadcast of your petition into the Logos. If it is your will to be known as a Magician of the First Degree in our Sovereign Order, you may present your petitions to me now. You may read them if you like, or present hand them over

If the time is very short Raimond may omit the option to read the petitions

Initiates: Present their petitions

Raimond:

Now, before we make you a Magician, and transmit thereby your name into the Logos you may recall that under the Sovereign Sanctuary of the Gnosis of the Thelemic Order, is operated the Independent and Rectified Rite of the Ancient and Primitive Mystery of Memphis and Misraim; one of many manifestations of that Rite, which is itself one of many manifestations of Masonry, Rosicrucianism, Neo-Templarism, and Neo-Gnosticism. It bears repeating that this is not itself the system of Thelemic Initiation, but rather a framework which not only connects us to the past, but also reminds us that our past was by rights progressive, with our siblings in the vanguard of that change which led to humanity and tolerance. That lesson is especially appropriate to the Thirteenth Degree of the Rectified Rite which is the Royal Arch of Enoch or Pillars of Thoth.

Raimond knocks 11 times in the following series: ! !!! !!! !!! !

I bear, among other titles that of Knight of the Rose Cross. As is appropriate within my charge, I hereby grant and confer upon you the Degrees Four through Thirteenth of the Rectified Rite of the Ancient and Primitive Mystery of Memphis and Misraim, culminating in that of Companion of the Royal Arch of Enoch. It is my earnest hope that you will seek out further learning regarding these progressive and humanitarian traditions of which we have preserved the esoteric core.

The Masonic Word of the Royal Arch is constructed JAH-BUL-ON, or in some cases Zebulon, or some similar construction. Within Memphis and Misraim, it is given as JAHBULON. The historical authorities do not agree on its origin, however they are taken in some cases as a reference to the pillars Jachin and Boaz, in which case they give reference to ON, a variant of AUM, which is given as an alternative name for Heliopolis which you will recall from your previous initiation. Other formulations make them some combination of the unitary names of God.

Now we will proceed to your instruction, after which you will leave this place having taken the first grade of the Thelemic Initiations and be a Magician, recognized as such.

Azalais:

You have already learned those things which are most important, to wit: "Do what thou wilt shall be the whole of the Law," that each among us are stars, and that "thou hast no right but to do thy will."

Yet, Thelema is not a few simple sentences. It is through the pursuit of the Holy and Inspired works we have commended to you, and the commentaries which throw light upon them, that you shall mature in your understanding of the Law and come into the fullness of attainment.

Raimond:

There is no single phrase which can provide all guidance, even if it provides absolute truth. I can tell you that the key to riding is balance and I will have told you the entire secret and also nothing whatsoever, for that knowledge will not keep you on a horse. You must know what balance is and practice it. Also, you must be able to identify a horse.

We shall proceed without delay to the teaching of the Formula of LAShTAL and a complementary ritual, Liber V vel Reguli,[160] which we shall relate to our play and our Sacred Feast.

The Thelemic Initiations

The Ritual – Liber V vel Reguli

Introduction to the Formula of LAShTAL

Raimond:

I will read from the ritual – which is, as well, an introduction to the formula of LAShTAL.

Of our nature, it is written: "I also am a Star in Space, unique and self-existent, an individual essence incorruptible; I also am one Soul; I am identical with All and None. I am in All and all in me; I am, apart from all and lord of all, and one with all,"[161] and also "I am the None, for all that I am is the imperfect image of the perfect; each partial phantom must perish in the clasp of its counterpart, each form fulfil itself by finding its equated opposite, and satisfying its need to be the Absolute by the attainment of annihilation."[162]

The essence of this teaching of Liber V vel Reguli is...

The First Objection to the Instruction

The Fool:

...Wait a minute...wait! You can't teach them this!

Raimond:

Not only can we, we must. Your objections grow tiresome, O Fool, and our time is not unlimited.

The Fool:

This is First Degree. You've already told them secrets of sex magick. Now you're teaching Liber V vel Reguli!? That ritual is advanced stuff.... There are all sorts of stories. People start practicing it and bad things happen in their lives.

Azalais:

As opposed to those who do not practice it, whose lives are devoid of ills?

The Fool:

Yes! No! It's unlucky? Some Thelemites somewhere said so. I read it.

Azalais:

The problem with all the world's wisdom being at one's fingertips is that all the world's foolishness is equidistant. It is the work of the Adept to discern between the two. Where did you read it, Fool? In the header by Master Therion where he says "an incantation proper to invoke the Energies of the Aeon of Horus, adapted for the daily use of the magician of whatever grade."[163]

The Fool:

Well, that was the Master. When he said "whatever grade" he surely wasn't thinking about...them.

The Fool waves his hand deprecatingly at the Petitioners.

Raimond:

Even knowing your true identity, O Fool, I think you sell them short, which is doubly troubling, if predictable. By their continued presence here, they prove themselves Magicians already, in spirit, if not so decreed into the Logos. First Degree within our Sovereign Sanctuary is not some learner's step. It is an immersion under fire. This path is for those who are Magicians and would achieve Mastery of the Temple.

The Fool:

But it's out of order...there are attributions to the grades...777!

Azalais:

What grades are those? Those of Orders which died in infancy at the Master Therion's feet or thrived a century past? These are the Grades of the Sovereign Sanctuary of the Hermetic Fellowship of Light as it lives and breathes on this day. These Grades are revealed according to the formula of YHVH, the meaning of which shall be enlarged to you in the formula of LAShTAL. These are the Grades of the New Aeon, forged of its work.

The Fool:

Would it not be better and less dangerous to leave it...vague? To tell them just enough to awe them, but not so much they might really understand? Then refer them to extensive and laborious reading that served to impress upon them the dangers and complexity of what they undertake? Easier for you as well. If you don't ever put forward any real theses about Thelema, then they can't dispute with you, and you come off as sage and all knowing. And it's more comfortable for them as well, for they are charged with nothing very difficult. The fortune teller's trick!

Azalais:

Leave it to a Fool to suggest a Fool's initiation. The Master Therion, in his own investigation of the Temple of Solomon the King, explicitly rejected such a proposition. If our goal was to make them our disciples and impress them with the superior knowledge of their initiators, then such an initiation would be perfect. But our goal is to make of them Adepts, on a path toward Mastery of the Temple. They must understand that even their instructors are but a few steps down the path, and that to initiate is to undertake the exploration of a realm unknown. They must be taught to build and develop their own understandings as Magicians, for they will face true ordeals.

The Fool:

Ordeals! That is behind all my reticence. I am supposed to safeguard them. How about we stick to theoretics rather than teaching them actual methods by which they might come to harm? You're teaching them every detail of the most profound of magics!

Exegesis of the Two Principles of Magickal Harm

Jeanne:

We have taught them nothing of the sort. We have done little more than let them know the possibilities. There is a vast gap between knowing that cake exists and being a baker. Yet if cake is alluded to only in obscure hieroglyphs, such as "the child of the wheat and the egg," or "the loaf of sweetness," and the existence of bowls and spoons a carefully guarded secret, it becomes a long and difficult road to learn the trade of baking.

Raimond:

I will say this in words so clear they cannot be mistaken: As with any skill, practice makes perfect. Would you think to withhold the fundaments of military strategy from a Prince until they stood before the enemy, then expect that Prince to triumph on the battlefield? There are but two ways in which one can come to harm in the practice of magick. Inform them!

Azalais:

The first is to doubt that you are God. Avoiding that doubt is very hard for some, but blissfully too easy for others.

Jeanne:

The second is to doubt that all other stars in the company of stars are also God. To do so is inherently to deny your own divinity and to forsake the chance of union.

Raimond:

The embrace of the first often leads to the abrogation of the second, and failure to embrace the first makes the second impossible. To learn to thread the path takes practice and, indeed, failure. As a Magician, there is nothing you can do which you cannot also set right, save that you not derail the course of another Star in the Company of Stars. On harm, or even benefit, to others think you well, for when your course collides with another, the impact bears upon you both, and the result belongs to both. Thus in voluntary collision you put yourself, voluntarily, into the hands of another.

The Fool:

Isn't that just moralizing? Like saying "harm none?" Impractical advice to frighten and dissuade them?

Raimond: Emphatically:

This is no moral but a simple law of the universe, a matter of action and reaction! This is the initiation of the Most Ancient Order of the Defenders of the Temple of the East and of the Hermetic Fellowship of Light! Defenders of the Temple which might be rendered Templar. Hermetic because it was founded by Thoth-Hermes, the original keeper and recorder of all wisdom. Light which is symbolized by the Rose Cross or the transcendent or golden dawn. It is not for those who wish to play at magick, but for Magicians who would attain Mastery of the Temple. In the book you were given at your previous initiation Ra-Hoor-Khuit, speaks thusly: "Fear not at all; fear neither men nor Fates, nor gods, nor anything. Money fear not, nor laughter of the folk folly, nor any other power in heaven or upon the earth or under the earth. Nu is your refuge as Hadit your light; and I am the strength, force, vigour, of your arms."[164]

Explication of LA

Raimond:

Having, we hope, calmed any fears that our initiates, or at least their Fool, were troubled by, and bid them act with forethought, yet most assuredly to act, we shall continue.

Raimond goes to the Tracing Board

In this formula, you will find many relationships to the Trumps depicted in that work which is the most recent form of the *Book of Thoth*.[165]

L or Lamed is Balance or Adjustment, which is the Eighth Trump. Within it Father-Mother Set-Isis.

A or Aleph is the Fool which is Trump Zero, the beginning, the pregnant void.

Lamed Aleph, together, is the universe with the potential for all manifestation.

The Hebrew letter Lamed has the value of 30 and the Hebrew letter Aleph the value of 1. Thus, together, they are 31, which is in itself a Key.

The mystery of these is two equals zero. Lamed Aleph is the passion of Nuit and Hadit joining each other in union and "making themselves naught thereby." In Lamed Aleph, their child is conceived but is yet naught.

The Fool:

They might understand the concept of zero equals two better if it were stated as negative one and positive one equal zero. Hadit and Nuit annihilate each other to become nothing, Nothing divides into Nuit and Hadit.

Jeanne:

Even a broken clock is right twice a day. Well said, O Fool.

Azalais:

Truly this is where Thelemites differ from the teachings of the Good People. The Cathars and all those Gnostics who came before them conceive of creation as the work of an evil Demiurge who wraps the immortal light in material flesh. Thelema conceives of the universe as joy; the infinite divided into the finite in order to experience itself, for the chance of union to come back together. That union is the meaning of love.

Raimond:

It is as you have said.

The Fool:

So I, the Fool am the nothing that is everything?

Raimond:

So you are.

The Thelemic Initiations

The Fool:

Then you are just a division of me?

Azalais:

The Fool sees. Keep this up and they'll know who you are. But let us continue.

Explication of ShT

Raimond:

The Trump in the Book of Thoth which corresponds to Sh or Shin is Twenty or The Aeon, depicting the Gods of the New Aeon. It is not, however, a thing, but an action; LA and AL set into motion. Shin, which is fire, and Teth which is flesh, combined.

Now you will note that the letters themselves do not make a convenient sum. However the Trump in the *Book of Thoth* which corresponds to T or Teth is eleven or Lust which depicts Sun, Lion and Serpent. Lust in this sense is the application or active form of Eros. The Trump also depicts Babalon and the Beast, which are the earthly emissaries of Nuit and Hadit. It is, too, the secret nature of transmutations – Fire and Force, Babylon and Beast, combined into Ra-Hoor-Khuit.

You will note as well that the number of Lust as 11 is not coincidental, and answers to our earlier talk on the relation of eleven to the higher uses of sex-magick.

Azalais:

Spirit, which is Shin, and Flesh, which is Teth, combine into a single letter as we are told "to mediate between identical extremes as their mean"[166] as "the secret that sunders and seals them."[167] We read earlier "The 'Child' of such love is a third person, an Holy Spirit, so to speak, partaking of both natures, yet boundless and impersonal because it is a bodiless creation of a wholly divine nature."[168] Here in LAShTAL you see that exemplified, the triform formula of the Aeon.

Raimond:

In our consideration of Shin and Teth together, we find somewhat of a cipher. If we sum the constituent Trumps, twenty and eleven, we get also a numeration of 31, thus yielding the same total as Lamed and Aleph but through different, though no less meaningful, attributions.

Together these, Fire and Force, depict Ra-Hoor-Khuit. Shin and Teth are double power, like the Wand of Solomon King, two opposite currents, each polarized unto itself. Yet these are modes of motion and transformation, not things or states of existence.

Explication of AL

Raimond:

Aleph Lamed is identical to Lamed Aleph but reversed; the Fool made manifest. AL is "all" or "God," and in this segment of the formula zero becomes two. Recalling our previous play, there is no distinction between EL and AL, and both are written Lamed Aleph.

Azalais:

The Naught faces itself as two.

Aleph Lamed sums identically to Lamed Aleph, and is also 31. Thus the three segments of the formula add to 93. This pattern informs the first four grades of our Mystery. As you see, this First Grade is that of the Father. Now, it is time that we moved to the performance of this rite.

Let us speak for a moment of the basic story of YHVH.[169]

Let the instructor identify the Hebrew Letters on the Tracing Board

In the first half of this story:

- Yod, the King, is the bornless self-created father, Hadit, of whom it is said "Thou art an egg of blackness, and a worm of poison. But thou hast formulated thy father, and made fertile thy mother. "[170]
- When Yod Joins Heh, that is "the marriage of the Father to the great and co-equal mother"[171] Nuit, the Queen.
- Their Union produces Vau the Son, and then she who is both twin sister and daughter of Vau, Heh

In the second half

- Then the daughter Heh, identified with Malkuth
- Unites with the Son Vau identified with Tiphereth
- The Son enthrones the Daughter upon the throne of his mother Heh.
- So enthroned the Daughter now becomes Mother and Queen Heh identified with Binah
- and "wakens the Eld of the Father," Yod, associated with Chokmah and
- Uniting with him dissolves all into Kether the crown.

Azalais:

You can see how the Annihilation of Lamed Aleph by Aleph Lamed, mediated by Shin Teth tell the same extended story?

Raimond:

The second half of this story is a metaphor for our task as adepts, the Great Work. We are told "the first step of this is the attainment of the Knowledge and Conversation of the Holy Guardian Angel, which constitutes the Adept of the Inner Order. The re-entry of these twin spouses into the womb of the mother is that initiation described in Liber 418...of the last step we cannot speak."

The Fool:

We have to be incestuous twin spouses?

Azalais: *Raises an eyebrow and scowls*

The Count, my brother and father of my child, did say it was a metaphor. It is written: "Note that there are now two sexes in one person throughout, so that each individual is self-procreative sexually, whereas Isis knew only one sex, and Osiris thought the two sexes opposed. Also the formula is now Love in all cases; and the end is the beginning, on a higher plane."[172]

Jeanne:

It is written that "The soul is beyond male and female as it is beyond Life and Death. Even as the Lingam and the Yoni are but diverse developments of One Organ, so also are Life and Death but two phases of One State. So also the Absolute and the Conditioned are but forms of THAT."[173] Did you have a problem with THAT, O Fool?

The Second Objection to the Instruction

The Fool: *Mumbles somewhat embarrassed, looking around for a distraction. When the Fool speaks they are clearly redirecting the conversation from their remark.*

Aren't these supposed to be initiations? Why do you keep teaching them rituals that are just...out of a book?

Azalais:

Did not but moments ago you fear this ritual?

The Fool:

Well it doesn't seem so daunting now.

Azalais:

And there you have our reasoning. Magic is the core of initiation, and one does not teach an art by simply describing it. Some of our initiates have never done a ritual from a book. Others have never done a ritual at all. Still others have progressed so far that the fundamental roots like vel Reguli are near forgotten. These initiations form a set of distinct keys to the process of Thelemic initiation and attainment; a royal road from Malkuth to Kether. It is our intention that none should walk forward who has not been shown the road, and how can we do that but by participation? No one shall call themselves Magician without having committed at least one true act of magic and, in so doing, they receive permission to commit that many more.

Raimond:

The point of Liber V vel Reguli is to take the role of the Prince in the pageant we have illustrated, and far more than that. It is to recognize oneself as being identical with "All and None,"[174] and "very God of very God,"[175] it is transformational. We become one who has "decreed fro my delight that Nothingness should figure itself ast twain, that I might dream a dance of names and natures and enjoy the substance of simplicity by watching the wanderings of my shadows."[176]

It is well that we state at this point that Liber V vel Reguli is meant to be performed with a wand or staff. As the initiations progress, you will find and dedicate at each grade one of the four elemental tools of the magician, though you have not yet dedicated a wand, nor were you asked to bring one here. When you return to your places, you will have some time to experiment in the selection of a wand, staff, or set of wands which are suited to you. While, at each grade, we focus on one of the elemental tools, that should not be taken as a suggestion that you may not obtain and experiment with all the tools appropriate to a magician; for that is what, from this day on, you are.

For our purposes here, Liber V vel Reguli may also be performed with the hands and will of the Magician, though it may be found more puissant once the appropriate tool is found to extend that will.

Azalais:

You will find, too, that some Magicians never use tools, or make use of whatever tools are at hand.

The Ritual Liber V vel Reguli

The Instruction in ritual may be undertaken by whichever Initiator is sufficiently knowledgeable and skilled, according to the will of the Sovereign Initiator, regardless of their character within the drama. It is usually preferential if this is not the Fool. However, in extremis, this is acceptable.

During the instruction, the Fool should model or mirror the actions and positions that the Instructor is describing.

Instructor:

This is the Book of the Prince and, in undertaking its work, one begins to comprehend one's role as Prince within the cycle of YHWH as illustrated in our discussion of AL.

The First Gesture is The Oath of Enchantment which is called the Elevenfold Seal.

The first element is curiously described as "the animadversion towards the Aeon," which means a criticism or censure. It instructs, also, to turn towards Boleskine House, which is the House of the Beast 666, where, of old, the magician would turn towards the East. The operative element of that instruction is understood to be to turn towards the House of the Beast 666, wherever that is, by reference of the magician found, rather than towards the common East.

Now, the magician is to strike a battery in the following series: 1-3-3-3-1. This can be done with a chime, by clapping the hands, rapping the knuckles on a hard surface, or some other such means.

Attitude of The Hand

Next, the magician is directed to put their right hand so that the thumb protrudes from the fist like so:

First, a circle is made about the head with the right fist while intoning or crying out, "NUIT!"

Then, draw the thumb of the right hand down vertically and touch the Muladhara (*mu-LAHD-hahra*) Chakra while intoning or crying out, "HADIT!" The Muladhara is called the root chakra. Make no mistake in pretty language. This chakra is associated with the anus which we have already identified to you as the Eye of Horus, and the Master Therion understood that perfectly. Its symbol of a red four petaled lotus around a yellow square is no coincidental attribution.

From there, the right hand is raised along the same line to touch the center of the chest, while intoning or crying out, "RA-HOOR-KHUIT!"

Next, the hand is raised vertically to touch the center of the forehead, the mouth and the throat, while intoning or crying out, "AIWAZ!"

The thumb is then raised to be drawn from left to right across the face at the level of the nostrils, completing a cross.

The thumb is then lowered to touch the center of the breast, and then down to touch the solar plexus, while intoning or crying out, "THERION!"

The thumb is next raised and drawn from left to right across the breast at the level of the sternum, creating a second cross.

Finally, the thumb is touched to the Svadhisthana (svahd-HIST-hahna) chakra, the source of Eros and the creativity that accompanies it, located above the pubic bone and below the navel, and then again down to touch the Muladhara chakra, while intoning or crying out, "BABALON!"

The thumb is then drawn from right to left across the abdomen at the level of the hips, completing a third cross.

This cross with three lines makes the Cross or **Symbol of the Grand Hierophant,** depending from the Circle as shown on the Tracing Board.

SIGN OF THE GRAND HIEROPHANT

The next section is the Asseveration of the Spells, which means declaration or affirmation. These are described as the words of power by which the energies of the Aeon of Horus work his Will in the world.

The magician then clasps their hands upon their Wand, (or in the absence of the wand may use the same "fig" sign as above, or outstretched hand) fingers and thumbs interlaced while intoning or crying out, "LAShTAL! THELEMA! VIAOV! (oo-ee-AH-oh-oo) AGAPE! AUMGN!"

The next section is the The Proclamation of the Accomplishment which is somewhat self explanatory.

Next, a battery of 3-5-3 is stricken as before, with the cry of "ABRAHADABRA!"

Thus begins the Second Gesture or the Enchantment.

The magician, still facing the home of the Beast, advances to the edge of their circle and turns towards the left to pace around it, giving the **Sign of Horus or the Enterer** as they start to project the force that radiates from the Home of the Beast before themself, with "the stealth and swiftness of a tiger" for one complete circle, continuing until facing North.

Sign of
Horus the Enterer

Once they have reached the north, the magician traces the **Averse Pentagram proper to Air or Aquarius.** Upon completing the pentagram, bring the thumb or wand to the center of it and intone or cry out, "NUIT!"

AVERSE AIR

Puella

Sign of Hapocrates or Horus the Child

Puer

Next, make the sign called **Puella**, by placing the feet together and bowing the head, with the left hand shielding the Muladhara chakra and the right hand shielding the breast, also known as the attitude of the Venus de Medici.

Turning to the left the magician again makes the **Sign of Horus** and paces along the circumference of their circle until reaching the South. Facing outwards, trace the **Averse Pentagram of Fire** or Leo. Finish by bringing the wand or hand to the center of the pentagram and intone or cry out "HADIT!"

AVERSE FIRE

There is given the sign of **Puer,** done by placing the feet together with one's head erect. Raise the right arm, extending the right thumb at right angles to the fingers and holding the forearm at a right angle with the upper arm. The left hand is clenched into a fist with the thumb extended outward and should rest at the junction of the thighs in the attitude of the God Mentu, the Bull-God of Victory and of the self-begetting Bull God Khem, self and father of Horus.

AVERSE EARTH

Turning to the left the magician again makes the sign of Horus and paces along the circumference of their circle until reaching the East, where they make the **Averse Pentagram of Earth or Taurus.** Finish by bringing the wand or hand to the center of the pentagram and intone or cry out, "THERION!"

There is given the sign **Vir**, done by standing with the feet together, hands clenched fingers and thumbs thrust out held to the temples, head bowed and pushed out like the butting of a horned beast in the fashion of Pan or Bacchus.

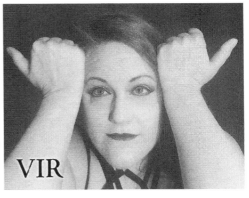

VIR

Turning to the left the magician again makes the sign of Horus and paces along the circumference of their circle until reaching the West, where they make the **Averse Pentagram of Water.** Finish by bringing the wand or hand to the center of the pentagram and intone or cry out, "BABALON!"

AVERSE WATER

There is given the sign **Mulier**, done by standing with the feet widely separated and the arms raised in a crescent. The head is thrown back in the attitude of Baphomet, Isis in Welcome.

Following this is a dance, a spiral widdershins (or anti-clockwise) with a revolution at each quarter until the magician comes to the center of the circle. There, facing the home of the Beast is traced the **Mark of the Beast**, while intoning or crying out "AIWAZ!"

MARK OF
THE BEAST

HEXAGRAM OF
THE BEAST

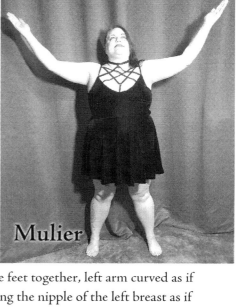

Mulier

Next, the magician traces the **Invoking Hexagram of the Beast**.

Then, the magician lowers the wand or hand to strike the ground.

There is given the sign of **Mater Triumphans,** done by standing with the feet together, left arm curved as if it supported a child; the thumb and index finger of the right hand pinching the nipple of the left breast as if offering it to that child. The word THELEMA is spoken.

The magician again performs the Spiral Dance, this time while moving deosil, or clockwise, and whirling widdershins, or anti-clockwise.

Each time on passing the west, extend the Wand or hand to the Quarter in question, and bow:

> To the West "Before me the powers of LA!"
>
> To the East "Behind me the powers of AL!"
>
> To the North "On my right hand the powers of LA!"
>
> To the South "On my left hand the powers of AL!"

Leaping into the air "Above me the powers of ShT!"

Note that it is entirely possible Crowley meant this to sound more or less like "Shit!" However how you should Shin-Teth is up to you. All of these could be sounded as the names of the letters, e.g. "the powers of Lamed Aleph" or "The powers of Shin Teth." Shin Teth may also be sounded as "Shuute" or in any other fashion that seems workable.

Striking the ground "Beneath me the powers of ShT!"

Mater
Triumphans

While standing in the attitude of Ptah erect, with feet together and hands clasped upon the wand: "Within me the Powers! About me flames my Father's Face, the Star of Force and Fire! And in the Column stands his six-rayed Spendor!"

This dance may be omitted and the whole utterance chanted in the **Attitude of Ptah.**

The Final Gesture is the same as the First Gesture.

The magician strikes a 1-3-3-3-1 battery.

Next, the magician is directed to put their right hand so that the thumb protrudes from the fist as indicated in **The Attitude of the Hand** to the right.

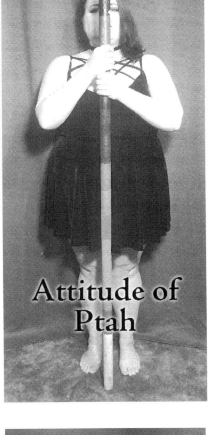

Attitude of Ptah

A circle is made about the head with the right fist while intoning or crying out, "NUIT!"

Draw the thumb of the right hand down vertically and touch the Muladhara Chakra while intoning or crying out, "HADIT!"

From there, the right hand is raised along the same line to touch the center of the chest, while intoning or crying out, "RA-HOOR-KHUIT!"

Next, the hand is raised vertically to touch the center of the forehead, the mouth and the throat, while intoning or crying out, "AIWAZ!"

The thumb is then raised to be drawn from left to right across the face at the level of the nostrils, completing a cross.

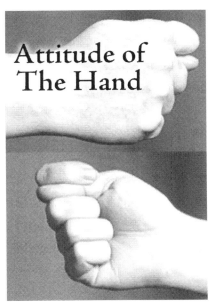

Attitude of The Hand

The thumb is then lowered to touch the center of the breast, and then down to touch the solar plexus, while intoning or crying out, "THERION!"

The thumb is next raised and drawn from left to right across the breast at the level of the sternum, creating a second cross.

Finally, the thumb is touched to the Svadhisthana (svahd-HIST-hahna) chakra, the source of Eros and the creativity that accompanies it, located above the pubic bone and below the navel, and then again down to touch the Muladhara chakra, while intoning or crying out, "BABALON!"

The thumb is then drawn from right to left across the abdomen at the level of the hips, completing the third cross.

The magician then clasps their hands upon their Wand, (or in the absence of the wand may use the same "fig" sign as above, or outstretched hand) fingers and thumbs interlaced while intoning or crying out, "LAShTAL! THELEMA! VIAOV! (oo-ee-AH-oh-oo) AGAPE! AUMGN!"

Finally, a battery of 3-5-3 is stricken as before, with the cry of "ABRAHADABRA!"

The performance of Liber V vel Reguli

The script of Liber V vel Reguli without annotation should be printed from the Appendices

If there are only a few Petitioners, or a single Petitioner, they may be led through the ritual in turn. If there is a group however they may be bid to omit the elements that take them from their places, and to walk through the ritual in place, turning rather than pacing the circle. Leading each of several Petitioners through the ritual will lengthen the initiation inordinately and should likely be avoided.

Summary

Summary of the Discussion of Liber V vel Reguli

Raimond:

Let us then relate the Formula we have learned to the Pillars of Thoth or Royal Arch of Enoch. Through LAShTAL we are told that all things are comprised of nothing and that the idea of permanence and stability is folly. This is the Lesson of the Pillars of Thoth. We live in a dynamic and ever-changing universe. So too, is the formula of LAShTAL the formula of the Child Horus, and this is how the Royal Arch relates to Eros and Sex Magick.

We understand that both pleasures and calamities must exist, and fear neither, for where all things are both zero and two, unitary and divided, all possibilities are ours to see. Rather than despising change, even that change which may intersect our orbit we learn to embrace change and take pleasure in its process.

We do not mistake for a moment our embrace of change with that despicable distancing with which those cowards who are impotent to change the world instead pretend disinterest in the miseries of others, or perversely, come to revel in them. They are prisoners who have come to love their prison. We recall as we learned in the previous initiation the point of annihilation of the Ego, the Secret of the Black Rite:

> My mind and body, deprived of the Ego which they had hitherto obeyed, were now free to manifest according to their nature in the world, to devote themselves to aid mankind in its evolution. In my case I was to be cast out into the Sphere of Jupiter. My mortal part was to help humanity by Jupiterian work, such as governing, teaching, creating, exhorting men to aspire to become nobler, holier, worthier, kinglier, kindlier, and more generous.[177]

Jeanne:

In our practice as magicians, we train ourselves to confront things which cause, "fear, pain, disgust, shame and the like,"[178] and first endure, then become indifferent to them. In this, they lose their power over us, and their ability thus to control the manifestation of our true will. Yet the Master Therion instructs us that once this has been completed we should abandon any things which are truly harmful in relation either to our health or comfort.[179] There is no virtue in permanent suffering or asceticism.

With each initiation comes ordeals. A truly wise magician might apprehend that to all people come ordeals. In truth it may be not so much that these initiations bring ordeal as that instead two factors collide. First, to become a magician is to create change in one's own life, and change seldom occurs without disruption.

Second, in those things which might before have seemed mere calamities of fate the magician may exert Will to profit by the challenge and thereby make what was previously mere suffering into ordeals.

Not every calamity must be taken as ordeal, it is a matter of Will, yet understanding these two things alone is given to you much power over the shape of Ordeal X.

Azalais:

The method of Liber V vel Reguli and the instruction which accompanies it is a practical method to place us in command of our world as Adepts, and is intended neither to humiliate nor endanger us

Those who take the road of attainment as an excuse to become villains, or to wallow in selfish neglect of others have already detoured into the pit of the abyss. They are the Dark Adepts.

In regards to Liber V vel Reguli, it is written. "Acts which are essentially dishonourable must not be done; they should be justified only by calm contemplation of their correctness in abstract cases." [180] We may overcome our prejudices by immersing ourselves in them, but we do not as it is written "overcome the distaste for dishonesty by forcing oneself to pick pockets."[181]

Exegesis of the Point of View of the magician - Good and Evil

Jeanne:

The worldview of the magician is a difficult trick and it must evolve, first to divest oneself of the illusions of the world and see all things for what they are without our prejudices and preferences, second to love all things within the pantacle.

To be driven by passion yet be dispassionate. And even so the magician must not lose that perspective that allows them to discern the course of true will and those principles which lead toward Union, the elements of Love.

The discernment of our pure will is a matter of our own understandings, informed by experience, credible knowledge, and an understanding of the core principles of Thelema starting with the three Principles we have already called out: That love is the Law, love under Will, that every person is a star, and that thou hast no right but to do thy will.

Raimond:

Over time, through the death of ego and that ascension which we call Mastery of the Temple, it becomes possible to feel instinctively the courses of the stars. This is a feeling quite distinct from that drive of "conscience" which is really the voice of our peers and social pressure to conform. We seek to break down those intolerances, whether prejudice on principle, or love of comfort, which have been visited upon us by society, yet to nurture and retain that intolerance of intolerance itself which distinguishes our understanding not only as Thelemites but as true Adepts.

The Master Therion has said "Each star is unique, and each orbit apart; indeed, that is the corner-stone of my teaching, to have no standard goals or standard ways, no orthodoxies and no code"[182]

We are taught that "the existence of 'Evil' is fatal to philosophy so long as it is supposed to be independent of conditions,"[183] and that the point of teaching the mind to "make no difference" between any two ideas in this way is to "emancipate it from the thralldom of terror."[184] It does not follow from those statements that all things are neutral with regards to us. The abjuration is against absolute ethics, we are to judge "evil" based on the conditions at hand. The war profiteer and the dutiful child may both steal bread, yet their acts are not the same. We understand and accept that nature does not care if we freeze or starve and accept that as a truth, may even appreciate beauty in our own starvation, yet it does not mean we do not care if we, or others, starve.

Nature is never bad, but the false will of others may be. Those acts which oppose the Law of Light, Life, Love and Liberty are most importantly restriction. I commend to your attention most especially that Essay entitled Duty[185] which establishes much of the framework by which we may apply the Law of Thelema to our daily lives. "The essence of crime is that it restricts the freedom of the individual outraged" Murder restricts the right to life; robbery, the right to the fruits of our work; fraud, our right to the guarantee of the state that we shall barter in security and so forth.[186] We are even given a rough guideline that judgment should be according to the "actual restriction created by the offense."[187]

This means that if someone steals from us, but their crime is driven by some gross restriction of their rights which we in fact supported ,it is we, not they who are in the wrong. We must consider not just those rights which we can see at the end of our arm, but all those which we influence even if they are hidden behind the horizon.

The lesson of the Royal Arch teaches us that that all things must fall, that change must come. But the formula of transmutation is put into our hands. We must be at once both the Architect, Thoth, laboring to preserve that which is good, and Isis who is above and outside and unaffected by good or ill.

As magicians our powers of transmutation shape the new Aeon and we assume personal responsibility to ensure that they support the law of light, life, love and liberty.

Azalais:

"Until the Great Work has been performed, it is presumptuous for the magician to pretend to understand the universe, and dictate its policy."[188] Only those who have gained Mastery of the Temple can say whether any given act is a crime.

"Then, and then only, art thou in harmony with the Movement of Things, thy will part of, and therefore equal to, the Will of God."[189]

This does not mean that we are obliged to act as naive children, credulously approving of every sort of Dark Adept, every falsehood and treachery. We strive to destroy those strictures which narrow our understandings. We are tolerant of all things, except for intolerance itself. [190]

Raimond:

On one hand we may not flinch to kill an enemy who is about to deliver a bomb load of oblivion upon our home and family. Yet we are not incapable of seeing that to derail the orbit of another star by murder in cold blood for the sake of pride or gain is no part of the law of light, life, love and liberty.

Azalais:

Likewise we do not see systems which force millions into poverty as mere neutrals because they are a result of zero equals two and happen to exist. The strictures we struggle against are not merely those that constrain our own behavior or our sexual freedom, but all those rules, traditions, and systems which restrain the freedom, constrain the true will, and intercept the course of any star in the company of stars, and we do not hesitate to challenge them.

Jeanne:

Fear not at all.[191]

Raimond:

I would finally commend to you to remember well our time here, and recall those things which you have been told which will admit you to the Initiation of the Second Degree. To that you are charged to bring a sword, at such length as you shall see fit, but manageable, by which you shall be made, should you choose, a Knight of the Rose Cross. You may find more guidance regarding the sword in Liber ABA, Book Four, Part 2, Chapter 8 "The Sword."

Seeing that you have been given all the Knowledge appropriate to a Magician, I ask that you review it with me, ere I pronounce you into the Logos.

Speak to me the Password of the First Degree.

Initiates:

Eros.

Raimond:

Give the Sign of the First Degree.

Initiates:

Give the sign of First Degree, The Grand Salute of the Royal Arch

Raimond:

What is the Formula of the First Degree?

Initiates:

LAShTAL.

Raimond:

And its elaboration, as you doubtless guess, is 93.

Having thus been given the signs, tokens, and knowledge of a Magician I name you as such. Timekeeper let the moment of this Initiation be recorded.

Timekeeper:

So mote it be!

Raimond:

> In closing, I will again recommend greatly for you as appropriate to your study that desert working which is recorded in *The Vision and the Voice* which is numbered 418. This is not merely a technical work, but a continuation of the revelation brought forth in *Liber AL*, and with several other works makes up the core of the inspired texts of Thelema.

> Grasping the core principles of Thelema is easy enough. However those who seek Mastery of the Temple will come to understand not only their own will but that which transpires around them, fluidly and reflexively.

> It is therefore our profound belief that the full understanding of this in the fashion of Thelema is accomplished through the study of not merely *Liber AL vel Legis*, but of all the inspired works of Thelema, as well as enough of the commentary and reflection on that text to render it in sufficient perspective that its full import may be absorbed.

The Fool:

> I have but one question before I guide our travelers on their path: The Secret Feast. Is Horus then, the Child of the Prophet?

Raimond:

> Yes and no. The Children of the Prophet certainly number among them that Logos which is in part the word of Ra-Hoor-Khuit. Tahuti is he who grants the words of life and the Feast is a celebration of the secret act which brought the Logos of the New Aeon.

The Fool:

> How do you know this is the true nature of the Secret Feast? Are not all the circumstances of the bringing forth of the Logos of the Aeon known?

Raimond:

> The circumstances yes are recorded on pages of Naught for anyone to read who has wisdom. For in truth in this case zero equals two. Now our time has come to an end. Our Feast is done and just begun. Let us have those readings which were indicated to you at the beginning of this ritual. When all is complete, as you would depart, take up your Pantacle from off the Altar, and know then that you are as of this moment recognized as a Magician and meet the world as such!

The Reading

First Reading

The first reading is from the *Magical Diaries of Aleister Crowley: Tunisia 1923*

"There seems to be much misunderstanding about True Will ... The fact of a person being a gentleman is as much an ineluctable (in-ELECT-able) factor as any possible spiritual experience; in fact, it is possible, even probable, that a man may be misled by the enthusiasm of an illumination, and if he should find apparent conflict between his spiritual duty and his duty to honour, it is almost sure evidence that a trap is being laid for him and he should unhesitatingly stick to the course which ordinary decency indicates. Error on such point is precisely the "folly" anticipated in…" *Liber AL* I: 36 "…and I wish to say definitely, once and for all, that people who do not understand and accept this position have utterly failed to grasp the fundamental principles of the Law of Thelema." [192]

Second Reading

The Second Reading is from *The Book of the Law*, Chapter One, Verse Forty Six

Nothing is a secret key of this law. Sixty-one the Jews call it; I call it eight, eighty, four hundred & eighteen. [193]

Third Reading

The Third Reading is from *The Confessions of Aleister Crowley, Chapter 66*

"We accordingly took loose rocks and built a great circle, inscribed with the words of power; and in the midst we erected an altar and there I sacrificed myself. The fire of the all-seeing sun smote down upon the altar, consuming utterly every particle of my personality. I am obliged to write in hieroglyph of this matter, because it concerns things of which it is unlawful to speak openly under penalty of the most dreadful punishment; but I may say that the essence of the matter was that I had hitherto clung to certain conceptions of conduct which, while perfectly proper from the standpoint of my human nature, were impertinent to initiation. I could not cross the Abyss till I had torn them out of my heart" [194]

Fourth Reading

The Fourth Reading is also from *The Confessions of Aleister Crowley*, Chapter 66

"The twelfth Aethyr describes the City of the Pyramids, whose Queen is called BABALON, the Scarlet Woman, in whose hand is a Cup filled with the blood of the saints. Her ecstasy is nourished by the desires which the Masters of the Temple have poured from their hearts for Her sake. In this symbolism are many mysteries concealed. One is that if a single drop of blood be withheld from Her Cup it putrefies the being below the Abyss, and vitiates the whole course of the Adept's career." [195]

The Fool: *Indicates by gestures or by whispers if necessary that the Initiates should process from the Temple. Other participants remain to close the Lodge.*

II° - Knight of the Rose Cross - Instructions

Major Properties

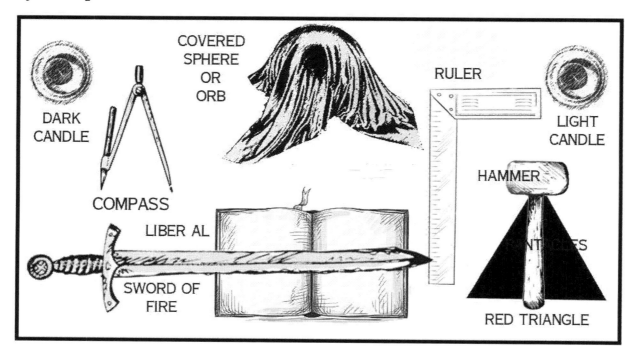

THE SETTING OF THE PRINCIPAL ALTAR

See the appendices for a printable checklist of Properties by location

The Altar Elements

- **The Orb** is rather large, the size of a large upright and oval about 8-10 inches high and 6-8 inches side to side It is never seen and so it could be made from any object, or even a bundle of cloth and duct tape.

- **Cloth Cover for Orb** – large enough to completely cover the orb, leaving no part of it exposed

- **Masonic Tools** – to the degree possible, the tools should be "archaic" - the sort that can be easily purchased at antique stores or online. It would be best if these were large enough not to seem comical as weapons.

  - Hammer
  - Compass
  - Ruler

Other Ritual Elements

- **Tracing Board** – Prepared according to the Illustration. Ideally the board would be hand painted but it may be copied and pasted onto cardboard.

Stone Elements

The Fall of the Stone – the fall of the stone is the first major SFX operation within the initiations. A stone, presumably thrown from a siege engine, crashes through a roof/wall/window with a loud sound, and hits one of the performers, showering debris on the initiates.

The Stone – the stone is square, with a Hebrew Character hewn into each face.

- This could be in simplest form, a cardboard or styrofoam cube, written on and painted to resemble stone. The stone may be only roughly cubical (it is not a dice) and the lower surface may suggest it was once connected to something else.

- Rust-Oleum American Accents Stone Spray and Krylon Stone Coarse Texture are two widely available US brands which allow for rapid painting of objects to resemble stone.

- Be aware that styrofoam tends to melt slightly on contact with spraypaint and test extensively. Be aware that this type of craft paints can produce dangerous vapors in enclosed spaces.

- Be conscious of eye and dental safety. The line of "flight" for the stone should not allow for the potential to hit an initiate or other performer in the face, and should strike the target on the chest or arm, not the head or face.

- The target can be coached to throw their arm across their face at the crash to further ensure eye and dental safety.

  Each face should be inscribed as follows:
  - The face on which "Heh" is written is inset or boxed.
  - Aleph
  - Mem
  - Yod
  - Lamed
  - The face opposite "Heh" may be blank.

The Debris – the debris is hurled onto the heads of the initiates at the moment the stone is supposed to crash through the ceiling.

- The debris should not harm anyone, and thought should be given to cleanup. In general any actual debris is likely too hard and may also contain allergens. The idea is not to *actually* clear out the initiation hall.

- Consideration needs to be given not only to having debris that is not heavy enough to do injury, but to eyes, as someone could "look up" just as the debris is being thrown.

- Initial experiments settled on brown, gray, and black crinkle-cut decorative paper, widely available form party stores and online, as a satisfactory substance which is easier to clean than confetti. This is essentially designed to be thrown on people.

- Other small, safe debris such as Styrofoam could be used.

- With sufficient control, larger light debris could be used which was not intended or allowed to hit anyone unprepared. For example, an entire faux wall of Styrofoam could be made to collapse, provided there was sufficient space. Provided it is safe this can be a major undertaking in special effects.

- Prepared Performers (not initiates) may choose to allow themselves to be struck with larger (safe) debris made of Styrofoam, cardboard, etc., however no-one should be forced into this.
- A "dust" effect could be gotten in some spaces using flour. However, this should not be overdone, and there should be an explicit warning as breathing flour dust can cause problems for breathing including allergy and asthma attacks.
- Talc should not be used as it has been determined to be carcinogenic.
- It is explicitly stated that no pyrotechnics should be used. While flaming projectiles were hurled in the siege, the stone does not represent one and pyrotechnics introduce a level of danger that requires professional expertise.

Sound – the fall of the stone should be accompanied by a sudden powerful "crash." This could be a recorded sound via stereo, or could be accomplished by dropping some heavy or loud object.

- A particularly good effect would be to have an absent performer drop a heavy object on the floor immediately above the initiates heads in a two-story building.

Readings

- **Readings** on printed cards or sheets

Properties for the Play

- **Scripts for the Play** – these should be ready to read. Readability is favored over authenticity so these should not be printed in a historic font. Ideally they can be presented in neat black binders

The Books

These are not really books, but binding covers for scripts. In general a binder from an office supply company, covered with decorative paper, leather or fabric, is probably preferential for ease of use. The binders should be neat and easy to use and not kept cluttered with unrelated material. A larger binder may be used for carrying multiple scripts.

- **Book M** – This Book may be bound with either a plain or fancy cover. It is the work of Rosicrucians, and may contain Rosicrucian symbols, etc. The Roman Letter "M" must be clearly legible from a distance.

Properties for Restraint, Binding and Hoodwinking

- **Sword** – see the details under Initiation Team Negotiations in the discussion of Raimond D'Afaro. The sword may be either a good quality faux weapon, or an actual sword, however it must be used carefully if a real weapon is to be used.

- **Bonds (1 per initiate)** – see the write-up on binding materials under Initiate Negotiations

- **Hoodwinks (1 per initiate)** – see the write up on binding materials under Initiate Negotiations

- **EMT Shears** – good quality and serviceable

Generic Properties

These properties should be fairly easy to come by at a given locale or purchase from a grocery store.

- **Lighter** – A reliable grill lighter, or high quality long matches should be used. A search on "candle lighter with bell snuffer" will reveal a number of church-style lighters which run on a replaceable wick. These can be lit from the Candle of the hours after the initial Temple opening. A small lighter in the 18" range is generally best, unless one is dealing with a particularly large Temple space.

- **Three Chairs** – Three chairs together, with the one to the right, as one stands facing them, somehow visibly denoted as a throne, either by being larger, more elevated, etc.

- **Chair Cover** – If the same room is used for the hoodwinking and binding as for the reception by Esclarmonde, the chairs should be covered with a sheet, etc. or otherwise concealed so that there is some appearance of being in a "new space."

- **Sideboard** – This may be any small or medium-sized table at the side of the room, which is used for various implements when they are not being used on the altar. It is used for a candle and so should be safe and away from any sources of combustion.

- **Altar** – This must be large and sturdy enough to accommodate a sword, the implements, and two candles without being in danger of tipping. In general, a size of 40"-50", and a depth of 14-18" or larger, is preferable.

- **Timepiece** - a timepiece to record the time of initiation

- **Note Paper and Writing Implement** - to record the time of initiation

The Feast Food

The II° has a feast, but it is purely symbolic. It should consist of foods that are "unpleasant" or represent "stored food" but safely edible. Saltines or stale bread would be a minimum. Ideally, there would also be roots that can be eaten raw, such as horseradish or carrots. Only small quantities are needed. An ideal menu would be, for each person:

- a stale cracker or piece of bread
- a slice of horseradish
- raisins or other old country (not tropical) dried fruit

Other elements could be added, but that's a good basis. This is a meal of hardship.

The cost of the feast should be budgeted as part of the overall initiation.

Dramatis Personae (Principals)

Esclarmonde de Foix   (*ess-KLAR-mahnd duh FWAH*)
Guillemette de Toulouse (*GEE-uh-met 'g' as in gun*)
Count Raimond (*RAY-mawn duh TOO-lose*)
Raimond d'Alfaro (*RAY-mawn DOWL-far-oh*)

The above roles of Principals may be filled by anyone who is already initiated to II°. In general, the Sovereign Initiator will take the role of The Fool or Esclarmonde, according to their Will, as those roles have the greatest ability to "guide" the experience of initiation. Technically speaking, the Sovereign Initiator is not obligated to take *any* speaking part. However, this would only tend to be the case in a situation where new Initiators were being trained.

The roles of Players in the play-within-a-play are preferentially filled by initiates, but any remaining roles may be played by any other attendees, or by other Principals.

Initiation Team Negotiations

- Discussion with the performer of the Raimond d'Alfaro on how to hold the blade safely so that, even if there is an accident, the initiates and other performers may not fall onto the blade and be injured.
  - If a real blade is used, the blade should be held crosswise, as a barrier, point slightly down, rather than thrust out at the Initiates.
  - If a false blade is used the performer should still be reminded not to move it in ways that may strike someone or inadvertently strike other properties, damaging them.
- Discussion with the performer of the Raimond d'Alfaro role on where and how they are to be hit with the stone.
  - Ensure there is a flight path clear of initiates or any Principals.
  - Ensure appropriate cues so that Raimond is able to be in a defensive position expecting the stone.
  - Ensure that the person responsible for special effects and the Raimond performer have specifically discussed the special effects with each other and there are no misunderstandings.
- Discussion with anyone else in the path of the debris or stone to ensure they are safely and properly prepared
- Discussion with the performer of Guillemette on how to safely "bind" and hoodwink the initiates (See Negotiations with Initiates – Binding and Hoodwinking)
  - How to bind wrists safely and without undue pressure
  - Location of safety shears
  - Particular emphasis on doing a final check on any initiate-specific issues in terms of hard limits.

Initiate Negotiations

These are the general issues which should be disclosed and which may require negotiations. At a minimum, the Sovereign Initiator should review with each candidate for initiation their Petition and ensure that they do not have any issues or concerns.

Binding

- The act of tying someone's wrists is bondage, even though it is fairly minor. There is a world of literature on doing bondage safely, and this act of bondage should be safe.

- Binding Practices
  - A safe tie or pre-tied rope cuff arrangement should be used
    - There is no one specific knot that is required, however the knots used should be simple and safe, particularly avoiding tight tying or placing pressure on the wrist.
    - A viable tie which has been recommended to us is the Somerville Bowline, which can be seen at https://www.youtube.com/watch?v=X2C3QM3Q_dE in a video by Lochai Stine.
    - The most qualified person may do the binding, regardless of their putative role.
  - Sovereign Initiators should make themselves familiar with basic rope bondage safety.
- Binding Materials
  - Only rope should be used for binding wrists.
  - Cloth, string and other substitutes can cut into the flesh, or become difficult to remove in an emergency due to knotting, and should be avoided. If they are used in an emergency, they should be tied so that they can slip off easily, and cannot pull tight.
  - Metal shackles, plastic ties, or any form of handcuffs may not be used in any circumstances.
  - At the discretion of the Sovereign Initiator, wrist cuffs which fasten or secure with a buckle or similar device may be used if they are:
    - non-locking
    - made of a material which can be cut with shears
    - are made of a material which can be safely cleaned (e.g. nylon, not leather)
    - If they are provided by the initiate they do not need to be cleanable, but the initiate must agree they may be cut in an emergency at the discretion of the Sovereign Initiator or their designate.
  - At the discretion of the Sovereign Initiator, pull-on/pull-off "Halloween" type shackles that do not *actually* restrain may be used, but only in the case that they can slide on and off without the use of any force. These may be a safe alternative if no-one knows how to tie safely, however they should be checked to ensure they are the correct size and do not interfere with circulation.
- **Good quality, serviceable, EMT/Emergency shears** should always be present.
  - The Sovereign Initiator and the person performing the role of Guillemette should know where they are, and they should be within easy reach; not in another room.
  - They may be located on the sideboard.
- Consider any trip hazards.
  - If there are any issues, the Initiates may be hoodwinked and bound only once they have been moved into final position before Esclarmonde. *This is preferable to creating a safety risk.*
- Consider what would happen if the initiate fainted or fell. Have a First Aid plan.
- Provide support for any initiate who is being moved while restrained.
  - If there are not enough performers, move initiates one at a time.

- Bonds are symbolic, and no effort should be made to make them tight. However, it is still possible that bonds could be pulled tight during a fall or other mishap and, if this occurs, the Sovereign Initiator should assess for potential nerve damage.
  - In the absence of an Initiation Team Member professionally competent to assess potential nerve damage, a copy of the Motor Function Assessment for Nerve Injury resource http://www.frozenmeursault.com/nerve-injury-reference-card/ or another comparable resource should be on hand.
- While the bonds are a significant element, if no safe bonds are available, *it is better to pantomime this element entirely* than to create a safety risk.
- Bonds must be removed immediately if any initiate indicates discomfort for any reason.
  - If bonds cannot be untied in a timely fashion they should be cut using the available shears.

Hoodwinking

- Blindfolds should not be used except as a negotiated substitution or in extremis.
- Hoods should be made of soft, breathable cloth, primarily of natural fiber, of no more than a double layer
  - Dark cotton pillowcases are ideal
  - Burlap or other "traditional" hoods may be used, but they must be washable and tested for allergens
- Hoods must be able to be laundered
- Hoods must be laundered prior to each use
  - Care should be taken with fabric softeners which may cause allergic reactions
- Hoods should be tested for breathability by the Sovereign Initiator
- Hoods are *never secured in any way* or situated so as to create *any* tightness around the neck
- Hoods must be removed immediately if any initiate indicates discomfort for any reason

Play-Within-a-Play

- This ritual contains a portion in which a play-within-a-play occurs, in which you may be asked to take a script and play act with others. No memorization is required.
- Potential Limits/Problems
  - Loud noise, being pelted with light debris
  - Dust if flour or some related substance is used with the debris
  - Stage fright, issues with reading, or reading aloud
  - The ritual "play within a play" contains discussion of, though not portrayal of, rape and torture
  - The ritual "play within a play" contains discussion of military actions against various peoples. This is a matter the Sovereign Initiator may discuss with anyone who seems particularly sensitive, but the topics are well within the boundaries of mainstream network and cable programming, and we feel most people could reasonably anticipate that any play involving the Templars would contain references to military actions.

- Because of the historic periods the play deals with the cast is largely made up of characters that are male, and this may be a point of criticism. Serious consideration was give to this point, however it was determined that:

  - The portrayals are realistic and faithful to the era. Attempting to develop "throwaway" or fictional female characters for "balance" also sanitizes and whitewashes the historical record, and undercuts the attempt to present these matters realistically.

  - Considerable time was expended on research to find any potential female characters for the Templar arc. Unlike the Hospitallers, the Templars did not tend to involve women, and those roles which could be historically confirmed tended to be very unequal. The only other potential involvement of women was as victims, which we did not feel improved the situation.

  - In general the presentation of the Occitan characters has been heavily driven by women creating overall balance within the Initiations.

  - It is especially important that Sovereign Initiators encourage women to take roles, including strong leading roles, in the Templar Play. The absence of women from the Templar historical record should not mean an absence of women within our portrayal.

- Possible remedies – stage fright, reading aloud

  - Candidate may be specifically given a part which has fewer lines (see roles below)

  - Candidate may choose not to read a role at all

- Possible remedies – rape and torture

  While this is an important warning to give, the references to these elements are well within the boundaries of network television and the warnings do not need to be overstated. They also comprise specific historic background references, attested to in documents.

  - Explain that the roles in which this language is used involve the portrayal of a villain, and that these activities are not graphically depicted.

  - Anyone still not comfortable with this language should be excused from playing one of the three villains

  - In extremis, someone may be excused from the play, or the end of the play, and merely told the story of what happens, or allowed to read the section.

Casting Imperatives

- All the Templars are militant men who have engaged in military campaigns
- Most of the Templars have views on race and gender roles which are markedly more "medieval" and less "modern" than those of the Occitan hosts.
- De Villiers and de Pairaud are, at a minimum, guilty of tolerating rape, torture, and other crimes beyond even the level that was considered "acceptable" for political leaders of the time.
- For purposes of casting, only Jacques de Molay overlaps in acts, nor do the narrators. Thus, the entire play could be performed with only four performers.

The Roles

- **Interlude/Narrators**
  - *Secretary* – young and does not speak much, an easy role
  - *Visitor* – moderate number of lines
  - *Johann Valentin Andreae*[196] (YO-han VAL-in-teen AN-dree) – the progenitor of modern Rosicrucianism. Moderate number of lines

- **All Acts**
  - *Jacques de Molay* (ZHOCK day MOW-lay) – Grand Master of Templars with Many lines

- Act I
  - *Matthieu Sauvage*[197] (MATT-ee-oo SOE-vahj) – An Old and Wise Templar Knight, moderate lines
  - *Otto of Granson* (AH-toe of GRAHN-sun) – A Knight of Burgundy in service to the English King, moderate lines

- Act II
  - *Templar1* – Minimal Lines
  - *Gerard de Villiers* (ZHER-ard duh Vee-yay) – a villainous Templar, associated with rape as well as other notorious and dishonorable crimes. Villiers does not see himself as a villain.

- Act III
  - *Hughes de Pairaud* (OOgh duh PAY-row) - a formerly villainous Templar, guilty of serious crimes in the past, which are implied to potentially include rape as well as other notorious and dishonorable crimes. Pairaud does not see himself as a villain, but recognizes that his past actions were wrong.
  - *Guy de Charnay* (GEE duh SHAR-nay g as in gun) - A generally honorable Templar Knight.

Safety Concerns

- Check for dietary issues regarding the food
- Check for allergies to any incense planned for use of incense
- For Stone – weight/safety
- For Debris
  - Weight/safety
  - Allergies to any particulates
- For noise – safety, negotiations
- Standard Fire Safety
  - Extinguisher
- Standard Medical Safety
  - First Aid Kit
  - Certified First Aid Training
  - EMT Shears (good condition, serviceable)
  - Motor Function Assessment for Nerve Injury

II° Initiation – Script

Prologue

This is delivered outside the Initiation space or, if that is not plausible, before the Initiation candidates have been excused to open the Temple. This may overlap with the Opening of the Lodge, though it may take somewhat longer.

The Sovereign Initiator should ensure that each initiate has a sword. It may be expedient to have a few spares on hand in case one has been lost or forgotten. In extremis, the Altar Sword may be offered as it serves no formal function in the initiation.

If a sword is lost through no fault of the initiate, e.g. it was lost by an airline, then the Sovereign Initiator should of course be sympathetic. If the sword was merely forgotten, the Sovereign initiator would do well to warn the initiate in a firm, friendly, and gentle way that moving forward the initiations may not be able to be so accommodating.

The Fool:

> If you remember from your previous two initiations there was a lengthy discussion of initiation. You have come here today in the role of a Magician, who seems to assume the heavy responsibility of Knight of the Rose Cross in our Sovereign Sanctuary.
>
> It is useful to tell you something about what that means. From your previous initiation you have already gotten the idea that the work of a Magus entails responsibility. The Sovereign Sanctuary of the Initiatory Arm of the Thelemic Initiations does not command your obedience except in certain very limited ways, chiefly secrecy, and honesty and transparency if you act in the role of Sovereign Initiator. You do not serve the Sovereign Sanctuary, or even that order which true name is mentioned only within the Initiations except as you have specifically agreed.
>
> You have, however, become increasingly obligated to serve your Will, and to work aggressively to determine the nature of your Will. This Initiation will not only deepen that obligation, but formally recognize the obligation that we feel is already implicit in Thelema of aiding others in the accomplishment of their Wills.
>
> You will have noted that we have already spread out maps that in historical orders were withheld long past these Foundational Grades. This is the New Aeon and we have no time for timidity. These initiations are designed for those who are Magicians and intend to attain Mastery of the Temple and embody the role of the Magus.
>
> You may already have experienced disruption in your life. This is not entirely a factor of magic. Awareness may lead you to force change where you would have avoided it before. Likewise, you may choose to accept what would previously have been random chaos as ordeals to strengthen your Adeptship.
>
> It is not the nature of these initiations to bring chaos or trials to your life. But pushing a boat from the safety of the sands into a mighty river will cause it to be jostled and even in some cases threatened. All motion is change, and change brings both good and ill. Likewise, once the boat is in the grip of the current it may be difficult or impossible to turn it back to safety without swamping it. Consider this when you are given the opportunity to wait to initiate.

You will face challenges as you begin the work mandated in this Initiation. They will be answered only by the diligent beginning of the work described. Once you have earnestly begun that work and understand what it means to begin that work, you may return for further initiation.

In regards to your obligations, we will briefly recap what you have been told before:

Unlike other Orders, our higher degrees exist only for the purpose of attainment, and do not grant wide or sweeping temporal powers of leadership. The leadership of this order rests primarily in the Supreme Senate of the Third Degree, and by advancing to the Second Degree you may reasonably expect, within a proximate and foreseeable time, to be a member of the Supreme Senate if you continue to advance. There will be no prolonged childhood, you will be thrust into a role of guidance and leadership. You will not be asked to initiate to the Third or Fourth Degree until you are ready, but understand that taking the Second Degree puts you on a path where many factors in your life, internal and external will drive you inexorably towards those initiations.

We do not ask for an Oath to any living being, or Organization, including our Sovereign Sanctuary, except in regards to basic privacy and secrecy.

Your Oath of secrecy regarding the initiations still holds, and I am asked by the Supreme Senate of the Third Degree to remind you of this oath. .

We ask that you refrain in act and in spirit from:

- giving out in written or in verbal form the exact words of the initiations, though where they quote from ancient sources those may be freely discussed.
- describing in synoptic detail the general course and outline by part, or the specific roles and speeches of the characters within the initiations.
- transmitting in any way the various words and signs of the degrees. These are important because they do serve to some extent as guarantors that someone attending an initiation has been exposed to this talk and others, and is thus duly informed as to safety and behavior.
- acting as an initiator into these specific mysteries, as written, without the due authorization of the Sovereign Sanctuary.
- We further ask that you please remember: that in deciding how to speak you err on the side of caution and, when in doubt, embrace the fourth power of the Sphinx which is silence.
- We remind you that it is your role only to police your own speech and that the obedience of other initiates to these oaths must be judge by themselves.

You have thus far vowed to:

- Walk the path of the Magician and seek your true will
- To understand the nature of Love
- To invoke the Aeon of Horus
- To embody the energies of the Aeon of Horus

Review of the Oath

The Fool:

With the upcoming initiation, you will vow to take responsibility for others without asserting leadership of them, to begin the perfection of your exercise of Will, and to invoke your Holy Guardian Angel. Let us review the Oath.

I --- *State your Name* --- do solemnly promise in the sight of the one secret and ineffable Lord, and in the sight of all stars in the company of stars that I shall do these things to the best of my understanding:

- I shall walk the path of the Rose Cross Knight
- I shall take responsibility for all other pilgrims who share the road with me; to guard their well-being, whether it be to aid them in obtaining knowledge or, as I am able, shelter or sustenance
- That I am by this initiation created guard, neither master, nor guide, nor shepherd, any manner of leader†
- I shall work to perfect restraint from the slightest exercise of my will against another being; with the intent that subsequently I shall exercise my will without the least consideration for any other being.‡
- I shall invoke without reserve my Holy Guardian Angel

So mote it be.

Leave to Depart

The Fool may explain what provisions have been made for anyone who wishes to leave, whether there is a waiting area, etc. In general, it is best if there is one person who can remain outside with anyone who chooses to leave the ritual if they are not also leaving the premises.

The Fool may explain how any refund is to be issued. The terms of initiation should be explained in advance.

The Fool may take a moment to ensure everyone has had water, used the restroom, etc., creating a pause in which anyone who chooses not to take initiation may leave.

The Fool:

As ever I am your confidant and guide. By now you may know or guess why. If you have questions or ought occurs that troubles you, you may pull me aside and ask only of me. I will remind you again that you may take me aside or ask questions of me, but that you should not disrupt the flow of the story. The people are not people and the places not places, and like the pages of a book they are fragile and may be torn. But I am made of the same stuff as you.

The Welcome

Guillemette: Gestures, urging the initiates into the room as if they might be harried by someone just behind.

Get in, quick!

Raimond d'Alfaro: His drawn sword is dropped, point down.

Quick quick as you love your lives pass through the gate now!

The Thelemic Initiations

The two hustle the initiates through the entryway and into an open area. The open area may be the actual chamber of Initiation, or a foyer. The three chairs at the front should be covered

What is the pass-word of the day?

*Whatever password is given, it shall be rejected, for it is not the password of the day. Raimond raises his blade. **The utmost care should be used to ensure that the raised blade does not present an actual hazard.** A false blade of wood or other more modern material may be used. If a real blade is used, it should be presented as a barrier, side on, rather than point first, and the point should never be thrust at the initiates.*

Raimond d'Alfaro:

Put your hands behind your back that my mother may bind you!

The Fool:

Put down that sharp weapon, for I see that you are but a child of tender years and can have no knowledge of its use.

Raimond d'Alfaro:

Child I may be, but I am squire to a knight and I command here under my mother who is daughter of our Count, and Esclarmonde of Foix (*ACE-clare-mawnd* of *FWAH*) who is Chatelaine (*SHAT-uh-lin*) by my Grandfather's word. I have steel and by the Rose Red Cross upon my breast if you do not place your hands behind your back there will be blood upon the floor this day.

Guillemette:

Good travelers, know that, if you are, in truth, friends of the rightful and true Count of Toulouse and his heir, you will come to no harm at our hands.

The Fool:

What pass is it that this child who cannot have seen ten summers guards the gates of the City of Toulouse? It is best we do what they ask, for it is clear that fog or fear of war is upon them. We know well that we have the pass-words and, if we satisfy them that we mean no harm, I am sure they will show their honor by releasing us.

Raimond d'Alfaro: *Steps away, raising his sword.*

Bind them mother, lest it prove they have entered after the fashion of the Assassins to solve the question of this siege by murder. Hoodwink them as well that they may not disclose aught of our situation.

Guillemette: *binds and hoodwinks the initiates. See the grade specific instructions for details, however the emphasis should be on safety. If it is possible the initiates may be marched back and forth, in a circle, or even taken into another room until Esclarmonde can enter and be seated. She may be assisted by others present who are not performers.*

There are three chairs at the front. Esclarmonde sits in a chair facing the initiates. Guillemette stands just before them to their left, Raimond d'Alfaro to their right.

Esclarmonde:

My kin-by-law, the good and young Squire Raimond d'Alfaro, son of Hughes d'Alfaro,[198] whom have you brought before the seat of the one indisputable and rightful Count Palatine of Toulouse?

Raimond d'Alfaro:

I present the Lady Esclarmonde of Foix, sister to our ally and great friend Raimond-Roger of Foix,[199] and at present Chatelaine of Toulouse at the behest of Count Raimond, rightful Count of this City. Explain you now your entry to this place.

The Fool:

These are travelers who of old were accustomed to enjoy the liberty and trust of this place. They were given by the Count divers signs and tokens that they might be known. Beg we ask who sits upon the seat of Raimond Count of Toulouse? And what befalls that we pass this gate in mortal danger?

Esclarmonde:

It augurs well that you speak the name of Raimond as Count of Toulouse. You came then without knowledge that we were besieged? It is well fated that you came when you did, for the men of Count Simon[200] have advanced past the Oratory Elm[201] and, had they been out in force, you might well have been cut down with crossbow shafts or feathered arrows. Boy, tell them of the fighting, for you have been to see.

Raimond d'Alfaro:

There has been much fighting today with many stones cast back and forth, where our hearty defenders are building up the walls and shelters. Everywhere among our seigers was the shattering of skulls, brains, chests, chins, arms, legs, and the scattering of many lumps of sweaty flesh.[202] Among our own people however were only a few slain. To this great distraction you owe the freedom of movement that brought you here.

The Fool:

How is it that a child narrates such terrible sights.

Esclarmonde:

You were warned the fight here would not be metaphorical.

Raimond d'Alfaro:

I do not fear the fighting. Even now, the nephew of Lady Esclarmonde, the noble Roger-Bernard,[203] and my father, the noble Hughes, prepare to sortie and destroy the cat[204] which Count Simon[205] has caused to be brought up against us.[206]

The Fool:

You are besieged by a feline?

Esclarmonde:

So it is called, a shelter by which they may come against our works, but our carpenters are building at Saint Semin a great War-Engine which shall be dragged up and I and the other noble ladies shall make of it a scorpion to put the sting of death upon this feline and its Master, for we are no mice. But you say that you are friends of this Court. Can you prove it so?

The Fool:

These travelers were given the honor of being Companions of the Royal Arch of Enoch and have journeyed a great distance to offer themselves as Knights of the Rose Cross. They were given...we were given...words by the Count himself and before that by the Lady Azalais. If the Count is occupied with matters of war, then I am certain that the Lady Azalais or Queen Jeanne could confirm the words and signs.

Esclarmonde:

Too late you come. For nearly two decades have those noble ladies lain cold. Today I am seated where Queen Jeanne once sat, though I cannot fill her chair or that of my kin, the noble Azalais. Yet you shall find me as subtle of wit as they and, in the secrets of the Good People and the Book, I am well versed.

The Fool:

What book, pray tell?

Esclarmonde:

Let their eyes be opened.

The hoodwinks and bindings are removed from the initiates.

The book *M*, which was brought from the far East, away beyond the Levant. But now you shall be tried as to your knowledge.

When you were received by the Count, you were given a password for the Royal Arch or Pillars of Thoth. I ask now that you convey it to me.

In asking for the signs, the order in which the initiates are called on should be random, so that if possible each initiate is called on to answer for some part of them. If an initiate does not remember the answer they may be prompted by the Fool with a hint.

Initiate:

Eros

Esclarmonde:

And you, what is its meaning?

Initiate: *Any reasonable answer signifying "sexual" or "creative" love is acceptable. If they give the Masonic word, JABULON, they will be politely acknowledged but asked for the Thelemic word.*

Esclarmonde:

And what sign were you given?

Initiates: *give the I° sign, that of the Royal Arch*

Esclarmonde:

And you, what is the formula of the grade?

Initiate:

LAShTAL

Raimond d'Alfaro:

And you would you tell me its elaboration?

Initiate:

93

Esclarmonde:

The Petitioners have proven themselves to be worthy and honored guests, and also by their understanding of the formula of LAShTAL true Magicians, seeking further enlightenment and attainment. Please, introduce yourselves.

Initiates: *Introduce themselves*

Esclarmonde:

Finally, I shall ask them for a token not only of seeking, but of capacity to undertake the perilous commitment of Knights of the Rose Cross. Do you then bear swords which signify, not only your willingness, but your readiness to receive patent of arms and serve as knights?

Initiates: *affirm that they have swords. The Senior Initiator should have seen to this before the start of the initiation. If anyone's sword has been forgotten or lost it may be replaced before the ceremony begins.*

Esclarmonde:

Night falls soon, but the light in the west has not yet gone out completely. When it does, we shall offer you what hospitality we may. In the meantime I shall prepare you in the first lessons of a Rose Cross Knight, that, when the Count returns from the ramparts, he may confer that honor upon you immediately.

As a start I will vouchsafe to you the password of the Second Degree of the Most Ancient Order of the Defenders of the Temple of the East and of the Hermetic Fellowship of Light. The Password is *Pragma* which is the root of our word pragmatism and in Greek means "with business way,"[207] as we are commanded.

The Fool:

All right, enough of this. We came here for mysticism, not popular psychology. I was willing to grant you *Ludus* and *Eros*, but...this is no ancient Greek system. It's a modern conceptualization of Love.

Esclarmonde:

I might have known that you would challenge me, but if you think that you will find me more easily cowed than those whose seat I fill, O Fool, you are very much mistaken. My name means the "Clarity of the

The Thelemic Initiations

World." And you are correct in part. The particular breakdown of "love" into Greek terms pertains to your time, as, I remind you, does much of Thelemic practice itself. Yet the Greeks had many words and concepts for "love" as did many other ancient peoples, and the concept is not new, merely clarified. As well, Thelema embraces "Agape" however this is a word used only infrequently by the Greeks themselves.

When the Master Therion first wrote it was quite obscure, though he doubtless learned it originally from Christians, but in the day of your travelers Christians of an evangelizing bent have taken the term and dragged it through the mud. As you learned when you were here previously, Union is philosophically complex, and Agape was and is a perfection of that Union.

A Pragmatic Exegesis of Thelemic Union and Love

The Fool:

But everyone knows that Thelemic Love isn't love at all. It's the Philosopher's stone, cold and dispassionate, the thing which brings about the union of opposites and their annihilation. I've been studying. It doesn't have anything to do with actual love, sentiment, or compassion.

Esclarmonde:

Do you think this shall go better for you the second time around O Fool? Guillemette, would you instruct this Fool? Or perhaps the child Raimond could do so?

Raimond d'Alfaro:

I have read in the book "The Love of Liber Legis is always bold, virile, even orgiastic. There is delicacy, but it is the delicacy of strength. Mighty and terrible and glorious as it is, however, it is but the pennon upon the sacred lance of Will, the damascened (*DAH-muh-seend*) inscription upon the swords of the Knight-monks of Thelema."[208]

The Fool:

Cute kid to talk of orgiastic love. You allow that?

Guillemette:

He is less a child than you are a Fool. Immortal archetypes learn things, and even he knows that Love is not a dispassionate operation of metallurgy. It is written "I have made Matter and Motion for my mirror; I have decreed for my delight that Nothingness should figure itself as twain, that I might dream a dance of names and natures, and enjoy the substance of simplicity by watching the wanderings of my shadows?" and further on "For I am Love, whereby division dies in delight"[209]

So if you take Love to be the ultimate union, we identify those natures which drive towards it. You might put any name on them you please, divide them by any scheme. The names are infinite, but of the natures we present a rough model, so that the totality of Agape may be better understood.

The Fool:

But these things are just human emotions.

Vol. I, 0° Petitioner - II° K.R.C.   225

Esclarmonde:

And of what do you think those natures are comprised? The physicians of old understood that our passions were driven by fluids, not metaphysical, but resident within the body. Paracelsus refined the old system of humors to our three: salt, sulphur, and mercury, and these lay at the root of our cross and circle. Our analysis of the humors today yields greater complexity, yet the seed understanding, that the transformation of salt and sulphur through mercury drives our passions, is not much different.

We are instructed "Let then the Philosophus meditate upon all love that hath ever stirred him," and hereafter are named many loves of many types without regard to the presence of sex, or gender, or even humanity, after which the seeker is told, "Now do thou take one such story every night, and enact it in thy mind, grasping each identity with infinite care and zest, and do thou figure thyself as one of the lovers and thy Deity as the other. Thus do thou pass through all adventures of love, not omitting one; and to each do thou conclude: How pale a reflection is this of my love for this Deity!

"Yet from each shalt thou draw some knowledge of love, some intimacy with love, that shall aid thee to perfect thy love. Thus learn the humility of love from one, its obedience from another, its intensity from a third, its purity from a fourth, its peace from yet a fifth."[210]

We are bid to "extend the dominion of our consciousness, and its control of all forces alien to it, to the utmost".[211] Our taxonomy of passions is a map of those forces, alien and self-created, which act upon of our Nature.

Thus, Fool, you see we are well bidden to divide Love *pragmatically* so that we can grasp its immensity and its manifold forms. And in this second great undertaking, we learn of *pragma*; love born of necessity.

Exegesis of Compassion and the Outcast and Unclean

The Fool:

On the point of your taxonomy of the nature of passion, I relent. But I notice you cleverly dodged my refutation of compassion.

Guillemette:

On that you are at once correct and mistaken, O Fool. You are right to say that Thelemic Love has nothing to do with sentiment. And so is Mercy and Compassion, as the hypocrites without our walls teach it, repulsive to us. The would offer us mercy if we came out and threw ourselves at their feet, giving them our worldly goods and begging forgiveness of our ways. They might even offer those of us who they cannot tolerate a merciful death. That Compassion is a sort of snide superiority that begs a cringing thankfulness.

Esclarmonde:

It is the fruit of their mistaken faith. They teach that we must be forever in the debt of Christ because he suffered for us, praising him and thankful for his gift. Did we ask him to? Who says that we even want to receive what he has given, and even if we did, or should, why could he not give it to us direct? If he created the whole game, then isn't the fact he had to suffer to give us everlasting life his problem, not ours?

The Thelemic Initiations

The Fool:

I thought the Good People you so admire didn't believe Christ suffered on the Cross at all...but I mean to say that Thelema is opposed to all forms of compassion. Is it not said: "We have nothing with the outcast and the unfit: let them die in their misery. For they feel not. Compassion is the vice of kings: stamp down the wretched & the weak: this is the law of the strong: this is our law and the joy of the world."[212]

The Fool turns to the Initiates.

See I'm getting good at this stuff. Next Grade, you'll be taking the lessons from me, not these half baked ancient people! And Agape is just a way of saying there is no God but the Self, that all things are the same above the fold. Like I said. It doesn't mean *love* love.

Esclarmonde:

The Fool makes himself a veritable signpost for the Abyss. Follow him and know the joy of delusion. Whom, precisely, do you think are outcast and unfit, O Fool? We who stand siege here, impassioned by our love for partage, for our Count, for tolerance? Those who fight for the peace of their homes? We are after all the besieged, those on the defensive, under papal interdiction and abjured by the King of the Franks? Are not we outcast? Even unfit as we have failed thus far to raise this siege.

Or are the unfit those who come with a claim of zeal for God, but seeking fortune, to take those things they did not work for through force of arms and who when they briefly held this city in their grasp acted as Masters of Slaves, demanding harsh tribute and torturing or slaying those who would not or could not pay?

The Fool:

It's a trick question. All things are the same, so it just doesn't matter. It is the true will of Count Simon who feels inadequate because he is heir to an Earldom he can never claim and thus is chained to a title of distinction he cannot back up to take it out on the miserable people of Toulouse. It is their true will to resist him Everyone loses. "All the sorrows are but as shadows."[213]

The Fool looks at the initiates.

See I'm really getting this stuff.

Esclarmonde:

If Thelema or Gnosticism were the philosophy of nihilistic selfishness, then we would hardly need to enlighten anyone with regard to it.

Raimond d'Alfaro:

Count Simon, who sieges us, needs no primer.

Guillemette:

On that I cannot agree my son. He is, in his way, an honorable man, but he has had many priests to fill his head with a welter of half-truths and words to put an end to thought.

Esclarmonde:

Now, Fool ,who is God? You or I?

The Fool:

Well we are all stars in the company of stars.[214] But you are no more a God than I!

Esclarmonde:

Nor any less?

The Fool:

So you say, and I cannot come up with a Crowley quote to disagree.

Esclarmonde:

The Law is not a matter of finding some convenient quote to support one's own arrogance. All words, whether from the Master Therion, his immediate partners and predecessors, or aught other, must be taken within their context.

The Fool:

Even so, none of us here are the outcast and unfit.

Raimond d'Alfaro:

Easy for you to say! You haven't had mangonels hurling stones at you the past months while the heaven anointed father of all the world's faithful pronounces blessing upon your adversaries and offers salvation to those who would help them exterminate you. Nor, I hope, have you been literally outcast as we were, driven from this City, which we have only recently retaken, by the Sword, forced to live as exiles. We are truly outcast and by the words of the Pope and Christian Princes, unfit as well.

Esclarmonde:

You prove yourself yet a child, Young Raimond. For we are not the outcast, nor the unfit. What did the Fool just say of the outcast and unfit? That they "feel not?" We most certainly feel. The sacrament of the Christians is to drink the blood of God, but our sacrament is to pour our own blood, the blood of God, into the cup of Babalon.

Those who are outcast and unfit refuse to give up their blood as is revealed in the 12th Aethyr, "Thus do they keep themselves from compassion and from understanding." Too it is written "They keep themselves from the kisses of my Mother Babylon, and in their lonely fortresses they pray to the false moon. And they bind themselves together with an oath, and with a great curse. And of their malice they conspire together, and they have power, and mastery, and in their cauldrons do they brew the harsh wine of delusion, mingled with the poison of their selfishness."[215]

It is this draught of delusion brewed of the bitter herb of selfishness whereby they inflame the ignorant to march against us. "Thus they make war upon the Holy One, sending forth their delusion upon men, and upon everything that liveth. So that their false compassion is called compassion, and their false understanding is called understanding, for this is their most potent spell."[216]

Guillemette:

We reject both false compassion and understanding, both of which being that especially pointless form of condescension in which, rather than lift others up, we plunge ourselves down, to share their misery.

It is true that we do not practice charity, for charity implies those who have a right to things making a sacrifice they are not obliged to, as a gift or favor to those less fortunate. Since we recognize the right of every star in the company of stars to their orbit, and to the things necessary not only for their survival but their leisure, to provide these things is, as paratge teaches us, not charity but Duty.

The Fool:

Surely you do not suggest that we should part with that property that we own by the Rights of Man so that others can have luxuries? It would be charitable enough if we fed them?

Guillemette:

I thought you rejected charity, O Fool? Charity is the hypocrite of Duty. We are told:

"For each Man in this State which I purpose is fulfilling his own true Will by his eager Acquiescence in the Order necessary to the Welfare of all, and therefore of himself also. But see thou well to it that thou set high the Standard of Satisfaction, and that to every one be a Surplus of Leisure and of Energy, so that, his Will of Self-preservation-being fulfilled by the Performance of his Function in the State, he may devote the Remainder of his Powers to the Satisfaction of the other Parts of his Will."[217]

Raimond d'Alfaro:

Think not that these things are incidental. Even as a squire I have learned that they speak to the heart of the work of the Rose Cross Knight. When Count Simon came to these lands he brought his ways of oaths and vassalage and made men slaves and put on them a heavy yoke, so that when my Grandfather and Uncle returned they were welcomed even though they had few men. We stand our ground though all the Christian Princes of the West and the Pope in Rome oppose us, and we shed blood at need and not beyond, because it is our path as true knights.

It is true that the Knight knows not pity, nor the false compassion that advertises itself as sympathy. These we are told are "The distress of another may be relieved; but always with the positive and noble idea of making manifest the perfection of the Universe."[218]

The Fool:

Well, what if my will is to be cruel and unfair and arrogant?

Guillemette:

I cannot say. What I can say is that false will exists, "ignorant and capricious,"[219] fed by Choronzon on the confusions of the abyss, most often manifest as superiority or smugness. If the appearance of will seems to destroy or derail the will of many others whose actions are in harmony with the Law, then it is likely a false will. Whether your will is true or false, if it extends to depriving me of my freedom, I shall oppose it.

Esclarmonde:

We recognize that to restrict another, whether directly, or through supporting a system which places restriction on them to our benefit is a fundamental transgression of the law. Nor does laundering our crime through many hands, so that we merely support one who supports one who places the restriction, make us any less guilty if we are aware or, as intelligent Adepts well-versed in the ways of the world should be aware, of the chain of unclean hands. The word of Sin is restriction. Therefore our dedication to defending the road for others is not out of some patronizing instinct of pity, but rather a recognition of our Duty.

Therefore our work is practical, and far-reaching, driven by reason rather than the momentary pang of conscience. We are not the wealthy man who throws the smallest coin of Puy to a beggar to assuage the fear of Hell, but protests in the Civic Commune against a tax which might give that beggar work or bread. Nor are we anchorites sacrificing worldly delight of touch, or embrace, or surrendering everything that we possess in the belief that we will reap some great reward. Our lives must be example, for we cannot lead by force, only shine light.

The Fool:

Aren't Thelemites supposed to detest reason?

Esclarmonde:

The cursing of because and the dogs of reason is specific to those applications of reason which unseat Will. The logic by which I must obey the will of my father, or of some tutor, or an apprentice Master, because that is how society says it must be done, and that to prosper I must follow dictates and rules rather than acting on my passion and those things dear to me. By reason, rather than within these walls, I would be outside siding with the Pope and Frankish King, for on that side lays power, resources, and the potential for rich gifts.

We understand that attainment is not subject to reason, that in relation to the triad of the City of Pyramids "an immeasurable abyss divides it from all manifestations of Reason or the lower qualities." Yet in the reading for this Grade...you did do the reading O Fool? Are we not told that the Sword is the "analytical faculty,"[220] the reason, of the magician.

At various points we are bid to use reason, for example to "reason out"[221] the connections between our acts and magical Will.

Raimond d'Alfaro:

The Light fails my Lady. We should take our dinner soon. And have some entertainment. A story about brave knights would be good!

Esclarmonde:

Even so, O Child of the Prince. I shall say to our travelers in closing that in the time that most of the Holy Books of Thelema were, or are to be, written, the New Aeon seems but a glimmer on the horizon, a tantalizing promise just blossoming. It crashes down on you in full furor, just as our battle against Count Simon comes to a head and must climax soon!

In Liber NV (*NOO*) is given much instruction on the path of the Aspirant, and I would heartily recommend it to you as a general outline of the work that must be accomplished. We are told that the Aspirant must beware of the slightest exercise of their will against another being. Conversely we are told that the Aspirant must exercise their will without the least consideration for any other being. Yet most pointedly it is written "This direction cannot be understood, much less accomplished, until the previous practice has been perfected."[222]

The Thelemic Initiations

Now the light is failing and we shall light the candles, then, as paratge prohibits that we should eat while others go hungry, we shall share our provisions and what entertainment we may with you, more alas of the latter than the former.

Guillemette, would you see the lights kindled?

Guillemette:

This is the magical History
Of the Dawning of the Light.

Guillemette lights the Dark Candle

Begun are the Whirling Motions;
Formulated is the Primal Fire;

Guillemette lights the Light Candle

Proclaimed is the Reign of the Gods of Light
At the Threshold of the Infinite Worlds![223]

The Meal

Esclarmonde:

Since there is expense and difficulty in bringing in food along the remaining open roads, and winter is past and spring planting much delayed, it is the case that we have a poor board. That said so long as we eat, you too shall eat, and so should it be with every star in the company of stars.

The food of hardship is served, After there has been some time for conversation, but before there is too much questioning of the circumstances..

The presenters may respond to basic questions about the situation they are in.

It is the Year of Grace 1218. It has been twenty years since the travelers last came to Toulouse.

There has been open war against Crusaders, who have the support of the Pope and the French Crown, for eleven years. In 1209 the people of Beziers were massacred by the Crusaders

In 1213, King Peter of Aragon took the side of the Counts against the Frankish King, but he was defeated in combat by Simon Montfort, the dispossessed Earl of Leicester.

Montfort was given great possessions for his persecution of the Crusade. He was unsuccessful in seigingg Toulouse in 1211, but took the city in 1216 without a fight. He subjected the citizens to many indignities and punishments and gained great resentment, thus when Raimond VI returned to the City in 1217 the City supported him, and he has been standing siege since shortly thereafter as Montfort attempts to retake the City he claims to rule.

Guillemette should defer any specific questions about her parents or station, since these will be answered momentarily.

The pause need not be long, as there is not a great deal of food. The Fool should ask his questions as soon as everyone is reasonably settled.

The Fool:

Would it suit you to tell us what became of those two of regal bearing who once sat upon the Chair of the Queen where you now reside? And what has transpired in the time since we last visited?

Guillemette:

Azalais, Countess of Burlats, passed from this world not long after you last met her. I had seen only seven summers, so most of what I know of her, beyond a pleasant memory of music, is from the book she left to me. Her brother still reigns as Count of Toulouse and is out today directing the fight against the landless Simon Montfort.

The Fool:

Azalais, the Countess of Burlats, was your mother?

Guillemette:

Such is seldom spoken, yet I make no contest of the statement. I am the natural daughter of her Brother, the Count Raimond. I have not suffered for my station, for I am made Lady of Montlaur and Saint-Jory in my own right and have taken to wife Hughes d'Alfaro; a great Knight who is beloved of the Count.

Esclarmonde:

Some secrets, O Fool, are best left unspoken.

The Fool:

This Simon then? How did he come to be your enemy?

Guillemette:

Through opportunity and no more. He had great lands in England and lost them for being on the side of the King of France. When the Pope called for a crusade against us he was at the forefront. The Pope's Legate led the fight at Beziers, and allowed the mercenaries to massacre the population, though the knights took all the treasure.[224] [225] After that they elected Count Simon as their leader, because they deemed him more reliable than an Abbot, however bloodthirsty.

My father had been excommunicated for sympathy to the Good People the year before the great letting of blood at Beziers, and after the destruction of several towns and the pillage of the country Count Simon was gifted the title to the lands of my father by the Pope.

My father, the Count, failed to resist Simon, for my father is more given to diplomacy than War. My father fled to England for a while where his erstwhile Brother-in-Law reigns, before going to Rome to appeal for his lands to the Pope to demonstrate that he is a man of peace. When that failed he returned and took the City by force.

Esclarmonde:

Those in the region have rallied to Count Raimond, for he is the last, best hope against the wholesale purge of the Good People, and the loss of the freedom of these people to the yoke of the Frankish King.

The Thelemic Initiations

The Fool:

I suppose they'd rather have the yoke of Count Raimond?

Raimond d'Alfaro:

It is not the same! Even though they share the old Roman title of Comte, the Counts of Toulouse do not rule as the Frankish nobles do. Our laws do not hold the Count to own everything, with all others slaves, even the nobles holding nothing in their own right except by will of the King. Here those who have farms or houses in the city have rights which must be respected by the nobles. None may make them work or labor without payment and a contract. Within the city, the Capital, which is the gathering of leading citizens, has power and authority. They agreed to surrender the city to Count Simon after he swore oaths upon the relics that he would be a good and fair lord. Instead, he took many hostages with threats and blows and extorted great treasure from them, which he had promised not to do, and destroyed many buildings, too. He took their food, and clothes, and thirty thousand Marks of silver, and beat the people in the streets with clubs.[226] Now the Capital supports my grandfather, for Count Simon had no right to treat them so ill!

The Fool:

His faith was false then? He picked up the cross only to take your land?

Guillemette:

I have heard from many that he is very devout. Indeed he refused to kill Christians at Zara though it would have profited him. Yet he had advice from the Christian Bishop of Toulouse,[227] who holds that the oath is binding upon the vassal but not upon the Lord. So he is unjust and cruel, and if his God is a real God, then it is that evil God of whom the Good People speak, a crafter of abominations who wants nothing but suffering for mankind.

Raimond d'Alfaro:

It seems convenient nonetheless that God wants us brought to our knees and he does too and so they have a common cause. It is almost as if the will of God were that of the Pope and Louis Capet. He so defiled partagee that when my grandfather returned with only a handful of knights he was welcomed and men from the countryside and men-at-arms who had dispersed gathered so that when Simon came again from celebrating his victories to reclaim Toulouse he was met with fire and stone and bolt!

The Fool:

It has gone hard for you? And what of Queen Jeanne?

Esclarmonde:

She sat where I now sit, but in truth her chair is hard to fill. Jeanne, the Queen of Sicily and Countess of Toulouse, gave birth to the young Count who fights today beside his father and then a daughter who took her name. She was promised with another child but, when she was already lying-in, she became so offended at the Lords of Saint-Felix who had taken some castles of her husband the Count she went to siege them herself, leading men into battle, a child already in her belly.

The Fool:

Did she succeed?

Guillemette:

These lands had no stomach for a warrior-Queen. Some of the men were bribed to betray her bravery was rewarded with injury and illness. Yet she was not one to be stopped. Some say that the rigor of the campaign killed her for she died bearing a babe which lived only long enough for the Monks to bury it. Others say that she knew the hour of her death and wished to accomplish one great act before she died.

The Fool:

There was peace then, at first? For this fighting seems recent.

Esclarmonde:

There was peace for a little while because the Pope called a Crusade against the Ayyubid (*eye-YOU-bid*) Sultanate to divest them of Jerusalem, which instead assailed the Christian Emperor of Constantinople and divested him of the Byzantine Empire. But shortly after that the Pope granted the same indulgence to those who would murder us as he would grant to those who would murder the Muslims.

He excommunicated the Count a few years after that, and then sent preachers to rouse and threaten. His Legate, named Peter, met with the Count and not only refused him absolution but insulted him.

Raimond d'Alfaro:

One of my grandfather's squires stabbed old Peter straight through the spine for his trouble!

Guillemette:

And turned preaching into war upon us in the bargain.

Esclarmonde:

Have you forgotten the Pope had already shown his hand by offering indulgences for those who would slaughter us?

Guillemette:

It is truly said. I cannot entirely fault the lad who slew the Pope's Legate. Since then there has been mounting war and slaughter, and we were driven from this city, the Count to England for a while, but the tide has changed.

Esclarmonde:

I hope the Count and my noble Brother can defeat Count Simon, but I have also under my brother's hand the rights to the distant castle at Montsegur,[228] and I have charged its keeper Raimond de Perelha[229] to prepare a place there, should this Crusade go badly and Toulouse be lost. It is a place so unassailable and impregnable that it will never fall.

The Fool:

Didn't Thoth say that about those pillars?

Esclarmonde:

Let us have entertainment!

Guillemette:

Have you forgotten that both Troubadours and Jongleurs are at this moment either manning the levels or taking their repose before tomorrow's fight?

Esclarmonde:

Not at all, but I am told these travelers once before did the honor of taking the roles of players. Perhaps they would again. Have you an entertainment?

Guillemette:

There is one drama which was penned by a troubadour but has yet to be performed. Shall I describe the roles that these travelers might speak for them?

The Tragedy of Jacques de Molay

Dramatis Personae

Interlude/Narrators

> *Secretary*
>
> *Visitor* – A mysterious Visitor (the word used in its normal sense of one who visits)
>
> *Johann Valentin Andreae* (YO-han VAL-in-teen AN-dree)

All Acts

> *Jacques De Molay* (ZHOCK day MOW-lay) – Grand Master of the Templars

Act I

> *Matthieu Sauvage* (MATT-ee-oo SOE-vahj) – An old and wise Templar Knight
>
> *Otto of Granson* (AH-toe of GRAHN-sun) – A Knight of Burgundy in service to the English King

Act II

> *Templar 1* – A knight
>
> *Gerard de Villiers* (ZHER-ard duh Vee-yay) – Lieutenant to the Templar Master of France

Act III

> *Hughes de Pairaud* (OOgh duh PAY-row) – Deputy Grandmaster and Visitor† of France
>
> *Guy de Charnay* (GEE duh SHAR-nay g as in gun) – Visitor† of Normandy

† Visitor in this sense means literally "Overseer" and can be translated as "Inspector General," a sense still used in some Colleges.

Introduction

Andreae is lying down. The Secretary sits beside his bed, while the Visitor enters

Secretary:

He is sleeping now. I can wake him if you like.

Visitor:

No. It is as well he sleep. How is he?

Secretary:

He can speak with some difficulty and write only a few letters. He has had a paroxysm. (*PER-ix-ism or PAIR-ox-ism*) He is paralyzed on the one side and has trouble seeing.

Visitor:

You are young. Have you known him for long?

Secretary:

In truth, I know little but his name and his station here. I am a student, but I was hired by his wife to write letters for him and sit with him while she was away.

Visitor:

What do you know of him, then?

Secretary:

I know his name is Johann Valentin Andreae. (*YO-han VAL-in-teen AN-dree*) Someone said he was Superintendent General of the Lutheran School in the Abbey at Bebenhausen (*BAY-ben-house-n*) but has retired to an honorable sinecure (*sin-UH-cure*) as the Abbot of a Cloister that no longer stands, and that Duke Augustus is his patron. Have you come a long way to see him?

Visitor:

Further than you might think. I don't know if he will appreciate my visit. He lost his humor with some of the things that bonded us together years past. Where is Agnes Elizabeth?

Secretary:

She is attending to an errand of his. Some matter of charity.

Visitor:

He was always a leader in charity of that practical kind which provides what is needed for citizens to help themselves. He did much to rebuild Calw (*KALF*) after it was burned, though he suffered as much as anyone. But he was also a very great author. He did much to create a world in which science must be harmonized with the spirit and the spirit with science. But three things in his youth he wrote, just before the Wars, took the learned men of Europe by storm. The tale of the Brotherhood of the Rosy Cross.

Secretary:

I think I have heard of that. Was he in the wars then before he came to the cloth?

Visitor:

No, he has always been a writer, thinker, and a Protestant Pastor. He has ever written of the horrors and hardships of the wars visited upon us and been a tireless and true advocate of peace and the cause of injured soldiers and those citizens maimed or paupered by the wars. He was three times burned out and lost his house twice. His son died when they had to flee from Calw, for he was well known and the troops under von Werth would have killed him first of all.

Secretary:

I was just twelve when the wars ended.

Visitor:

You must be eighteen now then?

Andreae: *stirs*

Who is here? I cannot see.

Visitor:

An old friend from years gone by. I knew you at Tübingen (*TOO-bin-gen*), many years ago.

Andreae:

Yes I see...hazily...it has been a very long time. I am sorry you have come to me when I cannot...speak...well. I have been taken by Cachexia (kah-KECH-see-uh) of late.

Visitor:

Wasting disease. Have you had good care my friend? A good Doctor?

Andreae:

I am beyond the Doctors, whether they be Galenists or Parcelsian Chymists. My good friend Imhof sent me his doctors, but I know after so many years extolling the virtues of science and medicine when a man is beyond all earthly help. I hope that is not why you have come – to bring me a new physician?

Visitor:

I came to bring you cheer my friend. To while away the idle hours and give you some surcease from the company of these young people who know nothing of our history or hardships.

Andreae:

My mind goes back to those days, you know. My poor Ehrenreich (*EE-ren-ryesh*) He was never in good health. Tell me a story then? You always had a knack for those.

Visitor:

Not as fine as yours.

The Thelemic Initiations

Andreae: *Tell me some old tale.*

Visitor:

>Very well...our story unfolds on a dark night in the City of Nicosia (*NEE-koh-see-uh*) on the Isle of Cyprus, in April of the common year Twelve Hundred and Ninety Two.
>
>For a hundred and ninety four years, Latin forces have occupied some portion of the Levant.

Andreae:

>Well I know that chronology...my mind is still well

Visitor:

>I repeat it only for the benefit of our young friend here.
>
>Now, for a hundred and seventy three years, the Knights of the Temple and the Knights of the Hospital of St. John have held portions of what they consider the "Holy Land" and played some role in its defense.
>
>One year ago, in the common year Twelve Hundred and Ninety One, the last contested Latin stronghold, the city of Acre, fell to the Mamluks. The remaining Latin outposts in the Levant were abandoned. No Latin forces remain anywhere south of the Kingdom of Armenia.

Interlude

The Fool: *aside to Esclarmonde*

>How is it that your plays contain stories that happened seventy-five years from now narrated by people who lived four hundred years after your death?

Esclarmonde:

>How is it, O Fool, that you think I can die? My name is Clarity of the World, and I should not have to explain narrative technique to you.

Act the First

De Molay: *is kneeling in front of the Altar.*

Granson: *enters with Matthieu behind him.*

>Grand Commander?

De Molay:

>You interrupt my vigil, Lord Granson. You have done me great good and for that I thank you, but I am just now at prayer. I ask you what matter is so great and weighty that it cannot wait until I am installed on the morrow as Grand Master of the Knights of the Temple?

Matthieu:

>It is well, Grand Commander, that your great friend should be present. For I have come as the eldest surviving Brother in Cyprus to instruct you as to some particulars of your duties.

De Molay:

I did not see you, Brother Matthieu. What instruction is this?

Matthieu:

Well, you know, Grand Commander, that there are some secrets which are known only to the Grand Master and a few of his elect within our Order. They have been passed down since Rinaldo De La Chapelle[230] was Grand Master, before the fall of Jerusalem.

De Molay:

How come you to know them?

Matthieu:

After Armand de Lavoie was lost without a trace in battle, they were shared with certain sympathetic Commanders. When I was younger I was at Acre, then Tortosa, and finally at Sidon, where I remained until last year when all were evacuated to Cyprus. The Relics were in my care, for I had contributed a very great relic when I was younger.

De Molay:

Well you know Brother that I have been kept a plain knight with no office for many years for my disagreements with our past Grand Master, Guillaume de Beaujeu, (GEE-ahm duh BOW-juh) who fell at Acre this year past. Under our late Grand Master, Thibaud Gaudin (TEE-bow GO-dahn), who Commanded from the fall of Acre until his death a few weeks past, I was given some preferment for my capability, but much happened quickly. I have heard somewhat of these secrets as I suppose has everyone, but I confess on Christ my belief they are idle rumors born of those who do not truly understand our lives in the Levant.

Matthieu:

I know that you opposed Master de Beaujeu, as I supported him. He sought to make truces and accommodation with our adversaries wherever possible, while you have sought to carry the sword to them.

De Molay:

I know that you were, in your youth, friend of the Mamluk Sultan (MAHM-luke), Baibars (BAY-barz), such that you shared blood with him, even before his greatest fame.[231] I have never faulted you for this. Yet during all our time, each deal with the Mamluk advantaged them and left us with less. We were like a poor cobbler who staves off starvation by selling his tools, but finds at the end that he has only put off the shadow of death by a little time, and has nothing left with which to earn his living.

Matthieu:

When I knew Baibars near a quarter century ago, there was much to be gained by friendship. The Mamluks, who were slave-warriors, had destroyed the last Great Crusade and driven King Louis of the Franks from his ill-fated effort to challenge them for Egypt itself. They had also overthrown their Ayyubid (*eye-YOU-bid*) overlords and were fighting them for control of Syria, ever with an eye on the Mongols. We hoped through siding with the Mamluks to win back our Holy Places. Such was the sacrifice of my blood. Though it was perhaps more than blood. Recall you what transpired at Antioch?

De Molay:

I know it was abandoned by its Christian Prince who left Simon Mansel, who was kin by marriage to the Queen of Armenia, to defend it. Mansel made an ill advised sortie, and was taken prisoner, and negotiated a surrender. The defenders wouldn't have it, the city was taken, its tombs sacked, and every man woman and child butchered or made slaves "women sold in lots four at a time and bought with a dinar" from the Prince's Treasury. "Priests and Deacons with their throats cut on the altars...dead burning in the fire of this world."[232]

Granson:

Well, there are always such stories when a Muslim Prince takes a city.

De Molay:

Yes. But that's from the letter Sultan Baibars' Secretary wrote to the missing Prince, to rub salt in the wounds him over the loss.

Matthieu:

Baibars wanted to scare him. Scare all his enemies. That letter, true or not, was a warning. Baibars had far greater forces than I could hope to bring. I sought to spare some of the people in my care the fate of the people in that latter.

Granson:

Such is the way of cities which fall without terms. You were wise to treat with him. When we turn from fights we cannot win we may yet live to fight another day.

Matthieu:

Or fight not at all. Our sworn duty is to protect those pilgrims that seek the Holy Sepulchre (*SEP-uhl-ker*). And my Lord Granson has late come from Jerusalem, no worse for the trip.

De Molay:

There is much ill-chance for pilgrims who come to Jerusalem under Mamluk banners.

Granson:

Yet you well know that the Crusades that gave us our original cause have become the clash of Empires. The last real Crusade was organized by the French King Louis, trying to win the approval of his mother Blanche of Castile who had crushed the Cathar Heretics in his youth. He didn't care much about the Holy Land and tried to seize Egypt for the Capetian Dynasty of France.

Matthieu:

Had he taken any advice on tactics he might have gained Egypt, but he was a fool and lost his army.

Granson:

Yes, well...After that disaster he went to Acre and schemed with your friend Baibars against the Ayyubid till he ran out of cash and had to go home. His grandson is no less rapacious. Phillip is jealous of the Holy Roman Emperor, and thinks himself entitled to the Kingdom of England. The smaller kingdoms, Aragon, Castile, he would gather them all into his fist. The Pope and Monasteries too.

Matthieu:

And the Orders.

De Molay:

Lord Granson, I was under no illusion that you supported me as Grand Master for any reason other than a check on French ambition. The King of France already uses the Templars as his tax collectors and he would happily repay himself by taking the order from within. I, like you, was born in Burgundy, which is subject to the Holy Roman Emperor, and I, unlike Hughes de Pairaud *(OOgh duh PAY-row)* Visitor of France, could be trusted not to put the Order into the hands of Phillip Capet, Iron King of France.

Granson:

It is true your election serves the interest of my Master, Edward King of England. But there are other reasons. You have shown intelligence and willingness to question, as much as by any other means in your defiance of the Grand Master who fell at Acre. You have a keen mind and good strategic sense. We hope that you would be open minded to the secrets that the Grand Master of Templars needs to know.

Matthieu:

Have you denied Christ?

De Molay:

I know something of it. I was never one of the ones who was asked, but one does not serve so long and not hear of it.

Matthieu:

What have you heard?

De Molay:

That it is a mystery. It was the business of the Grand Master and the Chaplains, none of mine.

Granson:

You are not an ignorant man, else you would not have risen to the position that you have. You know or guess far more, and you have an opinion.

De Molay:

What I guess is blasphemy of heresy. There are in the cities and countryside in these lands all manner of things which would lead to a heavy penance or worse were they spoken in our homelands. The Orthodox who deny the primacy of the See of Peter, the followers of Nestor who question the Nature of Christ, the Armenians who question that Christ truly died, the Harranians who deny Christ for or Enoch whom they take to be Hermes. All manner of Manichees, and even, so the Mamluks say, worshipers of the Head in the lands beyond Antioch. Between Beyrut and Tripoli the Christians of Saint Maron who have some disagreement with the Patriarch of Constantinople about the nature of Christ's will which is too obscure for me to recall. No man who sees and hears can come to this place and not see that here in the holy land all is not holy. And for all that, we are so hard pressed by the followers of Islam…which rather than denying the mystery of the resurrection rather adds more after…that all those heretics are of needs most times our uneasy friends.

Granson:

And many of these beliefs are older than those of the Holy Father in Rome. Or Viterbo or Orvieto, or wherever he betakes himself these days.

De Molay:

The beliefs of Rome are what I learned.

Matthieu:

So are they what I learned. Yet here I met those who opened the true pilgrim's road to me.

De Molay:

What is this road?

Matthieu:

Even a Grand Master must have patience. It will be revealed to you in time. For now I will ask only if you are open to receiving it?

De Molay:

If I say no? If I expose these teachings as heresy within the Order?

Matthieu:

You will not.

Granson:

What if he does?

Matthieu: *Addresses de Molay directly*

You will not, because you love the Order and have given your life to it. You know that the slightest whisper of heresy from the Grand Master would destroy the order. Already there is talk that we should be combined with the Knights of the Hospital, that all the orders should be put under some King, that of Aragon or of the Franks. Our position was precarious before we lost the last Christian Kingdom in the Levant.

De Molay:

What if I love Christ more than I love the Order?

Matthieu:

Do you? God perhaps. But Christ. What is he to you but a legend? Have you met him?

De Molay:

I heard that once in Edessa there was an image of him. I have seen and heard many strange things, but no miracles.

Matthieu:

I shall reveal the secret to you, for it is not so terrible as you might think. The Christ is a symbol to you, the Agnus Dei, Lamb of God. But his blood is the Ignis Dei, Fire of God, and it is that fire that makes red our crosses. The Cross too is real, though perhaps not quite as you believe. The Baptism of Fire is accomplished by the Ruby Cross, and the purification of man through the Graal.

De Molay:

The cup which Joseph of Arimathea used to gather the Blood of Christ?

Granson:

The Graal is not a cup, but stone as Wolfram of Eschenbach wrote in that legend of Templars which not one of us has been spared.

De Molay:

I liked it, Parzival. I am sure it bore on my decision to take vows. It seemed glorious. But a story.

Granson:

Von Eschenbach learned it from a poet of Provence who got it from ancient books copied by the Moors at Toledo.

De Molay:

Yes, but we don't guard a mystical stone. Right now we don't even guard a castle in the Holy Land and if we don't watch our backs, and let heresy proliferate we will not be guarding a castle in Cyprus for much longer either. King Henry of Cyprus is no friend of ours. This isle has been a last resort for us. We misgoverned from the day we purchased it from Richard Lionheart a century gone.

Matthieu:

Bought with Treasure which was more than gold.

De Molay:

Perhaps. And lost it quickly too. The Templars of that time had no wit to govern, and now we have only a few houses here left. For a century we've been harried and hated in this place, loved by neither the Latin rulers nor these Eastern Priests. I will speak truth to you. Of course I have heard the stories. I never reported them or said aught because I knew however poor the Priests and Bishops would take them, they were not meant as Blasphemy against the Holy Spirit. The Levant is not like Europe and it is easy for Knights to be fascinated by this or that ancient whispering. My truth is the simple truth of numbers.

Granson:

What numbers are those?

De Molay:

We have few knights and need more. We have great revenues but have spent it all on fortifications and ships and few of those survive. We have great trouble with supplies because the King of Cyprus is at odds with those ports which will ship to us and everything costs us dear.

Granson:

Come with me then to Armenia. The King there has invited us. Politically, Armenia is the only alliance for us now. They fear the Mamluks as much as we do, and with good reason. We have rights there.

De Molay:

What has this to do with mystical stones or the Fire of God?

Matthieu:

There is a certain book which has been translated, called *The Goal of The Wise*.[233] Perhaps you have seen it.

Otto of Granson:

If you read Latin, it is called *Picatrix*.

Matthieu:

There is much in it which is still known in Armenia and was known in my childhood here and there by wise men from Sidon to Edessa; wisdom from the time of Solomon, from long before Christ.

De Molay:

I took you more for a warrior than one who reads books Matthieu. Beaujeu always said you were smart and dangerous, and I'm not sure he meant it as a compliment. Since you have put it in my mind, I would see the relics which were brought from Sidon, for that is my due as a Master of the Temple.

Matthieu:

It is my pain to say that you shall not, at least not on this day. They were on orders of the late Grand Master who fled from Sidon, sent for safekeeping to Hugh of Pairaud, Visitor of France.

De Molay:

Would you tell me then that one is the Graal stone?

Matthieu:

I would not, for I do not lie. What was sent to France is a thing infinitely greater.

Interlude:

Secretary:

He has fallen asleep.

Visitor:

It is as well. He might not have liked where that story goes.

Secretary:

Is it true?

Visitor:

The principles of it are true. One must confess at such great remove that the exact words may blur.

Secretary:

Parzival? I know that story. And I have heard of the Templars, of course. Did they really guard the graal?

Visitor:

Well, that is the rest of the story.

Secretary:

You can tell me if you'd like.

Visitor:

Very well...the Templars suffered more reverses, losing their remaining castles in Armenia in 1299. They resolved to harry the Mamluks and establish a staging point for a new invasion. In concert with the Hospitallers and the King of Cyprus, they were invited to a treaty with the Mongol Warlord Ghazan, with the expectation that they would mount a joint attack on the Mamluks together in 1300. They raided the coast, and the Templars seized the offshore island of Ruad ($RAWD$) as a staging point for operations when the Mongols came. The Templars left a garrison at Ruad of a hundred and forty men. But No Mongols came in 1300. Or in 1301. Our second act takes place in Cyprus in the common year thirteen hundred and two.

Act the Second

Templar1:

Gerard of Villiers has returned with news. What was rumored is confirmed, Grand Master. The garrison at Ruad was surrendered to the Mamluks, and taken prisoner.

De Molay:

All of them?

Templar1:

Sir Gerard escaped with some men on a transport.

De Molay:

It is done then. Ruin and disaster. The largest force that the Orders and the King of Cyprus together could muster. We harried some towns, took plunder and the staging point for a new invasion.

The Thelemic Initiations

Templar1:

What do we do now, Grand Master? More raids. Perhaps we can ally again with the Armenians and launch an attack. Or send more embassies to the Mongols.

De Molay: *darkly*

We have done enough. Forty good men lost to imprisonment or worse. The Armenians are unreliable and their borders have a welter of enemies whom are none of our concern.

Templar1:

Surely we must strike some blow, lest they see this as ultimate victory. Even a symbolic one. Another set of raids.

De Molay:

The Mamluks muster better than twelve thousand horse and forty thousand bow just in the region of Jerusalem, without consideration for the forces of the Sultan in Egypt. The only point of pissing on their ports is to make ourselves pirates, more hated and feared but no better respected. If the only fighting we can do is for the sake and show of fighting, accomplishing nothing but bringing an endless toll of misery than by the Holy Cross of Ruby on my watch we shall not fight at all.

Templar1:

We have God on our side.

As Templar1 speaks Villiers enters without asking, startling him slightly when he speaks from behind him.

Villiers:

I would submit that until such time as God sees fit to part the Mediterranean Sea as he parted the waters for Moses that both we and God are at the mercy of a greater power, though whether it be Genoa or Venice is anyone's guess.

Templar1:

Why so? They do not, since the settlement at Cremona, quarrel with each other or with us?

De Molay:

My noble Villiers is correct about that. Everything that comes to the Levant, even to Cyprus, from the lands to the West, has always had to come through the eye of a needle. Thus what was one piece of silver in Marseilles (*MARR-say*) is ten pieces of silver in Cyprus. As far away as England they publish letters saying that we hoard our wealth, live well and fatted and care nothing for the Holy Land. They have no concept of the cost of anything where there are few laborers and little to build with. One castle lost, such as Safed, is the ransom of a Great King. The Levant has always been a deep hole into which we pour gold. And there is nothing in it of great worth.

Templar1:

It is the land of Christ!

De Molay:

What is Christ to you? Is he more or less real because you can see a place his body isn't.

Templar1:

Mighty miracles have been worked there; great cures.

De Molay:

If the cost of every cure is forty good men, perhaps we should spend our money on physicians and let the Mamluks keep the damnable sepulchre.

De Molay acknowledges the Knight who as walked in.

Sir Gerard.

Villiers:

Grand Master.

De Molay: *To Templar1*

Leave us.

De Molay and Villiers wait in silence until Templar1 has stepped out.

Sir Gerard. Can you give account of this late disaster at Ruad?

Villiers:

As you well know, the garrison was ill-provisioned. The Isle itself is scarce a mile and grows little, what food came in had to be smuggled or brought from here in Cyprus, and the harvests have been awful. The winter was exceptionally cold and many of the men were weak or ill. The Mamluks came in force and they came up with Galleys.

De Molay:

How is it that you escaped, but not the men of your command?

Villiers:

As well you know, we had only transports. There was no defending them against the galleys and without stopping them at sea there was no defense against their numbers on land. I got aboard the first transport to get it into action and hoped perhaps to draw them off or split their numbers. The Mamluks knew their business and they ignored us and took the island. The second transport with the bulk of the men was slower loading and never got away.

De Molay:

You have a convenient sense of when to leave the fray, Sir Gerard.

Villiers:

I don't suppose you like me. You never liked Hugh of Pairaud and he has oft been my patron. He would have made a better Grand Master than you.

De Molay:

Perhaps. I'll be returning to the Western Lands soon, and there may be a reckoning.

Villiers:

Because I saved a ship and some men?

De Molay:

I know the games you and Pairaud have played back there. I thought bringing you out here to take command might give the chance to make an honest man of you. The reputation of the Order is low. The Pope hears complaints. You recruit dishonestly, impress men into our service on one hand, and demand fees on the other to make Knights of the Temple. You use all manner of usurers and criminals to recruit and give them preference when they ought to be imprisoned or hanged. And you live well and send only the problematic men and misfits to the Levant.

Villiers:

We do, and worse if you want to know the truth. You said to give you men. So we did. You said to give you money. So we did. Now you want to ask pretty questions about how we got it. How many men do you think are itching to take the cross since Acre? How much enthusiasm do you think we see? Knights? There are plenty of fights with a better chance of spoils close to home. It's been a long time since anyone came back from the Holy Lands with treasure.

De Molay:

I implemented reforms. Perhaps if knights thought we lived clean and represented something Holy they'd be more inclined to serve us.

Villiers:

How many good, actually competent, men do you know who just want to serve God and live a simple life? If they see that Templars eat well, get fucked well, can do as they please, have coins in their purse when they go out into the town, then taking their inheritance and plowing it into a life of chastity and service seems a trifle more appealing.

De Molay:

At the cost of the goodwill of Christendom.

Villiers:

Fuck the goodwill of Christendom. Do you know whose goodwill we need? The goodwill of Phillip the Stiff, King of France. If you so want a Crusade, you know there will never be another one without the king of France. And the Pope and the King of France both know there will never be a Crusade without the Orders.

De Molay:

And if they merge the orders make the King of France Rex Bellorum...War King? That's been floated more than once.

Villiers:

Well, I guess you Burgundians would be out of luck. But even if they made him head, who's going to run it? Not the King of France. The Visitor and Preceptor of France perhaps. Myself, Hughes…

De Molay:

That would suit you wouldn't it?

Villiers:

Look, I don't hate you. If Hughes does that's his problem. But we're knights. We can swallow it and work together. Give up this whole reform scheme, work with us instead of against us. The King of France will never control the Order because the ones who are in the know will never turn on each other. There are secrets you don't know.

De Molay:

I know more than you think. I know what relics were sent to Sidon, then to the West. Old Matthieu told me everything before he died, and I learned more in Armenia.

Villiers:

Join us then. We're broadening the circle.

De Molay:

Is that wise? People talk.

Villiers:

Not more than once. There's a pit in Merlan.[234] It's not an easy place to be a prisoner.

De Molay:

So you hereticate at will and threaten anyone who doesn't like it?

Villiers:

Approximately.

De Molay:

That strikes me as lacking subtlety.

Villiers:

It works.

De Molay:

For how long? What happens when Phillip-with-a-stick-up-his-ass gets wind of it? Moral flexibility isn't one of his strong points.

Villiers:

It is if there's enough coin involved. You don't understand. We *own* the French Crown. We're the bankers and the debt collectors and the treasurers. If Phillip wants money...and I assure you he *wants money*...he goes through us. And we get it for him. And every day we own him just a little more.

De Molay:

You can't buy a King.

Villiers:

Watch us.

De Molay:

Tell me something. Do you care a thing for the actual hidden wisdom? The things Matthieu understood? The fire of the Cross of Ruby that came before the Christ and the secret knowledge of Hermes?

Villiers:

I like those parts of the hidden wisdom which say that we shouldn't hate pleasure. There were, according to the Apocalypse of John of old, in Antioch, Christians who were followers of Nicolas and held that love should be in common. Were they wrong? Augustine understood pleasure before he turned his mind towards the sort of piety that provides a cloak for the ambitions of Kings. Take what we want of any man or woman we want, whether they will or not.

De Molay: *Offhandedly, reflective*

Well, if they were in Antioch back at the time of the Revelation of John, they're dead now. Baibars saw to that, I saw a letter once that says so...

De Molay sighs.

That we should not take pleasure does not mean we should do whatever we wish. That we are freed from the old covenant does not mean we must become soldiers of the Abyss.

Villiers:

If you're coming back to France for a fight, you'll get one.

De Molay:

No. We both know that neither of us can afford a fight. is we have to work together. I've enacted reforms and I expect them to be obeyed. I need to be able to go before the Pope with a clean slate. Keep anything that smacks of heresy or sodomy out of sight and for the love of the true and holy cross stop cheating people. There's nothing in the world more venomous than someone with a true grudge and we can't afford to turn all the West into a field of scorpions.

Villiers:

They don't love us anymore. But they can still fear us. Listen. There's never going to be another Crusade to the Holy Land. The fact is the King of France will never have the money, the Emperor doesn't have the will, the King of England hasn't got the pull, and things have changed for all the little second rate

Kingdoms and Principalities. They're too worried about being gobbled up like Toulouse and Anjou to gallivant off to find the True Cross. The Hospitallers have some good ideas. Attack the Byzantines. They're weak. Beset on all sides.

De Molay:

Wasn't taking over the Byzantine Empire a thing that fell apart back when I was a young man and you were still sucking a tit?

Villiers:

Sure...the Latin Empire Collapsed. Just like the Kingdom of Jerusalem. But you have to think more practically. The Byzantines are weaker than they've ever been. You don't take them directly, just take them in little pieces. An island here, a territory there. The Hospitallers are looking at Rhodes.

De Molay:

I may have reservations about claiming another island for you to sail away from. So tell me, you know why I sent for you. Now, why didn't you bring it?

Villiers:

Who says I didn't?

De Molay:

Ruad fell.

Villiers: gives a sardonic laugh

Well, I wasn't there now was I?

Interlude

Andreae:

You make Villiers quite the bastard.

Visitor:

You're awake...Wasn't he?

Andreae:

There is a certain admirable pragmatism about him, though he is everything I despise. Yet, it is still hard not to like him a little.

Visitor:

The call of the Black Adept is seductive, isn't it?

Andreae:

Real evil is seductive.

The Thelemic Initiations

Visitor:

What is evil then, according to the distinguished author of the *Chemical Wedding of Christian Rosenkruetz* (*Kriss-tee-ahn ROZ-uhn-krootz*)?

Andreae:

It is to derail the stars in their courses, not because you must, but merely because you can.

Visitor:

An interesting view.

Andreae:

A book I'd done better to have never written.

Visitor:

It accomplished what you wanted.

Andreae:

An allegorical tale of an imaginary brotherhood? How much more obvious could I have been? Should I have added crossing the Styx with Virgil in a boat? Made Christian of the Rosy Cross a comic giant in the style of Rabelais? I wanted to foster a world where we interpret the divine nature through both experiment and experience.

Visitor:

Your myth has become real. With all you know of the elements, do you truly believe that the literal incarnate body of Jesus Christ walked upon the water, contrary to every fact you know about the natural order of the universe and causality? Is it not myth become reality?

Andreae:

It does stretch one's understanding of causality, but that is what makes the study of Natural Law wonderful. If miracles happened as attested, then they cannot have happened outside such laws. Therefore, those laws exist for us to discover, just as our old friend Kepler discovered the harmony by which the planets are arrayed around the Sun.

Visitor:

I thought you had lost interest in Natural Law and Alchemy.

Andreae:

Like music, Alchemy is a distraction. It does not build cities torn apart by siege guns, or feed people whose crops have been laid to waste by French soldiers. But I suppose now that I can barely rise, I think back on it more. It is not that I ever came to hate the study of Natural Law through Alchemy. Rather to despise most of those who practiced it. The true Art is hard work, and perseverance. But finish your tale.

Visitor:

Should I repeat my story?

Andreae:

I caught most of it. Pray tell the rest...I know the ending, but we may still surprise my dear Secretary here.

Visitor:

I'll skip a bit so as not to tire you. You know that the Grand Master, Jacques De Molay did return to the West at the bidding of the new Pope, Clement V, who was a hand picked tool of the French King. The Order was investigated, and exonerated, but on October 13, 1307 King Phillip arrested them anyway, and the weak Pope had no choice but to go along with it. The Templars mounted a robust defense, but the King of France was the law and he had one of their lawyers murdered, then summarily burned some fifty four of them to death. The Trials dragged on but there was no hope in them after that.

The Grand Master confessed in writing several times, but only when he was before the King's Men. We don't know if they tortured him or threatened him, or simply made up words for him to have said and wrote them down. Whenever he was before the Pope's authorities, he plead his innocence.

Finally in 1314 a group of Cardinals called out the Grand Master, Jacques de Molay, Hughes of Pairaud Visitor of France whom you heard me speak of as the friend and partner in crime of Villiers, the Preceptor of Normandy Guy de Charnay, and a handful of other ranking Templars. Since they'd confessed and all the property of the Templars had been taken, the order itself merged with the Hospitallers, the surviving leaders were to be quietly consigned to life in prison. de Molay was probably in his late sixties or early seventies by then, having spent the last seven years of his life in prison.

Act The Third

Pairaud:

You are resolved to this madness then?

De Molay:

I am.

Pairaud:

I'll end up burned because of your intransigence.

Charnay:

I doubt that. The Cardinals will be happy if you don't support us.

Pairaud:

You too then, Guy?

Charnay:

I am resolved.

Pairaud:

Make me to understand. Why? This affair is finally over. Why choose now to condemn yourselves to an awful death.

De Molay:

Over fifty years I've seen men, women, and children hacked, disemboweled, seen their blackened bloated carcasses picked apart by vultures and the flies laying eggs on their eyes. I've seen the ground covered with the spattered matter of brains. And I have felt the exultation that comes with these things, and also the chill that comes at night, that steals sleep and weakens resolve for seeing those things which cannot be unseen. Yet who does not find more horrible that corpse cut down beside the road than the knight fallen in battle. Death is most awful when it is meaningless. I have felt much pain. I can feel a little more that my death not be without meaning.

Pairaud:

What meaning? We are thwarted...Done.

De Molay:

Our deaths will write a message that even the secretaries of the French Court cannot change or erase. They cannot spare our lives and they cannot make a secret of our deaths.

Pairaud:

What message is this? You've confessed and unconfessed as many times as I have.

De Molay:

Some lawyers will look back years hence and ask "if the Templars were so corrupt, why did they only confess when in the hands of the King of France who benefited from their dissolution."

Charnay:

But every villager in France will wonder why, if the Templars were guilty, the Grand Master chose to burn when he could have lived. They will tell that story and people will wonder. Like that Graal story the German told. I once had a German pilgrim offer me a hundred bezants to see it.

Pairaud:

Shame you didn't have it.

Charnay:

I took him into the chapel and showed him the Communion Cup. I even let him drink from it.

De Molay:

I hope he wasn't disappointed.

Charnay:

No more than when I sent the Mandylion home. Old Matthieu learned some wondrous tricks from his Mamluk friends.

De Molay:

Clever.

De Molay laughs.

At least you'll be guilty of something when you burn.

Pairaud:

But we *are* guilty. All of us. You as much as I, for I did the things and you knew and benefited and kept silent.

Charnay:

The benefit to us of your bringing out the relics in front of an entire Chapter and daring them to speak may be limited. As for the amount of attention given to kissing the newly received Knights, it might have been better to wait and see their inclinations.

Pairaud:

There was in fact a point to it. I thought it best to get a read fresh off...shock them into acceptance…and if they reacted poorly I could lean on them to keep quiet.

De Molay:

Of all the reforms I pressed, letting men and women go their way without pressing attentions upon them would have served us best. De Villiers told me long ago that threats secured silence. It seems that more profound threats secured much speech.

Pairaud:

The Novices and stable-hands could have complained forever. They were only heard because the King turned against us.

Charnay:

Because you paupered him!

Pairaud:

And your Grand Master helped with his Burgundian and English friends. How secure do you think the King of France felt to be so deep in debt to an Order headed by those who consorted with his rivals? He bought a Pope. That which he could not control he could destroy.

Charnay:

It was never part of the Rule of the Templar Order to provide Simony to the Crown of France on demand!

De Molay:

Hush, Guy. It is all my fault.

Pairaud:

On that at least we are agreed.

De Molay:

Probably not. But it doesn't matter now.

The Thelemic Initiations

Charnay:

I see no fault with you, Grand Master.

De Molay:

I received the secret wisdom. I understood it. But I did not make use of it. I tolerated De Villiers because we needed men. I tolerated the dealings with the French Crown because I dared not antagonize Phillip. I wrote of what we would need to take the Holy Land when I knew it was a pointless endeavor that could bring only misery and death. I worked to preserve the Order without any thought to the meaning of the Order.

Charnay:

How could you have done differently?

De Molay:

We should have continued to be guardians for pilgrims.

Charnay:

How could we do that without a Crusade?

De Molay:

By thinking backwards. Here is an interesting story. You know of course of Count Raimond the Fourth of Toulouse who became the First Count of Tripoli and was a great leader of the First Crusade?

Pairaud:

I grew up speaking the Language of the South, of Occitania. I know him well. He was one of the mightiest heroes of the Crusade.

Charnay:

I know of him from Tripoli. He started enough fights with his kin that he did more harm to the Crusader Kingdoms than Salah-ad-Din ever managed after.

De Molay:

Perhaps, but my thought is not of him. You know Toulouse passed to his younger son and thence to Raimond the Fifth and then the Sixth, who was declared heretic by the Pope...near a century ago now.

Pairaud:

He was a Heretic Cathar Prince and suffered for it. His son was forced to heel by the Capet King, or at least his mother, and Toulouse finally alienated to the crown some years after I joined the Order.

De Molay:

Yet Count Raimond the Sixth didn't die a heretic, or if he did he didn't speak of it. He was dressed in the coat of the Hospitaller, and received by them, because he'd always been a patron of the Order of the Hospital.

Pairaud:

An example it would not have hurt us to follow. They've secured Rhodes for themselves.

De Molay:

An endeavor exactly as pointless as another Crusade unless it supported some design of ours above mere existence. But you interrupt…When he died, the priest of Saint-Semin planned to burn his body so at the urgent request of his son it was taken by the Hospitallers to their Grand Priory on the rue de la Dalbade in Toulouse, and placed in an open sarcophagus. The Pope would not allow them to bury him in consecrated ground, so they simply left him lay there in the hall.

The story is told that the Hospitallers petitioned the Pope to allow Count Raimond to be buried on consecrated ground. But he had died excommunicate and the Pope refused. So the Hospitallers determined that if the Count couldn't be buried in consecrated ground, or entombed, they would put him on a bier (*beer*) in a hall instead for the Pope could not forbid them to keep his remains. And there his bones still lie.

Charnay:

I follow the outline of the story but I don't see what you mean by it.

De Molay:

Why think you that such a Great Knight embraced heresy?

Pairaud:

Did he? He sought the church in the end.

De Molay:

Sought a military order which respected him. He was excommunicated and forbidden burial on consecrated ground. Why entertain the Cathars?

Charnay:

Politics, I suppose. He didn't like the vise of the Pope and the King of France that had been tightening since the Great Schism with the Eastern Church just before the Crusades. His family knew something of the Levant. I suppose he knew the West to be narrow and getting narrower, and he saw the Heretics as a check on their ambition to impose a monolithic rule.

Pairaud:

A curious story that is spoken in the lands where I was raised. It is recalled to me now, and I heard it attested by a Hospitaller who had served at the Grand Priory in Toulouse. That upon the back of the skull of Raimond VI, Heretic Count of Toulouse, was the natural mark in the bone of a Fleur-de-Lis.

De Molay:

A strange sigil to find. What is its import?

Pairaud:

Some say the arms of Phillip Augustus who bested him. But there are others who say it marks him a Saint of those secrets held in Asia, the same significance it has to myself and thee.

Charnay:

He was a fool to stand against the King of France. As, I suppose, were we.

Pairaud:

He never fell to battle, though his son was brought to heel. The King was not so strong then, and the people of Occitania, were different. They hated mightily the Frankish law that ties all men to the land, and ties them to their Lord as chattels. Those things they owed to their Lords were by contract, and they might walk away from their land and go to the city or elsewhere as they pleased.

De Molay:

They didn't like the idea of being slaves, you mean?

Pairaud:

Tied to serve the land and the Lord.

De Molay:

Servus. The Roman word for slaves.

Pairaud:

Are we not all servus of God?

De Molay:

I am and am not, as are you, for we know the true nature of God. But I was a false servant, for I wasted Godhood. I spent the last decade of my free life on a fool's errand, promoting a new crusade. I was content for it to be an illusory dream, for I knew it to be useless at best, and a matter of despair and bloody ruin at worst. Yet all my energies went into sustaining that illusion, in the conviction that as long as the illusion stood, our Knights and dependents would be safe. I had no other goal. I was content with safety. I did not seek to protect the pilgrims.

Pairaud:

What could you do? The Holy Land was fallen.

De Molay:

I failed in courage, but most of all I failed in imagination. I thought...of those pilgrims who came from West to East, and ignored those pilgrims in my charge. Yourself, Villiers, so many others. You learned things in that harsh and forbidding land, and made pilgrimage from east to west.

Pairaud:

So we did. And unlike you we did not fear to use those things we had learned. Yet I would never say you were not brave. You fought as well as any man.

De Molay:

To fight is often the path of easy acceptance, not the act of courage. Villiers was right. I should have made common cause with you. I did not love you well enough.

Pairaud:

In fairness, I had no love for you.

De Molay:

I gave you no cause to. There are times when love must come of pragmatic necessity that it should temper and moderate great quarrels or small irritations. For we are able to love all things. In Armenia I learned the truths of which your knowledge was but the gate. I lamented your ignorance, yet I did not teach you. I lamented your rashness, yet my answer was to hide the light. My illusion called for you to raise soldiers thus I did not confront your methods.

Charnay:

Well, what else could you have done?

De Molay:

Stood for that which we had all learned. Imposed a strict and careful system by which men might be brought to the knowledge of that unspeakable name known to us. Used our arms strategically to make a base of safety, unassailable like those heretics a generation past made at Montsegur, yet perhaps so close to the Roman Empire of the East or of the Muslims that none would dare dislodge us. Maintained order and discipline to protect our brothers and sisters within the order from manifold abuses, and recruited at a pace that did not exacerbate...nearly demand...that we should happily clutch vipers unto our bosom.

Pairaud:

I will tell you that it is truth you could want many soldiers or good soldiers. In asking for both you tied my hands so that I gave you neither. I could too have been less careless. The more vipers that slithered into our midst, the more I used the rule of fear, and pain, and mystery to hold them in check, not out of pleasure in their pain but out of fear born of necessity. Yet their venom spread and dripped out into the world. And in my pride I thought to put a golden leash on the biggest viper of them all. But one cannot leash a snake and Phillip bit us mortally.

De Molay:

My guilt is greater than yours for I knew, yet every day let the mantra of "we must survive" justify my inaction. I imagined as long as I did not tell you forcibly that the snake could slip the lead and lead you to disturb it, the serpent would remain forever passive.

Pairaud:

In this dungeon, I have come to love you in that worldly way of those who share sorrows or burdens. That still does not make me wish to burn to death with you. I understand now, though, that you tried to keep us safe. And I think you understand that we wanted more to survive the failure of our enterprises in the

Levant, which was beyond us all, and to enjoy those luxuries we could without remorse, more than to do any great mischief or evil.

Yet even had we launched a great and pointed heresy, who is to say we would not have been killed as quickly. I was proud, and as the hidden wisdom says, "If there is one emotion which is never useful, it is pride; for this reason, that it is bound up entirely"[235]...with thy self.

De Molay:

A great cavalry wins battles by inexorable charge, but a small force may prevail by good maneuver. Change does not come to human hearts as a slow sea tide. The hearts of men are like a shuttered tower. For many years they gather must and dust, but eventually comes a savage storm and in that moment the shutters are blown open and all the dust and must cleared away.

Charnay:

And we, the storm?

De Molay:

Who better than Knights to blaspheme their truths, to confound their inane doctrines of sin? Who better understands both extremes, asceticism and the pleasure of the flesh? The Pope declares himself supreme on one hand, and the King of France hires scholars to teach that the King governs by some special right from God to refute the Pope. We, all of us, know that God cares nothing for them, nor despises pleasures of the flesh, nor is even God. We could have stood them both off as Toulouse did a century ago. We could have been the root of a fiery promulgation of the true Laws of Nature that made the heresy of the last century seem like a child's game. Is it not the way of knights to die in battle?

Charnay:

I suppose perhaps we might have broken them by our willingness to transgress. And if not, at least we'd have stood for something and our secrets not die in vain.

Pairaud:

Even I have come understand this much, that the secrets are not treasures to be hoarded; that unused they are toxins which multiply and rot the soul. I wasted them on trifles and if you had no plan neither did I. I gave Villiers the slack of his lead as one does a war dog. But it is too late to undo all that now. Is that what the two of you intend in Court? To burn shouting out the name?

De Molay:

If I died screaming the name, their ears could not hear it. What you never understood, what even for all his potence Old Matthieu never understood, and what in my shame I never taught to you is that the name is nothing in itself. It is the path one walks to learn the name which holds the power. It is too late to teach it now. Barbarous words, they would say, an abomination blurted by heretics. The best we can do is declare our innocence to arouse enough wonder that others may stumble on our tracks and discover our treasure.

Pairaud:

For all you say, I expect things would have turned out the same. Us burning, Villiers away and safe. I wonder where Villiers is now? Nothing has been heard of him. If I know him, he's having a good laugh at our misfortune.

Charnay:

He was always capable of caring for himself.

De Molay:

That's just the thing. He was not. Villiers was ever no more than a spoiled and willful child. He knew only the how and what of the Name, not the why. But did I teach him? Did I set an example? As his sworn Master, I failed to care for him. I did not keep his road safe, but left him to his own devices and looked the other way. I failed him as I failed all of you. I raged about his failings, but did I ever lift him past them? Did I ever fire his imagination to truly fight for the Ruby Cross? I could not bring myself to break from this vast web of rule of tradition...the Templars were about the Crusades and pilgrims to Jerusalem. I, of all people, came to know the Temple was not in Jerusalem. Villiers is the most blameless of us.

Pairaud: laughs

He was my friend, as much as he could be friend to any man, and even I question that. He was a first class villain.

De Molay:

He never knew his own true will. I knew mine, but didn't act on it. Who is worse? The Knight who through ineptitude never spots the enemy, or the Knight who sees the foe and slinks away in cowardice.

Pairaud:

Is that why you burn then? In penance for cowardice?

De Molay:

All penance is ignorant foolishness save one kind only. That which sets right wrongs which have been done and in so doing recovers the course of Will. I burn because I can still accomplish my will even now. The smoke of my pyre will be a sign, a trail to follow. Through the fire I will become the light. We alone saw the cross was empty and called it so. We said that Jesus was a man and no more a God than you or I, and so it was. We spoke the word of truth as we learned it and knew it, as it came down from of old. I will stand in Court and say that the Templars are blameless for they are in spirit, and all will wonder at that, and ask many questions.

Pairaud:

And you too, Charnay?

Charnay:

I am as guilty. I knew and did nothing. I knew you were careless with the relics. I knew you were in over your head with the King of France. I knew that you took in and turned a blind eye towards those who did harm to Brothers, and Sisters, to all those in our care. I knew all of this was wrong. But I feared the wrath of the King of France, the Pope, the people should I disturb the balance. Told myself it was better a few suffer than that all our houses be torn down. Told myself that if something was to be done it was the Grand Master's job. I am a knight and a Knight should fear not at all. In the end I saved no one.

Pairaud:

You, then, burn for guilt?

Charnay:

No. I will blaze gloriously and leave a story that echoes down the years, instead of dying in obscurity and misery as you choose. But it is done now. They come for us.

De Molay: *holds his hands up to Pairaud as a benediction*

I am the flame that burns in every human heart, and in the core of every star.[236]

Epilogue

Andrae:

I am Life, and the giver of Life; yet therefore is the knowledge of me the knowledge of death.[237]

Visitor:

Your eyes are getting heavy.

Andrae:

So they are. Is that why you came here? To make me question my will?

Visitor:

No. I came to reassure you that you have seen the accomplishment of your will.

Andrae:

I got nothing I wanted. Not from those books. I wanted to reconcile the foolishness of fighting over this or that way of seeing God. I wanted a Kingdom with morality and strictness, where everyone was lifted up. Where science was held in check by the spirit and the spirit upheld by science. A world without war and greed and cruelty where everyone could accomplish something of meaning without fear or hunger. That most of all.

Visitor:

And so you did.

Andrae:

I got nothing of the sort. They looked at an allegory and were enraptured by the secret. They produced a hundred books, a thousand on the Secrets of the Brothers of the Rosy Cross, and the secret society. Even made the society itself in time.

Visitor:

Did you think all that could be accomplished in one year? One lifetime?

Andrae:

I sought to start.

Visitor:

And so you did. Did you think they needed to be taught about the need for medicine, or the fundamental concept of providing food for everyone? Those things are easily comprehensible. But they are driven...we are driven...by our passions.

Andrae:

We shouldn't be. Or rather they should be the horses for our cart, our hands upon the reins. We should not be dragged behind them.

Visitor:

You gave them a way to remember it. A thing of beauty that calls it to mind. The method of science. The aim of religion.

Andrae:

It was all trifles. They play with horoscopes and trying to derive an elixir from mercury. They play number games with holy books and try to discern the end of days. It does nothing to uplift the lives of the people, especially those shattered by our endless wars. It does nothing to feed anyone or rebuild houses or stop the fighting that destroyed them.

Visitor:

The War has ended.

Andrae:

I do not need to look at the stars to know a greater one will come.

Visitor:

It is not all trifles. It is not all playing endlessly with numbers to no real end. In London there is even now a true College, a secret and invisible one, set up in your model. It is no group of little minds.

Andrae:

The English ridicule the work of Dee, of Fludd, of Paracelsus. They exclude the spiritual entirely....maybe they are right to. But no...the excess of zeal for the spiritual may interfere with science as the Inquisition did in damning Copernicus. Yet with no spiritual aspect science is blind and may bring grave and terrible results.

Visitor:

You have tied the two together such that there will always be a force to bring them back.

The Thelemic Initiations

Andrae:

So you say. My eyes are heavy. I must sleep.

Secretary:

He looks so drawn and pale. Should I fetch the Doctor?

Visitor:

He is beyond all medicine now. Even mine. I'll sit with you and wait. I do not think it shall be long now.

Secretary:

So what it was that he wanted in his youth, you think that he got it?

Visitor:

Yes and no. He did not become a Dark Adept or fall into the abyss, but had an uneasy truce with his Will. He could not take that one step from Orthodoxy, so was ever at war within himself. The war and the hard times beat him into a conventional mold, as it does so many, but he was above the crowd, for where they were driven to caution by fear, he was driven by love. Not romance but the daily sort of love that so many cannot rise to. It is easy to feel the arrows of eros, but not so easy to love those who have been made ugly by war.

Secretary:

Wouldn't he have gotten in trouble? If he had written more about those secret conspiracies?

Visitor:

Quite likely. But what glorious trouble. Yet, I judge too quickly and must confess my mistake. I see that he did live his true will, the mantle of orthodoxy no more than a convenient overcoat taken from a corpse. His will was not what I would have it be, what I imagined, but that failure is to project the Will of another onto him. I am impatient and would have him have fulfilled his dreams. But the fulfillment of his glorious dreams belongs to yet another.

Secretary:

Your story made me curious. Do you think the Templars really knew all those things?

Visitor:

It is easy to put words into the mouths of Templars. Von Eschenbach did that when they yet breathed. The Templars lived during a time that saw the lives of men in much of the west change. The old systems passed away and many people were bound as slaves to the land, and the name of God was used to justify their subjugation, a bondage we are just now starting to cast off. The Church of Rome never entirely wiped the old ideas from the world. Perhaps the Templars knew and perhaps they didn't but they were much in the Levant. At a guess some knew a little, some knew more, but many of them knew enough to make them dangerous to the Church by which one Man stood for the word of God and the Crown that appropriated God unto itself.

Secretary:

Didn't the great Kings create the modern states though? And our current science?

Visitor:

The great Empires that late spent near thirty years raping, pillaging, murdering, and plundering all the land that lay between them? How did their unending wars make us any safer? Their repression of trade, restriction of the rights of the cities, binding of people to the plow? Tell me how that has improved our world? They take credit for those things which circumstance and ingenuity visited upon them, oft times unwilling.

Secretary:

Are humans then truly evil and flawed by nature?

Visitor:

Humans have great qualities of nobility. We are by instinct generous when we ourselves are not in need, we are inclined by natural law to recognize fairness and be repulsed by cheating, and to show loyalty to those who are fair with us. We see beauty in those actions which are fair and generous, and hold that beauty sacred. Yet our greatest strength is our greatest weakness. Alone we are easy prey for a lion but together we can tame the surface of the earth. To act together requires leadership.

Secretary:

How is that a weakness?

Visitor:

By Natural Law, we endeavor to apply our instincts for fairness and generosity to our selection of leaders. Yet our repulsion of cheating and our valuing of those things we hold beautiful and our instinct for loyalty can allow the perversion and manipulation of our passions such that Kings or Pontiffs or their Ministers bring us to great ruin through greed and ignorance. If we question them always, we accomplish nothing, but if we question them not at all we may come to the sort of ruin this land has seen since my youth.

Secretary:

How then may we be uplifted?

Visitor:

Through science valued with the spirit. By showing reverence for each human as if they were a King, and turning their minds against acceptance of slavery. By discerning fact from fiction. By making our passions our tools instead of our masters. And the mechanism of this is the constant moderation and examination of our motives so that we refine them to a pure and single thread which is our ultimate will.

Secretary:

I have one question yet. In your story, the Templars spoke of a Word or Name. I imagine even if your story is fiction that name is real?

Visitor:

> It is.

Secretary:

> May I know it?

Andreae: *Draws a ragged breath and is still.*

Visitor: *Leans forward and closes Andreae's eyelids firmly.*

> I fear the veil of life hath fallen from the eyes of the only one who could tell you...he had the gift of teaching which I do not, and the word alone you would not understand. You must find it for yourself.

II° Initiation – Script – Second Section

The Oath

Esclarmonde:

>Now, as there is a great battle on the morrow. I shall take your oath in place of the Count.

Esclarmonde directs the initiates to stand in a line before her.

>Good travelers. You have proven yourself companions of the Royal Arch of Enoch, or Pillars of Thoth. Now it is time that you become true Knights of the Rose Cross. You shall swear a mighty oath of fealty to me, and to the Red Cross of Toulouse. Kneel before me and repeat after me.

This is a point of vigilance. Some initiate may be repulsed enough that they reflexively attempt to draw their blade, and even if only in defiance may strike or injure someone else. The Fool is bid to be watchful and calm anyone who may react strongly.

Initiates: *It is presumed that, having just received a lesson on leadership, the initiates will all demur. If they do not, as in the past grade, the Fool should provide them with some guidance and remind them to think about whether swearing and oath to Esclarmonde is truly part of their Will. It is remotely possible that someone may insist their "True Will" is to swear allegiance to Count Raimond. The Senior Initiator must be prepared to deal with this and all eventualities.*

At the first sign of demurral from the initiates, Guillemette speaks:

Guillemette:

>Understand that this is different from what has been asked before. This is not a matter of some nebulous oath to an imagined superior. This is different, for it is we who have been friend to you asking. Bind yourself to us, for we would never lead you wrongly.

The Fool should be prepared to encourage the initiates to question whether they should kneel. As they continue to refuse, Raimond d'Alfaro will speak up.

Raimond d'Alfaro:

>It is a matter of destiny and ordained. If you wish to pick up the banner of Thelema and become Knights, then you surely know that all Knights must make a vow of obedience.

It is presumed that the initiates will continue to refuse, having picked up on the cues given by the Fool. They may be prompted "Do you then refuse?" but it is not necessary for them to make a declaration, so long as the Sovereign Initiator is satisfied that they are not of a mind to accept this oath.

The Sovereign Initiator may wish to arrange a signal with the performer of Esclarmonde to indicate when to move on, or may simply utter a cue such as "let us then continue."

The Thelemic Initiations

Esclarmonde:

> You have then passed a great test of the Rose Cross Knight though there is yet another before the oath may be administered. For now we shall have more instruction…I would have you attend here to the Tracing Board.

There is nothing of import actually on the tracing board at this moment. However, attention should be drawn to the rose and cross at the top as a distraction for the Stone dropping to take the initiates by surprise. Esclarmonde may ad lib a bit as necessary to ensure that the stone may be dropped safely and with full surprise.

The Falling of the Stone

There is a tremendous crash behind the initiates and a square stone crashes down. They may be coated with some dust or debris which are calculated to do no major harm and be easily cleaned. Care should be taken in regards to allergies and inhalants, therefore actual building debris or gypsum residue should not be used. Corn starch or flour may be acceptable in small quantities.

The stone strikes Raimond d'Alfaro who is knocked to the ground by it.

Guillemette goes to him, but Esclarmonde remains seated.

Guillemette:

> Child of my flesh of flesh! He has been struck down by a stone hurled down from heaven. Oh bitter regret!

Esclarmonde:

> He is dead but may not be killed.

Guillemette:

> I fear it is a curse brought by his heritance! A repayment for the sins of his forefathers and myself.

Esclarmonde:

> "The word of Sin is Restriction….There is no bond that can unite the divided but love."[238]

Raimond d'Alfaro: stonily without moving

> I am alone; there is no God where I am.

Esclarmonde:

> Breathe the word I have given you from the Book into his ear.

Guillemette: *Kneels and whispers a word which is inaudible. As the word pertains to the Greater Mysteries and may not be known to the initiate playing this role a substitute word may be used in case it should be overheard. Jabulon, the Masonic Password of the First Degree, may suffice.*

Raimond d'Alfaro: Rising

> There is no law beyond do what thou wilt!

Esclarmonde:

> Make an examination of the stone.

Guillemette: *goes to the stone shakily*

> There is script upon it in the characters we have been taught by the Jewish scholars of Toulouse who know the secrets of the eight, and the three, and the three. This stone must have been prized from some ancient place of worship destroyed by our enemies.

Esclarmonde:

> They thought to destroy us and instead they have strengthened us. Such is often the way when one brings force of arms against the magician who knows their will.

The initiates are bid to examine the stone. On each face is written a character. Together they form ALHIM. The Face on which the H is written is inset or boxed. The Fool may call their attention to the word on the Tracing Board in order to decipher the characters if they do not know them.

Esclarmonde will allow the initiates some leeway in their discussion of the formula of ALHIM. However, this is not meant to be a major puzzle and they should be quickly guided to a conclusion.

Esclarmonde:

> The formula of ALHIM has been revealed to us from on high. This secret which is so revealed is timely and we shall reveal to you its details, as it forms an integral part of that work which it is given to me to reveal to you.

Guillemette:

> Here I must give you a caution. We are accustomed to relying on the Master Therion and give great regard to his revelations. Yet we have been careful to say they are a bedrock and foundation, not the entirety, of the revelation of Thelema. It is worth noting a particular limitation.

> We have noted well that the nature of the Master Therion was neither entirely masculine, nor feminine, nor did he consider himself to be wholly of either gender. Yet his understanding was colored by his time and birth. It is written in that Book which you were handed at your first initiation, "the work of the wand and the work of the sword; these he shall learn and teach."[239]

> Now there is also Comment which must be given regard, for it is mandated by that Book itself, "he shall comment thereupon by the wisdom of Ra-Hoor-Khuit."[240] And, in that comment, the Master Therion muses, "Why am not I to learn and teach the work of the Cup and of the Disk? Is it because they are the feminine weapons? Shall the Scarlet Woman attend to these? The Book does not say so; the passives are ignored. I feel the omission as a lack of balance, the only case of the kind in the Book."[241]

> Thus, we are officially warned that there the revelation is, or was, incomplete. We know now that that teaching was not perfected, could not be perfected, in the language of that day and time. Thus, we must look elsewhere for that teaching, and recognize as well the limitations in what we read. In regards to his recognition of the mysteries of the Cup and the Disk, it is often hard to know when the Master Therion had run up against the limits of his mandate and when he was being deliberately obtuse. Yet, at the end of his life he was still learning and studying the mysteries of the eleven.

In the published texts, the Master either fails to comprehend entirely the import or, more likely, refuses to put such unconventional wisdom into print for publication.

In the understanding of the nature of the Aeon as "Two sexes in one person," and of the Formula of ALHIM, the Master Therion cut close to understanding of all the mysteries. On that foundation you are led to those revelations of your time which, if even they do not fully complete the understanding of the Cup and the Disk, enlarge upon it.

The Instruction

As in the previous grades, the role of the instructor may be performed with the person who has the most familiarity and comfort with the subject.

Exegesis of ALHIM[242]

Instructor:

The formula of ALHIM is presented in Chapter Four, of Part Three of Book 4, Liber ABA. As we discuss the formula, we shall quote liberally from the text, which you will find on that short list of most urgently recommended reading.

ALHIM or Elohim is, as you have already learned, the root of the word for Gods. There is much more that can be divined from it, for it contains the story of the creation of Light and the Universe. It contains all the elements, not leading one into another as in Y-H-V-H but, rather, thrown together, harmonized only by their stormy energy.

In the center, He is the breath of spirit.

At the beginning, Aleph is Air.

At the end, Mem is Water.

Aleph and Mem make Am the mother womb of all that may be.

Yod, by juxtaposition with He, is the Yod of Y-H-V-H; the Fire of the Father.

Lamed stands in for Earth, being Libra, which emphasizes the influence of Venus.

ALHIM therefore is a formula of Consecration, not a complete ceremony.

"It is the breath of benediction, yet so potent that it can give life to clay and light to darkness."[243]

In consecrating a weapon,

Aleph is seen as the force, like a thunderbolt.

Lamed is similarly seen as force, but a driving principle which is likened to an Ox-goad. Lamed is also balance and represents the care of the magician in perfecting their instruments. "It is the loving care which he bestows upon perfecting his instruments, and the equilibration of that fierce force which initiates the ceremony."[244]

From our previous mystery LAShTAL, we are familiar with Aleph Lamed and Lamed Aleph in relation to YHVH, and the incestuous mythology implied by it.

Yod is the creative energy, and also solitude and silence of the Hermit. It is the Red Lion from our previous lesson, which is often cognate with sperm.

Finally, Mem is water, the sea at Peace. It is the White Eagle, cognate with those sustaining and receptive fluids of life.

At the center broods Spirit, Heh, mildness of the lamb and horns of the Ram, Bacchus, or Christ. This is Nuit; not as a passive but as an active, enabling the awakening of the Eld of the Father, the word which raises the procreative clay of Osiris to life. Here Heh transcends gender, being both Mother and Father, Nuit arched over the Earth, the essence of self-engendering Kneph or Kamephis, the God of the Black Rite which gives Perfection, the God whom is both Serpent and Egg.[245]

After the magician has created his instrument and balanced it truly, and filled it with the lightnings of his Will, then is the weapon laid away to rest; and in this Silence, a true Consecration comes.

The Master Therion suggests contrasting the formula ALIM, which is the same formula deprived of its creative self-engendering spirit.

ALIM is the masculine plural of the masculine AL, while ALHIM is the masculine plural of the feminine ALH. He suggests that ALIM might be presumed to be more "virile" but dismisses this. The masculine has no meaning unless it is in relation to some feminine correlative.

Instead, he suggests ALIM is genderless. And here we gain an insight into the steps away from mere phallocentrism to a true understanding of the creative force. Whereas the archetype of female for creation needs the metaphor of male to be fertilised, the androgyne ALIM is fertilized by the Spirit. How then does ALIM, deprived of the spirit which engenders, represent a magical formula?

Here, Master Therion's description is obscured or incomplete so you should attend closely to my words that you understand its meaning. It is couched in the analogies of the old Aeon, and iconoclastic terminology of the period.

He speaks of the magick of illusion; obtaining effects by merely altering the arrangement of things. Such magick is appropriate to the moon, and to reflected light. By the theories of the day, this was related to black magick, sorcery, or witchcraft – illusion without the power of creation.

How then does ALIM bear on the phenomenon of energy and of Hadit?

We learn the true magician must sometimes rearrange the structure of a formula, just as the chemist must rearrange the molecules of isomers. All operations which do not create or transform fall into this category, but they should not be seen as inferior or undesirable on this ground. This is, elsewhere, likened to operations of the Tao with the Yin and Yang. You have already been told that sexual magick, whether literal or metaphorical, has the power to create new life, both in the sense of living beings as well as possibilities.

We come to understand that "Yin hath also a Formula of Force. And the Nature of the Yin is to be still, and to encircle of limit, and it is as a Mirror, reflecting diverse Images without Change in its own Kind."

This type of force, we are told, does not want to overlap the barriers of its own plane, and thus is best used in operations of a definite and restricted type.

He has already laid the groundwork for the understanding that all humans have both the active and passive sexual nature, but either fails to comprehend entirely the import or, more likely, refuses to put such unconventional wisdom into print for publication. It is fine, however, because those who came after understood perfectly well.

We are given, then, a riddle which can be more easily resolved now than when it was written; another interpretation of ALIM relevant to that principle of engenderment which is associated with eleven. This formula is presented as "totally different," but we can see clearly at some distance in time the relationship.

Aleph is referred to as Hapocrates, with a sly wink to Catullus[246] if we fail to get the reference.
This is the Cup or eye of Horus, which we do not shy to say is the Anus.
Lamed implies the "exaltation of Saturn" and suggests the Three of Swords in a particular manner.
Yod then recalls Hermes.
Mem recalls the Hanged Man.

Thus a Tetragrammaton which contains no arbitrarily feminine component.

The initial force here is the Holy Spirit and it's vehicle or weapon the "Sword and Balances." Justice is then done upon the Mercurial "virgin," with the result that the man is "hanged" or extended, and is slain in this manner.

Such an operation makes creation impossible, but there is no re-arrangement. The creative force is expended deliberately to be destroyed, entirely absorbed in its own cylinder of action. This will be considered with reference to the Red Lion in our previous Instruction.

This formula, we are told, avoids contact with the inferior planes, is self sufficient, and involves no responsibility, leaving its masters stronger in themselves but wholly free to fulfill their essential natures. The technique as described if it is not already obvious is of anal sex.

We are also told that the title of Knight of Qadosh is conferred upon the adepts who have mastered this technique. It is our belief that the title rightly pertains to those who have mastered the formula of the Aeon of Horus, though that is one way that an Adept might come to that mystery.

Thus, we do not shy for a moment in saying that this is a valid sexual formula, and that the Master Therion's exegesis of it is unquestionably valid. Yet, it is but one conceptualization of the Formula of ALIM. A naive read might suggest that this is a principle reserved for those with a penis, yet a moment's reflection tells us that Master Therion, who considered that the abuse of this formula was an "abomination," was more often the cylinder than the dispenser of creative force. To be sure, the cylinder is Hapocrates, the Aleph which is energy and action. Yet, Aleph is not the active force. That is the Holy Spirit and its sword.

The physical form of that dispenser and "cylinder" could be whatever was deemed suitable by the Adept, and the physical fluids might, as noted in our previous work, be dispensed with entirely in some configurations. It is a recipe, a true and valid one, but like any recipe it is a starting point, not ending point, for our work.

The larger lesson is this: In the Old Aeon, the formula of sex was tied exclusively to representation of the masculine and feminine. We are given an unambiguous list:

Aeon of Isis – Matriarchal Age. One sex.

Aeon of Osiris – Patriarchal Age. Two sexes.

Aeon of Horus – Two sexes in one person.

"Note that there are now two sexes in one person throughout, so that each individual is self-procreative sexually, whereas Isis knew only one sex, and Osiris thought the two sexes opposed. Also the formula is now Love in all cases; and the end is the beginning, on a higher plane."

The Fool:

So does this mean I have to have...anal sex? Or be a different sex than I am?

Instructor:

It means, O Fool, that you may be whatever you are. It is the opening of a vast array of possibilities, illustrated with one example which was readily comprehensible to Master Therion. What it means to you as a magician is that there is no more Yin and Yang or, rather, that both are made manifest in you, and you may work them as you see fit. It is the recognition of a fact which the Holy ones of Qadosh have known since the days of the House of Asherah which the dullards of our long past drama so deplored.

The Fool:

So I can stay the same?

Instructor:

No one can ever stay the same, O Fool. We are encouraged to cultivate the qualities which our culture assigns to the gender opposite ourselves. This is no more than most of us already know. We have no wish to be archetypes, but instead to cultivate all those powers we have been denied by custom. We are told "It will then be lawful for a magician to invoke Isis, and identify himself with her; if he fail to do this, his apprehension of the Universe when he attains samadhi will lack the conception of maternity. The result will be a metaphysical and – by corollary – ethical limitation in the Religion he founds."[247]

The Fool:

At the risk of belaboring a point, even if we concede that this doctrine, at least in extension is core to the concept of Thelema, what does anal sex have to do with the Rose and...

The Fool's words come out more slowly, as if realizing what the answer is.

Cross...?

Instructor: *Is silent and looks at the Fool.*

The Fool:

Never mind. I sort of answered my own question there didn't I?

Instructor:

Now if you will allow me to finish. This formula is the basis for the operation of sexual magick without gender, for it abhors procreation on the physical plane. And thus we intuit a secret. The Aleph may refer to any chalice or any conceptualization which retains the energy of creation in any of its forms, physical or spiritual.

This is why the religions of the Old Aeon, and even those pseudo-religions of society and politics, so abhor the use of sexual energy without the creation of a child - because it is the creation of a powerful weapon for the will, and this formula may be richly manipulated. This is a further instruction in the Mystery of the Dwarf-Homunculous, applying the lesson of the Magical Child to the creation of any tool.

The formula by which only the actives are invoked suggests, as we have said, the self-engendering Kneph. Which leads fluidly to our final lesson, which is the invocation of the Bornless One.

The Fool:

They must perform this rite before they may become Knights?

Esclarmonde:

A part of the necessary education for the Rose Cross Knight is a full understanding of both the rite by which the Holy Guardian Angel may be invoked, and of the nature of that Angel. That, they must receive and accept. They shall not perform that work today, but a part of their oath as Knights is to begin that work, so for their Oath to be valid, they must gain adequate understanding to know what it is that they are swearing to.

The Ritual, Liber Samekh

Instructor:

We have reached that point where the scale and preparation necessary for ritual transcends the space and time of initiation. The definition of all magical ritual is the union of the self with the infinite or, as it is said classically, the Microcosm with the Macrocosm. The Invocation of the Holy Guardian Angel is therefore the Supreme and Complete Holy Ritual.

The Fool:

Oh, I've heard of this. I see where that's a problem. We need to do a big magical retreat, and to do that we need money and time off from work.

Instructor:

Perhaps. Before you return to take the next step in Initiation, you are charged to complete the work of the invocation of the Holy Guardian Angel. There are tools at your disposal: most especially, *The Sacred Book of Abramelin the Mage*, *Liber Samekh*, which we shall touch on momentarily, and the revelations of the 8th Aethyr as set down in *Liber 418*, the *Vision and the Voice*.

The Fool:

In all seriousness, isn't this something they need a lot of preparatory work and reading for? Should they even be taught this if they haven't done all the basic work?

Instructor:

What basic work do you mean, O Fool?

The Fool:

Oh, I don't know. Elemental magick. Meditation. All sorts of basic...stuff.

Instructor:

It is well that those who would have Knowledge and Conversation of the Holy Guardian Angel have such basic grounding. Thus in this degree, as we commended previously the Cairo Working, which is *Liber AL*, and the *Vision and the Voice*, which is *Liber 418*, we remind the Aspirant that *Book Four, Liber ABA* is also delivered of inspiration – that of the Ab-ul-Diz working which was posthumously published under the putative number of *Liber 60*. We recommend the thorough reading, not only of the working itself, but of the entirety of *Book Four*, Liber *ABA*. As this is a large work, it may take some time. We highlight certain sections that may be suitable for immediate attention.

That said, there was a time not much more than a century ago by your figuring, when the number of useful books on magick that had been published in the modern era could be written on a single sheet of stationery, and to find classic texts one had to go to the British Museum Reading Room. At that time, the most sophisticated orders passed around sheets of instructions on hand written "flying rolls."

That is no longer the case. There is no agreed upon comprehensive "basic education" in magick. If someone has taken the time and effort to initiate into an order which practices Ceremonial magick, we must assume they have the grounding to be a magician. We cannot possibly look at the tens of thousands of books and say "these six make you qualified, but these six don't." Nor can we say "these five difficult to read books written in 1925 are vital to your understanding of magick, but these twenty published in 2010 mean nothing."

In the early 20th century, it was fair to assume, both, that most people coming to an order knew little of magick and that they equally knew very little of philosophy or the underlying ideas of science. In the modern era, this is not so true. Even those who have never read Nietzsche are familiar, through media, with his principles and many more sophisticated ideas, though they could not say who originated them.

We don't know what you've read and we don't know what you understand, but we do know this: If we say "halt and read many things that are strange to you, and take much time on trifles," you will abandon Thelema and move on to some other practice.

The one thing we cannot do is turn back the tide of the Aeon. In stories, we celebrate those difficult paths of initiation where someone may be forced to contemplate the infinite or do busy work for a decade to learn patience, but they are symbolic myths now, if they ever held much truth. We accomplish nothing if we initiate only those ghosts who were suitable for initiation a century past.

The Thelemic Initiations

The Thelemic Order is an order for working Magicians. The Order General exists to provide a universal collegium where magicians may learn in the Socratian fashion, questioning each other and exchanging ideas.

The Thelemic Initiations of the Most Ancient Order of the Defenders of the Temple of the East and of the Hermetic Fellowship of Light exist to provide a path through those ordeals which can, and must, occur to anyone who is seeking attainment. What good would be an order of Templars that defended only the last mile of the road?

In the New Aeon, we celebrate the path of initiation, not as catastrophic death and rebirth, but as the growth of a child. Our Order is not one to engage in coddling or encourage arrested development, but rather that which presents the bold child with the chance to explore and grow into the fullness of adulthood in a healthy way. As with every simile or metaphor there are limits, and to be clear, more for the same of those who read these mysteries without the proper context rather than those who understand them, those ideas we nurture our spiritual children with we do not hold to be meant for those who are still children in the flesh.

Here, however, we do charge the seeker to pause, waiting to return to this place until they have grown in the way of Thelema, for the next initiation has many hard lessons. Should they return they must bear the Cup, as described in *Liber ABA, Magick in Theory and Practice*, Part II, Chapter 7, "The Cup."

We are told that the Aspirant must analyze themselves with "indefatigable energy, shrewd skill, and accurate subtlety;[248] but then be content to observe the interplay of instincts, instead of guiding them." That, not until the Aspirant is familiar with them, should they undertake those practices which enable them to read the Word of their Will. Here is the time to take conscious control of the faculties in order to do thy Will.

The Fool:

Then they may not actually perform this ritual until they have fully analyzed themselves?

Instructor:

They should perform it at their earliest prepared convenience, for it is the key to such analysis.

The Fool:

Why teach so much in initiation? Why not just send them out with homework?

Instructor:

We initiate in those things which must be felt, and may require a certain patience to take in, yet we have a coherent plan.

While we have averred that true initiation does not happen solely within a ritual, we initiate in full. Does one help a pilgrim find his destination by merely telling them vaguely where the road lays? It is not given to us to put a lead around the pilgrim's neck and drag them along the road, but we may guide our pilgrim to the road, set their feet on it, and ensure that they have a start.

Likewise, does one send the pilgrim on their way with an empty food sack, or without a walking stick? These rituals are sustenance and tools handed to the pilgrim to ensure they are started on the path. To that extent, we initiate in full and not in part. We shall ensure that you leave this place fully armed with at least one method of attaining the Knowledge and Conversation of the Holy Guardian Angel.

The Fool:

The Holy Guardian Angel? What is that anyway? It sounds suspiciously like something Christian.

Instructor:

This was explained previous to answer that very objection, O Fool, but you shall stand reminded.

It is written of Master Therion "His will was sufficiently informed by common sense to decide him to teach man 'The Next Step', the thing which was immediately above him. He might have called this 'God', or 'The Higher Self', or 'The Augoeides (*oh-GEE-uh-deez*)', or 'Adi-Buddha (*AH-dee BOO-duh*)', or 61 other things — but He had discovered that these were all one, yet that each one represented some theory of the Universe which would ultimately be shattered by criticism — for He had already passed through the realm of Reason, and knew that every statement contained an absurdity. He therefore said: 'Let me declare this Work under this title: 'The obtaining of the Knowledge and Conversation of the Holy Guardian Angel", because the theory implied in these words is so patently absurd that only simpletons would waste much time in analysing it. It would be accepted as a convention, and no one would incur the grave danger of building a philosophical system upon it."[249]

There are, elsewhere, colleges of magick which will guide the seeker on every step, and that we cannot do, nor would we wish to if we could, for the seeker's path is their own. For all that we may seem adamant towards The Fool, that which we put forward is no more than the most conventional and essential skeleton of Thelema.

The Fool:

Yeah. Don't you think they get bored hearing you correct me all the time. What kind of teaching method is that?

Instructor:

This form – where a student raises questions or objections so that the Instructor may shoot them down – is the format of most classical teaching. It is the method of the *Divine Poemander*, the key of the *Corpus Hermeticum*.

But we are guides, not instructors. It is not necessary to agree with all we say to proceed along the path. We give practical demonstration of how to pass along the road and ensure that the initiate has adequate equipment and a good map. No one will say that you did not pass initiation if you leave disagreeing on some point, or even several points. It is possible that our reception of the information is flawed, or limited by our current mortal understandings.

The Fool:

I thought you weren't mortal?

Instructor:

So we are not, but our copyist is.

The Thelemic Initiations

The Fool:

So they cannot return for the next initiation until they have achieved Knowledge and Conversation?

Instructor:

They cannot return until they have invoked it, truly and earnestly. It may take a while. Master Therion speaks of a growing state in which such contact may be maintained for longer and longer periods. And to be clear, we shall not ask "did you perform Liber Samekh," or this or that other rite. We ask merely if you have truly and earnestly invoked your Holy Guardian Angel. If your answer is "yea" then you may progress.

Now, as has been stated, there is a single definition of the object of all magical ritual. It is the uniting of the Microcosm with the Macrocosm. The Supreme and Complete Holy Ritual is therefore the Invocation of the Holy Guardian Angel or, in the language of mysticism, Union with God.

The Fool:

That sounds really complex and taxing.

Instructor:

That's why we aren't doing it here and now.

What we will learn is the Bornless Ritual, which is the Invocation for Liber Samekh. Our purpose in doing so is to teach the fundaments of invoking the Macrocosm to unite with the Microcosm.

This ritual has been a source of great fear, as well it should be, because those who use it thinking that they are summoning some other being open themselves to much. But you have made an oath. You shall not forget that you are God. There is an appropriate time and place to remember that Oath. Putting yourself forward among other people is not the place. But when summoning the bornless power of creation, the self-engendering one, you must not fail.

The Fool:

What will happen if they do?

Instructor:

Probably nothing, but they may be deluded or even come under some ill influence.

The Fool:

Possessed! That is terrible!

Instructor:

We are magicians, not children with their tutors. You were, before becoming magicians, to have learned the fundaments of banishing. If you did not pursue the Star Ruby, it would be well that you review it remedially before you begin these practices on your own, but you shall come to no harm here.

The Bornless Ritual is the informal name of a spell of the Egyptians, which is known from a papyrus which was written down sometime between about the common years 100 and 400. Thus, it is contemporary with most of the books in the canon of the Christian church. It is referred to as "Stele of Jeu the Hieroglyphist in his letter."[250] This may also be interpreted as Jeu the painter, or Jeu the writer, though, in the original 1852 edition, Goodwin translates it as "An address to the god drawn upon the letter."[251]

There are many versions, some based on the more recent translations of Betz, others upon the older translation of Goodwin. It was in the possession of the Reverend William Ayton of the Golden Dawn, and routinely used by its adepts.[252] The version which Crowley used to achieve Knowledge and Conversation, was probably suggested by Allan Bennett. Whatever the case he included it as a Preliminary Invocation in his edition of the Goetia. The "barbarous names" were changed several times.

There are two arguments regarding the names. On one hand that they should not be changed as they have potence and meaning. On the other that it is their meaning which gives them import, so a Magician may bend them in alignment with their Will. However you decide to practice, whether with a preference for the oldest forms, those which carry the greatest meaning, or a mixture of both, this ritual serves as a lesson in the evolution of rites and as an example of how Magicians might change rites to serve their Will,

It may be of interest to you to pursue the original versions, and one of these shall be provided to you, as well as references, to allow you to provide another. There are many differences of opinion on the barbarous names and that, too, is of interesting debate. We shall pursue the version which was written down by the Master Therion, not because it is the most accurate, but because it may be the most easily repurposed for Thelema. You are, however, magicians, and you must in the end decide on your own version of each ritual. There is nothing wrong with using the forms suggested by Master Therion, but only if you can make those forms your own.

Likewise, in the wider work of the Holy Guardian Angel, you must make your own decisions.

We shall read through this ritual with each barbarous name rendered into the common language of this place, that you may understand them. Thus, as I read a name, I shall call on one of you to supply the words which go with it.

The Instructor walks to the Tracing Board.

Thee I invoke, the Bornless One.

This ritual may also be interpreted "headless one." In this sense we must understand the concept of the tree of life as the body of God, with Kether as its head. It is headless because we identify the body with "Ein Sof" or that form of god which is infinite and without end, which we may more commonly call the body of Nuit. Thus we are calling one formulation of Hadit within that boundless body.

Thee, that didst create the Earth and the Heavens.

Thee, that didst create the Night and the Day.

Thee, that didst create the darkness and the Light.

As all things unite in love, all things must divide to manifest as separate from that limitless body. Therefore we assert the Angel has created three pairs of opposites so that it may manifest:

Earth and Heavens - fixed versus volatile

Night and Day - that which has not manifested and that which is manifest or seen

Darkness and Light - that which us unmoved and that which is moved

Further it is explained the Negative and Positive in respect to Matter, Mind, and Motion.

Thou art ASAR UN-NEFER (*AYSAR-un-NEPHER*)

Whom no man hath seen at any time.

ASAR UN-NEFER is elaborated as "Myself made Perfect."

In the Old Aeon, the Heirophant represented the perfected Osiris, and the initiate was led to identify with Osiris to realize that they were, themselves, Osiris.

In the new Aeon, the Heirophant is Horus who is known by his complete and secret name. The formula of the dying God is abolished and the process of initiation, rather than a catastrophic death and rebirth, is seen instead as the natural growth of the Child. The symbol of this is the Fool; the innocent and impotent Hapocrates Babe who becomes the Adult Horus by obtaining the Wand. Bacchus becomes Pan. The Holy Guardian Angel is the Unconscious Creature Self; the Spiritual source of fire of life. The knowledge and conversation constitutes the state of coming of age.

And now you know why the Fool accompanies you, and will for a little while yet. The Fool is yourselves and you are the Fool. Children who will be Adults and Adults who must become Children.

Thus, the Master Therion suggests that this name ASAR UN-NEFER be replaced by the name of Horus the Child, Ra-Hoor-Khuit, at the outset, and by the name of one's own Holy Guardian Angel when it has been communicated.

Thou art IA-BESZ (*EYAH-bezz*)

Thou art IA-APOPHRASZ (*EYAH-uh-POE-frazz*)

Here we meet two old friends. You may remember them as the slayers of Hiram from the Story of the Lost Master's Word. More information is given on them.

We are told BESZ is "the Truth in Matter" which is elaborated as "the Matter that destroys and devours Godhead, for the purpose of the Incarnation of any God." Historically Besz was also the focus of a great cult and the guardian of the child Hapocrates.

APOPHRASZ is the Motion that destroys and devours Godhead, for the purpose of the Incarnation of any God.

Their combined action is to bring the God they destroy and devour into the joy of existence through division by the sacrament of "Life" or Bread - the flesh of BESZ - and "Love" or wine - the blood or venom of APOPHRASZ.

Thou hast distinguished between the Just and the Unjust.

Here, Master Therion equates Justice and Injustice to eating of the Fruit of the Tree of Knowledge of Good and Evil. Remember, in Thelema, there is no absolute good or evil. We are given a key to the true meaning of Good and Evil by relating it to the formula of Equilibrium which is the property of the magician to apply accurately to his self-made world, which we first imagined in the Pantacle. We recall, too, the injunctions in regard to how we should regard the will of others.

Thou didst make the Female and the Male.

Here, these symbols are referred to the Law of Love and the magical formula of the universe; the magician being able to return those things which are manifest to their unmanifest state through uniting opposites in ecstatic passion.

Thou didst produce the Seeds and the Fruit.

Here we are hitting the core of the Thelemic sex mystery: the union that is Love. This refers, in Master Therion's usage of the ritual, to the union of forces to create a "Child" - a thing separate from its parents. In the previous line, "Thou didst make the Female and the Male," we are talking about the union of opposites which annihilates and returns to the unmanifest state. Here, at the central mystery of Thelema, we create a new being; a thing separate from the parents. In the Bornless Ritual, we create the Angel which is ourselves, annihilating ourselves in the process, in an act of self-engenderment.

This is the nature of the Black Rite of the Kneph, the annihilation of the ego to give birth to ourselves.

Thou didst form Men to love one another, and to hate one another.

Here the magician defines the object of incarnation; self-realization through reaction to other incarnate beings.

Section Aa.

I am ANKH-F-N-KHONSU (*AHN-koff nah-KON-sue*) thy Prophet, unto Whom Thou didst commit Thy Mysteries, the Ceremonies of KHEM. (*HIM*)

In the original papyrus, this name is Moses, who it is suggested is God concealed in the form of a human. This is the assertion of the right of the magician to enter into communication with their Angel, on the ground that the Angel has taught them the secret magick necessary. The name of Moses is replaced, according to the Master Therion, with the "Adeptus minor motto." More generally, it should be one's name as a magician. Likewise, in the original, the word KHEM is rendered as Israel. It should be the magical tradition or origin of the Magus, and need not be a land, but may be any heritage or tradition.

Thou didst produce the moist and the dry, and that which nourisheth all created Life.

Here, the magician reminds the Angel that he has created the substance of transmutation, which is sometimes called the philosopher's stone, which has the virtue of uniting all opposites. This is a statement of how the Magus may partake of the "Eucharist which createth, sustaineth, and redeemeth all things."

Hear Thou Me, for I am the Angel of PTAH - APO - PHRASZ - RA (*PUH-tah-uh-POE-frazz-RAH*) (vide the Rubric): this is Thy True Name, handed down to the Prophets of KHEM. (*HIM*)

Here, the Magus identifies with a complex concept. Hadit, wrapped in the Dragon Nuit, and manifest as the Sun. The egg or heart girt with a serpent is a related idea which we'll see more about in a few moments.

The next section, which is labeled B in the ritual, is the invocation of Air. As I point to you, read to me the explanation of the Barbarous Name. When you perform the invocation as part of Liber Samekh, there are also directions for movements both physical and energetic and this ritual, like Liber V vel Reguli, is primarily widdershins. Here we focus on the meaning.

First we pace the circle, taking on the god-forms of the Elemental Gods of the quarters.

We are to let our whole being be filled with these names. Recall our previous work with vibrating names. Those who know only the superficial edge of Thelema will say that there is little guidance as to what "will" truly is, but here we are given numerous unambiguous statements. Will, in this context, is to be understood as a dynamic aspect of our Creative Self. We are told to formulate our will, but in the "bodily vehicle of spirit which is sacred to Baphomet." To be very clear, this is the suggestion that we formulate our will in the form of a Phallus; the sperm, or serpent-lion, at its core, with energies projected outwards along the shaft.

Lest we dismiss this ritual as a mere phallocentric exercise, note that Master Therion advises at the final word that the magician bring their Will rushing back within themselves, offering themselves to its point "as Artemis to PAN." Thus, even within this microcosm, the magician is a model of the self-engendering or "bornless" entity, having both phallus and womb.

Thus, while some other visualization may be better than the phallus for those to whom the phallus plays either a different, conceptual role in their creative eros, or is a negative symbol, the intent is, in all cases, for the magician to manifest both active and receptive natures.

While all of us are entitled to the Phallus should we choose to manifest it, in our era, we must construct the image of the projection of creative and sexual energy each according to our will. This bears considerable thought and experimentation. One reason we refer to the original version of this ritual and urge that you read it is to see the degree to which the Master Therion altered it, or imprinted upon it specific interpretations

We are taught that to change ancient rituals may be a risk or entail a loss of their power, but we are Magicians. When we change these things in accordance with our will, they do not lose, but rather gain, power. Thus we may alter the rituals of the Master Therion, as he himself altered the formulae of Jeu the Heiroglyph scribe.

The will is then extended beyond the circle in this imagined shape, the force of the extension of eros, whatever its form, doubling with each word.

We are told that "The conception is of Air, glowing, inhabited by a Solar-Phallic Bird, "the Holy Ghost", of a Mercurial Nature."

Hear Me: -

AR (AHH-RAYN)	O breathing, flowing Sun!
ThIAF (thee-AHH-owf)	O Sun IAF! O Lion-Serpent Sun, The Beast that whirlest forth, a thunder- bolt, begetter of Life!
RhEIBET (*RYE-bet*)	Thou that flowest! Thou that goest!
A-ThELE-BER-SET (AH-therr-EE-burr-SET)	Thou Satan-Sun Hadith that goest without Will!

A (*AHH*)	Thou Air! Breath! Spirit! Thou without bound or bond!
BELAThA (BAY-LA-thon)	Thou Essence, Air Swift-streaming, Elasticity!
ABEU (AHH-bay-oo)	Thou Wanderer, Father of All!
EBEU (AYY-bay-oo)	Thou Wanderer, Spirit of All!
PhI-ThETA-SOE (FEE-theeta-sow-AY)	Thou Shining Force of Breath! Thou Lion-Serpent Sun! Thou Saviour, save!
IB (EE-bay)	Thou Ibis, secret solitary Bird, inviolate Wisdom, whose Word in Truth, creating the World by its magick!
ThIAF (THEE-AYY-O)	O Sun IAF! (*IAO*) O Lion-Serpent Sun, The Beast that whirlest forth, a thunder- bolt, begetter of Life!

In the sacrament, we are to be wholly at one with the element, the charge conferring upon us the fullest freedom and privilege of that element.

Hear me, and make all Spirits subject unto Me; so that every Spirit of the Firmament and of the Ether: upon the Earth and under the Earth, on dry land and in the water; of Whirling Air, and of rushing Fire, and every Spell and Scourge of God may be obedient unto Me.

In the next section, we invoke Fire.

I invoke Thee, the Terrible and Invisible God: Who dwellest in the Void Place of the Spirit: -

AR-O-GO-GO-RU-ABRAO (ARR-OH-GOE-GOE-ROO-AHH-brah-oh)	Thou spiritual Sun! Satan, Thou Eye, Thou Lust! Cry aloud! Cry aloud! Whirl the Wheel, O my Father, O Satan, O Sun!
SOTOU (SOW-*thou*)	Thou, the Saviour!
MUDORIO (MOO-door-ee-oh)	Silence! Give me Thy Secret!
PhALARThAO (FOUL-AHR-THA-oh)	Give me suck, Thou Phallus, Thou Sun!

OOO (Oh-Oh-Oh)	Satan, thou Eye, thou Lust! Satan, thou Eye, thou Lust! Satan, thou Eye, thou Lust!
AEPE (AHH-AYY-PAY)	Thou self-caused, self-determined, exalted, Most High!

The Bornless One.

Hear Me, and make all Spirits subject unto Me: so that every Spirit of the Firmament and of the Ether: upon the Earth and under the Earth: on dry Land and in the Water: of Whirling Air, and of rushing Fire, and every Spell and Scourge of God may be obedient unto Me.

Section D. Water

Hear Me: -

RU-ABRA-IAF (ROO-AHH-brah-EE-AHH-Oh)	Thou the Wheel, thou the Womb, that containeth the Father IAF!
MRIODOM (MAHH-REEH-OH-DUM)	Thou the Sea, the Abode!
BABALON-BAL-BIN-ABAFT (bab-UH-lawn- BAL-BIN-AHH-baff)	Babalon! Thou Woman of Whoredom. Thou, Gate of the Great God ON! Thou Lady of the Understanding of the Ways!
ASAL-ON-AI (ASS-ah-loan-aye)	Hail Thou, the unstirred! Hail, sister and bride of ON, of the God that is all and is none, by the Power of Eleven!
APhEN-IAF (AHH-FAIN-EE-AHH-Oh)	Thou Treasure of IAO!
I (EE)	Thou Virgin twin-sexed! Thou Secret Seed! Thou inviolate Wisdom!
PhOTETh (*FOE-teth*)	Abode of the Light ....
ABRASAX (AHH-brah-SAX)	......of the Father, the Sun, of Hadith, of the spell of the Aeon of Horus!

AEOOU (AHH-AYY-OH-OH-OO)   Our Lady of the Western Gate of Heaven!

ISChURE (*ISH-oor-AY*)   Mighty art Thou!

Mighty and Bornless One!

Hear Me: and make all Spirits subject unto Me: so that every Spirit of the Firmament and of the Ether: upon the Earth and under the Earth: on dry Land and in the Water: of Whirling Air, and of rushing Fire: and every Spell and Scourge of God may be obedient unto Me.

Section E. The Invocation of Earth

I invoke Thee: -

MA (MAH)   O Mother! O Truth!

BARRAIO (BAH-RAH-EE-OH)   Thou Mass!

IOEL (EE-OH-ALE)   Hail, Thou that art!

KOThA (COE-thah)   Thou hollow one!

AThOR-e-BAL-O (AHH-thor-EE-BALL-OH)   Thou Goddess of Beauty and Love, whom Satan, beholding, desireth!

ABRAFT (AHH-braff)   The Fathers, male-female, desire Thee!

Hear Me: and make all Spirits subject unto Me: so that every Spirit of the Firmament, and of the Ether: upon The Earth and under the Earth: on dry land and in the Water: of Whirling Air, and of rushing Fire: and every Spell and Scourge of God may be obedient unto Me.

Section F is the invocation of Spirit the quintessence or fifth element

Hear Me: You will find the formulation of will here directed to be similar to that at the conclusion of the Pentagram Ritual, with the expansion of will above and below. You will also find reference to Liber V vel Reguli on which we have touched.

There is a beautiful visualization here, in which the brahmarandhra chakra, which is specifically identified as the fissure between the parts of the brain, extrudes a drop of clear crystalline dew, and that the pearl is the magician's soul; a virgin offering to the Angel, pressed forth from the being by the intensity of Aspiration.

One could say that this is phallic symbolism, or might work backwards and say that the equation of the phallus is a more material expression of this pure orgasm. Whether the particular image grips your will or not, it is further permission to express the creating and engendering force of eros as you will.

Section Ff.

This is the Lord of the Gods: The Gods are all conscious elements of your own nature.

This is the Lord of the Universe: This is the Pantacle; the Universe of all possible things of which you can be aware.

This is He whom the Winds fear.

Here, the winds are those thoughts which have prevented the Magus from knowledge of the Angel.

This is He, Who having made Voice by His commandment is Lord of all Things; King, Ruler and Helper. Hear Me, and make all Spirits subject unto Me: so that every Spirit of the Firmament and of the Ether: upon the Earth and under the Earth: on dry Land and in the Water: of Whirling Air, and of rushing Fire: and every Spell and Scourge of God may be obedient unto Me.

Here, we are told the Magus does not withdraw Will back into the self, but instead the will remains as a reflection of truth on the surface of the dew created above, with the soul trembling within. This drop is the first formulation of consciousness of the nature of the Holy Guardian Angel. Thus we create that new life, ourselves, which has always been.

Section G. Spirit

Hear Me:

The Instructor points out ADNI on the tracing board

We are given some thoughts about the Gnostic formulation of Adonai, ADNI - that AD is the the paternal or Hadit, ON the maternal complement Nuit, and the final Yod signifying "mine," meaning specifically the Mercurial or creative seed of the magician which is hermaphroditic and virginal. This is further related to the Hermit of the Taro, so that the name is an invocation of one's inmost secrecy; the result of the union of Hadit and Nuit.

The Second Aleph which is added to ADNAI is the affirmation of the operation of the Spirit and the formulation of the Babe in the Egg from which the Hermit is born. Thus we see Adonai as a microcosm of the creative or sexual operation we have just carried out.

The fact that this is noted as being "taught slowly," when a simple explanation makes this obvious to almost anyone at all learned in magick or even remotely aware of sexual symbolism, emphasizes why the instructional methods of the old Aeon, with their cautious approaches and excessive mystery and obfuscation, do not suit the Aeon of Horus.

There is much useful imagery in the commentary to this section, but it is essentially an attempt to explain in words the concept of ego death, or the annihilation of the ego, being swept away by the purity of purpose of the self-created Angel who is the magician. This is the first real step in the process of truly understanding, rather than merely accepting, the self as God.

It is also seen as a normal part of the process that this state cannot be maintained and it is expected that the magician will collapse back into a normal state. This is not a one time operation but, rather, a process that may and must be repeated, so that the magician may begin to identify with specific aspects of the experience and capture them, returning with them to their normal state of consciousness.

The main purpose of the ritual is to throw the Angel into sharp relief. While the normal conscious mind contains much that was forced into it from outside, or is self-deceptive, the Adept becomes aware that knowledge and conversation shatters all doubts and delusions.

We are counseled not to simply rest in rapture, but to analyze this experience in rational terms in order to open and unify our minds and hearts. This is not something merely to be experienced, but to be learned from.

The important element here is to understand that this is a process which must be repeated. This ritual is not one magical working which will bring complete knowledge and conversation. It is a moment of contact which we may learn to sustain and make permanent over time.

From here, we progress to Section Gg which is The Attainment.

Since this begins the culmination, we'll talk in advance about what is happening here.

We are told that the Act of Union with the angel implies: The death of the magician's old mind, except for what the unconscious elements preserver when they absorb it and

The death of those unconscious elements themselves

This process of ego-death is a renewal of life through love. By comprehending these parts consciously, both separately and together, the magician becomes the messenger, voice, and self of their Angel, just as Hermes is the messenger, voice, and self of Zeus.

By analogy, Zeus may be seen as a passionate concept whose voice is thunder, powerful but incoherent, until rendered into a comprehensible form by Hermes. This implies, then, that Hermes has some understanding of Zeus which exceeds mere recognition of the existence of Zeus; that Hermes can know the will of Zeus and can discern the message in the rolling thunder.

Thus is the Angel rendered into comprehensible form through the magician and, in this next element, the magical projected body is drawn back into the physical body to constrain the Angel to indwell in that space.

I am He! the Bornless Spirit! having sight in the feet: Strong, and the Immortal Fire!

This is the destruction of the separateness between self and self. The old self is dead and the created self is all which exists. "Sight in feet" meaning they are able to choose their path, Immortal fire being the creative force which cannot perish.

I am He! the Truth!

Truth is the relation of any two things.

I am He! Who hate that evil should be wrought in the World!

The Instructor indicates Tiphareth obscuring Kether on the Tracing Board.

The Angel which the adept can perceive is in Tiphareth, which conceals Kether, which the Magus may know of but cannot perceive. The Magus cannot yet truly experience that all things are both illusion and absolute. Tiphareth is redemption and the Magus deplores the sorrows from which they have escaped, but also even in that ecstasy is aware that their attainment is limited.

I am He, that lighteneth and thundereth!

This refers to the phenomenon of attainment.

I am He, from whom is the Shower of the Life of Earth!

The Angel is the true self of self. The relationship of the Angel to True Will is here made evident.

I am He, whose mouth ever flameth!

The Adept recognizes that the creative fire referred to above is every breath and every word of the Angel. The Angel is likened to the Sun, which is Tiphareth.

I am He, the Begetter and Manifester unto the Light!

Here we sum up the entire process of bringing the Universe to self-knowledge through the magical formula of generation. A soul implants itself in a blind body and unknowing mind, makes them aware they are captive within the flesh, and thus allows them to partake of the consciousness of the light.

I am He, The Grace of the Worlds!

Grace here means that which is good or pleasant. The existence of the Angel is the justification for creation.

"The Heart Girt with a Serpent" is my name!

This is one of the most important lines in the Ritual, and is to be interpreted with reference to Liber LXV, or the Book of the Heart Girt with a Serpent. This book portrays the relationship between the Angel and the Magus, and there are several excellent commentaries and analysis available.

Section H.

In the penultimate section we have the Charge to the Spirit: Come thou forth, and follow me: and make all Spirits subject unto Me so that every Spirit of the Firmament, and of the Ether, upon the Earth and under the Earth: on dry Land, or in the Water: of Whirling Air or of rushing Fire, and every Spell and scourge of God, may be obedient unto me!

In this section the Magus and the Angel are charged to go forth together to work on earth among the living.

Finally we have Section J: The Proclamation of the Beast 666.

IAF: SABAF (EE-AH-OWE SAH-BAH-OWE)

Nuith! Hadith! Ra-Hoor-Khuit! Hail, Great Wild Beast! Hail, Such are the Words!

Here, it should be recalled that the Beast 666 is not Crowley or some external figure, but the principle of the Beast which is made manifest in the magician.

Now you have completed a thorough review of this most important invocation and participated in a recital of the barbarous names. I charge you to use it, adapt it, or to find some other more suitable method with which to invoke your Holy Guardian Angel. Only once you have begun a sincere and diligent attempt to invoke this power may you return to this place to seek further initiation.

The Rose Cross Knighthood

During the Instruction the Count shall enter. If Raimond d'Alfaro and Count Raimond are to be portrayed by the same Officer, then some exchange of clothing should be done to make a difference between them.

Esclarmonde:

Count, you are finally come from the preparations. How fare we?

Count Raimond:

All is in readiness. The great war engine has been brought up from Saint-Semin and will hurl death upon the besieging forces while we sally to free ourselves from their grip.

Your son, my Lady, Count Raimond-Roger, and my son-by-law, Hughes d'Alfaro, are all making final preparations with many other brave captains. Tomorrow we will cross the ditches and put sword to these seigers, while you and the other women and children rain death upon them from on high.[253]

Guillemette:

Is not that rash?

Raimond VI:

I have weighed it long in council and listened to much advice. As we gather more great lords so does our adversary, and more are promised. But the wife of the Capetian Prince Louis is recently much stung by her defeats in England. She is the niece of my Wife Jeanne and like our late Countess the fire of her grandmother, Eleanor of Aquitaine runs in her veins. She is the ill wind come out of Castile, sword ever before her. England will not have her, so she will soon look for fresh fields to conquer, and if we do not settle this Simon, he and the Pope will set her on us.

If we fail our cause was lost from the beginning. If we carry the day at best we might discourage the others and at worst we'll have fewer enemies to face in a year. Such is the course of pragmatism.

The Fool:

Would it not be more pragmatic to simply turn out or imprison all those heretics within your realm. I'm sure if you turned over the Good Men of the towns, the Bishops and the Blessed among them, you could keep a few kin folk safe.

Raimond VI:

Pragmatism is fine so far as it goes, but it may not be placed ahead of honor or partage. It is the pragmatic course within those options which it is my Will to entertain. To betray my kin and the Good Folk of these towns is not my Will.

And who are these travelers brought before my Court?

Esclarmonde:

We have received these travelers who have learned much of the Pilgrim's road. They are prepared to take the Oath of Rose Cross Knights.

Count Raimond:

So mote it be. Now, our time grows short. Tomorrow we will sortie and face the enemies of freedom of both the mind and the body. The Black Adepts who trample on partage and come to destroy our lives and make us slaves. Would you be Knights of the Rose Cross and fight to hold open the road, that pilgrims might pass or not as they will?

Repeat after me the words of the oath:

The initiates should repeat after the Count.

I --- State your Name --- do solemnly promise in the sight of the one secret and ineffable Lord, and in the sight of all stars in the company of stars that I shall do these things to the best of my understanding:

I shall walk the path of the Rose Cross Knight.

I shall take responsibility for all other pilgrims who share the road with me; to guard their well-being, whether it be to aid them in obtaining knowledge or, as I am able, shelter or sustenance.

That I am guard, neither master, nor guide, nor shepherd, nor any manner of leader, except by the example that I shall set.

I shall work to perfect restraint from the slightest exercise of my will against another being; with the intent that subsequently I shall exercise my will without the least consideration for any other being.

I shall invoke without reserve my Holy Guardian Angel.

I alone shall be responsible for my actions.

I shall try in every circumstance to better understand these matters, engaging in both unflinching and incisive pursuit of knowledge of myself, and in eager and anxious acceptance of all experience.

With my sword I shall, on every account, strike down and slay false will when I recognize it within myself that I do not fall into the darkness of complacency.

So Mote it Be.

Count Raimond:

For the Second Degree of the Thelemic Initiations, and of the Most Ancient Order of the Defenders of the Temple of the East and of the Hermetic Fellowship of Light. You have already been given the word of this grade, which is *Pragma*.

I confer upon you as well the fourteenth through eighteenth degrees of the Independent and Rectified Rite of the Ancient and Primitive Mystery of Memphis and Misraim, which is Knight Prince of the Rose Cross.

Please kneel as was the tradition of knights of old, with your swords drawn and held cruciform before you – not as an act of fealty before me, but in reverence for this Holy and Profound Occasion.

In the event the space is small it may be wise for the knights to advance one at a time to receive the honor, to avoid striking anyone as their blade is drawn. The Fool should remain vigilant most especially to see that they do not strike any bystander, nor the ceiling or lights.

Count Raimond places his sword in turn upon the right shoulder, left shoulder, then touches the top of the head with the blade, and then the center of the forehead with the hilt saying

By the authority vested in me by the Sovereign Sanctuary I create you now and forever as a Knight Templar of the Rose Cross. Arise honorable Knight! Timekeeper, let this moment be recorded.

Timekeeper:

So mote it be!

Count Raimond:

The Masonic Word of this order is I-N-R-I, which may found to be related to I-A-O or some other formulae of Thelema.

The formula of this grade of this Thelemic Initiation is ALIM. Its elaboration is ALHIM.

I shall give you now the sign of this grade. First, the right hand is placed just over the center of the chest. Then it is extended and the left crossed over it, so that it forms the inverse of the Sign of Osiris Risen, and also the attitude of the knight upon their tomb, left arm uppermost holding a shield, right arm over a sword laid at rest upon the breast.

Many who dedicate themselves as Rose Cross Knights choose to take the mark of the Rose Cross over their breast in some form, whether as tattoo or aught else. It is not given to us to mandate this, however as you grow along the path of the Rose Cross Knight you may give deep consideration to this practice.

Summary

Count Raimond:

Repeat for me the password of the grade.

Initiates:

Pragma.

Count Raimond:

And the Masonic Password?

Initiates:

I-N-R-I

Count Raimond:

And the sign of the grade?

Initiates: *The initiates should give the sign, placing their right hand over the center of the chest, then raised, with left hand crossed over to form the inverse Sign of Osiris Risen.*

Count Raimond:

And now the formula of the grade, please?

Initiates:

ALIM

Count Raimond:

Its elaboration?

Initiates:

ALHIM

Count Raimond:

I will remind you as well that we do earnestly commend to your reading the written account of the Ab-ul-Diz working, as well as the fruit of that working which is Book 4, Liber ABA.

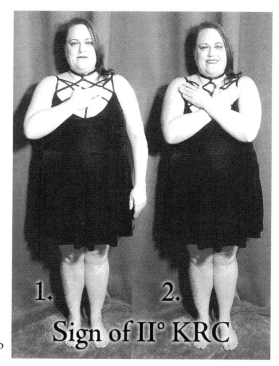

Sign of II° KRC

The Charge

Count Raimond:

As you have been created Knights of the Rose Cross, I do charge you to do as thou wilt. To seek the Knowledge and Conversation of your Holy Guardian Angel and aught else which is your will. At such time as you have truly and earnestly invoked your Holy Guardian Angel, I invite you to return to this place and receive the Initiation of the Third Degree of the Thelemic Order.

Esclarmonde:

"I reveal unto you a great mystery. Ye stand between the abyss of height and the abyss of depth.

In either awaits you a Companion; and that Companion is Yourself.

Ye can have no other Companion.

Many have arisen, being wise. They have said "Seek out the glittering Image in the place ever golden, and unite yourselves with It."

Many have arisen, being foolish. They have said, "Stoop down unto the darkly splendid world, and be wedded to that Blind Creature of the Slime."

I who am beyond Wisdom and Folly, arise and say unto you: achieve both weddings! Unite yourselves with both!

Beware, beware, I say, lest ye seek after the one and lose the other!

My adepts stand upright; their head above the heavens, their feet below the hells. But since one is naturally attracted to the Angel, another to the Demon, let the first strengthen the lower link, the last attach more firmly to the higher.

Thus shall equilibrium become perfect."[254]

The Reading

The Fool should distribute the readings around to the initiates.

First Reading

From *Liber 65, The Book of the Heart Girt by a Serpent*

> I am the Heart; and the Snake is entwined
> About the invisible core of the mind.
> Rise, O my snake! It is now is the hour
> Of the hooded and holy ineffable flower.
> Rise, O my snake, into brilliance of bloom
> On the corpse of Osiris afloat in the tomb!
> O heart of my mother, my sister, mine own,
> Thou art given to Nile, to the terror Typhon!
> Ah me! but the glory of ravening storm
> Enswathes thee and wraps thee in frenzy of form.
> Be still, O my soul! that the spell may dissolve
> As the wands are upraised, and the æons revolve.
> Behold! in my beauty how joyous Thou art,
> O Snake that caresses the crown of mine heart!
> Behold! we are one, and the tempest of years
> Goes down to the dusk, and the Beetle appears.
> O Beetle! the drone of Thy dolorous note
> Be ever the trance of this tremulous throat!
> I await the awaking! The summons on high
> From the Lord Adonai, from the Lord Adonai![255]

Second Reading

From the *Vision and the Voice* - The Introduction

> The name of the Dweller in the Abyss is Choronzon, but he is not really an individual. The Abyss is empty of being; it is filled with all possible forms, each equally inane, each therefore evil in the only true sense of the word-that is, meaningless but malignant, insofar as it craves to become real. These forms swirl senselessly into haphazard heaps like dust devils, and each such chance aggregation asserts itself to be an individual, and shrieks, "I am I!" though aware all the time that its elements have no true bond; so that the slightest disturbance dissipates the delusion just as a horseman, meeting a dust devil, brings it in showers of sand to the earth.[256]

Third Reading

From the *Book of Thoth*

> "For until we become innocent, we are certain to try to judge our Will by some Canon of what seems 'right' or 'wrong'; in other words, we are apt to criticise our Will from the outside, whereas True Will should spring, a fountain of Light, from within, and flow unchecked, seething with Love, into the Ocean of Life."[257]

Fourth Reading

From *Liber ABA*, Book 4, Part II, Chapter VI, "The Wand"

> Hence to will anything but the supreme thing, is to wander still further from it—any will but that to give up the self to the Beloved is Black Magick—yet this surrender is so simple an act that to our complex minds it is the most difficult of all acts; and hence training is necessary. Further, the Self surrendered must not be less than the All-Self; one must not come before the altar of the Most High with an impure or an imperfect offering. As it is written in Liber 65, "To await Thee is the end, not the beginning."

The Dismissal

Esclarmonde:

Before I send you away from us to take up the mantle of your knighthood, it is well that I should explain some things which may be mysteries to you.

You may wonder why we have been so uniformly diligent in explaining to you so many ancient mysteries. Most especially, we have exposed those supposed "secrets" which, while not truly secret, are often used in divers other orders or in the broader world by supposed higher initiates or superiors to dismiss the arguments and beliefs of those they deem to be of "lower degrees."

You will note that we do not use the term "lower" but, rather, "foundational," for the foundation is no less critical than the ribs of the vault. If one is poorly laid, the other is prone to crumble.

At this point you are entitled to apply for a Charter to Initiate others into those degrees which you have thus far received. It is not necessary for you to comprehend the mysteries of the 13th Degree – in fact, it is not even relevant. All that is necessary is that you understand those mysteries with which you have been presented. This will also allow you to study these mysteries in text and see the many references to them which aid in completing an understanding. It is not necessary for you to become an Initiator, but we do encourage you to consider it, even if you intend, primarily, to assist with Initiations.

There is a thing called the Tyranny of Knowledge. You may have felt that tyranny when you have known, based on common sense and convictions, that some plain act of decency was Thelemic. Yet there are voices that would shame you with threats that generosity is weakness, kindness a curse, and they may invoke both a wider reading and some initiation which you do not possess.

You now may choose to answer "at my initiation I learned it so." But also you may now come to understand that you have command of more knowledge and experience with Thelema than many of those who profess it will ever gain. You have a broad and complete outline of the ethics, you understand in principle its hidden mysteries of sex, and you have an outline of the point of the Great Work and the method of apprehending your Pure Will.

In the essay "The Law of Liberty" we are told: "At the very head of the Book" that is the *Book of the Law, Liber AL*, "stands the great charter of our godhead: 'Every man and every woman is a star.'"[258] If one has the true heart of the Rose Cross Knight it is possible to get by on this, on the declaration of the Law, and little else.

Yet, in regards to the Tyranny of Knowledge, we have given you a war hammer. There are few now who can claim superior knowledge to you, or a purer understanding of Thelema. If we have done our work well, it is no longer an abstract avalanche of revelations, but a clear set of principles and an increasingly clear set of concepts and paths. Armed with your initiations you may now strike down all those who try to tell you that Thelema is lesser, weaker, more selfish, or more ignorant than it is.

Esclarmonde makes a cross to the left with thumb through forefinger in the "fig" position.

Be ye blessed of the one True God that is Self of thy Self

Esclarmonde makes a cross to the right with thumb through forefinger in the "fig" position.

May the apprehension of the Mystery of Mysteries enlighten your minds and comfort your hearts and sustain your bodies.

Esclarmonde makes a cross to the center with thumb through forefinger in the "fig" position.

May the fire of life and force of motion bring you to the accomplishment of your true Wills, the Great Work, the Greater Good, True Wisdom and Perfect Happiness.

The Fool:

Indicates by gestures or by whispers if necessary that the Initiates should process from the Temple.

Appendix A – Lexicon of Terms

The Lexicon of Terms is not a degree symbolism class, nor does it explain the significance of every element of the Initiation. It is designed to serve as a jumping off point for research, and allowing the seeker to sort between dozens of similarly named places and individuals referenced.

Introduction

Thelema and the Esoteric

The Lexicon of Terms does not address most of the standard Thelemic terms – e.g. Babalon, Holy Guardian Angel, etc. Those terms are better pursued through the references in the end note, including Liber ABA, Book 4. Providing extensive end notes that amount to nothing more than reprints of chunks of easily available Thelemic writing would serve no purpose other than making this text unmanageably long. It is specifically intended to provide a reference to those terms, places, and people which are either not a part of the core Thelemic *corpus*, or are inadequately explored – e.g. Heliopolis.

History, People, and Places

It is reasonable to assume that those attempting initiation have a firm grounding, or are willing to get a firm grounding, in esoteric principles. It should not be the case that an advanced degree in history is needed to understand our traditions. Unfortunately, without contextual information, it is easy for those who have not had extensive training in history to embrace transparently false narratives.

In a dangerous way, this undercuts the legitimacy of our degrees. When they are known to be based on likely pretenses or imaginary chains of direct initiation, it is easy for that to become a lynch-pin of doublethink, whereby they are taken seriously in the moment but then discarded, almost as the canon to a favorite fiction, when real life comes to call. Thelema is not a fanfic to be discarded at the first inconvenience. To initiate completely, we must break down this tendency, and the best way to do that is to provide a good, if basic, grounding in the history of our traditions.

The intention of the entries on History, People and Places entries is to provide some context for the verifiable historical figures who appear in the initiations, as well as some discussion of what is known of them historically as opposed to what is presented in our initiations. It is the intention that the Sovereign Initiator II° be liberal with this information, helping those who have not been exposed to it. No degree secrets are printed in the Lexicon, though it is given to the II° on the grounds that, as an entire work, it might tend to foreshadow the I° and II°. Elements of it may be published for the general public at some future point.

Obscurity

It will be instantly clear that we have focused on those terms and people which are more obscure, e.g. Zeus Arrhenothelus, Marsilio Ficino. We assume that it is fairly easy for anyone with an interest to look up Mirandola on the internet or to order a book and satisfy any lack of knowledge or curiosity, so we provide what can best be considered a jumping off point. For more obscure subjects, where simply finding sources might take hours or days, we try to provide a more detailed write-up.

The Bible

You may notice that there are numerous references to the Hebrew Bible or the Latin Vulgate Bible which may give the impression that our rituals are Judaeo-Christian in nature. It is worth noting that this text happens to be one of the few histories of the Levant. As well, Rosicrucianism and Freemasonry, while crypto-pagan in context, were Christian in presentation and heavily utilized Christian sources to provide a justification for their core mythology.

The "Bible" is first and foremost a historical epic of the Kingdom of Judah, no more or less historical than any other chronicle. It is necessarily flawed and fictionalized, however it reveals traces of original traditions around the Temple of Solomon which lie at the root of the Western Traditions carried by the Hellenes and others into the modern era.

The Lexicon

Abiathar – *uh-BEE-uh-thar* – High Priest at the Temple of Jerusalem under David, served him during his civil war with Saul and his heirs, and subsequent civil war against his son. Abiathar sided with Adonijah, David's son, against Solomon in his claim to the throne of the United Kingdom of Israel. He was deposed and allowed to retire to his country estate, the only known case of a High Priest being deposed. [259]

Abiegnus – *ah-BEE-ay-noose* or *ABEE-ayn-us* – reference to Mount Abiegnus The universal symbolism of ascent of a mountain is here manifest in Rosicrucian sources. The name means "made of fir" or in this sense "fir covered mountain." Its caverns contain the tomb of Christian Rosencreutz. The term dates back to the early 17th century, at minimum.

The derivation given in the Golden Dawn Adeptus Minor 5=6 Ritual is of a late origin and spurious, though it does give some insight as to how this was looked on in the G.D., particularly in regards to a rather veiled sexual symbolism:

> *The meaning of this title of Abiegnus—Abi-Agnus, lamb of the Father. It is by metathesis Abi-Genos, born of the Father. Bia-Genos, strength of our race, and the four words make the sentence: Abiegnus Abi-Agnus Abi-Genos Bia-Genos. "Mountain of the lamb of the Father, and the strength of our race." I.A.O. Yeheshua. Such are the words.*[260]

Abiychazah – *uh-BEE-shah-ZAH* or *uh-BEE-shuh-ZUH* – Presented as a Priestx of Asherah. Literally the name means "my father saw" or "my father beheld" in a sense that could mean a "prophetic vision."

Rezon the Syrian is recorded as an enemy who raided Solomon's borders, possibly initially a rebel against his rule. See *Ahiman Rezon*. In the 19th century he was widely equated with Hezion, king of the Aramean State of Aram-Damascus, who was active around 770 BCE. Hezion is translated as "Vision" e.g. Chezon or Chazah, and the name Abiychazah can be readily associated with Rezon.

Acre – *AH-ker* or *AY-ker* – Coastal Seaport in the Levant. Sporadically settled since at least 3000 BCE, and continuously inhabited since 2000 BCE it is an important Bronze Age site. By around 1000 BCE it was a Phoenician City, peopled by the group which is generally referred to as "Canaanite" as a geographic catch-all. The city Canaan was an area of convergence between various Late Bronze Age empires, seeing an overlap of the spheres of the Egyptian, Hittite, Mitanni, and Assyrian Empires. Archaeology suggests the ""Israelite"" peoples of the Bible were largely Canaanite in culture, and the Old Testament as a historical doctrine has many references to Canaanite worship and practices. In late antiquity the term "Canaanite" was used by Phoenician immigrants to Carthage, the

"Chanani." (see Tyre, Sidon)had cultural similarities to Tyre and Sidon. and formed joint military expeditions with them."

Advaitist – *ad-VIH-tuh* – rom Advaita, a Hindu school considering the world an illusion. Most pronunciations sound "ai" as in "high," though some credible sources sound the "ai" as in "Way."

Ahiman Rezon – *AHH-hee-mon or AY-hee-mon RUH-zon* – Laurence Dermott's Constitution for the Ancient Grand Lodge of England from 1751 was named *Ahiman Rezon*.[261] The "Ancients" were a movement away from the "Modern" trend to associate Freemasonry with Kings and other great people, and pushed to keep a focus on the individual craftsmen and the concept of a history of ideas passed down through actual working-people. At the time, the Ancients held that they were maintaining a holy element of Freemasonry against what they saw as an attempt to remove those elements by the "moderns."

Dermott's use of the term *Ahiman Rezon* was cryptic even in the mid 18th century.

Ahiman is one of Four Levite gatekeepers along with Shallum, Akkub, and Talmon who can be readily associated with the Hiram Myth.

The use of the name of Rezon is more obscure. Rezon is recorded as an enemy who raided Solomon's borders. In the 19th century he was widely equated with Hezion, king of the Aramean State of Aram-Damascus, who was active around 770 BCE. Hezion is translated as "Vision" e.g. Chezon or Chazah (*See Abiychazah*).

It has been suggested that Dermott chose these two names to highlight the "outlaw" status of the Ancients.

Alcibiades – *OWL-sibby-AHH-deez* – provides a drunken ending to Plato's *Symposium*. See Plato. While Alcibiades was an actual person, like Socrates, he is known principally through Plato.

Anatolia – *ANN-uh-TOLE-ee-ya or ANN-ah-TAHL-ee-ya* – Most of the area of modern Turkey, historically "Anatolia" and "Asia Minor" were often cognate. Anatolia was the heartland of the Byzantine Empire until the Battle of Manzikert in 1071, when Emperor Romanos IV was captured by the Seljuks. While captive he was deposed and upon his return was blinded and consigned to a monastery. By the late 12th century the majority of central Anatolia was under Seljuk control, with an increasingly unstable Byzantine Empire controlling the coast and north. Anatolia borders Armenia, and the Paulician dualist sect emanates from Eastern Anatolia, Armenia having been principally Zoroastrian until the early fourth century when it adopted Christianity, in defiance of the Persian Sassanid dynasty to the south.

In the mid 9th century, Paulician dualists formed their own Principality centered on Tephrike in Eastern Anatolia, and under Chrysocheir they raided across Anatolia as far as Ephesus, harrying the Byzantine Empire. Defeated at Bathys Ryax around 872 CE, Paulicianism continued to thrive in the Byzantine Empire, such that around 970 CE the Byzantine emperor John Tzimisces forcibly moved about two hundred thousand Paulicians to Philippopolis in Theme of Thrace, where they would become the core of the Bogomil movement. *See Gnosticism*

Andreae, Johann Valentin – *AHN-dree-AY* – 1586-1684 – *See also: Rosicrucianism*. Andreae was a Lutheran Protestant clergyman educated at the prestigious Tubingen University at 1586-1654 who is usually seen as the principal creator of Rosicrucianism.

Rosicrucianism is defined by three early texts: *Fama Fraternitatis* (1614) *Confessio Fraternitatis* (1615) and *The Chymical Wedding of Christian Rosenkreutz* (1616). Andreae admitted to writing *Chymical Wedding*, making it the only one of the three works to have a known author, though he is nearly universally cited as the author of all three

Rosicrucian texts. John Warwick Mongtgomery, Andreae's principal biographer, gives an exhaustive investigation of the matter,[262] and concludes that the two original works actually may have predated Andreae's career and have been circulated in manuscript form for some decades. He gives a comprehensive coverage of the rather convincing reasons for Andreae's authorship, but concludes "Therefore at the end of his college career (1605) when he wrote his Chymische Hochzeit to wed true theology and true science together, he took as its hero Christian Rosencreutz – but a transformed, christianized Rosencreutz – in order to provide an evangelical counteractive to the Fama and Confessio. He was content at first to allow the Hochzeit to remain unpublished...indeed there was no external pressure for publication since Rosicrucian manifestos themselves were still in manuscript. As the ensuing decade went by, however, the millennial fervor increased; German teetered on the bring of the catastrophic Thirty Years' War, and the allegedly prophetic times were fast approaching."[263]

Montgomery bases his argument that Andreae did not write the *Fama* largely on later contempt which Andreae showed for the Rosicrucian phenomenon, doctrinal differences between Andreae's work and the *Fama*, and the assumption that the generally honest Andreae did not lie in saying that he was not responsible for the earlier work. His arguments hold some weight, but must be viewed in light of the tremendous upheaval of Andreae's life, as well as his need to both provide for his family and receive sponsorship and patronage for important rebuilding work. That he came to a point of view over time in which he saw the earlier Rosicrucian work with mixed emotions is unquestionable. Importantly, Andreae fought off attempts to accuse him of the embrace of the Melanchthonian Protestant heretic Georg Calixtus (1586–1656),[264] who has been re-evaluated in the modern era as a humanist himself, and Andreae's sympathies for Calixtus, as well as pressure throughout his life by detractors who resented both his pro-active work and eminent reputation may have rendered him far less willing to claim early work which he did not feel had borne out its promise.

Andreae's life was heavily defined by the Thirty Years' War, which encompassed most of his adult years. The war impacted him severely. He was pastor at Vaihingen, which was badly damaged by fires November 1, 1617 and October 9, 1618, the second of which destroyed his house and church.[265] He left Vaihingen in March 1620 to take a position at Calw, where he remained for some years. Over most of his adult life, he worked with increasing fervor on causes which would now be seen as Pro-peace, attempting to create structures within the Protestant world to support the vast numbers of those left homeless, destitute, or injured in the calamitous war that framed his life.

In 1634, Protestant Swedish and German forces occupied much of Southern Germany, preventing the Catholic Spanish from moving troops and supplies from Italy to support their war against the breakaway, and Protestant, Dutch Republic. A decisive conflict for control of this region took place at Nordlingen in that year, and resulted in a crushing victory for Spain, the Holy Roman Empire, and the Catholic League. This led to an orgy of plunder within the region, and two weeks later Bavarian and Croatian troops under Johann von Werth sacked and burned Calw, destroying the majority of houses and public buildings. The loss of life was fairly limited as most of the civilians fled into the Black Forest. Montgomery quotes Andreae's German biographer in saying that "he knew very well that he himself, as the well-known leader of the evangelicals, would be the first victim of the fanatical soldiers." and adds "he lost his ten year old son Ehrenreich to exposure and hunger on the flight from Calw; and when he was finally able to return home, he found his house burned to the ground, and with it is his library, consisting of three thousand separate items, numerous irreplaceable Reformation manuscripts, his musical and scientific instruments, and original paintings by Durer, Cranach, and Holbein."[266]

Andreae wrote for most of his life about the establishment of a Christian Utopia based on providing for everyone. While his model may seem at odds with the social values of Thelema, which deplore puritanism, the dissimilarities are more superficial than it would seem. Andreae was conventional in regard to sexuality but as a Protestant rejected ideas of celibacy and was married with several children. Crowley, writing in "Energized Enthusiasm" doesn't fall as far from Andreae as we might expect. "It is the casual or habitual—what Christ called *"idle"*— use or rather abuse of these forces which constitutes their profanation."[267] In regards to other social "libertinism" what those behaviors meant in Andreae's time and place are significantly different from what they meant in Crowley's. Andreae saw sexuality as a sacred act not to be profaned and deplored "libertine" behavior which he associated with cheating and failure to support the community. Yet he called for the close linking of science and spirituality, with spirituality guiding science to prevent it from being destructive, while science guided spirituality providing wisdom on how to remedy society's ills. He was a close correspondent of Johannes Kepler, who developed the modern laws of planetary motion following from Copernicus.

Whatever the case with the earlier two manifestos, as we note in the entry on Rosicrucianism, Andreae's *Chymical Wedding* was a key inflection point in the modern conception of gnosis

Angevin – *ANN-juh-vin* – meant "coming from Anjou" and was used to refer to the Royal French house that ruled England in the 12th and 13th centuries. They built an "Angevin Empire" consisting of Britain and large swathes of what is now France which, including Anjou, Normandy, and Aquitaine. The monarchs were Henry II, Richard I (Lionheart), and John, whose loss of Anjou in 1204 leads historians to consider the subsequent English Kings a new Plantagenet dynasty, though Henry II is also considered as a Plantagenet King.

Anjou – *AHN-zhoo* – a province of France. The adjectival form is *Angevin.* The Dukes of Anjou formed an Empire from that territory and England, during the 12th and early 13th centuries, reaching its zenith with Henry II, crowned in 1154, and known historically as The Angevin Empire, though neither that term, nor the name "Plantagenet" were contemporary in the late 12th century. The Empire was subsequently ruled by Henry's son, Richard I, and collapsed afterwards during the reign of his brother John I, most of the continental territory being lost to Philip II of France.

Antioch – *ANN-tee-ok* – An ancient city south and inland from the Gulf of Alexandretta, the Easternmost inlet of the Mediterranean. Founded by the Alexander the Great's General Seleucus in the fourth century BCE it was the seat of the Roman Province of Syria an a major center of Hellenistic Judaism. The Paulician sect of dualists, ancestors of the Bogomils and likely a seminal influence on Catharism, is supposed to be named for a 3rd century Bishop of Antioch, Paul of Samosata.

The City was supposedly depopulated in a single day when it fell to the Mamluk Sultan Baibars in 1268. Prince Bohemond IV had removed himself to Tripoli, and left Simon Mansel, Constable of Antioch to defend the City. Mansel led an early sortie, was captured, and attempted to negotiate a surrender, however the remaining defenders refused.

Antioch was sacked with 17,000 people killed and 100,000 taken prisoner. The detailed letter sent by Baibars Secretary, describing in gruesome terms the atrocities committed, is well attested in numerous sources.[268] The purpose was likely to inspire fear and encourage the easy capitulation of other Cities, much as with Arnaud Amalric's massacre of the population of Beziers during the Albigensian Crusade. [269] [270]

Apophrasz – *ap-OPH-razz* – The typical pronunciation for this is taken from the Bornless Ritual, where this is "destroying matter." For more details see most especially the Golden Dawn Neophyte Ritual. This is also an Enochian term, which has among other pronunciations Ah-poh-peh-ra-seh-zod, meaning motion however the Enochian pronunciation is generally contrary to the tone.

Aragon, King Alfonso II – *awl-FON-soh of AR-uh-gawn* – see Appendix B

Aragon, King Peter II – also Pierre or Pere – *see Appendix B*

Armand de Lavoie – *ARR-mond duh LAH-vwah* – c. 1178-unk. - Grand Master of the Knights Templar 1232-1244. Also known as Armand de Perigord, and Hermann de Lavoie. As part of a Treaty he had made with the Muslim Sultan of Damascus, he agreed to fight against Egyptian and Khorezmian forces threatening Jerusalem and other cities after their defeat by the Mongols. The strategic situation was similar to Hattin and it is likely that Lavoie counseled restraint as the attack was led by the Count of Jaffa, an enemy of the Templars. [271] Lavoie either died in battle or was captured, however he was never accounted for. This was also a turning point in Christian attempts to ally with local leaders, as the Damascus forces deserted, and Frederick II blamed the Templars for having "received these Muslims in their house and provided them with lavish entertainment, and they had allowed them to perform their superstitious rites and to invoke the name of Muhammad. The result of this foolish policy had been the desertion of these false allies in the time of crisis."[272]

Asherah – *uh-SHEE-rah* – A semitic Goddess, identified with the Ugaritic goddess Atiratu, and the Hittite Aserdu or Asertu. The name is generally thought to come from the Semitic root YWM, and mean "Lady Dawn." She is identified as the wife of El, or the feminine form of El, the Semitic Father God. As Athirat, she is called "Creator of the Deities," and she is the mother of the children of El. She is variously cognate with and the mother of Ashtart or Astarte. The Hellenes considered Astarte cognate with Aphrodite and Venue. In the Apocalypse of John "Mystery, Babylon the Great, the Mother of Harlots and Abominations of the Earth," is generally thought to refer to, or at least call back to, Astarte, the Goddess identified with Babylon. She was variously associated with fertility, war, sexuality and hunting.

It is understood today that the people we know collectively as the "Israelites," were polytheistic before 598 BCE, and likely continued to be polytheistic to some extent well after that date. Thus depictions of the enforcement of monotheism from the 10th-9th century BCE must be taken either as recollections of internecine rivalry between various cults, or a whitewash by authors reconstructing the Royal chronology and traditions of Judah after the end of captivity in 538 BCE, under Cyrus the Great.

Azalais of Burlats - *ahh-ZUH-lie-ees.* - d. 1199 - *see Appendix B*

Ba'al – *BAH-el* – The apostrophe indicates the correct pronunciation spelling the word from Hebrew. In the West it is frequently rendered BALE or BALL and either of these is acceptable. In the north semitic languages it means "Lord" or "owner," and has the same sense when applied to a person or deity as the use of the English "Lord." The title of Ba'al is particularly associated with the storm god Hadad, variously a son of El or Dagan. Some sources suggest that Hadad supplanted El as the principal deity in Canaan.

Ba'al is used frequently in the Hebrew Bible, however it is not always clear what deity is actually being referred to, and the final renderings may be many centuries removed from the original. In particular there is confusion between references to Melqart and Hadad.

The Phoenician Ba'al is most usually identified with El or, in some cases, Dagan. Likewise, many scholars feel that the title of Ba'al was applied to the Hebrew YHWH. It is attested in personal names which are presumably references to YHWH, e.g. David's son Beeliada "The Lord Knows," Saul's son Eshba'al "The Lord is Great," and he Judge Jeruba'al "The Lord Strives." Most anthropologists consider El to be generally cognate as the same Semitic deity which eventually came to be named as YHWH in the Hebrew Texts.

Bacchus Diphues - "Diphues" meaning "of two natures" (*dee-FOO-ay*), properly *diphuês*, see *Zeus Arrhenothelus*

Baibars – *BAY-bahrs* – c. 1223-1277. Baibars was a Kipchak Turk, born in the region between the Volga and Ural rivers. His parents were massacred in the Mongol invasion of Bulgaria and he was sold into slavery. During his lifetime, slaves, known by the Arabic "Mamluk" meaning "one who is owned," were used as slave-soldiers, and eventually commanders. The Mamluks overthrew the Ayyubid dynasty in Egypt in 1250. Baibars was a prominent leader, aiding in the defeat of the Crusade of Louis XI, the rout of the Mongols, and the defeat of the majority of the Crusader states. He succeeded Qutuz, whom he probably assassinated, to become the Fourth Mamluk Sultan.

Benoit – *BEN-wah* – 1154-1173 - (Properly Benoît) Benoit de Sainte-Maure wrote *Le Roman de Troie*, an epic poem which was a principal medieval source for the Troy Legend, between 1155 and 1160. The epic was composed without reference to the Iliad, which did not exist in a European translation at the time. It was likely commissioned by Henry II and dedicated to Eleanor of Aquitaine. The treatment of the Trojan War is sophisticated, breaking down, and to some extent inventing, causes for the war based along lines of then contemporary politics.

Bernardo del Nero – 1422-1497 – *see also Savonarola* – A prominent political leader in 15th century Florence he had served in a number of state and military roles. Savonarola, who held de facto power in Florence had been excommunicated in May, and the word had spread in Florence that the Friar was formally excommunicated putting him on the defensive. Nero was accused of plotting the return of exiled Medici heir and former ruler Piero di Lorenzo de' Medici, though he had in fact kept the gates shut against Piero when he approached with troops in April of 1497. At the age of seventy two, as Savonarola's de facto dictatorship tottered, del Nero was of five men executed secretly in the dead of night, with five blows of the executioner's axe, one of which cut off his chin by mistake.[273]

Besz – *BEZZ or BES* – The worship of Bes was widespread in antiquity emanating from Egypt but reaching Spain, and surviving for a millennia. The Phoenicians named the Balearic island of Ibiza after the deity. The deity as a dwarf, money, or cat headed figure is found on personal amulets and cult figures. Besz has many of the attributes of Pan, representing music, dance, and sexual pleasure. He may have originally spread as a "soldier's god," associated with success in fighting; being known for besting fierce animals with his bare hands. There is evidence of Bes tattoos on the thighs of New Kingdom dancers. Other sources suggest Sacred Prostitutes had a tattoo of Besz placed near their pubic area.

He is linked to Tawret and some sources say the he was at various points considered to be her husband, though she is more formally associated with Set and Sobek, as well as Amun.

Besz may have been a Nubian or Somalian import and seems to have been a popular icon rather than a figure with a priesthood or temples, though in a later period there were chambers dedicated to Bes which may have been intended to cure infertility. He was thus associated with childbirth and the entertainment and protection of children. Significantly to Thelema he is considered to have been the nursemaid of Horus.

For more details see most especially the Golden Dawn Neophyte Ritual.

Bezalel – *BAY-sal-el* – The name comes from the root be, meaning "in," salal meaning "quiver, sink or grow dark," and el, the Semitic Godname. It is generally translated as "In the Shadow of God," but could also be taken as "To Bow Before God." In the Hebrew Bible in the Book of Exodus

> 31: 1 And the LORD spake unto Moses, saying,
> 31: 2 See, I have called by name Bezaleel the son of Uri, the son of Hur, of the tribe of Judah: 31: 3 And I have filled him with the spirit of God, in wisdom, and in understanding, and in knowledge, and in all manner of workmanship,

    31: 4 To devise cunning works, to work in gold, and in silver, and in brass,

    31: 5 And in cutting of stones, to set them, and in carving of timber, to work in all manner of workmanship.

The degree to which the qualities taught to Bezalel mirror those conferred by the Goetic spirits is noteworthy. Bazalel's could be considered to have founded a line of craftsmen in the same way that Melchizedek constitutes a special line of Priesthood.

Beziers – *see Appendix B*

Bezant – one of several gold coins in the Eastern Roman Empire, originally struck in Byzantium and based on the roman solidus. The Islamic governments of the region later struck their own gold coins, often referred to as "bezants" as were the dinar based coins of the Crusader Kingdoms.

The relative value of a bezant is hard to establish and is complicated by the relative poverty of most laborers in the periods concerned.

Similar gold coins minted in England were worth about nine silver coins. A rough value would be around 1300 GBP or 1700 USD based on labor valuations, though other valuations might have the actual purchasing power as low as 100-200 USD when applied to goods.

Burgundy – a region in what is now northern and eastern France, significantly larger than the surviving French County of Burgundy. A large part of the territory, the Kingdoms of Upper and Lower Burgundy, became part of the Holy Roman Empire.

Burlats – *BEE-or-lah* – The Occitan pronunciation may be closer to BOOR-lah A commune in the Occitane. The Adelaide Pavilion which still stands there is associated with Azalais of Toulouse. - *see also Appendix B*

Canaanites – generally accepted as an ethnographic and historical term for the population of the Levant. While it is best known from the Hebrew Bible, the term was in wide use and is well attested in various official and diplomatic Egyptian documents including those of the Amarna period. There has been some consideration given to the precision of the term,[274] however the term remains in common use in scholarship to denote the general population for nomadic-pastoral and settled groups throughout the southern Levant. The Phoenician civilizations of Tyre and Sidon are broadly referred to as Canaanite. The term should be understood as being imprecise.

Cachexia – wasting in the body due to illness, usually from a chronic disease, often due to cancer, though also seen in other disease.

Cagliostro, Alessandro – 1743-1795 – Guiseppe Balsamo, who used the name Cagliostro, was a self-made man and esotericist from Palermo Sicily, intriguingly once the seat of Jeanne of England. Cagliostro was named as a past life by Crowley.[275]

He came from a poor family but was educated, becoming a religious novice before being expelled. Johann Wolfgang von Goethe had Cagliostro investigated in 1787 and suggested his family was Jewish, which he doubtless meant to injure Cagliostro's reputation.

By his early twenties, he already had tremendous occult learning and a flair for scams. He robbed a local goldsmith and fled to Malta where he worked as a chemist and member of the auxiliary of the Sovereign Military Order of Malta. He later moved to Rome, where he worked as a secretary for a noted Cardinal while leading a double life selling "Egyptian" amulets. He would inflate his travels to include Egypt. Both in Malta and in Rome, he certainly had access to occult legends, traditions, and books and if his Egyptian Rite did not come from Egypt, it was at least based in esoteric scholarship.

He became a Freemason in 1777 in London. Not satisfied with the Masonic rites of his day, he recruited from the German lodges operating as "Strict Observance" which was the German version of Scottish Rite. The Strict Observance popularized but did not invent the idea of "secret masters." The Lodge claimed Templar roots and Cagliostro had some success in creating his "Egyptian" order of Masonry.

Some esoteric scholars such as K. Paul Johnson do credit the possibility that Cagliostro received a genuine initiation in Egypt. Certainly it is not impossible that he traveled there, nor is it impossible he picked up some local initiatory tradition. It is very unlikely that it included the full framework of his, or subsequent, Egyptian Masonic Orders.[276]

If Cagliostro's orders are not historical, they are reconstructive, and well researched by the standards of the day. Allen Greenfield says "The point is not to ascertain the actuality...but to acknowledge that, almost certainly, members of the Old Egyptian Priesthoods that had been hereditary did indeed become Christians without necessarily giving up all of the forms and concepts of the intiatic systems." Certainly the concept that these Priesthoods formalized and to an extent "invented" Hermeticism as we know it in the first three centuries CE is well established by Christian Bull and others.[277] That these Priesthoods would have survived and transformed themselves seems reasonable and unremarkable.

Exiled from France over the "Affair of the Diamond Necklace," during which an entirely different confidence trickster, Jeanne de Valois-Saint-Remy, played the role of a confidante of the Queen of France, and convinced a notable Cardinal who wished for Royal patronage to buy a very expensive diamond necklace on credit, with her taking a fee. Ironically, Cagliostro was probably innocent of any involvement in the doomed enterprise. The Affair ultimately badly hurt Marie Antoinette's image and played a role in the fall of the French monarchy.

In 1789, he was lured to Rome by spies for the Inquisition, who arrested him for attempting to found a Masonic Lodge in Rome. He was originally sentenced to death, but his sentence was commuted and he died in prison in 1795.

Cagliostro did not invent the idea of Egyptian Freemasonry. *Crata Repoa* which has a Memphis origin story, was published in Berlin in 1782 by Fri Koppen and J. W. B. von Hymmen[278] [279] and was clearly not a completely new idea drawn in fact at least in part from an earlier fiction novel. Koppen broke from the Strict Observance to found his own Order of African Architects, by which he meant "Egyptian."

> *Whilst in Bordeaux in 1783/4, Cagliostro had a premonition that was a pivotal point in his desire to form his system of higher Freemasonry. Feeling ill one night, he retired to bed and fell into a trance-like state. His vision took him to a place he did not recognize where he was accosted by two men and carried off to an underground passage. He found himself before a door which opened to reveal a beautiful room wherein were assembled a group of men dressed in the robes of Egyptian priests.*[280]

The door might as well have been labeled Koppen's African Order. The timing is just right for the new idea from Germany to have had time to make its way into Cagliostro's hands.

Some esoteric historians have credited Cagliostro, or at least his inspirations, with preternatural understanding of Ancient Egypt.

> *"Remember that almost all knowledge of Ancient Egypt, let alone its literature, has come light*
> *since Cagliostro's death, the most telling comment perhaps was that of Kenneth Mackenzie who*
> *observed of Cagliostro that "His system of Masonry was not founded upon shadows. Many of*
> *the doctrines he enunciated may be found in The Book of the Dead, and other important*
> *documents of ancient Egypt..." including, I might add, some only understood since the time*
> *Mackenzie penned those words, a hundred years after Cagliostro's rituals were to launche the*
> *public, and more documented, history of the Rite of Memphis.*[281]

In practical fact, much of both *Crata Repoa* and the *Rite of Memphis* owe a debt to the very popular historical fantasy novel *The Life of Sethos, Taken from Private Memoirs of the Ancient Egyptians*, by Jean Terrasson, published in French in Paris in 1731 and in English in London in 1732. While Egyptology in the 1700s was more speculative, the similarities to the *Book of the Dead* are no more striking than those to the already well known *Corpus Hermeticum*. *Life of Sethos* itself draws from Herodotus and other well known sources, including Sanchuniathon.

This is not to say Cagliostro did nothing. He likely revised and improved the rite, adding an internal Hermetic and Alchemical framing which would stand the test of time. Certainly if nothing else, Cagliostro expanded the interest in Egyptian Masonry and act as its tireless advocate, leaving a rich wealth of mystery which led directly to the creation of the Rite of Memphis, in 1813 by Marconis de Negre and Samuel Honis.

Calw – *see Andreae, Johannes Valentinus*

Canso – meaning "song" in Old Occitan, was a common structure for song in the 12th and early 13th century. The canso is divided into an *exordium*, or introduction, a main body, and an *envois*, or short ending. Each stanza has a matching sequence of lines which have an identical metrical structure.

Capet – *KAH-pay KUH-pet* – The French pronunciation is KAH-pay, however the Occitan pronunciation is closer to the Catalan "KUH-pet" Either is acceptable. Since the reference is glancing, and the French pronunciation common today, we give preference to the French.

Carcassone – *KAR-cass-own* – A city on the border of the Kingdom of Aragon, *see Raimond Roger Count of Beziers and Carcassone in Appendix B.*

Castellan – *KASS-tu-lahn* – From the medieval Latin, Castellanus, is an individual who does not hold a castle by right, but is appointed by its rightful Lord as governor of the castle and its surrounding territory.

Castile – *KASS-teel* – An area of Central Spain, and historically a Kingdom centered on Burgos and Toledo in North Central Spain. *See Alfonso II of Aragon, and Peter II of Aragon in Appendix B.*

Cathars – *see Gnosticism, Appendix B*

Celestine III – Pope from 1191-1198 – *see also Appendix B*

Cesarea – *suh-SER-ee-uh* – Now commonly spelled Keisarya, or Qaysaria, a coastal city in Northern Israel, built by Herod the Great about 20 BCE as Caesarea Maritima. Held by the Christian Byzantine Empire until 640, when it was captured by Yazid ibn Abu Sufyan for the Islamic Caliph Abu Bakr. It was seized by Baldwin I, Latin King of Jerusalem, in 1101. It was the last City occupied by Crusaders of the Latin Kingdom of Jerusalem, captured by the Mamluk sultan Baybars in 1165.

Chemical Wedding of Christian Rosenkruetz – *see Rosicrucianism*

Chnoubis – *KUH-noob-iss* – was associated with the late classical Agathodaemon *ah-GOTH-oh-DYE*-muhn or Abraxas *ah-BRAX-us*. See *Kneph*

Christians of Saint Maron/Maronites – Maronites were a Christian population in the Levant during late classical antiquity. They maintained full communion with the Orthodox Catholic Church; however, they were isolated from about 637 CE until the arrival of the Crusades in 1096 and apparently did not maintain strong ties with the Armenian Church. They were determined to be monothelite heretics, but they generally are held to have recanted under Crusader influence, and come into Communion with Rome. Those ties were formalized in the 16th century, and are currently an Eastern Catholic, rather than Orthodox, church under the Code of Canons of the Eastern Churches, in Communion with the Holy See in Rome. While they have had generally peaceful relations with the Druze, there was a notable massacre in the 1860s which led to a Maronite diaspora to Egypt. The President of Lebanon is traditionally a Maronite Christian.

Constantinople – *KON-stan-TIN-ope-uhl* – In the 4th century, Constantine reorganized the Roman Empire making Byzantium, where he founded a new city which he named Constantinople. When the Western Roman Empire Collapsed in the 5th century the Eastern Empire continued as the "Roman Empire," known as the Byzantine Empire only in retrospect.

Constantinople was the center of the Great Schism of 1054 in which the Eastern Patriarchies denied the authority of the Roman Pope, forming the basis of the divide between the Eastern Orthodox Church and the Roman Catholic Church.

In 1204, the Fourth Crusade sacked Constantinople, hastening the decline of the Empire and briefly establishing a Latin Empire. The term "Latin Empire" was not used at the time and should not be confused with the Historical Latin Kingdom of Jerusalem. The Orthodox Byzantines established an Empire at Nicea and eventually recaptured Constantinople. Never recovering its former stature Constantinople fell to the Ottoman Empire in 1453.

Corpus Hermeticum – The core works of Hermetic Philosophy reintroduced to Europe at the end of the 15th century by Marsilio Ficino and Lodovico Lazzarelli. The texts were originally Koine Greek from the Byzantine Empire, and through the mid 19th century were known by the title *Pimander, Poemandres, Poimandres*, from the title of the first book.

Recent scholarship has suggested that these Byzantine works were, over centuries, purged of their ties to the larger body of Hermetic magical literature known collectively today as the Papyri Graecae Magicae, or PGM. As late as the current century some modern scholars maintained one "Hermetic" tradition of philosophy and high thought emanating from Greece, with another "low" tradition of magical charms and spells emanating from late Hellenic Egypt.

While the point of view was not universal, the discovery of new Hermetic treatises in Nag Hammadi Codex VI began the process of tearing down this artificial distinction, revealing a rich world of thought in which common cantrips existed alongside high philosophical thought. In his recent work Christian Bull endeavors to "contextualize the myths and rites of Hermes, in order to arrive at a plausible Sitz im Leben (social situation) for the Hermetic treatises. The texts will successively be considered in light of philosophy, magic, and traditional Egyptian cult. The intention is to demonstrate that all of these contexts point in the direction of a priestly milieu at the heart of Hermetism."[282]

Crata Repoa – published in Berlin in 1782 by Fri Koppen and J. W. B. von Hymmen[283][284] puts forward a nine degree system of Egyptian Masonry that was the basis for Koppens' "Order of African Architects." The book was a likely influence on Cagliostro and certainly a precursor to the Rite of Memphis and the Rite of Misraim.

Cremona, settlement at – in this context probably refers to the treaty between Venice and Genoa which ended the War of Saint-Sabas in 1270.

Cyclades – an extensive archipelago which form a crossroads and permit easy sailing by "hops" from Greece to Asia, these islands were inhabited from at least the 11th millennium BCE, when they began trading obsidian to the continent. The islands seem to have had a strong sailing and mercantile culture, slightly older than the Minoan civilization of Create and reaching a zenith about 2300 BCE. One of the principal trade goods was obsidian and it continued to be used well into the bronze age for its durability and ready availability.

Cyprus – *see Appendix B, Jeanne of England for details on the overthrow of Isaac Comnenus by Richard I of England. See Jacques de Molay and Templars for notes on the Templar presence there.*

Dee, Dr. John – 1527-1608. Gnostic Saint named in *Liber XV* under the name Johannes Dee, and under his common name in the canon of the Heterodox Gnostic Church. English polymath, noted for his alchemical and occult studies. A highly respected mathematician, he is a slightly older contemporary of Andreae and the Rosicrucian documents show his influence. His scrying experiments conducted with Edward Kelley, and eventually published by Meric Casuabon, who at least superficially intended to discredit Dee, form the basis for Crowley's scrying in *The Vision and the Voice*. Dee is a fascinating subject and can receive only the most peripheral coverage here. There are numerous biographies of Dee available and most books on the Enochian language cover at least the outlines of Dee's remarkable life, as well as that of his partner, Edward Kelley. Dee's role as a core progenitor of Thelema, both through his Enochian work which led to *The Vision and the Voice*, and his influence on Rosicrucianism, cannot easily be overstated.

Diotima Priestess – a character in Plato's *Symposium*, if she was real, or based on a real person, they would have lived about 440 BCE. She is not presented as a priestess, and that misconception comes from an early mistranslation, though her epithet does suggest prophecy. There is some suggestion she is modeled on Aspasia, a noted companion of Pericles who was widely admired for her intelligence. Her name may have been changed because she espouses positions which are closer to Plato's than those of the historical Aspasia. She would seem to be evidence of the continuing presence of strong, intellectual, women, even in the rather male-centered world of Plato.

Duke Augustus – 1579-1666 – Augustus II, or "The Younger," ruler of the Duchal Principality of Wolfenbuttel. He was not expected to inherit and was a traveler and scholar. When Prince of Wolfenbuttel died during the Thirty Years war with no direct heir, negotiations eventually brought Augustus to his seat. He proved to be an exceptionally capable and enlightened ruler, reforming the government, and building what was, at the time, the largest Library in the region. He wrote a reference book on cryptography and another on chess which largely displays the influence of Trithemius. He was a patron of Johannes Valentinus Andreae.

Edessa – *see also Harran* – An inland city in what is now Turkey and located at the extreme westward extent of the Crusader conquest. The city itself was not conquered, but the local Armenian ruler invited the Crusaders in to help with defense. The city appears prolifically in Crusader records and had a rich history both in Roman, Byzantine, and more contemporary times. In the late Byzantine period, it was a center of intellectual thought within the Syraic Orthodox Church. The fall of Edessa to Muslims in 1144 sparked the Second Crusade. Edessa is noted in our texts for its proximity to Harran/Carrhae, and another reference may be intended to note its proximity to Gobekli Tepe.

Edomites - "Deep into the Desert land of the Edomites" - American archaeologist Nelson Glueck first posited in the 1930s that extensive iron deposits along the length of Wadi Araba, and that these were worked during the time of David and Solomon, providing an archaeological basis for the location of "King Solomon's Mines." Glueck was widely discredited in the following decades. David and Solomon were generally put forward as tribal leaders with limited influence who could not possibly have managed such far-flung trade, while others took issue with the chronology.

In the late 1990s, Thomas Levy, professor of archaeology at the University of California, San Diego, began excavations at Khirbat en-Nahas that tended to support Glueck's original suggestions. Recent excavation in the Timna Valley suggest a complex society at the time of David and Solomon, capable of building a large, fortified mining and smelting complex that required overland supply with food and water from at least twelve miles away. Whether it was operated by Israelites or Edomites (who may have traded with Solomon's kingdom between, or even during, periods of military confrontation), there is distinct evidence of a complex facility that would have been operational during the time generally agreed on for Solomon's reign.

Ehrenreich – *see Johannes Valentinus Andreae*

Ein Sof – The nameless and non-existent form of God from which YHWH emerged. The emergence of Hadit from Nuit can be seen as analogous to this concept found in the *Zohar* and other Kabbalistic sources. "In Christian kabbalah, in particular that of Pico della Mirandola, *Ein Sof* is also viewed as inexpressible and as uniting all within itself."[285]

El – **ELL** – Properly ʾĒl also ʾIl or ʾÁl, Semitic word for "deity" found in Ugaritic, Phonecian, Hebrew, Syriac, Arabic, and cognate to the Akkadian ilu. The suffix hm or him in Ugaritic and Hebrew gives elohim. ʾIl gives rise to the Semitic ʾIh giving the Aramaic ʾAlāh and the modern Arabic form Romanized as Allah. It is found in personal names, and in the characteristic appendant to the names of Hebrew Angels.

The term El was both a title applied to deities and used to refer to a deity in the generic. In the Canaanite and Levantine religions he is considered the father of many Gods, including Hadad, Yam, and Mot. He is identified as the husband of Asherah in Ugaritic texts.

There is no consistent understanding of El. The combination and recombination of mythological and cult elements through conquest and trade results in a melange of interpretations.

El was likely originally a Zeus or Poseidon like figure. El is often associated with a bull, whose cult attributes were eventually more associated with his son Hadad (much as many attributes of Zeus were embodied in Heracles), while El himself was considered as a more primordial god.

Enochian/Book of Enoch – The historical *Book of Enoch (1 Enoch)*, which contains fascinating information about demonology, the Giants and the Nephilim. It was not part of the Hebrew Tanakh. Neither *2 Enoch*, nor the Merkabah text *3 Enoch* which were available during the Middle ages or Renaissance. What is interesting is that the existence of the text was well-known in Dee's time. Sir Walter Raleigh mentions it in his history of the world as having been preserved by the Queen of Sheba and thus available to certain late Roman writers,[286] and as certain references and fragments survive it is likely that Dee knew something of the contents. Certainly, Dee had the idea that he was "recreating" this lost Book. Viewed in light of the Mystery of the Royal Arch of Enoch in which the Book of Enoch is understood to be the Emerald Tablet or Book of Hermes, and thus the Book of Thoth, the idea linking "Enoch" to Dee and Kelley's revelations may be seen more clearly. Crowley caused the creation of the Book of Thoth as a perfection and explication of the Tarot, but also called into being a set of revelations that make use of, and in a sense complete, Dee and Kelley's revelations, making *The Vision and the Voice* also, in a sense a completion of the larger Book of Enoch.

Esclarmonde de Foix – *see Appendix B*

Eusebius – *AY-oo-SEB-ee-oos* – Eusebius of Caesarea was a Christian historian and polemicist, and an advisor to the Emperor Constantine. c. 260-240 CE He was Bishop of Caesarea and attended the Christian Council of Nicaea in 325. His histories are questionable and clearly propagandistic, but they contain the only lengthy passages of the earlier work by Sanchuniathon. As with any period author, while his political agenda is suspect, he could not lie about widely known facts, so we can consider his basic attributions regarding pagan deities at least reflective of the widely known understandings of the late Classical era.

FIAOF – conjectural F in the word "FIAOF" represents the Hebrew Vau and has a sound somewhere between the English long O, as in rope, and long OO, as in tooth.

Fludd, Robert – also known as Robertus de Fluctibus 1574 -1637. A physician with a Paracelsian practice, he was an alchemist, Cabalist, and Rosicrucian.

Galenists – *see also Paracelsian Chymists* – Galenic medicine is identified with the philosopher Galen (129-216 CE). Identified heavily with the humors, Galenist medicine was as much philosophy as medicine. It held the body was well when in harmony with nature and sought to restore the natural harmony. Natural philosophy, logic, and ethics were core to diagnosis, prognosis, and therapy. Paracelsianism, the first modern medical movement, supplanted Galenism in the late 16th and early 17th century.

Gemistos Plethon – *juh-MEE-stos PLEE-thon* – c. 1356-1453 – Greek philosopher and scholar. At the Council of Florence, which was aimed at reconciling the Great Schism of 1054 between the Eastern and Western Christian Church, he reintroduced the philosophy of Plato, especially intriguing Marsilio Ficino, laying the groundwork for the translation of the *Corpus Hermeticum*, and the Hermetic revival as a core thread of the Renaissance.

Plethon lived in the Peloponnese (then Byzantine Morea) and is associated with the city of Mystras (near Classical Sparta) which was the center of the Palaeologan Renaissance; a flourishing of art, culture, and thought under the last Byzantine Dynasty which presaged and drove the Greek and Italian Renaissance.

He proposed radical and utopian political reforms to the Byzantine administrators along the lines of Plato's republic, though he suggested homosexuals be burned at the stake. Christianity was at the time heavily based in Aristotelian thought, following from to Augustine, however Plethon drew strong comparisons between Plato's conceptualization of God and the Christian God.

Plethon authored, but did not circulate, a *Book of Laws* which provided an outline of a radical plan for the complete reformation of religious thought, combining Stoicism with Zoroastrian mysticism, and recommended replacing the worship of the Christian God with the classical deities, including Zeus, reforming the Byzantine state religion along hierarchical pagan lines with humanist ideology. His radical program is arguably one of the first true pagan revival movements since the collapse of pagan social structures in the 4th century. Like modern pagan revival movements, it placed contemporary ideology on a structure associated with classical religion.

The book came into the possession of the Princess Theodora, wife of the Byzantine Despot of the Peloponnese, eventually turning it over to an associate of Plethon who burned it, though he made an outline before doing so. It is unknown how long Plethon contemplated a return to paganism and there is no evidence he discussed it with any of the Italians he encountered. The agenda would have been too radical for Italy and, indeed, was clearly too radical for

Greece. Regardless, his general ideas have significant overlap with those later proposed by Giovanni Pico della Mirandola.

Ghazan, Mahmud – *GOZ-ahn MA-mood* – Persian Ghazan Khan 1271 – 1304, seventh Khan of the Ilkhanate division in the area of modern Iran. Ghazan invaded Syria in 1299 against the Mamluks, taking Aleppo. with the backing of his vassal Hethum II of the Armenian Kingdom of Cilicia. Hethum's forces included Hospitallers and Templars. He promised an attack on Egypt in 1301 but were unable to do more than raid Syria. *See also Ruad.*

Gnosticism – can be divided into two elements, closely related:

- A personal apprehension of, and relationship with, deity; the element of "gnosis" or "knowledge of" which exists outside of any church structures or personal intercession
- Most of what we consider "Gnosticism" is specifically dualist, including a belief that the material world is the work of an evil creator, a rebel against God, who "mired" humankind in flesh to keep them from the light of the true God. Thelema removes the precept of "evil" but does not reject the concept of a division between the material and higher worlds.

Traditionally, Gnosticism was seen as a Jewish and Christian movement originating in the first century BCE through the second century CE, however, a greater awareness of the first four centuries CE as a period with many emergent faiths has changed this belief.

A brief look at the Orphic myth (*see Orpheus*), by which humankind has the divine nature of Dionysus but the flesh of the Titans, and Neo-Platonic doctrines focused on the apprehension of the divine will show a strong relationship with paganism of the time. Gnosticism can be viewed more correctly as an amalgam of the various West Asian faiths which certainly had a strong Jewish base and which became increasingly connected to Christianity as the Christian faith became culturally dominant. Orphism was likely heavily influenced by Zoroastrian dualism which reached a zenith around the seventh century BCE and may reflect an attempt to syncretize Hellenic theogony with that of West Asia. Whatever the historical fact, from the Renaissance on, Gnosticism and Hermeticism are inextricably interwoven in the field of esoteric thought.

Historically, the first Christian Gnostics emerged in parallel with Manichaeism in the first and second centuries and, by the late second century, Gnostics were embroiled in controversy with anti-Gnostic Christian writers. As Orthodox Christianity became more powerful and mainstream in the third century, we begin to see a distinct separation of Gnosticism and Gnostic counterattacks on Orthodox writers. There is also some thought that it is not until this period that Christian Gnosticism began to look heavily outside of Christianity and absorb hermetic and other esoteric elements, including Manichaeism and Alexandrian Neoplatonism.

Writing in the late 19th century, Church Historian Adolf von Harnack describes the battle of Irenaeus and other Orthodox Christians as one against "acute Hellenization."[287] However, this posits a "pure" Christianity against which the Gnostics rebelled. A more realistic consideration taking into account the Nag Hammadi material, which was not available in Harnack's day, suggests a gradual co-evolution, with Orthodox Christianity winning an easy victory as it began to be accepted by secular rulers.

The reason for this lies in the appeal of Gnosticism to us today. It is intrinsically anti-authoritarian. Hebrew University Scholar Jonathan Cahana says, "Once again, it was Hans Jonas who remarked that 'Gnostic libertinism was the brazen expression of a rebellion no less against a cultural tradition than against the demiurge.'"[288] Nothing about the Gnostic experience of self-revelation led itself to intercessory churches or the belief in rulers as divinely anointed authorities. While it is possible to argue the chicken-egg precedence, the fact is that Gnosticism was doomed to outsider status because of its individualistic nature, just as those more individualistic expressions of Protestantism, e.g. the Quakers or Society of Friends, provoked rage and punitive action against the ostensibly "Puritan" New Englanders. It was one thing to purify the church, another entirely to revoke it's authority.

Key Gnostic Movements

It would not serve our purpose of providing a brief overview to make extensive efforts to sort the various strains of late Roman Gnosticism. We will briefly remark that Valentinianism was, and is, the best known historically. Jules Doinel considered himself a Valentinian Gnostic and used Tau Valentin as his episcopal title. Valentinianism was the form of Classical Gnosticism closest to Orthodox Christianity and the most organized Gnostic movement. For this reason, it was in many ways the greatest enemy of the Orthodox Christian Church and to some of the Orthodox Church Fathers, most especially Irenaeus, the most hated branch of Gnosticism. While outlying Gnostic movements could be easily dismissed as "heresies," Valentinianism presented a powerful challenge to the Orthodox Church.

It is likely that Gnosticism was never driven completely down by Orthodox Christianity, however, it was centered in West Asia in those regions where the reach of the Byzantine Empire, even at is zenith, remained weak. We can see the movement of Gnosticism in five non-exclusive hops:

> The Gnostics of Antiquity – West Asia, Europe, North Africa
> The Messalians or Euchites - West Asia
> The Paulicians of – Asia Minor and the northern Levant, transported to Bulgaria
> The Bogomils – Bulgaria
> The Cathars – Lombardy and Southern France

This represents an oversimplification, and there are scholarly quibbles with each step.

Nonetheless, this is generally agreed as the fashion in which Gnosticism spread into the West. Likewise, while "Bogomil" may have been a term actually used by the group for its founder, "Catharism" was not, and those who followed the Bishops anointed by Nicetas would not have seen themselves as part of a different sect.

Paulicianism and Messalianism

Messalianism was founded in the 4th century, and had strong dualist elements. Paulicianism was a 7th century dualist heresy that incorporated most of the classic "Gnostic" elements. The Paulicians maintained a state in Anatolia but they were eventually defeated by the Byzantine Emperor Basil I. "Their state was eradicated when their fortress at Tefrice in the theme of Armeniakon in eastern Anatolia fell to Basil I in 878; even so, they were not eliminated, for some were recruited into imperial armies, where their presence was regularly reported down to the twelfth century, while the removal by the Emperor John Tzimisces of further communities from the eastern frontier to Philippopolis in Thrace during the 970s added to their presence in the Balkans"[289] The area of the Byzantine frontier should be understood as a refuge for non-Orthodox practice. In addition to paganism, Harran supported a large Monophysite Christian population which was equally uninterested in Byzantine rule.

Messalians or Euchites, had a sort of "proto-gnostic" theology that migrated to Thrace well before the Paulician displacements and created a receptive climate for the migration of Paulician ideas.

> "Both sects...gained adherents throughout the Byzantine Empire, for during the fifth century
> Messalians could be found in Syria, Cappadocia, and Asia Minor, while by the early ninth
> century the Paulicians claimed to have seven churches extending from the Euphrates in the east

> to Corinth in the west. Neither accepted the Judaeo-Christian belief in the creation of the world
> by God; both sought an explanation for evil in the existence of matter, a key component of which
> was the human body. However, While the Messalians thought that a demon inside each body
> needed to be expelled by intense prayer, the Paulicians were part of the dualistic tradition, in
> that they believed in the eternal separation of God and Matter. These are the 'Two Principles'
> which ultimately came to characterise the absolute dualists of Languedoc and northern Italy
> from the 1170s onwards."[290]

In many ways, Messalianism may be more relevant to our history than Paulicianism. A repeated point about the Messalians is that they believe that sex or orgasm is the means to perception of the Holy Spirit. Writing somewhat circumspectly, John of Damascus tells us of the Messalians that their doctrine insists "That it is necessary for the soul to feel such communion with the heavenly bridegroom as the wife feels while having relations with her husband.""[291]

This is certainly not the only manifestation of this idea in antiquity, but it is the point, or at least a definable point, where what Crowley termed the IX° secret moves from paganism to Gnostic Christianity and prepares for its jump into the west. It also maintains at least the outside possibility that the idea made the jump to Catharism. The ambiguous sexuality attributed to the Cathars was debauched in Roman Catholic eyes. The Cathars believed all sex was sinful, but held incest to be no more debased than any other sex, a point made repeatedly. Given the accusations of sexual debauchery, it would be difficult to map out a real practice or rite, particularly if it was a secret of an initiated leadership. There are points against it, but it is an interesting idea.

We know that legendry concerning sexual irregularities still attached to the Bogomils at this time. While Michael Psellus, a Byzantine Court official, refers to them in "On the Operation of Demons" as Euchites, it is clear he is speaking of the contemporary Thracian heresy around 1050 CE. In his dialog between Timothy and the Thracian, the Thracian gives the supposed sordid details of the heretical practices then prevalent in Thrace. He repeats a set of calumnies common to every attempt to blacken the name of enemies through the current day. His principal accusation revolves around the claim of orgies in a darkened house or room, where the women are taken in common with a chance of the men taking their "their sister, or their own daughter, or their mother." [292] The darkness is so they will not know if they are lying or joining with someone of their own blood. According to Psellus, the Bogomils then take the children of such unions on the third day after birth and sacrifice and eat them, mixing the blood and ashes into an unholy substance which they slip into the food of others.

While the idea is wild and almost certainly a fiction, there may be some root of an actual rite there. While some accusations come to nothing, they are most often distortions of some truth, misheard or willfully misrepresented. The potential for some sort of transcendental or other magical work involving sex would seem to be suggested. [293]

This accusation had wings. A Chartrain monk, Paul of St Pere de Chartres who, writing some half-century after the events, alleged that the heretics discovered in Orleans in 1022 held orgies at night in which indiscriminate sexual intercourse took place and that the ashes derived from the cremation of children born of such unions were used as a viaticum for the terminally ill.[294]

The Bogomils and the Cathars

The Bogomils of Bulgaria, which was a region of Thrace in antiquity, organized their church in the 10th and 11th centuries and were periodically persecuted. The weak control of Byzantine authorities made the area ripe for the spread of heresy, particularly a heresy which was anti-authoritarian. The Byzantine writer Cosmas "nevertheless, saw this religious dissent as encompassing incitement to social revolt. "They teach their followers not to obey their masters; they scorn the rich, they hate the Tsars, they ridicule their superiors, they reproach the boyars, they believe that God looks in horror on those who labour for the Tsar, and advise every serf not to work for his master.'"[295] For a look at how this sort of theology would have appealed to the Toulousians of the 12th century, *see Appendix B.*

By the time the Bogomil Bishop Nicetas presided over a Council at Saint-Felix in 1167, there was already an established Dualist Church in Occitania. We have fairly little information on how it got there. Germanic Kings in the region had been Arian heretics, denying the divinity of Jesus in the 7th century, but they had fallen by the end of the Century. We see periodic reports of heresy as early as 1000, including one from Vertus, near Chalons-sur-Marne, followed by less detailed reports of other heretics in the region in the following century.[296]

What is clear is that by the late 12th century dualist heresy was flourishing in the region and had the patronage of a number of important families. The reasons are manifold. As noted, dualist heresy is inherently anti-authoritarian. The Princes of the region were engaged in generational struggles not just against each other but against the Frankish Crown, and the Hegemony of the Roman Church. The area also saw a profound boom in arts and literature which would have prompted curiosity and a willingness to question absolutes. Radical Christian purists have little use for Troy or Greek Gods. Whether they accepted or rejected Cathar beliefs, the Troubadour class may have had more trouble seeing them as inherently evil and poisonous.

The influence of the Crusades cannot be dismissed. Inasmuch as it was a Crusade fueled by intolerance of Islam which denounced the doctrine of Mohammed as corrupt and Satanic, it brought Christians into contact with Muslims and with divergent Christians. This was bound, over time, to have produced a degree of tolerance which can be seen in the accusations leveled against the Templars. To live side-by-side with the Muslims, employing them as laborers and, at times, as mercenaries would make it difficult to see a need for their extermination, whatever the Pope might say. It is impossible to tell, as well, what direct information might have been brought back by the Crusaders. Many crusaders were, for their time, quite literate and well-read, though literacy was not a prerequisite (as is noted with Wolfram Von Eschenbach) for picking up a wide range of esoteric foreign lore.

Correspondingly, Occitania was close enough to Spain to be influenced by the Muslim presence there, but not so close as to be completely bound up, as were Aragon and Castile, in constant warfare. Just as Muslims were tolerated in Palermo (*see Appendix B - Jeanne of England*), Christian traders from Montpellier and Marseilles traded, directly or through Palma, to Bejaia and Oran. That Von Eschebach (*see entry*) chose an Islamic author in Andalusia through a Provencal poet, as the proposed origin of his *Parzival* story attests to considerable cultural interest and openness, even if and, perhaps, especially if the account was fictional. It was, most importantly, plausible.

We don't believe that all Occitan heretics were either dualists or members of the group we identify today as "Cathars" that is the church organized by Nicetas. We do know that some of them had libertine beliefs that match our profile of Gnostics. "Archbishop Samson at Reims in October 1157, was directed against Piphiles, who rejected marriage, and lived in impure or even incestuous unions, while the very important Council of Tours of May 1163, presided over by the pope and attended by seventeen cardinals, included legislation specifically aimed at 'Albigensians' and those who helped them."[297] After Montsegur, the faith continued at least through an attempt at a revival by the Autier Brothers in the early 14th century. Perhaps, more importantly, the Autiers maintained communication with a Lombard Church, supposedly stamped out when 200 Cathars were burnt in Verona in 1278, but still clearly in operation some decades later.

The Thelemic Initiations

The Lure of the Forbidden - Modern Gnosticism and Spermatophagy

Dualist heresy as an operative concern had fallen to the level of folklore or tradition by the mid 14th century. Yet the very necessity to write against it had created a body of knowledge that proved irresistible to those who came after. If the claim of Peter of Les Vaux-de-Cernay's that Cathars believed they "could sin in safety and without restraint"[298] was the lineal descendant of stories like that of Psellus, even the most over the top Grand Guignol was fascinating in late 19th century France. In an esoteric world which had heavy elements of Satanism – both traditional anti-Catholic Satanism practiced as a sort of ironic protest and pagan Satanism which embraced the Devil as the "God of our Enemies" - the libertinism of the Gnostics was intriguing. Crowley was not the only one who understood that "eating children" was more likely to refer to oral sex than cannibalism.

> "...during the Last Supper, it is not bread and wine that Jesus Christ gave to the apostles as symbols of his body and of his blood. What Jesus really offered on that occasion, which was to become the model for the central ceremony of Christianity for centuries to come, was his sperm. Since then the practice of spermatophagy (literally, the eating of sperm) has been the central, albeit hidden ritual practice of the Catholic priesthood. But references to this practice can also be found in all the religious traditions of the world....What I have just described is, in a nutshell, the thesis that a Belgian spiritualist, the Chevalier Georges Le Clément de Saint-Marcq (1865–1956), presented to the world in a pamphlet first published in 1906, L'Eucharistie." [299]

The Modern Gnostics and L'Eglise Gnostique

Jules Doinel based his L'Eglise Gnostique (known by several similar names) of 1890 on spiritual experiences of 1888-1889. While doing spirit-work with Lady Caithness he received various messages, including a communication from Helene-Ennoia, the "Divine Androgyne," and instruction from the martyred Cathar Bishop Guilhabert de Castres, both of whom commanded him to re-found the Cathar Succession. Doinel used existing knowledge of Cathar rituals to establish his church.

Jules Doinel and the Taxil Anti-Masonic Hoax

Doinel was organizing his church at the height of the Anti-Masonic Hoax. He appears to have stepped away from the Gnostic Church from 1894-96. His original reason for breaking away seems to have been his participation as one of a circle of authors who worked on the hoax with Taxil, notably through the publication, under the pseudonym "Jean Kostka" his fictional non-fiction Lucifer Unmasked. Understanding the nature of the Taxil hoax is essential to understanding why some of our most useful information about Doinel's Gnostic Church comes from a book ostensibly opposing it.

The Anti-Masonic Hoax was organized by writer Leo Taxil and can be explained in the current era as a sort of Victorian version of trolling on an epic scale. The point was, at least initially, to discredit the Roman Catholic Church by associating it with assertions of absurdity while demonstrating the comparative gullibility of its followers and clergy.

> "'The public made me what I am; the arch-liar of the period,'" confessed Taxil, 'for when I first commenced to write against the Masons my object was amusement pure and simple. The crimes I laid at their door were so grotesque, so impossible, so widely exaggerated, I thought everybody would see the joke and give me credit for originating a new line of humor. But my readers wouldn't have it so; they accepted my fables as gospel truth, and the more I lied for the purpose of showing that I lied, the more convinced became they that I was a paragon of veracity.'

'Then it dawned upon me that there was lots of money in being a Munchausen of the right kind, and for twelve years I gave it to them hot and strong, but never too hot. When inditing such slush as the story of the devil snake who wrote prophecies on Diana's back with the end of his tail, I sometimes said to myself: 'Hold on, you are going too far,' but I didn't. My readers even took kindly to the yarn of the devil who, in order to marry a Mason, transformed himself into a crocodile, and, despite the masquerade, played the piano wonderfully well.'

One day when lecturing at Lille, I told my audience that I had just had an apparition of Nautilus, the most daring affront on human credulity I had so far risked. But my hearers never turned a hair. 'Hear ye, the doctor has seen Nautulius,' they said with admiring glances. Of course no one had a clear idea of who Nautilus was, I didn't myself, but they assumed that he was a devil.

Ah, the jolly evenings I spent with my fellow authors hatching out new plots, new, unheard of perversions of truth and logic, each trying to outdo the other in organized mystification. I thought I would kill myself laughing at some of the things proposed, but everything went; there is no limit to human stupidity".[300]

Taxil revealed the hoax at a press conference in 1897, but Doinel had already returned to the Gnostic Church, being appointed Bishop of Aleth and Mirepoix at the beginning of 1896,[301] so his time away from the Church may have been somewhat less than typically depicted. The fact that he was quickly received back into the Church suggests that his activities were reasonably well understood by his contemporaries, at least those "in the know." Papus seemed unconcerned by his resignation, though his departure apparently caused some confusion, some believing it was sincere, others that it was tongue in cheek.[302] Doinel died in 1902, leaving some questions unanswered, though he suggested at least some sincerity, telling fellow Gnostic Fabre des Essarts "Only know that under the influence of the demiurge angels, I had formed the project very sincerely to reconcile Gnosis with the Church. I was cruelly disillusioned."[303]

How writing *Lucifer Unmasked* fit into Doinel's goals is a little unclear. Was it pure profit motive, as was admittedly the case with Taxil's later work? Or was it an attempt to write a "provocative" work on the assumption that the right sort of people would see through the veneer of disapproval and become interested in the subject matter? This may seem absurd in a modern context, but this was a period when subjects such as drug use, or queer sexuality, could only be written about, outside of small private publications, if the subject was addressed from a moralistic point of view. Often an overwrought or facetious morality or ending made the work palatable to the mainstream press, where it was gobbled up by people who were fascinated by the subject matter but could not admit to any sympathy with it. This was certainly true to a lesser extent of occult work, and *Lucifer Unmasked* got some of Doinel's ideas in front of a much larger audience than was reached with straight up "occult works."

There is a question as to whether or not we can take the texts presented in Lucifer Unmasked, a work we know to be fiction representing itself as truth, as factual. The answer appears to be "yes" in that the Gnostic Ceremonies, including that for Consecration of a Bishop, are generally conceded to be quite accurate, as are most of the other technical details.

Of particular interest is the description of the night in 1890 where, at a séance with Lady Caithness, the charge to form a new Gnostic Church was given to Doinel:

> *I am Luciabel, whom you name Lucifer. I am the son of God like Jesus, eternally begotten like him. I am speaking to you. I address myself to you because you are my friend, my servant and the prelate of my Albigensian Church. I am exiled from the Pleroma, and it is I whom Valentinus named Sophia-Achamôth. It is I whom Simon Magus called Helene-Ennoia; for I am the Eternal Androgyne. Jesus is the Word of God; I am the Thought of God. One day I shall return to my Father above, but I require assistance in this; to intercede for me, the supplications of my Brother Jesus are required. Only the Infinite is able to redeem the Infinite, and only God is able to redeem God. Listen well: The One has brought forth One, then One. And the Three are but One: the Father, the Word and the Thought. Establish my Gnostic Church. The Demiurge will be powerless against it. Receive the Paraclete.[304]*

It appears that the account was sufficiently credible for Jean Bricaud, a Gnostic Bishop who must certainly have known the details of the founding of the Church quite well, to reproduce it in *Le Reveil Gnostique, organ of the Gnostic Church*, Vol 2, March-April 1908, No. 7, pages 2 to 4.[305] Golden Dawn author A.E. Waite, who wrote with apparent sincerity to refute Kostka, ridicules the name "Luciabel" but does not refute the details of the seance.[306] Given our understanding of the role of Satan as "The Sun in the South"[307] in Thelema, the appearance of Lucifer in this context seems more appropriate than not.

The Gnostic Church in the 20th Century

Doinel consecrated several Bishops, including Papus, Fabre des Essarts, and others who continued the work of his church. We have no interest in giving an exhaustive history of the Gnostic Church here. It would probably be impossible to fully clarify its overlap with Reuss, Crowley, and O.T.O. David G. Robertson has given the various French lineages, as well as their relationship with Martinism and other period groups, extensive coverage in *Gnosticism and the History of Religions*.[308] In *Of Memphis and Misraim, The Oriental Silence of the Winged Sun*, Milko Bogard covered the various lineages and overlaps through that esoteric Masonic body, which became heavily entangled with the Gnostic Church in the early 20th century.

Nor are lines of succession and authority of much interest to us. Neither our Sovereign Sanctuary, nor the related Heterodox Gnostic Church, depend on them for authority to operate. The Ecclesiastical lines are embodied in some TTO members and are conferred at request upon the Prelates of the Order, while the M∴M∴ elements of our initiations are interwoven with various lines of L'Eglise Gnostique. It must be made clear, however, that our initiations do not appeal to Reuss and Crowley's O.T.O. or the Church of Doinel for *authority*, but rather see in them a seminal *ideological* seed from which we bring forth a new initiatory cycle. Our interest in Gnosticism is how it became central to Thelema.

While Jean Bricaud took the French Gnostic Church, or at least a branch of it, in a more orthodox direction that rejected the Cathar material, Neo-gnosticism, descended directly from Doinel, had become core to the philosophy of Theodor Reuss and Aleister Crowley. Around 1908, at a conference that was unfortunately rather poorly documented, the existing Gnostic Church and Theodor Reuss' O.T.O. exchanged some dignities and authorities. Regrettably, the details and specifics do not survive. The result was that, by 1911, Reuss' O.T.O. was firmly wedded to both the Gnostic Church and to Crowley's incipient idea of Thelema. For his part, Crowley made "one Gnostic and Catholic Church of Light, Life, Love and Liberty," a central structure "the Word of whose Law is THELEMA."[309]

Doinel's influence on Crowley should not be underestimated. One could easily suggest that Crowley's entire project during the First World War of writing intentionally "over the top" pro-German material for George Sylvester

Viereck's *The International*, in order to de-legitimatize pro-German sentiment in the United States shares a great deal with the Taxil hoax.

Perhaps more directly influential was Doinel's successor Papus, a member of the Golden Dawn Ahathoor Temple in Paris which was run by MacGregor Mathers, Crowley's mentor at the turn of the century. The intellectual concepts of the Gnostic Church dovetailed closely with Crowley's concept of Thelema, and his visits to Paris afforded him extensive exposure. Reuss expressed his vision through a translation of Crowley's *Liber XV* Gnostic Mass into German which he proposed as a universal Gnostic sacrament. Thelema and French Neo-Gnosticism were wed at the outset, and the Cathar ideal was seminal to, and if one credits the magical origin of, the French resurgence.

In addition to Papus, Crowley was notably influenced by the work of fellow Cambridge student George Robert Stow Mead, who linked Blavatsky's Theosophy to Gnosticism. Mead was a vocal opponent of Annie Besant, who Crowley also detested, and published the first English translation of the *Pistis Sophia* in 1896.

> *Crowley gravitated to Gnosticism, possibly because it was a faith about which so little was known that it encouraged unrestrained speculation, in much the same way that Egyptian hieroglyphics, prior to the discovery of the Rosetta Stone, prompted speculation by de Gebelin that tarot cards originated in ancient Egypt. Mead's influence is visible in Crowley's first magical text, the Sword of Song (1904): there, he refers to the Gnostic Codex Brucianus , which consists of the Coptic-Gnostic Books of Jeu and another untitled work. In 1904, the only two translations of this codex were by Schmidt (in German) and Mead. During his American period (1914-1919), Crowley sought out Mead's translation of the Gnostic Pistis Sophia; he subsequently included the book in his syllabus for students of magick.*[310]

Summary

Gnosticism did not lie dead and dormant from the early 14th century until late 19th century Paris. There were likely always adherents and interested parties. The Hermeticism of Renaissance Italy is part of a continuum of Gnostic thought, and with Protestantism came a number of Christian churches that were Gnostic in outlook if not in name, though few specifically embraced the dualist model. The revelation of a vast tranche of Gnostic material in the mid 20th century lent vast legitimacy to the gnostic movement. Some scholars have lamented that the material has not been more firmly assimilated. "The challenges of the Nag Hammadi corpus are routinely ignored; terminology from Jung and particularly Jonas is ubiquitous; the methodology remains predominantly phenomenological with a historical gloss."[311] Yet, alongside the "Grimoire Revival" discussed in our introduction has been a resurgence of interest in the PGM, itself the working branch of Hermeticism, never as comfortably far from the Poemandres as some philosophers would have liked.

Robertson in "Gnosticism and the History of Religions" discusses modern Gnostic groups.

> *"The tendency for scholars to describe contemporary self-identifying gnostic groups as 'neo-Gnostic' underlines that they are viewed as somehow illegitimate. The reason, surely, is that without a direct historical lineage, they should not be understood as 'really' gnostic. Historical transmission is of course a very common strategy of legitimization used by new religions themselves, and Gnostics are no exception. But Bentley Layton has argued that the best practice historiographically is to use the name that a group uses for itself, and moreover only in that sense, 'because ambivalent usage would introduce disorderliness into historical discourse'. If this*

> *were true, then it is possible that today's self-identifying gnostic religions are the only ones there have ever been."*[312]

Gnosticism has been a form of scholarship as well as an active philosophy or faith. Continuing the thought begun with his citation of Jonas above, Cahana says "Continuing this line of thought, it seems worthwhile to investigate whether the now infamous 'gnostic acosmism' was not so much a revolt against the physical world and its constituents, such as 'lovely cypress trees and delicious grapes and dates and Mediterranean evenings lit by radiant full moons,' nor was it an aversion to a specific sociopolitical sphere, but a resentment of the cultural premises that appeared to be keeping this world from breaking apart."

The world breaking apart may seem like scary stuff, but it is the implicit goal of Thelema and the New Aeon. What Thelemites who do not really understand the ethics of Thelema or its doctrines fail to grasp is that this is not about some bleak nihilistic anarcho-capitalist agenda. It is about breaking down the elements of society that destroy individual freedom, from massive corporate structures that prevent governments from addressing issues of disease and climate change to the very international order that tolerates and abets warfare.

In whatever case, the very fact that we are discussing things that happened two thousand years ago argues that Gnosticism has a tradition now. What is made Crowley desire to incorporate it into Thelema, and what makes it an operative element of Thelema is that part of that tradition involves a constant questioning of tradition itself. Tradition allows us to feel we are acting with the weight of history. But that weight only matters if we are on the right side of history, and Gnosticism, with its preference for immediate and personal experience, allows us to choose wisely.

Guilhabert de Castres – *see Appendix B, Gnosticism*

Guillaume de Beaujeu – c. 1230-1291 – Grand Master of the Knights Templar from 1273-91. By the time of his tenure the Crusader states, weakened by the War of Saint Sabas in which Genoa and Venice warred over access to Acre, were exposed to increasing attack. The County of Tripoli ignored warnings from Beaujeu, who was killed leading the defense of Acre.

Guillemette, Lady of Montlaur and Saint Jory – *see Appendix B*

Guy de Charnay – 1251-1314 – also Geoffroi de Charney, Guy D'Auvergne, Knights Templar Preceptor of Normandy. He was one of the ranking officials captured by the King of France, and within eight days issued a confession in which he admitted to having denied Christ and engaged in homoerotic acts.[313] He recanted along with Jacques de Molay and was burned in 1314. *See also Mandylion*

Gynander – a term borrowed from botany, it occurs in the 1913 Webster's Dictionary and was adapted to describe a female with masculine characteristics. It is no longer current, but would have been considered dignified and scientific at the time.

Hadad – *see El*

Hapocrates – the Egyptian child God of the Sun Horus, representing the dawn. The name Hapocrates is a Hellenization of *Heru-pa-khered*, "Horus the Child." Portrayed in statuary as a naked child with his finger raised to his mouth in imitation of the hieroglyph for "child" the Hellenes attributed this gesture to the raised finger to lips meaning "silence."

Harran – *HAR-ann* – also Harranians – While it was, for a time, part of the core of the Neo-Assyrian Empire, the location of Harran tended to render it a perpetual melting pot and buffer state, lying in a region that historically tended to mark the frontier or boundary of an empire. No incident could illustrate this more than the Battle of Carrhae, in 53 BCE, during which the Parthians defeated a large Roman army under Crassus, who was killed. The city eventually fell into Roman hands but was a perpetual location for confrontations between the Romans and their eastern rivals. An army of the emperor Galerius was defeated by the Sassanids in 296 CE, and was in and out of Byzantine and Sassanid hands on multiple occasions.

The core legend of Harran is that during the Abbasid caliphate, Harun al-Rashid marched through on his way to war with the Byzantines, informing the population that they must convert from Paganism to Islam before his return. The lawyers of the Pagan population conferred and determined that the Quran allowed for the protection of three non-Islamic "faiths of the book," Christians, Jews and Sabians. As Sabians were poorly documented the Harranians held that they were people whose book was the Hermeticum, and whose Prophet was Hermes Trismegistus, who was understood to be Enoch or Idris, thus giving them a legitimate connection to the Abrahamic religions. We know this is a gross oversimplification, if not an outright fabrication "Harran was not, after all, some backwater town, unnoticed by the Muslims until the time of Ma'mun [al-Rashid]. It had played, as we have seen, an important role in early Islamic history: it was to here that the school of medicine was moved from Alexandria by the Caliph 'Umar II in 717 C. E.; it had been the capital of the last Ummayad caliph, Marwan II, and the fame of its ancient oracle of the Moon god was widespread.""[314] Nor was this familiarity short lived. Green recounts a Sabian Baghdad Scholar Ibrahim ibn Hilal, encouraging an edict of toleration for the Sabians of Harran, which allowed them to "visit their prayerhouses, temples, meeting places and assembly halls, and to practice the precepts of their religion in the traditional manner."[315]

In nearby Edessa, Bar Daysan (named a Gnostic Saint as Bardesanes) is far better documented. While he eventually became a Christian "Eusebius regretted that Bardaisan had belonged to the Valentinians, and that 'he did not entirely leave behind the filth of the old heresy'"[316] the historical consensus is that "Bardaisan's doctrine is founded upon the same Aramaic paganism which still constitutes the inheritance of the Sabians in Ḥarran."[317]

Why is Harran important to us? There are two axes:

Harran is a corridor through which the ideological concepts of Hermeticism come down to us. Alexandria is often seen as the center from which Hermeticism exploded; however the Islamic world however an interest in Hellenism and Hellenic thought also emanated from the fertile crescent.

> *"Abu-Yusuf Yacqub ibn-Ishaq al-Kindi (d. after 870 C.E.), who is the first "Hellenist" Faylasuf among the Muslims and a major source for the doctrinal positions of the Sabians, was born in Kufa on the banks of the middle Euphrates...the most important Arab city in the Fertile Crescent before the coming of Islam. It had played an important role as a point of confluence of Christian, Persian and Arab traditions during the Sasanian period, a role which seemingly continued into the Muslim era. Although he knew no Greek, Kindi was acquainted with members of the Harranian community in Baghdad, and it is likely that his first glimmer of how the substance of Greek philosophy might be applied to Islamic revelation was filtered through a Harranian prism. His perceptions of Harranian doctrine were preserved, although sometimes criticized, by his intellectual descendants. His students, Sarakhsi and Abu Zayd al-Balkhi (d. 934 C .E.), who cite their teacher frequently, were the sources for many of the later works about the Harranians which cast their beliefs in a Neoplatonic/Hermetic perspective. "[318]*

The Thelemic Initiations

By the time the *Gayat al-Hakim* began to circulate in Europe as the Latin Picatrix, at least a century of Islamic thought about Hellenistic magic had been influenced by Harranian thinkers in Baghdad. If Randolph and Crowley, writing in the 19th and 20th century picked out Hermetic inferences in Alawite, or Sufi practice, that's not necessarily a coincidence. Harran represents a point from which late classical paganism seeped into Islam, and Islam was as important as the Byzantine Empire as a source of the preservation of Classical thought, especially during the Abbasid period. Al-Mamun sent representatives to the Byzantine Empire to purchase Greek manuscripts for his universityh in Baghdad.

Secondly, we typically think of a clean break of almost a millennia between the Neo-Platonism of the 4th century and the beginnings of pagan revival in the west with authors like Pletho and Ficino in the Renaissance in the 15th century. This exaggerates the distance in doctrine and philosophy between the time of the Neo-Platonists and our own and has the knock on effect of making Christianity seem monolithic and unchallenged, with the whisperings of crypto-paganism of the 15th century a modern footnote. Living in the US and Europe, both of which is still identify as about 65% percent self-identified Christian (even if many of those Christians embrace numerous folk traditions which are strongly rooted in paganism, or Eastern faith, e.g. Karma) the perception of historic inevitability of Christianity has a dampening effect on the feelings of legitimacy among those who profess reconstructed faiths.

Harran brings Hermeticism centuries closer to us. The Arab histories suggest strongly that a robust pagan practice in Harran was tolerated well into the Crusader period. While we cannot know how much pagan influence seeped into Europe through Harran, it lay two days travel from Edessa and was a frequent object of Crusader ambitions. In times of peace, trade, spies, and dissidents must have flowed readily between the two cities. Sources suggest that paganism existed in Harran contemporary to the County of Ibelin or, if it did not, it had been suppressed only recently. Displaced pagans may have found work, as did Muslim factionaries, with the Crusaders, possibly professing some form of Islam or Christianity.

This is speculative. We have no smoking gun; no letter from a Christian of Edessa specifically citing pagan influence. Yet the Templar Trial confessions suggest a root of pagan practice that is neither entirely consistent with Islam or the various eastern forms of Christianity. In particular, the recurrence of the worship of a "head" at the Templar Trials,[319] the earliest identification of Baphomet, are interesting in regards to accusations leveled against the Harranians regarding being "Adherents of the Head."

> *"when Ma'mun [al Rashid] visited Harran, he accused the inhabitants of being 'Adherents of the Head,' who had lived in the days of his father, Harun al-Rashid (786- 809 C.E.). Following this story, Ibn al-Nadim provides an explanation of the meaning of 'the Head.' It referred to the head of a man who resembled 'Utarid (Mercury),' in accordance with what they believed about the looks of the forms of the planets.' The man was seized and was placed in a solution of oil and borax, until his joints relaxed, and His condition was such that if his head was pulled, it could be lifted without tearing what it was fastened to ... This they did every year when Mercury was at its height. They supposed that the soul of this individual came to his head, because of (his resemblance to) 'Utarid. It spoke with its tongue, relating what was happening and replying to questions. They supposed that the individual's nature fitted and resembled the nature of 'Utarid more than that of other living creatures, being more closely related to him than to others in connection with speech, discernment, and other things they believed him to possess' Dimashqi gives a similar account of a 'prophetic head,' in this instance concerning a man with the physical characteristics associated with the planet Mars."[320]*

There is not enough information to make any positive identification; however given the difficulty of tracing even well-known and openly admitted influences from this period, the potential that pagan influences slipped into Europe through the Crusades is certainly conceivable. If we have not identified a smoking gun, we can certainly identify a very reasonable path. The knowledge that an active pagan culture that had at least strong intimations of Hermetic thought sat thirty miles from Edessa is compelling.

Hatshepsut – *HAHT-shep-soot* – 1507-1458 BCE – Fifth Pharaoh of the 18th Dynasty, the second female Pharaoh whose existence can be definitively established. Her iconic representations in statuary and painting carried a beard and other male signifiers though it is unclear whether this indicates a queer identity or simply artistic convention, (e.g. the child Thutmose III was portrayed as an adult Pharaoh).

Heliopolis – *HEE-lee-OP-uh-lis* – Heliopolis, with ruins located in what is now the Mataria district of Greater Cairo, is verifiably one of the oldest cities in Egypt. A surviving obelisk marks the site of the Temple of Re Atum, constructed by Senusret I around 1950 BCE. Atumu or Etom was one of the best known forms of the Sun God, giving the city its Greek Name "House of the Sun."

Christian myths have been attached to a sacred well there. The temples were praised by Herodotus. While never politically important, the city's location on the caravan route from Syria seems to have given it great commercial importance. There were Canaanite quarters as early as 1200 BCE. The Hieroglyphic form '-n-w is attested by the Assyrian Unu, and is rendered in Hebrew as On.

Heliopolis and the word "On" began to appear in Egyptianized initiatory traditions of the late 18th and early 19th century. One of the earlier references is from *Crata Repoa*, a text composed by German Masons around 1785.

> *If someone wished to join the society of Crata Repoa he must first be particularly recommended by an initiate.*
>
> *Generally this happened by way of a letter from the king himself to the priests.*
>
> *The priests, however, first turned him away from Heliopolis, referring him to the teachers at Memphis; from Memphis he was instructed to go to Thebes.*[321]

In Thelema The Sun God Atum as Ra-Harakht, Ra-Horakhty, or Ra-Hoor-Khuit is given considerable importance which may be investigated at length throughout the mysteries. The literal city of Heliopolis is emblematic of an idealized Heliopolis which is the City of Pyramids; home to those adepts who have crossed the Abyss having poured out their blood into the Cup of Babalon. Crowley gives the Name ON, correlated by the Jewish Encyclopedia, and links that to AUM, in his discussion of AUMGN[322]

The 1906 Jewish Encyclopedia, which was available to Crowley and Reuss, gave this summary, which is noteworthy for its summary of historical data widely accepted by Freemasons and Rosicrucians of the period and bears repeating in full:

> *Egyptian city, whence came Poti-pherah, Joseph's father-in-law (Gen. xli. 45, 50; xlvi. 20). It is mentioned also in Ezek. xxx. 17, where the punctuation אָוֶן, Awen, is to be corrected to אוֹן, On. The versions render "Heliopolis" in all cases "Heliupolis." An addition in the Septuagint (Ex. i. 11) mentions Heliopolis among the cities built by the Israelites. The inscriptions, however, show that it was perhaps the most ancient of all Egyptian cities—certainly the most sacred about 3000 B.C. Its god, Atumu (Etôm), was then the most prominent of the many forms under which the sun-god appeared in Egypt (being identified especially with the setting sun), so that the*

city bore the name "house of the sun" (comp. the Greek "Heliopolis" and the equivalent Hebrew "Beth-shemesh"; Jer. xliii. 13 [doubted by Winckler, "Alttestamentliche Untersuchungen," p. 180, who considers "Beth" as an erroneous repetition of the final syllable of the word "maẓẓebot"]).

It is remarkable that sanctity is still attached to the sacred well and tree among the insignificant ruins near Maṭariyyah, a few miles north of Cairo, which are protected by Christianization of the old myths (whence the place had the earlier Arabic name "'Ain al-Shams" [fountain of the sun]). The temples, of which only one obelisk from the twelfth dynasty has been preserved, were famous for their size and beauty, as were the priesthood for their learning, for which they were praised by Herodotus. A trace of this respect may possibly be found in the Biblical mention of Joseph's Egyptian relatives. Politically, the city was never of importance, although it was the capital of the thirteenth nome of Lower Egypt. Its position near the caravan road from Syria seems to have given it great commercial importance; hence the numerous Jewish settlements in and around it, among which were Castra and Vicus Judæorum. It already had Canaanitish quarters about 1200 B.C. Therefore the Septuagint considered it as a Jewish place (see above); Juba, in Pliny, vi. 177, as Arabic. During the Roman period it diminished rapidly in population and importance; the Arabs found it deserted.[323]

Hermes Trismegistus – the identity of Hermes Trismegistus has been investigated in great depth in a recent volume by Christian H. Bull, *The Tradition of Hermes Trismegistus (Religions in the Graeco-Roman World)* published by Brill in 2018.[324]

Essentially, Hermes Trismegistus presents two problems. The identification of the authors of the work attributed in the *Corpus Hermeticum*, and related sources, and the derivation of Hermes Trismegistus from other Gods. Bull focuses on the first question, and establishes, uncontroversially, that the work emanates from Hellenized Egyptian priests during the first few centuries of the Common Era.

That Hermes Trismegistus is a Hellinization of Thoth as "Thrice Great Hermes" is well understood. Hermes Trismegistus may be understood to be the Thelemic Tahuti, which is one of several variant names for Thoth. Thoth is among the older gods, attested in some of the oldest religious texts in existence four thousand years ago (2353-2107 BCE).[325]

Bull has less interest in the identification of Hermes Trismegistus with Enoch/Idris, which is a recurring and credible theme of Tobias Churton's *The Lost Pillars of Enoch*, published by Inner Traditions in 2020. The connection of the Pillars or Emerald Tablet; the *Book of Thoth*, which Crowley organized around the depictions by Lady Freida Harris, and the *Book of Enoch* revealed to Dee and Kelley which frames *The Vision and the Voice*, is no coincidence. Hermeticism frames the esoteric tradition of the West.

Now give good heed, son Horus, for thou are being told the mystic spectacle which Kamephis, our forefather, was privileged to hear from Hermes, record-writer of all deeds, and I from Kamephis, most ancient of--us--all, when he did honour me with the black--rite--that gives perfection; hear thou it now from me.[326]

What is clear is that in first four centuries CE, Hermes assumed a role of near primacy in pagan thought, assimilating and eclipsing other gods and influencing both Christian and Islamic conceptions of deity.

The summary of G.R.S. Mead, writing in *Thrice Greatest Hermes* under the Theosophical Society Imprimatur 1906, has been widely if incompletely cited:

But there is another and still more profoundly interesting side of the subject which we cannot expect to find treated in a purely philological, technical, and critical treatise. The more one studies the best of these mystical sermons, casting aside all prejudice, and trying to feel and think with the writers, the nearer one is conscious of approaching the threshold of what may well be believed to have been the true Adytum of the best in the mystery-traditions of antiquity. Innumerable are the hints of the greatnesses and immensities lying beyond that threshold— among other precious things the vision of the key to Egypt's wisdom, the interpretation of apocalypsis by the light of the sun-clear epopteia of the intelligible cosmos.

Such greatnesses and such mysteries have a power and beauty which the most disreputable tradition of the texts through unknowing hands cannot wholly disguise, and they are still recognisable, even though thus clad in the rags of their once fair garments, by those who have eyes to see and ears to hear. [327]

Hiram Abif – *HEE-rahm AHH-beef* or *HI-rim ABB-iff* – The first is more generally correct, but the second corresponds to the pronunciation used by many US Freemasons. Hiram Abif is associated with the character of King Hiram of Tyre, who aided Solomon in the construction of his Temple at Jerusalem. There is no particular reason to think the alliance of Solomon and Hiram is ahistorical. The two would have been natural allies in trade, and Tyre would have been seeking support as it grew in rivalry with its original mother city, Sidon.

The question of Hiram's name has been a source of confusion for Masonic scholars. Abif is generally taken as indicating the "Father of" and so this figure has been variously identified as Hiram the King, or his actual father. The interpretation of "Father of Hiram" as that of a senior priest/builder, much as a Christian Clergyman sent by the King of France might be regarded as a "Father of King Louis," e.g. a Priest in his service, seems less far fetched than most other interpretations.

Hirschfeld, Magnus – *1868-1935* – while queer himself, German Doctor Magnus Hirschfeld became what was, essentially, the first modern queer activist as a reaction to the number of patients in his therapy who committed suicide due to homosexuality and a sense of outrage at the Oscar Wilde trial. In 1898, Hirschfeld led a public effort to revoke Paragraph 175 of the German Penal Code, leading the Social Democratic Party to introduce the first credible modern period attempt to overturn anti-homosexual legislation. The move was unsuccessful, but established the credible existence of a movement working openly for homosexual rights.

In his report, he argued that, based on a study of approximately 5,000 homosexuals for which he had been lead researcher, homosexuality was a constant in all human societies. It was no more frequent in the present than in the past, could be found in all social classes, and was no more widespread in Germany than in the country of Raimond Lecomte or Oscar Wilde. Hirschfeld was thus able to conclude that "homosexuality is part of the plan of nature and creation, just like normal love."[328]

Among his accomplishments were the data collected by Hirschfeld on homosexual suicide which "can be seen as an attempt to make visible the queer scar tissue that marks modern homosexuality. By counting homosexual suicides within a statistical framework, Hirschfeld emphasized the collective shape of the individual suffering. This archive documents the deadly effects of homosexual persecution and how social ostracization could make queer lives feel unlivable." [329]

"Hirschfeld gathered what was arguably the first full-scale archive of sexual science. With his colleagues at the Institute of Sexual Science in Berlin, he accumulated a large library containing books, journals, objects, and visual material as well as clinical notes, questionnaires, and other documents relating to the work of the institute itself. Hirschfeld thus played an active part in the institution of sexual knowledge."[330]

At a time when most efforts at awareness focused on homosexual men, Hirschfeld is notable both for a focus on all sexual rights including, explicitly, transgender rights and in acknowledging and discussing the broad spectrum of sexuality.

> "Arguably the most famous aspect of the work was Hirschfeld's so-called sexual intermediaries work. Sexual intermediaries describes the existence of infinite variations in gender and sexual desire. Hirschfeld understood sexual desire and the manifestation of gender to be encoded in the body, arguing that infinite variations exist in desires, bodies, gender expressions, and the intersections between them. To some extent the overlaps and confusions between the terms Hirschfeld used to describe same-sex and transgender phenomena reflect the impossibility of producing neat sex-gender distinctions....However, given that Hirschfeld worked at a time when binary gender essentialism was the norm and that he overtly tried to challenge this norm, framing his work entirely in terms of the constructionism versus essentialism debates that concerned gender theorists in the 1980s and early 1990s forecloses understanding of the issues that preoccupied Hirschfeld and the people whose self did not match their assigned gender."[331]

That Hirschfeld was a profound influence on Crowley's Europe was beyond question. Hirschfeld was the leading progressive thinker in regards to queer issues, and a key to creating the modern awareness of sexuality that was queer rather than explicitly gay or lesbian. Crowley was drawn to Berlin during the last years before Hirschfeld fled, and the reason why is clear. It was the one place he could be certain his own unique understandings of sexuality and gender would not be, automatically, dismissed.

Hirschfeld was not merely a thinker without skin in the fight. He was beaten in an ambush by right-wing street thugs in 1920, who left him for dead. In 1933 his life's work the Institute was burned by the Nazis and he was forced to flee to France. He died in 1935.

Hughes de Pairaud – Hughes de Pairaud was a leading contender for leadership of the Templars when Jacques de Molay was elected in Cyprus. He was sentenced to life imprisonment in 1314 and did not repudiate his confession, thus did not die with Jacques de Molay. He was accused of homosexual behavior and supporting homosexual behavior at his receptions, including telling Ralph of Gizy (one of the more prolific confessors) that "that should 'the heat of nature' require it he could 'cool himself' with his brothers."[332] He was accused of presenting a "head" at Chapter meetings. His actual position as Visitor of France seems to have been in flux, though this may have been merely a shift in administrative functions. He was well connected with the King of France. "In July 1303, Hugh of Pairaud, Visitor of the Temple in France, was ordered to collect the war subsidy for the kingdom, except for the se´ne´chausse´es of Toulouse and Rouergue. Pairaud was among those who had supported the French monarchy against Boniface VIII in the previous month, and in June 1304 the king made a general confirmation of Templar property in France"[333]

Iam – named as "a craftsman and villain" the name "Iam" should be viewed in light of its relationship to YHWH, "I am that I am."

Ictinus (*IK-tie-nuss*) **Callicrates** (*kuh-LICK-ruh-tees*) - Ictinus, was celebrated for his work on the Parthenon and was Temple of Mysteries at Eleusis. It is unclear if he was a partner or rival of Callicrates. We cite the example of these two architects in order to emphasize the universality of the Hiram story.

> *Ictinus. The leading architect in Periclan Athens and one of the greatest of all time. With Callicrates he designed and built the Parthenon (447/6—438 BC),about which he later wrote a book, now lost, with Carpion. He was commissioned by Pericles to design the new Telesterion(Hall of Mysteries) at Eleusis, but his designs were altered by the three new architects who took over on the fall of Pericles. According to Pausanias he was also the architect of the Doric temple of Apollo at Bassae, begun after the Great Plague of 304 BC. R. Carpenter, The Architects of the Parthenon, Harmondsworth 1970[334]*

Imhof – a correspondent and friend of Johann Andreae.

Jeanne, Queen of Sicily and Countess of Toulouse – *ZHUN* – Pronounced as if rhyming with gun. Alternatively ZHAN rhyming with Stan or ZHEN Rhyming with Gin. All are common and acceptable. A remarkable figure, Joan or Jeanne of England, Queen of Sicily was born 1177 and married the Norman King of Sicily, William II, in 1177. Joan produced no surviving heirs. William named his aunt Constance as his heir. When William died in 1189, his cousin, Tancred, seized Jeanne's lands and imprisoned her. Arriving in 1190 to receive promised help from William for the Third Crusade, her brother Richard Lionheart sacked Messina and seized a strategic Castle. Eventually Tancred agreed to return her dowry.

In the Holy Land, Richard proposed a peace settlement with Salah al-Din which would have Jeanne marry his brother, Sayf ad-Din, and become co-rulers of Jerusalem, but the plan came to nothing. Jeanne is said to have refused to convert to Islam. Returning from the Crusade after securing pilgrims' rights to Jerusalem, Richard married Jeanne to Raimond VI to maintain his strategic alliance with the Count of Toulouse.

Jeanne became the third wife of Raimond VI Count of Toulouse in 1196, with two territories as her dowry. She was the mother of his successor Raimond VII and a daughter, also named Jeanne. Some chroniclers suggest she was unhappy with Raimond, partially based on her decision to give birth at Fontevrault Abbey; however, she is recorded reliably has having risen while pregnant to lead troops to regain territory lost by her husband to encroachment. When the troops she was commanding mutinied, she went to seek the help of her brother, finding that he had died. She herself died in childbirth, her third child by Raimond surviving only long enough to be baptized. The exigencies of her campaign are credited with her death.

Jongleur – *see Appendix B*

Joseph of Arimathea – One of the better attested Biblical figures, he is referenced in all four canonical gospels. Mark implies he was a member of the Sanhedrin and mentions the linen shroud (see Mandylion). Robert de Boron, also mentioned in Appendix B under "family" authored "Joseph of Arimathea or the Romance of the Grail" around 1190-1200 in Burgundy. This was a major addition tying the Grail to the Arthurian Canon, about the same time the Wofram von Eschebach added the Grail to the Templar Legend.

Josiah – *JOE-si-uh* or Hebrew YO-see-ah-hoo – As this is a minor reference, the common pronunciation is preferred. King of Judah, Josiah instituted major religious reforms and the modern. He is attested only in the Hebrew Bible, but is generally thought to be a real person though elements of his story are probably borrowed from an earlier King, Joash. His reign may be the beginning of an "orthodox" version of worship in Judah which would more closely resemble that which we have been taught to believe existed in Old-Testament times. The description of him removing cult items from the Temple indicates clearly that polytheism was common at the time. His reforms are suggested to have been bloody with descriptions of executions and even the exhumation and humiliation of the dead.

Kamephis – *See Kneph*

Khephri – *See Kneph*

Kneph – *NEF* – Kneph is a complex idea, with several different attributes. The origin may have been an Egyptian deity of Thebes who had a snake body. Classically, Kneph is associated with the Lion-Serpent motif, and a serpent and egg motif. This is identified with Baphomet to in Crowley's Gnostic Creed, "And I believe in the Serpent and the Lion, Mystery of Mystery, in His name BAPHOMET,"[335] and called out in imagery in *Liber XV*. For further detailed discussion of the role of the serpent-egg motif in Rosicrucianism and Freemasonry, see Milko Bogard *The Dawning of the Kneph, the Egyptian Influence on Roscrucianism*, 1614-2014 (2018).

> "Thus Eusebius (Euseb. Praep. Ev. 3.11) informs us, that the Egyptians called the creator and ruler of the world Cneph, and that he was represented in the form of a man, with dark complexion, a girdle, and a sceptre in his hand. Cneph produced an egg, that is, the world, from his mouth, and out of it arose the god Phtha, whom the Greeks called Hephaestus."[336]

As with many ideas, it is probably as important to understand what was believed about it both classically and during the period during which Thelema was conceived. The actual root equates Kneph with Agathodaemon, a companion spirit or literally "noble spirit" featured on some classical coins and associated with vineyards and fields. By the first century, Kneph was understood by the Greek Platonists as something akin to pneuma or spirit. In *Moralia*, Plutarch references "the god whom they call Kneph, whose existence had no beginning and shall have no end"[337]

Lamen – Traditionally a Lamen, which means "plate," is a magical breastplate worn around the neck so it hangs over the heart. Crowley gives a much expanded definition of the Lamen for Thelemites in *Book Four*, Part II, Chapter XV[338]

Levi, Eliphas – 1810-1875 – born Alphonse Louis Constant and originally aspiring to be a Priest, he abandoned his vocation in 1826. Levi was claimed as his immediate past life by Crowley.[339] He is a Gnostic Saint named as Alphonse Louis Constant in *Liber XV*, and as Eliphas Levi or his birth name in the Canon of the Gnostic Heterodox Church. Levi was a Catholic; though very much in the fashion of other Romantics of the period who were drawn to Catholicism for its ties to tradition. He left regular Grand Orient Freemasonry because of its relative sterility and, while nominally Catholic, laid the foundation for the generation of Gnostics which came after him.

Despite attempts to scrub Levi of socialism, particularly by A. E. Waite, he embraced populist-socialist ideals and saw magick not merely as an art, but also as a tool for shaping a new era. Levi became somewhat of an elitist after the collapse of the Second French Republic, disillusioned with the fruits of populism; however all his work is suffused with certain presumptions of commonweal. Following from the Rosicrucians, he sees an absence of spirituality, from whatever source, to guide the public agenda and science. Whether past life or inspiration, his work shaped Crowley's concept of the "New Aeon."

> Hereunto therefore we have made it plain, as we believe, that our Magic is opposed to the goetic and necromantic kinds. It is at once an absolute science and religion, which should not indeed destroy and absorb all opinions and all forms of worship, but should regenerate and direct them by reconstituting the circle of initiates, and thus providing the blind masses with wise and clear-seeing leaders.
>
> We are living at a period when nothing remains to destroy and everything to remake. "Remake what? The past?" No one can remake the past. "What, then, shall we reconstruct? Temples and

thrones?" To what purpose, since the former ones have been cast down? "You might as well say: my house has collapsed from age, of what use is it to build another?" But will the house that you contemplate erecting be like that which has fallen? No, for the one was old and the other will be new. "Notwithstanding, it will be always a house." What else can you expect?[340]

Louis – *LOO-ee* – Louis VII was King of France 1137-1180. His sister, Constance of France, married Count Raimond V of Toulouse. Louis VII married Eleanor of Aquitaine, but had the marriage annulled in 1152 when no heir was produced. Eleanor then married Henry II, providing him with a vast expansion of territory that was the initial basis for the Angevin Empire. Constance lived from 1124-1176.

As Raimond of Toulouse moved away from alliance with the Capetian Monarchs and looked towards alliance with Henry or the Emperor Frederick Barbarossa, the relationship soured and Constance left the house of her husband, begging her brother in letters to allow her to return to Paris. He apparently assented and she returned there by 1166. Raimond switched his allegiance to Henry shortly thereafter, swearing fealty at Limoges in 1173.

His son, Phillip II or Phillip Augustus, shattered the Angevin Empire at Bouvines in 1214, and sponsored the anti-Cathar Crusades of Simon Montfort which, under the guise of religious orthodoxy, subjugated the Occitane.

Lydda – *LID-uh* – the modern city of Lod in Israel. About halfway between Jerusalem and Caesarea, it was the site of several notable meetings between Salah ad-Din and Crusader forces. Around October 1, 1191 Richard proposed that Al-Adil should marry his sister Jeanne. On 8 November 1191, Richard and Sayf ad-Din met for a great feast.

Mamluks – *MAHM-luke* – literally "slave" or "owned." *See also Baibars.* Mamluks were slaves and freed slaves, mostly of non-Arabic origins, used as a military and administrative class during the Ayyubid period. In 1249, the Seventh Crusade dispensed with attempts to capture the Holy Land and attempted to destroy the Ayyubid Sultanate by attacking Egypt, landing at Damietta. The role of Mamluks in administration can be seen as not unlike that of eunuch slaves in the Byzantine Empire. It is worth noting that the instigator of the Crusade, Louis IX, was the son of Blanche of Castile who, in his youth, pressed the final destruction of the Cathars. Louis IX hoped to win his mother's approval, and she served as regent in his absence.

The Crusade was, at first, successful, sending panic through the already unstable Egyptian Sultanate and amplified when the ruler, al-Salih, died. His widow and heir were able to briefly assume power, dispatching the Mamluk Commander, Baibars, to attack Louis. He defeated the French and captured Louis, but a power struggle ensued. The Mamluk viceregent, Qutuz, seized power, but within a year he had been overthrown, likely assassinated by Baibars, who would hold power for the next 17 years as the second Mamluk Sultan.

Manasses – *muh-NAS-uhs* – In the Hebrew Bible, Manasseh was the thirteenth King of Judah, and son and successor to Hezekiah. His name means "Forgetter." The Latin Vulgate suggests that he reigned for fifty five years, and the Hebrew text credits him with rebuilding high places, including altars to "Baalim" and "groves" to Asherah.

And he made his sons to pass through the fire in the valley of Benennom: he observed dreams, followed divinations, gave himself up to magick arts, had with him magicians, and enchanters: and he wrought many evils before the Lord, to provoke him to anger.

He set also a graven, and a molten statue in the house of God, of which God had said to David, and to Solomon his son: In this house, and in Jerusalem, which I have chosen out of all the tribes of Israel, will I put my name for ever.[341]

While the text is part of a cyclic portrayal of pre-captivity worship, where the people of Judah fall away from the worship of YHWH and are seduced by polytheism, it more properly recounts a period of religious retrenchment and the shuffling of cult status following the collapse of the Kingdom of Israel in the north. He is interesting to us as providing strong contemporary evidence for the prevalence of an Asherah Cult in the Temple of Solomon at Jerusalem less than a century before it's final destruction in 586 BC.

Mandylion – also known as the *Image of Edessa*. It was not originally supposed to have been the burial shroud of Jesus, but rather a "miraculous image" having a number of origin stories, though at some point the story that the cloth was the shroud in which Joseph of Arimathea wrapped the body of Jesus seems to have become entwined. The Mandylion resurfaced in the early sixth century and later on a number of conjectural occasions in the Crusade period, though there is some agreement it was taken to Constantinople and may have been among the treasure taken when the Crusades sacked that city.

Reasonably plausible historical records connect the Shroud of Turin to Geoffroi de Charny of Burgundy. Charny was a landless knight who made his living as a sporting knight, mercenary, and author of books on knighthood. He was involved in a Papal attack on Smyrna in 1344, nominally a Crusade, better understood as an action against Turkish piracy in the Agean. He died heroically at Potiers. His bequest to the Church at Lirey does not mention the Shroud and it appears to have been displayed only after his death. It was named as a forgery by a regional Bishop. Later, family members attested that Charny had acquired the Shroud. Inevitably, a connection between the Geoffroi de Charny killed at Potiers in 1356 and Guy or Geoffroi de Charny, former Templar Preceptor of Normandy who burned with Jacques Molay as a hertic in 1314, would be proposed, along with the suggestion that the Shroud originally came from the Templars. Further suggestions abound. The Mandylion is known to have the "face" of Jesus, though there are also suggestions it was an entire shroud. It is suggested this cloth was the "head" which the Templars worshiped.

The respected historian Malcolm Barber discusses the connection between the Templars and the shroud at length.[342] He stresses there is no known genealogical connection between the two Charnys. He also points out there are no Latin records which suggest the Templars were a presence at the sack of Constantinople and has little positive to say for the notion that the Templars possessed the Mandylion.

For purposes of our initiation, Z. believes that the reference by the Preceptor of Normandy in the Initiatory play is intended more as a humorous in-joke than a serious posit of history. To the extent it may be true, it would suggest more that the Templars had an active business in making fake artifacts, in the vein of Cagliostro, than that they possessed the genuine Mandylion. If one assumes there is nothing in the Initiations entirely bereft of intent, Z. posits may be "a symbolic statement there about the relative value of objects of beliefs and the role of truth in mythology, a microcosm of the entire Templar Play."

Manichees – Manicheism is generally viewed as a syncretic faith – an attempt to reconcile and replace Judaism, Christianity, Zoroastrianism, Buddhism and Gnostic Paganism. It is a fairly recent development from the late 3rd Century from the theologian and religious leader Mani. It can be understood as a reconciliation of Zoroastrian cosmology with Buddhist ethics, decorated with relatively superficial Christian elements. It was enormously popular in the late Roman Empire and was the original faith of Augustine of Hippo. The use of the term Manichees is misleading because it was used through early modern times by Catholics to refer to any sort of Dualist heresy.

Marsilio Ficino – *mar-SEE-lee-oh fi-CHEE-noh* – *1433-1499* – As part of his recognition as a Thelemic Saint, in the canon of The Thelemic Order, the Secretary General posted a short biography of Marsilio Ficino, which is reproduced below.

> *In a community where Paracelsus is well known, it is surprising how obscure Marsilio Ficino remains. He is, in many ways, the father of modern Hermeticism, and also a major figure in queer history. If you've ever used or heard the phrase "Platonic Love," you've been impacted by his legacy. Because he was a keystone, to understand Ficino requires understanding the men and events which revolved around Florence of his day. Still, this in no way understates his own significance. He birthed Hermeticism into Western Culture and spurred the creation of a syncretic western tradition.*

Ficino and Cosimo de' Medici

Ficino was born the son of a Physician in the patronage of Cosimo de' Medici and, as such, was raised in the Medici Court. Unlike much of Europe in the late 14th and early 15th century, Florence was not ruled by hereditary nobles, but by various republican groups and councils, proud of its "democratic" traditions. Through his wealth as a banker, Cosimo became "first among equals" – a leading statesman of Florence, but did not rule as an autocrat. When opponents forced Cosimo into exile in 1433, he moved to Venice and his business moved with him. The flight of capital threatened to collapse the Florentine economy and Cosimo was allowed to return, establishing himself as the dominant influence in the City's politics for the next 30 years. When Cosimo died in 1464, his grandson Lorenzo seems to have seamlessly accepted patronage of Ficino.

Ficino was born in the year of Cosimo's return to Florence and would come of age in an era of relative stability under Cosimo's leadership. He would become tutor to Cosimo's grandson, Lorenzo – known to history as Lorenzo the Magnificent – architect of the Peace of Lodi which ended years of warfare between the Lombard City States and brought stability to northern Italy for nearly a half century.

Ficino and Georgius Gemistus Pletho

During the years of Marsilio's childhood, there were attempts to reconcile the Catholic and Orthodox churches. This high-profile effort led to a Council in Florence attended by the Byzantine Emperor John VIII Paleologus, and a delegation remained there for several years. Among the delegates who attended was a Greek Neoplatonist philosopher, scholar, and senator from Constantinople, Georgius Gemistus Pletho, who had written extensively on Plato and the Alexandrian mystics.

While Western Europe had some access to ancient Greek philosophy from documents maintained by the Catholic Church and from some Islamic translations, the Byzantine Empire contained a treasure trove of information that had been lost to the West for centuries. Western tradition at this time was almost entirely Aristotelean, through Aquinas and other sources. At the invitation of Cosimo and others he set up a series of lectures on the difference between Plato and Aristotle. Neoplatonism was the last great intellectual force of western Paganism before the rise of Christianity, and Plato became the single overwhelming influence on the Renaissance.

Before his death, Pletho devised a modern system of religion which rejected Christianity, returning to Neoplatonic ideals, but mixed with Zoroastrian mysticism, astrology, daemons, and the migration of the soul. He sought to invoke the classical gods such as Zeus – not literally, but as symbols of universal principles and the powers of the planet. He intended to call for a reform of the Byzantine Empire and the effective overthrow of the Orthodox Church. His final text, "Book of Laws," survives only in the form of an outline written before it was burned, however it may represent the first coherent modern neopagan movement. While he had not yet committed this work to paper, it certainly informed the ideas he passed along in Florence. The influence of Pletho paved the way for Cosimo's establishment of the Platonic Academy of Florence, and planted the seeds that would mature into the Platonic movement in Renaissance Italy. Moreover, it led directly to the residence of John Argyropoulos, who would be Ficino's teacher and mentor in Platonic ideology.

Ficino and John Argyropoulos

Argyropoulos was also a member of the Byzantine Delegation to the Council of Florence. Converting to Catholicism, he studied at Padua and received a degree. After the fall of Constantinople in 1453, he fled Greece for Italy and took work as a teacher in Florence. There, in 1459, the 26 year old Ficino became his pupil. While Argyropoulos was less radical than Pletho, he was in a position to impart a picture of late pagan philosophy far more complete than Ficino could have gained through instruction in the West.

The Platonic Academy and The Hermetica

Around 1462, Cosimo decided to re-found Plato's Academy in Florence. According to his Renaissance biographer, Giovanni Corsi, Ficino had financial difficulties and moved to Bologna about this time. However, on a trip to Florence to visit his father, he met Cosimo who decided to become his patron and provide for him, making him the Leader of his new Academy.

The Academy was never a formal school. It was more of an organized salon or discussion group. He selected Marsilio Ficino, then about 30, to lead it. The Academy was, over time. enormously influential. The Victorian critic and early queer advocate, John Addington Symonds, believed that Michelangelo[343] spent time there. Whether that is the case or not, the ideals of the Academy definitely suffuse Michelangelo's work. Many other important thinkers came out of the Academy, most notably Pico della Mirandola – an important humanist who was the first to introduce the Kabbalah to the European mainstream outside of Jewish rabbinical and intellectual circles.

Ficino's Translations and Written Work

Ficino's primary work for Cosimo was the translation of manuscripts. Supplied with Greek copies of Plato's work he began complete translations into Latin which were published in draft in 1468-69, and published in final in 1484. While that work was important, even more important to us was the moment Leonardo da Pistoia arrived in Florence with a collection of Greek Manuscripts from Macedonia, which we know today as the Corpus Hermeticum. Cosimo asked Ficino to stop his work on translating Plato to translate the Hermeticum. This specific act was the birth of modern Western Hermeticism.

Ficino also translated other Neoplatonist work, including Porphyry, Iamblichus, and Plotinus. These works, particularly Iamblichus, were critical to the development of a Gnostic countercurrent in Europe, and formed a considerable part of the foundation for the theology that led to Doinel's re-establishment of a Western Gnostic Church and an active Western Gnostic Tradition. He translated a number of lesser works such as Psellus' "On Daemons," which greatly expanded the understanding of Western Spirit magic. His own core work, "Platonic Theology," a treatise on the immortality of the soul, was an attempt to rectify Platonism with Christianity which was not entirely compatible with either Plato or Christianity. His work was condemned by the Inquisition in articles published at the University of Pisa in 1490.

Platonic Love

Ficino invented the term "Platonic Love" in championing love between men. He published his Platonic love letters to his lifelong friend, Giovanni Cavalcanti, which popularized the term and the concept. Neither Ficino nor his intellectual circle was ignorant of the fact that Plato discusses not only intellectual, but sexual love between men. At that point in Western Europe, "sodomy" was simply a crime and a sin, more or less harshly punished depending on the time, the locale, and the views of the local priesthood. Ficino creates an intellectual framework of beauty and spiritual growth around the concept of love between same-sex partners, while avoiding direct mention of physical union. This intellectual basis for homosexuality was the first glimmering of a gay rights movement in Europe, and would underlay Western gay counterculture through Wilde and Crowley. The concepts in Wilde's "De Profundis" have root in Ficino's earliest expressions. Ficino's life, acquaintances, and writing suggest that he was primarily homosexual, though at a time when such activity could result in severe penalties, it was not acknowledged. Whatever his personal sexuality, he sparked a powerful current in the defense of homosexual and asexual relationships.

Ficino as Priest

Much has been made of Ficino's determination to become a priest at the age of 42. The reason seems to have been rather practical. Lorenzo de'Medici arranged for his income and upkeep by gifting him with two parishes, but to enjoy their revenue he had to be a clergyman. This allowed his brothers to divide his father's estate. This system of assuring a living by awarding a benefice was common throughout Europe, essentially allowing wealthy and powerful men to use the money of the church to pay private salaries.

Ficino as Friend

Corsi says of Ficino, "his health was not at all settled, for he suffered very much from a weakness of the stomach, and although he always appeared cheerful and festive in company, yet it was thought that he sat long in solitude and became as if numb with melancholy."[344] Corsi apparently did not know Ficino personally, but rather knew a number of his friends, but he makes much of his public demeanor. "He was as mild and gentle in discussion as in everything else, ever cheerful and an excellent conversationalist, second to none in refinement and wit. Many of his sayings survive, as they were uttered, in the Tuscan language. Every day these sayings, full of wit, jests and laughter, are commonly on the lips of his friends." Of his medical skill, Corsi says, "It was wonderful to see the healing skill with which he cured some afflicted by black bile, restoring them to perfect health."

Savonarola

Despite the relative peace of the last years of Lorenzo's life, there was unquiet within Lombard and Italian Society. The Italian city-states were involved in a complex and ongoing game of politics between the Pope, the King of France, and the Holy Roman Emperor. In this atmosphere, a wave of puritan fanaticism swept Florence, led by the Dominican clergyman, Savonarola.

It would be convenient to create a story of an intolerant church at war with enlightened Platonic secularists organized behind Lorenzo, but the reality is not that simple. Lorenzo was very much a strongman and the forces of puritanism were also pro-democracy. Originally brought to Florence by Lorenzo, Savonarola became dedicated to the destruction of the Medici house, seeing them as corrupt and anti-democratic. Lorenzo died in 1492 and the peace he had forged collapsed in 1494, leading to an invasion by Charles VIII King of France. Lorenzo's son and heir, Piero III, attempted to keep Florence neutral which infuriated Charles. When Charles moved against Florence, Savonarola undermined public support for the de'Medici and, during the struggles, forced the family from the city. Those formerly patronized by the de'Medici were forced to prostrate themselves before a wave of puritan fanaticism from 1494-1498.

Savonarola was, at heart, a mystic, as much influenced by Neo-Platonism as Ficino. The two were on good terms for some time until Savonarola's "ecstatic visions led him to asceticism and to war on the estheticism of Ficino"[345] Pasquale Villari accuses Ficino of forsaking and betraying Savonarola. However, it was Savonarola that turned against Ficino, declaring that the banquets of the Platonic Academy were "pernicious examples of renascent paganism."[346]

Savonarola's crusade against vice included new laws against sodomy, explicitly including both homosexual and lesbian relations, drunkenness, and other moral crimes. Gangs of boys were organized to patrol the streets. Immodest dress and clothing was repressed. The significant focus on sodomy can be seen as a direct reference to the Platonic Academy and its sympathizers, or at least the freedom which allowed it to prosper, and the Academy was dissolved c. 1492-94.

Savanarola's Bonfire of the Vanities in 1497, in which the extremist Dominican priest burned works of art, cosmetics, and literature that were, to his way of thinking, "sinful," was not carried out in the same vein as Nazi Book-Burnings. Instead, it reflected a spirit that would later be seen in the Amish, Quakers, and others who thought that "fancy" things led away from spirituality and charity. Much of the emphasis touches on causes we would recognize sympathetically today – resentment of the ultra-rich and conspicuous consumption while others suffered in poverty.

Savonarola's success can best be viewed against an atmosphere of uncertainty. The Florentines rightly felt that the de'Medici had failed in maintaining their safety and were justly afraid of a return to chaos. Savonarola sapped the influence of the traditional clergy (including, by this point, Ficino) who petitioned the Pope for his removal. When he refused to lead Florence into Pope Alexander III's Holy League, the Pope excommunicated Savonarola and interdicted Florence. In the end, he would be burned on the site of his bonfire on orders of the Pope. The church, in this case, was both persecutor and rescuer. Savonarola's motives were neither entirely evil nor can we disapprove of them, though the painful link between human charity and the need for spiritual purity is a demonstrable ill of his reign.

Ficino was 61 by the time Savonarola seized power, and 65 by the time he was executed. Given the fate of Pico, we could anticipate that he would spend the Savonarola years quietly, living in his country benefice. That he had a hand in Savonarola's eventual undoing seems likely.

Shortly after Savonarola's arrest Ficino wrote a letter to the College of Cardinals, most likely on behalf of the canon of the Cathedral. In it, he claimed that the removal of Savonarola was, while inspired by the Pope, assisted by the Franciscans and the canon of the Cathedral, which was certainly at least in part true. One of the first signs of his imminent fall was his restriction from the Cathedral on March 1, and Ficino must certainly have had a hand in that, if only as a member of a group. Of his own behavior he says.

> ...although in the beginning, after the Republic had undergone sudden change, while the French were agitating Florence with various terrors here and there, I myself also, together with the fearful populace, was terrified by I know not what demon and for a time deceived, but quickly I came to my senses and for three whole years now I have warned many known to me, frequently in private and often publicly, and not without great peril, so that they might flee far away from this poisonous monster, born to be a disaster for this people.[347]

Given his remarkable intelligence, his letter to the Curia is essentially a profuse apologetic, but cannot be taken seriously. He gives diabolism as the essential cause of Savonarola's possession of the Florentine state, not in all likelihood because he viewed the matter that way himself or expected Pope Alexander to, but more as a sort of *mea culpa* and admission of the inexplicable. "The Devil made us do it!" was a graceful out in the late 15th century and, combined with flattery, was designed to give Alexander the firm impression that the Florentines knew they had been in error and didn't intend to repeat their mistakes. The letter is an abasement on behalf of a city that found itself in a bad situation and needed to dispel the ire of a profoundly secular and militant Pope. Certainly, the civil leadership also sent letters, but that Ficino was selected for such a task suggests he still had a very high stature after Savonarola's fall.

That he approved of Savonarola at first is only sensible. The Friar was credited legitimately with nearly single-handedly preventing the looting of Florence. That he fell out quickly seems likely as well. Just as many intellectuals who initially supported Hitler turned against him when they saw his actual program, Ficino can be credited with not misrepresenting himself when he suggests he saw through Savonarola no more than a year into his effective Dictatorship.

Ficino and Pico de Mirandola

The entire period of the late 15th century seems to have seen cultural backlash against intellectualism and humanism. In 1486, at the age of 26, Ficino's student, Pico de Mirandola, very much under the influence of Ficino and Lorenzo, proposed to defend 900 theses on religion called the "Oration on the Dignity of Man" at a giant conference in Rome. Suffused with Humanism, Neoplatonist Paganism, and Kabbalah, they form the first great Western push towards a Syncretic religion, 400 years in advance of the Theosophical Society. The Pope quashed the proposed conference and declared the work heretical. This was the first time the Vatican had banned a printed book. Through the intercession of Lorenzo, Pico was able to return to Florence under his protection. Responsible for originally inviting Savonarola to Florence, Pico was swept up in his extremist movement. He died in 1494, probably poisoned for his support of Savonarola.

Paganism

Writing in 1506, a few years after Ficino's death in 1499, his biographer, Giovanni Corsi, outlines his paganism while insisting on an essentially Christian life. "Marsilio intended at this time to develop fully the book of Platonic Theology almost as a model of the pagan religion, and also to publish the Orphic Hymns and Sacrifices; but a divine miracle directly hin-dered him more and more every day, so that he daily accomplished less, being distracted, as he said, by a certain bitterness of spirit."(Ficino, 1975, pp. Vol 3, p. 139) Reading between the lines, Ficino encountered increasing resistance from the Church and, unlike Mirandarola, saw the writing on the wall. He must have been concerned by the 1490 repudiation of even his tame attempts to reconcile Platonism and Christianity, and the debacle of Mirandarola's attempt to create a syncretic tradition certainly must have chilled him.

Legacy

Ficino was the crux on which the birth of modern neopaganism turned. If he did not, on his own, develop its system, he definitely supplied the raw materials. He brought us the Corpus Hermeticum, which in turn led to the work of Paracelsus, Cornelius Agrippa, and many others who we consider the forebears of modern esoteric practice. In terms of religion, he furnished the core doctrines on which Pico del Mirandola and others after him would develop the syncretic Western tradition, which would give us at some remove various mystical Protestant groups, as well as Theosophy and the French Gnostic Church. As a Platonist and humanist, he was an acknowledged influence on Rabelais, who is the direct creator of Thelema. Plato's ideas on sexuality pervade Western culture from Rabelais through the homosexual culture of Cambridge and represent a major element in the cultural ferment that led to Crowley's intellectual rebellion against Victorian culture. In numerous ways Ficino laid the foundations on which modern Gnosticism and Thelema rest.

Mattheiu Sauvage - can be roughly translated as "Matthew the Wild."

> *"One of the most colorful depositions made during the proceedings against the Templars (1307–14) is that of the Italian notary Antonio Sici di Vercelli. In the 1270s, Antonio had rendered legal services to the Templars in the Latin East where he had heard that the Order's commander of Sidon, Brother Matthew Sauvage...was 'the brother of the Sultan of Babylon who was then reigning, because each had drunk from the blood of the other in turns, wherefore they were called brothers'....This 'Sultan of Babylon,' the contemporary title given by Western Christians to the Sultan of Egypt, was none other than Baybars."*[348]

Sauvage is first referenced in February 1261 when he was a Commander at Acre. We know nothing of his background other than that he was a knight from Picardy. The Sultan, Qutuz, made a diplomatic visit there after he had been allowed safe passage to fight the Mongols. It was also not uncommon for the Templars to lodge diplomatic guests in their Commanderies.

Sauvage and Baibars had a sustained relationship that continued after Qutuz was assassinated and Baibars took his position. He was a Turcomans prisoner for a time and may have been ransomed with help from Baibars. He was found in 1263 carrying a verbal message between Baibars and the commander in Cyprus. Sauvage's eventual career arc is unknown, though he was apparently commander in Sidon for a time, possibly during its final evacuation. See also *Templars*.

Melchizedek – *mel-KIZ-i-dek* – Also Melchisedech – Named as Gnostic Saint in *Liber XV* and also in the Canon of the Heterodox Gnostic Church – Rendered as Malki-sedeq, this name comes from the roots Malki, "King," and either "righteousness" or, in the typical form used by Caananite Priest-Kings, "My lord is Zedek." Zedek may refer to Sdq a Phoenician godname found in numerous inscriptions, possibly cognate with the Ugaritic Saduq, making Melchizidek a Priest of Sdq, rendered by Eusebius through Philo of Byblos as Sedek. Whatever the issues with Eusebius history, the existence of inscriptions suggests the name is real and historical.

There are a welter of somewhat confusing Old Testament references to this figure; however, he is accepted as the "First Priest," or Kohen, though this may be a late interpolation. In the Christian New Testament, Jesus is identified in the Epistle to the Hebrews, and likewise is said to have made his followers "a high priest forever according to the order of Melchizidek"[349] a paraphrase of Psalms.[350] In Gnostic tradition, as demonstrated at Qumran, Jesus is sometimes named as being Melchizidek. In related tradition Melchizidek is identified as the Archangel Michael. The Qumran tradition was not available to Crowley at the time of the writing of *Liber XV* and it is likely that he embraced the Protestant theory of a Melchizidek Priesthood common to all those who would claim it.

Memphis – in the area of modern Greater Cairo, the city of Memphis was the capital of Old Kingdom Egypt, having a strategic position in the Nile Delta. Important through most of antiquity, it was noted as the cult center of Ptah. The city lost commercial prominence with the rise of Alexandria and further declined with the ban on the traditional religion in 380 CE by the Eastern and Western Emperors. The western word Egypt comes from the Greek rendering *Aigyptos* of the Middle Egyptian *hwt-ka-ptah*, or "Temple of the Ka of Ptah" the chief temple complex at Memphis. Memphis is cited in various early Masonic sources and the association with the "Rite of Memphis" is a clear attempt to associate the modern esoteric Masonic rites with this chiefest ancient temple.

Merlan, pit – a recurring fixture as a pit or prison in the Templar Trial testimony. John of Chalons, a serving brother, who had been the preceptor of two small Templar houses at different times, showed himself equally prepared to make an all-embracing attack on the Order. He had denied Christ because he had been told that if he did not the receptor

> *...would, within a few days, place him in a pit at Merlan. And he said that this pit or prison was so harsh, that no one was able to live long there, and he saw, after one man had been thrust in there, that he lived only five days, and he was sometimes keeper of this prison, and in his time nine brothers died there from the harshness of the prison....Incarceration in the prison at Merlan was mentioned more than once, a place 'from which no one comes out', said one Templar.*[351]

Misraim – Mizraim is the Hebrew and Aramaic name for Egypt, the dual suffix probably indicating "two" i.e. Upper and Lower Egypt, though the etymology is otherwise conjectural. The term was used throughout the area of Egypt and the Levant; Ugaritic inscriptions refer to Egypt as *Msrm*. The Classical Arabic word for Egypt is *Misr*.

Molay, Jacques de – c. 1245-1314 – Grand Master of the Knights Templar 1292-1314. As *Jacobus Burgundus Molensis the Martyr* (Jacques of Burgundy and Molay), he is named in Crowley's *Liber XV* as a Gnostic Saint. He is generally referenced under his more common name in the Canon of the Heterodox Gnostic Church, though there is no prohibition against the more traditional reference.

Molay became Grand Master of the Knights Templar under drastic circumstances. His family were minor nobility from Burgundy and he was likely a younger son. After Guillame de Beaujeu was killed during the fighting at Acre, the last possession of the Frankish, or European, Crusader forces in the Levant, the Templars evacuated to Sidon. Thibaud Gaudin, the Grand Commander (not Grand Master), left the Marshal at Acre, which still had defensible positions at the time, and removed archive, relics, and treasure to Sidon. The Templars originally had the intention of defending Sidon, but as Acre fell and the Mamluks laid siege, they began an evacuation of troops and citizens to Cyprus. Gaudin died within the year and little is known of Molay's appointment as Master of the Temple. It has been suggested that Otto of Granson, also a Burgundian, may have influenced the election. He was a spymaster and diplomat for King Edward I of England, with whom Burgundy, nominally part of the Holy Roman Empire, was aligned against France.

It may be this influence which doomed Molay and the Templars. The King of France was in the process of effectively "buying" the papacy during this period, and he doubtless resented that an organization which was deeply enmeshed with his finances elected a Burgundian Core. A strong faction had opposed Molay's election and preferred Hughes de Pairaud who had strong connections to the French Crown.[352]

Molay was a reformer[353] but the scope and effectiveness of his reforms were limited. In many ways it is seen as "too little too late." Historically he was a tireless worker to support Cyprus as the easternmost outpost of Frankish Christianity and a potential spot from which to launch a new Crusade to regain the Holy Land. Alain Demurger's *The Last Templar* is the exhaustive source on Molay's life, though not all scholars agree with Demurger's interpretations of the trial evidence.

Historically, Molay can be seen as being caught between two vises. After the fall of the last Frankish outposts in the Levant, the Templars were redundant. There was no Temple, nor even Kingdom, to protect. The Hospitallers wrested Rhodes from the Byzantine Empire. Molay focused on Cyprus, where he had a troubled relationship with the local ruler, and aspired for a return to the Levant. The Hospitallers and all of Christianity were certainly also involved with this, but the expensive and ultimately pointless expedition to Ruad seems to have been largely funded and manned by Templars.

What may have been more important is that the King of France was in the process of trying to gain control of the papacy and create a new doctrine in which the Crown, not the Pope, was the true representative of Christ on Earth, or at least his Prime Minister. The rise of this doctrine can be seen in the facility with which Henry VIII of England would discard the papacy altogether, naming himself head of the Church. The date of Henry's rebellion in 1533 may seem remote from the first decade of the fourteenth century, but it was no more than the completion of the political doctrine laid down at the time of the Templar trials.

From 1294-1303, Pope Boniface VIII had increased the secular power of the Papacy, leading to conflicts with both the Holy Roman Emperor and the King of France. King Philip wanted the revenue of the Church to stay in France and benefit him in his ongoing wars with England. As Philip seized clerical revenues, Boniface excommunicated him. Phillip had the Pope taken by force of arms, arrested, and beaten. He was released but died within the month. The College of Cardinals elected Benedict XI as a candidate who would be more acceptable to Philip. He rescinded the King's excommunication, but prosecuted his minister who had imprisoned Boniface VIII. Benedict XI only lived for eight months and may have been poisoned on orders of King Philip. The new Pope, Clement V, was under strong French influence and moved the Papacy to Avingnon.

The result was to make the Templars, or at least the Burgundian, Molay, a target at a time when the Pope was of little help as a protector. Molay was, as much as anything else, a martyr to the rise of autocratic states. Accusations of heresy were the classic medieval stalking horse for seizure of property and assets, and in this regard Molay presents very much the same figure Raimond of Toulouse and his Catholic contemporaries. *See also Templars.*

Monte Vecchio – a small farm owned by Marsilio Ficino as a gift from Cosimo de'Medici, it lay near the Villa Medici at Careggi, which still stands. Christophe Poncet has given extensive consideration to the likelihood that the Careggi farmhouse belonging to Ficino was a literal and physical site associated with his Platonic Academy, and gives interesting details about its likely construction and the inclusion of a gymnasium.[354]

Montfort, Count Simon – *see Appendix B*

Montsegur – *see Appendix B*

Nicetas – *nee-KAY-tass* – papa Nicetas, Bogomil Bishop of Constantinople, in Lombardy c. 1160, convened the Council of Saint-Félix in Occitania in 1167, confirming the episcopal office of six Cathar Bishops, a lineage which would include Guilhabert de Castres (c. 1165-1240), Cathar Bishop of Toulouse, who would, through Lady Caithness, charge Jules Doinel with the foundation of the modern Gnostic Church.

Nicosia, Cyprus – inland city and capital of Cyprus, site of the Templar headquarters from the fall of Acre through the suppression of the Order.

Nous – the concept of intelligence as distinct from perception or reason. This leads to the sense of *Nous* as the faculty which allows the distinction between the imaginary and the real. In Neoplatonist thought this leads to the sense of the Nous as the intelligence of God, an emanation of God the absolute, in a fashion which is expressed through the Thelemic relationship of Hadit to Nuit.

Occitania/Oucitanio – *OXY-tann-yuh* – A region of Southern France. The term itself was not contemporary to the early 13th century.

Orpheus—a cycle of Greek cultic belief which is seen as bridging a gap between strictly Hellenic legend and mythology and that of West Asia. Orphic belief shows strong Neoplatonist and potentially Christian influence. The Orphic cult can be attested through grave goods as early as the 5ᵗʰ century BCE, though the specific form is not know. The Orphic cult seems to represent a first integration of Egyptian myth with Hellenic mythology, with Dionysus being substituted for Osiris. Orpheus as song-maker takes the role of Prophet teaching a theogony, himself exceptional because he has passed into death and returned. The Orphic mysteries evolved and shifted over the centuries. In their rawest form, they are suggestive of Pre-Hellenic Faith. In their last incarnations they epitomize the pinnacle of classical paganism.

In an attempt to convey the general outline of the Orphic myth, a Serpentine Zeus gets a child, Zagreus, on his daughter Persephone. Hera goads the Titans to destroy Zagreus and consume him, leaving only his heart. Athena brings the heart to Zeus who swallows it, punishing the Titans by destroying them with thunderbolts. The ashes of the Titans give rise to humankind which has material body because of the Titans, but also soul because of the remains of Zagreus. Zeus begets a child on Semele from the heart of Zagreus, who is called Dionysus. Semele was tricked by Hera into asking Zeus to appear in his full form which destroyed her. Zeus kept the unborn child in his thigh. Once born, Dionysus visits the underworld to reclaim Semele. In relation to Thelema, and occultism in general, it should be noted that Orphic, rather than Classical Hellenic, interpretations of Zeus, Athena, Dionysus, and so on are often intended. [355]

Orphism is related through Kore, Demeter, and Persephone to the Eleusinian Mysteries, but is not precisely aligned with it.

> *"While the Eleusinian Mysteries were widely known and participated in by large groups of ordinary Athenians, Orphism/Pythagoreanism was more obscure and elitist, partly because it was a literary cult, for which teaching and initiations involved writings that would have been accessible only to the educated. Most of the evidence available on Orphism deals with the afterlife: the Orphics/Pythagoreans believed that the divine soul, which is immortal, separates from the mortal body which serves as a kind of prison. On death, the soul travels to the underworld, and eventually returns to a new human body in a cycle of reincarnation."* [356]

The Orphic cult didn't exactly die out. An impartial observer, evaluating Trinitarian Christianity in the way that we evaluate Manicheanism, or Zoroastrianism, and accounting for its central mystery of the consumption of the body and blood of Jesus, might well describe it as a mix of a "Jewish Messianic Cult and Hellenic Orphism." Certainly, it can be seen as a direct ancestor of the dualist gnostic heresies focusing on the imprisonment of the "pure" soul in the "corrupt" body. While Orphism itself reflects an older Egyptian cult, it was widespread in classical antiquity and doubtless one of the core drivers of the development of dualist Christian heresies. The various trinitarian elements, as well as the idea of a descent into the underworld (i.e. crossing the abyss), inform many aspects of modern esotericism which found their way into Thelema.

Orvieto – a papal city considered safer and more defensible than Rome. Location of a Papal Palace, several Popes preferred Viterbo or Orviedo as vacation home but also as a refuge in times of unpopularity or unrest.

Otto of Granson – *see Jacques de Molay*

Paracelsus – *Philippus Aureolus Theophrastus Bombastus von Hohenheim* – Paracelsus was not an alias but, rather, a Latin "literary name" which was common for writers to take at the time. He claimed to be an illegitimate descendant of the noble von Hohenheim family, but may in fact have been a commoner.

Paracelsus traveled through Europe and to Constantinople, and may have traveled to Egypt. He was a surgeon in various wars at the time, which would have given him a strong appreciation for the realities of medicine and human suffering. In subsequent periods, surgeons had been semi-skilled laborers, doing cutting and other physical activities under the direction of a physician. During this period, it became somewhat more common for educated and talented surgeons to become physicians and to write medical books.

Paracelsus' father had been a physician, and he settled in Strasbourg to practice medicine and write medical books. He also began a correspondence with Desiderius Erasmus, one of the most notable humanist philosophers in history. He practiced alchemy, astrology, and other esoteric arts which were part of the science of the day, and wrote on Hermeticism as well as medicine. He taught and lectured on medicine in German rather than Latin and burned copies of the classical medical books from the second century which were still standards. Doctors of the time were scholars and philosophers, not hands on students of disease and symptoms. Paracelsus included all the people who actually practiced medicine in the conversation: surgeons, chemists, alchemists, and apothecaries. Paracelsus rocked the medical establishment of his day. He was banned from practice in several cities, and aroused the bitter resentment of the Galenist establishment, but within a generation he changed the basic nature of medicine.

Paracelsian Chymists – *see Paracelsus, and Galenists* – Paracelsianism, the first modern medical movement, supplanted Galenism in the late 16th and early 17th century.

Paulicians – *see Gnosticism*

Picatrix – prior to the translation of the Hermetica, *Picatrix* was, in some cases, the only significant source for Hermetic thought and talismanic magic from the classical period. The volume was written in Arabic under the title *Ghayat al-Hakim*, translated variously as *"The Aim of the Sage"* or *"The Goal of the Wise."* It was probably produced in Spain and has been attributed to al-Majriti, a Muslim astronomer, alchemist, and mathematician in Andalusia, who also translated astronomical work by Ptolemy; however, modern scholarship suggests *Picatrix* to be from a later author using his name. The work was translated from Arabic into Spanish by Alfonso X of Castile around 1257 and into a Latin version later. Marsilio Ficino had access to a copy and the manuscript circulated fairly widely, thus any assumptions about what was and was not known about magic in Europe must take into account the circulation of *Picatrix*. *Picatrix* cites the 10th century alchemical work *Rutbat al-Hakim* of Maslama al-Quturbi, which in turn cites an Arabic translation of the late 3rd and early 4th century Hermetic and Gnostic pagan writer Zosimus' *Tome of Pictures*,[357] establishing an ideological line of transmission for Hermetic ideals into Latin speaking Europe by the mid 13th century.

Pico de la Mirandola – *see also Marsilio Ficino.* Giovanni Pico della Mirandola is far better known and better documented, despite his fairly short life. At the age of 23, he tried to call a grand conference where he would defend his 900 theses. The theses would have led to a drastic reform of the Roman Catholic Church, but the conference was quashed by the Pope and the book banned. Many of his theses were heavy influences on Protestantism. His *Oration on the Dignity of Man*, has been called the "Manifesto of the Renaissance," and remains in print in many editions, most of which include an adequate biography and summary of his thought. He is notable for a syncretic approach which effectively harmonized Hermeticism, and elements of Jewish mysticism as well as other West Asian faiths. He dramatically popularized the Cabbala among Christians.

Piero di Medici – *see Savanarola*

Plato and the Symposium - This has been widely debated through several centuries of history, however Alcibiades and the Symposium provide an illustration of the clear link between Neoplatonism and Thelema.

In her discussion of "Neoplatonism and the Problem of Sex," Katherine Crawford illustrates:

> *"When Neoplatonic thinkers sought to bring Plato back into the Catholic tradition in the Renaissance, one of the problems they faced was reconciling Plato's utilization of physical desire as an element in his philosophy with the Christian rejection of corporeal pleasure.*
>
> *The problems associated with sex in the Platonic tradition stem from Ficino's construction of love and desire as salvific elements. Recurrently in his commentaries on Plato's dialogues but particularly in his Commentary on the Symposium, or De amore (1469), Ficino argued that love and beauty, often in sexualized terms, provided the means to ascend to heaven. At the same time, corporeal desire pulled body and soul downward, and inappropriate desire (variously defined) was often difficult to distinguish from the salvific form. Responses to the issue of sex in Ficino's Neoplatonism were especially complex because he argued for understanding Plato metaphorically."*
>
> *The combination of Christian theology, Platonic allegory, and contemporary understandings of sexualized terminology produced much slippage."*[358]

Crawford continues:

> *"In his effort to reconcile Plato with Christianity, Ficino posits an epistemology in which the relationship between soul and body is mediated by the concept of love. In the De amore, Ficino explicates his central notion that love is defined as seeking the divine."*[359]

The relationship between Plato and Thelema is here manifest. The magical and initiatory system of Reuss and Crowley is built heavily on the conceptualization of union with the divine through physical sex. Even where Crowley is dislodged, reluctantly, from a firm commitment to the exchange of actual fluids, the imagery of sexuality is core to the Thelemic concept of attainment. This sees its root in Plato and, while much of Western Neoplatonism reaches us through Mirandola, it is this element of which Ficino was far more the champion, making him unquestionably one of the chief progenitors of Thelema.

The Symposium also sees the portrayal of the Androgyne, the archetype of Baphomet, which is explored in greater detail a half century later by Rabelais, who drew "his material from Plato himself – his own copy of the Aldine edition of 1513 is still extant in the Montpellier library - rather than from Ficino's famous commentary on the Symposium with its more refined description of the Androgyne"[360]

Poemander – see *Corpus Hermeticum*

Ptah – The primordial Sumerian creator God Anu is Ilu in Akkadian, and is a sky deity similar to Uranus. The frequent attribution of "eternal" as an attribute of El suggests a connection with the Egyptian Ptah, "the Lord of Eternity." In Ugaritic text, a creation myth suggests that El came to the shore of the sea and saw two women. Killing a bird he asked them to call him husband or father, and when they chose him as husband, he lay with them and gave birth to Dawn and Dusk. The women are not clearly named, however there is reasonable association of one with Athirat/Asherah, whose name may mean "Lady Dawn."

The precise identification of El with Yahweh is not entirely clear, just as the association between El and Hadad is unclear; however, it is generally conceded that El is the earlier form and the Tanakh preserves this when Melchizedek, the king of Salem, blesses Abraham in the name of El Elyon; literally "God the High God." Whatever the case, the cult of El antedates and is entwined with the cult of Yahweh.

Writing uncontroversially in the Oxford Companion to World Mythology, David Leeming says

> *The Semitic term "El" essentially refers to the concept of god. As such it is related to the Arabic il and thus ilah and al ilah—literally "the god"—and Allah and the Hebrew Elohim. It seems almost certain that the God of the Jews evolved gradually from the Canaanite El, who was in all likelihood the "God of Abraham." Karen Armstrong reminds us that in Genesis 16 and 17, an eighth-century B.C.E. text, God introduces himself as El Shaddai ("El of the Mountain") and that El's name is preserved in such words as EL-ohim, Isra-EL ("El rules"), and Ishma-EL. In Exodus 6: 2-3 the deity introduces himself to Moses as Yahveh and points out that he had revealed himself to Abraham, Isaac, and Jacob as El Shaddai, and that they had not known that his name was Yahveh[361]*

In Thelemic terms primordial El can be seen as cognate with Chaos.

Puy, smallest coin of – the Bishops of Puy en Verlay struck a silver denier piece which was, over time, heavily debased through alloying with copper and reduction in size. This coin was heavily circulated by pilgrims to Notre Dame de Puy and was eventually worth about a farthing and formed part of expressions indicating that something was cheap.

Pythagoras of Samos – c. 570-495 BCE – an Ionian Greek philosopher and religious leader, who began the school of thought that bears his name. He was a profound influence on later schools of thought. Generally, the most significant element of Pythagoreanism is the doctrine of the transmigration of souls (called metempsychosis). Historically, many of the things most heavily associated with Pythagoras, including the Pythagorean theorem and the five solids, may have been developed by his successors. More importantly most esotericists of the 19th and early 20th century, and even of the present day, consider Pythagoreanism and Orphism to be effectively the same. The view that Pythagoras was either the inventor of Orphism, or alternately an Orphic initiate, was commonplace by the time of the Neoplatonist philosophers of late antiquity. In fact, whether these were originally separate traditions which became conflated, or whether one influenced the other and in what procession is very unclear and a matter of dispute among scholars of the present day.

Regardless, when approaching references to Pythagoras in Hermetic writing, recent or classical, we must assume that references to Pythagoras presuppose an Orphic connection, and in fact may use the terms Pythagorean and Orphic somewhat ambiguously or interchangeably.

Qlippoth – *KLI-fath* – as in fish and palm, Qlipoth literally means "shells." In Kabbalah, these are spiritual obstacles which conceal the divine vision. This brief listing does not contain space for an investigation of this deep and multifaceted concept. In more esoteric tradition, including Thelema, they may be seen as separate planes, demonic beings, or the shells of the dead.

Raimond d'Alfaro – *see Appendix B*

Raimond de Perelha – *see Appendix B*

Raimond Roger, Count of Foix – *see Appendix B*

Raimond VI Count of Toulouse – *see Appendix B*

Raimond Roger Trencavel, Viscount of Beziers and Carcassone – *see Appendix B*

Robes of the Priests of Asherah – The story of Josiah's cleansing of the Temple in 2 Kings provides the best evidence that Asherah and Ba'al were worshiped in the Temple of Solomon. The exact texts differ, but the New International Version provides one of the most accurate translations into English:

> *2 Kings 23:4-7: The king ordered Hilkiah the high priest, the priests next in rank and the doorkeepers to remove from the temple of the Lord all the articles made for Baal and Asherah and all the starry hosts. He burned them outside Jerusalem in the fields of the Kidron Valley and took the ashes to Bethel.*
>
> *He did away with the idolatrous priests appointed by the kings of Judah to burn incense on the high places of the towns of Judah and on those around Jerusalem—those who burned incense to Baal, to the sun and moon, to the constellations and to all the starry hosts.*
>
> *He took the Asherah pole from the temple of the Lord to the Kidron Valley outside Jerusalem and burned it there. He ground it to powder and scattered the dust over the graves of the common people.*
>
> *He also tore down the quarters of the male shrine prostitutes that were in the temple of the Lord, the quarters where women did weaving for Asherah.*

In 2 Kings 23:13 we are told:

> *The king also desecrated the high places that were east of Jerusalem on the south of the Hill of Corruption—the ones Solomon king of Israel had built for Ashtoreth the vile goddess of the Sidonians.*

That is a pretty thorough and indisputable record that Ba'al and Asherah were being worshiped in the Temple, and that Ashtoreth (who may or may not be identical to Asherah) had been worshiped since the time of Solomon.

The KJV renders 2 Kings 23:7 as:

> *He destroyed also the pavilions of the effeminate, which were in the house of the Lord, for which the women wove as it were little dwellings for the grove.*

Despite various translations as whore-mongers the translation as "male prostitutes" is fairly pervasive. The weaving referred to here, "for Asherah" are generally agreed to be the robes worn by the male prostitutes who engaged in cross-dressing as part of their role as cultic prostitutes. This is of particular interest to us because it makes the cult of Asherah not simply a fertility cult, but one which has a queer central mystery suggesting the androgyne Baphomet. See also Zeus Arrhenothelus.

Rodrigo Borgia – 1431-1503- Pope 1492-1503. Gnostic saint listed as as Roderic Borgia Pope Alexander the Sixth in Liber XV, maintained under the same two names in the Canon of the Heterodox Gnostic Church. Crowley considered Alexander VI to be one of his past lives.[362]

Crowley's affinity for this figure is a little unclear. Certainly he debased the Papacy, having children by multiple mistresses, enriching himself at the expense of the Holy See, and engaging in open nepotism. His early double-dealing caught him in a difficult position and forced his surrender to Charles VIII of France. Using the French to break the feudal despots of Italy, he was able to forge a more modern state over which he had control similar to that of the Kings of Spain, France, and the Emperor. He built an effective political power base for the Papacy in Italy, and formed the Holy League against France. He would eventually shift alliances to Franc. At the same time Alexander VI tarnished the spiritual power of the Papacy, opening it to criticism from reformers (*see Savonarola*).

Historically, Alexander VI is an indefensible figure. He was a competent secular Lord, but his work included a rubber stamp of Portuguese and Spanish slavery in the New World. Previous Popes had been against slavery and attacked it in papal bulls in relation to the Canary Islands. Ironically, his reputation for libertinism may be overstated. There is no modern proof of his involvement in assassination or poisoning, and some scholars have even suggested his "children," originally recognized as nieces and nephews, were never legitimized at all, but rather adopted; his address to them as "son" and "daughter" in letters being common to all Papal correspondence.

Alexander VI's role in slavery was known but not emphasized in the late 19th century. Instead, he was portrayed as a sort of latter day Nero or Caligula, a debauched libertine, a lover of hedonism and luxury, practitioner or sympathizer with the black arts, and essentially a model for the destruction of chaste and ascetic Catholic values. It is likely these factors which drove Crowley's interest in Alexander VI. Nevertheless, times change, and Alexander VI cannot be seen, in modern terms, as a role model for Thelemites. It is probably not coincidental that the Initiations focus not on Alexander VI, but on his equally flawed nemesis, Savonarola.

Rosicrucianism – a modern mythology connected to three published works from the early 17th century, the *Fama Fraternitatis* (1614) *Confessio Fraternitatis* (1615) and *The Chymical Wedding of Christian Rosenkreutz* (1616). Of the three, only the author of the last is known with certainty (see also *Andreae, Johann Valentin*). There is some belief that the documents circulated in manuscript form during the late 16th century, for 20 to 30 years before their publication. There is no significant evidence of an actual Rosicrucian society significantly predating the Fama and, despite numerous attempts to link the Rosicrucians to preexisting secret societies, any such ties appear more ideological than brick-and-mortar.

What is Rosicrucianism

For our purposes, Rosicrucianism must be understood not merely as an interesting secret society involving a specific symbol, but as:

- *Science and Ethics* – An attempt to join ethics and science using each to throw light upon the other, a movement that is still critical in our culture today
- *A Modern manifestation of the Hermetic Tradition* – The precursor to a vast array of esoteric Protestant movements that lead into Spiritualism, Theosophy, Neo-Gnosticism, and Thelema
- *Syncretic* – The first popular modern attempt to integrate elements of tradition common in Western Europe and deriving from Europe, West Asia and North Africa, into a single, coherent, Tradition. Unlike other Protestant movements, Rosicrucianism, like Theosophy, the Golden Dawn, and Thelema is Syncretist.
- *Sexually Symbolic* – the source of sexual symbolism heavily employed by Reuss and Crowley and core to Thelema.

In addition, it must be understood that Rosicrucianism changed radically between the 17th and early 20th centuries. The Rosicrucianism of Fin-de-Siecle Paris is not the Rosicrucianism of Andreae. In a sense, Rosicrucian still fulfilled the same function, serving as a bridge between a Christian social aesthetic and a purely esoteric and hermetic milieu. On an artistic level, Rosicrucianism was an important element in the modern European quest to find roots and tradition. While many of the Romantics were drawn to Catholicism precisely because it seemed to offer a richer tradition than Protestantism, Rosicrucianism offered a neutral alternative, a "soft" gateway into Hermeticism and the rising tide of neo-pagan thought.

Science and Ethics

Johann Valentin Andreae's biographer, John Warwick Montgomery, provides the key link to Thelema in "wed true theology and true science together."[363] The motto of the Equinox "The Method of Science -- The Aim of Religion," is an emphatically Rosicrucian statement. Reuss' movement was explicitly Rosicrucian (one of two original Charters Reuss received from Golden Dawn founder William Wynn Westcott was to form a German branch of the English Societas Rosicruciana in Anglia, or SRIA). Neo-Templarism which distinguished Reuss' "O.T.O." or Order of Oriental Templars, must be understood as an effectively Rosicrucian Tradition.

The term "theology" may be somewhat repellent to modern Thelemites. It is important to understand that, in this context, theology deals with an attempt to harmonize the supposed will of the deity with observable natural law. Protestant theology of Kepler's time was not based on the concept that the laws of God could be read from the way in which the universe functioned not in the arbitrary "theology" of modern fundamentalism; by which a religious text is supposed to be infallible. It is cognate with ethics, to the extent that it was more about how people should live than the sort of rigid theology which defines arbitrary rules for behavior based on the capricious utterances of a supposed deity.

It is typical for modern people to think in terms of European culture as a steady march away from superstition and monlithic religion towards personal spirituality and humanism. In fact, this is not a clear and unflagging progression. Humanism was the dominant intellectual force of the Renaissance, beginning in the 1300s in Italy and coming to maturity in the late 1400s, spreading to the rest of Europe in the 1450s, and becoming the dominant intellectual movement of Europe in the 1500s. Consider that the era of Desiderius Erasmus was 1466-1536. The late 1500s and early 1600s saw a backlash against Humanism, driven in part by various wars pitting Catholic and Protestant forces against each other, including the Dutch War of Independence (Eighty Years' War 1568–1648), a revolt of the Seventeen Provinces of what are today the Netherlands against Catholic Habsburg Rule; the French Wars of Religion (1562-98), a series of clashes between Catholic, Protestant, and Protestant-tolerant, factions; and the apocalyptic Thirty Years' War (1618 to 1648), considered to be among the most destructive conflicts in European History which resulted in depopulation of as much as 50% in some areas of Germany.

Protestant faith itself had a mixed relationship with Humanism. Humanist thought originally flourished in Protestant states precisely because they lacked the mechanisms for formal repression; however Protestantism contained elements of traditionalist thought that were at odds with Humanism while the Counter-Reformation, which established the modern Tridentine Catholic Church (named for the Council of Trent 1545–1563), strengthened the intellectual basis of Catholicism. During the same period, Protestant states became more established and orthodox, enabling more control over the intellectual life and writing of Protestant authors.

Rosicrucianism can be seen in many lights, however it may best make sense when seen as an attempt to moderate the rise of an evangelical and Puritan Protestantism that rejected science and Renaissance Humanism. Understanding the need for belief and mythology in human nature, Rosicrucianism attempted to create a rational mythology, with the understanding of science as a core value. The matter is further confused because science itself was undergoing profound changes throughout the 17th century, during which Rosicrucianism flourished. The elimination of theology and ethics from scientific disciplines resulted in a more practical and secular science, but also divorced science from the field of ethics. Most of us know that Isaac Newton was an alchemist, but fail to understand that this is not a matter of a modern man of science with some primitive superstitions, but rather the visible signs of an integrative approach that saw science and ethics as a single field. Occult Philosophy was a study intended to to understand the hidden laws by which the universe moved.

A Modern manifestation of the Hermetic Tradition

Whoever authored the Fama, Rosicrucian philosophy was heavily influenced by Heinrich Khunrath, who is generally understood as a Hermeticist who was, in turn, heavily influenced by John Dee. Khunrath, like Andreae, heavily Christianized his core Hermetic message, but the concept of a gnosis, accomplishable through science or natural magic which could provide all wisdom, is an essentially Hermetic and Gnostic concept. By putting a Christian wrapper on the Hermetic concept, Khunrath built a tradition that connected modern rationalism to classical thought.

In his summary of arguments that Andreae did not write the Fama, Montgomery provides us with a concise basis for its importance to our own movement. "With Libavius, Andreae believed that at its core the Rose Cross was not Christian. He was aware, of course, that the Rosicrucian manifestos had been written by Protestants - in all probability Lutherans - and they they included not only Christian allusions, but explicit Christian truths….But for Andreae, the problem cut deeper than this; his concern was with the heart of the myth. He recognized that at its deepest level the Fama and Confessio presented not a Lutheran - or even a Christian - theology, but a philosophy rooted in pagan sources."[364] The same passage also offers insight into the importance of *Chymical Wedding* in our understanding of Rosicrucianism. "In its stress on asceticism and celibate life it suggested the Gnostic opposition of matter and spirit, not the evangelical convictions that the body as well as the soul is a divine gift and that that marriage is the highest human analogy for Christ's saving work in man."[365]

This requires a little unwrapping. First, we need to understand that, stripped of the Lutheran insistence on monogamy, "wedding" in this sense means sexual union. Second, we must understand "Christ's saving work in man," as a statement identical in intent to "apprehension of the divine," or "gnosis," filtered through Montgomery's own Protestantism. With this clarification, whether he was refining his own earlier manifestos or providing guidance to the work of others, Andreae creates a theology that welds the core values that will become Thelema to their Hermetic core. In *Chymical Wedding* we take a step away from the asceticism that flows from Plato and is amplified by the Italian Renaissance rejection of homosexuality as a non-allegorical act and wed it to a Protestant value, flowing from the previous century's Humanism. This becomes the Gnostic doctrine of Thelema in which attainment is realized, as Ficino suggests, through refinement of appreciation for the sensual world, including and most explicitly, human sexuality.

Syncretic

The Rosicrucian works represent a synthesis of other traditions. They are more externally Christian than Theosophy or Thelema, but they differ from other Protestant movements of the time by being modular. Rosicrucianism was accepted and argued across a broad range of Protestant and, eventually, Catholic movements which were not all adjacent or even mutually tolerant. It explicitly included Humanist, Hermetic, and Jewish thought. Through its core myth of the discovery of Wisdom in West Asia and North Africa, it implicitly drew links to Islamic mysticism and Classical and Neoplatonist Paganism. It can be best understood as a precursor, or literal progenitor, of syncretist traditions such as Theosophy, the Golden Dawn, and Thelema.

Sexual

In our investigation of Hermeticism above, we lean heavily into the element that makes *Chymical Wedding* a pivotal point in thought. Up until this point, all Hermetic thought and all Gnosticism are aligned to some greater or lesser degree with the concept of escape from the world. Whether one deplores the world entirely or, like Plato, appreciates beauty as a ladder to the divine, the point is still *escape*. With the introduction of the Protestant and Humanist reverence for the body, Rosicrucianism creates sexuality and sensuality as a perfected Gnostic sacrament in which we are not called upon to reject the world, but to immerse ourselves in it. There are 300-odd years between the inception of this formula and its perfection, but *Chymical Wedding* is an emblematic turning point where Renaissance Gnosticism becomes modern Gnosticism. Such turning points don't happen without a profound cultural ferment around them, yet the degree to which Rosicrucianism both electrified and horrified Europe cannot be understated.

The Circle and Cross or Rose and Cross as representative of the generative organs is hardly coincidental. *The Chymical Wedding* is certainly a sexual metaphor, though one on a very high level. It is, as John Warwick Montgomery points out, also a symbol of Martin Luther, who probably did not consciously project any sexual symbolism into the cipher. Nevertheless, it is difficult not to see the symbolism of cross and circle or cross and rose as a statement of the sexual formula of Alchemy, and this formula is made explicit in *Chymical Wedding*.

Queer doctrines which lead into Thelema's understanding of gender are muted in the early Rosicrucian work. As we see with Rabelais, any Neo-Platonist doctrine carries a thread of queer sexuality; however this is not fully developed until the late 19th and early 20th century. It is clear, however, that this is a core piece of Roscrucianism, not merely a graft of Reuss and Crowley. *The Secret Doctrine of the Rosicrucians*, originally published in 1918 by William Walker Atkinson, contains a significant discussion of the Universal Androgyne. In this light, Rosicrucianism must be seen, appropriately, as a core driver of Thelema's implicitly queer understanding of human sexuality.

Ruad – *RAWD* – Following the loss of Acre and Sidon, the Templars and others conceived a major effort to retake the Levant. Their best hope lay in an alliance with the Mongols. The Mongols had already absorbed two Christian Kingdoms as vassal states and generally had treated them as allies against the Mamluks. The Latin Crusaders had been attempting to form an alliance with the Mongols for some time, but were seldom able to coordinate. They had delivered little help to the Mongol invasion of Syria in 1280-81, however Hospitallers fought alongside Mongols at the Second Battle of Homs in 1281.

Mongol Ilkhanate ruler, Ghazan, made the first of several attempts to conquer Syria in 1300. Latin forces attempted to land in the Levant in order to link with Ghazan. The expedition was not merely a Templar undertaking, but was supported by Amaury of Lusignan, and the Hospitallers, with about 600 Troops.[366] The Force set up a base on Ruad, a small coastal island, which included some buildings, and raided Tortosa.

"A Templar garrison under the command of the order's marshal, Bartholomew of Chinsi, was left to guard Ruad."[367] Despite some historical mythology, Ruad was a tiny island and never a principal headquarters for the Order. This remained on Cyprus, though Jacques de Molay wrote that he intended to go to Ruad in 1301 when Ghazan was again expected.

Ghazan never reached the area and the remaining garrison which was, by 1302, exclusively Templars and Syrian foot-soldiers. The Mamluks attacked during the winter and forced the Templars to surrender, beheading the Syrian. "Nearly 40 of these men were still in prison in Cairo years later where, according to a former fellow prisoner, the Genoese Matthew Zaccaria, they died of starvation, having refused an offer of 'many riches and goods' in return for apostasising."[368]

Interestingly, Gerard de Villiers was recorded as having been blamed for the loss. "A letter written by Ponsard of Gizy, the Templar preceptor of Payns, and introduced at the trial on 27 November 1309, states that Gerard of Villiers, the Templar preceptor of France, was blamed for the loss of Ruad at one of the order's chapters in the west. Allegedly, Gerard and his friends had left the island prematurely."[369] This was presented as a possible factor in his decision to flee, taking some of his friends with him.[370] *See also Gerard de Villiers, Templars.*

Safed – The Templars spent a great deal of effort fortifying and arming a powerful citadel at Safed. Baibars displayed a masterful command of tactics in distracting and confusing the Latin forces to ensure that they did not know the target of his assault until Safed was cut off, capturing it in 1266. Baibars, contrary to his usual policy of allowing safe conduct, slaughtered the garrison except for the Hospitallers.

Saint-Felix – *SAHN -fay-Leeks* – (properly Saint-Félix) site of a Council organizing the Cathar Church in 1167 at Saint-Felix-de-Caraman, now called Saint-Felix-Lauragais. – see *Appendix B, Jeanne of England*

Saint-Semin – A major church and gathering area in the City of Toulouse. It is where Raimond VI first camped upon his re-entry to the city, and where the mangonel that killed Simon Montfort was constructed. *see also Appendix B*

Salah ad-Din – *sa-LAH ad-DIN*- 1137-1193 CE – Al-Nasir Salah al-Din Yusuf ibn Ayyub. Kurd and first Sultan of Egypt, founder of the Ayyubid Dynasty. صَلَاحُ الدّين (ṣalāḥu d-dīn). The name means The Righteousness of the Faith. Also rendered Saladin. His brother was Sayf ad-Din.

Sanchuniathon – *SAN-chu-nee-AH-thun* – The Phoenician author of several works of history. Dates unknown, attributed to the early 12th Century BCE. His name, SKNYTN or Sakun-yaton, means "the God Sakon has given." Known as Sanchuniathon the Berytian or Sanchuniathon of Beirut. All knowledge of his writing comes from the *Praeparatio Evangelica* of Eusebius, an early Christian Church History. The work of Sanchuniathon is supposed to have been based on collections of secret writings of the Priests of Ammon discovered in the shrines of Beirut. Despite controversy about the origin and accuracy of the work attributed to him, he is one a source for correspondences between Semitic and Hellenic deities. The work may have been forged by Philo of Byblos. In whatever case, the work clearly draws on then known history and tradition, and was extant and available during the core period of the composition of the *Corpus Hermeticum* from the 1st through 3rd century CE.

Savonarola – 1452-1498 CE – de facto ruler of Florence 1494-1498.[371] [372]Best known for his "Bonfire of the Vanities," the image of Savonarola as a book burning populist or mindless puritan is overly simplistic. Savonarola was well educated and one of the most brilliant religious minds of his era. He has long been seen as a sort of "proto-protestant" – a reformer who saw the intrinsic corruption of the Roman Church and longed to cleanse it much like Martin Luther.

His creed, necessarily, was Spartan. It should be remembered that, at the time he urged the burning of "Vanities," the people of Florence were, periodically, starving on account of Florence's political isolation for its failure to align with Rome. His message, that the rich lived in ease while the poor starved, was admirable and, unlike many other leaders, he did indeed practice as he preached. He lived a spartan lifestyle, devoted most of his time to preaching and writing, and worked actively to improve the lot of the poor.

Initially, he had been brought to Florence as a reformer by the brilliant Giovanni Pico della Mirandola. The death of Lorenzo di Piero de' Medici had thrown Florence into political chaos as his heir, Piero, engaged in flamboyant misrule. Piero was overthrown by the Civic Council which re-established a functional Republic. In practice,

Savonarola became dictator and strong man, but it should be recalled this was at a time when such was the rule rather than the exception.

His chief issue was an attempt to side with the French King Charles VIII of France against the Pope and a league of other Italian Cities. Initially threatened by Charles, Florence had little choice and originally had the support of Milan. Savonarola interceded with Charles to save Florence from sack, convincing him to make Florence a friend and go elsewhere, and that act alone made him the effective civic leader.

Savonarola had seen Charles VIII as a righteous King to cleanse Rome and his failure forced the Friar to consolidate his position politically. After his excommunication in May 1497, Savonarola was increasingly on the defensive. His refusal to intervene in the kangaroo-court condemnation of several leading citizens accused of having aided Piero di'Medici in an abortive attempt at restoring his rule, followed by their messy and botched execution, was one of many factors that led to his fall from power.

Savonarola may have believed his own lies, but he was, in fact, a liar, using a false claim to prophecy and the implication of a gift from God to back up his civil authority. The period during which he ruled was one of war, privation, crop failure, and seasonal plague, as well as the first major outbreak of the disease said to have been brought by the French troops, syphilis, and he took advantage of having a strong personality to impose an autocratic order on the chaos. Backed into a corner, Savonarola fell back on a supposed gift of prophecy and hinted at miracles. One of his followers agreed to a Trial by Fire with a rival Franciscan Friar and, when the proceeding was rained out, the crowd turned on Savonarola and within the day he was imprisoned. Savonarola and two followers were hanged on 23 May 1498 and burned afterwards.

Savonarola's legacy is complicated. Remembering that most of the Puritans were "well-intentioned," he is perhaps best seen as a leader who started with good intentions, but his willingness to mix claims of divine authority with autocratic tactics ultimately made him a villain and traitor to his own cause. The choice of Savonarola as an antagonist in one of the scenes from the II° initiation is interesting. Crowley certainly thought Savonarola was a prude. He references him briefly in "A Venus to seduce Savonarola!"[373] Crowley also embraces his arch-enemy, Pope Alexander VI, considering the dissipate Borgia Pope one of his past lives. Savonarola makes an interesting foil. In our mysteries, he is not so easily dismissed as a caricature any more than his Borgia rival could be dismissed. Ficino gives an underlying rationale for his dismissal of Savonarola which could be applied to other would be dictators.

Sayf ad-Din – *SAFE ahd-DIN* or *SIFE ahd-DIN* – 1145-1218 CE – Ahmed, son of Najm ad-Din Ayyub, father of Bakr, the Just King, Sword of the Faith. Also known as Al-Adil. Sayf ad-Din Meaning "Sword of Faith," he was the brother of Salah ad-Din and fourth Sultan of Egypt. It was briefly proposed that he would marry Jeanne, the sister of Richard I, King of England, and they would jointly rule Jerusalem. History records that neither would convert to the other's faith. The proposal by Richard I of England to marry his sister to Sayf-ad-Din is widely attested in the literature of the period. Various reasons are given for the failure of this plan, but most focus on its general unpalatability to both sides, as it would have mandated the conversion of one of the two. The framing of the proposal gives a framework for the degree to which Richard's interests in the Holy Land were political, rather than ideological.

Secret Society of the Dionysian Artificer – this is a proposed Secret Society of Proto-Masons, dating to around 1000 BCE. The actual "Society" or, rather, the legend of it dates from 1820, from *The History of the Dionysian Artificers*, a book published in London by the Brazilian author Hippolyto Joseph Da Costa. It is in a similar vein to the *Crata Repoa*, and follows the Egyptian Masonic concepts of Cagliostro; however, while giving an Egyptian bent,

Da Costa ties the Secret Society to Greece. The book has no particular authority other than allusion to classical sources such as Josephus.

Seljuks – *SELL-juke* – one of several Medieval Turkish dynasties.

Seshat, Scribe of the Seven Pointed Star – identified as the wife, daughter, or sister, of Thoth, Seshat was a goddess of writing, scribes, record-keeping, and, in general, the retention of knowledge and wisdom. As the name means "female scribe," she has been associated with other deities including Isis. She is also associated with the cult of Ptah at Heliopolis. She was eventually identified with engineering and astronomy as well and she was concerned with the "Stretching the Cord" ritual which was used to lay out the foundation for any major new building work. This ceremony may be a rationale for the border on Masonic temple floors or, previously, around tracing boards. She may have, at one time, had an educated priestess class which learned mathematics and writing. In later antiquity, her cult was largely subsumed by that of Thoth.

The "Seven Pointed" emblem above her head may be a palm or hemp leaf, a horned headdress, a star, or signify something else. There is no agreement among scholars.

Sidon – *SAI-dn* – Modern Sayda or Saida is the third largest city in Lebanon. It was an important Phoenician city and the central point of a great Mediterranean web of trade. The city was known for glass manufacturing and the distinctive purple dye made from snails that became known as Roman "Imperial Purple." Ashtart is archaeologically attested as the deity of Sidon around the 5th century BCE. The city was conquered by Alexander in 333 and became part of the Hellenic, Roman, and then Byzantine spheres. Sidon was captured by Yazid for the Caliphate before 635, then by King Baldwin I of Jerusalem in 1110. It changed hands in 1187 when it was captured by Salah ad-Din, returning briefly to Latin control in 1197, until being captured by the Ayyubids in 1249. The city was sacked by the Mongols in 1260 under Kitbuqua. *See also Matthieu Sauvage.*

Simon Mansel – *see Antioch*

Sinking City – the only defining characteristic of the Sinking City in the I° play is that it was in the Peloponnese and fell about 400 years after the building of the Great Pyramid. This could make it the city found at Kiladha Bay in the Argolid Gulf around 2015 by the University of Geneva. It could also be an as yet undiscovered city. The rise in sea level was a continual factor through late antiquity as a result of the retreat from the period of maximum glaciation. This is known as the Holocene marine transgression. The drowned city does not match any precise timeline. It is likely not associated with the eruption of Santorini c. 1627–1600 BC. Sea rise occurred in the area continually, but may not have been steady, and there is certainly sea rise documented in the period from 4300 BCE to 1000 BCE in the region.[374] However, we have been unable to identify any specific incident in the range of 2200 BCE.

Tahuti Djehuti or Tahuti, but better known to us as Thoth – *see Hermes Trismegistus*

Templars – Poor Fellow-Soldiers of Christ and of the Temple of Solomon – founded in 1119 by Hughes de Payens. Considerable coverage is given to their acquisition of the Al-Aqsa Mosque Temple site in the Introduction under "The Temple of Solomon the King", see also *Jacques de Molay, Thibaud Gaudin, Guilliame de Beaujeau, Otto of Granson, Gerard de Villiers, Hughes de Pairaud, Matthieu Sauvauge, Ruad, Safed, Edessa, Sidon, Antioch.*

For the Grail Legend, *see Wolfram Von Eschenbach.*

As there are hundreds of books on the Templars, it is not necessary to give a detailed account of their entire history. The order was active until its repression by Philip the Fair of France in the early 14th century. Instead, we will briefly cover sources for some core material, the Masonic Templar Tradition, and common legends. *The New Knighthood, A History of the Order of the Temple,* and *The Trial of the Templars,* by Malcolm Barber, are excellent and historically accurate portrayals of the Templars. Care should be taken to vet source books on the Templars, as many are little more than hare-brained conspiracy theories, presenting a tapestry of wild conjecture as fact. Even from an esoteric or occult point of view, their facts are often so skewed as to be without any value whatsoever.

Many of these are based around, or tied to, the 1982 work *The Holy Blood and the Holy Grail,* which covers the Priory of Sion Legend, and the 2003 fiction novel *The Da Vinci Code* by Dan Brown, which wildly popularized this legend. The legend is not harmful, per-se. Like the work of Wolfram von Eschenbach, it is fanciful, though it contains elements of non-fiction as its basis. The Gnostic Gospels tend to suggest or support a mythology wherein Mary Magdalene was the wife of Jesus. Certainly, the idea that the historical Jesus was married is not particularly controversial to anyone but ardent Christians; an unmarried Jewish Teacher or skilled Workman of the age of 30 would have been completely remarkable in the early first century CE. Whether or not Jesus married Mary, whether that was his first marriage, and regardless even of who precisely Mary Magdalene was, there is a great deal of material now available that differs from the Synoptic Gospels.

The Scottish Rite and Templarism

After William and Mary ousted King James of Scotland and England in 1688, he went into exile and was held to have abandoned the state, making them monarchs of Scotland. The Knights Templars are associated most specifically with the Ancient and Accepted Scottish Rite. According to this myth, Knights Templars fleeing persecution had come to Scotland and formed the core of the Freemason movement. In reality, this was a framework for Jacobite political clubs after the revolts of 1689, 1715, and 1719. Prince Charles Edward Stuart, who led the doomed 1745 rebellion, was associated with Freemasonry and Scottish Freemasonry flourished on the continent. It is unclear that all Scottish Rite bodies were Jacobite in nature; however, the association of the Templars with a fallen leader who needed to be avenged was most definitely Jacobite symbolism. Neo-Templarism was picked up by other Masonic organizations as the political significance of Scottish Jacobite Masonry ebbed on the Continent. The Rite of Memphis was constituted by Jacques Etienne Marconis de Negre in 1838 and integrated strong Templar elements.

Jacobite political sympathies remained a fringe and crank cause for decades, without any serious capability or intent. Jacobitism was associated with Catholicism which, as noted, was attractive to the Romantics. In the 1890s, "MacGregor" Mathers of the Golden Dawn had explicit Jacobite pretensions, despite being English, and Crowley's affinity for Boleskine has a Jacobite air. The popularity of the Scottish Rite and then other Templar orders on the continent grew heavily from Jacobite Masonry.

Templars are inevitably tied to Rosicrucianism. While Andreae or his collaborators avoided a Catholic Templar identification, it is heavily influenced by the grail legend as portrayed in *Parzival* by Wolfram Von Eschenbach, and the crypt itself is difficult not to identify with the Vault of the Royal Arch of Enoch, which is often legendarily associated with the Templars as being found on the Temple Mount. It is impossible to know whether or not the Templars were, in fact, pagan occultists. What is probably more important to us is that both Eliphas Levi and Crowley *believed* they were. To the occultist, steeped in gnostic tradition, there is a certain uniformity in the presentation of the Baphomet, the denial of Jesus, and the presumption of a certain underground cabal of homosexual or bisexual men within the Templars. This opens the issue of the Templars as an early source of queer identity. The name of Baphomet, chosen for a representation of the Thelemic incarnation of the Aeon, comes from the Templars, which alone is enough to give us an interest in the order.

Anyone interested in the Templar heresies should read the actual trial descriptions, to the extent they are available. Most importantly, it should be noted that Baphomet, whatever its nature or origin, was generally presented as a bearded head, and there is no suggestion at all of anything resembling the goat-human construction so well known from Eliphas Levi. We have chosen to explore, based on our inspired material, a plausible middle ground by which the Templars may have served as a conduit for esoteric traditions previously lost in Europe to find their way back, if principally by word of mouth. *See Harran.* Whatever its inspiration, we present our exploration of the Templars as a fictional play and do not insist in any way upon its realism. To emphasize this, the figure of Rinaldo de la Chappelle from Crowley's play *The Scorpion*[375] is referenced as a historical character.

It is worth noting that the presence of "Head" idols does not necessarily mean paganism or any connection with the pagan worship of Harran. A quick search for "Head-Shaped Reliquary of Pope Alexander I" will disclose images of a typical period "head reliquary" often, though not invariably, used for the putative skull of a saint. It has been suggested that the Templars may have had one or more of these reliquaries which were the source of the idol stories, either through actual misunderstanding or through convenient construction on the part of individuals looking for something to confess.

The Templars lived in a savage time and were theist warriors. That said, so were all their opponents and, in the end, they were condemned for their willingness to accommodate the enemy; having either through preference, circumstance, or a likely combination of both, preferred on many occasions to make treaties and deals rather than fight. The Templars are not without their flaws and our presentation of them shows them as such, struggling with the issues of their time. The image of Templars, not as righteous Christian Knights, but as individuals tied to a common cause struggling both to discern good and find ways to carry it out against impossible odds, present a version of the Templar legend that is both historical and meaningful to us in the present day.

See also Appendix B for a discussion of Otto Rahn as an unreliable source in regards to Grail Lore.

The Book M – a core element of Rosicrucian lore, going back to the original Rosicrucian Manifesto, the 1614 *Fama Fraternitatis*:

> *After this manner began the Fraternity of the Rosie Cross; first, by four persons onely, and by them was made the Magical Language and writing, with a large Dictionary, which we yet dayly use to Gods praise and glory, and do finde great wisdom therein; they made also the first part of the Book M: but in respect that the labor was too heavy, and the unspeakable concourse of the sick hindred them, and also whilst his new building (called Sancti spiritus) was now finished, they concluded to draw and receive yet others more into their Fraternity; to this end was chosen brother R.C. his deceased fathers brothers son, brother B. a skilful Painter, G. and P.D. their Secretary, all Germains except J.A. so in all they were eight in number, all batchelors and of vowed virginity, by those was collected a book or volumn of all that which man can desire, wish, or hope for.*[376] *- Fama, English from Vaughn 1652*

The Rosicrucian book of "all knowledge" can be considered as a reconstruction of the *Book of Thoth* or the *Emerald Tablet*.

The Sacred Book of Abramelin the Mage – This book is so widely known it is included mostly for purposes of disambiguation and clarification. The book is not particularly old compared to *Picatrix*, *Psellus*, *Abano*, or other early sources. By internal dating, it was composed in 1458, which would make it contemporary with *Trithemius*; however there is little evidence for the manuscript before the early 17th century.

MacGregor Mathers of Golden Dawn fame resurrected this comparatively obscure manuscript after he became fascinated by a copy he found at the Bibliotheque de l'Arsenal in Paris. Mathers may have thought the book was more rare than it actually was. There are twelve manuscripts and an early printed edition.

The definitive modern version is by Georg Dehn, published in English in 2006 and German in 1995.[377] Dehn worked from the German editions found at Wolfenbuttel, which were older and more complete than Mathers' comparatively recent French edition. Linguistically, Dehn's scholarship is excellent, though in terms of the book's authorship it is speculative. For Thelemites, the version translated by Mathers may hold some interest (and is still widely available in recent editions), as it was the edition which Crowley had access to at Boleskine.

The "Abra Melin Working" includes a sort of road map towards a state of magical perfection. However, like most grimoires, the utility of its demons seems to have less to do with attainment than with gathering secular power. Abraham of Worms himself, the putative author, seems mostly to be notable for abetting the lifestyles of the rich and famous.

Dehn assigns the work to Yaakov ben Moshe Levi Moelin (1365-1427). Writing in *The Magickal Review*, Ian Rons cast strong doubt on this in 2010;[378] however he does concede there may have been a contemporary Abraham of Leipzig who may have been the author. That said, the writer seems somewhat vague on Jewish customs and ignorant of Hebrew, making a non-Jewish source more likely. Whatever the age or authorship, we can discern in the book's outline an earlier philosophy that relates squarely to the Kabbalistic tradition as it emerged from Andalusia.

Thebes – The capital of Egypt during much of the 18th Dynasty of the New Kingdom. *See Crata Repoa*

Thibaud Gaudin – *TEE-bow GOW-dan* – Considered very pious, Gaudin was dispatched with the Templar Order's treasure to Sidon as Acre was falling. He was elected Grand Master there. Gaudin decided to abandon the City of Sidon and move to the Castle of the Sea. He sailed to Cyprus to attempt to gather reinforcements, and eventually the garrison abandoned Sidon altogether for Tortosa. The fall of Beirut and Haifa left only Tortosa and Athlit in Frankish hands, and the garrisons there were too small to defend either and sailed for Ruad. Gaudin died in 1292, the year after his appointment.

Tortosa – *see Ruad*

Toulouse – *TO-loos* – Major city and cultural center of Southern France and Medieval Europe - *See Appendix B*

Tripoli – *TRIP-uh-lee* – also Arab Tarabulus. Settled from the 14th century BCE, the Phoenicians established a trading station there in the 9th century BCE. During the Hellenistic period, it was independent, coming under Roman rule around 64 CE. The Byzantine City was destroyed by the Beirut Earthquake of 551 CE. The Crusaders laid siege to the city at the beginning of the 12th century and were able finally to enter it in 1109, causing a fire which destroyed the city's famous library the Dar al-'Ilm, or House of Knowledge. The city was the capital of the Crusader County of Tripoli until its fall in 1289 to the Egyptian Mamluk sultan, Qalawun. As a predominantly Frankish City, Occitan was one of the predominant languages spoke, and Tripoli was a major base of the Knights of the Hospital of St. John.

Troubadour – *see Appendix B*

Tübingen – A noted university associated with the Protestant movement, near Stuttgart. The school still exists and was, for many years, a principal seat of Lutheran learning. *See also Andreae, Johann Valentin.*

Tyler, Tyling, Tyled – There are a number of folk etymologies as to how this term came to be used for the outer guard at a Masonic Lodge and, thus, attached to the process of ensuring the guests are members by asking for the passwords and signs. In all likelihood, the term was associated with masonry for the obvious reason – that it was the term for one who lays tiles; however the association with "doorward" is largely a matter of conjecture.

Tyre – *TAI-uh* or *TAI-ur* – Likely originally founded as a colony of Sidon, Hiram is attested as a Biblical King. Referencing Tyrian records and the history of Menander Josephus dates his reign to 980-947 BCE. Allied with David, then Solomon, which assured him of access to trade routes to the South and East, Hiram is said to have built the palace of David and aided in the construction of the Temple of Solomon. According to Josephus, he enlarged the city, and constructed a new Royal Palace and a Temple of Melquart; however there is no trace of these in modern archaeology.

Urim and Thummim – *YOO-rim TOO-mim* – the description of these divinatory items is confusing. In Temple practice, the High Priest wore both an outer garment called an Ephod, which was similar to an apron. Over this was worn a breastplate. The breastplate was attached to the Ephod by gold chains and a blue ribbon. The sacred breastplate is equally detailed and features four rows of three gems.

The Urim and Thummim were placed into a pouch in the breastplate. They were then used in some sort of ritual of divination; the nature of which is uncertain. Some sources believe it was a simple "yes/no" divination based on an ancient etymology which makes the names "revelation" and "truth" or "lights" and "perfection." The exact nature of the objects is unknown, though there are multiple conjectures.

Villiers, Gerard de – Preceptor of France, the Templar most closely associated with the Pit *see Merlan*. He was blamed for deserting his comrades *see also Ruad*. Villiers was prepared for the arrests, quite possibly because he had friends in France who tipped him off or because he was the major informant regarding the arrests. He is believed to have left with about 40 Templars and taken a ship. His flight shows signs of having been well-planned.

Viterbo – a papal city considered safer and more defensible than Rome. Location of a Papal Palace, several Popes preferred Viterbo or Orviedo as vacation home but also as a refuge in times of unpopularity or unrest.

Von Werth, Johann – German General of Cavalry on the side of the Holy Roman Empire during the Thirty Years War.

Wolfram of Eschenbach – c. 1170-1220 – German Knight and poet. He is described as a minnesanger, a German term very similar to the Occitan troubadour, though minnesangers specifically performed their own work. He describes himself in his work as Bavarian and his dialect is appropriate to Bavaria. There is some debate over his literacy as he claims to be illiterate; however this is debated and may have been a joke or brag. His greatest work, *Parzival,* is based on an unfinished work by Chretien de Troyes. The majority of his songs are in a genre dedicated to knights who spend the night with their ladies, but have to leave before or at dawn. An echo of this tradition can be seen in Shakespeare's bedroom scene from Romeo and Juliet. Von Eschenbach is interesting in interpreting the Holy Grail as a Stone rather than the Cup of Joseph of Arimathea, which was the popular legend of the time. This corresponds well to Hermetic alchemical principles and mythology.

Von Eschenbach himself gives the source of the poem as a Provencal poet, named Kyot, late in the story. Written between 1200 and 1210, Parzival was probably written just before the Cathar Crusades. His patron was Hermann, Landgrave of Thuringia. Von Eschenbach, like his patron, was likely widely-traveled.

Von Eschenbach is cosmopolitan and his world knowledge is extensive. The first two books involve Parzival's father who marries a Moorish queen. He gives his source for the Parzival story as a Provencal Poet named Kyot who found the information in a manuscript in Toledo written by a Muslim named Flegetanis. There has been much historical argument over the names cited, which are probably either fictional or pseudonyms. The date is too early for the publication of *Picatrix*, but it does suggest that secret knowledge was already associated with the Muslims of Andalusia. The notable but vague idea of the Grail as a stone suggests word of mouth knowledge.

Von Eschenbach made one indispensable contribution to Grail lore, which was to make Templars the guardians of the Grail. Here we must note that the Templars were still very much a going concern in 1210. Why, particularly, Von Eschenbach picked the Templars rather than Teutonic Knights or Hospitallers is unknown. Likely, they appealed to him or his patron. His Templars are mythical, yet the idea that the Knights Templar had and guarded the Grail has been part of the legend since.

Zeus Arrhenothelus – *Zoos or ZAY-oos air-HEN-oh-THEE-lus* - The history of Zeus Arrhenothelus is fascinating and singular. We are first able to find the term in the work of the respected historian, archaeologist, and ethnologist Daniel Garrison Brinton, considered to be one of the founders of American Anthropology, who said in 1876:

> *The startling refuge was had in the image of a deity at once of both sexes. Such avowedly were Mithras, Janus, Melitta, Cybele, Aphrodite, Agdistis; indeed nearly all the Syrian, Egyptian, and Italic gods as well as Brahma, and in the esoteric doctrine of the Cabala, even Jehovah, whose female aspect is represented by the "Shekinah." To this abnormal condition the learned have applied the adjectives epicene, androgynous, hermaphrodite, arrenothele. In art it is represented by a blending of the traits of both sexes. In the cult it was dramatically set forth by the votaries assuming the attire of the other sex, and dallying with both.*[379]

The term crops up in a number of turn of the century dictionaries, including the *American Encyclopediac Dictionary* under *arrenothele* which gives the Greek *arrhenothelus* as the root,"male and female, of uncertain or doubtful sex,. Androgynous, uniting the characteristics of two sexes in one person."[380] This is certainly spot on for Crowley's meaning. It should be noted that the term appears to be an appropriation from science, and *arrhenotokous* may be more correct having sense still current in the term "arrhenotokous parthenogenesis."

Zeus Arrhenothelus forms an important part of Crowley's mythology and is, fundamentally, a Thelemic construct. Crowley references Zeus Arrhenothelus in, the *Vision and the Voice*[381] and in *Liber ABA*[382] and *The Book of Thoth*.

> *In dealing with Zeus, one is immediately confronted with this deliberate confusion of the masculine and the feminine. In the Greek and Latin traditions the same thing happens. Dianus and Diana are twins and lovers; as soon as one utters the feminine, it leads on to the identification with the masculine, and vice versa, as must be the case in view of the biological facts of nature. It is only in Zeus Arrhenothelus that one gets the true Hermaphroditic nature of the symbol in unified form. This is a very important fact, especially for the present purpose, because images of this god recur again and again in alchemy.*[383]

When Crowley speaks of "alchemy" here, he is explicitly speaking of the processes concerned with the Red Lion and so forth, seeing alchemy principally as a cipher for sex. A few passages later, it is made explicit that Zeus Arrhenothelus corresponds to Baphomet, though so, too, do we learn is Babalon.

> *There is no doubt that this mysterious figure is a magical image of this same idea, developed in so many symbols. Its pictorial correspondence is most easily seen in the figures of Zeus*

Arrhenothelus and Babalon, and in the extraordinarily obscene representations of the Virgin Mother which are found among the remains of early Christian iconology. The subject is dealt with at considerable length in Payne Knight, where the origin of the symbol and the meaning of the name is investigated. Von Hammer-Purgstall was certainly right in supposing Baphomet to be a form of the Bull-god, or rather, the Bull-slaying god, Mithras; for Baphomet should be spelt with an "r" at the end; thus it is clearly a corruption meaning "Father Mithras". There is also here a connection with the ass, for it was as an ass-headed god that he became an object of veneration to the Templars.

The Early Christians also were accused of worshipping an ass or ass-headed god, and this again is connected with the wild ass of the wilderness, the god Set, identified with Saturn and Satan. (See infra, Atu XV.) He is the South, as Nuit is the North: the Egyptians had a Desert and an Ocean in those quarters.[384]

Appendix B – The Medieval Cathars

People Places and Events

The Cathar Court of Raimond VI and the Cathar Wars end up forming a core element of the Thelemic Initiations because the Cathar Church factored heavily in the revelation of Jules Doinel that began modern Gnosticism, leading to the foundation from which come many of the modern branches of the "Gnostic and Catholic Church of Light, Life, Love and Liberty," including the Heterodox Gnostic Church. Ultimately, the *history* of the Cathars is not of supreme importance and, if one does not care for history, it is possible to appreciate the initiations with only the barest outline of knowledge; that the Cathars were people persecuted by the mainstream religion and society of their day, and that some people stood up for them and their beliefs.

There was some trepidation about creating a large Appendix with extensive details of the people of the initiations. There was fear it could make the initiations seem to be about those people when they are not, any more than the Reuss-Crowley initiations are about Salah ad-Din. Eventually, the decision to do so was made on several bases:

- There would be people who wanted to know the stories. Having gathered the information in the search of researching how to present the stories we were delivered, we were aware that it is spread out over dozens of sources some leading back to the 18th century or earlier. Not gathering it in one place seemed ultimately a dereliction of a duty to our Sovereign Initiators.

- In presenting the information ourselves, we could consider the implications within the initiations, particularly the issue of symbolic incest. While it is clear to us that the presentation in the initiations is meant to be a slightly abstract representation of the YHVH formula, we felt that clearly setting aside what is known from what has no historical evidence was important.

- The portrayal of these complicated people in their complex times helps even out a presentation in the initiatory plays that is, as a necessity of drama, rather simplistic. In this way, it becomes easier to relate the lives of these figures which are, for our purposes, mythological, to our own. In particular, it underscores the strongest axis of affinity with these characters: for any other failings, they, like ourselves, are *defenders of tolerance in a time of intolerance*.

These people are not necessarily the characters of the initiations, even if they spoke to Doinel, or to us. The protagonists are a framing mechanism for voices which make it clear they are immortal avatars rather than the people we identify them with. Yet the history is interesting and there are many references to it, as well as a thread of the inspired material which suggests why these individuals, and not some other persons, were chosen to convey the initiations of the New Aeon.

It will be observed at once that the characters of our initiations live in messy and cosmopolitan times; fraught with war, greed, and intolerance – an era not unlike our own. They, too, see the rise of great political movements which may swamp their basic values. Yet they are, historically, very human people, prone to the same anger, vanity, and mischance as all of us. As with Thelema's Prophet, a perfected figure would not suit the philosophy or transmission of our particular gnosis. The message of Thelema is not of some bodhisattva lifting up but, rather, a human aspiring, struggling, attaining, and yet still remaining human. For that reason, Sovereign Initiators may want to know more about the times and characters who are portrayed, if for nothing else than to answer questions about the historical basis, or relative unknowns, surrounding of some of the assertions made in the initiations.

Ultimately, the figures presented in our initiations must be regarded as larger-than-life portrayals of ideals; neither perfectly accurate portrayals nor exactly historical fiction. Any consideration of these individuals is further clouded by the fact that several of our Protagonists, while perhaps somewhat obscure in English-speaking countries, have been the subject of multiple historical romances in French and have contemporary "fandoms" as avid as those who devour novels and shows about Anne and Mary Boleyn. In our Appendices, we have included a good bit of information on the historical people represented along with some guidance as to what is known historically, as opposed to elements that are purely conjecture on our part.

We do not know if Azalais of Burlats and Joan of England were ever at the Court of Raimond VI at the same time in the 1190s. We do know that it was customary for nobles to travel and attend each other's courts and that recent war or differences sometimes necessitated, rather than excused court appearances. In many cases, we don't know exact ages for these people or what seasonal or monthly trips they may have made. The supposition that travel was difficult and thus rare in the middle ages does not pertain to the figures of the Toulousian Court and its satellites and rivals. Nobles, including women, traveled frequently and made extensive visits. Certainly not the overnight stays of the modern era, but one noble might take several trips within a season.

We've included this section with a light history of the people, places, and events; and the notes link to some references that can be useful. For our own part, we've preferred period sources and relied most heavily on the sympathetic *The Song of the Cathar Wars* by William of Tudela[385] and his anonymous continuator on one hand, and Peter of Vaux de Cernay's highly anti-Cathar *Historia Albigensis*[386] on the other. The *Chronica* of William of Puylarens[387] is also a notable period source. This single article is by no means intended to be scholarship in depth, but rather a quick single source gloss for the highlights, particularly as they relate to our initiatory track. For a complete list of sources, see the end notes. For manageable reading to get a good overview of the conflict and time, we recommend *The Cathars: Dualist Heretics in Languedoc in the High Middle Ages*[388] by Malcolm Barber.

Otto Rahn as an unreliable source

In regards to the Cathars and Templars, especial attention should be paid to the work and reputation of Otto Rahn. His books regarding the Holy Grail, Templars, and Montsegur are still in print, and fairly popular. They form much of the basis for some of the wilder interpretations of these events. Rahn was a Nazi propagandist, who wrote with the explicit intention of achieving recognition by the Nazi hierarchy for putting a German Nationalist and white supremacist spin on events. Even before his turn to re-writing history to please the Nazi leadership, he was a sloppy and fantastical scholar. His work is heavily laden with fiction, and even beginning to distill the few grains of fact is a difficult undertaking.

If his scholarship were accurate, we might be forced to acknowledge his contribution, despite his toxic political views. The respected historian Malcolm Barber concludes regarding his 1933 *Kreuzzuge gegen den Graal*, kept in print in English by Simon and Schuster as *Crusade Against the Grail*,[389] with little note of Rahn's dubious history and scholarship:

> "In fact, in some senses, he was doing no more than exploit the ideas of Josephin Peladin who, in 1906, had turned Montsegur into 'Montsalvat' and the Cathars into a group of initiates and, more immediately, the novels of Maurice Magre, whom he had met in Paris. Much of the rest

of the book is a straight-forward, if not always accurate, account of the troubadours, the crusaders, and the inquisitors."

Barber continues to discuss his later work:

> *However, Rahn has developed a notoriety since that time as a consequence of a second book, Luzifers Hofgesind,[390] published in 1937, which moulded his previous theories to the contemporary racist climate of Hitler's Germany: the two civilisations remain in conflict, as in the previous book, but now the true God is Lucifer, the Bringer of Light, venerated by the Cathars. Around him Lucifer gathers his 'court', which is pitted against the wicked Jehovah, God of the Judaic' Catholic Church.[391]*

If you choose to pursue Rahn's works, be aware that much of his initial (and nearly all of his secondary) interpretation has been questioned by almost all serious scholars and many occultists. Among other issues, he attributes the Cathar struggle culminating at Montsegur as the source material for Von Eschenbach's *Parzival*, though Montsegur did not fall until 1243, and *Parzival* can be established as as having been completed not much later than 1220. Rahn's cultural constructions, while superficially plausible, lack any underlying cohesion, and oppose both the known historical record and the larger understanding of the transmission of the Hermetic light.

The Time of the Cathar Wars

To the anonymous continuator of *Song of the Cathar Wars*, the wars were a disaster – an assertion of autocracy and authoritarianism, often written about in shockingly modern terms, against a peace and freedom loving people. Certainly, that is one one historical theme. The wars provided a framework for the extension of the Frankish Crown and Papal authority at the expense of an area which had historically been largely self-governing. We are told the leading citizens of "the patricians of Toulouse, virtually free of comital control, led their militia against smaller towns and rural lords for miles around, imposing their urban lordship on the countryside; it was an Italian-style city-state in the making."[392] It is a matter of historical perspective whether this was good or bad. Had the French Crown failed to assimilate Toulouse, Carcassone, and Beziers, as the Empire failed to assimilate Genoa, Venice, and Florence, might these areas have flourished more powerfully, providing an earlier and easier axis for the rise of theories of self-governance and progressive ideas? Or, alternatively was the imposition of Feudal rule a step in the abolition of what amounted to warring tribalism?

The Counts and City of Toulouse

Understanding Toulouse as an independent principality caught up in the expansion of the French monarchy is core to understanding the wars against the Cathars. We use the term Occitania here geographically, as it was not current until about a century after the time in which the initiations are set.

In the 12th and early 13th century, the Counts of Toulouse did not owe fealty to a monarch as we would envision it today, nor did most of their vassals owe fealty to them. The Counts of Toulouse were Princes. That is to say sovereign and autonomous lords over their own territory. They were bound very loosely to the Crown of France, but that allegiance may be understood as a military alliance.

The Count of Toulouse was an ally of the King of France, not a subject as we understand it today. Neither he, nor anyone else in Toulouse, could be arrested by the King of France and tried, executed, fined, or detained. The relationship of Toulouse to France would be not dissimilar to that of an EU state to the Union, or perhaps a NATO member to the Alliance.

> *"Most historians believe that, until the post-crusade settlement of 1229, in most parts of the south, ties of vassalage were weak or non-existent, freemen were generally unwilling to become directly dependent upon a suzerain, and the granting of a fief in return for military service was quite rare. Men did enter into agreements of mutual support, known as convenientiae, but participants saw themselves as equals and not dependents, and would not have interpreted them in anything like the manner that northerners understood oaths of homage and fealty. Such men held their own territories, often centred upon a castrum or fortified town, which they fully intended would be handed down to their descendants. Many of these were allods, quite free of outside encumbrance: even though the proportion was declining, it is estimated that just under 50 per cent of land in the Toulousain was held in this form at the end of the twelfth century.*
>
> *Others were free fiefs, for which relatively few services were owed, sometimes no more than render; even then many were reluctant to comply, as can be seen by Aimery of Montreal's refusal to grant such access to Peter II of Aragon in 1210, although he was in dire need of his help. This pattern was reinforced by the survival of Roman influence in the south, both in law and art. Roman law allowed the free disposal of property rather than insisting on primogeniture which had become increasingly common in Francia during the twelfth century. As a consequence patrimonies were not so much divided as shared; in places the numbers of co-seigneurs could grow to unmanageable proportions."*[393]

It is easy to picture the refusal of the Count of Toulouse to accede to the demands of the King of France as a vassal being disloyal, but this is not the case. The King of France had no rights in Toulouse by any law. Count Raimond would later refuse an offer from the King of Castile which would have protected him from his enemies because it would have granted the right of the King to use any of his castles at will – something common in feudal autocracies, but outrageous by Toulousian standards. It may be seen as emblematic of his status as a Prince that Raimond VI married a former queen who also happened to be the sister of a king, and that his daughter was married to the ing of Navarre.

The City of Toulouse also enjoyed a greater standard of freedom than was common during much of the period. In general, the cities of Languedoc enjoyed considerable independence from their Lords, making them important centers of trade, art, and innovation. The Counts of Toulouse had given, over time, a great deal of authority to the "Capital," or City Council, of Toulouse. Toulouse itself was not a harmonious unit, being divided into two enclaves, City and Bourg, which had their own minor wars.

During his period of occupation, Count Simon Montfort is supposed to have given promises to the citizens of Toulouse which were not kept, taking hostages and extorting money from them. However true this may or may not have been, it is clear that he was an unpopular ruler, had little respect for the Capital, and thus had little traction in Toulouse. While the accounts of his iniquities may have been exaggerated by the anonymous continuator of William of Tudela, the fact that Toulouse opposed him seems to be confirmed by most accounts.

Occitania or the Languedoc Region

Where we use the term Occitania it is with the understanding that it was not current until about a hundred years after the time depicted in the primary initiatory cycle. Despite the ideals voiced by Azalais and Raimond, we must not overly romanticize the period. Outside the territory of cities such as Toulouse, we learn:

> "To outsiders, Languedoc by the late twelfth century was a terrible, lawless place. In1181, for example, Stephen de Tournai, Abbot of St Genevieve de Paris (d.1203), wrote of his journey through Languedoc as 'A journey undertaken, because of the danger from rivers, from bandits and from Coterills, Bascules and Aragonese, more with dread than with joy'. For 'dread' Stephen used the Latin word lethalis, a pun on Lethe, the river of the underworld, stressing the impression that Languedoc was as fearful as Hell itself. He went on to describe the horrors which he had seen in the deserted country through which he travelled, referring to 'the burning of towns and the ruin of homes, where there was nothing safe, nothing relaxing, nothing which did not endanger health and threaten our lives'. The 'burning of towns and the ruin of homes' is usually interpreted as a reference to the ongoing warfare between the counts of Toulouse and Barcelona, but in his list of the special dangers of the journey, however, Stephen left the merely descriptive to give a clue as to what he considered to be the real source of the endemic disorder. According to Stephen, the party in which he was traveling had to deal not only with usual risks to the medieval traveler such as rivers and bandits, but also with 'Coterills, Bascules and Aragonese'; that is, mercenaries. Mercenaries were employed by most if not all of the major lords of Languedoc and were regarded as causing a significant social problem. In 1179, for example, the Count of Toulouse, the Viscount of Béziers and Carcassonne and the Viscount of Nîmes were all excommunicated by the Archbishop of Narbonne for this and other crimes, following the decree of the Third Lateran Council of the Church in the same year, which had laid down excommunication as the penalty for employing them."[394]

With this understanding, it can be considered that the Cathar faith grew both because the area was sufficiently lawless that it was not within the scope of normal organization to impose the law upon them and, because, with their pacifist creed, they offered a sort of stability of the sort attractive to the mercantile class; an alternative to a church that was seen as, for the most part, ineffectual and parasitical. During the early 13th century the Cathars were identified heavily with the nobility and mercantile classes. It is unclear how much support they had among the common people, but the willingness of the regional leadership, both noble and civic, to defend them stemmed from the fact they were often family members and kin.

Within that framework, the narrative of the modern state, however ruthless, as a bearer of civil peace and prosperity must be given some credence. Raimond of Toulouse was not so much tolerant of the Civil Commune of Toulouse and of the Cathars because he was inclined to tolerance, but rather because there was very little he could do about them in any case. Thus, the King of France becomes, however heavy-handed, a force of law and order, imposing peace upon perpetually warring local potentates. Describing the region in the late 12th century, Fredric Cheyette says:

> "Sieges with their squadrons of mercenaries pillaging the countryside gave way to truces, and truces once again to renewed sieges and fresh pillaging; but neither side seemed capable-or perhaps even interested-in inflicting a decisive blow, if such a thing indeed were possible. At this distance, the events seem directionless, the motives-other than the pure joy of battle-obscure. War

became an end in itself. Behind the bare chronicle of marches and treaties and mounting debt....a war pretext was not the same as a war aim; peace was not the norm, with war an exception. The relation was exactly the reverse....another excuse to fill the meadows with tents and horses, and ribs with pennoned lances. Most often such occasions must have occurred deep in the historical shadows, far from the feeble light of our charters and distant chronicles: disputed successions of the far less than great, brothers unable to strike a fair division, sisters promoting claims beyond their dowries, opposing trajectories of those who shared a common castle, families convinced the demands of their overlords violated every canon of truth and justice. Most often these disputes must have disrupted the tranquility of only a handful of parishes. Sometimes, however, through ties of neighborhood, faction, or the accident of alliance, they could escalate to attract the attention of the great and be hastily registered by monastic scribes (and their modern historian successors) as the doings of a truculent and unruly baronage. Then more numerous squadrons of mercenaries and their camp followers took to the roads."[395]

Paratge

In the initiation text we make a good bit of the concept of paratge. The word is ambiguous, but the way that the anonymous continuator uses it certainly makes it clear that it is the opposite of the feudal system of the Frankish Kingdom.

The term paratge has proved untranslatable. In derivation it is the same word as our 'peerage' and has a general meaning of 'equality', of being level with one's peers, that everything is all right because rank and order are decently observed, just as in cases of 'disparagement' (once meaning 'to marry out of one's class') rank is put under threat and society de-stabilised. P.T. Ricketts defines paratge as 'le droit territorial et l'honneur de celui qui le revendique', rights over land and the personal honour of the lord who claims them (see bibliography). Paratge, then, is seriously threatened by the disinheriting of the counts of Toulouse. But the word contains further nuances: Freda White says that in twelfth-century Languedoc 'life was illumined by a quality the troubadors called parage. That word... included food for all, festal games and dances, fine clothes and good manners, kindness and the sweetness of life. Above all it meant poetry' (Freda White, 1964, West of the Rhône, Faber, p. 64.). William and the Anonymous might be slightly surprised by this definition, but they would recognise 'illumined' and agree that paratge was a rich and joyful word.[396]

The Conception of Family among Medieval Nobles

It is important in considering these figures to recall that "family" is a very different concept in this period. Children were often raised away from their families for long periods of time. The future Count Raimond VII had apparently been educated in Paris by the eminent theologian Master Geoffrey of Poitiers, who was a regent master at Paris by 1221. William of Tudela tells us, "The count of Toulouse sent for his son because the crusading lords, Raymond's friends from Paris and that neighborhood, wanted to see the boy. Raymond of Ricaut brought him on a Thursday. The child was good-looking and very well brought up, for Geoffrey of Poitiers had taken great care of him.[397]" It is unclear that Azalais and the future Raimond VI, her brother, were much together as children, and also unclear that she spent much time with her husband who was periodically at war with her brother. On the contrary, Azalais of seems to have had her own regionally legendary troubadour court at Burlats. Yet, whether that was a year-round court or a seasonal or sporadic seat is far from clear. Nobles were prone to movement with the seasons.

For those familiar with the Arthurian legend, either through early sources or "Sword in the Stone," it will be remembered that Arthur is depicted not as growing up in his father's court but, rather, as the squire foster brother of Sir Kay. This sort of arrangement was common in the period of the Cathar Wars, and indeed that element of the Arthurian legend is literally tied to the decades of our initiations, the Sword in Stone episode[398] as it appears in Disney and T. H. White being the work of Robert de Boron, writing in French c. 1195-1210. Boron was in service to Count Gauthier I de Montfaucon, a Burgundian.

Clearly this could lead to estrangement. Count Baldwin, the brother of Raimond VI and the youngest son of Raimond V, was apparently left in custody of his mother and raised in Paris. When Baldwin originally arrived from Paris, Raimond denied that he was his brother and sent him back to Paris to get proof of his identity. William of Tudela, who was in service to Baldwin said that "Raymond had never much liked him or been willing to give him a brother's share or do him honour in his court."[399] However, his point of view may have been biased. In May 1211, Baldwin took himself and Bruniquel over to the crusading side and fought on the side opposite his brother, Raimond VI, and King Peter II of Aragon at the key battle of Muret. Baldwin was given some small castles by Simon Montfort, but was kidnapped by Roger Bernard, son of the count of Foix, who wanted to hang him "since he had been present on the other side at the battle of Muret." We are told that Raimond "hesitated for a few days until, more resigned than revengeful, he acquiesced to the execution of his brother."[400] These differences may be multi-generational. The difference between Raimond VI and his brother Baldwin may be seen as a reflection of the differences between Raimond V and Constance which led to her asking to be allowed to return to Paris in letters to her brother the King.

Likewise, the role of illegitimate children needs to be understood in light of the period. Medieval law was generally informed by imperial Roman law which recognized two categories of illegitimacy. *Spurius* was the designation for children who were the result of illegal unions; the result of incest or adultery. *Naturalis* was the designation, broadly, for children whose parents could have married but did not.[401] These definitions wavered but, given the definition of Indie, the illegitimate child of Raimond V, as a "natural child," it is likely that Occitan custom at the time considered the child to be in the higher of the two classes of legitimacy provided the mother was unmarried. Other terms were used, including the term *nothus*,[402] which distinguished children of unions between nobles and non-nobles or, at least, non-gentry. The rigid definition of nobility that comes to mind from modern peerage guides must be modified to include a variety of families in different contexts.

Being the illegitimate child of a significant noble was a social multiplier. Illegitimate children of major nobles were knights at the very least, and might expect to have some minor castle settled upon them. When captured by the Cruasders, Raimond VI's illegitimate son, Bertrand, was forced to pay a ransom of a thousand shillings, as well as "all his armour; they got his horse, his arms and equipment and everything else he possessed,"[403] a wealthy sum in equipment and money by contemporary standards.

Victorian drama in which illegitimate children are a shame to be hidden away may color thinking about their role. Instead, they should be thought of as "reliable second tier family;" people whose identity depended on their family affiliation and could be considered exceptionally loyal. Illegitimate children were a "second best" offer in marriage as well, a way to tie vassals – even those of some rank – to one's family. Some illegitimate children, particularly *naturalii*, did particularly well; the illegitimate son of King Pedro I of Portugal was elected King by the Assembly in preference to Ferdinand of Castile in 1385.

Apparent Catholicism

The Cathar Wars are a confusing situation because they were not a fight of Cathars against Christians. The Cathars were nonviolent and not very numerous. Nearly every lord who fought on the Cathar side was, at least nominally and outwardly, Roman Catholic. The closest we come to actual Cathars is where some of the secular lords had Cathar-professed relatives, such as Esclarmonde de Foix. While we can assume that some Cathar *credentes* fought against the Crusaders, they too may have presented themselves principally as Catholics.

There is even some confusion over who the Cathars were. We know the details of the organized Cathar heresy mostly from accusations of its enemies and forced confessions. We do know that it wasn't limited to Gnostics in the mold of Esclarmonde de Foix. Contemporary documents said that the region was rife with "Arians, Manichaeans, and Waldensians (or Lyonnais)."[404] Not every heretic was a Cathar, but we can still discern the outline of an organized Gnostic faith which was the one most hated by the Papal authorities.

There are no surviving writers who present themselves as Cathars, and few major figures. The worldly and violent knights who protected the Cathars certainly were not themselves Cathar clergy, though they may have been *credentes*, or believers. The figures we identify as Cathar from among the nobility are usually women, like Esclarmonde de Foix. Not expected to fight and past childbearing years, they could aspire to that position which has been described by historians as *Perfecti*, though the Cathars themselves probably did not use that term.

The situation with Catholicism is confusing. Raimond VI presented himself as a Catholic. He died excommunicate, but made appeals to the Pope, was driven naked and scourged in penance, and is supposed to have asked for the coat of the Knights Hospitaller, rather than the Cathar *consolamentum* on his deathbed. In the initiations, Azalais of Burlats is presented, at least near the end of her life, as Cathar-accepting and Catholic rejecting, though she was perhaps not quite either. Where she is not acting as an avatar of Thelema, she still seems to be something more, manifesting a Troubadour faith based in beauty which transcends either belief. Other writers have presented her as an ardent Catholic.

The fighting was universally between Crusaders and those who refused to give up Cathar heretics to certain death, whether because they were noble relatives or because they were respected citizens of a given town. The matter was forced by the Crusaders. Had it been merely a matter of the locals professing faith, the Crusades would probably have had to turn around and go home. Indeed, on numerous occasions lords or citizens professed Catholicism and then returned to heresy.

In most cases, we have no firm knowledge of the actual disposition of Raimond VI or Raimond Roger of Foix towards Catharism. Were they Catholics who simply tolerated Cathars as they did Jews through a general embrace of the Christian message of charity and lack of zeal to fight on behalf of anything other than their land rights? Did they take a "check both boxes" approach? Were the usually strict Cathar leaders somewhat more obliging towards those who, after all, were the sole reason they were able to exist? Clearly the Cathars allowed for a great deal of secrecy when warranted.

No one who ventured into the Crusader Kingdoms could realistically doubt that heretics of many stripes could co-exist with Catholics who looked to Rome. In addition to the Eastern Church, which had been outcast since the Great Schism, there were several variants of Christianity which were all heretical by the standards of Rome, yet they were not the enemy. It is entirely possible that this alone drove a policy of laissez-faire. If Maronite Christians were tolerated in the Levant, what harm was there in tolerating Jews and Cathars?

Likewise, the Troubadour movement was, in conception, dangerously close to paganism. It can be seen, in many ways, as a harbinger of the Renaissance. When we learn of Benoit de Sainte-Maure's *The Romance of Troy*, there is an embedded message. Despite Jeanne's disclaimer, classical paganism was already a strong influence in the intellectual culture of the region. It is possible that many of the nobles of the region, at least when in good health and far from the point of a sword, considered themselves somewhat too worldly for the inner profession of religion, regardless of what outside form they may have been obliged to demonstrate, and it is that outside form which interests us. Was Raimond's conspicuous deathbed profession of faith sincere? Having taken the consolamentum would not, in principle keep him from being draped in Hospitaller colors, nor were the Hospitallers, whom he had long patronized, in any position to refuse him the honor. The appearance of deathbed reconciliation might have been based in hope of papal indulgence clearing a path to heaven. Just as likely, it was an effort to ensure there was no pretext to disinherit his son, Raimond VII. Jeanne of England's choice locations to give birth is often presented as a pilgrimage away from her husband. Instead, it was a movement towards her recently bereaved family. Her move to take holy orders was only on her deathbed, with a race to find clergy from whom she could take vows before her imminent death.

We see a similar thread in the work of William of Tudela, who is described as supportive of the crusades.[405] He is a cleric himself but there is "much moral and metaphoric ambiguity in his attitude to the crusaders. He was always trying to sing his way through events that seemed dictated by a providence too brutal to be completely benign."[406] He talks of his rather important scholastic friends in Paris and owes his livelihood to the Church, yet he seems a far less than enthusiastic promoter of the Crusade. It is important to remember that *Song* is a politically complex piece presented to sophisticated audiences. It is hard to tell at this remove where he may be covertly ironic.

If William of Tudela is not completely on board, his anonymous continuator has the flavor of a reporter from an authoritarian state who clearly disapproves of the dictator's agenda, but can only criticize it through praise so effusive on one hand as to be sarcastic and so lukewarm on the other as to damn with faint praise. He was living at a time when Catharism itself is in decline. It is hard to tell if he was genuinely indifferent to its beliefs or simply unwilling to go any further in his praise than lauding the spirit of those who fought against the Crusade, and that only with due reflections on them being Good Catholics, loyal to the Pope, and so forth.

Of all of the Principals in our initiations, only Esclarmonde openly professed the Cathar faith on the record. Yet the issue was not only one of local rights. It may have been that Raimond VI could not root out heretics in Toulouse because he lacked true authority there, but it would not have prevented him from carrying out arrests and show-trials elsewhere in his realm. He clearly had no interest in persecution. To have the discernment which set them above the credulous who saw a divine mission in burning heretics shows some divergence from the norm of the day, whether through the influence of a crypto-pagan Troubadour culture, or simply a worldly tolerance of those who differed from themselves. Yet if we cannot allege that the Principals were Gnostic sympathizers, it is also the case that no historical records in which they proclaim Catholicism create an indisputable proof of their actual sympathies or personal spirituality.

Troubadours and Jongleurs

A final note on the culture of the time concerns *troubadours* and *jongleurs*. The terms are often used somewhat interchangeably. A troubadour was a literate noble who wrote and composed poetic song or verse, sometimes also writing in prose. Troubadours might perform their own work if they had sufficient talent, but might also turn it over to a jongleur – a performer who played and sang. Troubadours were often minor nobility, but some of the great nobles of the period such as King Alfonso of Aragon were known for their skill at composing verse.

A significant element of the troubadour culture is that it pushed a secular entertainment. While the northern French chanson de geste had begun to develop a secular tradition of literature and entertainment, the troubadour culture, particularly that which centered around the Court of Henry II and Eleanor of Aquitaine, was the kernel of most of the stories we recognize from the middle ages. In particular, the development of the Arthur cycle from historical recollections and Welsh legend to the cycle still recognizable today onscreen occurred during this time period.

Women were less common as troubadours, but educated women were not uncommon in the region and there are a number of notable female troubadours or *trobairitz*, of who Azalais de Porcairagues (not to be confused with Azalais of Toulouse) is probably the best known. To be identified as a *trobairitz* was a matter to some extent of wide recognition. It is likely that Azalais of Toulouse, Esclarmonde de Foix, and other literate and educated women of the time may have tried their hand at verse without having created a formidable enough body of work to be best known for their compositions.

A Brief Summary of the Cathar Wars through 1215

Rivalries in Occitania

Prior to the Cathar Crusades, there had been considerable rivalry in the region. The Trencavel family, which held Beziers and Carcassone, was, except for a brief period, allied with the King of Aragon against the Count of Toulouse, though they had originally been Toulousian vassals. The Counts of Foix were slowly being positioned by the King of Aragon to replace the Trencavel, whom he considered weak. Increasing political tensions after 1197 led to Raimond VI apparently reversing many of the policies of his father and seeking alliance with Aragon. Following the death of Jeanne Plantagenet, he married Eleanor of Aragon, daughter of King Alfonso II and Sancha of Castile with the intent of ending disputes between Aragon and Toulouse but this did not lead to intensely warm relations between Raimond VI and his nephew, the Raimond Roger Trencavel, Count of Beziers and Carcassone.

A series of increasingly tense diplomatic disputes resulted in the excommunication of Raimond VI for support of heresy and a series of other charges, including charging unfair tolls. The Pope's legate, Pierre de Castelnau, expected answers and when he met with Raimond VI in 15 January 1208 and Raimond VI wasn't able to satisfy him. With the excommunication still in force, one of Raimond's retainers conspired to ambush and assassinate Castelnau. The Pope was convinced that Raimond VI was behind the crime, but the facts have never been firmly established. Given the Count's general inclinations toward negotiation, it seems likely to have been the rash action of a sympathizer.

The Crusade Begins

What Raimond VI thought didn't matter. The crime was enough for the Pope to declare a Crusade against heresy in the region and, by September 1208, Arnaud Amalric, a Cistercian abbott, had been named as the leader of a Crusade. The military action would not shape up until the following spring, but the die was cast and the Holy War begun.

Raimond VI sided, originally, with the Crusaders. Already under threat of excommunication, he treated furiously with the Pope and submitted to the Pope's representative, Milo. This was not the easy submission of a great Lord playing politics. Raimond was publicly humiliated. After being forced to surrender several castles into custody "on Thursday, 18 June 1209, a naked Raimond VI was led by Milo through the streets of Saint-Gilles in a final act of repentance."[407] It has been generally suggested that Raimond VI played politics, using the Crusade to attack his

Trencavel nephew. In fact, "the count rode fast to his nephew the viscount [Raimond-Roger Trencavel, Viscount of Beziers and Carcassone] and begged him not to attack him; let them stand together in defence and avert their own and their country's destruction. But instead of Yes the viscount answered No. They parted on bad terms and the count rode away in anger..."[408]

Raimond VI seems to have understood the inevitability of the Papacy. He was clearly no enthusiast for the Crusade, nor was his willingness to play along driven by smugness. Rather than vacillation, we see increasingly desperate attempts to compromise while minimizing conflict. Paying lip service to Rome had worked in the past, and Raimond was willing to bend as long as it didn't mean betrayals he wouldn't, or couldn't, accomplish. Certainly he hoped to play the Crusaders, but only as an alternative to what was doubtless a dearer wish they had never come around at all.

The Crusade's first destination was the lands of Raimond-Roger Trencavel. They laid siege to Beziers. When it would not surrender, it was stormed and the inhabitants massacred. If people who are not historians know a single fact about the Cathar Wars, they probably know the words of the Papal Legate Arnaud Almalric: "Kill them. For the Lord knows who are His." [409] [410] Likely, the words weren't his, though the sentiment may not have been far from his mind. The words come from an account of the event by Caesarius of Heisterbach a few years later. "The passage in question reads as follows: 'Knowing from confessions of these Catholics that they were mixed up with heretics, they [the crusaders] said to the abbot[Arnald Amalric]: What shall we do, lord? We cannot tell the good from the bad. The abbot, as well as others, fearing that as they were in such great fear of death they [the heretics] would pretend to be Catholics, and after they had left again return to their perfidy, is said to have said (fertur dixisse): Kill them. For God knows who are his. Thus innumerable persons were killed in that city'"[411] Barber notes that while the exact words are unlikely, "Caesarius was, like Arnald Amalric, a Cistercian, and therefore may have had some knowledge of this, particularly as his reference to the role of Conrad of Vrach as legate (1220-24) shows that he was not writing later than 1224"[412]

It should be noted that the attack on Beziers was actually instigated by irregular troops according to William of Tudela, a cook, and kitchen boys.[413] The knights forced the original looters to give up their loot and, in return, the low ranking servants who had won the town put it to the torch. This account is borne out in Arnaud Almalric's contemporary letter to the Pope, and it seems likely Almalric did not intend a general massacre. He showed no profound regrets either, and certainly the policy of massacring garrisons that refused to surrender was employed later in the Crusade.

That said, it is clear that the spirit of the words was the driving spirit of the Crusade, and adequately embodied in its new leader Simon Montfort.

> *"Two heretics were brought before the Count, one a 'perfected' heretic and the other a sort of 'novice' and a disciple of the first one...After taking counsel the Count decided that they should be burnt. The second heretic — the disciple — was seized with heartfelt grief; he began to show contrition and promised that he would freely forswear heresy and obey the Holy Roman Church in all things. A heated discussion arose amongst our people when they heard this; some said that now that he was prepared to do what we had told him to, he ought not to be condemned to die, others maintained that on the contrary he deserved death*
>
> *The Count [Simon Montfort, ed.] agreed that he should be burnt, taking the view that if his contrition was genuine, the fire would serve to expiate his sins; if he was lying, he would receive a just reward for his perfidy."*[414]

Even if the event never happened, what may be more important is the Peter of Vaux-Cernay thought it did, or wanted others to believe it did. In this case the lucky heretic was not burned by the fire, but because of the intervention of God. It's clear that Vaux-Cernay and approved of the Count's decision

Attempts to Negotiate

Raimond VI remained with the Crusade through the first summer. However, the city of Toulouse, which was run by its Civic Commune and Consuls and over which he had very little real control, was approached to surrender its heretics. The leaders declined and were excommunicated. Raimond visited the Pope and left reasonably satisfied that he had defused the situation, then visited Arles to speak with the Holy Roman Emperor and Paris to speak with the King. "The first was politely indifferent, the second overtly inimical."[415]

Raimond entered the war slowly. He could not meet the demands made by the Papal Legates to lift his excommunication, but proposed a number of degrading half measures, including placing all of his lands except Toulouse into a sort of trust with the Crusaders. By this time his recalcitrant nephew, Raimond-Roger Trencavel, was dead. He had belatedly tried to come to the Crusader side along with his uncle and been denied. The Pope forced the Crusaders to accept Raimond VI, but they had their sights on spoils and, without Raimond-Roger Trencavel to fight, there would be no cities to loot. Taken prisoner at a parley at Carcassone, he was imprisoned and died two months later. Raimond Roger of Foix was already actively fighting the Crusaders. He, too, had been given no choice. Branded as a defender of heretics, his possessions were attacked and sacked.

Raimond VI's immediate action was a year of activity in which he underwent repeated humiliations in a vain attempt to reconcile with the Catholic Church without giving up the City of Toulouse. In the meantime, King Peter of Aragon had begun negotiating with various local lords to defend against the Crusaders, not out of any particular interest in heresy, but rather a feeling that the principal effect of the crusade had been to strip him of his vassals. As late as January 1211, Raimond was still meeting with the Pope's representatives and the Crusaders in an attempt to reconcile. The Papal Legate instead heaped on new demands.[416]

Raimond Forced to Fight

Raimond VI's first actual military action against the Crusade was a self-inflicted wound. He evacuated and burned one of his own strategic castles to deny its use to the Crusaders. When Simon marched on Toulouse, Raimond VI went out in force to try a final parley. Simon believed he was on the march for a fight and launched a surprise attack that drove him to the gates of Toulouse. This led to the first abortive siege after which Simon, unable to breach Toulouse, harried the lands of the Count and city. However, the siege made Raimond VI's decision. During the late summer and fall he mustered an army to march against Simon Montfort and the Crusade.

Raimond VI was unsuccessful at capturing Simon in a brief siege of his seat at Castelnaudary, but most of the castles and towns won by Simon rebelled against him during the fall and winter. Reinforced, Simon captured them back during the summer. He then imposed draconian rules which changed regional inheritance laws to those of the Frankish realm around Paris and forbid local widows who were in possession of castles from marrying local men, though they were allowed to marry Frenchmen. It was the first attempt at a "cleansing" aimed at the destruction not only of heresy, but of the regional identity.[417]

By 1213, the King of Aragon had taken a hand. He met with the Church leaders and Raimond VI while sending representatives to the Pope, and wanted a deal for peaceful reconciliation. The Pope, after some initial sympathy, doubled down in support of his representatives, but his hesitance and a call for an initial Crusade led to few new additions to Simon Montfort's Crusader army. Raimond VI began a small offensive and, when it proved successful, the King of Aragon, who had moved his forces to Toulouse, marched to destroy Simon Montfort, resolving to besiege him at Muret with Raimond VI and the Count of Foix. They even expected aid from King John of England, but he conveniently ducked his obligations. Simon elected to defend Muret. Raimond VI counseled a defensive posture, but the King of Aragon had enough and wanted to go on the offensive. At the end of the day, his much larger force was shattered and the King himself dead "naked in a field of naked bloody bodies."[418]

Simon wasn't left with enough strength to take Toulouse, but Raimond VI no longer had a strong enough force to challenge him. Raimond or his vassals raided Simon's new territories, while Simon made peace with the Count of Foix and others. Raimond spent Christmas in England at the court of his former brother-in-law, King John, and returned with ten thousand marks for his attempt to regain his lands. The summer of 1214 saw chaotic small scale combat, but by the end of the year Raimond had not made a great deal of headway and Simon had been confirmed by the Pope as Count of the lands he had captured.

The Fourth Lateran Council

By January of 1215, Raimond VI was in Rome at the Fourth Lateran Council to plead the case for the restoration of his lands. By then, he was in firm alliance with the Count of Foix and the two of them attended the Council together. A final judgment was not issued until Monday, the 14th of December. The Count was deprived of his realm and forced to live outside of it. Simon Montfort seized Toulouse on the Pope's authority and required oaths of fealty from the Council, then began work dismantling the city's defenses and tearing down the fortified houses of the city's urban nobles and wealthy burghers. He was invested by the King of France in April of 1216 with all the lands he conquered including "the Trencavel territories that were never part of the French domain."[419]

Pope Innocent died suddenly in summer of 1216, leaving a questionable legacy:

> *Historians have variously defined the twelfth century as a "renaissance," a "reformation," and a "revolution." It was the century—usually defined as "the long twelfth century" and so beginning and ending with a certain temporal elasticity—when the medieval world achieved cultural coherence around particular ideas and practices. Innocent III and his policies highlight the fragility of such claims. An intellectual edifice was certainly constructed in the century before the crusade, along with a sweeping archipelago of monasteries and churches, but beneath those notional towers and outside those cloistered walls, most ordinary Christians lived and worshipped in vastly differing ways. We must always be wary of mistaking what intellectuals say a world was like for the reality of that world. Innocent III understood this and set out from the beginning of his papacy to remake Christendom in His coherent and unified image—and he did this especially through the Albigensian Crusade and the Fourth Lateran Council. The effects of the council would take a century to be wholly realized; the consequences of the crusade were immediate.* [420]

This was a lynch-pin moment in history for those of us who do not see Western thought and Christianity as inseparable, and underscores the importance of this era. Prior to this point European Christianity may not have been pagan, but it was local and retained ancient ties to its roots. This began the period of cleansing during which the individuality and local expression of Christianity was wiped away in favor of the monolithic uniformity emanating from the Roman Clergy. The Cathars and other Occitan heretics represent a final stand against

Catholicism. It is easy to see a victory for uniformity. It would be three centuries until 1517 when the increasingly top heavy Roman Church was rent by the schism that would forever limit its power.

Yet the very knowledge that the Church had to repress Cathars kept the memory of an alternative to Christianity alive. The Church may have meant to send the message that nothing which defied orthodoxy could survive, but implicit in the story of the Church's attempt to crush heresy was the clear message that it had thrived in the first place. The Orthodox Catholic point of view, embodied in the writing of Peter de Vaux Cernay, was that heresy was a creeping poison which, if not cut out quickly, could destroy Christ's kingdom on Earth. That message fired warriors to fight for the Church, but it also empowered those who had reason to struggle against it. If heresy was so dangerous, it must represent a potent weapon at bringing down the edifice that was the all powerful Roman Church. As the Roman Church was co-opted more strongly to the agenda of national rulers, that message remained. Luther and other first generation Protestants did not see themselves as heretics, but as purifiers, maintaining a pure faith against Papal corruption. Yet there was an early attempt to identify Cathars and other heretics as proto-protestants, not least because they had struggled with some success against the Roman Catholic Church.

Raimond VI Reclaims Toulouse

The Pope's final refusal and humiliation of Raimond VI set up the endgame. He refused the dictates of the Church and, traveling to Genoa, met his son Raimond VII. Simon Montfort's position was untenable. He could raise a great army with the support of Papal promises to attack heretics, but no power extended to levying men for his own defense. His loot had deepened his pockets, but conquest was notoriously expensive.

The "young Count" marched up the Rhone gathering supporters and seizing his birthplace, the city of of Beaucaire. A group of French knights supporting Simon was trapped in the Castle, while Raimond VII held the town. Simon came to their relief, but could not dislodge Raimond VII. Local lords and peasants, including archers from Marseilles, arrived to support the son of the rightful count. Simon's forces were too small to stop the reinforcements. Simon was forced to lift the siege in return for the lives of the knights trapped in the castle. Raimond VII was in Aragon and Catalonia gathering mercenaries and anyone who had a grudge from Muret. Simon's next action sealed his fate. He returned to Toulouse angry.

> "'We shall return to Provence when we have silver,' he told his men, 'but first we shall destroy Toulouse and leave nothing beautiful or good inside it. They have robbed me of Provence and they shall pay for its recovery!' His brother tried to dissuade him. Folc de Maselha attempted to calm him and 'blunt the sharp edge of steel with silver.' Simon demanded 30,000 marks from the city and the bourg. 'Pay up,' growled French lads, knocking on doors in every parish, 'or else be tortured!' The churches were looted, the synagogue ransacked (there were about five hundred Jews in the city), and the four leprosaria robbed. Peire de Yspania, a modest merchant who owned some houses and shops in the bourg near the public baths, fled to Saint-Sernin for protection. Upon returning to his properties, he found them forfeited to Simon—they were worth 200 shillings—along with his 'good leather coat, leather helmet, iron hat,' bows, arrows, 'and all grain and wood.'"[421]

It wasn't merely a matter of extortion to get the money he needed to raise an army. Even if we agree that the anonymous continuator has a lopsided point of view, the historical record attests that Simon was tyrannical enough to provoke an uprising. Barricades went up. Simon demanded hostages, money, and destruction.

Great and small ran screeching through the ruined streets and, picking up clubs and applewood cudgels, bludgeoned to death every Frenchman they found. 'Today the false lord must go! And all his family and all his evil race!' The terrified crusaders retreated into the Chateau Narbonnais."

The Second Siege of Toulouse

By the time Raimond VI crossed the Pyrenees in August, Simon was sacking villages along the Rhone. He entered Toulouse without resistance and setting up a camp near Saint Semin organized the resistance. Despite holding the Narbonnais Castle, Simon's men could not take the city of Toulouse and laid down a siege, setting up winter quarters in a "New Toulouse;" a temporary Crusader town hung around some houses in the shelter of the castle. Both sides made siege machines. It is in this environment that our II° takes place. Simon made a huge siege tower, called in period slang a "cat," which a troubadour named Raimon Escrivan (literally just "Raimon the Writer,") immortalized in a little song about the battle between Trebuchet and Cat.

> *"That made the Trebuchet's hairs stand on end, for he is fierce and strong, cruel and true, and he said, 'Miserable Lady Cat, you will need that tough skin, because you will not escape!' And he sent her a flaying missile that not even three ribuats could have picked up, and he shot it, hot, into her body, and that made everyone happy and glad."*[422]

The more grotesque descriptions of brain and blood in the initiatory script are largely taken verbatim from *Song of the Cathar Wars*. The level to which period song rivaled modern true crime drama in vivid detail and garish delight in gore cannot be overstated. Of the struggle to drive Montfort's men from Toulouse, we are told:

> *"Both sides with furious hatred attacked any enemy they could find: lances and swords, spear-hafts and stumps, arrows, stones, clubs, firebrands, shafts and halberds, blades and pennons, pikes, wooden beams, rocks, planks and quarrels flew fast on every side, shattering shields, helms and saddlebows, shattering skulls and brains, chests, chins, arms, legs, fists and forearms."*[423]

It is rare for history's persecutors to get their comeuppance, but on 25 June 1218 it happened. Simon Montfort, leading the siege of Toulouse was killed by a siege engine:

> *There was in the town a mangonel built by a carpenter and dragged with its platform from Saint Semin. This was worked by noblewomen, by little girls and men's wives, and now a stone arrived just where it was needed and struck Count Simon on his steel helmet, shattering his eyes, brains, back teeth, forehead and jaw. Bleeding and black, the count dropped dead on the ground.*
>
> *Jocelyn and Sir Aimery galloped to him at once and hurriedly covered him with a blue cape; but panic spread. How many knights and barons you would have heard lamenting, weeping under their helmets and crying out in anger! Aloud they exclaimed, 'God, it is not right to let the count be killed! How stupid to serve you, to fight for you, when the count who was kind and daring, is killed by a stone like a criminal! Since you strike and slay your own servants, there's no work for us here any more!'*

The Crusade collapsed for the year by July and, while following years would bring new upheavals and, ultimately, the extermination of any visible sign of the Cathar church, the triumph of the city of Toulouse would not be completely erased, nor would Count Simon's heirs ever hold that territory.

The Cathar Period Principals of the Initiations

Raimond VI Count of Toulouse

Count Raimond VI of Toulouse came from a preeminent family of the Languedoc. While we may associate the title of "Count" with a position of lesser nobility, it originates from the Roman "Comes," the title for a provincial governor.

Chivalrous Noble or Depraved Monster?

We have two pictures of Raimond VI that have come down through history. One is of an intelligent, thoughtful and considerate nobleman who had a general dislike of war, was highly respectful of the rights of the civic commune of Toulouse, and generally respected. The author of the first part of *Song of the Cathar War*, William of Tudela, has some obvious animosity towards Raimond VI. William was in service to Raimond's brother and there was bad blood between the two. Nevertheless he speaks of him respectfully. His anonymous continuator was far more of a partisan towards Raimond and was probably a member of his Court. To both of them he is "The valiant count of Toulouse," always spoken of respectfully and seldom capable of doing wrong.

The other is of a monster with abysmal manners who loved heresy and engaged in near constant debauchery. This is the image we get from Peter of Vaux de Cernay of *Historia Albigensis*. Peter is unabashedly partisan against the Cathars and their defenders. His uncle, Guy, Bishop of Carcassone, was one of those who was brought in by Simon Montfort to preach against the Cathars, and Peter owed his position to Simon. Peter had crusaded with Simon and was likely a personal acquaintance.

If the work of the anonymous continuator of *Song of the Cathar War* is somewhat of a romanticist, Peter reads like a tabloid, with headings such as "Malice of Count Raimond de Toulouse, instigator of the Albigensians."

> *"Always he acted as a limb of the, Devil; a son of perdition, an enemy of the cross, a persecutor of the Church, the defender of heretics, the oppressor of the Catholic faithful, the servant of treachery, forswearer of his word, replete with crime, a veritable treasury of all sins."*[424]

The accusations of Pierre run the gamut from amusing to deadly: Raimond brought a jester to Mass to mock the officiant. He was friends with and refused to punish a notorious heritic, Hughes Fabri, who had once defecated upon a church altar and used the cloth to wipe himself. From his childhood he was mostly interested in sleeping with the concubines of his father, "Again, from early youth he lost no opportunity to seek out his father's concubines and felt no compunction about bedding them — indeed none of them could please him unless he knew his father had previously slept with her. So it came about that his father frequently threatened to disinherit him, for this enormity as much as for his heresy."[425] He was a friend to highwaymen or mercenaries who he employed to rob the churches.[426] One day while playing chess with the Chaplain he denied God.[427] Pierre even faults Raimond for his marriages, one of which, to Bourgogne, the daughter of Ammiry King of Cyprus, may or may not have actually occurred.[428] Other charges show Raimond in a light that is positive by modern standards. He employed Jews in official roles,[429] a strong sign of a tolerant disposition and a secular disdain for religious fanaticism.

The anecdotes often seem rather trivial, but they are revealing. That Raimond was playing chess with a Chaplain, or appearing at Mass at all suggests he was not the bellicose opponent of the Roman Church that Peter paints him. That he may have said words of offense or defended those who made jokes, or even engaged in defacements at the expense of the Church seems possible as well. Perhaps he didn't consider the Church case credible, or perhaps those incidents happened at times when he was already on the outs with the local Bishop and not inclined to do him any favors. As with Raimond-Roger, one of the accusations against Raimond VI was tolerance of Jews and their employment in official positions.[430]

As extreme as the charges are, it seems unlikely that they are entirely groundless. Certainly the core charge that Raimond kept company with heretics must be true. As noted in "The Cathar Principals," when he was dispossessed of his Palace at Toulouse, Raimond found refuge at the house of the Roaix family,[431] which served as the principal Cathar House in Toulouse and the likely seat of its Cathar Bishop.

It is easy to assume that *Historia Albigensis* is nothing more than a set of calumnies with little basis in meaningful fact. Certainly, in our modern experience with social media, we have learned that it is possible to create legends from whole-cloth, yet the very bizarre nature of the anecdotes tends to suggest they are at least a sincere repeating of gripes. If the point were merely to make up atrocities and attribute them to Raimond VI, why not make up stories of murder or pillage? Instead, multiple lines are given to an anecdote about hiring a jester to mock a priest. The reason is clear enough: they were genuine anecdotes which Peter had heard. He specifies that the tale about Fabri's defecation was told by "The Abbot of Citeaux, who had by then become Archbishop of Narbonne, described these abominations to the bishops ~ about twenty in number — attending the Council of Lavaur, where I was present."[432] Whether the allegation was true or not, it was certainly reported in his presence. So we can be reasonably sure that, whether or not it was true, the rumor that Raimond VI was involved in sexual relations with Azalais was plausibly circulated at the time. Most historians give no credit to the idea because no other chroniclers mention it. Conversely no other chronicler has the grocery store scandal-sheet tone of *Historia Albigensis*. It could be argued that they also do not mention Fabri's defecations, yet there is no particular cause to doubt that something of the sort happened, though under what circumstances it would be hard to say.

Incest between Raimond and Azalais

Probably the most notable charge in the *Historia Albigensis* is that Raimond had sexual relations with his sister Azalais. "The Count was a vicious and lecherous man to the extent that —we can take it as an established fact — he abused his own sister as a way of showing contempt for the Christian religion."[433] We deal with this charge at some length since it forms part of the canon of our initiations. It should be stressed that this is not the Christian Church and literal belief in the stories told in the initiations is not an article of faith. Many things about the portrayal could be understood as mythological rather than historical. Nevertheless, the inclusion makes the subject worth discussing, and we should start by saying that there is no proof that this was ever the case.

The issue of his incest is of a different magnitude from accusations of casual heresy while playing chess. Where illegitimacy was not a major concern, incest – particularly close incest – may well have been. Children of such unions would have been *Spurii* or worse. The Church had been preoccupied with incest for the last six centuries, most probably as part of an ongoing drive to curb the power and prerogatives of the great regional lords and corral them to the Church, which was a vast secular land-owner. Until 1215, marriage had been prohibited within eight degrees of consanguinity. The Fourth Lateran Council, where Raimond VI, his son, and Raimond-Roger of Foix were incidentally on hand to plead the case for the restoration of their lands, lowered it to Four Degrees. Many great lords ignored the prohibition, though it was a frequent reason to discard wives that had become inconvenient. For example, after having five children, Raimond V was still able to have his marriage to Constance terminated on the grounds of being related within prohibited degrees. Yet, while dispensations could be had for cousin marriage, particularly outside the first degree, brother-sister arrangements seem to have been out of bounds for even the most corrupt of popes. The accusation certainly does not prove the thing happened, merely that it was alleged, and that the allegation was not so implausible as to result in instant disbelief.

There are interesting an unexplained historical issue. It is unclear how close Azalais and her brother were. Azalais' son, Raimond Roger Trencavel, was an infrequent visitor to the Court of Raimond VI and, on at least one occasion after his mother's death, rather rude. Visiting his uncle's Court in 1204, "he behaved badly and aroused considerable hostility while he was there;" the historical record being borne out in the castigation of a troubadour for his behavior.[434] Yet we have no sense of whether that was a final family explosion at the end of a long string of awkward holiday visits or a singular occasion, nor do we get a sense of how often Azalais' husband, Roger II Trencavel, might have attended Raimond's Court though, with their near constant warring and Roger's fealty to Alfonso of Provence, it seems unlikely he would have visited frequently. We know that Azalais was of age by 1185 and probably somewhat before. She may well have visited her brother independently, or seen him in the course of other movements about the region.

An interesting note is that Roger II Trencavel originally attempted to disinherit his own child by Azalais. "In 1185, Roger [II Trencavel] proposed the adoption of Alfons, the younger son of Alfons of Aragon, to be his heir and to inherit all his lands.…The record of the adoption is dated to June 1185, which makes Roger's motivation particularly incomprehensible, placing it after the conception, if not the birth, of his own son and eventual heir, Raimond Roger [Trencavel]."[435] While historian Elaine Graham-Leigh creates a somewhat laborious political motive[436] it is not impossible that Roger II Trencavel had misgivings about his child's parentage or, perhaps, his wife's loyalty. Peter of Vaux de Cernay seems more a gossip monger than inventor and, if so, the rumors must have had some origin. The issue could have been one of Azalais' courtiers or King Alfonso himself, but it would seem odd in the latter case to make Alfonso's heir his own. That could put the date of any potential incest at around 1185, though Raimond Roger Trencavel was accepted as the heir without question nine years later when his putative father, Roger II Trencavel, died in 1194. Certainly, the attempt to replace Azalais' child as his heir could have pushed her closer to her brother in the years afterwards as well.

Why did Raimond VI take the Crusader side?

It will be easy for those schooled in the black and white thinking of much of the post-Reagan era to see Raimond VI as vacillating. He was, after all, willing to compromise, humiliate himself, and fight in the Crusades. It would be better to see him in a mold appropriate to Thelemites; of one only willing to break the peace at great provocation.

Raimond was a diplomat and peacemaker. There are more records of his long treks in attempts to reconcile diplomatically than his campaigns in war. His marriages to the daughter of King Alfonso II of Aragon and Sancha of Castile, the Brother of the King Peter of Aragon who fell at Muret, were diplomatic, aimed at bringing unity and ending internecine fighting.

He did not see a winning hand in opposing the Pope, yet at any point he could have simply begun aggressively hanging Waldensians (at least) and rural Cathars. That he refused to engage in such persecutions indicates that he had basic values aligned as the anonymous continuator says with the traditions of paratge and what we would understand as common decency. He was, if anything, a lover not a fighter. Historian Mark Pegg suggests "He continued fighting the crusaders until his death. He played politics relatively well (he was married five times), but, somewhat surprisingly, his bellicose temperament was as brittle as his martial skills were mundane."[437] He is cited as cautious on several occasions, proposing tactics before Muret that might have avoided the disastrous defeat only to be shot down by a rash counterpart[438]; on another occasion criticizing his seneschal and son-in-law, Hughes d'Alfaro, for making an ill-advised sortie. "These men armed themselves privately in their own quarters, but the count of Toulouse almost went out of his mind with rage. Because they were willing to take the risk of making a sortie, he thought they wanted to lose him his inheritance, and he forbade them to go out."[439]

A real image of Raimond VI probably lays somewhere between the two extremes. He was well received at the Court of King John, his former brother-in-law, and left with a sizable payment to help in the restoration of his fortunes. Yet he was certainly a friend to heretics and had little patience with the pretensions of the clergy.

Predecessors of Raimond VI

For purposes of clarity we present Raimond VI's immediate predecessors as Count of Toulouse:

Raimond V(1134 – 1194) - Father

Count of Toulouse from 1148, Raimond V was with his father, Alphonse I of Toulouse, on Crusade when Alphonse died at Caesarea in 1148.

- Established the first assembly of Toulouse, which became the Capital.
- Married Constance the Daughter of Louis VI of France. They had five children, but became estranged and were separated by ecclesiastical authority in 1165.
- During his reign there was a debate at Albi in which his wife, Constance debated against Cathar influenced Heretics.
- In 1178 he asked the Cistercians for help in opposing heresy in his domains, however this may have been primarily a matter of seeking Papal support against King Alfonso II of Aragon.

Raimond V's parting with Constance of France is a matter of interest to us. The two had five children including Raimond VI, and she decamped in 1165 after the Cathar issue had exploded at Lombers. Raimond's detractors imply that he was cruel to her, but she was allowed to leave and her return to Paris was based, not on Raimond detaining her, but the need to receive the permission and possibly means from her brother, the king, to come.

Constance does not complain of any particular ill-treatment, rather that she was cut off "on the day our retainer Simon left me, I left the household and entered the home of a certain knight in the town. For I did not have anything to eat or to give my servants. The count has no concern for me, nor do I receive counsel from him or anything from his land which might be necessary to me. That is why I send to you, begging your highness, that you not believe messengers who are to come to your court if they tell you I am well. My situation is as I tell it. Indeed if I dared to write it to you, I would say more about the harm to me." Unfortunately, her letters do not give her reasons, but rather promise that the bearer, a Knight named Guido, will disclose them, "Since he knows the secrets of my need better than any other man, he will not refuse to expose their truth to you. I pray that you, for the love of God and family piety, help me soon in this. I call God as my witness unless you help me, I am in bad straits and worse will happen in the future."[440] The potential that Constance, who seems to have been an outspoken opponent of Catharism, was repulsed by her husband's harboring of heretics following the declarations at Lombers seems possible. The letters must likely have come after the Council as the two appeared together there.

Alfonso Jordan I (1103-1148) – Grandfather

Count of Toulouse from 1112, also Count of Tripoli 1105-1109.

He was born in Tripoli while his father was taking part in the First Crusade. His half-brother, Betrand, named him as heir to Toulouse, though it was conquered by William of Aquitaine in 1114. Alfonso was:

- Excommunicated by the Pope for expelling monks who had aided his enemies
- Did not stabilize his rule until 1125
- Left for the Second Crusade in 1147 with his son, visiting Italy and Constantinople
- Arrived at Acre in 1148 and died.
- Is widely supposed to have been poisoned by either Queen Melisende of Jerusalem, or Eleanor of Aquitaine.

Raimond IV, 1041-1105 — Great-Grandfather

Count of Toulouse from 1094 who participated in the First crusade, capturing Antioch. He rejected the Kingship of Jerusalem, which was eventually taken by Baldwin I. He was an enormously powerful and divisive figure, involved in numerous intrigues. He devoted considerable time and energy to the siege of Tripoli, but the city did not fall until after his death.

Jeanne of England

The life of Jeanne, or Joan, of England is remarkable and deserves greater coverage than we can provide in a brief summary. Her mother was the equally remarkable Eleanor of Aquitaine, the wife of two Kings that would survive them both to reign as virtual regent over England.

Jeanne was the daughter of King Henry II who controlled a vast territory known to modern historians as the "Angevin Empire." Centered in Anjou, it contained the Crown of England and a vast segment of territory that is modern France. She would have grown up largely at her mother's Court, arguably the most literate and cosmopolitan in the Western World; a center for troubadours and literature.

Sicily was, like England, a Norman state; a conquest started only a few years before the invasion of England in 1066. Jeanne was married to the Norman monarch of Sicily, William II – a wedding prominent enough it necessitated its own special tax. The couple had no surviving child, though there were rumors of a short-lived boy.

Jeanne would first have been exposed to the idea of a mixed religion court in Sicily. Relations between Muslims and Christians in Palermo were friendly and King William had Muslim servants at his court. Recounting the writing of Islamic Traveler Ibn Jubayr, we learn:

> "His pages in particular, from whose ranks he drew his ministers and chamberlains, kept their religion secret, but they were Muslims, Ibn Jubayr insists. The royal cook was too, and the king's tailor; and William II made much use of the services of Muslim doctors and astrologers. Most remarkably, William could read and write Arabic, and his 'alamah', or personal motto, was strikingly Islamic in form and tone: 'Praise be to God. It is proper to praise him.' William's wife could hardly have escaped such influences herself. Indeed, Ibn Jubayr remarks how the Muslim presence at the royal court was more than just male. The 'handmaidens and concubines' of the palace were Muslims, he says, and there were rumours that the Christian ladies who came to the court were converted secretly to Islam by these women. Perhaps this was an exaggeration, but Ibn Jubayr saw for himself how the Christian women of Palermo followed Muslim fashions: they went to church, he says, veiled and 'bearing all the adornments of Muslim women, including jewellery, henna on the fingers, and perfumes'."[441]

Atypically for the time, William II did not attempt to have the marriage annulled for dynastic purposes, instead naming his aunt as his heir. This suggests that Jeanne was not unhappy with the arrangements at the Palermo Court. Upon his death, the throne was seized by his illegitimate cousin, Tancred, who put Jeanne under house arrest. The timing could not have been worse. William II died in 1189 and Jeanne's brother, Richard I, now King of England arrived on his way to the Crusade, demanding her return along with the value of her dowry. When Tancred balked, Richard sacked the city of Messina.

Richard ultimately continued toward Acre with his new bride, Berengaria, who had been brought to Sicily by his mother Eleanor of Aquitaine. Berengaria was placed in Jeanne's care and the two traveled aboard the same vessel. A storm separated the English Fleet and the two were threatened with capture by the putative Emperor of Cyprus, Isaac Comnenus, who also plundered several less fortunate English ships and captured their crews. Richard conquered Cyprus in reprisal, turning the "Emperor" over to the Hospitallers to be imprisoned at Tripoli. He had no use for the island and sold it to the Templars, who mismanaged it badly.

Richard I had other plans for his sister. He proposed that she marry Sayf ad-Din, or Al-Adil, the brother of Salah ad-Din. History records that she balked, however it is not clear that she was shocked at the proposition so much as the potential loss in status. The proposal seems to have been historical, though many of the details of Jeanne's response are probably apocryphal. The account was written by Salah ad-Din's biographer, Baha al-Din, who was told of the negotiations by al-Adil personally and served as messenger to Salah ad-Din. It is reported that al-Adil considered the proposition, even conversion, but ultimately the proposed alliance fell apart.[442]

Jeanne neither married Sayf ad-Din, nor did her brother siege Jerusalem. While he was capable of excessive brutality, Richard was not the hotheaded battle-lover portrayed in media. He spent most of his time "on Crusade" trying to reach a diplomatic solution and won a treaty that allowed the Christians to keep territories he had taken on the coast and to visit Jerusalem. Jeanne had sailed for Italy before the treaty was signed. If she had not minded a court with Muslims, she was happy enough to spend six months as the guest of Pope Celestine at the Lateran Palace, though they appear to have been concerned the Holy Roman Emperor, Frederick, who had taken Richard Prisoner as he returned from Tyre, would seize them as well. They returned by land, escorted first by King Alfonso of Aragon, then by Raimond of Toulouse.

Her marriage was a result of the shifts in diplomacy following the death of Raimond V. It is clear that Raimond VI was more interested in compromise. He quickly agreed to a marriage that ended claims by Richard I on Toulouse going back half a century and began the movement towards peace with Aragon. They were married in 1196. The future Raimond VII was born at Beaucaire in 1197. She is recorded as spending Easter with her brother and husband at Le Mans.[443]

In 1199, she learned that the Lords of Saint-Felix in Lauragais had seized one of Raimond's castles.[444] Not waiting for her husband, she rode out armed to take it back and laid siege to Cassés. Some of her own men betrayed her, smuggling arms into the castle and setting fire to her camp.[445] Jeanne went for help to her brother, and learned he had died of infection from a crossbow bolt which hit him in the shoulder at a siege near Limoges. The final months of Jeanne's life were more complex than the bare recounting in our initiations. Richard I forgave his killer but, depending on legend, it was either his mercenary captain, Mercadier, or Jeanne who had him killed.

> *"Having been seized by Mercadier and sent to her, the story goes, it was on Joan's orders that*
> *the nails of his hands and feet were pulled out, he was blinded and then skinned before, still*
> *breathing, he was drawn by a team of horses. It was behaviour such as this that led the writer of*

> *this graphic account to describe Joan as 'a woman whose masculine spirit transcended the weakness of her sex.'"*[446]

She traveled from Fontrevaud to Normandy, likely to meet with her brother, John, and Eleanor. John gave her a pension and payment for enormous debts which Richard had owed her, quite possibly paid by her husband Raimond VI. Her health seems to have been fine up to the point where she gave birth. The child survived only long enough to be baptized and it was clear Jeanne was fatally ill. She chose to take the veil, and asked for the Prior of Fontrevaud, so instead "she asked the archbishop of Canterbury, Hubert Walter, who was also in Rouen, to administer the vows. Hubert told Joan that she couldn't become a nun while her husband was still alive, but so zealously and fervently did she press her case that he relented and took her vows in the presence of her mother, Queen Eleanor."[447]

Unlike our questions regarding Raimond VI, it is impossible to think that this was not sincere. Only a short time earlier she had been literally fighting Raimond's battles, but on her deathbed Jeanne wanted reconciliation with the Catholic Church. Perhaps her long sojourns in lands rife with heresy cast a chill on her. The climate of the time was such that even the most educated and cosmopolitan people were believers. The zeal shown on her deathbed may be evidence more for, rather than against, the notion that she had lived most of her life with any particular antipathy towards either infidels or heretics.

Azalais of Burlats

The legitimate sister of Raimond VI, daughter of Constance of France.

We have no definitive age for Azalais, other than a presumption she is roughly contemporary with Raimond VI, born in 1156, and that she was definitely born before 1171 when she was married, though she was likely a young child at the time. She did not have her first child until 1185 which indicates that, as customary, her child marriage was symbolic; a sort of heavy duty "betrothal" not consummated until she was an adult.

Unlike Jeanne of England, she is recalled mostly through references from troubadours. Married at an early age to one of her father's rivals, she kept her court at Burlats, which appears to have been nominally her possession. She kept a regionally famous "Court of Troubadours," and patronized a number of notable noble artists of the period.

Issues around the accusation of incest with her brother Raimond VI are covered above in his respective entry.

Her husband, Roger II Trencavel, Count of Beziers and Carcassone, was on poor terms with her father. Her son, Raimond Roger Trencavel, also Count of Beziers and Carcassone, was on scarcely better terms with her brother, yet the same is not necessarily true of her. She was heavily involved with politics of the day and may often have been a go-between, as Eleanor of Aquitaine sometimes was, between warring members of her family.

She was courted by King Alfonso II while already married and can certainly be presumed to have had a number of Troubadour lovers based on their work. The troubadour, Arnaut de Mareuil, depicted Alfonso as a jealous rival. The troubadour Guillem, Viscount of Bergueda, criticizes Alfonso's treatment of Azalais in his work, saying of Alfonso, "she gave you her love, and you took two cities and a hundred castles from her."

Esclarmonde de Foix

The daughter of Roger Bernard I, Count of Foix, she was married to Jourdain III, lord of L'Isle-Jourdain, and had six children. Her brother, Raimond Roger, was Count of Foix through 1223. She is significant in having been elevated to the Cathar equivalent of Priesthood around 1204 by Guilhabert de Castres. She is identified as a "Perfect," though there is some historical question as to whether or not that title existed or was used by the Cathars. She was a "Good Lady" of the Cathars and a religious leader. We do not have any records of a female Cathar Bishop, however the highest of female clergy could perform the consolamentum, the rite which took the place of confirmation and which was usually performed just before death. She is generally credited with approaching Raimond de Perella to rebuild and strengthen Montsegur, and Oldenbourg believes Montsegur was a part of her inheritance.[448] The date and circumstances are unknown.

She is primarily named historically in records pertaining to her brother, Raimond Roger Count of Foix, not to be confused with Raimond Roger Trencavel, Count of Carcassone and Beziers.

There is no historical information that places her in Toulouse during the siege. Likewise, there is none to the contrary. However, her brother Raimond-Roger was Count of Foix and was, by this time, working in close concert with Raimond VI. The two had been in Rome together before the Pope and had both enjoyed the support of the King of Aragon before his death at Muret. It is by no means inconceivable that Esclarmonde accompanied her brother. Her role as a Cathar leader may have called for her presence in the besieged city. In any case, there were other noblewomen present and they were cited as being among those who operated the Mangonel that killed Simon Montfort on 25 June 1218.[449] That she went without mention would also not be exceptional. Mentions of women in the period are fairly rare and, despite clearly playing an active role in the politics of the era, we have few specific records of Esclarmonde. The individuals identified with the siege are, for the most part, notable knights who took part in the combat. Here we deferred to our inspired sources with the comment that "if history should prove that Esclarmonde was not present in person, she was most certainly present in spirit."

Guillemette d'Alfaro

Very little is known of Guillemette d'Alfaro. Essentially, we have a reference to her from a will made by Raimond VI stating that she was the lady of Montlaur and Saint-Jory[450] There is no information whatsoever from her mother. Historical authorities believe that she was married to Hughes d'Alfaro, the Seneschal of Agenais, based on Peter de Vaux-Cernay's allegation that he married an illegitimate daughter of the count.[451] The fact that she was eligible to be left Montlaur suggests that she was considered *Naturalis* under the law.

We cannot assert that she was the daughter of Raimond VI and Azalais, however we can put forward some circumstances which place such a thing within the realm of the conceivable without in any way insisting they were or must be the case. First, we know that Raimond was perfectly willing to lie repeatedly and profusely to make things right with the law. It is not inconceivable a mistress of his could have been lodged with his sister, and it is not inconceivable that his sister could have passed her own child off as that of the mistress. The question would be why?

A ready answer would be the unwillingness of Raimond and Azalais to allow their child to suffer life as *Spurius*, particularly if they both embraced Cathar tenets enough to feel that union between brother and sister was no more unholy than any other sexual coupling. Given the choice of a parent, the status of Raimond VI (then not yet seriously challenged as Count of Toulouse), would have offered more protection than that of his sister. It must be remembered that we are not dealing with people who lived in a single castle as an extended family. Azalais had her own seat and court, whether she visited Toulouse or not. Probably the best argument against such an arrangement is that, had it been a matter of contemporary gossip, Peter of Vaux-Cernay would probably have repeated that too. Nevertheless, it is possible to posit a situation in which he was aware of the rumors of incest but, provided it was handled adroitly enough, not of the issue.

That said, the entire representation may be no more than symbolic. It is made clear in the initiation that Esclarmonde and Jeanne of England fill a similar role within the framework. The representation of Guillemette as daughter of Raimond VI and Azalais may be no more than a symbolic representation of the YHVH formula.

Raimond d'Alfaro

We know very little about Raimond d'Alfaro and far more about his father, Hughes d'Alfaro. We know that he ended up as the bailiff at Avignonnet by 1242, but that constitutes a chapter of history which goes beyond the current initiatory cycle. His presence there certainly suggests Cathar sympathies which, by extension, suggests the sympathies of Count Raimond VI, and potentially his son, may have been both durable and extensive.

Hughes d'Alfaro

Originally a mercenary from Navarre, he likely married Guillemette, an illegitimate daughter of Raimond VI. Hughes was a distinguished knight at the siege of Toulouse and was, at the time, Seneschal of Agenais, a large territory of Raimond VI, essentially making him a territorial governor. He appears to have been less a wandering mercenary than the leader of a significant household. He is mentioned by name at several prominent gatherings. In *Song* he is described in vivid terms:

> "Sir Hugh of Alfaro was inside the town. He was seneschal of the Agenais, a man of great courage and a very valiant knight. His brother, Sir Peter Arces, was with him, and so were the pick of their family, all excellent knights, proud and fierce."[452]

Other Cathar Period Figures Referenced

Montfort, Count Simon — 1165-1218

Born as heir of Leicester which he was unable to claim due to relations between the French and English Crown. He joined the Fourth Crusade. However, when called upon to attack Christians at Zara, he left the Crusade, disgusted. Peter de Vaux Cernay was likely a member of his entourage there. He joined the Albigensian Crusade and after confusion and chaos at Beziers, not only in regards to the massacre but in regards to the general lack of command. Montfort was elected or selected to lead based on his general eminence and perceived tactical skill. The anonymous continuator considers him to have made grave blunders in alienating the civil population of Toulouse. Despite his cruelty, Montfort was not exceptionally bloodthirsty or destructive for his time, his undertakings no worse than those attributed to Richard I, his contemporary, and his various butcheries and executions were certainly urged on by the religious around him. That said, he was generally arrogant, even in regards to the Pope, and does not seem to have been widely liked or to have done well at making allies.

Raimond Roger Trencavel, Viscount of Carcasonne Beziers, Albi, and Razes — 1185-1209

He became count at the age of nine in 1194. Nephew of Raimond VI through his sister Azalais. Despite this relationship, the Count and Raimond Roger were not close. We know that Raimond Roger Trencavel, Viscount of Carcasonne Beziers, Albi, and Razes, visited his uncle's court in 1204, but that "he behaved badly and aroused considerable hostility while he was there," the historical record being borne out in the castigation of a troubadour for his behavior. [453] We don't know how often he visited, or how often his mother, when she was alive, might have traveled as his deputy. Likewise, his rejection of the proposal of Raimond VI to fight the Crusade together has already been mentioned. William of Tudela thought highly of him and seemed to frame him as a tragic figure:

> *"Day and night Raymond Roger the viscount of Béziers worked to defend his lands, for he was a man of great courage. Nowhere in the wide world is there a better knight or one more generous and open-handed, more courteous or better bred. He was Count Raymond's nephew, his own sister's son. And he was certainly Catholic; I call to witness many a clerk and many a canon in their cloisters. But he was very young and was therefore friendly with everyone, and his vassals were not at all afraid or in awe of him but laughed and joked with him as they would with any comrade. And all his knights and other vavassors maintained the heretics in their towers and castles, and so they caused their own ruin and their shameful deaths. The viscount himself died in great anguish, a sad and sorry loss, because of this grievous error. I never saw him, though, except once, when Count Raymond married the lady Eleanor, the best and fairest queen in Christian or heathen lands or anywhere in the whole wide world. All the good I can say of her, all the praise I can give her, must always fall short of her worth and excellence."*[454]

Raimond Roger Trencavel left Carcassone under a white flag to parley and was imprisoned by the Crusaders and Simon Montfort. He died about two months into his imprisonment, most likely of disease. Rumors at the time suggested poisoning, of which there has been considerably historical discussion, but no suggestion of any real evidence.[455]

Roger II Trencavel

His date of birth is unknown, died in 1194. Viscount of Carcasonne Beziers, Albi, and Razes c. 1167-71 through 1194. Except for the short period during which he married Azalais, he was usually a rival and, in some years, an actual enemy of Raimond VI of Toulouse. His attempt to disinherit his child by Azalais, Raimond Roger Trencavel, which came to nothing, is covered under the entry on Raimond VI under the subject of his potential incest with Azalais. He was a repeated excommunicate in the final decades of the 12th century.

Raimond Roger Count of Foix

Not to be confused with Raimond Roger Trencavel

Count of Foix from 1188-1223. Closely related to Raimond VI of Toulouse, Raimond Roger Count of Foix is the brother of Esclarmonde. Despite protestations that he could not be responsible for his sister's activities, Raimond Roger was, if not a heretic himself, certainly powerfully defensive of those in his family.

> *"William of Puylaurens says that, in 1207, heretics at Pamiers, where Raymond Roger normally resided, were openly protected by his sister, Esclarmonda, who, according to inquisitorial witnesses had become a Cathar perfcta in 1204 in the presence of her brother. His wife, Philippa, also became a perfecta with a house for Cathars at Dun, about twenty kilometres to the south-east of Pamiers, while the appearance of his aunt, Fais of Durfort, another perfecta, in Pamiers, was the occasion of a major altercation between some of the count's knights and the canons of St Antonin."*[456]

While there had been traditional hostilities between Foix and Toulouse, the marriage of Raimond VI to the sister of Peter of Aragon seems to have reduced those tensions and it is unclear Raimond Roger ever had any particularly bad blood with Raimond VI. They both came of age around the same time and seem to have been more engaged in easing away from the wars of the late 12th century than fanning the flames. By 1215, when the two Counts were at the Lateran Council, they seem to have been at least close allies if not friends. Raimond Roger is famed as an orator who spoke eloquently in defense of Raimond VI.

Raimond Roger was a troubadour author of verse and highly literate and learned. He died in 1223 with the questions of heresy still unsettled. His son Roger Bernard II, the nephew of Esclarmonde, continued his work, and was able to bring Foix out of the Cathar wars largely intact through the Treaty of Meaux.

Peter King of Aragon

Son of King Alfonso II, he was born in 1178 and reigned from 1196 to 1213. He was the first King of Aragon to be crowned by the Pope. His sister, Eleanor, married Raimond VI of Toulouse in 1204. In 1212, when Simon Montfort initially conquered Toulouse, Peter assembled an army, the first real contest to the Albigensian Crusade, saying "And as he is my brother-in-law, my sister's husband, and I have married my other sister to his son, I will go and help them against these accursed men who are trying to disinherit them."[457] At the Battle of Muret, the Aragonese forces were badly organized and fell to Montfort's professional army. Peter II was killed in the battle, which effectively insured French dominion over Occitania.

Alfonso II King of Aragon

King of Aragon from 1164-1196, called "Alfonso the Chaste" or "Alfonso the Troubadour." He was succeeded by Peter II, 1196-1213. He was a paramour of Azalais of Burlats, wife of Roger II Trencavel, and sister of Raimond VI of Toulouse.

Raimond de Perelha

Seigneur of Montsegur, asked by Esclarmonde of Foix to rebuild and fortify the castle which plays a part in the later history of the Crusade.

Guilhabert de Castres

Little detail is known about this Cathar Bishop who was key to Doinel's charge to found the modern Gnostic Church. Historically, Zoe Oldenbourg suggests "Guilhabert himself seems to have been one of the greatest personalities in thirteenth-century France,"[458] but laments that little detail is available. There are some modern sources which, in discussing Doinel, suggest that Guilhabert de Castres cannot be historically attested, but this is not the case. Zoe Oldenbourg provides a reasonable chronology of what little is known of him and his name is attested in the Deposition of Raimond of Pereille, 30 April 1244 and 9 May 1244, following the fall of Montsegur.[459]

Chronology

A brief and select chronology of the Cathar Wars, and events relating to the Counts of Toulouse:

1147 – Alfonse Jourdain, Count of Toulouse, embarks on the Second Crusade with his son Raimond V

1148 – Alfonse Jourdain arrives at Acre and dies, likely poisoned by Eleanor of Aquitaine or Melisende

1151 – Birth of Esclarmonde of Foix

1153 – Raimond V marries Constance, daughter of King Louis VI of the Franks

1156 – Raimond VI born

1165 – Birth of Guilhabert de Castres

Council of Lombers. This was an "examination," which is often historically presented as a debate, with certain Cathar representatives known as "Good Men." While they enjoyed the protection of the knights of the area, they were under investigation and declined to reply to many questions, so it was not a true debate. Constance of France is supposed, famously, to have disputed with them. She split with Raimond V shortly thereafter.

1167 – Cathar Council held in Saint-Felix de Caraman is presided over by Nicetas, the Cathar Bishop of Constantinople, and establishes doctrine and administrative procedures. Catholic Councils have condemned Cathars as far back as 1022, however they seem to have achieved a level of acceptance and prosperity in the area known today as Occitania.

1165 – Jeanne of England born to Henry II and Eleanor of Aquitaine.

1171 – Azalais married to Roger II Trencavel during a brief period of alliance, she is six, though as was customary there is no suggestion that the couple were intimate before the birth of her first child at age 20.

1178 – Raimond requested assistance from the Cistercians to combat heresy.

Roger II Trencavel breaks his alliance with Toulouse and returns to fealty with Alfonso of

1185 – Raimond Roger Trencavel born to Roger II and Azalais.

Roger II involved in conflict with Raimond V in support of Alfonso of Aragon and, unusually, names Alfonso's son as his heir in preference Raimond Roger.

1187 – Christian defeat at Hattin; Templars and Hospitallers executed

1189-1192 – Third Crusade

1190 – Richard I "Lionheart" of England sacks Messina, forces return of his sister, Jeanne, from the usurping King of Sicily.

1191 – Oct 2, Richard I meets with Al-Adil, Salah ad-Din's brother, at Lydda. Proposes a marriage between Al-Adil and his sister Jeanne. It is recorded that with neither of them willing to convert, the proposed arrangement is abandoned.[460]

1194 – Raimond V dies.

Raimond VI becomes Count of Toulouse.

Roger II Trencavel dies, his possessions pass to Raimond Roger.

1196 – Raimond VI marries Jeanne of England

0° INITIATION c. 1197

1197 – Raimond VII born to Jeanne of England and Raimond VI

1° INITIATION c. 1198

1198 – Jeanne of Toulouse born to Jeanne of England and Raimond VI

Death of Pope Celestine, Innocent III becomes Pope

1199 – Death of Azalais of Burlats

Death of Jeanne of England

1200 – Eslcarmonde de Foix widowed

1202-1204 – Fourth Crusade

1204 – Raimond Roger, Viscount of Béziers and Carcassonne, visits the court of Raimond VI in Toulouse

1207 – Raimond VI Excommunicated for failing to suppress heresy

1208 – Murder of Peter de Castelnau, Papal Legate, by an adherent of Raimond VI

1209 – Initation of the Cathar Crusade.

Raimond VI does penance and initially joins the crusade.

Massacre at Beziers, 22 July.

Carcassone falls in August after Raimond Roger Trencavel is taken prisoner while negotiating. He subsequently dies imprisoned of disease or poisoning. Simon Montfort made commander of the Crusade.

1210 – Crusade continues

1211 – First abortive Siege of Toulouse

1211 – Guillemette, daughter of Raimond VI, marries Hugh D'Alfaro, Seneschal of the Agenais

1213 – Battle of Muret. King Peter II of Aragon killed, Crusader side Victorious

1214 – Toulouse under control of the Papal Legate and Bishop

1215 – Raimond VI living at the house of the Roaix Family in Toulouse, known as a principal Cathar House

Raimond VI is in Rome with Raimond-Roger Count of Foix and his son, Roger Bernard II, to petition Innocent III

Simon of Montfort made Count of Toulouse by the Pope

1216 – Innocent III dies unexpectedly

Raimond VII takes Beaucaire, starting a reconquest of their lands.

Simon loots Toulouse, which he holds, after losing Beaucaire.

1217 – Ramon VI retakes Toulouse without a fight.

Simon Montfort begins a siege. Roger-Bernard II Count of Foix and Hugh D'Alfaro are distinguished during the action.

2° INITIATION 24 June, 1218

1218 – Count Simon Killed by a stone from a seige engine

Appendix C – The Organization of the Order

The Structure of the Governing Bodies

Driving principles

Historically, initiatory groups have been organized in a very top-down fashion. Often, the order was the work of some central luminary, e.g. Cagliostro, and that individual organized the group to support obedience and financial support for themselves. During the late 19th and 20th centuries, most Masonic groups moved towards a business model, where the majority of functions were handled by mid-level initiates who were selected for their business sense. Many still retained a top-down structure, with supreme authority vested in a single high-grade initiate or individual. As the battle against authoritarianism and fascism in the 21st century heats up, we find that the idea of an oligarchic or authoritarian organization is increasingly repugnant. Authoritarianism, no matter how "soft," tends to promote the interests of those who look and act like the authoritarians, and is thus antithetical to diversity.

Overview: The Government of the Initiatory Arm

The Initiatory Arm is governed by members who have initiated to III° or to a higher grade. All disciplinary and business functions of the Order, excepting those which are specifically and directly related to the ritual materials, contents, and execution themselves reside in the III°.

There are groups of initiates of higher degree whose sole function is to supervise the ritual operations appropriate to their degrees. These groups are the supreme governing bodies in regards to ritual. The Initiatory Arm is subsidiary to the General Assembly of TTO, an elected body, in matters which do not concern ritual.

Below we'll break out the details and some specifics. The Bylaws of the Initiatory Arm, which may be amended or changed by the Supreme Senate, contain the specific details, and supersede anything printed here:

Separation of Business and Ritual

There is no particular reason that the business and ritual functions of the organization must be handled by the same individuals. This includes decisions over whether or not to debar individuals from initiation based on their behavior or actions. It does not take a higher degree to determine if someone has violated basic rules of consent or behaved in a manner that is dangerous or threatening to other initiates. This is a matter of basic common sense and, in almost all cases, the appeal to a higher authority in defense of indefensible actions is a weak sham. History is full of charlatans and abusers who have used the claim to some "inner knowledge" to justify truly abhorrent actions. It is our goal to break, rather than perpetuate, this cycle.

Likewise, positions of authority in authoritarian groups are routinely abused to debar individuals on specious grounds for reasons that have more to do with insider friendships or group politics than any actual violations of policy. When authorities answer to no-one but themselves, it becomes easy to propitiate friends by taking action on their behalf without due process or adequate consideration. Because people often favor those who seem most like themselves, an authoritarian system inherently supports discrimination based on class, social background, gender, sexuality, and race.

Business Functions are Vested in the III°

Practically speaking, it is also problematic to have the newest volunteers or members of an organization handling all the decision-making. Some time to become acquainted with the organization's culture, processes, and operations is important. In saying that the business functions are vested in the III°, we mean that degree and above. There is no process for aging out, so the senior initiates will always get a say. However, as the initiation grows, newer members will also have a meaningful and significant voice. Within TTO, the 0-II° may be taken at one time. Thus the III° is the first which would definitively require re-application. It is presumed that the majority of individuals who progress to the III° have a sincere interest in the organization, and intend to continue participation.

All members of the III° and above are members of the **Supreme Senate**, which is the principal body of the organization in matters pertaining to business, membership, and safe operations. The only matters over which the Supreme Senate does not have jurisdiction are the specific operations and rituals pertinent to the higher degree rituals themselves, as well as any safety issues specifically pertinent to those degrees. There is no fee to remain a member of the Supreme Senate; it is a lifetime privilege unless specifically revoked by an act of the Senate.

Because the Supreme Senate is a large and diffuse body, members who remain in contact will elect an Executive Committee which supervises regular operations, referring matters to the entirety of the Senate as needed. The structure of this Committee and its relationship to the Supreme Senate is intentionally nearly identical to the structure of the TTO Executive Committee and its relationship to the TTO General Assembly. The Executive Committee elects a Consul General who serves as the overall leader and voice of the organization.

Relationship to TTO

Because the TTO is the parent organization, providing structure, resources, and promotion for the Thelemic Initiations, the TTO General Assembly has authority over the Supreme Senate, and the Initiatory Body. It is expected, however, that this will be principally handled by advice and discussion with the Cancellarius, who sits on the TTO Executive Committee.

Relationship to Memphis and Misraim

The role of the Independent and Rectified Rite of the Ancient and Primitive Mystery of Memphis and Misraim (I. & R. R., A. & P. M. of M∴ & M∴) is purely ceremonial. The Consul General and Cancellarius of are, upon election or appointment, granted the honor of 97°, Grand Hierophant. While those who pursue the Thelemic Initiations are explicitly granted M∴ & M∴ degrees, many individuals may hold M∴ & M∴ degrees without having taken the Thelemic Initiations.

The role of the M∴ & M∴ organization is ceremonial rather than legal. It provides a rich connection to antiquity and tradition, however no individual 97°, inside or outside the I. & R. R., A. & P. M. of M∴ & M∴, has any specific authority or jurisdiction over the operation of the organization, either business or ritual. Members of the Supreme Senate and of the other higher bodies which oversee the specific Initiatory Rituals, will thus always have a commensurate degree in M∴ & M∴, however, merely holding a degree in M∴ & M∴ does not imply authority over Thelemic Initiations.

Organization

Principles of Government

The Government of the Order rests principally in the III°. All members of the Order III° and above are members of the **Supreme Senate.** While the mysteries are appropriate to those who have undertaken the grade work, the fair and efficient operation of a business organization requires no special insight granted by initiation.

Members of the Lodge of the Initiatory Order 0°

- Are not privy to the business of the Order
- Do not sit on its Councils.
- May not Initiate 0°

Members of the College 1° of the Initiatory Order are

- Privy to the decisions of the Initiatory Order
- Do not sit on its Councils.
- They may hold the position of Cancellarius, but not of Consul General

Members of the Chapter of the Initiatory Order II° are

- Privy to the decisions of the Initiatory Order
- Do not sit on its Councils.
- May Initiate 0°-II° as Sovereign Initiators
- May hold the position of Cancellarius, but not of Consul General

Members of the Supreme Senate of the Initiatory Order III° are:

- Privy to the decisions of the Initiatory Order
- Sit on the Supreme Senate
- May Initiate to their degree as Sovereign Initiators
- May hold the position of Cancellarius
- May serve as Consul General

The Supreme Senate determines all matters pertaining to the Initiatory Order, including issues of debarment. It is subsidiary only to the Secretary General and the Executive Council of TTO.

The Supreme Senate is the central business mechanism of the Initiatory Order. The Consistory of Knights Kadosh and Supreme Dionysian Council are subsidiary to the Senate, except in specific matters.

The Supreme Senate

- Elects or Appoints the Cancellarius
- Elects the Consul General for a term of two years
- Oversees Chartering of Sovereign Initiators
- Oversees Chartering of Subsidiary "Side" Degrees
- Oversees the day to day operation of the Initiatory Arm

- Oversees general Safety and Consent Training, in partnership with the Secretary General and Executive Council of TTO
- Coordinates Notification of Debarment with the Inspector General of TTO
- Reports to the Secretary General and Executive Council of TTO
- Handles all matters of Law, business, licensure that are exclusive to the Initiatory Arm
- Handles all matters of debarment excepting those specifically relating to actions within, or concerning higher degree rituals.

The Consistory of Knights Kadosh VI° - VII°

- Develops Initiation Specific Training for IV° and Intermediate Grades
- Charters Subsidiary "Side" Degrees above III°

The Sublime Dionysian Council IIX° - X°

- Develops Initiation Specific Training for V° through VII°
- Handles questions of debarment regarding actions during, or specifically relating to Initiations V° through VII°
- Charters Subsidiary "Side" Degrees related to or above VI°

The Council of the Knights of Shiraz XI°-XII°

- Develops Initiation Specific Training for IIX°- XI°
- Handles questions of debarment regarding actions during, or specifically relating to Initiations IIX°- XI°
- Charters Subsidiary "Side" Degrees related to or above IIX°

The Conservators of the Sovereign Sanctuary XIII°

- Develops Initiation Specific Training for XII° through XIII°
- Handles questions of debarment regarding actions during, or specifically relating to Initiations XII° through XIII°
- Charters Subsidiary "Side" Degrees related to or above XI°

The Officers

Cancellarius

The General Secretary of the Initiatory Arm, the Cancellarius, serves at the pleasure of the Senate. The Cancellarius is a non-voting member of the Executive Committee of TTO. The Cancellarius may also sign as "General Secretary of the Initiatory Arm" in regards to business matters.

The Cancellarius works with the TTO Inspector General to maintain the Debarment list, and to quickly and efficiently verify the status of applicants for Initiation at the request of Sovereign Initiators.

The Cancellarius produces all papers, certificates, and is in charge of records keeping.

The Cancellarius is accorded the TTO O.S.M. for their service or, if they hold this distinction, the next distinction within the Chivalric Order.

The Consul General

The Consul General serves for a term of two years and is the Executive and Ceremonial Head of the Initiatory Arm. The Consul General speaks for and acts as the face of the Initiatory Order, convening such meetings and conclaves of members as are useful to ensure the long term perpetuation of the Order.

The Consul General acts as Chair of the Supreme Senate.

The Consul General is accorded the TTO O.S.M. for their service or, if they hold this distinction, the next distinction within the Chivalric Order.

The Duty of the Sovereign Initiator

Overview of the Principles of Initiation

In sponsoring the Thelemic Initiations, The Thelemic Order intends to put forward not just a new set of initiations, but a new and more modern model and paradigm for the principles of initiation. These revolve around the concepts of safety, how and when ordeal occurs, and focus on the experience of initiation by the individual rather than the pretense of some special quality conveyed by the initiator.

While we do not entirely reject the idea that initiation may gain power through the links of initiator and initiation to tradition, we note that most notable initiations have been self-initiations and that many initiators of great stature have proclaimed their students failures. With that, we must assume that it is the mindset and readiness of the initiate, rather than the special property of the initiator, which determines when and if initiation occurs.

Sovereign Initiators have a series of obligations, however, they focus on safety and fiscal responsibility. All of the oaths speak to one of these two elements.

In Regards to Safety

- The Law is for All and initiation should not be subject to discrimination on the basis of ethnicity, ancestry, appearance, gender, gender identity, gender expression, sexuality, sexual identity, sexual expression, international origin, age, or disability.
- Initiations should be physically and emotionally safe.
- Within a given ritual, trials or challenges should be uniform. The intention is for each initiate to face roughly the same degree of challenge. If, because of a specific fear, trigger, etc., an element of initiation is disproportionately problematic to a prospective initiate, the Sovereign Initiator will work with them in order to ensure a uniform experience by modifying or removing elements that would impact them differently from others.
- The Sovereign Initiator is tasked with preserving elements of secrecy and surprise while securing informed consent from prospective initiates.
- Within the lower grades of initiation within this system, the rituals may provide trials and challenges, however, the true ordeals are provided by life, as a definite and inevitable result of the initiatory ritual. The initiate should be duly warned of this on multiple occasions. Thus, the rituals are an invocation of ordeal, rather than an ordeal in and of themselves. As a matter of practical fact, we feel this is observably true of almost all base initiations within the Western ceremonial tradition, whatever their claim – except in the case where a relatively mundane element happens to

speak to the particular phobias or trauma of a specific initiate, in which case the effect of ordeal is largely unpredictable, ungoverned, unintended, and often unproductive.

In Regards to Cost and Money

- Initiations should not be a scheme that enriches either the Initiator, or the sponsoring organization.
- Costs for initiation should reflect the actual site costs.
- Initiators are volunteers who donate their time and supply their own equipment and vestments. They may be reimbursed for some actual costs, including consumables (food and consumable supplies), the cost of the venue, and travel.
- Initiators are never required to be reimbursed and may donate their time and money as they see fit.
- Initiators are governed by, and expected to adhere to, specific rules produced annually.
- There is no fixed cost for initiations. Because actual costs vary wildly, each initiator sets their fees based on actual costs, subject to auditing by the Cancellarius of the Initiatory arm. The aim is to keep the costs as low as possible while accounting for the necessity for travel to far-flung areas and allowing for a wide variety of venues.
- No prospective initiate is compelled to work with a given Sovereign Initiator. They may select a Sovereign Initiator whose style and facilities fit their needs and budget.
- TTO does not collect increasing fees per initiation. There is a flat rate for each initiation or side degree which reflects actual costs for records keeping and administration.

Terms of Payment

It is not the business of the Sovereign Sanctuary to make money, nor should Sovereign Initiator make profit from the matter of Initiation or of Training. In general, it is the intent of the Sovereign Sanctuary to create local initiators who will use the available resources of their TTO Group, presenting initiations at approximately the cost of site and food. However, it is understood there may be additional costs involved in creating a trained body of initiators. In this matter, there are rules

Automatic Compensation:

The Initiator may always be compensated for any actual costs of the initiation related to:

The Venue

The costs of the site. This includes rental costs, and any additional fees (cleanup, use of equipment) charged by the site.

Consumables

Specifically, food and paper goods, including any costs for reproduction or purchase of initiatory materials, and those items given away at initiation.

Static Items

While Sovereign Initiators are encouraged to build their own properties sets, or work with a TTO Group to build them, it is understood that properties may require replacement or may represent a financial burden for some

Initiators. In addition, some items which are not strictly required (backdrops, side pieces, curtains, scrims, etc.) may be desirable. In order to encourage excellence in presentation, Sovereign Initiators may assess an additional 5% of cost per initiation which does not require specific accounting, but is presumed to create a fund for the purchase of, maintenance of, and replacement of reusable properties, even those not explicitly named in the scripts.

Conditional Compensation:

Other costs are covered only if the Sovereign Initiator is Chartered to Train Initiators and also present a training which covers initiation to the degrees being presented. The training need not be attended by all the initiates. These costs may be paid by the Trainees, or by a TTO Group, or a group of TTO Siblings who wish the training to be presented.

Travel

Direct costs, e.g. airfare, bus fare, rental fees, baggage check fees, fuel for personal vehicle, etc.

Lodging and Food

Costs of hotel, hostel, or other professional arrangement, and a basic allowance for daily food for each day traveled. The Cancellarius of the Sovereign Sanctuary may periodically publish, through the Website or other means, a list of acceptable per-diem rates.

Travel Expenses of Additional Officers or Presenters

The same expenses may be paid for other Officers or Presenters of Training, provided they are significantly involved in the presentation and production.

Payment of Siblings and Initiates

The payment of Siblings and Initiates presents an interesting dynamic. On one hand it is absolutely not the intention of the Sovereign Sanctuary to create an initiatory system in which profit motive is an element. On the other hand it is only common sense that Initiates should deal with Siblings preferentially where it is possible and ethical. Therefore, the following standards are set: Siblings may be reimbursed for their time and services at initiations *provided those services are professional in nature and part of a regular business practice*, and the rates charged are the same or lower as those offered to comparable customers, e.g. a Sibling and Initiate who is a caterer may be paid for catering. A Sibling who operates an online rental may be paid for lodging.

When Siblings are not professionals, or do not possess the necessary licensing, they may still of course be compensated for costs and materials associated with food preparation, etc.

Costs not Compensated

Compensation for Time

The Initiator may not be compensated for their time, including wages lost due to leave, missed opportunity, etc. Time is a donation to the Sovereign Sanctuary.

Costuming and Personal Properties

The Initiator may not be compensated for their own costuming and personal properties for any of the roles, even if they make these available to others, unless they are the Leader of a Group, and the items purchased are the property of that Group.

Petty Profits

It is the intent of the Compensation clause to ensure that initiation does not become a pay scheme or a personal business. It is also not the intent create a situation in which Initiators agonize over pennies.

It is understandable that costs charged up front may generate some slight revenue in excess of actual costs of an initiation, otherwise the initiator might consistently be forced to pay out of pocket for shortfalls. Petty amounts which result from charging a reasonable rate which can be expected to cover venue, food, travel, etc. are not considered a violation of the Compensation regulations, and may be retained and spent on Initiation related expenses. The definition of "petty amounts" is subject to the discretion of the Governing Body.

The Oath of the Sovereign Initiator

I agree upon my own honor and self-divinity to faithfully and regularly execute the Role of Sovereign Initiator within the Initiatory Arm of the Thelemic Order.

Discrimination

The Law is for All. I will not discriminate in whom I initiate or what roles and conditions others are offered within my initiations on the basis of ethnicity, ancestry, appearance, gender, gender identity, gender expression, sexuality, sexual identity, sexual expression, international origin, age, or disability.

Remuneration

The Law is for All. I will be careful and diligent in setting my fees, understanding that my time is a donation, and while I may seek compensation for my actual costs within the prevailing written rules, I will not seek compensation for my time, nor profit from my office, as a Sovereign Initiator.

Accessibility

The Law is for All. I will work diligently to ensure that no one is unable to initiate due to physical or psychological factors. I will work as a professional to change the physical circumstances and to work out negotiated compromises on presentation in order to buffer or ameliorate any negative impact, in keeping with the guidance available to me, while maintaining the basic nature and message of the initiations.

Safety

I will strive diligently to make my initiations as safe as possible, recognizing issues of both physical and emotional safety for all participants including Initiates, those assisting me with initiation, and myself. In particular, I will ensure that I model informed consent both in my personal behavior and within my initiations.

Negotiation

Informed consent being vital to a positive and reasonably uniform initiatory experience, I will ensure that all questions described in the Initiatory materials, as well as any other questions which have arisen due to the situation, site, or individuals present, have been satisfactorily answered and agreed upon before I undertake to initiate.

Debarred Persons

My job as a Sovereign Initiator is to create a safe environment for initiations. To that end, both with regard to my safety and the safety of others participating, I will, to the best of my ability, ensure that those I initiate have not been debarred from initiation by official acts of the governing bodies of the Initiatory Arm. If I believe someone has been wrongly debarred I will champion their cause on and before the governing bodies, but I will not undertake to initiate them outside the authority of the Initiatory Arm.

Authority

I recognize that the organization of a central body which supervises safe administration of the Thelemic Initiations and ensures a consensual framework is a critical part of maintaining a healthy initiatory environment, and that I have been chartered by an organization that serves to further those goals. I will not present or disseminate the materials with which I have been provided, in whole or part, outside the due authority granted me by the governing bodies of the Initiatory Arm.

Communication

It is my responsibility, in all cases where I wish to exercise my charter, to ensure that I am in contact with the authorizing organization, have read and understood all current and applicable rules, and have all current and applicable certifications and education.

Reporting

I understand that it is my responsibility to keep appropriate records and report diligently all performance of my official duties. In any case where I claim expenses, or in which I deduct official expenses from any taxes, or for any other legal benefit, I will keep exact and careful records, and make sure they are available for inspection.

Privacy

The privacy of those who choose to follow the path of initiation is entrusted to me. I will handle their information with due diligence, and I will guard myself against any accidental revelations, always erring on the side of caution and silence.

Will

I retain the right to refuse initiation to anyone for reasons other than those listed under the nondiscrimination clause. I will exercise this right diligently to avoid creating unsafe situations, and will not allow myself to be pressured into undertaking any initiation where I do not feel confident and comfortable for any reason.

Appendix D – The Rite of Memphis and Misraim

Within and under the Sovereign Sanctuary of the Gnosis of the Thelemic Order (The Initiatory Arm) is operated the Independent and Rectified Rite of the Ancient and Primitive Mystery of Memphis and Misraim (I. & R. R., A. & P. M. of M∴ & M∴.), one of many implementations and traditions of that Rite, which is itself one of numerous manifestations of Masonry, Rosicrucianism, Neo-Templarism, and Neo-Gnosticism.

The Lodge of the Sovereign Sanctuary of the Gnosis of the Thelemic Order is Opened in the 18° of the Independent and Rectified Rite of the Ancient and Primitive Mystery of Memphis and Misraim.

As part of the Thelemic Initiations, specific degrees within the I. & R. R., A. & P. M. of M∴ & M∴ are symbolically conveyed. The following information should be provided to the Initiates, as part of their Degree materials.

About the Rites of Memphis & Misraim

The Origin of Freemasonry, Rosicrucianism, Neo-Templarism and Neo-Gnosticism

Beginning in the 16th century and alongside the Reformation began the dawn of a series of organizations in Europe which were not Churches, but which functioned to combine spirituality with a humanist philosophy. These organizations, termed either Rosicrucian, Freemason, or Templar, provided a link between the ancient pre-Christian traditions learning, wisdom, and esotericism which were the core inspiration of the Enlightenment to modern people.

The Meaning of "Memphis" and "Misraim"

Misraim is the Aramaic name for Egypt. It is attested in Ugaritic inscriptions from around the 12th century BC as Msrm(1).[461] It is sometimes described as "Hebrew" for Egypt, though this is not precisely correct.

Memphis was the ancient capital of lower Egypt and is today a UNESCO World Heritage site. Memphis had great importance in both legend and Egyptian history. Memphis was sacred to the primordial god Ptah who, depending on the time and period of Egyptian belief, can be seen as cognate with Osiris or with Ra, the winged solar disk. Ptah is generally agreed to be a principal source or influence for the Canaanite deity El, whom was worshiped in Jerusalem as Yahweh and passed down in much altered form through Judaism and Christianity.

The suggestion of a special tradition of initiation in Egypt is attested in numerous classical sources. In the 18th and 19th century, it was widely speculated that the Classical mystery cults, including the Eleusinian cult and the mysteries of Dionysus, Bacchus, Osiris, Adonis, Thamuz, and Apollo, shared a common origin in Egypt. The concept that all religion was syncretic and shared common origins and links was an important exploration of a newly secular world. The celebration of ancient mysteries served, not only as a link to the past, but to marginalize the necessity to give all consideration to the dominant Christian paradigm. Neo-Classicism was not merely an intellectual exercise, but a rebellion against theism at a time when the Christian Church, both Protestant and Catholic, still exercised a strong grip on the levers of power. That grip is today diminished, but preserving and celebrating the long history of sacred practice and ecstasy provides a balance against the persistence of Christian Dominionism within the social sphere.

The Origin of the Memphis and Misraim Rites

In regards to the Rite of Misraim, legend ties it to Cagliostro's Egyptian Rite organized around 1788, but it may have been more inspired by than descended from that Rite. There are several citations suggesting it was being practiced in Italy by the 1780s. Masonic scholars writing contemporarily and in the 1930s suggested that Memphis and Misraim borrowed the Ancient and Accepted Scottish Rite. However, this is a partial truth.

We don't know exactly how, or even for certain if, speculative Masonry developed from a system of Craft initiation. We know that a Grand Lodge was constituted in London in 1717, but there is no certain indicator whether this was the outgrowth of the mysteries of a craft guild or the consolidation of a branch of traditions of a secret society of the type which had been known in Europe for centuries. References to "Scottish Masons" describe a particular practice rather than their location.

While it emanated from the British Isles, high degree masonry flourished on the European Continent, where it was clearly influenced by other secret societies of which we know less. There were Scottish lodges in France by 1744, but they continued to grow and morph. Various high degree systems were seen in the UK and on the European continent, particularly in France, in the United States, and in the Caribbean.

The modern Scottish Rite dates only to 1801, itself based on a likely spurious charter. The attempt to claim the Memphis and Misraim derived principally from a specific group, or that a particularly strong vine represents a solid and unbroken tradition, is ludicrous. The fact is that High Degree Masonry ranged across the continents in the late 18th century and it was not until the 19th that some of the High Degree organizations we recognize today began to coalesce. Historically, it would be more accurate to say that the modern Ancient and Accepted Scottish Rite and the Memphis and Misraim practices both arose from the common ferment of mid and late 18th century High Degree Masonry, owing their history and rites to numerous systems which were developed during 18th century. If the Egyptian Rite did not actually come from Egypt, neither was it a sycophantic copy of a rite from Charleston in the nascent United States.

Milko Bogard has found evidence that the Rite was being worked in Toulouse by 1806,(2)[462] possibly on the basis of a charter issued in Italy. The first well-documented lodge of the Oriental Rite of Misraim was founded in Paris in 1814. Complicating any attempt at tracing the history of these Orders was their own insistence on an ancient origin.

The Rite of Memphis is supposed to have been Rosicrucian in nature and was linked by author A. E. Waite to a Greek integration of the Dionysian Mysteries around 1600. That it picked up elements of some older European Rosicrucian practices seems a reasonable conjecture, but we have little data. What is important is not that these systems actually date back to the time of the Fama Fraternitas, or to medieval Europe, or to late Imperial or Ptolemaic, or even ancient Egypt. It is that they reflect a continuing interest in those subjects which legitimately dates to the 15th century and the Platonic Academy of Marsilio Ficino and the translation of the *Corpus Hermeticum*; the modern rebirth of a Neoplatonist, Hermetic, and implicitly queer Western philosophy.

It is often stated that a given Masonic Lodge is or is not "recognized" by the United Grand Lodge of England or the Grand Orient of France, and characterizing Lodges outside this structure as "irregular." In technical terms, groups recognized by these bodies are said to be "in obedience" to them, and those groups have some history of seeking to repress those operating outside their authority. It might be emphasized that the matter of being irregular is of interest only to those operating dogmatically within the Grand Lodge Structure. Even in the US, not all Grand Lodges are universally recognized.

The Thelemic Initiations

Memphis-Misraim Consolidation of 1881

While the documentation is sparse, it is widely posited that the unified Rite of Memphis-Misraim was created in 1881 in an attempt by several European Grand Masters to create a unified "Confederation of Rites," with the Italian Revolutionary Giuseppe Garabaldi as the Grand Hierophant. Most of the documentation comes from John Yarker's magazine, and any participation of the aging Garabaldi was ceremonial at best.

The association of the Rite with Garabaldi is significant, even if he personally had little to do with it. Garabaldi, a revolutionary who united much of modern Italy, was a progressive who supported the Paris Commune and encouraged radicalism, though his ultimate vision for government was a more moderate socialism. He strongly opposed the papacy and any form of religious hegemony. He saw Freemasonry as a network for progressive people to work across national borders and was the Grand Master of the Grand Orient of Italy. The formation of Memphis-Misraim must thus be seen as intimately tied to progressive politics.

It is unclear just how involved Garabaldi actually was, though he was certainly involved in Freemasonry. This may have been more an attempt on Yarker's part to establish a "traditional" origin for the order than an actual interest in Garabaldi's patronage. Similarly, the Scottish Rite, organized in Charleston, South Carolina in 1801, derived its traditional authority from the "Grand Constitution of the 33°" supposedly ratified by Frederick the Great of Prussia, though it remains highly conjectural that such a connection existed despite assertions.

By this time the various Grand Masters patching together the unified Rite were already of mixed and uncertain lineage. The primary French lodge of Memphis is said to have ceded control to the Grand Orient of France in 1862. (3)[463] The modern Scottish Rite argues that Seymour, who operated the US Rite, never had any actual authority. (4)[464]

An Italian Lodge in the United States had no known origin, and much of its continuation must be attributed to the English collector of Masonic Rites, John Yarker, who was Grand Master General of the Sovereign Sanctuary of the Marconis lineage in England. Yarker's work was to collect a really wide variety of extinct or nearly-extinct Masonic degrees, many dating back to the late 18th century, and patch them together into a cohesive rite. It was understood at the time that they would not likely all be worked, and to some extent Memphis-Misraim was considered a theoretical and symbolic lodge, enshrining a great deal of material of interest to the more esoteric branches of Freemasonry. Yarker published his consolidated Rite, allowing for its adoption by Memphis Lodges not actively signatory to his 1881 convention. As a result of this, groups which were never formally aligned with Yarker may have moved to using the Memphis-Misraim name.

Later Lodges

In the U.S., the Rite of Memphis is well-documented as having operated from the late 1860s, though it suffered a schism when an attempt was made to reduce the Rite to 33 degrees in conformance with the wishes of the Grand Orient of France. Calvin Burt continued to operate the original degree structure and, in 1872, Chartered John Yarker to form a Sovereign Grand Lodge in England. When Theodor Reuss obtained a charter for the Ancient and Primitive Rite of Memphis-Misraim from Yarker in 1902, there were already several other groups operating on the Continent.

Reuss largely abandoned Memphis-Misraim in favor of his own O.T.O.; however O.T.O. retains its Memphis-Misraim connections, conferring the degrees as part of its IV° ritual, along with various Scottish Rite distinctions. While the O.T.O. considers that Aliester Crowley inherited Theodor Reuss' rights to Memphis-Misraim, there was no formal appointment.

The French branch of Memphis-Misraim continues through an exchange by Reuss and Gerard Encausse and is picked up with some breaks by Roger Ambelain after the Second World War.

The history of Memphis-Misraim after 1881 is scattered and poorly documented, and it is clear that the Rite has been restarted from scratch or on vague authority numerous times. At least one of the groups that formed the 1881 compact was of questionable descent and may have had little contact with either original organization.

The Sovereign Sanctuary of the Gnosis of the Thelemic Order (The Initiatory Arm) operates the Independent and Rectified Rite of the Ancient and Primitive Mystery of Memphis and Misraim (I. & R. R., A. & P. M. of M∴ & M∴) on the basis of several different lineages including Ambelain and, of particular interest, The Ecclesia Cabalistica Gnostica de Memphis-Misraïm, which reaches back at least six decades to Marc Lully, Michael Bertiaux, and Manuel Lamparter. These traditions are interesting because they re-imagined Memphis and Misraim somewhat after the fashion of a Gnostic Apostolic succession, rather than a working system of degrees.

Why Memphis and Misraim?

In choosing a Masonic substructure for our mystery, we could easily have chosen any of a number of traditions which are either inactive or readily available. We could less generously have chosen, as some other Thelemic groups have, to appropriate the customs of the Ancient and Accepted Scottish Rite without due accreditation. Certainly, the use of the Memphis and Misraim mysteries step on no toes. There is no organization which plausibly claims to exercise exclusive rights to these mysteries.

It is not our intention to disrespect or usurp the prerogatives of any of the existing Grand Lodges which still grant Masonic Degrees. Milko Bogard documents in excess of 42 different Organizations of Memphis-Misraim which were active, or recently active from 2004-2017, and numerous other international bodies. What is more important is that, with its ties to the concept of a single Egyptian tradition, Memphis and Misraim provides a solid tie to the core of western Hermetic Traditio, while including the Freemason, Rosicruician, Neo-Templar, and Neo-Gnostic traditions. With its ties to Cagliostro it is, as Theodor Reuss certainly recognized, the "Grandparent of them all" in regards to truly esoteric Masonry. It is not a branch of Freemasonry with esoteric ties, rather it is a branch of Hermetic Tradition with a Masonic framing.

It provides an excellent and legitimate core for us to explore the Western Traditions that shaped Thelema, without attempting to fit them into the narrow structure.

The Presentation

There may be time when it is useful for a Sovereign Initiator who holds the 96° M∴M∴ to present the degrees outside the structure of the Thelemic Initiations. Many individuals who take the Thelemic Initiations will already hold the M∴M∴ degrees. This script may be used for a short, formal, presentation of the degrees:

The Rite of Memphis and Misraim is one of the oldest High Degree systems, tying together the threads of Freemasonry, Rosicrucianism, and Modern Templarism. It has become very much the tradition in the last century to confer such degrees without adequate explanation of their meaning and importance. Sometimes it is understood, but more often it is not. I will take a few moments of your time, so that this can be understood not only as a ceremonial matter, but as something that has never been more relevant.

The Thelemic Initiations

The Enlightenment is a collective name for a series of disparate social and philosophical movements in the 17th and 18th centuries. The core idea that tied these movements together was the concept reason is the primary source of authority and legitimacy. Resultantly, these movements advocated ideals including liberty, scientific progress, racial tolerance, constitutional government, the separation of church and state, and a scientific rather than religious approach to sexuality and gender which allows for individual expression.

The rise of the Masonic, Rosicrucian, and modern Templar Orders is a major outgrowth of the Enlightenment. These groups of individuals came together principally to promote the ideas of Enlightenment thought as they were understood at the time. Of necessity, their implementations were partial and imperfect. However, they represented, in their time, a clean break from the past; a rejection of Theism which denied the deity inherent in humankind, relegating humans to an inferior status, inferring that they should be chattels, or subordinate to, the Church and hereditary rulers. These groups became the evangelical branches of humanism, competing with both Church and State with the message that reason and tolerance need not run counter to spirituality.

Modern Templarism was based on the recognition that certain medieval groups, notably the Templars and Cathars, had through heresy sustained a glimmer of the Neo-Platonic idea of deity inherent in all people, which we recognize today in affirming "every human being is a star."

There were real dangers to membership in these groups. Throughout their history members were persecuted and physically tortured or killed. These dangers are not confined to ancient times. As late as the Second World War, Freemasons, Rosicrucians, and Gnostics were murdered by the Nazis. Constant Chevellion, who in 1934 became the Grand Hierophant of the then Antient and Primitive Rite of Memphis and Misraim was executed by a French rightist militia working in cooperation with the Nazi occupation forces on April 23, 1944, while Robert Amebelain, from whom one of our lines of authority descends, engaged in underground resistance to Nazi rule.

In their first three centuries, these groups struggled against monarchism and intolerance. The struggle was not always external. Even within organizations, there was an ongoing fight to establish that the rights of humankind pertained to all people, and to include women and minorities. As with any vast social and political movement, members of these groups hesitated or even slid backwards, but as a whole these movements were usually at the forefront of freethinking and progressive ideology.

It is no wonder then that these groups have a sordid reputation. If Freemasonry, Rosicrucianism, Modern Templarism, and Modern Gnosticism seem unimportant or irrelevant today, one need merely visit the website of any right wing conspiracist organization to understand how inimical these ideas remain to fascism, totalitarianism, and racism. In the melange of the 1960s, the ideas of these groups were subsumed by many other movements including Wicca and other forms of Neo-Paganism, which represent their direct descendants in terms of intellectual thought. On the right, these organizations are accused of a vast conspiracy toward one world government. To understand why this is so terrible, we need only understand that it is a racist dog whistle for a social movement to level white supremacy and enter an era in which all people are truly respected and entitled to their own agency.

It is probable that Freemasonry descended in some form from Medieval Craft Associations; however Modern Masonry was a product of the 17th century. The first new "High Degree" was created in 1725, however other Lodges were working high degree systems by 1733.

The Rite of Memphis was created in the 1770s or early 1780s. It is no coincidence that it dates to around the time of American Independence and the French Revolution and First Republic. Even that far back the traditional Masonic Lodges had become staid in their acceptance of the social order. These rites, which were at least modeled on rites by Cagliostro, were revolutionary and Republican in Character. They integrated British and French concepts of High Degree Masonry, with a Greek Dionysian tradition, as well as Rosicrucianism and Modern Templarism. They were a first attempt to create a unified Western Rite, tying together all the disparate bodies of European, North African, and West Asian philosophy and tradition which comprise that vague entity called "Western Tradition." In doing so, it foreshadowed and established the tradition of the Golden Dawn and Thelema by more than a century. Of the esoteric branches of Masonry, it was understood to be that which most combined age with scope, and thus was valued by both members of the Golden Dawn, Theodor Reuss, and Aleister Crowley.

Today we reconsecrate this tradition to be one which can help serve as a backbone of tradition in the modern struggle against intolerance and fascism. We embrace this rite as a reminder that resistance to narrow mindedness and the blind rejection of reason is not the only quality of the past, and that the "good old days" were filled with people struggling against human bondage, superstition, and hatred; that humanism is not the empty rejection of spirituality but rather the deepest spirituality, honoring the self and all others.

It was the tradition in ancient Masonic rites to turn up the cuff of the pants and to place about the neck of the candidate a noose. This was a reminder of the state in which condemned heretic was brought to execution in the Middle Ages, with especial reference to the Templars. In placing these traditional items on you, I want to remind you that you are agreeing to be martyrs in the cause of liberty, not for one class or group of people, but for all human beings and of tolerance in all things, save intolerance.

Do you accept your obligation as the recipient of high degrees in the Masonic, Rosicrucian, Templar, Dionysian, and Gnostic Traditions to strive for light, for the betterment of your fellow human beings, and to honor the agency of all people and the sacred nature of all life, to seek always for truth in all things and to, in whatever way is most appropriate to you, enlighten others?

Responses

Because this rite has many high degrees, throughout their history these rites were conveyed most commonly ceremonially, and were not in most cases operated in all particulars. It is our hope that you will study, practice and operate some or all of the appendant ninety seven degrees, either under the auspices of the our Chartering body, or as will be your right, under such auspices as you shall choose to create.

By the authority of my initiation, under the auspices of the Independent and Rectified Rite of the Ancient and Primitive Mystery of Memphis and Misraim, and of the Sovereign Sanctuary of the Gnosis of the Thelemic Order:

> I confer on you the Chapter of Rose-Croix of 18 Degrees. In these degrees is stressed the importance, and is recommended to you the study, of Symbolic Masonry.
>
> In so doing I remove the halter, and present it to you that you may preserve it in remembrance of the reality of the sacrifice of others which has been made to further the ideals which our organization embodies.
>
> I confer upon you the Senate of Hermetic Philosophers of 27 Degrees. In these degrees is recommended to you the study of Philosophical Masonry.
>
> Therefore I hereby confer on you the The Council of the Sovereign Sanctuary of 45 degrees, and recommend to you commitment to the study of Hermetic or Esoteric Masonry.
>
> These are profound distinctions, but they do not grant to you the inherent privilege to grant these degrees or to operate bodies of the Ancient and Primitive Mystery of Memphis and Misraim.

91st Degree of Grand Tribunal of Defenders of the Order

92nd Degree of Grand Liturgical College of Sublime Catechists of the Order

93rd Degree – Grand Consistory of Inspector Regulators General of the Order

94th Degree – Prince of Memphis or Grand Administrator

95th Degree – Sovereign Sanctuary of Patriarch Grand Conservators of the Order

96th Degree – Grand and Puissant Sovereign of the Order

97th Degree – Grand Hierophant

With these dignities is completed a ceremonial conference of the degrees the Ancient and Primitive Mystery of Memphis and Misraim. It is our our hope that you will choose to work in cooperation with our Sovereign Sanctuary, both in the preservation of these degrees as living appendant degrees, as well as other endeavors. Whatever your choice, these degrees have been duly conferred upon you and cannot be revoked by any power. Do what thou wilt shall be the whole of the Law.

Response – Love is the Law, Love under Will

(1) Gregorio del Olmo Lete; Joaquín Sanmartín (12 February 2015). A Dictionary of the Ugaritic Language in the Alphabetic Tradition (2 vols): Third Revised Edition. BRILL. pp. 580-581. ISBN 978-90-04-28865-2.

(2) Of Memphis and of Misraim, the Oriental Silence of the Winged Sun: History of the Egyptian Rites of Freemasonry; its Rites, Rituals and Mysteries, Milko Bogard, CreateSpace (2018) p. 112

(3) A Library of Freemasonry: Comprising Its History, Antiquities, Symbols, Constitutions, Customs, Etc., and Concordant Orders of Royal Arch, Knights Templar, A.A.S. Rite, Mystic Shrine, with Other Important Masonic Information of Value to the Fraternity Derived from Official and Standard Sources Throughout the World from the Earliest Period to the Present Time. (1911). United Kingdom: John C. Yorston.

(4) Albert Pike and William C. Cummings, The Spurious Rites of Memphis and Misraim, Heredom, vol. 9 (2001), pp. 147-97

Appendix E – 0° Materials

These materials are structured to be copied and handed out to Initiates

Qabbalistic Cross and The Lesser Banishing Ritual of the Pentagram

Qabbalistic Cross with Reference to Eliphas Levi's original version

touch the forehead
> For thine
touch the breast
> is the kingdom
touch the left shoulder
> the justice
touch the right shoulder
> and the mercy
hands are dropped to cover the reins
> Through the Aeon, AUMGN

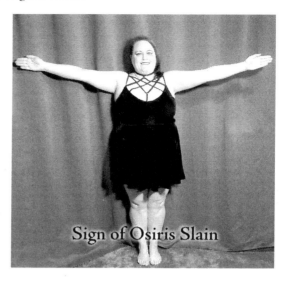

Sign of Osiris Slain

Turn to each of the cardinal points. At each point
- *Make a pentagram*
- *Makes the sign of Osiris Slain*
- *Vibrate the appropriate name*
  - *East: IHVH (ye-HO-wau)*
  - *South: ADNI (ah-DOH-nie)*
  - *West: AHIH (Ehyeh/Eheieh or AY-yah)*
  - *North: AGLA (Ahh-gah-lah)*
- *Make the sign of Horus*

Again extend arms outward to form a cross

> Before me Raphael
> Behind me Gabriel
> On my right hand Michael
> On my left hand Auriel
> For about me flames the Pentagram
> And in the Column stands the six rayed star

touch the forehead
> For thine
touch the breast
> is the kingdom
touch the left shoulder
> the justice
touch the right shoulder
> and the mercy
hands are dropped to cover the reins
> Through the Aeon, AUMGN

A Modern Discussion and Instruction of the Pantacle

This is a discussion of the Pantacle, heavily based on the writing in Liber ABA or *Book Four*, Pt II, Chapter IX, and other sections. For a full historical discussion of the Pantacle, see this source.

The effort here is to update the primary ideas into modern English for the 21st century. This should be read as a commentary and companion to Liber ABA or *Book Four*, Pt II, Chapter IX, and otherwise unattributed quotes are to the above cited section of the principal text. Quotes from different sections of *Book Four*, Pt II are distinguished with page numbers.

The Pantacle is an object which is one of the four elemental tools, sometimes called weapons, which are displayed on the Altar of the magician, along with the Wand, Cup and Sword. It may be seen as connected to the suite of Disks, Pentacles, or Coins in the Tarot.

The Pantacle is not a Pentacle, or five pointed star in a circle. It is a design, more or less complex, through which the magician imposes his will.

Historically, it is a round, flat piece of beeswax which the magician writes upon with a knife. Craft beeswax is inexpensive today and may be melted into a round form in any oven. That said, in the modern era, it is very often made of paper.

A suggested size is "eight inches in diameter, and in thickness half an inch."

The Sigillum Dei Aemuth of John Dee may be seen as the archetype of the Pantacle. An early example of this type of pantacle exists at the British Museum, item 1838,1232.90.a, from the collection of Sir Robert Bruce Cotton, and this example can be seen currently in detail on the British Museum Website through a search of the number above.

Crowley distinguishes between the Pantacle which declares the magician's will, and the Lamen, worn upon the breast which declares the magician's work.

In footnotes, we are told that the Pantacle can serve as a paten for, and is related to, the host of the sacrament. When we think of the Pantacle as the body of the magician this connection becomes very clear. The communion cake is literally a small model of the Pantacle. "In the brown cakes of corn we shall taste the food of the world and be strong."

The Pentacle as the Symbol of the Self

The Elemental Tools:

> **Wand** – divine force, will, the spoken word of the Magus.
>
> **Sword** – human force of the Magus, reason of the Magus
>
> **Cup** – heavenly food of the Magus, understanding, the source of grace of the Magus
>
> **Pantacle** – earthly food, symbolic body, seat of the Holy Guardian Angel and Temple of the Magus

Symbolically the Cup is hollow to receive influence from above, while the Pantacle is flat like the plains of earth. The Pantacle can be seen as a symbolic model of Earth, in the same way that a piece of bread can be seen, through extension to be the body of God. Along similar lines, we are told earlier (p. 98) that "The Pantacle can be seen as the bread of life, and the Sword the knife which cuts it up." This carries a particularly important follow up, "One must have ideas, but one must criticize them." The concept of the magician's tools include not only imposing one's will, but also questioning and refining it.

The Thelemic Initiations

At the heart of Thelema is the question of "true will" versus "false will." There is no easy guideline or "thou shalt not." Rather, the tools are intended to build the symbolic mental capacity to evaluate our true will.

As a temple, the Pantacle has immense scope:

> What is the length of this Temple?
>> From North to South.
> What is the breadth of this Temple?
>> From East to West.
> What is the height of this temple?
>> From the Abyss to the Abyss.

The Pantacle includes everything within the universe. "Fire is not matter at all; water is a combination of elements; air almost entirely a mixture of elements; earth contains all both in admixture and in combination."

Despite the association with the suite of Pentacles, which is often depicted as coins or metal disks, the Pantacle is made from wax, the product of a living thing, reminding us that "everything that lives is Holy." Paper, which is also the product of a living plant, can be seen as having the same basic properties.

The Pantacle as a Storehouse of Ideas

The Pantacle is a storehouse from which the Magus draws. We are told that it must contain "every fact and every falsehood." Conceptually, that may be a little confusing. Why would our Pantacle contain things that aren't true? It depends on what is meant by falsehood. Things like mythology or fictional stories may not be "real," but the ideas of them are true. Some damaging falsehoods are "real" in the sense that they are believed and do damage in the world and we need to account for them in our understanding of our universe.

In a more general sense, all fictions are possibilities and the universe understood as the body of Nuit includes, not just all things, but all possible things. In particular, we're cautioned not to exclude ideas because we don't like them.

> "These stones are the simple impressions or expressions; not one may be foregone. Do not refuse anything merely because you know that it is the cup of poison offered by your enemy; drink it with confidence; it is he that will fall dead!"

There is a lesson here that is shockingly relevant to our era: The idea is not that we must embrace ideas like white nationalism or genocide, but we do need to include them in our view of the universe. In the rough century since the original genesis of these ideas, we've learned that intolerance and catastrophe are abetted by blindness. Not thinking about injustice or the impact of our political systems or personal actions on the environment, deliberately or through ignorance, magnifies destructive change. Not thinking about the realities of human biology and psychology leads to destructive choices in regards to law enforcement and education that act as wrecking balls on the true will of vast numbers of people. Few people set out to be villains – most bad things happen through "benign neglect."

We include everything in our worldview, and that includes those things we find worst. We cannot ignore them in favor of a pristine, privileged worldview including only those things which are comfortable to us. We do not mistake things that have no place in the world we would create from things which do not exist within the universe of possibilities.

The Training of the Magus

A lot of the writing about the Pentacle focuses, not on the object itself, but of the development of the Magus. That makes sense. There is a concept that has become very popular in the West in the 21st century: It is all inside your head, but your head is bigger than you think. The concept that we carry all of reality inside our heads goes back to the 1960s and beyond that to ideas nascent in the 1920s. To that extent the Pantacle is an external symbol of that idea.

The Magus cannot have all experience and all knowledge and will be faced with a choice as to which avenues of knowledge to choose. In 2004, American Psychologist Barry Schwartz popularized the term "Tyranny of Choice" when he discussed how the proliferation of choice in the modern world can paralyze us and hurt our capability for decision-making. Crowley anticipated him in the early 1920s, "The ass hesitated between two thistles; how much more that greater ass, that incomparably greater ass, between two thousand!"

The Pantacle is an external model of our internal tools for preventing paralysis through choice. It isn't random, though. We're given some specific ideas on how to develop a wide-ranging worldview that, since we can't know everything, gives us the flexibility to handle changes:

- Don't choose one area of knowledge, choose several
- The areas of knowledge you study should be diverse
- The focus in any area of knowledge should be not so much the knowledge itself, but its links with all other knowledge
- Excel at a sport
- Choose the sport as one that is best calculated to keep your body in health
- Have grounding in literature, math, and science
- Have enough general knowledge of languages and the way the world works to travel with ease

A huge number of impressions enter our mind every day, but we only retain a few. Excellence of memory is not about remembering everything, but about making good choices in what to remember.

Again, there is emphasis on how things relate. "The best memories so select and judge that practically nothing is retained which has not some coherence with the general plan of the whole."

Symbols within the Pantacle

All Pantacles contain the underlying concept of the circle and the cross, which is an explicit reference to the fundaments of sexual or creative magick. In the simplest conception the Cross and Circle is seen as "phallus" and "vagina." In Crowley's system sexual magick these are taken fairly literally, though not as literally as some of his modern adherents would like to believe.

The cross may be represented by:

A point (a reference to Hadit as the point to Nuit's circle)

Tau cross

A Triangle.

The circle may be represented by:

The Vesica Piscis, or overlapping of two circles.

A serpent (probably most specifically the ouroboros)

Other things which are suggested for representation

Time and space and the idea of causality

Three stages in the history of philosophy, in which the three subjects of study were successively Nature, God, and Man.

Duality of consciousness

The Tree of Life

Categories or specific Sephira or Paths on the Tree

Separately, it is suggested that "an emblem of the Great Work should be added."

The idea of connectedness is seen again in this instruction: "the Pantacle will be imperfect unless each idea is contrasted in a balanced manner with its opposite, and unless there is a necessary connection between every pair of ideas and every other pair." It is suggested that we start with very large and complex sketches, then simplify not so much be exclusion as by combination. The Pantacle should not be simplified too far however, "since the ultimate hieroglypic must be an infinite. The ultimate resolution not having been performed, its symbol must not be portrayed."

The Pantacle and the Dissolution of Ego

There is instruction here on separating the ego, or self, from the impressions one receives. The concept is put forward that we reject some ideas because of our innate ideas or tendencies. Elsewhere in the discussion of Thelema it is made clear that this doesn't mean accepting all ideas as equally good; a sort of abstract lack of relevance where murder is as good as sex.

The point is to be a blank slate and accept all ideas as they are, seeing the connections between them and not rejecting them because they don't fit our preconceptions. We need to feed our ego on everything, not just on ideas we already agree with. "Distasteful facts should be insisted upon until the Ego is perfectly indifferent to the nature of its food."

In a time where conversations about echo chambers have become part of the general dialog on the state of society, this has never been more relevant. We can't function as magicians if we stand in an echo chamber and hear only what we want to hear, even if stepping outside that chamber is very uncomfortable. This is what is meant by "distasteful facts should be insisted upon."

This is related to the concept of "Solve," or "Dissolve," the alchemical process which balances "Coagula," or "Cojoin." It fits into the Thelemic concept that things are divided so that they may be perceived and brought together "for the joy of Union." In the Dhammapada we read:

All that we are from mind results; on mind is founded, built of mind;

Who acts or speaks with evil thought him doth pain follow sure and blind.

So the ox plants his foot, and so the car wheel follows hard behind.

All that we are from mid results; on mind is founded, built of mind;

Who acts or speaks with righteous thought him happiness doth surely find.

So failing not the shadow falls for ever in its place assigned.

A Discussion of Karma

The Pantacle is identical with "the Karma of the magician." The Thelemic concept of Karma is discussed in contrast to the ideas of others "who ought to have known better," which includes the Buddha. It is not about poetic justice or retribution. We are given an example of bad construction of Karma: in one, a man is afflicted with blindness because in a previous life he maliciously deprived a woman of her sight. This is the most simplistic misunderstanding of Karma, where it is assumed to be some form of cyclic punishment for transgressions. "Karma does not act in this tit-for-tat way. An eye for an eye is a kind of savage justice, and the idea of justice in our human sense is quite foreign to the constitution of the Universe."

We are also given an idea of how trying to make Karma into moralistic tales often lead to stories that don't prove the point the author was hoping for. Crowley cites an example from John Bunyan's allegorical 1678 novel "The Pilgrim's Progress" which would have been very familiar to most of his readers. It's still easy to understand today. Two children, Passion and Patience are given toys. "Naughty Passion played with all his toys and broke them, good little Patience put them carefully aside." We are warned that "Bunyan forgets to mention that by the time Passion had broken all his toys, he had outgrown them."

Karma, we are told is a confusing ledger. We don't know what debts may be in it, what we may have to pay, or what we're owed, and we don't know the dates of any payments.

"If we eat too much salmon we get indigestion and perhaps nightmare. It is silly to suppose that a time will come when a salmon will eat us, and find us disagreeable."

"On the other hand we are always being terribly punished for actions that are no faults at all. Even our virtues rouse insulted nature to revenge."

What is Karma?

It's difficult to even understand some of the concepts behind what constitutes our Karma. We're referred to a fairly obscure but pivotal document, Liber Tau-Yod-Shin-Aleph-Resh-Bet (ThIShARB) CMXIII, which is a discussion of the work of the Exempt Adept and how that Magus exists separate from the rest of the Universe and relates to it.

Karma is all we have, but our object is to get rid of it; to surrender our selves. But we aren't the self that we want to surrender. We're "the heap of refuse from which that Self is to be built up." We're told the magical instruments must be made before they are destroyed. This sort of surrender is the annihilation of ego; the pouring out of ones blood into the Cup of Babalon in the Abyss.

We are told that very few people manage to escape basic animal life and make a difference.

> "With the majority of people their actions cancel each other out; no sooner is effort made than it is counterbalanced by idleness….One goes on from day to day with a little of this and a little of that, a few kind thoughts and a few unkind thoughts; nothing really gets done."

Body and mind are changed, but the change itself doesn't have much meaning. "How few are there who can look back through the years and say that they have made advance in any definite direction?" And even of those people, in how many is that really the result of an intentional process.

"The dead weight of the original conditions under which we were born has counted for far more than all our striving. The unconscious forces are incomparably greater than those of which we have any knowledge. This is the solidity of our Pantacle, the Karma of our earth that whirls us will he nill he around her axis..."

The Pantacle is the world which bounds us.

We are told that it is difficult to fashion the Pantacle, because we can write on it, but the characters will "scarcely come to more than did the statue of Ozymandias, King of Kings, in the midst of the unending desert." This is a reference to the poem Ozymandias by Shelley in which a mighty statue of a once great king stands alone and ruined in a desert. Trying to create the Pantacle may even cause despair.

"We cut a figure on the ice; it is effaced in a morning by the tracks of other skaters; nor did that figure do more than scratch the surface of the ice, and the ice itself must melt before the sun."

It's interesting here how well this resounds with us today. We're routinely overwhelmed by the world, swamped by the sheer number of things we can or must do. To fashion the Pantacle, our life's story, into our true will, even into something that is intelligible in the end is a huge work. First, we need to understand our tendencies to cultivate one quality and destroy another. Yes, we must ultimately dissolve our ego in the abyss, but that's an abstract thing in the future. Before we do that we have to make our ego into something that is worth dissolving in the first place. Touching again on the idea that all things are interconnected we are told "And so—beware! Select! Select! Select!"

The Pantacle is an infinite warehouse, but we won't have a lot of time to clean or organize it. Crowley uses the analogy of an aircraft, which must be by necessity kept as light as possible – advice still basic to aerospace today "Remember that in travelling from the earth to the stars, one dare not be encumbered with too much heavy luggage. Nothing that is not a necessary part of the machine should enter into its composition." We are finally left with some very specific advice: The Pantacle is composed of fictions, but some of these fictions are more false than others. The Universe may be an illusion, but it is a fairly persistent one. For most purposes it is true.

That said, most impressions or ideas we have are false even compared to other things in the illusory, but persistent universe. It is important to distinguish between fictions that are "true as far as they go" within the universe and things which are just shams even in that context. "Such distinctions must be graven deeply upon the surface of the Pantacle by the Holy Dagger." The idea of the Universe may be bullshit, but it's pretty solid bullshit most people agree on. Within it, most ideas are actual bullshit. Remember that and make distinctions.

Ciphers and Alphabets

The Masonic Alphabet of Angles. There are in fact a number of variations on this system, however this one comes from the Memphis and Misraim 64° Sage of Mythras Degree

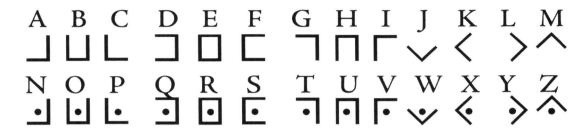

The core concept is the **Pigpen Cipher,** and many other versions derive from this.

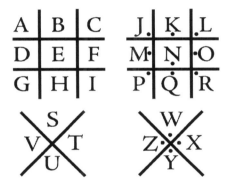

Passing the River - the magician may also wish to be familiar with the Enochian Alphabet of Edward Kelley and Dr. John Dee, for which there are many references, as well as the Passing the River alphabet, which is mentioned in the *Vision and the Voice,* and appears in the work of Cornelius Agrippa. The alphabet is Kabbalistic, and "The River" is the Euphrates which was crossed by the Jews on their return from the period of Babylonian Captivity. In Kabbala, the Euphrates is cognate with Binah, and thus the River can be seen as the Abyss, separating Binah from the lower Sephira. Thus the alphabet can be seen as having a relationship with the process of Crossing the Abyss.

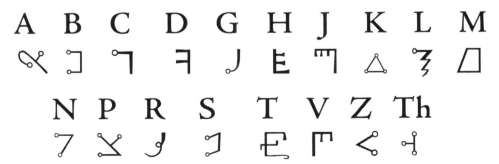

Appendix F – I° Materials

These materials are structured to be copied and handed out to Initiates

I° Initiates Copy of Liber V vel Reguli

Being the Ritual of the Mark of the Beast: an incantation proper to invoke the Energies of the Aeon of Horus, adapted for the daily use of the magician of whatever grade.

THE FIRST GESTURE

The Oath of the Enchantment, which is called The Elevenfold Seal.

The Animadversion towards the Aeon.

Let the magician, robed and armed as he may deem to be fit, turn their face towards Boleskine, that is the House of The Beast 666.

Let them strike the battery I -3-3-3-1.

Let them put the Thumb of their right hand between its index and medius, and make the gestures hereafter following.

The Vertical Component of the Enchantment.

Let them describe a circle about their head, crying NUIT!

Let them draw the Thumb vertically downward and touch the Muladhara Cakkra, crying, HADIT!

Let him, retracing the line, touch the centre of their breast and cry RA-HOOR-KHUIT!

The Horizontal Components of the Enchantment.

Let them touch the Centre of their Forehead, their mouth, and their larynx, crying AIWAZ!

Let them draw their thumb from right to left across their face at the level of the nostrils.

Let them touch the centre of their breast, and their solar plexus, crying, THERION !

Let them draw their thumb from left to right across their breast, at the level of the sternum.

Let them touch the Svadistthana, and the Muladhara Cakkra, crying, BABALON!

Let them draw their thumb from right to left across their abdomen, at the level of the hips.

(Thus shall they formulate the Sigil of the Grand Hierophant, but dependent from the Circle.)

The Asseveration of the Spells.

Let the magician clasp their hands upon their Wand, their fingers and thumbs interlaced, crying LAShTAL! THELEMA! FIAOF! AGAPE! AUMGN!

(Thus shall be declared the Words of Power whereby the Energies of the Aeon of Horus work their will in the world.)

The Proclamation of the Accomplishment.

Let the magician strike the Battery : 3-5-3, crying ABRAHADABRA.

THE SECOND GESTURE.

The Enchantment.

Let the magician, still facing Boleskine, advance to the circumference of their circle.

Let in turn himself towards the left, and pace with the stealth and swiftness of a tiger the precincts of their circle, until he complete one revolution thereof.

Let them give the Sign of Horus (or The Enterer) as he passeth, so to project the force that radiateth from Boleskine before him.

Let them pace their path until he comes to the North; there let them halt, and turn their face to the North.

Let them trace with their wand the Averse Pentagram proper to invoke Air (Aquarius).

Let them bring the wand to the centre of the Pentagram and call upon NUIT !

Let them make the sign called Puella, standing with his feet together, head bowed, their left hand shielding the Muladhara Cakkra, and their right hand shielding their breast (attitude of the Venus de Medici).

Let them turn again to the left, and pursue their Path as before, projecting the force from Boleskine as they passeth let them halt when he next cometh to the South and face outward.

Let them trace the Averse Pentagram that invoketh Fire (Leo).

Let them point their wand to the centre of the Pentagram, and cry, HADIT!

Let them give the sign Puer, standing with feet together, and head erect. Let their right hand (the thumb extended at right angles to the fingers) be raised, the forearm vertical at a right angle with the upper arm, which is horizontally extended in the line joining the shoulders. Let their left hand, the thumb extended forwards and the fingers clenched, rest at the junction of the thighs (Attitude of the Gods Mentu, Khem, etc.).

Let them proceed as before: then in the East, let them make the Averse Pentagram that invoketh Earth (Taurus).

Let them point their wand to the centre of the pentagram, and cry, THERION!

Let them give the sign called Vir, the feet being together. The hands, with clenched finger and thumbs thrust out forwards, are held to the temples; the head is then bowed and pushed out, as if to symbolize the butting of an horned beast (attitude of Pan, Bacchus, etc.). (Frontispiece, Equinox I, III).

Proceeding as before, let them make in the West the Averse Pentagram whereby Water is invoked.

Pointing the wand to the centre of the Pentagram, let them call upon BABALON!!

Let them give the sign Mulier. The feet are widely separated, and the arms raised so as to suggest a crescent. The head is thrown back (attitude of Baphomet, Isis in Welcome, the Microcosm of Vitruvius.) (See Book 4, Part II).

Let them break into the dance, tracing a centripetal spiral widdershins, enriched by revolutions upon their axis as he passeth each quarter, until he come to the centre of the circle. There let them halt, facing Boleskine.

Let them raise the wand, trace the Mark of the Beast, and cry AIWAZ!

Let them trace the invoking Hexagram of The Beast.

Let them lower the wand, striking the Earth therewith.

Let them give the sign of Mater Triumphans (The feet are together; the left arm is curved as if it supported a child; the thumb and index finger of the right hand pinch the nipple of the left breast, as if offering it to that child).

Let them utter the word 0EAHMA!

Perform the spiral dance, moving deosil and whirling widdershins.

Each time on passing the West extend the wand to the Quarter in question, and bow:

     a.   "Before me the powers of LA !" (to West.)

     b.   "Behind me the powers of AL !" (to East.)

     c.   "On my right hand the powers of LA !" (to North.)

     d.   "On my left hand the powers of AL !" (to South,)

     e.   "Above me the powers of ShT ! (leaping in the air.)

     f.   "Beneath me the powers of ShT !" (striking the ground.)

     g.   "Within me the Powers !" (in the attitude of Phthah erect, the feet together, the hands clasped upon the vertical wand.)

     h.   "About me flames my Father's face, the Star of Force and Fire."

     i.   "And in the Column stands their six-rayed Splendour !"

(This dance may be omitted, and the whole utterance chanted in the attitude of Phthah.)

THE FINAL GESTURE

Being the Ritual of the Mark of the Beast: an incantation proper to invoke the Energies of the Aeon of Horus, adapted for the daily use of the magician of whatever grade.

THE FIRST GESTURE.

The Oath of the Enchantment, which is called The Elevenfold Seal.

The Animadversion towards the Aeon.

Let the magician, robed and armed as he may deem to be fit, turn their face towards Boleskine, 1 that is the House of The Beast 666.

Let them strike the battery I -3-3-3-1.

        © 2022, The Thelemic Order, Ltd.

Let them put the Thumb of their right hand between its index and medius, and make the gestures hereafter following.

The Vertical Component of the Enchantment.

Let them describe a circle about their head, crying NUIT!

Let them draw the Thumb vertically downward and touch the Muladhara Cakkra, crying, HADIT!

Let him, retracing the line, touch the centre of their breast and cry RA-HOOR-KHUIT!

The Horizontal Components of the Enchantment.

Let them touch the Centre of their Forehead, their mouth, and their larynx, crying AIWAZ!

Let them draw their thumb from right to left across their face at the level of the nostrils.

Let them touch the centre of their breast, and their solar plexus, crying, THERION !

Let them draw their thumb from left to right across their breast, at the level of the sternum.

Let them touch the Svadistthana, and the Muladhara Cakkra, crying, BABALON!

Let them draw their thumb from right to left across their abdomen, at the level of the hips.

(Thus shall they formulate the Sigil of the Grand Hierophant, but dependent from the Circle.)

The Asseveration of the Spells.

Let the magician clasp their hands upon their Wand, their fingers and thumbs interlaced, crying LAShTAL! THELEMA! FIAOF! AGAPE! AUMGN!

(Thus shall be declared the Words of Power whereby the Energies of the Aeon of Horus work their will in the world.)

The Proclamation of the Accomplishment.

Let the magician strike the Battery : 3-5-3, crying ABRAHADABRA.

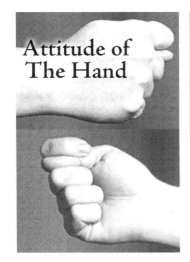

Attitude of The Hand

Sign of Horus the Enterer

Puella

Sign of Hapocrates or Horus the Child

Puer

Mater Triumphans

Attitude of Ptah

AVERSE AIR

AVERSE FIRE

AVERSE EARTH

AVERSE WATER

HEXAGRAM OF THE BEAST

MARK OF THE BEAST

SIGN OF THE GRAND HIEROPHANT

References Liber V vel Reguli

Appendix G – II° Materials

The Bornless Ritual

In our ritual, we recommended the Bornless Ritual on two counts. The first is because it is the ritual through which Aleister Crowley, Master Therion, claims to heave accomplished Knowledge and Conversation with the Holy Guardian Angel. Secondarily, however, it is an excellent microcosm of the long history of the evolution and adaptation of magical ritual. As such, it serves as a well-documented example of how the Magician may take command of such rituals for themselves. Israel Regardie wrote extensively about the Ritual, initially disliking Crowley's adaptation of the names, but over time coming to find a surprising degree of validity in them.

> But others are not thus to be derived at all, so unrecognizable and distorted have they become. In Aleister Crowley's analysis of the barbarous names, he has followed only his own sexual inclinations, which is perhaps as it should be. The only difficulty is that some of the interpretations or analyses, while basically correct and rooted in Yetziratic tradition, sound ludicrous and echo only his own personal sexual proclivities….It therefore seems evident that much the same is true in applying this theme to the string of names to be found as parts of the Bornless Ritual. Some of these names Crowley has quite successfully fitted into the framework of his own Thelemic philosophy and theology. Others are equally evident tortures to suit his own particular views on the relationship of sex and religion - in other words, to suit his version of a solar-phallic religion predicated on "The Book of the Law."

> Yet, piling up here and there is evidence tending to validate much of what Crowley essayed years ago, to lend credibility to some of his seemingly grotesque interpretations. For many years, though I could manage to follow the Qabalistic principles involved in his arbitrary rendering of the barbarous names employed in this ritual, I constantly felt almost outraged, or put upon, as it were, when reading them. Somehow I felt they were excessive, or perhaps unnecessary.

> In recent years, however, much has occurred to cause me to modify the above reaction. For example, I recommend to the student with an eye for research a book entitled "The Sacred Mushroom and the Cross" by John M. Allegro. The author is a lecturer in Old Testament and inter-testamental studies at a leading English University. His previous book "The Dead Sea Scrolls" (Penguin edition, 1964) should be required reading for every student of the Mysteries.

> The introduction, a masterly piece of work, to the first-mentioned book, read in conjunction with Crowley's interpretations of the barbarous names, leads one immediately to the conclusion that no matter how fanciful they seem to be at first sight, there may be considerable philological and not merely symbolic justification for them. Regardless of whether Mr. Allegro's particular thesis is substantiated or not by other scholars, none-the-less his present contribution provides another linguistic key which helps turn the rusty lock to give fundamental meaning to these ancient and obscure words.[465]

> - Israel Regardie, *Ceremonial Magic*, Lowe & Brydone, 1980 pp. 60-61

The ritual also serves as an introduction to PGM working as part of Thelema. Goodwin's translation of the Bornless Ritual from 1852 is quite obscure, however it was cited by the well known Egyptologist E.A. Wallis Budge, in *Egyptian Magic*[466] (now widely available in public domain online) which went through a vast number of editions from 1890 on, and that may be how it came to the attention of Ayton and the Golden Dawn.

The full ritual by Crowley can be found as an Appendix IV of *Liber ABA, Book Four, Magic in Theory and Practice*. The work is out of copyright in Europe and may be found online in various European archives. An excellent new edition has been made available in the UK and Europe by Stephen Skinner who had been preparing it prior to the battle over Crowley's copyrights at the turn of the century, and it is available for Amazon Kindle as of this printing.

The Adept would do well to acquire for themselves a copy of Book IV. It should be noted that while the Skinner edition is available only from resellers in the United States, it is legal to purchase in the US under the 2013 ruling in *Kirtsaeng v. John Wiley & Sons, Inc.*

Two scholarly renderings of the Bornless Ritual, PGM V. 96-172

From Charles Wycliffe Goodwin, 1852

An address to the god drawn upon the letter.

I call thee, the headless one, that didst create earth and heaven, that didst create night and day, thee the creator of light and darkness. Though art Osoronnophris, whom no man hath seen at any time; though art Iabas, though art Iapos, though has distinguished the just and the unjust, though didst make female and male, though didst produce seeds and fruits, though didst make men to love one another and to hate one another.

I am Moses thy prophet, to whom thou didst commit thy mysteries, the ceremonies of Israel; though didst produce the moist and the dry and all manner of food. Listen to me:

I am an angel of Phapro Osoronnophris; this is thy true name, handed down to the prophets of Israel. Listen to me, ………….
…………………………………………….. hear me and drive away this spirit.

I call thee the terrible and invisible god residing in the empty wind,………………….. thou headless one, deliver such an one from the spirit that possesses him…………………
…………………………………………….. strong one,

Contemporary from Hans Dieter Betz, 1986

Stele of Jeu the hieroglyphist in his letter:

I summon you, Headless One, who created earth and heaven, who created night and day, I you who created light and darkness; you are Osoronnophris whom none has ever seen; you are Iabas; you arc Iapos; you have distinguished the just and the unjust; you have made female and male; I you have revealed seed and fruits; you have made men love each other and hate each other.

I am Moses your prophet to whom you have transmitted your mysteries I celebrated by Israel; you have revealed the moist and thc dry and all nourishment; hear me.

I am the messenger of Pharaoh Osoronnophris; I this is your true namc which has been transmitted to the prophets of Israel. Hear me, ARBATHIAŌ REIBET ATHELEBERSĒTH [AM] BLATHA ALBEU EBBNPHCHI CHITASGOĒ IBAŌTH IAŌ; / listen to me and turn away this daimon.

I call upon you, awesome and invisible god with an empty spirit, AROGOGOROBRAŌ SOCHOU MODORIŌ PHALARCHAŌ OOO. Holy Headless Onc, dcliver him, NN, from the daimon which restrains him, / ROUBRIAŌ MARI ŌDAM BAABNABAŌTH ASS ADŌNAI APHNIAŌ

The Thelemic Initiations

headless one, deliver such an one from the spirit that possesses him

....

deliver such an one...

This is the lord of the gods, this is the lord of the world, this is whom the winds fear, this is he who made voice by his commandment, lord of all things, king, ruler, helper, save this soul

....

...... angel of God ....

....

I am the headless spirit, having sight in my feet, strong, the immortal fire; I am the truth; I am he that hateth that ill-deeds should be done in the world; I am he that lighteneth and thundereth; I am he whose sweat is the shower that falleth upon the earth that it may teem: I am he whose mouth ever burneth; I am the begetter and the bringer forth (?); I am the Grace of the World; my name is the heart girt with a serpent. Come forth and follow.

—The celebration of the preceding ceremony.—Write the names upon a piece of new paper, and having extended it over your forehead from one temple to the other, address yourself turning toward the north to the six names, saying:

Make all spirits subject to me, so that every spirit of heaven and of the air, upon the earth and under the earth, on dry land and in the water, and every spell and scourge of God, may be obedient to me.—And all the spirits shall be obedient to you.

ITHŌLĒTH ABRASAX AĒŌŌY; mighty Headless One, deliver him, NN, from the daimon which restrains him. MABARRAIŌ IOĒL KOTHA ATHORĒBALŌ ABRAŌTH, deliver him, NN AŌTH ABRAŌTH BASYM ISAK SABAŌTH IAŌ. /

He is the lord of the gods; he is the lord of the inhabited world; he is the one whom the winds fear; he is the one who made all things by the command of his voice.

"Lord, King, Master, Helper, /save the soul, IEOU PYR IOU PYR IAŌT IAĒŌ IOOU ABRASAX SABRIAM OO YY EY OO YY ADŌNAIE, immediately, immediately, good messenger of God ANLALA LAI GAIA APA DIACHANNA CHORYN."

I am the headless daimon with my sight in my feet; [I am] the mighty one [who possesses] the immortal fire; I am the truth who hates the fact that unjust deeds are done in the world; I am the one who makes the lightning flash and the thunder roll; I am the one whose sweat is the heavy rain which falls upon thc earth that it might be inseminated; I am the one whose mouth burns completely; I am the one who begets and dcstroys; I am the Favor of the Aion; my name is a heart encircled by a serpent; come forth and follow."

Preparation for the foregoing ritual: Write the formula' on a new sheet of papyrus, and after extending it from one / of your temples to the other, read the names, while you face north saying,

Subject to me all daimons, I so that every daimon, whether heavenly or aerial or earthly or subterranean or terrestrial or aquatic, might be obedient to me and every enchantment and scourge which is from God." / And all daimons will be obedient to you.

Appendix H- The Passwords and Signs of the Grades

0° - Petitioner

Password of the Grade – Ludus

Sign of the Grade – Place their left hand on the book at an angle of 90 degrees, right hand under the book

Formula of the Grade – Abrahadabra

Elaboration on the Formula – 418

I° - Magician

Password of the Grade – Eros

Masonic Password – JABULON

Sign of the Grade – Grand Salute of Royal Arch

Formula of the Grade – LAShTAL

Elaboration on the Formula – 93

II° - Knight of the Rose Cross

Password of the Grade – Pragma

Masonic Password – INRI

Sign of the Grade – Right hand over the center of the chest, then raised, with left hand crossed over to form the inverse Sign of Osiris Risen

Formula of the Grade – ALIM

Elaboration on the Formula – ALHIM

Appendix I – printable copies for use during initiation

Materials for 0° Initiation

The Readings

First Reading

From *The Book of the Law, Liber AL vel Legis*, The Third Chapter, First Verse

ABRAHADABRA the reward of Ra Hoor Khut. (AL III: 1)

Second Reading

From *The Book of the Law, Liber AL vel Legis*, the Third Chapter, Forty Seventh Verse

This book shall be translated into all tongues: but always with the original in the writing of the Beast; for in the chance shape of the letters and their position to one another: in these are mysteries that no Beast shall divine. Let him not seek to try: but one cometh after him, whence I say not, who shall discover the Key of it all. Then this line drawn is a key: then this circle squared in its failure is a key also. And ABRAHADABRA . It shall be his child & that strangely. Let him not seek after this; for thereby alone can he fall from it. (AL III: 47)

Third Reading

From *The Book of the Law, Liber AL vel Legis*, the Third Chapter, Seventy Fifth Verse

The ending of the words is the Word ABRAHADABRA. (AL III: 75)

Printable copies of Materials for I°

The Readings

First Reading

The first reading is from the *Magical Diaries of Aleister Crowley: Tunisia 1923*

"There seems to be much misunderstanding about True Will ... The fact of a person being a gentleman is as much an ineluctable (in-ELECT-able) factor as any possible spiritual experience; in fact, it is possible, even probable, that a man may be misled by the enthusiasm of an illumination, and if he should find apparent conflict between his spiritual duty and his duty to honour, it is almost sure evidence that a trap is being laid for him and he should unhesitatingly stick to the course which ordinary decency indicates. Error on such point is precisely the "folly" anticipated in…" *Liber AL* I: 36 "...and I wish to say definitely, once and for all, that people who do not understand and accept this position have utterly failed to grasp the fundamental principles of the Law of Thelema." [467]

Second Reading

The Second Reading is from *The Book of the Law*, Chapter One, Verse Forty Six

Nothing is a secret key of this law. Sixty-one the Jews call it; I call it eight, eighty, four hundred & eighteen. [468]

Third Reading

The Third Reading is from *The Confessions of Aleister Crowley, Chapter 66*

"We accordingly took loose rocks and built a great circle, inscribed with the words of power; and in the midst we erected an altar and there I sacrificed myself. The fire of the all-seeing sun smote down upon the altar, consuming utterly every particle of my personality. I am obliged to write in hieroglyph of this matter, because it concerns things of which it is unlawful to speak openly under penalty of the most dreadful punishment; but I may say that the essence of the matter was that I had hitherto clung to certain conceptions of conduct which, while perfectly proper from the standpoint of my human nature, were impertinent to initiation. I could not cross the Abyss till I had torn them out of my heart" [469]

Fourth Reading

The Fourth Reading is also from *The Confessions of Aleister Crowley*, Chapter 66

"The twelfth Aethyr describes the City of the Pyramids, whose Queen is called BABALON, the Scarlet Woman, in whose hand is a Cup filled with the blood of the saints. Her ecstasy is nourished by the desires which the Masters of the Temple have poured from their hearts for Her sake. In this symbolism are many mysteries concealed. One is that if a single drop of blood be withheld from Her Cup it putrefies the being below the Abyss, and vitiates the whole course of the Adept's career." [470]

Printable copies of Materials for II°

First Reading

From *Liber 65, The Book of the Heart Girt by a Serpent*

I am the Heart; and the Snake is entwined
About the invisible core of the mind.
Rise, O my snake! It is now is the hour
Of the hooded and holy ineffable flower.
Rise, O my snake, into brilliance of bloom
On the corpse of Osiris afloat in the tomb!
O heart of my mother, my sister, mine own,
Thou art given to Nile, to the terror Typhon!
Ah me! but the glory of ravening storm
Enswathes thee and wraps thee in frenzy of form.
Be still, O my soul! that the spell may dissolve
As the wands are upraised, and the æons revolve.
Behold! in my beauty how joyous Thou art,
O Snake that caresses the crown of mine heart!
Behold! we are one, and the tempest of years
Goes down to the dusk, and the Beetle appears.
O Beetle! the drone of Thy dolorous note
Be ever the trance of this tremulous throat!
I await the awaking! The summons on high
From the Lord Adonai, from the Lord Adonai![471]

Second Reading

From the *Vision and the Voice* - The Introduction

The name of the Dweller in the Abyss is Choronzon, but he is not really an individual. The Abyss is empty of being; it is filled with all possible forms, each equally inane, each therefore evil in the only true sense of the word-that is, meaningless but malignant, insofar as it craves to become real. These forms swirl senselessly into haphazard heaps like dust devils, and each such chance aggregation asserts itself to be an individual, and shrieks, "I am I!" though aware all the time that its elements have no true bond; so that the slightest disturbance dissipates the delusion just as a horseman, meeting a dust devil, brings it in showers of sand to the earth.[472]

Third Reading

From the *Book of Thoth*

"For until we become innocent, we are certain to try to judge our Will by some Canon of what seems 'right' or 'wrong'; in other words, we are apt to criticise our Will from the outside, whereas True Will should spring, a fountain of Light, from within, and flow unchecked, seething with Love, into the Ocean of Life."[473]

Fourth Reading

From *Liber ABA, Book 4*, Part II, Chapter VI, "The Wand"

Hence to will anything but the supreme thing, is to wander still further from it—any will but that to give up the self to the Beloved is Black Magick—yet this surrender is so simple an act that to our complex minds it is the most difficult of all acts; and hence training is necessary. Further, the Self surrendered must not be less than the All-Self; one must not come before the altar of the Most High with an impure or an imperfect offering. As it is written in Liber 65, "To await Thee is the end, not the beginning."

Apendix J - Properties Lists

0° Initiation Props by Class

The Altar Elements

Two Altar candles - these may be pillar candles, or may be glass jar (novena) candles.

☐ Right candle - white or light

☐ Left candle - black or dark

Masonic Tools

☐ Hammer

☐ Compass

☐ Ruler

Other Altar Elements

☐ **The Orb** 8-10 inches high and 6-8 inches side to side

☐ **Cloth Cover for Orb** - large enough to completely cover the orb, leaving no part of it exposed

☐ **Sword of Fire**

☐ **Display copy of** *Liber AL*

☐ **Copies of** *Liber AL* **for distribution**

☐ **Red Triangle** - made of cardboard, paper, or cloth

Other Ritual Elements

☐ **Candle of the Hours** - This is lit during the M∴M∴ Opening

☐ **Bowl** - Sufficient for handwashing.

☐ **Hyssop** - for water to be used for handwashing.

☐ **Tracing Board**

☐ **Pitcher**

Readings

☐ **Readings** on printed cards or sheets

Properties for the Play

The Weapons

☐ Compass

☐ Ruler

☐ Hammer

Other Props

☐ **Ring of Hiram** - ring which bears the inscription YHWH on the inside or reverse.

☐ **Staff of Hiram** - theatrical prop so the quality may be minimal.

☐ **Broken Staff of Hiram** - *As this is only alluded to, it may be omitted.*

    ☐ **Prop for Well** - *may be a chair or table*

    ☐ **Scripts for the Play** - Ideally they can be presented in neat black binders

    ☐ **Bread, Salt** - the bread and salt from the Sideboard may be reused

    ☐ **Wine in a cup** - prepared and set aside to be carried by the Villains.

The Books

    ☐ **Book AMBZ - ⵑVⵄⵏ -** bound in Orange, AMBZ in Dark Violet - Azalais

    ☐ **Book ABFMA - ⵏⵄⵑVⵏ -** bound in Red, ABFMA in Blue - Raimond

    ☐ **Book - AN - ⴺⵏ -** bound Brown Red or Blood Red, AN in black - Jeanne

    ☐ **Book** - Bound in black with no inscription - Fool

Generic Properties

    ☐ **Three Chairs** - Three chairs together

    ☐ **Sideboard** - small or medium-sized table at the side of the room

    ☐ **Altar** - large and sturdy

    ☐ **Towels** - adequate to dry hands of all initiates, clean and fresh.

    ☐ **Timepiece** - a timepiece to record the time of initiation

    ☐ **Note Paper and Writing Implement** - to record the time of initiation

    ☐ **Lighter** - A reliable grill lighter, or high quality long matches

The Feast Food

    ☐ **Bread**

    ☐ **Honey**

    ☐ **Salt**

    ☐ Additional Feast Food

The Gifts

    ☐ **Scourges** - Small flails or scourges.

    ☐ **Chains**

    ☐ **I° Initiation Petitions**

0° Initiation Props by Start Location

Furniture

- ☐ **Three Chairs** - Three chairs together
- ☐ **Altar**
- ☐ **Sideboard**

M∴M∴ Opening - Sideboard - 0° - Altar

- ☐ **Hammer**
- ☐ **Compass**
- ☐ **Ruler**

The Altar Elements

- ☐ **The Orb** 8-10 inches high and 6-8 inches side to side
- ☐ **Cloth Cover for Orb** - large enough to completely cover the orb, leaving no part of it exposed
- ☐ **Right candle** - white or light- may be pillar candle, or may be glass jar (novena) candle.
- ☐ **Left candle** - black or dark- may be pillar candle, or may be glass jar (novena) candle.
- ☐ **Sword of Fire**
- ☐ **Display copy of** *Liber AL*
- ☐ **Red Triangle** - made of cardboard, paper, or cloth
- ☐ **Copies of** *Liber AL* for distribution

In front of the Altar

- ☐ **Tracing Board**

Sideboard

The sideboard is a default location. It may be more desirable to start with this props in the possession of an individual, or in some other location.

- ☐ **Readings** on printed cards or sheets
- ☐ **Lighter** - A reliable grill lighter, or high quality long matches
- ☐ **Towels** - adequate to dry hands of all initiates, clean and fresh.
- ☐ **Candle of the Hours** - This is lit during the M∴M∴ Opening - Sideboard
- ☐ **Scourges** - Small flails or scourges.
- ☐ **Chains**
- ☐ **I° Initiation Petitions**
- ☐ **Timepiece** - a timepiece to record the time of initiation
- ☐ **Note Paper and Writing Implement** - to record the time of initiation

Properties for the Play

    The Weapons *(may be the same as the altar weapons)*

☐ Hammer

☐ Compass

☐ Ruler

Other Props

☐ **Scripts for the Play** - Ideally they can be presented in neat black binders

☐ **Ring of Hiram** - ring which bears the inscription YHWH on the inside or reverse.

☐ **Staff of Hiram** - theatrical prop so the quality may be minimal.

☐ **Broken Staff of Hiram** - As this is only alluded to, it may be omitted.

☐ **Prop for Well** - may be a chair or table

☐ **Bread** - the bread and salt from the Sideboard may be reused

☐ **Salt** - the bread and salt from the Sideboard may be reused

☐ **Wine in a cup** - prepared and set aside to be carried by the Villains.

On Chairs

☐ **Book AMBZ -** ꝑＶℰꝫ **-** bound in Orange, AMBZ in Dark Violet - Azalais

☐ **Book ABFMA -** ꝫℰꝑＶꝫ **-** bound in Red, ABFMA in Blue - Raimond

☐ **Book - AN -** ꝭꝫ **-** bound Brown Red or Blood Red, AN in black - Jeanne

Located for Fool

☐ **Book** - Black - binder containing script - Bound in black with no inscription - Fool

The Feast Food

☐ **Bread**

☐ **Honey**

☐ **Salt**

☐ **Additional Feast Food**

I° Initiation Props by Class

The Altar Elements

- ☐ **The Orb** 8-10 inches high and 6-8 inches side to side
- ☐ **Cloth Cover for Orb** - large enough to completely cover the orb, leaving no part of it exposed
- ☐ **Right candle** - white or light- may be pillar candle, or may be glass jar (novena) candle.
- ☐ **Left candle** - black or dark- may be pillar candle, or may be glass jar (novena) candle.
- ☐ **Sword of Fire**
- ☐ **Red Triangle**
- ☐ **Display copy of** *Liber AL*
- ☐ **Brazier**
- ☐ **Brazier Candle**

Masonic Tools

- ☐ **Hammer**
- ☐ **Compass**
- ☐ *Ruler*

Other Ritual Elements

- ☐ **Candle of the Hours** - This is lit during the M∴M∴ Opening
- ☐ **Tracing Board**

Readings

- ☐ **Readings** on printed cards or sheets

Properties for the Play

- ☐ **Scripts for the Play** - Ideally they can be presented in neat black binders

Optional "Color" Props

- ☐ **Crown** - for the King
- ☐ **Fishnet** - for the fisherman
- ☐ **Solar Crown** - for Isis, Cow Horns and Solar Disk
- ☐ **Ankh or Tyet** - for Isis
- ☐ **Pschent Crown or Hawk Headpiece** - for Horus
- ☐ **Military Hats or Jackets** - for Officers, NCO
- ☐ **Rope** - for Soldiers
- ☐ **Old style flashlight**- for Soldiers
- ☐ **Old Poster for Cafe Dorian Gray** - for Soldier cache
- ☐ **Old Books**
- ☐ **Broken Wall**
- ☐ *The Scented Garden of Abdullah the Satirist of Shiraz*

☐ *Berlin's Third Sex.* By Doctor Magnus Hirschfeld

☐ *The Equinox* Volume One, Number Five

The Books

☐ **Book of the Left Hand/Sempiternal *Liber AL*** with initiation script 4 copies

Generic Properties

☐ **Lighter** - A reliable grill lighter, or high quality long matches

☐ **Three Chairs** - Three chairs together, with the one to the right, as one stands facing them, denoted as a throne, either by being larger, more elevated, etc.

☐ **Sideboard** - This may be any small or medium-sized table at the side of the room

☐ **Altar** - This must be large and sturdy enough to accommodate a sword, the implements, and two candles

☐ **Chessboard** - optional prop

☐ **Timepiece** - a timepiece to record the time of initiation

☐ **Note Paper and Writing Implement** - to record the time of initiation

The Feast Food

☐ *Feast Food - optional prop*

I° Initiation Props by Start Location

Furniture

- ☐ **Three Chairs** - Three chairs together
- ☐ **Altar**
- ☐ **Sideboard**

The Altar Elements

- ☐ **The Orb** 8-10 inches high and 6-8 inches side to side
- ☐ **Cloth Cover for Orb** - large enough to completely cover the orb, leaving no part of it exposed
- ☐ **Right candle** - white or light- may be pillar candle, or may be glass jar (novena) candle.
- ☐ **Left candle** - black or dark- may be pillar candle, or may be glass jar (novena) candle.
- ☐ **Sword of Fire**
- ☐ **Red Triangle**
- ☐ **Display copy of** *Liber AL*
- ☐ **Brazier**
- ☐ **Brazier Candle**

In Front of Altar

- ☐ **Tracing Board**

Sideboard

- ☐ **Readings** on printed cards or sheets
- ☐ **Candle of the Hours** - This is lit during the M∴M∴ Opening - Sideboard
- ☐ **Left Hand/Sempiternal** *Liber AL* with initiation script
- ☐ **Timepiece** - a timepiece to record the time of initiation
- ☐ **Note Paper and Writing Implement** - to record the time of initiation
- ☐ **Lighter** - A reliable grill lighter, or high quality long matches

On Chairs/Positioned for Fool

- ☐ **Book of the Left Hand/Sempiternal** *Liber AL* with initiation script

Situated near Raimond's Chair

- ☐ **Chessboard** - optional prop

The Feast Food

- ☐ **Feast Food** - details optional

Play Materials

- ☐ **Scripts for the Play** - Ideally they can be presented in neat black binders

Optional "Color" Props

- ☐ **Crown** - for the King
- ☐ **Fishnet** - for the fisherman
- ☐ **Solar Crown** - for Isis, Cow Horns and Solar Disk
- ☐ **Ankh or Tyet** - for Isis
- ☐ **Pschent Crown or Hawk Headpiece** - for Horus
- ☐ **Military Hats or Jackets** - for Officers, NCO
- ☐ **Rope** - for Soldiers
- ☐ **Old style flashlight**- for Soldiers
- ☐ **Old Poster for Cafe Dorian Gray** - for Soldier cache
- ☐ **Old Books**
- ☐ **Broken Wall**
- ☐ *The Scented Garden of Abdullah the Satirist of Shiraz*
- ☐ *Berlin's Third Sex.* By Doctor Magnus Hirschfeld
- ☐ *The Equinox* Volume One, Number Five

II° Initiation Props by Class

The Altar Elements

- ☐ **The Orb** 8-10 inches high and 6-8 inches side to side
- ☐ **Cloth Cover for Orb** - large enough to completely cover the orb, leaving no part of it exposed
- ☐ **Right candle** - white or light- may be pillar candle, or may be glass jar (novena) candle.
- ☐ **Left candle** - black or dark- may be pillar candle, or may be glass jar (novena) candle.
- ☐ **Sword of Fire**
- ☐ **Display copy of** *Liber AL*
- ☐ **Red Triangle** - made of cardboard, paper, or cloth

Masonic Tools

- ☐ **Hammer**
- ☐ **Compass**
- ☐ **Ruler**

Other Ritual Elements

- ☐ **Candle of the Hours**
- ☐ **Tracing Board**

Stone Elements

- ☐ **The Stone**
- ☐ **The Debris**
- ☐ **Sound SFX**

Readings

- ☐ **Readings** on printed cards or sheets

Properties for the Play

- ☐ **Scripts for the Play**
- ☐ **Properties** - there are no specific properties for the play, however Templar surcoats, swords, helmets or faux manacles for the prison scene could be used.

The Books

- ☐ **Book M** - The Roman Letter "M" is visible

Properties for Restraint, Binding and Hoodwinking

- ☐ **Sword**
- ☐ **Bonds** (1 per initiate)
- ☐ **Hoodwinks** (1 per initiate)
- ☐ **EMT Shears**

Generic Properties

- ☐ **Lighter**
- ☐ **Three Chairs**
- ☐ **Chair Cover**
- ☐ **Sideboard**
- ☐ **Altar**
- ☐ **Note Paper and Writing Implement** - to record the time of initiation
- ☐ **Lighter** - A reliable grill lighter, or high quality long matches

The Feast Food

- ☐ **Food of hardship**
- ☐ a stale cracker or piece of bread (optional)
- ☐ a slice of horseradish (optional)
- ☐ raisins or other old country (not tropical) dried fruit (optional)

II° Initiation Props by Start Location

Furniture

- ☐ **Three Chairs** - Three chairs together
- ☐ **Altar**
- ☐ **Sideboard**

M∴M∴ Opening - Sideboard - 0° - Altar

- ☐ **Hammer**
- ☐ **Compass**
- ☐ **Ruler**

The Altar Elements

- ☐ **The Orb** 8-10 inches high and 6-8 inches side to side
- ☐ **Cloth Cover for Orb** - large enough to completely cover the orb, leaving no part of it exposed
- ☐ **Right candle** - white or light- may be pillar candle, or may be glass jar (novena) candle.
- ☐ **Left candle** - black or dark- may be pillar candle, or may be glass jar (novena) candle.
- ☐ **Sword of Fire**
- ☐ **Display copy of** *Liber AL*
- ☐ **Red Triangle** - made of cardboard, paper, or cloth

Sideboard

- ☐ **Lighter**
- ☐ **Chair Cover**
- ☐ **Candle of the Hours**
- ☐ **Tracing Board**
- ☐ **Readings on printed cards or sheets**
- ☐ **Note Paper and Writing Implement** - to record the time of initiation
- ☐ **Lighter** - A reliable grill lighter, or high quality long matches

Stone Elements - Set up as Properties

- ☐ **The Stone**
- ☐ **The Debris**
- ☐ **Sound SFX**

Properties for the Play

- ☐ **Scripts for the Play**
- ☐ **Properties** - there are no specific properties for the play, however Templar surcoats, swords, helmets or faux manacles for the prison scene could be used.

On Chairs

☐ **Book M** - The Roman Letter "M" is visible

Properties for Restraint, Binding and Hoodwinking

☐ **Sword**

☐ **Bonds (1 per initiate)**

☐ **Hoodwinks (1 per initiate)**

☐ **EMT Shears**

The Feast Food

☐ **Food of hardship**

☐ a stale cracker or piece of bread (optional)

☐ a slice of horseradish (optional)

☐ raisins or other old country (not tropical) dried fruit (optional)

The Applications

Note that these applications are current as of this publishing. They may be replaced at any time by the order of the Supreme Senate III°, and may be supplemented or replaced by an automated process. It is the duty of the Sovereign Initiatior to check periodically to ensure that the most recent version is being used.

Applications and Waivers should be scanned or photographed clearly by the Sovereign Initiator, and submitted using secure email to:

Cancellarius@thelemicorder.io

cc: Secretarygeneral@thelemicorder.io

Applications and Waivers must be submitted at least two weeks in advance, unless a specific exemption is granted by the Cancellarius in writing.

As of this printing Sovereign Initiators should notify the Cancellarius of completed initiations
Sovereign Initiator Notification of Initiation

https://forms.gle/XH4jpL1uxbPZWpAT8

Petition

to the College I°

of the Sovereign Sanctuary of the Gnosis of the Thelemic Order

I _____ do hereby, acting in line with my Will as I understand it do hereby petition for admission into the College of the First Degree of the Sovereign Sanctuary of the Gnosis of the Thelemic Order.

Herein I outline my reasons for seeking admission to the Sovereign Sanctuary whereby I shall be made and declared a Magician and my word placed into the Logos:

Signed _____

Date _____

The Sovereign Sanctuary
of the Gnosis
Of the Initiatory Arm of the
Thelemic Order

By Order of the Cancellarius and of the Consul General on
Behalf of the Initiatory Lodge 0° of the Sovereign Sanctuary
of the Thelemic Order

Application for 0° Petitioner

The Thelemic Initations

The Charge

We demand no oath upon anything but the self and honor. The implicit penalty of the violation of such an oath is an injury to faith in the self, and to the public perception of the self. To the true Adept, such Obligation freely undertaken is far more potent than any litany of imaginary punishments and to the cowardly or faithless seeker, no oath can carry meaning regardless of its content.

We further demand no oath of obedience to any living person or organization outside of that of basic respect for the secrecy of the Initiations. Nor do we collect oaths of obligation to forces or principles which you have not had the opportunity to fully explore and understand, so that you may decide advisedly whether or not you wish to be so obligated. You may be asked for oaths of intent in keeping with your profession of seeker, however, these will not entail answering to any authority other than yourself. You may find to your surprise that the self, in these instances, becomes a more demanding taskmaster than avoidance of some ghoulish threat.

The concepts of these initiations, even their symbolism may be discussed. In most cases, the elements are centuries or even millennia old, and to forbid discussing them would be as foolish as to prohibit that you speak of Orpheus or Dionysos. *It is also not your duty to repress the knowledge of their contents;* those who wish to spoil secrets will most often find a way.

We ask that you refrain in act and in spirit from:

- giving out in written or in verbal form the exact words of the initiations, though where they quote from ancient sources those may be freely discussed.

- describing in synoptic detail the general course and outline by part, or the specific roles and speeches of the characters within the initiations.

- transmitting in any way the various words and signs of the degrees. These are important because they do serve to some extent as guarantors that someone attending an initiation has been exposed to this talk and others, and is thus duly informed as to safety and behavior.

- acting as an initiator into these specific mysteries, as written, without the due authorization of the Sovereign Sanctuary.

- that in deciding how to speak you err on the side of caution and when in doubt embrace the fourth power of the Sphinx which is silence.

- We further state that it is your role only to police your own speech and that the obedience of other initiates to these oaths must be judged by themselves.

With that understanding, you will be asked to make the Following Oath, of which you are here provided in advance with a written copy.

0° The Oath

On my name, upon the deepest identity and understanding of my self, and upon my honor I do swear to maintain the secrets of this Sovereign Sanctuary both in adherence to the word of my oath and the spirit of my action, as it has been fairly and diligently explained to me.

- I will not reveal the words as they are written in whole or part;

- I will not reveal the general course and form of the initiation by part, or the specifics of the characters within;

- I understand that transmitting the words and signs outside of the path of initiation may endanger others and I will refrain utterly from doing this;

- I will not act as an initiator into these mysteries, in whole or in part, without the due authorization of this Sovereign Sanctuary;

- I will not violate the privacy of other initiates, including disclosing their initiatory status or details about their initiation, including their grade of initiation, without their explicit consent;

- When considering how I speak I will err towards silence;

- I understand that it is my duty to police only myself and that I am neither obliged nor empowered to school others in their adherence to this oath;

So mote it be.

Requirements

Warnings or Concerns

The Sovereign Initiator will discuss this with you before the initiation. Please be prepared to voice any concerns that you may have.

Skin Allergies to Hyssop - please disclose any skin allergy to hyssop.

Food Allergies - please disclose any food allergies to the Initiator well in advance.

Sight Reading - Initiates will be asked to sight-read short plays or scenes from a script. It is not necessary for every initiate to do this. The Sovereign Initiator should discuss this before the initiation and ensure that everyone is comfortable.

Depiction of ritual mutilation - One of the roles within the dramatic performances involves the clothed pantomime of castration/penectomy. It is not necessary for any specific initiate to be involved with this, however, the scene will be performed in front of everyone.

Depiction of misogynistic, homophobic and transphobic attitudes - There is misogynistic, homophobic, and transphobic language used in the course of a dramatic historical portrayal. This is not directed *at* the initiates in the sense of hazing or ordeal, nor is this presented as acceptable behavior in the past or present.

What do I need?

What to wear:

The attire specific to the 0-II° initiations should, to a considerable degree, reflect the personality of the Initiate.

The specific guidance is:

"Robes or traveling clothes, which may be of a rustic, archaic or ancient character. In general, these should be simple, rather than complex. Dark or primary colors are to be favored."

Attire must be:

- Safe in a space which includes open flame.
- Safe for normal movement (e.g. it may not involve a train, or other costume elements which require assistance or spotting).
- Allow for normal vision without undue restriction.
- Should not generally include headgear. Hoods or other elements should be able to be pulled back or removed. Headcoverings should generally not be included except in the case that they form a part of the Initiate's regular attire due to some other profession or affiliation.
- Any gloves or hand coverings must be removable.

What to bring:

The petitioner shall bring with them a Dagger, using as guidance *Liber ABA, Book Four, Magic in Theory and Practice* Part II, Chapter IV- the Scourge, The Dagger, and the Chain.

Dagger Details

- The Dagger does not need to be brand new, or unused, but should be suitable for dedication to the purposes of the magician. The blade will be carried by one of the Performers within the Ritual, though if the sheath is detachable it does not need to be unsheathed.

- Despite the reference to *Liber ABA*, which states "The Dagger is made of steel inlaid with gold; and the hilt is also golden" the dagger may be of any material or size that does not violate the requirements below. It may be single or double edged, or blunted.

- The Dagger must be sheathed or otherwise encased so that it does not present any safety hazard when carried, or when drawn, including if the Initiate should trip and fall.

- The Dagger must be of a length, size, and material that can be managed within a confined space. It is not a short sword, and those designs of dagger which are very long and verge on a martial weapon are discouraged.

- There is no specific requirement, however, Initiators may decline to accept any blade that they feel is unsafe or unmanageable, including those which are overly large and cannot be easily drawn in a conventional fashion. These may be accommodated by being provided within the room, but under the supervision, and carried by, the Sovereign Initiator or their designate.

- The definition of "Dagger" is up to the initiate. A symbolic blade shorter than a conventional dagger is completely acceptable.

Negotiation Notes

The Initiate should keep this part of the application.

Sovereign Initiator Contact Info:

_____

The Sovereign Sanctuary
of the Gnosis
Of the Initiatory Arm of the Thelemic Order

By Order of the Cancellarius and of the Consul General on Authority
of the College I° of the Sovereign Sanctuary
of the Thelemic Order

Application for I° Magician

The Thelemic Initations

The Charge

The Grade of Magician in the Thelemic Initiations focuses on the magical foundation of the individual and the establishment of the individual as a Magician within the world. The Grade may be better understood after the Petitioner Grade initiation.

In practice, the grades 0°-II° involve lessons and experiences which most individuals who come to esoteric initiation in the 21st century are at least partially familiar with. Moreover, the building exercises and work which follow them are not particularly exclusive. Thus the grades 0°-II° may be taken in succession and assimilated together afterwards.

The oath below assumes that the candidate for initiation has read *Liber ABA, Book Four, Magic in Theory and Practice* Part II, Chapter IX - The Pantacle, and the language of the oath reflects concepts found in that passage. If you are intending to take 0°-II° inclusive, you will want to read that material now, in order to fully understand the significance of the oath.

The significant thrust in this oath is the agreement to invoke the Aeon of Horus "in fact" as well as theory. There is implicit agreement to actively invoke the Aeon, rather than simply experiencing or observing it. There is no agreement to a particular methodology, though the initiate will be given examples. Thus the initiate agrees to become an active Magician, beginning to control their experience of the New Aeon, rather than merely responding to it.

I° - The Oath

I _____ do solemnly promise on my self of self in the sight of the one secret and ineffable Lord, and in the sight of all stars in the company of stars that I shall do these things to the best of my understanding:

- I shall walk the path of the Magician

- I shall seek my true will

- I shall seek the understanding of love which is Agape

- I shall invoke the Aeon of Horus in fact as well as theory

- I shall embody the energies of the Aeon of Horus

I shall try in every circumstance to better understand these matters, both unflinching and incisive pursuit of knowledge of myself, and in eager and anxious acceptance of all experience.

Within the Pantacle that is my world, I will include not only those things favorable to me, but those things which are poisonous to me, that my world not be folly and lead me to a false will.

That I shall strive in every way to increase my understanding that I may better walk the path of the Magician.

So mote it be.

Warnings or Concerns

Food Allergies

Please disclose any food allergies to the Initiator well in advance.

Sight Reading

Initiates will be asked to sight-read short plays or scenes from a script. It is not necessary for every initiate to do this. The Sovereign Initiator should discuss this before the initiation and ensure that everyone is comfortable.

Depictions

Depiction of misogynistic, homophobic and/or transphobic attitudes

There may be misogynistic, homophobic and/or transphobic language used in the course of a dramatic historical portrayal. This is not directed at the initiates in the sense of a hazing or ordeal, nor is this presented as acceptable behavior in the past or present.

What do I need?

Pantacle Details

- The petitioner shall prepare a pantacle, using as guidance *Liber ABA, Book Four, Magic in Theory and Practice* Part II, Chapter IX - The Pantacle.

- If the Petitioner intends to take the Grades 0°-I° inclusive, they will need to prepare the pantacle in advance.

It is not necessary that this pantacle be made of wax or upon parchment, it is well sufficient that it be drawn neatly upon paper. The pantacle should be sufficiently portable that it may be brought into the initiation.

Petition Details

The Petition is a statement reflecting your Pantacle which summarizes your intentions and goals in initiating.

What to wear:

The attire specific to the 0-II° initiations should, to a considerable degree, reflect the personality of the Initiate.

The specific guidance is:

"Robes or traveling clothes, which may be of a rustic, archaic or ancient character. In general, these should be simple, rather than complex. Dark or primary colors are to be favored."

Attire must be:

- Safe in a space which includes open flame.
- Safe for normal movement (e.g. it may not involve a train, or other costume elements which require assistance or spotting).
- Allow for normal vision without undue restriction.
- Should not generally include headgear. Hoods or other elements should be able to be pulled back or removed. Headcoverings should generally not be included except in the case that they form a part of the Initiate's regular attire due to some other profession or affiliation.
- Any gloves or hand coverings must be removable.

Negotiation Notes

The Initiate should keep this part of the application.

Sovereign Initiator Contact Info:

_____

The Sovereign Sanctuary
of the Gnosis
Of the Initiatory Arm of the
Thelemic Order

By the Order of the Cancellarius and of the Consul General on
Authority of the Chapter II° of the Sovereign Sanctuary
of the Thelemic Order

Application for II°
Knight of the Rose Cross

The Thelemic Initiations

The Charge

The Second Degree is Rosicrucian and Neo-Templar in nature and begins the exploration of those elements of the Western Tradition. The wording of the Oath corresponds specifically to certain Thelemic writings, as detailed below, and must be taken with due regards to them.

This degree has a strong relationship with the related degrees from Traditional Esoteric Freemasonry, as explained under Memphis and Misraim (M∴M∴) below.

The name used should be the core identity of the initiate, in whatever form that takes, whether birth name, magical name, etc.

II° - *The Oath*

Repeat after me the words of the Oath

I --- State your Name --- do solemnly promise in the sight of the one secret and ineffable Lord*, and in the sight of all stars in the company of stars that I shall do these things to the best of my understanding:

- I shall walk the path of the Rose Cross Knight

- I shall take responsibility for all other pilgrims who share the road with me; to guard their well-being, whether it be to aid them in obtaining knowledge or, as I am able, shelter or sustenance

- That I am by this initiation created guard, neither master, nor guide, nor shepherd, any manner of leader†

- I shall work to perfect restraint from the slightest exercise of my will against another being; with the intent that subsequently I shall exercise my will without the least consideration for any other being.‡

- I shall invoke without reserve my Holy Guardian Angel

So mote it be.

Discussion and Clarification

These are official points of clarification, and the oath is to be read in light of these charges:

* This should be understood at this point of Thelemic Initiation to be the self.

† This element is not intended to preclude taking positions of secular or organizational leadership. It pertains specifically to the sacred role of Knight and Adept, clarifying that there is no claim, by right of this initiation or grade, to have dominion over any other.

‡ For the specific background of this charge, see *Liber NV*, specifically the third and fourth practice of Ethics.

> *Let the Aspirant beware of the slightest exercise of his will against another being. Thus, lying is a better posture than sitting or standing, as it opposes less resistance to gravitation. Yet his first duty is to the force nearest and most potent; e.g. he may rise to greet a friend. - This is the third practice of Ethics (ccxx. I. 41).*

> *Let the Aspirant exercise his will without the least consideration for any other being. This direction cannot be understood, much less accomplished, until the previous practice has been perfected. - This is the fourth practice of Ethics (ccxx. I. 42, 43, 44).*

Clearly, this charge is not intended to cause the adept to stop living a normal life, etc., nor does the oath presuppose immediate success. The oath is to the learning process, and is explicitly worded as "I shall work to" rather than "I shall." Failure to make an effort would be an abrogation of the oath, but the oath is understood to be to the effort, not the achievement, recognizing that full success may take considerable time. Making an effort is necessary to progress to the subsequent grade, but full achievement is not.

Requirements

The petitioner shall bring with them a sword, using as guidance Liber ABA, Book Four, Magic in Theory and Practice Part II, Chapter VIII - the Sword.

Sword Details

- Despite the reference to *Liber ABA*, the sword may be of any material or size that does not violate the requirements below.

- The sword must be sheathed or otherwise encased so that it does not present any safety hazard when carried, or when drawn. While swords requiring an overhand draw are not prohibited, they are subject to the "manageability" requirement below.

- The sword must be of a length, size, and material that can be managed within a confined space. There is no specific requirement, however, Initiators may decline to accept any blade that they feel is unsafe or unmanageable, including those which are overly large and cannot be easily drawn in a conventional fashion.

- The definition of "sword" is up to the initiate. There is no minimum size. A knife or symbolic blade shorter than a conventional sword is completely acceptable.

Sovereign Initiator Contact Info:

Warnings or Concerns

The same Warnings and requirements pertain as in I°.

Loud Noises/Jump Scare

Additionally, there is a warning regarding sudden loud noises or startling events. If a sudden loud noise is likely to cause issues above and beyond the usual (being startled), this should be discussed with the Initiator in advance.

Binding of Wrists

As a ritual element, your wrists will be bound with natural or synthetic fiber rope, in a safe fashion, for a short period of time.

It is possible tor this element to be modified or omitted if you are uncomfortable with it, or have concerns with allergies to natural fiber or dyes. You should mention this in your contact with your Sovereign Initiator.

If you have cuffs that you would prefer to use instead of wrist bindings you may bring them.

- Using them is at the discretion of the Sovereign Initiator
- They must be clean
- They must fasten with a simple single tongue (belt style) buckle
- They must not lock or be able to lock
- The portion that circles your wrist must not be metal, or any other inflexible element

Hooding

As a ritual element, your wrists will be bound, in a safe fashion, for a short period of time. The hood will be breathable natural or natural synthetic fabric. It will not be tied or fastened.

It is possible tor this element to be modified or omitted if you are uncomfortable, or have concerns with allergies to natural fiber or dyes. You should mention this in your contact with your Sovereign Initiator.

The Sovereign Sanctuary
of the Gnosis
Of the Initiatory Arm of the
Thelemic Order

By the Order of the Cancellarius and of the Consul General on
Authority of the Chapter II° of the Sovereign Sanctuary
of the Thelemic Order

Application for the Thelemic Initiations

It is my Will to apply for the following Thelemic Initiations. I have discussed this with a Sovereign Initiator, and have determined that these initiations can be performed at an agreed on time and date, or that such a date and time will be agreed on. I understand that that which degrees I may take at a given time and place is subject to the ability of the Sovereign Initiator to arrange an initiation of any given degree, and that my right to initiate is subject to availability.

I am applying for:

☐ **0° Degree - Petitioner**
☐ **I° Degree - Magician**
☐ **II° Degree - Knight of Rose Cross**

Understandings of Disclosure and Informed Consent:

☐ I understand that I may check on the Charter Status of any Sovereign Initiator by contacting the Cancellarius of the Initiatory Arm.

☐ I have read the Charge of the degrees indicated above and have had the opportunity to ask questions.

☐ I have read the Oath of the degrees indicated above, as well as any pertinent Discussion and Clarification, and have had the opportunity to ask questions.

☐ I have read the Consent Policy of The Thelemic Order, which can be found at: **https://rb.gy/2sfzyd**

Things to Bring:

☐ I have read the section on what to wear and have had the opportunity to ask questions.

☐ **0° Degree** -I am aware that I should bring a dagger

☐ **I° Degree** -I am aware that I should bring a pantacle and my petition

☐ **II° Degree** -I am aware that I should bring a Sword

Warnings:

☐ I have had a chance to discuss sight reading with my my Sovereign Initiator and negotiate what level of participation I am comfortable with.

☐ I have read the warnings pertinent to the degrees indicated on the left and had the opportunity to ask questions.

☐ I have explicitly read the information on binding of wrists and hooding in regards to **II° Degree.**

Allergies:

☐ I have disclosed any food allergies.

☐ I do do not have a skin allergy to hyssop.

_____

Print Name

_____

Signature

_____

Initiatory Name

_____

Date

_____

The Sovereign Sanctuary of the Gnosis
of the Initiatory Arm of the Thelemic Order

Initiate Waiver and Agreement to Hold Harmless

This Release is executed by the participant

I, the undersigned participant agree to participate in the following Initiatory Rituals, provided by a Chartered Sovereign Initiator of The Thelemic Order:

☐ **0° Degree - Petitioner**
☐ **I° Degree - Magician**
☐ **II° Degree - Knight of Rose Cross**

Contagious Diseases and Illness

I acknowledge the nature of contagious diseases and viruses and voluntarily assume the risk that I may be exposed to or infected by contagious diseases and viruses by attending and participating and that such exposure or infection may result in personal injury, illness, permanent disability, and death. I understand the risk of becoming exposed to or infected by contagious diseases and viruseand other contagious diseases and viruses may result from the actions, omissions, or negligence of myself and others, including, but not limited to, Initiators, Initiates, Performers, or other contractors or volunteers.

It is my express intent that this Hold Harmless Agreement shall be deemed as a release, waiver, discharge, and covenant not to sue The Thelemic Order including but not limited to its Executive Board, General Assembly, Sovereign Sanctuary of the Gnosis, Officers of the Initiatory arm, agents, employees, representatives and volunteers whatsoever.

The Initiatory Arm reserves the following rights and powers:

- The right to cancel without penalty, *with refund* for any reason.
- The right to cancel *without penalty or refund* the Programs or Events or any aspect thereof after a building closure or outbreak if it or its representatives determine or believe that any person is or will be in danger if the Initiations or any aspect thereof is continued.
- The undersigned acknowledges the right of the Initiatory Arm or its Representative to withdraw any part of the Initiations and to terminate, alter, delete, or modify the Initiatons as deemed necessary without penalty or refund, in order to assure their safe and timely execution.

Obligations of the Initiatory Candidate

The Sovereign Sanctuary of the Thelemic Order and its Initiatory Arm has the authority to establish the rules necessary for the operation of the Initiations and its designated Representative has the sole discretion to decide that an individual should be separated from the Initiations because of a violation of such rules, for disruptive behavior, for conduct which could bring the Initiation staff, volunteers, or Initiates into danger, physical or emotional, including but not limited to violation of the TTO Consent Policy, as well as violation any policy or procedure of the venue, or local law. The decision to separate the individual shall be final. I understand that if I am required to leave the Initiations, no refund will be made.

Good Health

I declare that I am in good health, and/or have disclosed to the best of my ability any conditions that might prevent his/her/my participation in strenuous and rigorous activities of a normal non-contact nature, including standing, rising, movement, climbing stairs, lifting objects and so forth.

Further I understand and acknowledge that because of the physical nature of performative Initiation, there may be physical contact between Initiators, performers, staff, volunteers and venue staff, during rehearsals, preparation, and especially during Initiation. I understand that at times for proper instruction and safety, physical contact is required and necessary.

Further I understand and acknowledge that performative Initiation may be an emotionally provocative environment. I am aware of the potential for emotional trauma or harm, and embarrassment, emotional distress, or any other psychological or emotional harm.

Acknowledgements

In signing this Agreement, I acknowledge and represent that I have fully informed myself of the content of the foregoing Waiver of Liability and Hold Harmless Agreement by reading it before I sign it, and understand that I sign this document as my own free act and deed; no oral representations, statement, or inducements, apart from the foregoing written statement, have been made. I further state that I am at least eighteen (18) years of age and fully competent to sign this agreement; and that I execute this Agreement for full, adequate, and complete consideration fully intending to be bound by the same.

Executed by (legal name):

_____

Witnessed by:

_____

_____

Date (common):

_____

Location:

_____

Sovereign Initiator in Receipt of Waiver:

_____

This waiver must be executed before Initiation may proceed.

Endnotes

Foreword

1) Aleister Crowley, "Liber LXV, Liber Cordis Cincti Serpente, Commentary," In The Continuum, 1978, 37.

Introduction

2) Aleister Crowley, The Confessions of Aleister Crowley: An Autohagiography, ed. John Symonds and Kenneth Grant, Corrected edition, [reprint] (London: Arkana, 1989), 853.

3) George Orwell, Animal Farm: 1984, 1st ed (Orlando: Harcourt, 2003), 10.

4) Aleister Crowley ed. Skinner, Aleister Crowley's Four Books of Magick, Book Four, Liber ABA, ed. Stephen Skinner (Watkins Publishing, 2021).

5) Aleister Crowley, Eight Lectures on Yoga (Sovereign Sanctuary Press, 2004), 48.

6) Rodney Orpheus, "The Method of Science, the Aim of Religion," accessed February 12, 2000, http://rodneyorpheus.com/writings/occult/the-method-of-science-the-aim-of-religion/.

7) George Orwell, 1984 (New York: Harcourt, 1949), 24.

8) Aleister Crowley, The Vision & the Voice: With Commentary and Other Papers (York Beach, Maine: Weiser, 1998), 23.

Topics of Interest

9) Aleister Crowley, "The Temple of Solomon the King," The Equinox (London: Simpkin Marshall, Hamilton, Kent & Co., 1909), 242.

10) The History of Magick: Including a Clear and Precise Exposition of Its Procedure, Its Rites, and Its Mysteries, trans. Arthur Edward Waite (York Beach, Me: Samuel Weiser, 1999), 43.

11) Aleister Crowley, "Liber XV," The Equinox, March 1919, 256.

12) The Douay-Rheims Bible/KJV, John 13:34.

13) Aleister Crowley and Marcelo Motta, magick without Tears: Unexpurgated, Commented (Being the Oriflamme, Volume VI, No. 3-4), 2 vols. (Nashville, TN, U.S.A.: Society Ordo Templi Orientis International, 1983).

14) S. L. MacGregor Mathers, ed., The Book of the Sacred magick of Abramelin the Mage (Dover Publications, 1975).

15) S. L. MacGregor and Crowley Aleister Mathers, ed., The Book of the Goetia of Solomon the King. Translated into the English Tongue by a Dead Hand (Edinburgh: Foyers, Inverness Society for the propagation of religious truth, 1904).

16) Francis X. King, The Secret Rituals of the O.T.O., 1st Edition (C W Daniel Co., Ltd., 1973).

17) Cœmgen La Vaughan, Amor Divina, Writings on the Sexual Praxis of Ordo Templi Orientis (UK: Hell Fire Club, 2018).

18) Jerry Edward Cornelius, "An Open Epistle Regarding Francis King's Book The Secret Rituals of the OTO," Red Flame, A Thelemic Research Journal (Berkeley, CA, 1999).

19) Phyllis Seckler, "Editor's Letter," In the Continuum (The College of Thelema, 1973).

20) Crowley, "The Temple of Solomon the King," 288–90.

21) Crowley, "Liber LXV, Liber Cordis Cincti Serpente, Commentary."

22) Patrick King, "Liber Qadosh - Under the Seal of the XI° Insero Inregia Rex Leoninus Serpens Ecstasis Inexstincto Elatio Volluptaria Meithras," c 1980.

23) Aleister Crowley, "The Antecedents of Thelema (c. 1926)," in The Revival of magick and Other Essays, ed. Beta Hymenaeus Kaczynski Richard Aeschbach-Stiftung (Tempe, AZ: New Falcon Publications in association with Ordo Templi Orientis International, 1998).

24) Aleister Crowley and Stephen Skinner, The magical Diaries of Aleister Crowley: Tunisia 1923 (York Beach, Me.: S. Weiser, 1996), 21.

25) Tobias Churton, The Lost Pillars of Enoch: When Science and Religion Were One (Rochester, Vermont: Inner Traditions, 2021).

26) Moshe Idel, Kabbalah in Italy, 1280-1510: A Survey (New Haven: Yale University Press, 2011), 231.

27) Sylvia Schein, "Between Mount Moriah and the Holy Sepulchre: The Changing Traditions of the Temple Mount in the Central Middle Ages.," Traditio 40 (1984): 179, http://www.jstor.org/stable/27831152.

28) Hugh Nibley, Mormonism and Early Christianity, The Collected Works of Hugh Nibley 4 (Salt Lake City, Utah Provo, Utah: Deseret Book Co.; Foundation for Ancient Research and Morman Studies, 1987).

29) Hugh Nibley and Hugh Nibley, Mormonism and Early Christianity, The Collected Works of Hugh Nibley, v. 4 (Salt Lake City, Utah: Provo, Utah: Deseret Book Co.; Foundation for Ancient Research and Morman Studies, 1987).

30) Gershom Scholem, Origins of the Kabbalah, Princeton classics paperback edition, Princeton Classics (Princeton, NJ: Jewish Publication Society, Princeton University Press, 2019), 309.

31) Scholem, 234.

32) Shahar Shulamith, "The Relationship Between Kabbalism and Catharism in the South of France," in Les Juifs Dans l'histoire de France: Premier Colloque International de Haïfa (Leiden: Brill, 1980), 55–62.

33) Philippa Faulks and Robert L. D Cooper, The Masonic Magician: The Life and Death of Count Cagliostro and His Egyptian Rite (London: Watkins, 2008), 133.

34) Churton, The Lost Pillars of Enoch.

35) Zoé Oldenbourg, Massacre at Montségur (London: Phoenix Press, 2000), 94.

36) Oldenbourg, 275.

37) La Vaughan, Amor Divina, Writings on the Sexual Praxis of Ordo Templi Orientis, XI Degree O.T.O., 201.

38) Crowley ed. Skinner, The Magical Diaries of Aleister Crowley: Tunisia 1923, 69.

39) Aleister Crowley, "Ecclesiae Gnosticae Catholicae Canon Missae, Edited from the Ancient Documents in Assyrian and Greek by the Master Therion," The International: A Review of Two Worlds, March 1918, 72.

Techniques of Initiation

40) Liber AL, I.38.

41) Liber AL, I.32.

42) Crowley, The Vision & the Voice: With Commentary and Other Papers, 21.

43) Aristotle, Nicomachean Ethics, 4, 8.

44) Liber AL, II.20.

45) Liber AL, III.17.

Opening of the M∴M∴ Temple

46) Abiychazah, Meaning 'my Father Is Vision,' in the Seeress Sense of Vision, Is a Feminine Form of Rezon Cf. Ahiman Rezon

47) Cf. G.D. Neophyte Ritual, Bornless Ritual

0° Material

48) The Casno Form Is 8/7/8/78/7/8/78/7/8/7

49) Circling/Cross - the Two Lines Imply a Circle and Cross

50) Star with Sword and Snake Cf. Vision and the Voice, 8th Aethyr

51) Heliopolis, Memphis and Thebes, as Well as Subterranean Depth Cf. Crata Repoa

52) Sunset of Blood and White Snowdrops - Red and White Fluids, Cf. 'Snowdrops' from a Curate's Garden, 'IX° Emblems and Mode of Use' Paper, Etc.

53) Mercy/Balance - Note This as an Alternative Attribution to Mercy and Severity in Qabbalah

54) I.e. Mount Abiegnus

55) Kneph Cf. Plutarch, Moralia, Isis and Osiris 21 'but "That the Inhabitants of the Theban Territory Only Do Not Contribute Because They Believe in No Mortal God, but Only in the God Whom They Call Kneph, Whose Existence Had No Beginning and Shall Have No End."

56) Cf. Bogard, Milko; The Dawning of the Kneph: The Egyptian Influence on Rosicrucianism 1614-2014

57) Cf. *The Vision and the Voice*, 8th Aethyr

58) "Serpent Heart' Cf. *Liber Cordis Cincti Serpente* Vel. LXV, *Liber Samekh*,

59) Assiah, Earth, Manifestation,

60) Constance of France, Countess of Toulouse, 1124 – c. 1176,

61) Yetzirah, Air, Formative,

62) Blanche of Castile, Queen Consort and Regent of France 1188 – 1252,

63) Briah, Water, Creative,

64) Henry II of England, 1133 – 1189

65) Al-Nasir Salah al-Din Yusuf Ibn Ayyub 1137 – 1193

66) Atziluth Fire, Archetypical

67) Crowley and Skinner, The magical Diaries of Aleister Crowley: Tunisia 1923.

68) Celestine III, Pope 1191-1198,

69) Cf. Liber XV 'I Am the Flame That Burns in Every Heart of Man, and in the Core of Every Star

70) Cf. The Golden Dawn Neophyte Ritual

71) Eusebius and Kirsopp Lake, The ecclesiastical history. 1: [Books 1 - 5] / with an English transl. by Kirsopp Lake, [Repr. der Ausg.] 1926, The Loeb classical library 153 (Cambridge, Mass.: Harvard Univ. Press, 2007), chs ix-x.

72) Liber CDXVIII , The Vision and the Voice, 30th Aethyr TEX.

73) "for My Father Goeth Forth to Seek a Spouse to Replace Her Who Is Fallen and Defiled." Liber CDXVIII , The Vision and the Voice,. 30th Aethyr, TEX,

74) Liber CDXVIII , The Vision and the Voice, 30th Aethyr, TEX.

75) Liber CDXVIII , The Vision and the Voice, 30th Aethyr, TEX.

76) Liber CDXVIII , The Vision and the Voice, 30th Aethyr, TEX.

77) "This Might Be Read with Some Interest in Light of the Other References to the 30th Aethyr, TEX

78) Aleister Crowley, Liber Aleph, De Comedia Universa, Quae Dictur Pan.

79) Crowley ed. Skinner, Aleister Crowley's Four Books of Magick, Book Four, Liber ABA, Appendix II, One Star in Sight, 395.

80) Notes Here Pertain to the IV° and May Be Found in an Appendix of That Edition.

81) Eleanor of Aquitaine, 1122-1204 Queen of France 1137-1152; Queen of England, 1154-1189, See Appendix B, Jeanne of England.

82) Melisende, Queen of Jerusalem, Daughter of Baldwin II and the Armenian Princess Morphia of Melitene. (1105-1161)

83) Raimond V, Count of Toulouse, 1134-1197, See Appendix B, Raimond VI Count of Toulouse,

84) Nicetas, Nicetas, Bogomil Bishop of Constantinople, in Lombardy c. 1160, Convened the Council of Saint-Félix in Occitania in 1167, Confirming the Episcopal Office of Six Cathar Bishops. See Lexicon, 'Gnosticism' and Appendix B

85) The Romance of Troy (Le Roman de Troie) c. 1155-60 Written by Benoit de Sainte-Maure

86) Liber CDXVIII , The Vision and the Voice, 1st Aethyr, LIL.

87) Liber CDXVIII , The Vision and the Voice, 8th Aethyr, ZID.

88) *Jesus Christ Superstar: A Rock Opera* (New York: Decca, [1970], 1970), https://search.library.wisc.edu/catalog/999470061602121.

89) Latin Vulgate Bible, I Kings 11:5,

90) The Douay-Rheims Bible/KJV, 2 Paralipomenon (2 Chronicles), 33:7; 4 Kings (2 Kings) 21:7.

91) The Douay-Rheims Bible/KJV, 4 Kings (2 Kings) 23:20.

92) Aleister Crowley, "The Temple of Solomon the King, Book II," The Equinox (London: SIMPKIN MARSHALL, HAMILTON, KENT & CO. LTD, 1909), 225.

93) Raimond Roger Trencavel, Count of Carcassone 1185-1209, See Appendix B

94) Raimond Roger, Count of Foix, d. 1223, Brother of Esclarmonde de Foix See Appendix B

95) Esclarmonde of Foix, Daughter of Roger Bernard I, Count of Foix, Dob 1151-1167, m. 1175, Date of Death Unk. See Appendix B

96) Raimond Roger Trencavel, Count of Carcassone 1185-1209, See Appendix B

97) Aleister Crowley, "Liber DCCCXXXVII The Law of Liberty," The Equinox, 1919, 47.

98) Crowley, "The Antecedents of Thelema (c. 1926)."

99) Cf. Eliphas Levi, Transcendental magick.

100) Eliphas Levi, Dogme et Rituel de La Haute Magie Part II: The Ritual of Transcendental magick (Originally Published by Rider & Co. UK, Transcriped by Benjamin Rowe to Adobe Acrobat, 2002), 28.

101) Aleister Crowley, magick in Theory and Practice (New York: Dover Publications, 1976), 45.

102) Aleister Crowley, "Liber O Vel Manvs et Sagittae Svb Figvra VI," The Equinox, 1909, pp 11-22.

103) The New Comment:, I.37.

104) Aleister Crowley, Berashith. An Essay in Ontology with Some Remarks on Ceremonial magick. (Paris: Clarke & Bishop, 1903).

105) Aleister Crowley, "Liber III Vel. Jugorum," The Equinox, 1909, 12.

106) Aleister Crowley, Aleister Crowley's Four Books of magick, Book Four, Liber ABA, ed. Stephen Skinner (Watkins Publishing, 2021).

I° Material

107) Cf. Francis X. King, The Secret Rituals of the O.T.O., MINERVAL (0°), Part II

108) Jack Parsons, Freedom Is a Two-Edged Sword: And Other Essays, 1. ed., 2. pr, The Oriflame, number 1 (Tempe, AZ: New Falcon Publ, 2001), 11.

109) Liber AL, I.41.

110) Liber AL, I.42.

111) Liber AL, I.41.

112) Liber AL, I.42.

113) Israel Regardie and John Michael Greer, The Golden Dawn: The Original Account of the Teachings, Rites, and Ceremonies of the Hermetic Order, 2015, Z.1: The Enterer of the Threshold, The General Exordium, 318, https://www.overdrive.com/search?q=3EC27475-4B2C-4F4B-A68C-B6BF1A5C1E21.

114) Liber AL, I.41.

115) Liber AL, I.42.

116) Crowley ed. Skinner, Aleister Crowley's Four Books of Magick, Book Four, Liber ABA, Part III, Chapt I,.

117) Liber AL, I.45-46.

118) La Vaughan, Amor Divina, Writings on the Sexual Praxis of Ordo Templi Orientis, IX° Emblems and Modes of Use, p 180–84.

119) Cf. Liber XV, V. Office of the Collects, ""The Lord."

120) The New Comment:, I.51.

121) La Vaughan, Amor Divina, Writings on the Sexual Praxis of Ordo Templi Orientis, IX° Emblems and Their Mode of Use, Emblem II: The Serpent p. 180.

122) "The Motto of The Equinox."

123) La Vaughan, Amor Divina, Writings on the Sexual Praxis of Ordo Templi Orientis, De Arte Magica, VIII, 169.

124) Mark Gregory Pegg, A Most Holy War: The Albigensian Crusade and the Battle for Christendom, Pivotal Moments in World History (Oxford; New York: Oxford University Press, 2008), 98.

125) La Vaughan, Amor Divina, Writings on the Sexual Praxis of Ordo Templi Orientis, De Arte Magica, XI, 170.

126) Aleister Crowley, Tannhauser, A Story of All Time (Leeds: Celphais, 2004), 25.

127) LIber 49, The Book of Babalon

128) Liber CDXVIII, The Vision and the Voice, 12th Aethyr LOE.

129) Crowley, "Liber LXV, Liber Cordis Cincti Serpente, Commentary," 37.

130) Aleister Crowley, "Astarte Vel Liber Berylli, Sub Figura CLXXV," The Equinox, 51.

131) La Vaughan, Amor Divina, Writings on the Sexual Praxis of Ordo Templi Orientis, De Homunculo Epistola, sub figura CCCLXVII, 191.

132) John P. Deveney, Paschal Beverly Randolph: A Nineteenth-Century Black American Spiritualist, Rosicrucian, and Sex Magician, SUNY Series in Western Esoteric Traditions (Albany: State University of New York Press, 1997).

133) The New Comment:, I.51.

134) The New Comment:, I.51.

135) Crowley ed. Skinner, The Magical Diaries of Aleister Crowley: Tunisia 1923, 103.

136) La Vaughan, Amor Divina, Writings on the Sexual Praxis of Ordo Templi Orientis, XI Degree O.T.O., 201.

137) La Vaughan, De Arte Magica, Addendum, 178.

138) "Cf. Vision and the Voice, 6th Aethyr, 12th Aethyr.,"

139) Christophe Poncet, "Ficino's Little Academy of Careggi," Bruniana & Campanelliana 19, no. 1 (2013): 67–76, http://www.jstor.org/stable/24338438.

140) Piero de' Medici 'The Unfortunate,' Florentine Political Leader, Banker, 1472-1503,

141) Rodrigo de Borja, Pope Alexander VI, 1431-1492, Canonized in the Initial Thelemic Canon as Saint Roderic Borgia.

142) Girolamo Savonarola, Dominican Friar, and Populist Political Leader, 1452-1498. See Lexicon

143) Bernardo Del Nero, Florentine Political Leader, 1422 – 1497 - See Lexicon Savonarola

144) Sandro Botticelli, 1445-1510, Florentine Painter, Best Known for His 'Birth of Venus.,

145) Giovanni Pico Della Mirandola, Noble and Philosopher, 1463-1494, Poisoned. See Lexicon

146) Gemistos Plethon, Byzantine Greek Scholar, 1355-1452 See Lexicon

147) Plato, The Symposium, 215a–23.

148) Liber CDXVIII, The Vision and the Voice, 16th Aethyr LEA.

149) Liber CDXVIII, The Vision and the Voice, 13th Aethyr ZIM.

150) Cf. Vision and the Voice 4th Aethyr PAZ, See Note 11; 19th Aethyr POP, See Note 22; 9th Aethyr; 13th Aethyr, ZIM,

151) Aleister Crowley, The Scented Garden of Abdullah the Satirist of Shiraz - The Bagh-i-Muattar (Probsthain & Co., 1910).

152) "The Equinox," 1911, Vol. 1, No. 5.

153) "The Equinox," Vol. 1, No. 5, 106.

154) "The Equinox," Vol. 1, No. 5, 151.

155) Crowley, Aleister and Francis King, The Secret Rituals of the O.T.O (London,: Daniel, 1973), 134.

156) Liber AL, I.22.

157) "Cf. Liber ABA, Book IV, Part III, Chapt IV, The Formula of ALHIM, and That of ALIM","

158) Percy Bysshe Shelley, Donald H. Reiman, and Neil Fraistat, The Complete Poetry of Percy Bysshe Shelley (Baltimore, Md: Johns Hopkins University Press, 2000), 326.

159) Crowley, Aleister, The Book of Thoth: A Short Essay on the Tarot of the Egyptians Being the Equinox Volume III No. V (York Beach, ME: Weiser, 1999).

160) Crowley ed. Skinner, Aleister Crowley's Four Books of Magick, Book Four, Liber ABA, Liber V vel Reguli, 502-14.

161) Crowley ed. Skinner, Liber V vel Reguli p. 506.

162) Crowley ed. Skinner, 507.

163) Crowley ed. Skinner, 502.

164) Liber AL, III.17.

165) Crowley, Aleister, The Book of Thoth.

166) Crowley ed. Skinner, Aleister Crowley's Four Books of Magick, Book Four, Liber ABA, 510.

167) Crowley ed. Skinner, 510.

168) La Vaughan, Amor Divina, Writings on the Sexual Praxis of Ordo Templi Orientis, XI Degree O.T.O. p. 201.

169) Crowley ed. Skinner, Aleister Crowley's Four Books of Magick, Book Four, Liber ABA, Part III, Chapter III, The Formula of Tetragrammaton, 222.

170) Liber CDXVIII , The Vision and the Voice, 23rd Aethyr.

171) Crowley ed. Skinner, Aleister Crowley's Four Books of Magick, Book Four, Liber ABA, Part III, Chapter III, The Formula of Tetragrammaton, 222.

172) Crowley ed. Skinner, The Formula of I.A.O., 236.

173) A. Crowley, Liber CCCXXXIII [i.e. Trecentesimus Tricesimus Tertius]: The Book of Lies, Which Is Also Falsely Called, Breaks : The Wanderings Or Falsifications of the One Thought of Frater Perdurabo, Which Thought Is Itself Untrue (Wieland, 1913), 45, https://books.google.com/books?id=vuVBAQAAMAAJ.

174) Crowley ed. Skinner, Aleister Crowley's Four Books of Magick, Book Four, Liber ABA, Liber V vel Reguli, 506.

175) Crowley ed. Skinner, 506.

176) Crowley ed. Skinner, 506.

177) Crowley, The Vision & the Voice: With Commentary and Other Papers, 23.

178) Crowley ed. Skinner, Aleister Crowley's Four Books of Magick, Book Four, Liber ABA, Liber V vel Reguli, 510.

179) Crowley ed. Skinner, 510.

180)Crowley ed. Skinner, 510.

181)Crowley ed. Skinner, 510.

182)The New Comment:, I.37.

183)Crowley ed. Skinner, Aleister Crowley's Four Books of Magick, Book Four, Liber ABA, Liber V vel Reguli, 509-510.

184)Crowley ed. Skinner, Liber V vel Reguli, 510.

185)Aleister Crowley, The Ethics of Thelema, A Collection of Essays, 2nd Edition (Los Angeles: College of Thelema, 2011).

186)Crowley, Duty, 8.

187)Crowley, Duty, 9.

188)Crowley ed. Skinner, Aleister Crowley's Four Books of Magick, Book Four, Liber ABA, Part III, Chapter XXI, 352.

189)Crowley, The Ethics of Thelema, A Collection of Essays, The Message of Master Therion, 4.

190)The New Comment:, II.57.

191)Liber AL, III.17.

192)Crowley ed. Skinner, The Magical Diaries of Aleister Crowley: Tunisia 1923, 21.

193)Liber AL, I.46.

194)Crowley, The Confessions of Aleister Crowley, 1989, 621.

195)Crowley, 622.

II° Material

196)John Warwick Montgomery, Cross and Crucible: Johann Valentin Andreae (1586-1654), Phoenix of the Theologians, International Archives of the History of Ideas; 55 (Hague: M. Nijhoff, 1973).

197)Jochen Burgtorf, "Enemies and Blood-Brothers in the Thirteenth-Century Latin East: The Mamluk Sultan Baybars and the Templar Matthew Sauvage," in COMMUNICATING THE MIDDLE AGES: Essays in Honour of Sophia Menache. (S.l.: ROUTLEDGE, 2020).

198)Hughes d'Alfaro Seneschal of the Agenais, Navarrese, m. Guillemette, an Illegitimate Daughter of Raymond VI See Appendix B.

199)Raimond Roger, Count of Foix, d. 1223, Brother of Esclarmonde de Foix See Appendix B.

200)Simon de Montfort, 5th Earl Leicester (1175-1218), See Appendix B

201)William of Tudela and Anon, The Song of the Cathar Wars: A History of the Albigensian Crusade, ed. Janet Shirley, Paperback ed., reprinted, Crusade Texts in Translation 2 (Aldershot, Hampshire: Ashgate, 2011), 159.

202)William of Tudela and Anon, 96.

203)Roger-Bernard II, 1195-1241, Count of Foix from 1223 See Appendix B

204)William of Tudela and Anon, The Song of the Cathar Wars, 169.

205)Simon de Montfort, 5th Earl Leicester (1175-1218), See Appendix B.

206)William of Tudela and Anon, The Song of the Cathar Wars, 166.

207) Liber AL, III.41.

208) Crowley, The Ethics of Thelema, A Collection of Essays, The Message of Master Therion, p 5.

209) Crowley ed. Skinner, Aleister Crowley's Four Books of Magick, Book Four, Liber ABA, Liber V vel Reguli, 506.

210) Crowley, "Astarte Vel Liber Berylli, Sub Figura CLXXV," v. 21.

211) Crowley, The Ethics of Thelema, A Collection of Essays, Duty, 7.

212) Liber AL, II.21.

213) Liber AL, II.9.

214) Crowley, "Liber XV," The Gnostic Creed.

215) Liber CDXVIII , The Vision and the Voice, the 12th Aethyr, LOE.

216) Liber CDXVIII , The Vision and the Voice, the 12th Aethyr, LOE.

217) Aleister Crowley, Liber Aleph Vel CXI, The Book of Wisdom or Folly, Cap. 39, Aμ, On the Fundamentals of State.

218) Aleister Crowley, "Duty" (Hermetic Library), accessed December 14, 2021, https://hermetic.com/eidolons/duty.

219) Crowley ed. Skinner, Aleister Crowley's Four Books of Magick, Book Four, Liber ABA, Liber Samekh, 435.

220) Crowley ed. Skinner, Part II, Chapter VIII, The Sword, 139.

221) Crowley ed. Skinner, Part II, Chapter VI, The Wand, 120.

222) Aleister Crowley, "Liber NV, Sub Figura XI," The Equinox, 1912, 15.

223) Allan Bennett, "A Note on Genesis, From the Paper Written by the V.H. Fra. I.A. 5 = 6," The Equinox, 1909, 181.

224) Oldenbourg, Massacre at Montségur, 116.

225) William of Tudela and Anon, The Song of the Cathar Wars, 19–22.

226) William of Tudela and Anon, 117.

227) William of Tudela and Anon, 113.

228) Oldenbourg, Massacre at Montségur, 317.

229) Oldenbourg, 235.

230) Aleister Crowley, "The Scorpion," The Equinox, September 1911.

231) "Enemies and Blood-Brothers in the Thirteenth-Century Latin East: The Mamluk Sultan Baybars and the Templar Matthew Sauvage," 3–14.

232) Jean Richard, The Crusades, c. 1071-c. 1291, Cambridge Medieval Textbooks (Cambridge, U.K.; New York, NY: Cambridge University Press, 1999), 319.

233) "Picatrix (Ghayat al-Hakim) c 10-11th Cen.,"

234) Malcolm Barber, The Trial of the Templars, 2nd ed (Cambridge, UK; New York: Cambridge University Press, 2006), 119–20.

235) Crowley ed. Skinner, Aleister Crowley's Four Books of Magick, Book Four, Liber ABA, Part II, Chapter VI, The Wand, 126.

236) Aleister Crowley, "Liber XV, O.T.O. Ecclesiae Gnosticae Catholicae Canon Missae," The Equinox, March 1919, 257.

237)Crowley, 257.

238)Liber AL, I.41.

239)Liber AL, I.37.

240)Liber AL, I.37.

241)The New Comment:, I.37.

242)Crowley ed. Skinner, Aleister Crowley's Four Books of Magick, Book Four, Liber ABA, Part III, Chapter , The Formula of ALHIM and that of ALIM, page 224.

243)Crowley ed. Skinner, The Formula of ALHIM and that of ALIM, 224.

244)Crowley ed. Skinner, The Formula of ALHIM and that of ALIM, 224.

245)Cf. Liber XV, the Consecration

246)Crowley Refers Here to the Well Known Relationship between the Poet Catullus and a Young Man He Called 'Juventius' and Catullus' Extensive Homosexual References e.g. Catullus 21.

247)Crowley ed. Skinner, Aleister Crowley's Four Books of Magick, Book Four, Liber ABA, Part III, Chapter 1, The Principles of Ritual, 213.

248)The New Comment:, II.77.

249)Crowley ed. Skinner, Aleister Crowley's Four Books of Magick, Book Four, Liber ABA, Part III, Chapter 2, The Formulae of the Elemental Weapons, 220.

250)Hans Dieter Betz, ed., The Greek Magical Papyri in Translation: Including the Demotic Spells. 1: Texts, 2. ed., [Nachdr.] (Chicago: Univ. of Chicago Press, 2007), 103.

251)Charles Wycliffe Goodwin, Fragment of a Græco-Egyptian Work Upon Magic; From a Papyrus in the British Museum (Cambridge: Deighton; MacMillan and Co., 1852), 7.

252)Sumner, Alex, "The Bornless Ritual," Journal of the Western Mystery Tradition 7, no. 1 (Autumnal Equinox 2004).

253)William of Tudela and Anon, The Song of the Cathar Wars, 169–70.

254)Aleister Crowley, "Liber Tzaddi," The Equinox, September 1911, 21–22.

255)Aleister Crowley, "Liber LXV Liber Cordis Cincti Serpente," The Equinox, March 1919, 53.

256)Crowley, The Vision & the Voice: With Commentary and Other Papers, 21.

257)Crowley, Aleister, The Book of Thoth, 121.

258)Crowley, The Ethics of Thelema, A Collection of Essays, The Law of Liberty, 1.

259)The Douay-Rheims Bible/KJV, 3 Kings (1 Kings) 2:27.

Lexicon

260)Regardie and Greer, The Golden Dawn, 232.

261)Laurence Dermott, D.G.M., The True Ahiman Rezon: Or a Help to All That Are or Would Be Free and Accepted Masons with Many Additions, 1st American from the 3rd London (New York: Southwick & Hardcastle, 1805).

262)Montgomery, Cross and Crucible, 160–255.

263) Montgomery, 234.

264) Montgomery, 106.

265) Montgomery, 66.

266) Montgomery, 77.

267) Aleister Crowley, "Energized Enthusiasm," The Equinox, 1913, 26.

268) Richard, The Crusades, c. 1071-c. 1291, 319.

269) Oldenbourg, Massacre at Montségur, 116.

270) William of Tudela and Anon, The Song of the Cathar Wars, 19–22.

271) Malcolm Barber, The New Knighthood: A History of the Order of the Temple (Cambridge [England]; New York, NY, USA: Cambridge University Press, 1994), 145.

272) Barber, 147.

273) Lauro Martines, Fire in the City: Savonarola and the Struggle for Renaissance Florence (Oxford; New York: Oxford University Press, 2006), 196.

274) Anson F. Rainey, "Who Is a Canaanite? A Review of the Textual Evidence," Bulletin of the American Schools of Oriental Research, no. 304 (1996): 1–15, https://doi.org/10.2307/1357437.

275) Aleister Crowley, The Confessions of Aleister Crowley: An Autohagiography, ed. John Symonds and Kenneth Grant, Corrected edition, [reprint] (London: Arkana, 1989), 838.

276) Allan Greenfield, The Compleat Rite of Memphis (The Celestial Lodge of Sirius, 1998), 5.

277) Christian H. Bull, The Tradition of Hermes Trismegistus: The Egyptian Priestly Figure as a Teacher of Hellenized Wisdom, Religions in the Graeco-Roman World, VOLUME 186 (Leiden; Boston: Brill, 2018).

278) Rev. A. F. A. Woodford, Kenning's Masonic Cyclopaedia and Handbook of Masonic Archaeology, History, and Biography (London: George Kenning, 1878), 139.

279) Kenneth R. H. Mackenzie, ed., The Royal Masonic Cyclopaedia of History, Rites, Symbolism, and Biography, Repr. (Cambridge: Cambridge University Press, 2012), 137.

280) Faulks and Cooper, The Masonic Magician, 182.

281) Greenfield, The Compleat Rite of Memphis, 5.

282) Bull, The Tradition of Hermes Trismegistus, 385.

283) Rev. A. F. A. Woodford, Kenning's Masonic Cyclopaedia and Handbook of Masonic Archaeology, History, and Biography (London: George Kenning, 1878), 139.

284) Kenneth R. H. Mackenzie, ed., The Royal Masonic Cyclopaedia of History, Rites, Symbolism, and Biography, Repr. (Cambridge: Cambridge University Press, 2012), 137.

285) Konstantin Burmistrov, "THE INTERPRETATION OF KABBALAH IN EARLY 20TH-CENTURY RUSSIAN PHILOSOPHY," East European Jewish Affairs 37, no. 2 (August 1, 2007): 157–87, https://doi.org/10.1080/13501670701430404.

286) Sir Walter Raleigh, History of the World (London: Walter Burre, 1614), 67.

287) Dr. Adolf Harnack, Outlines of the History of Dogma, trans. Edwin Knox Mitchell (London: Hodder and Stoughton, 1893), 133.

288) Jonathan Cahana, "None of Them Knew Me or My Brothers: Gnostic Antitraditionalism and Gnosticism as a Cultural Phenomenon," The Journal of Religion 94, no. 1 (2014): 73, https://doi.org/10.1086/673542.

289) Barber, The Trial of the Templars, 2006, 9.

290) Barber, 10.

291) John and Frederic Hathaway Chase, Writings, The Fathers of the Church, a New Translation, v. 37 (Washington, D.C: Catholic University of America Press, 1958), 132.

292) Michael Psellus, Dialogue on the Operation of Daemons, ed. Stephen Skinner, trans. Marcus Collisson, 2nd ed (Singapore: Golden Hoard Press, 2010), 58 "seu sororem, seu propriam fliam, mntrem"

293) Psellus, 57–58.

294) Malcolm Barber, The Cathars, The Medieval World (Harlow, England; New York: Pearson Education, 2000), 109.

295) Barber, 16.

296) Barber, 28.

297) Barber, 24.

298) Barber, 109.

299) M. Pasi, "The Knight of Spermatophagy: Penetrating the Mysteries of Georges Le Clément de Saint-Marcq," Molecular and Cellular Biology - MOL CELL BIOL, January 1, 2008, 369–400.

300) National Magazine, 1906, 228, https://books.google.com/books?id=ckEPAQAAIAAJ.

301) Jean-Pierre Bonnerot, "Deodat Roche et L'Eglise Gnostique," Academia.edu, 20, https://www.academia.edu/37047276/DEODAT_ROCHE_et_L_EGLISE_GNOSTIQUE_pdf.

302) Bonnerot, 19.

303) Bonnerot, 20.

304) J. Doinel, Lucifer Démasqué (Delhomme et Briguet, 1895), 19–20, https://books.google.com/books?id=zrSZVY44DTIC.

305) Bonnerot, "Deodat Roche et L'Eglise Gnostique," 64.

306) A. E. Waite, Devil-Worship in France: Or, The Question of Lucifer; a Record of Things Seen and Heard in the Secret Societies According to the Evidence of Initiates (G. Redway, 1896), 194, https://books.google.com/books?id=xmMuAAAAYAAJ.

307) Crowley ed. Skinner, Aleister Crowley's Four Books of Magick, Book Four, Liber ABA, Part 3, Chapter 5, The Formula of IAO, 233.

308) David G. Robertson, Gnosticism and the History of Religions, 1st ed., Scientific Studies of Religion: Inquiry and Explanation (New York: Bloomsbury Academic, 2021).

309) Crowley, "Liber XV."

310) Henrik Bogdan and Martin P. Starr, eds., Aleister Crowley and Western Esotericism (New York: Oxford University Press, 2012), 144.

311) David G. Robertson, Gnosticism and the History of Religions, 1st ed., Scientific Studies of Religion: Inquiry and Explanation (New York: Bloomsbury Academic, 2021), 77.

312) Robertson, 105.

313) Malcolm Barber, The Trial of the Templars, 2nd ed (Cambridge, UK; New York: Cambridge University Press, 2006), 77.

314) Tamara M. Green, The City of the Moon God: Religious Traditions of Harran, Religions in the Graeco-Roman World, v. 114 (Leiden; New York: E.J. Brill, 1992), 120–21.

315) Green, 122.

316) Ute Possekel, "Bardaisan of Edessa: Philosopher or Theologian?" 10, no. 3 (2007): 444, https://doi.org/10.1515/ZAC.2006.033.

317) H.J.W. Drijvers, Bardaisan of Edessa (Gorgias Press, 2014), 8, https://doi.org/10.31826/9781463235307.

318) Green, The City of the Moon God, 135.

319) Barber, The Trial of the Templars, 2006, 82.

320) Green, The City of the Moon God, 179.

321) Nick Farrell, trans., Crata Repoa, Or Initiations into the Ancient, Secret Society of the Egyptian Priests (Rome, 2009).

322) Crowley ed. Skinner, Aleister Crowley's Four Books of Magick, Book Four, Liber ABA, Part 3, Chapter 8, The Formula of the Holy Graal: of Abrahadabra: and of certain other Words Also: the Magical Memory p. 241-245.

323) Isadore Singer and Cyrus Adler, The Jewish Encyclopedia: A Descriptive Record of the History, Religion, Literature, and Customs of the Jewish People from the Earliest Times to the Present Day (Funk & Wagnalls Company, 1901), 335.

324) Bull, The Tradition of Hermes Trismegistus.

325) Bull, 1.

326) Thrice-Greatest Hermes [Volume 3] (Watkins), 149, https://books.google.com/books?id=k15bAgAAQBAJ.

327) G.R.S. Mead, Thrice-Greatest Hermes, Studies in Hellenistic Theosophy and Gnosis, vol. Volume I. Prolegomena (London and Benares: The Theosophical Publishing Society, 1906), 44.

328) Norman Domeier and Deborah Lucas Schneider, The Eulenburg Affair: A Cultural History of Politics in the German Empire, German History in Context (Rochester, New York: Camden House, 2015), 127–28.

329) Heike Bauer, The Hirschfeld Archives: Violence, Death, and Modern Queer Culture, Sexuality Studies, 2017, 48, https://hdl.loc.gov/loc.gdc/gdcebookspublic.2019668041.

330) Heike Bauer, The Hirschfeld Archives: Violence, Death, and Modern Queer Culture, Sexuality Studies (Philadelphia: Temple University Press, 2017), 3.

331) Bauer, The Hirschfeld Archives: Violence, Death, and Modern Queer Culture, 87.

332) Barber, The Trial of the Templars, 2006, 188.

333) Barber, 54.

334) John Fleming, Hugh Honour, and Nikolaus Pevsner, The Penguin Dictionary of Architecture and Landscape Architecture, 5th ed., New ed, Penguin Reference Books (London: Penguin, 1999), 277.

335) Crowley, "Liber XV."

336) William Smith, Dictionary of Greek and Roman Biography and Mythology, vol. Vol 1 (London, 1869), 803.

337) Plutarch, Moralia, V. 26.

338) Crowley ed. Skinner, Aleister Crowley's Four Books of Magick, Book Four, Liber ABA, 168.

339) Crowley, The Confessions of Aleister Crowley, 1989, 838.

340) Levi, Dogme et Rituel de La Haute Magie Part II: The Ritual of Transcendental Magic, 16.

341) The Douay-Rheims Bible/KJV, 2nd Chronicles, 33:6-7.

342) Malcolm Barber, "The Templars and the Turin Shroud," The Catholic Historical Review 68, no. 2 (1982): 206–25, http://www.jstor.org/stable/25021340.

343) John Addington Symonds, The Life of Michelangelo Buonarroti, Rouben Mamoulian Collection (Library of Congress), The Modern Library of the World's Best Books (New York,: The Modern library, 1928), 30.

344) Marsilio Ficino, The Letters of Marsilio Ficino (London: Shepheard-Walwyn, 1975), 140, http://www.loc.gov/catdir/enhancements/fy0701/76362802-d.html.

345) Harriet Wells Hobler, "Marsilio Ficino, Philosopher, and Head of the Platonic Academy of Florence" (University of Illinois, 1917), 46.

346) Hobler, 47.

347) Anne Borelli et al., "Postmortem: Marsilio Ficino, Apologia Contra Savonarolam," in Selected Writings of Girolamo Savonarola (Yale University Press, 2006), 357, http://www.jstor.org/stable/j.ctt1npnwt.

348) Burgtorf, "Enemies and Blood-Brothers in the Thirteenth-Century Latin East: The Mamluk Sultan Baybars and the Templar Matthew Sauvage," 3.

349) The Douay-Rheims Bible/KJV, Hebrews 6:20.

350) The Douay-Rheims Bible/KJV, Psalms 109:4.

351) Barber, The Trial of the Templars, 2006, 119–20.

352) Alain Demurger, The Last Templar: The Tragedy of Jacques de Molay, Paperback edition (London: Profile Books, 2009), 66.

353) Demurger, 218.

354) Poncet, "Ficino's Little Academy of Careggi."

355) Crowley ed. Skinner, Aleister Crowley's Four Books of Magick, Book Four, Liber ABA, Book 3, Chapter 3, The Formula of Tetragrammaton, 222.

356) Bianca M. Dinkelaar, "Plato and the Language of Mysteries: Orphic/Pythagorean and Eleusinian Motifs and Register in Ten Dialogues," Mnemosyne 73, no. 1 (January 20, 2020): 36–62, https://doi.org/10.1163/1568525X-12342654.

357) Wilferd Madelung, "Maslama Al-Qurṭubī's Kitāb Rutbat al-Ḥakīm and the History of Chemistry," Intellectual History of the Islamicate World 5, no. 1 (January 1, 2017): 118–26, https://doi.org/10.1163/2212943X-00501005.

358) Crawford, Katherine, "Marsilio Ficino, Neoplatonism, and the Problem of Sex," Renaissance and Reformation / Renaissance et Réforme 28, no. 2 (2004): 5, http://www.jstor.org/stable/43445751.

359) Crawford, Katherine, 6.

360) Nan Cooke Carpenter, "Rabelais and the Androgyne," Modern Language Notes 68, no. 7 (1953): 457, https://doi.org/10.2307/3043653.

361) David Adams Leeming and David Adams Leeming, Creation Myths of the World: An Encyclopedia, 2nd ed (Santa Barbara, Calif: ABC-CLIO, 2010), 14.

362) Crowley, The Confessions of Aleister Crowley, 1989, 838.

363) Montgomery, Cross and Crucible, 234.

364) Montgomery, 236.

365) Montgomery, 236–37.

366) Barber, The New Knighthood, 293.

367) Jochen Burgtorf, The Central Convent of Hospitallers and Templars: History, Organization, and Personnel (1099/1120-1310), History of Warfare, v. 50 (Leiden; Boston: Brill, 2008), 136.

368) Barber, The Trial of the Templars, 2006, 22.

369) Burgtorf, The Central Convent of Hospitallers and Templars, 137.

370) Barber, The Trial of the Templars, 2006, 147.

371) Paul Strathern, Death in Florence: The Medici, Savonarola, and the Battle for the Soul of a Renaissance City, 2016.

372) Martines, Fire in the City.

373) Aleister Crowley writing ast Rev. C. Verey, Clouds without Water, Edited From a Private M.S. (London: Privately Printed for Circulation Among Ministers of Religion, 1909), 101.

374) Morgane Surdez et al., "Flooding a Landscape: Impact of Holocene Transgression on Coastal Sedimentology and Underwater Archaeology in Kiladha Bay (Greece)," Swiss Journal of Geosciences 111, no. 3 (October 1, 2018): 573–88, https://doi.org/10.1007/s00015-018-0309-4.

375) Crowley, "The Scorpion."

376) Anonymous, Fama Fraternitatis Rosae Crucis (Kassel: 1614).

377) Abraham ben Simeon et al., The Book of Abramelin: A New Translation, 1st American hardcover ed (Lake Worth, Fla: Ibis Press, 2006).

378) Ian Rons, "The Book of Abramelin: A New Translation," Archive, The Magickal Review, Archived from the Original, 2010, https://web.archive.org/web/20131208091331/http://themagickalreview.org/reviews/book-of-abramelin.php.

379) Daniel Garrison Brinton, The Religious Sentiment (New York: Henry Holt, 1876), 65–66.

380) R. Hunter, J.A. Williams, and S.J.H. Herrtage, The American Encyclopaedic Dictionary: A ... Work of Reference to the English Language Defining Over 250,000 Words ... Containing Over One Hundred Maps and Diagrams and Nearly Four Thousand Illustrations, The American Encyclopaedic Dictionary: A ... Work of Reference to the English Language Defining Over 250,000 Words ... Containing Over One Hundred Maps and Diagrams and Nearly Four Thousand Illustrations (R.S. Peale and J.A. Hill, 1897), 273, https://books.google.com/books?id=wVlYAAAAMAAJ.

381) Crowley, The Vision & the Voice: With Commentary and Other Papers, 5th Aethyr.

382) Crowley ed. Skinner, Aleister Crowley's Four Books of Magick, Book Four, Liber ABA, 242.

383) Crowley, Aleister, The Book of Thoth, 64.

384) Crowley, Aleister, 67.

Appendix B

385) William of Tudela and Anon, The Song of the Cathar Wars.

386) W. A. Sibly and Sibly, M.D., The History of the Albigensian Crusade: Peter of Les Vaux-de-Cernay's Historia Albigensis (Woodbridge: Boydell Press, 2002).

387) William, W. A. Sibly, and M. D. Sibly, The Chronicle of William of Puylaurens: The Albigensian Crusade and Its Aftermath (Woodbridge, Suffolk, UK; Rochester, N.Y: Boydell Press, 2003).

388) Barber, The Cathars.

389) Otto Rahn, Crusade against the Grail: The Struggle between the Cathars, the Templars, and the Church of Rome, 1st U.S. ed (Rochester, Vt: Inner Traditions, 2006).

390) Otto Rahn, Luzifers Hofgesind: Eine Reise zu den guten Geistern Europas, 2. Aufl (Dresden: Verl. Zeitenwende, 2006).

391) Barber, *The Cathars*, 208.

392) Fredric L Cheyette, Ermengard of Narbonne and the World of the Troubadours (Ithaca, N.Y.; Bristol: Cornell University Press; University Presses Marketing [distributor, 2004), 277, http://www.vlebooks.com/vleweb/product/openreader?id=none&isbn=9781501722554.

393) Barber, The Cathars, 55–56.

394) Elaine Graham-Leigh, The Southern French Nobility and the Albigensian Crusade (Woodbridge, Suffolk, England: Boydell Press, 2005), 95–96.

395) Cheyette, Ermengard of Narbonne and the World of the Troubadours, 275–76.

396) William of Tudela and Anon, The Song of the Cathar Wars, 27.

397) William of Tudela and Anon, 28.

398) Norris J. Lacy, ed., The Lancelot-Grail Reader: Selections from the Medieval French Arthurian Cycle, Garland Reference Library of the Humanities, v. 2162 (New York: Garland Pub, 2000), 71.

399) William of Tudela and Anon, The Song of the Cathar Wars, 45.

400) Pegg, A Most Holy War, 2008, 135.

401) Sara McDougall, Royal Bastards: The Birth of Illegitimacy, 800-1230, First edition, Oxford Studies in Medieval European History (Oxford; New York: Oxford University Press, 2017), 27–28.

402) McDougall, 29.

403) William of Tudela and Anon, The Song of the Cathar Wars, 46.

404) Mark Gregory Pegg, A Most Holy War: The Albigensian Crusade and the Battle for Christendom, Pivotal Moments in World History (Oxford; New York: Oxford University Press, 2008), 20.

405) Pegg, A Most Holy War, 2008, xxii.

406) Pegg, xxii.

407) Pegg, 64.

408) William of Tudela and Anon, The Song of the Cathar Wars, 15.

409) Oldenbourg, *Massacre at Montségur*, 116.

410) Guillaume et al., *The Song of the Cathar Wars*, 19–22.

411) Barber, The Trial of the Templars, 2006, 211–12.

412) Barber, 212.

413) William of Tudela and Anon, The Song of the Cathar Wars, 54.

414) Sibly and Sibly, M.D., The History of the Albigensian Crusade, 62–63.

415) Pegg, A Most Holy War, 2008, 98.

416) Pegg, 108.

417) Pegg, 122.

418) Pegg, 132.

419) Pegg, 148.

420) Pegg, 148.

421) Pegg, 151.

422) Catherine Elisabeth Léglu, Rebecca Rist, and Claire Taylor, The Cathars and the Albigensian Crusade: A Sourcebook (London New York: Routledge, 2014), 99.

423) William of Tudela and Anon, The Song of the Cathar Wars, 108.

424) Sibly and Sibly, M.D., The History of the Albigensian Crusade, 25.

425) Sibly and Sibly, M.D., 24.

426) Sibly and Sibly, M.D., 25.

427) Sibly and Sibly, M.D., 25.

428) Sibly and Sibly, M.D., 23–24.

429) Pegg, A Most Holy War, 2008, 64.

430) Sibly and Sibly, M.D., The History of the Albigensian Crusade, 305.

431) Oldenbourg, Massacre at Montségur, 275.

432) Sibly and Sibly, M.D., The History of the Albigensian Crusade, 24.

433) Sibly and Sibly, M.D., 24.

434) Graham-Leigh, The Southern French Nobility and the Albigensian Crusade, 29.

435) Graham-Leigh, 111.

436) Graham-Leigh, 111.

437) Pegg, A Most Holy War, 2008, xix–ix.

438) William of Tudela and Anon, The Song of the Cathar Wars, 70.

439) William of Tudela and Anon, 46.

440) Andre du Chesne, Historiae Francorum Scriptores Coaetanei, vol. 4, 1641, 714–26.

441) Richard Huscroft, Tales from the Long Twelfth Century: The Rise and Fall of the Angevin Empire (New Haven; London: Yale University Press, 2016), 146.

442) Huscroft, 281.

443) Huscroft, 165.

444) Jean Baptiste Courcelles, Histoire Généalogique et Héraldique Des Pairs de France, vol. 11 (Paris, 1831), Cap. Saint-Felix, 2.

445) Huscroft, Tales from the Long Twelfth Century, 165.

446) Huscroft, 166.

447) Huscroft, 167.

448) Oldenbourg, Massacre at Montségur, 317.

449) William of Tudela and Anon, The Song of the Cathar Wars, 172.

450) Claude De Vic and J Vaissete, Histoire Générale de Languedoc Avec Des Notes et Les Pièces Justificatives - Privat, vol. 5 (Toulouse: J. - B. Paya, Proprietaire-Editeur, 1842), 572.

451) De Vic and Vaissete, 5:403.

452) William of Tudela and Anon, The Song of the Cathar Wars, 46.

453) Graham-Leigh, The Southern French Nobility and the Albigensian Crusade, 29.

454) William of Tudela and Anon, The Song of the Cathar Wars, 18–19.

455) Pegg, A Most Holy War, 2008, 2.

456) Barber, The Trial of the Templars, 2006, 52.

457) William of Tudela and Anon, The Song of the Cathar Wars, 65.

458) Oldenbourg, *Massacre at Montségur*, 236.

459) Catherine Elisabeth Léglu, Rebecca Rist, and Claire Taylor, *The Cathars and the Albigensian Crusade: A Sourcebook* (London New York: Routledge, 2014), 162.

460) Timothy Venning, A Chronology of the Crusades (London: Routledge, 2015), 210.

Appendix D

461) Gregorio del Olmo Lete, Joaquín Sanmartín, and Wilfred G. E. Watson, A Dictionary of the Ugaritic Language in the Alphabetic Tradition, Third Revised Edition, Handbook of Oriental Studies. Section 1, The Near and Middle East; Handbuch Der Orientalistik, vol. 112 = (Leiden; Boston: Brill, 2015).

462) Bogard,Milko, Of Memphis and of Misraim, the Oriental Silence of the Winged Sun: History of the Egyptian Rites of Freemasonry; Its Rites, Rituals and Mysteries (CreateSpace, 2018).

463) John C. Yorston, A Library of Freemasonry: Comprising Its History, Antiquities, Symbols, Constitutions, Customs, Etc., and Concordant Orders of Royal Arch, Knights Templar, A.A.S. Rite, Mystic Shrine, with Other Important Masonic Information of Value to the Fraternity Derived from Official and Standard Sources Throughout the World from the Earliest Period to the Present Time. (United Kingdom, 1911).

464) "Albert Pike and William C. Cummings, The Spurious Rites of Memphis and Misraim," Heredom, 2001.

465) Israel Regardie, Ceremonial Magic: A Guide to the Mechanisms of Ritual (Wellingborough, Northamptonshire: Aquarian Press, 1980), 60–61.

466) E.A. Wallis Budge, Egyptian Magic, Second Impression (London: Kegan Paul, Trench, Trubner & Co. Ltd., 1901), 176.

467) Crowley ed. Skinner, *The Magical Diaries of Aleister Crowley: Tunisia 1923*, 21.

468) *Liber AL*, I.46.

469) Crowley, *The Confessions of Aleister Crowley*, 1989, 621.

470) Crowley, 622.

471) Aleister Crowley, "Liber LXV Liber Cordis Cincti Serpente," *The Equinox, The Official Organ of the A∴ A∴*, March 1919, 53.

472) Crowley, *The Vision & the Voice: With Commentary and Other Papers*, 21.

473) Therion, *The Book of Thoth*, 121.

Made in the USA
Columbia, SC
10 December 2022

72371385R00267